THE WARD LOCK GUIDES
SCOTTISH VOLUMES

Illustrated editions

ABERDEEN, Deeside, Donside, etc.

EDINBURGH and District.

THE HIGHLANDS.

INVERNESS, Strathpeffer, etc.

NORTHERN SCOTLAND.

OBAN, Fort William, Skye and Western Scotland, etc.

WESTERN SCOTLAND.

WARD LOCK LIMITED
116 BAKER STREET, W.1

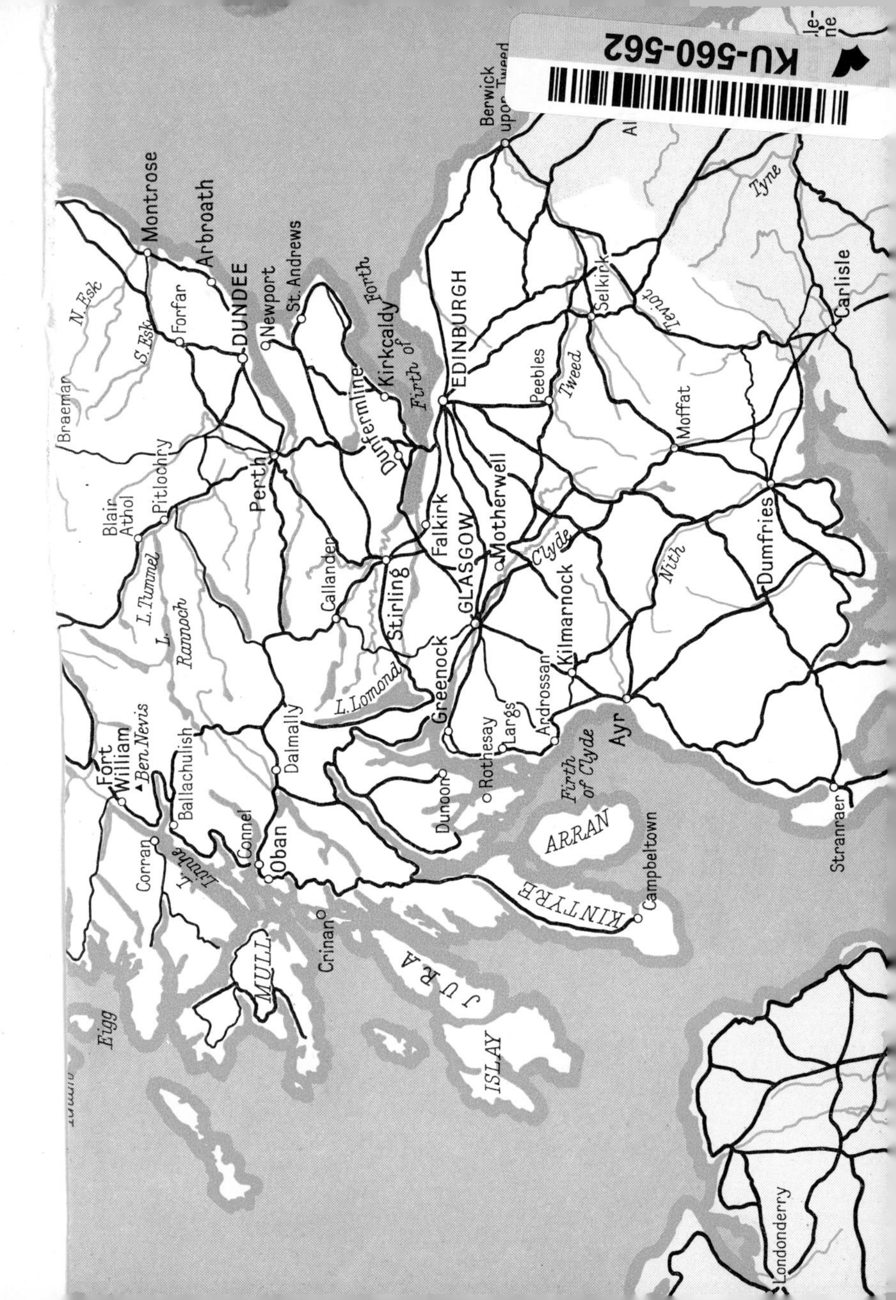

SCOTLAND

RED GUIDE

THE COMPLETE SCOTLAND

A COMPREHENSIVE SURVEY, BASED ON ROAD, WALKING, RAIL AND STEAMER ROUTES

Edited by Reginald J. W. Hammond

TENTH EDITION

WARD LOCK LIMITED
116 BAKER STREET, LONDON, W.1

ISBN 7063 5071 5

Printed in Great Britain by Butler & Tanner Ltd., Frome and London

CONTENTS

CENTRAL SCOTLAND.

MAPS

PLANS

INTRODUCTION.

CREDIT for making Scotland known to the outer world has been given to Dr. Johnson, to Sir Walter Scott and to many more recent writers, but greater credit is perhaps due to General Wade for the roads he engineered, early in the eighteenth century, into the then inaccessible Highlands and to David MacBrayne for the steamboat services with which a century later he brought the most remote places on the west coast into intimate touch with Glasgow. The railways also played their part, but it is only in recent years, with the rise of motoring and the revival of walking and cycling, that tourists have penetrated in any numbers into those out-of-the-way corners beyond the railways and hitherto served by an infrequent steamer or coach.

This Handbook has been written in recognition of the fact that the revolution in travel methods necessitates what is virtually a reassessment of Scotland from the tourist's point of view. Places which a few years ago were almost unknown are now popular resorts ; on the other hand a number of places which have too long been allowed to pose as good holiday centres have in recent years been forced to shed this false glamour and relegated to positions more in accordance with their relative touristic importance. The book as a whole is written from the point of view of those who see the country from the roads. While adequate notes are given respecting railway and steamer services, the roads provide the greater part of the itineraries upon which our descriptive chapters are based ; where roads fail, the hill-paths are utilized, and in districts where the customary mode of progression is the steamer or the railway our notes are written accordingly.

THE HIGHLANDS.

A line drawn more or less directly from near Glasgow to Aberdeen divides the Highlands from the rest of Scotland, and it is curious to reflect that until the beginning of the nineteenth century this line also marked the border between what was condescendingly regarded as " civilized " Scotland and a savage land of mountains and wild passes through which (said gossip) roamed hordes of barbarians whose intentions towards tourists only just stopped short of sheer cannibalism. Closer acquaintance has given the Highlander his share in the high national reputation for courtesy and kindliness, but although roads, railways and walking routes traverse the Highlands in all directions the wildness of the scenery is still its distinguishing feature—a wildness on too grand a scale to be spoiled by man, vast areas now being safeguarded as National Forest Parks or Nature Reserves.

The mineral wealth of the country is for the most part disposed along or near the narrow belt of land connecting the Firth of Clyde, on the west, with the Forth on the east. Down the south-west coast are a few outlying coal-mines, and Galloway and Fort William are noted as the seats of great hydro-electric installations and for the preparation of aluminium, but the great industrial towns of Scotland will mostly be found within a few miles of Glasgow or Edinburgh. The reason is not far to seek. Here the Clyde and the Forth penetrate far inland to give unrivalled facilities for water transport, and this same penetration is also responsible for the coming together of all the main road and railway routes between the north and the south.

Mills for the manufacture of tweeds and woollens will be found in various parts of the country (but seldom in the Highlands, where whisky distilleries are more characteristic), and all round the coast are ports which in the aggregate carry on a stupendous trade in fish—herring, cod, haddock, hake, etc., much being cured, frozen or made into fish-meal. It is around the coasts, too, that the oldest towns are generally to be found—St. Andrews, Aberdeen, Inverness and so on. On the West Highland coast Inveraray is the place which most successfully conveys an atmosphere of age ; yet it is only two hundred years old, and Oban as a town is even more youthful, having grown from a small fishing hamlet during the last century as a result of the increase of touring. Scattered through the Highlands are a number of ruined keeps and castles of ancient date, but with the exception of these nearly all the inland centres are places of relatively modern build, a feature which is in many cases emphasized by the unsullied appearance of the granite so widely used as building material. In this connection the visitor will be struck by the almost uniform manner in which the Highland village is built around a central Square. Though useful nowadays for the annual Games Meetings, these open spaces were designed with a more sinister end in view by those who encouraged the rise of law and order after the '45.

Although the Highlands comprise almost entirely mountainous scenery—

THE LOWLANDS.

are by no means flat. For miles north of the Border are hills which, if less lofty than those beyond Stirling, are in their way no less picturesque : indeed, some of the Lowland scenery attains a very high order of beauty. At the same time, whereas the Highlands are interesting mainly on account of their grand natural scenery, in the Lowlands and the Midland belt one has on every hand evidence of man's endeavours to work and rule, to love and play. Castles, battlefields, abbeys, palaces are encountered with such profusion that even a cursory pilgrimage would give one a very clear insight into the tortuous passages of Scottish history. Ayr, Alloway and the south-west are to Burns-lovers what Warwickshire is to Shakespearians ; in many circles the Braes of Yarrow are at least as important as Abbotsford and the Eildons, and Moffat has its memories of "Ossian" Macpherson.

Lying apart from the rest of the country in more than one sense are the **Islands**. Air and boat services keep them in touch with the mainland and every summer carry increasing numbers of visitors across the intervening waters, but habits—especially Scottish habits—are slow to change, and to visit some of these isolated communities is to step into a past century. The scenery is varied, but of a very high average, culminating in the magnificent mountains of Skye. To geologists many of the islands are of supreme interest, as is shown on later pages.

MOTORING.

Scotland has a well-merited reputation for good roads, and active steps are being taken not only to retain this reputation but even to enhance it. Just prior to the war saw completion of a vast scheme which had for its object the construction of a great highway from central and southern Scotland to Inverness, and involving the engineering of an entirely new road between Tyndrum and Bridge of Orchy, across the western edge of Rannoch Moor and through Glencoe, and the virtual rebuilding of the road through the Great Glen from Ballachulish to Fort William and Inverness. In 1936 a new road bridge over the Forth at Kincardine was opened ; in 1964 the colossal road bridge at Queensferry, and in 1966, the new Tay road bridge, have stimulated north-bound traffic.

In the Highlands especially the valleys are so deep and steep-sided that the roads run through them and round, rather than over, the intervening mountains and ridges. This results in an extraordinary absence of dangerous hills : Scotland, for all its mountainous character, has fewer really steep main roads than North Devon. Moreover, the manner in which the roads tend to follow the valleys has an important result on their picturesqueness. The outstanding feature of Scottish Highland scenery is the combination of rocks and water—mountains, lochs and rivers—and it is a fact that almost every one of the lochs has a road running along its rim, enabling the motorist to taste the cream of Highland scenery from the seat of his car. Many of the sea-lochs exhibit this feature even more strikingly, and very delightfully for those who like everything about the sea but its motion. Up and down the west coast are roads along which it is possible to drive for mile after mile within a few feet of the salt water. Thus from Ardrishaig, a considerable way up long Loch Fyne, to Campbeltown and back is a run of nearly a hundred miles, and throughout the entire trip one is rarely out of sight of the salt water and for a greater part of the way one is actually within range of the spray which blows up over the road on a windy day.

As might be expected, with such an indented coastline, **ferries** play an important part in certain of the road communications. Many of these are equipped for the transport of cars and on other pages we indicate the facilities available. Those proposing to use the outlying ferries on the wild west coast should bear in mind that their operations are subject to tidal conditions and that occasionally a fairly long wait is necessary before one can make the crossing.

A very useful ferry is that across the Clyde between Erskine and Old Kilpatrick, a few miles downstream from Glasgow.

Those touring Scotland will find it a wise plan to start the day's run fairly early in the morning and to finish it quite early in the afternoon wherever possible, especially if no arrangements have been made for hotel accommodation, since hotels are liable to become full up towards evening and it may be difficult to find shelter for the night if such arrangements are left too late. An early start has the further advantage of avoiding the crowd, for certain parts of Scotland are so famous that the roads serving them during the season are very busy indeed and drivers must attend closely to their task.

A TEN-DAY TOUR.

On later pages of this book will be found descriptions of practically every road of importance in Scotland (*see* Index). The following tour has been designed to include as many of the scenes of prime importance as can well be visited in ten days' comfortable travelling with some allowance of time for sightseeing (those for whom the daily runs are too short can of course vary the daily allowance to suit themselves); but it is capable of indefinite extension, as, for instance, northward to John o' Groats, south-westward into Galloway, eastward into Fife and Forfar and "over the sea to Skye" in the west.

1. Cross the Border at Carter Bar (p. 60) and so by Jedburgh to Melrose (330 miles from London), where the day's journey, presumably a fairly long one, may well be concluded. If time allows, a detour may be made to Dryburgh, otherwise—

2nd Day.—From Melrose, having seen the Abbey, visit Dryburgh and Abbotsford and continue by Peebles to Edinburgh (about 60 miles).

3rd Day.—Leave Edinburgh by the Queensferry Road, which leads to the Forth Bridge, but continue by Linlithgow and Stirling to Callander (55 miles), whence visit the Trossachs.

4th Day.—Callander to Pitlochry by Lochearnhead, St. Fillans, Comrie, Crieff and Dunkeld (or Perth). Unless time is very limited, turn off from main road at Ballinluig, between Dunkeld and Pitlochry, and go up the Tay valley to Aberfeldy and Kenmore, beside Loch Tay. Hence to Fortingall, with a glimpse into lovely Glen Lyon, and then northward again over the hills to Tummel Bridge and so to Pitlochry by the road overlooking Loch Tummel. Just before this road rejoins the main Great North Road, the river Garry is crossed at the foot of the Pass of Killiecrankie. About 90 miles.

5th Day.—From Pitlochry to Blairgowrie, either by main road and Dunkeld or the quieter road starting through Moulin. From Blairgowrie to Braemar is 35 miles over the mountains by the highest motoring road in Great Britain, a height of 2,199 feet being reached at the Cairnwell Pass. Total mileage from Pitlochry about 60.

6th Day.—Braemar to Aberdeen (about 60 miles), by Balmoral, Ballater and the Dee Valley.

7th Day.—Aberdeen to Inverness (about 110 miles). From Aberdeen go northward to Dyce, Old Meldrum and Turriff and so to the coast at Banff and Macduff. The remainder of the route follows the coast westward for about 60 miles. A most remunerative detour is that inland from Forres to Ferness by the lovely Findhorn valley. From Ferness one can regain the main road at Nairn, as explained on page 387. The main road between Nairn and Inverness is one of the straightest in Scotland, but it misses Culloden Moor and the gorgeous views therefrom, and on the whole a preferable route for those coming from Ferness is to turn off on the left about two miles short of Nairn by a secondary road which passes Cawdor Castle and comes up to Culloden Moor near the Cumberland Stone and the battlefield cairn. Hence to Inverness is only 5 or 6 miles. (The rebuilt roads north of Inverness are described on pp. 406–30.)

8th Day.—Inverness to Oban by Fort William and Glencoe. The reconstruction of the road through the Great Glen and Glencoe makes this one of the finest runs of its kind in Scotland. The route is unmistakable as far as Fort William and Onich, whence Loch Leven is rounded (for ferry, however, *see* p. 224). On the south side of the Loch is the entrance to Glencoe and from the upper end of the Glen the road continues over Rannoch Moor to Bridge of Orchy and Tyndrum, where turn right for Dalmally, near the head of Loch Awe, and continue to Oban (about 140 miles).

9th Day.—Oban to Glasgow (130 miles). To Lochgilphead (30 miles), where turn sharp to left, thence follow the road round the head of Loch Gilp and up the northern side of Loch Fyne to Inveraray, whence the loch is still skirted. At Cairndow, however, turn off on the left and so by way of " Rest and Be Thankful " to Arrochar, on Loch Long. From Arrochar strike up left for Tarbet, on Loch Lomond, and follow the loch-side road all the way down to Balloch—one of the prettiest roads in Scotland. From Balloch to Glasgow is a matter of some 18 miles, through industrial suburbs which are singularly unattractive after the beauties through which we have recently passed, and those who have already visited Glasgow may prefer to cross the river by Erskine Bridge (p. 150).

10*th Day.*—To Kilmarnock and Ayr, the capital of "The Burns Country," and thence to Cumnock, Sanquhar, Thornhill, Dumfries and the Border at Gretna Green. If one has lingered overlong in Glasgow, Ayr and Kilmarnock may be omitted and the Border regained by the more direct route passing Hamilton, Abington and Lockerbie; alternatively one can diverge to Dumfries or to Moffat and St. Mary's Loch.

PUBLIC MOTOR SERVICES.

It would perhaps be too much to say that where there is a road in Scotland there is also a motor service, but it can safely be stated that practically every clachan, however remote, is within hail of a motor service (frequent or otherwise) to and from the nearest town. In addition to the purely passenger traffic, there are a number of carriers' cars which are often very useful. They do not, however, figure in the published time-tables and the best source of current information is usually the local hotel-keeper or the station-master at the market town.

Additional to the local bus services, more or less long-distance coaches run from Edinburgh, Glasgow and other centres to various places of interest. Some of these make extensive tours occupying several days. The chief bus company operating in south-east Scotland is *Scottish Omnibuses, Ltd.*; in the south-west, *Western S.M.T. Company*; in the north-east, *W. Alexander and Sons*; and north of Inverness, *Highland Omnibuses.*

As with trains and steamers, some of the motor services are withdrawn on Sundays.

Time-tables.—British Rail (Scottish Region) and the bus and steamer concerns issue time-tables of their own services.

STEAMERS.[1]

In no other part of Britain does the steamer play such an important part in the daily life of the community as along the western seaboard of Scotland. Not only the islands are thus brought into touch with the cities of the mainland, but countless villages dotted beside the lochs

[1] See footnote, next page.

or on the peninsulas which alternately characterize the storm-beaten west coast. Many of these places are far more easily reached by boat than by motor—some of them are so tucked away that for long months of the year the weekly steamer is the only contact, other than radio and television, they have with the outer world.

The greater number of the west coast services are controlled by *David MacBrayne Ltd.* (302 Buchanan Street, Glasgow). The Caledonian Steam Packet Co. Ltd., Gourock, also run services between various ports in the Firth of Clyde. The motor ships of *Burns and Laird Lines Ltd.* (82 Oswald Street, Glasgow) connect Scotland (Ardrossan) with Ireland (Belfast).

On the east coast, the Orkney and Shetland services are in the hands of the *North of Scotland, Orkney & Shetland Shipping Company Ltd.* (Head Office: Matthew's Quay, Aberdeen), running from Aberdeen and Thurso.

RAILWAYS.[1]

Scottish railways form part of the British Rail system, and the services between London and Glasgow and Edinburgh in particular are among the best in Britain.

Through trains or carriages are run between the principal Scottish centres and all parts of England; restaurant-cars are attached to most of these trains and attached to the night trains are sleeping-cars, berths in which can be obtained on payment of a supplement in addition to the normal fare (both first- and second-class available). At all times it is advisable to book such accommodation in advance, but it is decidedly necessary during the season from July to October, and during this period seats should also be booked in advance.

Travel in Scotland is encouraged by the issue of cheap circular tour and weekly "runabout" tickets.

It should be noted that on Sundays many services are curtailed.

AIR SERVICES.

In vivid contrast to the simple, almost primitive, life of some of the outer islands are the air services which keep them in close touch with the mainland. Barra has been brought within two hours of Glasgow, Lewis is within an hour of Inverness. Regular services connect Glasgow with Tiree and Barra, with Benbecula and

[1] It should be understood that all references in this book to travel facilities, as also to admission to show places, require confirmation from current announcements.

Stornoway, with Islay and with Campbeltown. B.E.A. and Aer Lingus give daily communication with Ireland (Belfast and Dublin). Other services link the mainland with Orkney and Shetland, while airports at Edinburgh, Aberdeen, Inverness, and Wick expedite journeys to and across Scotland. Details of services are too variable to be quoted here ; they can be ascertained from current time-tables or at any tourist office.

HOTELS.

One of the surprises of Scottish touring is the size of many of the outlying hotels. Often it happens that one travels for miles through a country so sparsely populated as to seem utterly deserted, and on arrival at journey's end the destination is found to be a solitary large hotel. During the summer and autumn most of these establishments are usually fairly busy, but for long months they stand unvisited, and if one bears these unremunerative periods in mind, the charges are very reasonable. The service is generally good, and as indicated below the sportsman can usually rely upon finding the best local assistance at his hotel.

Except in the cities, there is a wide gap between these large and almost palatial establishments and the humble boarding-houses and private hotels. The gap is disappearing, but it is there ; meanwhile, it must be said of the smaller establishments that they compare very favourably indeed with places of similar size in England, particularly in point of cleanliness. The majority of these smaller hotels do not provide evening dinner, but offer instead a high tea with fish or eggs, etc.

Elsewhere in this book we mention the principal hotels and add the number of bedrooms at each establishment. When touring it is difficult to be sure where one may be at a given time, but for an extended stay it is always advisable to book well in advance.

SPORT.

Superlatives are apt to defeat their own object, but it may fairly be stated that Scotland is as nearly a sportsman's paradise as any part of Europe. Every burn, river and loch yields trout ; the salmon fishing is famous, and those who prefer sea-fishing have a wide choice of centres and styles. A considerable amount of the stream and loch fishing is entirely free ; much more is in the hands of the hotel-keepers, who (freely or at a nominal rate) provide boats, men and advice for their guests. Other waters, again, are either private or are kept exclusive by the very high rents charged for fishing. It is always advisable to inquire as to possible restrictions before beginning to fish.

References to the fishing from various centres will be found in our descriptive notes on other pages of this book ; but in many cases it would obviously be misleading to include precise details in a volume of this character. Among other handy books of reference is *Scotland for Fishing*, issued annually by the Scottish Tourist Board. The trout-fishing season in Scotland is from March 15 to October 6 (both dates inclusive). Salmon fishing (rod) generally is open February 11 to October 31, but begins and closes earlier or later on several rivers and lochs.

Many of the hotels also provide shooting for their guests, but some of the best shootings are now let to small syndicates, membership including residence at a shooting lodge. Shootings, whether for grouse or for deer-stalking, are frequently advertised in the daily and other papers, or inquiries could be made from an hotel-keeper, for in many areas the hotel-keeper is the sportsman's best friend.

Golf established itself as the national game as early as the fourteenth century, and it soon obtained such a hold upon Scotsmen that it became necessary to suppress golf by law in order that proper attention might be paid to archery, which at that time was a matter of some national importance. But the game was not to be denied, and in the fifteenth century we find a Bishop of St. Andrews concerned in a Royal Charter which enabled the inhabitants of St. Andrews to play golf for all time on their common links.

It is a far cry indeed from the St. Andrews of those days to the Gleneagles of our own, and all that the transition implies, but Scotsmen have retained their enthusiasm for the game, and have sent missionaries into all parts, so that now the influence of St. Andrews is felt all over the world. Every village, hamlet and town in Scotland boasts a course of some kind, and the visiting golfer is not likely to experience difficulty in getting a game.

Among other sports, bowls and tennis have made great

strides in Scotland of late, and at all the larger centres will be found public or semi-public courts and greens. Highland and Lowland hills and moors are ideal for hiking and pony-trekking, as are the many lochs and bays for boating and water-ski-ing.

In recent years attention has been directed to the facilities in Scotland for Winter Sports. Skating and curling have of course for very many years been national pastimes (Scotland, indeed, may claim to be the home of curling) and in most winters there is very little difficulty in securing suitable ice, most of the large towns having one or more clubs with their private ponds.

For thoroughly experienced skiers also Scotland can provide some good sport from about the end of January, but those accustomed to the thick blanket of soft snow to be found in Switzerland and Norway at this season must not expect anything of the kind in Scotland, and it is often dangerous for beginners to attempt ski-ing in such conditions. Weather-reports and statements regarding the depth and condition of snow are published in the press, at railway stations and broadcast by the B.B.C.

The Highland Gatherings.

A unique feature of the Scottish season is the series of " Gatherings " or " Games," many of which have a world-wide celebrity. At these gatherings one sees the Scot in all the pride of kilt and tartan ; the pipes are heard from morn till eve and the national dances take a prominent part in the programme. The sporting events include tossing the caber—the stem of a fir tree—putting the weight and other feats requiring not only strength but skill for their proper performance. Sheep-dog trials are also a feature of the season.

The " Games " season extends from June to September, and includes the Braemar Gathering—usually attended by Royalty—in September, like the Argyllshire Highland (Oban) ; Fort William in July ; Cowal Games (Dunoon) and those at Edinburgh (during Festival time) in August. Skye Week is late in May.

CYCLING.

The ubiquity of the bicycle in Scotland is such that cyclists might well be referred merely to the accompanying notes on motoring and walking. Certainly the motor tour on pp. 13–15 displays to best advantage all that is best in Scotland, and as for the walking routes, one encounters bicycles on the most unlikely tracks, though it is not always clear that they are being used for cycling. There are good walkers who consider that the tramp over the Corrieyairack from Laggan to Fort Augustus is a very full day, even when unhampered by heavy rucksacks, and yet each season one meets an increasing number of cyclists, pushing or carrying their machines over the rough places which form such a high proportion of the whole route; and cycles have even been taken through the boggy path between Rannoch and Glencoe.

Much depends upon the standard set, but if good riding over good roads through beautiful scenery is required, then Scotland is a cyclist's Paradise. Except on the wild north-west coast (where one learns anew the meaning of "off the beaten track") the hills are for the most part long and well graded and capable of being ridden by any good cyclist unhampered by a headwind. The cyclist, too, can use many of the ferries which are not big enough to carry cars, and in various other ways he has a greater freedom. He can penetrate into many parts of Western Scotland that are inaccessible to the motorist, and can explore quite a number of islands on which no car has yet been landed. And for those who prefer country that has responded more closely to the influence of progress, we would remark that much of the Lowlands is still unexplored country for the tourist.

WALKING.

With the exceptions of the alternative route up Ben Nevis and the ascents of the Coolins in Skye, all the routes described in this book are available for walkers of ordinary capacity, but some of them provide a very long day's march and the going is often terribly rough. The map, for instance, gives no indication of the chaotic condition of the Larig Ghru Pass through the Cairngorms, and the tramp over the Corrieyairack Pass will give one increased respect for the army of Bonnie Prince Charlie, which marched this way from Fort William to Dalwhinnie in two days.

Boots should be nailed—rubber soles are apt to be treacherous on wet rock or on grass. Carry a reliable compass and in reading the map do not attend only to details of route but study the conformation of the ground over which you pass—such information may be invaluable in helping you to "feel" your way down in case of mist. Also in case of mist or other causes of delay, it is always well to carry an emergency ration—such as a good slab of chocolate—and to *reserve it* at least until one is definitely on a beaten track.

Midges, clegs and other winged pests are apt to prove a trial and it is well to carry a repellent such as that recommended by the Scottish Tourist Board.

For many reasons, June is the best month for walking in Scotland. Later in the year routes are apt to be restricted by grouse-shooting, deer-stalking, and similar sports. Against these restrictions the Scottish Rights-of-Way Society have fought with much success, and their signpost is a familiar and welcome feature, but strangers should note that the right on such routes is confined to the actual paths and does not assume leave to wander at will.

Walkers will find the hostels of the *Scottish Youth Hostels Association* of great service. There are now nearly 100 hostels in the Lowlands and Highlands, particulars of which are given in the Annual Handbook of the Association (7 Glebe Crescent, Stirling).

Most of the routes in general use are indicated elsewhere in this volume, but for the benefit of those desirous of seeing the best of Scotland afoot we outline :

A Walking Tour in Scotland.

The following tour is divided into daily walks of about 8–12 hours, according to difficulty of country. The general direction takes one from the pretty, wooded hill country around Loch Lomond and the Trossachs by rugged Glen Lyon and barer Glen Tilt to Braemar, among the Cairngorms. The excursion over Lochnagar shows some magnificent rock-precipices, and the tramp over the Larig Ghru Pass, below Ben Macdhui, is rugged and grand—and rough going over the Pass.

From near Laggan Bridge the long and desolate Corrieyairack Pass crosses to Fort Augustus, and if the scenery onward is on a less impressive scale, the mountainous country west of the Great Glen is unmatched for its wildness, which is in many places enhanced by contrast with lovely wooded glens which are at least equal to the over-run Trossachs.

The Coolin Mountains in Skye offer some of the roughest

walking—and the finest mountain scenery—in Europe. From the ferry at Kyle of Lochalsh there is a grand route by Glen Affric, Struy and Kilmorack to Inverness; but if time allows it is worth while exploring the rough and wild road running up the north-west coast.

Those setting out on a walking tour from Glasgow should ride to Balloch, on Loch Lomond, and thence from Balmaha or Inversnaid walk (as indicated on other pages, *see* Index) to the Trossachs and so to Callander.

Callander to Killin by Lochearnhead.

Killin by Ben Lawers to Glen Lyon (magnificent scenery) and on by Fortingall to Loch Tummel and Pitlochry. (A longish day, but easy going most of the way.)

From Pitlochry through Killiecrankie Pass and then by Glen Tilt to Braemar. Another long day; ride as far as Blair Atholl is recommended.

Motor down Deeside from Braemar past Balmoral to Ballater and return on foot over Lochnagar to Braemar.

Over the Larig Ghru Pass from Braemar to Aviemore.

Bus (or walk) up Speyside and to Laggan Bridge; thence walk over the Corrieyairack Pass to Fort Augustus.

From Invermoriston through Glen Moriston and Glen Shiel to Loch Duich and on by Dornie to Kyle of Lochalsh. Or alternatively from Invergarry through Glen Garry to Kinlochhourn and on by Arnisdale to Glenelg and Kyle of Lochalsh (by steamer) or to Broadford (by crossing the Kyle Rhea ferry).

Ferry to Skye. The parts most worth doing are the Coolins and the Quiraing, which is north of Portree. Each requires one full day at least.

Back by Kyle of Lochalsh Ferry to the mainland, then:

(*a*) By Glen Affric or Glen Cannich to Glen Affric Hotel, and next day continue by Struy and Kilmorack to Inverness; or

(*b*) Zigzag northward up the West coast. The region teems with beauty spots, such as Loch Torridon, Loch Maree, Gairloch, Gruinard Bay and Ullapool, with glorious scenery ahead. (Bus from Ullapool to Garve and rail to Inverness.)

From Inverness there is a good bracing walk, with fine sea views but few mountains, over Culloden Moor to Cawdor Castle (south of Nairn). It is best to do much of this by motor, and then strike southward to Ferness and go down the Findhorn Glen to Forres; or if accommodation can be obtained near Ferness, one can explore the finest part of the Findhorn Glen and then make southward to Grantown —a walk which gives magnificent views of the Cairngorms.

THE HISTORY OF SCOTLAND

By Professor J. D. MACKIE, M.C., M.A.

SCOTLAND in many ways is very like England. Both countries are contained, for the most part, in the same island. They use, for the most part, the same speech. They are far more akin in race than is usually recognized, for although the Anglo-Saxon stock predominates in England, both countries share in common a Norse strain, a " Celtic strain," and a well-marked strain which was in these islands before ever the Celtic speakers came. And both countries have had very much the same political development; in both there arose, out of contending tribes, a monarchy, whose growth was conditioned by the influence of successive waves of culture from the south—Christianity, Feudalism, the Renaissance, for example.

But, despite all this, Scotland and England are two quite distinct countries. Alongside the similarities, differences are to be noted, and these differences, operating down the ages, have meant that the collective experience of the people to the north of " The Border " has been different from that of the people to the south. Scottish nationality has developed as a thing apart from English nationality.

How has this come about? What are these differences which have made the collective experience, the nationality, of Scotland distinct from that of England?

Many explanations might with justice be given. The factors of race, of speech and of geography admittedly entered, though none of them would in itself account for the existing " Border." Geographically, the southern boundary of Scotland might have been the " Highland Line," the line of the " Firths " or even the Humber.

Yet a consideration of geography will go far to solve the problem. Scotland was more remote from the great world than was England, and the waves of culture which rolled in from the Continent reached the north of Britain only after long delay, and with diminished force. The early drifts of population, Roman imperialism, Anglo-Saxon invasion, feudalism—it was the same with them all. Each of these great movements had exhausted much of its power before it came to the land which is now called Scotland, and each met, as it moved north, an increasing resistance from the elements already in possession. Long before one wave had over-run the whole of Scotland, its successor was already pouring into England, and some of the waves never reached the north of Scotland at all.

What was the result ?

One might say that Scotland lagged behind England in her political development, that she became the home of lost causes. It would be fair to add that she retained much of value, and that the old causes, defended with virility, were not utterly lost. Defending them, Scottish nationality was born.

The spirit of nationality was emerging before Scotland was called to encounter the full force of the English attack. Already it had taken political expression in the form of a monarchy. This monarchy, strengthened by borrowings from the south, proved to be strong enough, if only just strong enough, to survive repeated assaults from the south, and by the very fact of survival was itself consolidated. Often defeated, the Scots managed to hold their own until accident of dynasty produced the Union of the Crowns in 1603. A Scottish king ascended the English throne, and Scotland, feeling that she entered the partnership, not as a bondswoman but as a sister, moved reluctantly, but inevitably, towards the Parliamentary Union of 1707. O that union, the outstanding merit was that Scotland, the smaller and the poorer of the contracting parties, was able to preserve her nationality ; and in spite of two centuries of union with England, Scotland maintains her nationality intact at the present day.

This is the history of Scotland in a nutshell. To give the details of the long development is impossible, but at least the various stages can be made clear.

The Beginnings.

Scotland has always been proud of her antiquity. When England alleged a descent from Brut, the mythical grandson of Æneas, Scotland replied by deriving the names "Gael" and "Scot," from the marriage between a Greek prince Gaythelos, and Scota, daughter to that Pharaoh who was drowned in the Red Sea. Save that they may enshrine some vague recollection of an old connection with the Mediterranean, these stories mean nothing.

The discoveries made in the cave of Inchnadamph in Sutherland show that man was in Scotland towards the close of the Ice Age. From the shell-mounds of Oronsay and the Oban caves it can be proved that Scotland was still inhabited during the long centuries during which the primitive "old-stone" (Paleolithic) culture gave place to the "new-stone" (Neolithic). In the Neolithic Age Scotland carried a fairly big population, as the numerous traces of settlements show. Part of this population, at least, had drifted in from the south—a short, dark, long-headed folk, who brought with them the habit of erecting great stone monuments which they had first practised in their Mediterranean home.

The Circles of Callernish in the Lewis, and the Ring of Brogar in the Orkneys, are not unworthy of comparison with Stonehenge itself.

Soon after the arrival of this Mediterranean race, another stream came in, this time from the Rhineland—a taller, broad-headed people who probably introduced the use of bronze. Much later the use of iron came in, perhaps with a people speaking some form of Celtic. Certainly about the year A.D. 100 there were in the south of Scotland people who spoke a language akin to modern Welsh. There is no need to assume that each wave of invaders exterminated the peoples whom it found. The evidence of archæology is that it did not. In the north we find the "dun," which in its latest development became the majestic "broch," a great stone tower; in the east-central area the "earth-house"; in the south and south-west the "hill-fort" and the "crannog," or artificial island. And all four types seem to have been occupied at the time when the Romans came to Scotland.

Certainly the people of the south-west Strathclyde were Britons. The names of the other peoples are variously given. The term "Pict," which has given rise to such controversies, was not used till A.D. 297, and then by an ill-informed Latin author. It is no more than a label on a closed box, and is best defined as a name given by foreigners to some of the inhabitants of Scotland between the third and the ninth centuries A.D.

The Visit of the Romans.

To the Romans Scotland was never more than a troublesome border state, part of which was sometimes held for the purpose of defending the province of Britain to the south. In A.D. 80 Agricola entered Scotland, and in 84 he routed the inhabitants at Mons Graupius, probably in the south of Perthshire or in Angus. Some of the forts he built were long maintained, and about the year 142 a wall of turf, on a stone foundation, was carried from the Firth of Forth to the Firth of Clyde. Garnished with 19 forts, this rampart was 39 miles long. It was built by legionaries, whose " distance-slabs "—records of the lengths of wall built by the various units—may be seen in the Hunterian Museum at Glasgow, but it was held by auxiliaries who came from many lands—Gauls, Belgians, Rhinelanders, Syrians and Thracians, whose business was rather to police the frontier than to wage aggressive war. But the Roman hold was weak. The wall was abandoned about 185 and thereafter Roman interference in Scotland was limited to punitive expeditions such as those of Severus (*c.* 210). Doubtless the contact with the great empire left some faint trace upon Scottish history, but it is essential to notice that Scotland, unlike England, felt hardly at all the shaping hand of Rome.

The Four Peoples.

With the departure of the Romans a curtain drops upon the history of Scotland, and when, about the middle of the sixth century, the scene reappears, four peoples may be distinguished.

The **Picts**, perhaps not even a single race, were as yet hardly a single nation. Apart from tribal distinctions there was a well-marked division into North Picts and South Picts.

The **Scots**, a Gaelic-speaking people who had been associated with the Picts in the attack on the waning power of Rome, had drifted across from Ireland in small numbers, and about 500 a definite colony was founded by Fergus Mac Erc and his brothers. The struggling kingdom of Dalriada which emerged was in constant danger from the Picts, and in 559 it was almost destroyed by Brude Mac Maelchon. In Strathclyde the **Britons** maintained their kingdom, in close relation with their kinsfolk in Cumbria and Wales, and with the Anglo-Saxon invasions a fourth element appeared when the Angle kingdom of Northumbria stretched north and embraced part of the Lothian, especially Berwickshire.

A United Scotland.

Out of these four discordant elements, two of them parts of groups which lay mainly outside the limits of modern Scotland, a united monarchy emerged. This was due to the co-operation of three factors—the common acceptance of Christianity, the Norse attacks, and the rise of the Scoto-Pictish monarchy to a position of dominance.

Ever since, about A.D. 400, Ninian founded his *Candida Casa* at Whithorn, Strathclyde, and possibly other parts of what is now "Scotland," had had a tincture of Christianity. About the middle of the sixth century St. Mungo or Kentigern was settled at Glasgow, and the victory of the Christian forces at the battle of Arthuret (573) made the position safe for the new religion. The Scots in Ireland had nominally been Christians ever since the day of St. Patrick, but Christianity took a firm hold in Dalriada only with the arrival of Columba (563). Of princely birth, eloquent and enthusiastic, Columba founded a community at Iona, and from this centre started a missionary enterprise which restored the waning fortunes of Dalriada and "converted" Pictland. His successors carried their banners into Northumbria, but there the Irish form of Christianity was met and routed by the Roman form at the Synod of Whitby (664). The victorious Church advanced into Scotland, and about 710 the Pictish king himself gave his adhesion.

What a common faith began, a common peril expedited. The Norse attacks were dangerous to Scotland, for they established in the Islands a power which was sometimes as great as that of the Scottish king. But on the other hand they furthered the process of union in two ways. They drove Scotland in upon herself and hammered the reduced area into one. They also disintegrated the kingdom of Northumbria, and removed, for centuries, the danger of an English conquest. The union of Scotland and Pictland under Kenneth Mac Alpin (843) provided a strong nucleus round which a vague national sentiment could rally. In 1018 Malcolm II beat the Northumbrians at Carham, and annexed Lothian; and the death of the last King of Strathclyde in the same year gave that country to his heir

Duncan, who was Malcolm's grandson. When Malcolm died in 1034 he handed a united Scotland to his successor. He was the first king to bear the title of King of Scotland; his successors were generally known as Kings of Scots.

The Development of the Monarchy.

The monarchy was at first very weak—the machinery was primitive, and the very rule of succession uncertain. For some time the throne had been held alternately by the Atholl and the Moray lines of the House of Alpin, and Malcolm had secured his grandson's succession only by violence. The slaying of Duncan by Macbeth (1040) was a vindication of the rights of Moray, and although Atholl recovered the crown with Malcolm Canmore's victory in 1057, Moray rebellions occurred sporadically until 1230. The great earls, it must be added, were also prone to rebel. The Norse, too, were a constant danger, and it was not until 1266, after the attack of the Norwegian King Haakon had been repulsed at Largs (1263), that Scotland secured the Hebrides in return for an annual tribute. The Orkneys and Shetlands remained Norse till 1472.

That the monarchy triumphed over all these difficulties was due in part to the help it obtained from England both directly and indirectly. There was much intermarriage between the royal houses; the Scottish kings came to hold land in England, and many English families were established in Scotland to become supporters of the Crown against uncertain "Celts."

From England also came the organization of the Anglo-Norman monarchy. The King's household was used for administrative work, and in the twelfth and thirteenth centuries, the land was divided into sheriffdoms, each with a royal castle (of a very simple kind) in its midst. The close relationship with England, however, inevitably led the stronger country to claim suzerainty over her weaker sister, and between the years 1174 and 1189, Scotland, owing to the capture of her king William the Lion (1165–1214) by the English, was compelled to acknowledge herself a vassal state. In 1189 Richard I sold Scotland her independence in order to get money for his crusade, but later English kings showed themselves very overbearing. Alexander II and Alexander III were married to English princesses as a matter of course, but a plain English nobleman was considered good enough for a Scots princess.

Scotland saw the danger, and both Alexander II and Alexander III married French brides *en secondes noces.*

The Struggle for Independence.

The death of Alexander III, thrown from his horse over the cliff near Kinghorn, gave to Edward I of England an opportunity after his own heart. He at once betrothed his son to the baby " Maid of Norway," the dead king's grand-daughter and heiress ; and when that project was ruined by the death of the little girl in the Orkneys on her way from Norway to Scotland (1290), he found a fresh means to his end in the quarrels of the thirteen " Competitors " who sought the Scottish crown. Appointed arbitrator, he coerced the claimants into acknowledging his suzerainty and, in 1292, selected as king John Balliol, whose claims were certainly the best according to feudal ideas. But he treated Balliol with a deliberate arrogance which drove the vassal king into revolt. In 1296 Edward suppressed the revolt and took the administration of Scotland into his own hands. He met, however, with a general resistance, in which plain William Wallace of Elderslie in Renfrewshire played a leading part. In 1297 Wallace and Andrew de Moray defeated the English at Stirling Bridge with great slaughter, but next year Edward himself came up and routed Wallace at Falkirk. In the next few years the English king steadily warred down the Scots who opposed him, and in 1305 Wallace was executed as a traitor, though he had never given allegiance to the oppressor.

Scotland, however, quickly found a new champion in Robert Bruce, grandson of one of the " Competitors." Bruce had met another hero of Scottish liberty, John Comyn, at Dumfries, possibly to concert rebellion, and, old hate having flared up, had slain him in the precincts of the church of the Grey Friars. Driven to desperation by this deed of blood, Bruce boldly assumed the crown, or rather the plain circlet of gold which alone was available, and after many defeats and escapes, gradually began to make headway. Whether or no he saw the celebrated spider, he certainly displayed a noble resolution, and he was fortunate in that the slack Edward II succeeded his father in 1307. The castles were steadily recovered—Edinburgh itself by a marvellous escalade in 1314—and in 1314 an English expedition to relieve the last stronghold of Stirling ended in the great Scottish victory of Bannockburn. By the Treaty of Northampton in 1328, Scotland gained formal recognition of her independence, and to her independence she clung, though David II (1329–71) came near to losing by folly all that his father had won by wisdom and manhood.

The Stewart Monarchy.

David II left no heirs, and the crown passed to his nephew Robert Stewart, son of Marjorie Bruce and Walter, sixth hereditary High Steward of Scotland. The House of Stewart held the throne until the death of Anne in 1714, but the reigns of the earlier kings were filled by an unceasing struggle against a baronage which had grown too strong in the English wars and which regarded the Stewart as little more than one of themselves. The quarrels of the nobles, and the efforts of the Crown to assert itself, provided some of the most dramatic incidents in Scottish history. The Battle of the Clans, thirty against thirty, at Perth (1396); the mysterious death of Rothesay in prison at Falkland (1402); the kidnapping of James I at sea by the English (1406); the murder of James I at Perth (1437); the death of James II, killed by a bursting gun at Roxburgh (1460); the hanging of James III's favourites at Lauder Bridge in the face of an English attack (1482), and that monarch's tragic end in the rout of Sauchieburn (1488)—all these things tell the same tale.

Conspicuous amongst the rivals to the royal power were two great houses, each able to count on English support—the "Black" Douglases of the Border, and the Macdonald chiefs who bore between 1350 and 1493 the proud title of "Lord of the Isles." Heroes of Otterburn (1388) and of many another struggle with the English, the Douglases became very arrogant, and only by brutal and dishonourable action were they suppressed. In 1440 the sixth earl was murdered in Edinburgh Castle by the regents of James II, and in 1452 the eighth earl was slain by the King's own hand in Stirling Castle, whither he had come under safe-conduct. Three years later the King made a grand attack upon the Douglas strongholds, which ended in the forfeiture and exile of the proud men of the "Bleeding Heart."

The attempt of the second Lord of the Isles to gain the earldom of Ross led to the battle of Harlaw in 1411, which saved Aberdeen from the sack; but it was not until 1476 that the Lords were compelled to surrender Ross, and not till 1493 was the Crown able to abolish the haughty title. This is significant. It was in the reign of James IV (1488–1513) that the Crown gained undisputed supremacy.

England versus France.

United by the strong hand of James IV, Scotland entered the arena of European politics. Ever since the day of John Balliol (1295) Scotland had maintained an "auld alliance" with France, and at the beginning of the sixteenth century France was encircled by a ring of enemies which included England. Almost inevitably therefore Scotland tended to become a battlefield where French and English influences contended. Cautious Henry VII married his daughter Margaret to the Scottish king, but Henry VIII displayed the old Plantagenet ambition, and James, somewhat against his own will, was led by French pressure into the disastrous adventure of Flodden (1513), where he was killed and most of the Scots nobles with him. During the minority of James V the balance swung this way and that between the French and English parties, but the Anglophil "Red" Douglases behaved so arrogantly that James, when he grew up, was entirely French in sympathies. He married Madeleine of France, and on her death Mary of Lorraine, and with them he espoused the cause of Rome as well as the cause of France; for by this time Henry VIII had achieved his remarkable Reformation, and the duel between England and France was merging into a war between the new and the old faiths.

Slain by the shame of the defeat at Solway Moss, James handed on to his baby daughter a most unhappy realm (1542). The long struggle went wearily on. In 1546 Cardinal Beaton, a courageous persecutor, was murdered by a handful of adventurers, who held the castle of St. Andrews against all Scotland until July, 1547, when the walls were beaten down by French guns, and the garrison, which by this time included John Knox, was taken off to row in the French galleys. A few weeks later the Scots were routed by Somerset at Pinkie, but the result of the English success was to drive Scotland entirely into the arms of France. Mary was sent to France for safety, and in 1558 she married the Dauphin; Scotland was governed almost as a French province between 1550 and 1560, Mary of Lorraine assuming the regency in 1554.

The Scottish Reformation.

February 29, 1528, is reckoned the birthday of the Scottish Reformation, for on that day the learned and well-born Patrick Hamilton was burned at St. Andrews ; but the movement was really the outcome of deep spiritual, social and economic causes. Its actual course was shaped by two political forces already noted—the quarrel of England with France and the quarrel between the nobles and the King. The nobles made common cause with the third estate against the King and the Church, and success came to them in 1560, when England sent effective aid and France did not. By the Treaty of Leith French troops evacuated Scotland, and the title of Elizabeth to the English throne was recognized. Immediately afterwards a hastily summoned Parliament abolished Roman Catholicism as the religion of Scotland.

The Title to the English Throne.

To most Catholics, the legitimate heir to the English throne was not Elizabeth, daughter of Anne Boleyn, but Mary Stewart, grand-daughter of Margaret Tudor ; and Mary herself, repudiating the arrangement made at Leith, spent her life in trying to make good her title. She had two alternative policies. She might come to terms with Elizabeth, abandoning her present claim in return for formal recognition of her right to succeed if Elizabeth left no heir ; or she might make herself champion of the Counter-Reformation which had already begun in Europe. She tried both courses.

Returned to Scotland as a fascinating widow of eighteen in 1561, her first thought was to placate her jealous cousin. She let the Protestant settlement stand, tolerated the admonitions of Knox, and endeavoured to marry to Elizabeth's pleasure. Elizabeth replied by delays and covert insolence. In 1565 Mary lost patience, married her Catholic cousin Darnley, himself possessed of a claim to the crown of England, and made overtures to Spain and other Catholic powers. Tragedies followed in quick succession —the murder of Secretary Rizzio almost in Mary's sight, by assassins introduced through her husband's bedroom ; the murder of Darnley at Kirk o' Field ; the hasty marriage with Bothwell, commonly regarded as the " first murderer " ; the collapse, imprisonment at Lochleven and forced abdication ; the escape and failure at Langside ; the flight to England. And in captivity in England Mary remained till in 1587 she was executed for complicity, probable but not proved, in the Babington plot.

Her son James VI, whose long minority was vexed by the bitter wars between "King's Men" and "Queen's Men," showed himself, when he grew up, equally resolute to obtain the English throne. Like Mary he bargained with both Catholics and Protestants, but in 1586 he came to terms with England at Berwick, and thereafter, despite much intrigue with Elizabeth's enemies, his policy was really fixed. He tolerated his mother's death (which he could not have prevented) ; he married a Protestant bride, Anne of Denmark ; he endured the rebukes of the ministers, until, with English support, he succeeded in breaking the power of the Kirk, even though Andrew Melville was its leader. In 1603 he had his reward. Elizabeth died at last, and he became, "King of Great Britain, France and Ireland."

Crown and Covenant.

The removal of the monarchy to England damaged the prestige of Scotland, but it increased the power of the Crown. Far in the south country, beyond the reach of kidnapping nobles and rebuking ministers, James was able to rule Scotland, as he boasted, with his pen. He used his new authority to complete the overthrow of the Kirk, making its government episcopal, and effecting some alterations in its ritual, though he was wise enough not to push things too far. His son, Charles I, himself tactless and advised by tactless Laud, soon succeeded in uniting all parties in the Church against his policy, and the **National Covenant** of 1638 was the expression of a universal opposition. Its signatories bound themselves to defend both King and Kirk, but the Kirk was to be Presbyterian. The "Bishops' Wars" which resulted (1639–40) ended in the defeat of the King, and proved the prelude of the Great Civil War in England between Charles and the Parliament. The opinion of Scotland was divided. The Covenanters sided with the Parliament, but they forced their allies to accept the **Solemn League and Covenant** (1643), enforcing upon all the British Isles a religious settlement which could only be Presbyterian. Montrose, on the other hand, abandoning the Covenant, rose for the King, and in 1644–5 won some astonishing victories before he was defeated at Philiphaugh. Charles was utterly beaten by 1646. But the Scots had no desire to get rid of their king; they only wanted him to be a Presbyterian, and at the end of 1647 made the compromise known as "The Engagement." This led only to the utter defeat of the Scots army by Cromwell and to the execution of the King. The Scottish reply was at once to acknowledge Charles II as King, and as the ruling party still adhered to the Covenant, the accommodating Charles came to Scotland as a "Covenanted King" in 1650. Cromwell's practical sword put a bloody end to that evil pretence in the battles of Dunbar and Worcester, and his gay majesty, after astounding escapes, went "on his travels again." Scotland, for her part, enjoyed eight years of humiliation and good government at the hands of the triumphant Cromwell, who forced a complete parliamentary union, and sweetened the bitter pill by a grant of free trade between the two countries. When, in 1660, the King came back to enjoy his own again, he remembered nothing of the Covenant save the coercion he had had to endure. Episcopacy was established by force, and the Covenanters, goaded into rebellion in 1666, became ever more bitter in their opposition. In 1679 Archbishop Sharp was brutally murdered at Magnus Muir near St. Andrews. The rebellion which followed was promptly suppressed at Bothwell Bridge, and the Covenanters suffered a persecution which became worse than ever when James II succeeded his brother in 1685.

The Union of the Parliaments.

This "Killing Time" produced an effect on Scotland which may be seen to-day, and in 1688 the resentment against James was so fierce that hardly a hand was raised to defend him when the English rejected him in favour of William of Orange. Gallant and ambitious John Graham of Claverhouse, "Bluidy Clavers," was true to his salt, and won a dashing victory at Killiecrankie in 1689, but he fell on the field, and the King's cause fell with him. But though Scotland followed England in accepting William, the son of one Stewart princess and the husband of another, she did so without undue enthusiasm, and she took the opportunity not only to restore Presbyterianism, but to establish for the first time Parliamentary government. This achieved, it became plain that a mere personal union of the crowns would no longer suffice. William's policy of constant enmity to France meant that some Scots money and much Scots blood was spent in a quarrel against Scotland's oldest ally, and while Scottish trade suffered in consequence, the English were careful to exclude Scotsmen from any share in their own Colonial commerce. Worse still, William as King of England helped to suppress the "Company trading to Africa and the Indies" whose best-known venture was the "Darien Scheme," which as King of Scotland he had actually legalized (1695), and the venture ended in utter ruin (1698–1700). Public opinion, already aroused by the "Massacre of Glencoe" (1692), was thoroughly inflamed. There was nothing for it but a more complete union or a complete severance. Chance provided the solution.

William and Mary left no heir, and it was clear that Anne would leave none either. Scotland made it plain that she would not accept the Hanoverian succession already adopted by England unless the conditions of Union were revised. The result was the Act of Union of 1707, whereby Scotland, accepting a somewhat inadequate representation in a British Parliament to sit at Westminster, kept her Church and her legal system, and was given a share in the splendid commerce of England and her colonial empire. "There's ane end o' ane auld sang," said Chancellor Seafield when the "Honours of Scotland" —the crown, sceptre and sword—were borne for the last time from the Parliament House in Edinburgh.

The Jacobite Risings.

Economic prosperity did not at once follow the grant of free trade with England, and the obvious disregard of Scottish affairs by English statesmen was another cause of discontent. This discontent showed itself in the "Malt Riots" in Glasgow in 1725, and in the Porteous affair in 1736, but its main expression may be seen in the Jacobite risings. "The 'Fifteen" promised well, but it came to nothing because Louis XIV, dying in bankruptcy, could send no real aid, and because the "Old Pretender" was an uninspiring leader. The one action of importance was at Sheriffmuir, and that was indecisive. A landing of Spanish troops near Glenshiel in 1719 did not accomplish anything, and did not deserve success, being only a sidewind of ambitious Spanish policy. "The 'Forty-Five," on the other hand, had more success than it deserved, since the Young Pretender, " Prince Charlie," produced it by his own rashness and personal charm in the face of the universal opposition of his supporters. France could send no troops for the moment ; the Highland chiefs were most reluctant to call out their men ; the Lowland Jacobites were most unwilling to rise. The action was dramatic ; victory at Prestonpans, occupation of Edinburgh, advance to Derby, retreat, success at Falkirk and ruin at Culloden. The Prince, after desperate adventures in the Highlands and Islands, at length escaped to France, and later to other adventures less reputable (d. at Rome 1788). Scotland remained to pay the penalty. The nobles lost their hereditary jurisdictions ; the Highlands were ruthlessly policed ; the wearing of the kilt was forbidden (till 1782). The hanging of James of the Glens (*see* R. L. Stevenson's *Catriona*) is a commentary on the justice of the government. It seemed as if even the echo of the " auld sang " was dead. This was not so.

Modern Scotland.

After the failure of the Jacobite attempts, the development of Scotland was more in line with that of England. Economic prosperity came with the increase of the American trade, and with the so-called Industrial Revolution. With England, Scotland advanced along the path of political reform, and the ardent spirit of her people expressed itself in ecclesiastical controversies—neither dull nor foolish—and in military service under the Hanoverian king. The Lowland regiments were already old in the British service, and the Black Watch had fought at Fontenoy before the outbreak of " The 'Forty-Five." But it is worth noting that when Wolfe took Quebec in 1759, one third of the British casualties were borne by Fraser's Highlanders, a regiment recruited from an old Jacobite stronghold. During the Napoleonic wars, fresh Highland regiments were created, and in the wars and the adventures which created the British Empire of to-day, Scotsmen have played no mean part.

Though now a part of the United Kingdom, Scotland is still keenly conscious of her own individuality, hopeful of her future and proud of her past. The National War Memorial in Edinburgh Castle is not only a monument to the brave dead ; it is the expression of a living spirit.

GEOLOGY AND SCENERY.

By T. M. FINLAY, M.A., D.Sc., F.R.S.E.

A STUDY of the map of Scotland shows that topographically the country is divided into three distinct regions, the Scottish Highlands, the Southern Uplands, and the broad Midland Valley which lies between. Towards an understanding of the origin of these features and of the scenery to which they give rise a brief account of the geological history of the country may be helpful.

The Highland area is, for the most part, occupied by metamorphic rocks, rocks primarily of igneous or sedimentary origin which have been so subjected to pressure and heat, so folded, fractured, sheared and crushed, that it is impossible in many cases to tell what they were originally. They have been thoroughly reconstructed; the granite, sandstone or clay has become the gneiss, quartzite or schist respectively. Three divisions are recognized, the Lewisian Gneiss of the North-west Highlands and the Outer Isles, the Moine Series of the Central Highlands, and the Dalradian Series of the Eastern Highlands.

The oldest rocks in Scotland, the foundation on which the later superstructure has been erected, are the Lewisian, sometimes spoken of as the Fundamental Complex. The series includes gneisses and schists, the metamorphosed representatives of ancient granite rocks, or of fragments of the cover into which they were intruded. Since their formation they have been subjected to earth pressures time and again; they have been repeatedly invaded by igneous rocks, and the result is a tough, grey, durable gneiss, the "Old Boy" of Scottish geologists.

The scenery to which this ancient rock gives rise is likewise characteristic. It nowhere rises into a hill of any considerable height, but presents a monotonous landscape of grey rock, now rising through the heather in rounded hummocky knolls, now sinking into hollows occupied by lochans. Without doubt this smoothness of contour as well as the freshness of the exposed rock is a legacy of the Ice Age, but for its monotonous uniformity another explanation must be supplied.

In striking contrast to the grey gneiss on which they rest, the red hills of Torridonian Sandstone rise above, and seem to dominate the Lewisian plain. They are mere remnants of erosion, but they tell how the present Lewisian fragments formed part of a more extensive land, of how this was carved by erosion into mountain and valley, and worn down to an irregular plain. Submergence followed and the old land surface was buried under at least 10,000 feet of strata, the Torridonian Series. These were in turn elevated, and have been largely stripped off, and with their removal this primeval landscape is once more exposed to view.

The Torridonian strata are mainly red sandstones, and they still lie in practically horizontal beds. The pyramidal hills into which they have been carved add a needed touch of form and colour to the gneissic landscape. Some like An Stac and Suilven are crumbling rapidly in ruins, others like Coul More or Slioch are more resistant, but in every case their form and architecture make them striking features of the landscape. They rise tier on tier of massive sandstones, carved by erosion into mural precipices, receding along joint-planes into gullies and chimneys, or projecting into craggy bastions.

With the Torridonian uplift, the movements which affected this ancient land were not yet at an end. Capping many of the Torridon hills and sometimes resting directly on the gneiss is a white quartzite which yields readily under weathering, littering the hill-tops with screes of angular fragments. From a distance these screes gleam in the sunshine, and seem to envelop the summits in a mantle of snow. This quartzite is the lowest member of the Cambrian formation. The Torridonian sandstones had been upheaved, and partially stripped off, when the area was once more submerged beneath the waters of the Cambrian sea, and a series of sandstones, shales, and limestones deposited, of which in spite of subsequent elevation and erosion, 2,000 feet still remain. Three successive land surfaces are thus evident in the north-west, the surfaces of Lewisian and Torridonian times and that of the present. Such mountains as Ben Arkle, Ben Eighe, Quinaig, Ben

More, Assynt and Liathach are especially notable in this respect.

One more chapter of geological change in the north-west has yet to be added. The normal upward succession is Lewisian, Torridonian, Cambrian. Sometimes however Torridonian, Moinean, or even Lewisian may be found resting on Cambrian, the youngest member of the succession. This apparent inversion presented a problem which long baffled solution until it was shown conclusively to be due to a series of gigantic overthrusts whereby great sheets of strata had been torn from their native beds, and pushed bodily westwards for a distance of at least ten miles, over-riding and surmounting the unmoved strata to the west. Such overthrusts where folded strata snap under powerful pressures are to be found in all mountain ranges, notably in the Alps, and their early recognition in the North-west Highlands makes this classic ground. The best localities for examples of these thrusts are the cliff of the Knockan, and the Stack of Glencoul (Moines on Cambrian), Ben Liath Mhor (Torridonian on Cambrian), and Loch Glencoul (Lewisian on Cambrian).

The Origin of the Highlands.

The traveller who climbs the winding path that leads to the summit of Ben Nevis is well rewarded for his labour in the magnificent panorama that lies spread around him. Ranging into the distance ridge follows ridge and peak succeeds peak, with " many a darksome glen and gleaming loch," the wide sweep of the Highlands, " a tumbled sea of hills." But if he should be so unfortunate as to make the climb when the valleys are filled with mist, with the dark hill-tops peeping through their filmy shroud, then is he doubly rewarded, for the origin of the Highland hills is made clear. All these peaks are seen to rise to the same general level, so that if the straths and glens were infilled, the surface would be that of an elevated plain, highest in the west, and sloping gently towards the east. Out of this plain has been carved the varied form of hill and strath and glen ; the Highlands are the remnants of a dissected plateau.

In this landscape the most arresting physical feature is the hollow of Glen More—the Great Glen—with its chain of lakes ; a great cleft which runs from the Linnhe Loch north-eastwards to the Moray Firth and which provides the route of the Caledonian Canal. It lies along a line of fault, the extent of which is still unknown ; of great antiquity, movement along it has not yet ceased, and earthquake shocks occasionally occur. By it the Highlands are cut in two and a marked effect is produced upon the drainage system. Prior to its initiation the rivers flowed eastwards in response to the slope of the ground, as consequent streams. West of the Great Glen they still do so without any regard to the underlying geological structure, the main lines of which run N.E.–S.W. They must therefore have begun to dig their valleys before the present structural folds were impressed upon the rocks, or at least before they were exposed at the surface, and the trend of their valleys shows the remarkable persistence of a river when it has once entrenched itself. East of the glen the faulting has diverted the drainage so that the rivers flow north-east, more in accordance with the underlying structure.

Ben Nevis.

Turning now to his immediate surroundings, let the traveller observe the mountain on which he stands. The summit of Ben Nevis is composed of volcanic rocks, lava-flows erupted as long ago as Old Red Sandstone times, and they rest on schists, a fragment of the old land surface over which they flowed. It is to be noted that the lavas are ringed round on every side by granite. The explanation of this structure reveals an interesting phenomenon in the mechanics of igneous intrusion. The molten rock may burst its way to the surface, and give rise to a volcano ; or it may simply uparch the overlying cover, and, occupying the cavity, cool quietly *in situ*. In this instance, however, the pressure exerted by the uprising liquid has rent the overlying roof, and a sinking block has forced the molten rock up along its margins to form the granite rings. Erosion has once more exposed the sunken roof, and the tough lavas, more durable than the granite, now tower above it and give rise to the mural precipices which form the northern aspect of the mountain.

The above phenomenon is termed a " cauldron subsidence," and a second example may be cited, that of the Glencoe region. Glencoe has a sinister reputation in Scottish history, and to the wayfarer it may present itself in sinister garb, its darksome corries and gloomy recesses veiled in mist. To the lover of scenery in its wilder aspects Glencoe makes a strong appeal. The glen itself is a relic of the time when the rivers flowed east before the formation of the Great Glen Fault, but widened and deepened by glacier action. Above it tower grand mountains, Aonach Eagach on the one hand, on the other the "Three Sisters of Glencoe," and Buachaille Etive Mhor, the "Herdsman of Etive." These hills are built up of lava flows contemporaneous with those of Ben Nevis. They rest on and are almost entirely surrounded by schists. They have been preserved through a cauldron subsidence, the sinking of an elliptical block 9 miles long by 5 wide. The lavas which once surrounded the cauldron, and a portion of the softer schists underlying them, have been planed away, and the resurrected fragment carved into its present form.

The Cairngorms.

Turning eastwards from Ben Nevis, the eye dwells on the Cairngorm massif. The best viewpoint for this group of mountains is from the north or north-west; from the south they fail to impress. From Aviemore (*see* the panorama on pp. 328–9) their structure is apparent—an extensive plateau with a slight eastward slope, cleft in two by the through pass of the Larig Ghru, and dissected by valleys into the six Cairngorms. Farther to the south-east rises the mass of dark Lochnagar.

The plateau origin of these mountains is shown by their uniformity of height (all in the neighbourhood of 4,000 feet), and by their level summits, littered with granite debris. For the Cairngorms are of granite, one of several masses in the Eastern Highlands now exposed through the removal of the thick cover into which they were injected. They show the varied forms of mountain scenery to which granite from its jointing and composition lends itself, but in these northern regions it is the evidence of glacial erosion that impresses most. Braeriach and Lochnagar possess magnificent corrie basins; there are glacial lakes, moraine-dammed like Loch Callater, or resting in over-deepened valleys like Loch Avon or Loch Muick, while the scree-littered hill-sides bear evidence to the shattering action of frost.

The Southern Uplands.

The scenery of the Southern Uplands is of a different order. To one fresh from the rugged grandeur of the Highlands, they bring a sense of quiet restfulness and peace. Their dearth of lakes, their treelessness, the smoothness of their grassy slopes, broken here and there by scaur or ravine, their level summits, are in strong contrast to the Highlands; only in the west do the granite hills of Galloway recall some of the features of Highland scenery, and these are the parts least visited. It is at certain seasons of the year when they are ablaze with colour that they present their most attractive aspect. To this must be added the charm of romance, enshrined as they are in song and story.

The Midland Valley.

The Midland Valley of Scotland is a wide tract of country faulted down against the Highlands on the one side and the Southern Uplands on the other. The somewhat abrupt front of the Southern Uplands forms one fault scarp, another rises north of the valley of the Forth in the steep face of the Ochils, while to the north the fertile vale of Strathmore ends sharply against the Highland Boundary Fault. As occasional earthquake shocks show, this fault is still in progress of adjustment. The faulted territory consists of strata ranging in age from Silurian to Permian; it contains the seams of coal which have made this the industrial belt of Scotland. Composed mainly of softer sediments giving rise to a low gently-rolling plain, such scenic features as it possesses are all due to the presence of igneous rocks. The Pentland Hills are mainly Old Red lavas ridged up and denuded till their core of Silurian rocks has been exposed; so also is the long line of the Ochils and Sidlaws, cut through by the valley of the Tay. Such relict volcanoes as Arthur's Seat, the Binn Hill, Largo Law and North Berwick Law, to name but a few, bring vividly before the mind a time when the valley of the Forth was girdled with fire, pouring forth the lavas that went to form King Alexander's Crag, Inchkeith, the hills of Stirlingshire and the Lothians, or injecting the sills and dykes that now rise as prominent crags above the surrounding plain. Such features are eloquent of the power of vulcanism in creating scenery and of long-continued erosion in modifying it.

The Western Isles.

Passing now to the Western Isles we see vulcanicity once more active in landscape formation. Unhappily fragments only of its work remain, but they include the finest scenic fragments to be found in Scotland. No one can know Scotland who has not explored Arran or the Coolins, or wandered over what were once lava wastes in Mull, Staffa, or Skye. These lavas, the "Plateau Basalts," were erupted in Tertiary times during the latest period of vulcanism to which these islands have been subjected. Sheet after sheet of molten rock issued forth, flowing far and wide, burying and preserving beneath it fragments of Mesozoic strata, elsewhere destroyed. In some cases sufficient time elapsed between successive flows for the formation of a soil and the growth of vegetation, the remains of which, preserved beneath a subsequent flow, have helped to fix its age. Most of that ancient land has disappeared through subsidence or erosion, but in what remains the scenic features due to the basalts are well displayed. In the west of Skye they rise tier on tier, to form cliffs upwards of 1,000 feet high, sometimes forming a level capping to a hill (Macleod's Tables), or cleft by erosion into isolated spires and pinnacles (Old Man of Storr, Macleod's Maidens). The regular jointing assumed by the central part of each flow during cooling is everywhere apparent, but is best seen in the caves and cliffs of Staffa.

As to the origin of the plateau basalts there are two theories. According to Judd they were emitted from central volcanoes. Sir Archibald Geikie, from his knowledge of the plateau basalts of the western United States, referred them to fissure eruptions, the quiet upwelling of lava from lengthy fissures formed in the earth's crust; and in the multitude of dykes ("dyke swarms"), which cut the region, he saw the sources of these lavas. Both theories are possible, but the tendency is to return to Judd's original conception, and to regard the "ring complexes" of Arran, Mull, Rhum, Ardnamurchan, and Skye as the basal wrecks of volcanoes from which the lavas flowed.

For geology and scenery combined, Arran has long been noted. Within its small compass are compressed representatives of all the geological formations in Scotland from the Dalradian to the Cretaceous. Through these the granite mass of the north was intruded, rising above, and dominating the landscape. The island has been riddled with dykes and injected with sills of various igneous rocks, dolerites, porphyries, and the pitchstones for which Arran is famous. Out of this complexity of rocks erosion has carved a varied series of scenic features, of granite peak and ridge, of mountain corrie and glen, of rock scarp and waterfall.

Arran possesses two examples of "ring complexes," the granite intrusion of Goatfell, and the so-called "vent" lying to the south of it. Such structures may be summed up as consisting of one or more injections of molten rock, presumably round the margin of a sinking block (cauldron subsidence), since their outcrops when exposed at the surface are ring-shaped or arcuate. Such intrusions necessarily imply strains and tensions in the surrounding country rock, and they are accompanied by a vast number of sheets and dykes intruded along lines of weakness thus developed. They may even have reached the surface, and appeared as lava flows, but owing to subsequent erosion such evidence has almost everywhere been destroyed. The Arran intrusion consists of an outer ring surrounding a central core, but in the examples exhaustively examined, those of Mull and Ardnamurchan, a shifting of the focus of intrusion has been noted, with a wide variation in the nature of the rocks successively intruded.

Skye.

In Skye the structure of its chief scenic feature, the Coolins, suggests a "ring complex" but this has yet to be proved. The region is unique in the attractions it offers to the mountaineer, the geologist, the artist, or the mere lover of nature. In an area 6 miles across are contained no fewer than fifteen peaks exceeding 3,000 feet in height, with numerous lesser hills, none of which deserves the epithet bestowed by Ruskin of "inferior." So varied is their scenery according to the geological structure and so variable from day to day and from season to season that the hills of Skye have become the Mecca of all true mountain-lovers. The two types of hills, the gabbroic and the granitic, the Black Coolins and the Red Hills, stand out in strong contrast. Marsco and Glamaig, of granite, are conical in shape with smooth outlines and scree-covered slopes; the sweeping arc of the Coolins presents a serried array of peak and pinnacle, of ridge and gully, of corrie and rock-basin, of bare, black rock and scree-covered slope. The contrast is intensified by light and shade from hour to hour. In the soft light of a summer's evening the Red Hills lie bathed in the warm rays of the sinking sun while the Coolins stand out grim and forbidding, their corries shadowed in darkness, their deep lochans like pools of ink. In winter they seem even more forbidding, their craggy summits seen for a moment through the swirling mists; yet in winter they attain their greatest beauty, their blackness veiled, their scars hidden beneath a soft canopy of snow.

The final chapter in this brief review of the origin of Scottish scenery opens with the Ice Age. During that period when north-western Europe was buried under ice, the high grounds of Scotland nourished their individual icefields from which ice moved outwards in all directions, until by the union of neighbouring streams it was directed along certain defined channels, reaching as far south as the Thames valley and moving westwards into the Atlantic as an unbroken wall of ice. Since the highest hills are glaciated almost to their summits, the total thickness of this sheet (taking the depths of the valleys and fiords into account), cannot have been far short of 5,000 feet. The passage of this huge rasp produced great changes in the landscape, the extent of which may be gauged if we form a mental picture of Scotland in pre-glacial times. The solid rock was capped with weathered debris probably to a considerable depth, the ruggedness of the uplands was intensified by crag and tor and scree-covered slope, the smoothness of the valleys accentuated by down-wash from the hills. Lakes, ever evanescent features of the landscape, were absent, their sites occupied by alluvial flats or marshes. Contrast with this the present topography of Scotland. The smooth, flowing outlines of the hills; the rounded, hummocky knolls (*roches moutonnées*), still bearing on their polished surfaces the scratches and grooves made by the ice; the over-deepened U-shaped valleys, the multitude of lakes, some resting in rock-basins scooped out by the passing glacier, others still dammed behind morainic ramparts, yet others resting black and sullen, in deep hollows beneath corrie walls; the huge erratics, often carried many miles; the sheets and mounds of boulder-clay; these among other features everywhere meet the observant eye, and bear witness to the transforming power of ice. For ice is the instrument that rounds off the work, rather than the chisel that creates it. Its finer touches are fast being removed, and the land is returning to its pre-glacial condition.

Since the disappearance of the ice, the unstable character of the earth's crust has been emphasized in certain Scottish areas. Up the eastern and western coasts there are "raised beaches" which indicate successive uplifts of the land to a height of 100 feet or more. These may be represented by a rock shelf, a shingly slope, or a rock cliff hollowed by the waves when the land stood at a lower level. In the Orkneys and Shetlands, and in the Outer Isles, there is as strong evidence for subsidence. Narrow valleys floored with peat are being invaded by the sea, sounds are widening, and even buildings are disappearing. While uplift may in part be due to crustal rebound on the removal of its load of ice, there is evidence of a warping movement, involving Scotland and Scandinavia in upheaval, while the intervening area is being depressed.

BERWICK-UPON-TWEED TO EDINBURGH.

THROUGHOUT this, the final stage of the East Coast Route to Edinburgh, the railway keeps the road close company, throwing out a branch to North Berwick from Drem.

BERWICK-UPON-TWEED.

Distances.—Edinburgh, 58 m.; Dunbar, 30 m.; Newcastle, 63 m.; London, 336 m.; Kelso, 24 m.
Car Parking Places.—Castlegate, Parade, Bridge Street and Walkergate.
Early Closing.—Thursday.
Hotels.—*King's Arms, Castle, Old Hen and Chickens, Salmon, Waterloo, Turret, Villa, Tweed View*, etc.
Sports.—Bowls, tennis, bathing, boating, golf. Good fishing for brown and sea trout in Tweed and Whiteadder.

Geographically speaking, the crossing of the Tweed at Berwick should take one from England into Scotland or vice versa. Actually, although it stands on the north side of the Tweed, Berwick is accounted part of England (itself a county, it is included for administrative purposes in Northumberland), and at one time it held an even more anomalous position, since it claimed to be neither in Scotland nor in England.

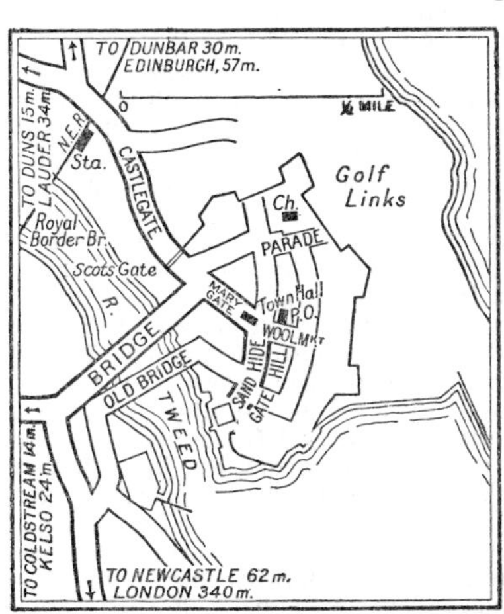

The town is spread over the western flank of the tongue of hilly land which turns the Tweed south in the last mile of its course to the sea. On the seaward side of the promontory are golf links, sands and bathing pool; the town itself looks down upon the river and bridges, and the military strength of its position in olden times, when it hung like a portcullis over the Great North Road, led to incessant sieges and changes of ownership. Of those days the principal memorials are the relics of the walls built by Edward I and those built to enclose a smaller area in Elizabeth I's time: the narrow Scotsgate which so sorely hampers traffic in mid-season is part of the Elizabethan defences. The most historic spot in Berwick—the Castle—was demolished to make way for the railway station, and in view of the Castle's bitter story one is inclined to wonder whether Stephenson had only the building of the railway in mind when he caused the words "The final act of union" to be inscribed over the station.

Certainly the history of the Castle tells of deeds best forgotten. With the town, the stronghold was burnt by the English during William the Lion's invasion of England in 1174, and subsequently formed part of his ransom. Henry II rebuilt the Castle; Richard Cœur de Lion sold it back to William the Lion and a few years later Richard's son John captured it anew, the town being burnt in the process. In 1292 Edward I from the Castle hall gave his decision concerning the rival claims of Bruce and Balliol to the Scottish throne, and four years later Balliol rebelled and held the Castle against the English. When Edward took and sacked Berwick, the Castle surrendered, though the garrison marched out with military honours, and there in 1306 he imprisoned the Countess of Buchan, for her offence in crowning Robert Bruce. Tradition asserts that the lady was hung in a cage outside the wall, but Edward's instructions make it plain that the cage was a device for solitary confinement inside a turret. The Castle was recaptured by Bruce in 1318, after the town had been taken in a brilliant night-attack by Douglas and Randolph. In 1333 Edward III, in a vain attempt to induce the governor, Sir Alexander Seton, to surrender, hanged his son Thomas, whom he held as hostage, within sight of the walls. The town and Castle were surrendered to him after the Scottish defeat at Halidon Hill. In 1461 Henry VI, a refugee in Scotland, gave up town and Castle to the Scots, but in 1482 they were regained, for Edward IV, by his brother Richard "Crookback," later Richard III. And Berwick remained a pillar of the English defences against Scotland till the Union of 1603, when these defences became unnecessary. Berwick later obtained a peculiar status as an independent town, belonging to neither country. This was its condition until the Reform Act of 1885, and until that time all Acts of Parliament, etc., contained the special allusion "and to our town of Berwick-upon-Tweed."

The Bridges of Berwick are interesting sentimentally and historically. The river-crossing here was responsible for the rise of the town and has been the cause of the greater part of its history down to the present day, when motors and vehicles of all kinds pour continuously across the two road bridges—the many-arched seventeenth-century bridge and the severely practical structure of reinforced concrete built in 1928—and trains rumble over the lofty viaduct.

The walk along the Elizabethan walls is most pleasant, and more or less extensive fragments of the earlier Edwardian fortifications also remain, but the glamour of Berwick the Border town is to be recaptured rather from a perusal of its history than by walking its streets. Of these the principal is the broad street known as Marygate, extending from the Scotsgate to the Town Hall. Eastward of Marygate lie the Parish Church, the Barracks and bastions ; on the other side various streets lead down to the riverside, whence one can walk round to the Pier.

Across the wide mouth of the river Tweed is **Spittal**, the borough's seaside suburb ; at the western end of the bridges is the more industrial suburb of **Tweedmouth**.

The salmon of Tweed are famous, and Berwick is a good centre both for the angler and for those interested in watching the proceedings of the net fishers.

Although Berwick has been deprived of its state of splendid isolation between England and Scotland, the County of the Borough and Town of Berwick-upon-Tweed is still an entity, and its landward boundary, running from sea to Tweed some 3 or 4 miles north and west of the centre of the town, still serves as the Anglo-Scottish border. The coast-road and the railway cross the Border by **Lamberton**, which once had a reputation among runaway couples akin to that of Gretna (*see* p. 83).

In a narrow valley running steeply to the sea a mile or so from Lamberton is the primitive fishing village of **Burnmouth**. Like the railway, the main road (A1) to Edinburgh keeps inland (by Ayton, Reston and Grantshouse) as far as Cockburnspath, missing a picturesque stretch of coast. A bus service from Burnmouth runs three miles north to the fishing port of **Eyemouth** (*Home Arms*), which has bathing, boating and golf among its holiday attractions. At one time the local alternative to herring-fishing was smuggling, and it has been said that the secret cellars and subterranean passages were so numerous that only a half of the town appeared above the surface, the other half being underground.

On again is **Coldingham** (*Anchor ; St. Veda's* (pte.) ; *St. Abb's Haven* (pte.)), a quiet village famed for the remains of a Norman Priory and frequented in summer on account of the allurements of Coldingham Sands.

Coldingham Priory was founded in 1098 as a Benedictine establishment on the site, it is said, of a nunnery founded some centuries earlier by that St. Ebba whose name is commemorated in that of the neighbouring St. Abb's Head. The site is a little east of the village cross. There is an isolated archway, but the most noteworthy remnants of this once extensive establishment are what now form the north and east walls of the parish church. The tragic episode concluding the second Canto of *Marmion* was suggested to Scott by the discovery, at Coldingham, of a female skeleton standing upright built into the wall. In bygone days apostate nuns were buried alive in this position.

St. Abb's Head is the most striking promontory on this coast, rising more than 300 feet above the sea. The Lighthouse, 224 feet above the waves, flashes every ten seconds and is visible 20 miles. Hardly less striking than this headland is the spot known as **Fast Castle,** 4 miles westward. Little remains of the Castle, which was built on a precipitous crag connected with the mainland by a narrow ridge. It must have been wellnigh impregnable : a miniature Dunnottar or Tintagel.

The road from Coldingham to **Cockburnspath** (colloquially " Co'path ") rejoins the main road shortly after passing above the charmingly wooded *Pease Dean* by a lofty bridge from which the stream can be heard but not seen as it rushes through the woods below. The main road winding across this eastern end of the Lammermuirs suggests the origin of the name Cockburnspath. A nearby ruined Tower is supposed to be all that is left of " Ravenswood Castle " in the *Bride of Lammermuir*, Fast Castle being the original of " Wolf's Crag."

Siccar Point, near Cockburnspath, is of interest to geologists as the site of Hutton's famous unconformity, where gently inclined Old Red Sandstone beds rest on the upturned edges of the Silurian.

From Cockburnspath to Dunbar the coast is seldom

out of sight. The tall white lighthouse at Barns Ness is away on the right; then on the left is the field where Leslie's men found themselves on the morning of September 3, 1650, a sight which, according to Bishop Burnet, moved Cromwell to cry, "The Lord hath delivered them into our hands!" The main road now bypasses Dunbar.

DUNBAR.

Amusements.—Cinema, dancing, motor tours, pony trekking, etc.
Caravan Sites.—Kirk Park; Winterfield.
Distances.—Berwick-on-Tweed, 30 m.; North Berwick, 10½ m.; Edinburgh, 28 m.
Early Closing.—Wednesday (except from May 16–Sept. 15).
Hotels.—*Bellevue* (43 rooms); *Roxburghe* (37 rooms); *Royal Mackintosh* (15 rooms); *Craig-en-Gelt* (23 rooms); *Bayswell* (15 rooms); *Golden Stones* (13 rooms); *St. George* (13 rooms); *Lothian* (16 rooms), etc.
Sports.—Bathing, open-air pool, boating, bowls, golf, tennis, sea-fishing.

Famed for centuries on account of its almost impregnable Castle, and afterwards as an agricultural and fishing centre, Dunbar is to-day highly regarded as a holiday resort. There are golf (two first-class courses), tennis, bathing, fishing, etc., and the inexhaustible attractions of the harbour. The chief feature of the long, wide street around which the town groups itself is the old Town House with its tower. The large building at the end of the street was originally a seat of the Lauderdale family; but is now used for civic and cultural purposes. From this wide street one turns off for the Harbour and the Castle ruins or for the modern promenade overlooking Bayswell Beach, with its boating lake and swimming pool.

Of the Castle—"built upon a chain of rocks stretching into the sea and having only one passage to the mainland, which was well fortified"—there are sufficient remains to kindle the imagination of those who know their Scottish history. Here Edward II, fleeing from Bannockburn, sheltered until a boat took him on to Berwick; here, in 1338, in the absence of her husband, the Earl of Dunbar, "Black Agnes" defied the Earl of Salisbury for nineteen weeks, until the siege was raised on the arrival of supplies by sea; here, too, Mary Queen of Scots sought sanctuary after the murder of Rizzio in 1565. Two years later she was brought there, willing or unwilling, by her abductor, Bothwell; a third time she returned, this time to prepare for the disastrous encounter on Carberry Hill. Not without reason, the Regent Moray ordered the dismantling of such a favourite refuge, and to-day only the crumbling red sandstone walls remain to tell of one of the most formidable strongholds in Scotland.

The direct road from Dunbar to Edinburgh runs *viâ* East Linton and Haddington. In the vicinity of **East Linton** (Sir John Rennie was born at Phantassie House, near the east end of the by-pass, in 1761) are *Preston Mill*, a charming seventeenth-century meal-mill (National Trust for Scotland), and **Hailes Castle** (*Open Summer 10–7, Sundays from 2 ; winter, closes at 4. fee*), once a stronghold of the Earl of Bothwell. On **Traprain Law,** a hill which assumes striking proportions when viewed from east or west, was discovered in 1919, along with other antiquities, a pit, 2 feet deep and 2 feet wide, filled with a rich collection of fourth-century silver plate, crushed and broken as if destined for the melting-pot. It is supposed that the plate (now restored and exhibited in the National Museum of Antiquities of Scotland, Edinburgh) was concealed by Angle or Saxon pirates in the early fifth century.

Seventeen miles from Edinburgh is **Haddington,** a royal burgh of the time of David I. It has associations with John Knox and Edward Irving, and in its churchyard —the ruined choir of " the Lamp of Lothian " (destroyed by the English during " The Burnt Candlemas " of 1356) —is buried Jane Welsh, wife of Thomas Carlyle.

DUNBAR TO EDINBURGH VIÂ THE COAST.

The road for Tantallon and North Berwick turns northward from the main highway about 4 miles west of Dunbar, running across the woods and rich pastoral lands of Tynninghame to **Whitekirk,** with its interesting Parish Church, burned by suffragettes in 1914, but since restored.

The place was the scene of the labours of the eighth-century St. Baldred, but owed its early importance to a well credited with miraculous powers of healing. The Countess of March, fleeing in 1294 from Edward I at Dunbar, drank of its waters and was cured of a wound, and in gratitude built a chapel in honour of Our Lady. So famous did the well become that upwards of 15,000 pilgrims came to it in 1413 ; while in 1435 the future Pope Pius II walked barefoot from Dunbar, a feat which so convinced James I of the worth of the well that he took the place under his care, added to the buildings and changed the name from Fairknowe to White Chapel.

About 2 miles north of Whitekirk and 3 miles east of North Berwick are the magnificent ruins of—

TANTALLON CASTLE.

(Open from 10 a.m. to 7 p.m. on weekdays, and 2 p.m. to 7 p.m. on Sundays. In winter, 10-4 and 2-4. Admission charge.)

Tantallon was a stronghold of the Douglases, and dates back to the latter part of the fourteenth century. The Castle occupies a striking position on a rocky promontory overlooking the North Sea. Readers of Scott will recall the well-known lines in *Marmion* :

> " Tantallon's dizzy steep
> Hung o'er the margin of the deep."

Hugh Miller's description is also worth quoting : " Tantallon hasthree sides of wall-like rock and one side of rock-like wall."

The impregnable character of the stronghold gave rise to a local legend : " Ding doon Tantallon ! Mak' a brig to the Bass "—feats considered equally impossible of achievement. In 1528 the Earl of Angus successfully defied James V and even captured the King's artillery. But in 1639 the Covenanters compelled the small garrison of the 11th Earl (1st Marquess of Douglas) to surrender ; in 1651 the Castle was captured from the Scots by General Monk, after a heavy bombardment, and never again did it rank as a fortress, though it has since been in some parts restored.

Opposite the Castle and 1½ miles out to sea is the **Bass Rock** (313 feet), about a mile in circumference, its sides in many places rising perpendicular from the water for some 300 feet. In summer there is a frequent service of motor launches from North Berwick harbour, and the trip is certainly one that should not be missed. The island was a favourite haunt of St. Baldred (*see* p. 52, under Whitekirk), and those whose visits are made on days when the tide permits landing on the rock may search the vicinity for the saint's well, cradle and cobble—the last-named a great rock which " at his nod " was transplanted from a position off the island where it was dangerous to shipping. In later times the island was used as a prison for the Covenanters. Nowadays the rock is the haunt of innumerable sea-birds, notably the gannet or solan goose, which line the cliffs in such numbers as to give them at a distance the appearance of chalk. It will be remembered that David Balfour's adventures on the island form an exciting episode in Stevenson's *Catriona.*

The conical **North Berwick Law** (612 ft.) is a conspicuous landmark in the southern outskirts of the town.

NORTH BERWICK.

Distances.—Berwick-upon-Tweed, 40 m.; Dunbar, 11 m.; Edinburgh, 23 m.
Early Closing.—Thursday.
Hotels.—*Royal* (43 rooms), *Marine* (74 rooms), *Imperial* (24 rooms), *Dalrymple, Golf, Redan, Westerdunes*, etc., etc.
Motor Launch Trips in season from harbour to Bass Rock and other islands off the coast.
Population.—4,161.
Sports.—Tennis, bowls, swimming pond, yachting, and golf on a dozen courses, including some of the best in Britain. Sunday play on both the West Links (18 holes) and the Burgh Course (18 holes). There are also excellent putting courses along the front.

In modern times the name and fame of North Berwick have been so linked with golf that one looks almost with surprise upon the ruins of a twelfth-century Church and of a nunnery of like antiquity. North Berwick is a prosperous little town with splendid sands and other natural facilities for holiday-making, to which have been added tennis courts, bowling greens, swimming pool and yacht pond—and the golf links. Golf was played at North Berwick in the early seventeenth century, and to-day there are two full-sized links and a shorter course, while within a few miles are a dozen or more courses of varying characteristics. Of these the most famous is that at **Muirfield**, 4 miles south-west (18 *holes : no ladies on Saturday and Sunday afternoons*). The way to it passes through pretty little **Dirleton** (*Open Arms*), with a formidable ruined Castle and enchanting garden (*open*, 10–7 ; *Sunday*, 2–7 ; *winter*, 10–4 and 2–4 ; *admission charge*).

Gullane (*Queen's* (14 *rooms*), *Bisset's* (29 *rooms*), *Gables, Mallard* (13 *rooms*), *Greywalls* (21 *rooms*) etc.), another famous golfing centre, adjoins the Muirfield links. There are three courses (*with various charges and Sunday play*), and also a (*free*) children's course. At **Kilspindie** is yet another course (*also with Sunday play*) ; in fact, the road from North Berwick towards Edinburgh is a veritable golfer's progress, so numerous are the links. Some miles away to the south the Hopetoun Monument on Garleton Hill is prominent ; in the other direction are views across the Forth.

Beyond **Aberlady** the road runs close to the coast—a favourite neighbourhood with picnic parties. **Longniddry** is known for its long golf course, and then comes **Port Seton**, in the vicinity of which are **Seton Chapel and House**, the latter erected in the eighteenth century on the site of Seton Palace, where dwelt the fifth Lord Seton, the staunch adherent of Queen Mary, who with Bothwell spent a week here after Darnley's murder. The Chapel, a sixteenth-century collegiate building, consisting of choir, transepts and tower, is of much archæological interest.

The final syllable of the word **Prestonpans** is a reminder of that local industry concerned with the abstraction of salt from seawater, but the name also introduces us to a small area which for various reasons became the site of three important battles.

Chronologically, the first of these was the **Battle of Pinkie**, fought a few miles south-west of Prestonpans in 1547, when the Protector Somerset, with 18,000 men, utterly routed a very much larger Scottish force, slaying at least 10,000, though the English losses were only about 200.

The next affair in point of time hardly merits the name of battle in comparison with Pinkie, but its effects were at least as momentous, for it was at **Carberry Hill** in 1567 that Mary Queen of Scots, after leaving Bothwell, surrendered to the insurgent nobles, to enter upon that long term of imprisonment which began at Lochleven and was to last almost without interruption until her execution (1587).

The **Battle of Prestonpans** was probably one of the most heartening incidents of Prince Charlie's 1745 adventure. The English under Sir John Cope had failed to engage his ragged force in the Highlands, and had therefore been shipped from Aberdeen to Dunbar in order to encounter them from the south, and so the two forces met at Prestonpans on the afternoon of September 19, 1745. Each side prepared for battle on the morrow; but the English placed too much confidence in a morass between them and their foes, who found a way through it during the night and at break of day staged such a surprise that in the brief space of fifteen minutes Cope's army was utterly routed.

The village of Preston boasts a fine seventeenth-century Mercat Cross.

At **Musselburgh** the Esk is crossed by a venerable bridge generally alluded to (incorrectly) as "Roman." Across the river is **Fisherrow,** which as its name implies is absorbed in fishing; and then come **Joppa** and **Portobello,** exceedingly popular seaside resorts. Portobello beach—and the open-air swimming pool—on a busy day must be seen to be believed.

Beyond Portobello the rugged heights of Arthur's Seat are seen beyond the houses to the left as we run through Restalrig, and as the road climbs the shoulder of Calton Hill to enter Edinburgh a glimpse will be caught on the left of the Palace of Holyroodhouse.

For **Edinburgh** *see* pages 107–34.

Dunbar to Edinburgh viâ Gifford.—An alternative route skirts the northern slopes of the Lammermuirs. It runs below Whittinghame (Earl Balfour's home, now school), Traprain Law to Garvald. Nunraw monastery was of old a fortalice as well as a Cistercian nunnery. At **Gifford** are Yester House (Marquess of Tweeddale) and ruined Yester Castle, with Goblin Ha', a rock-hewn chamber of the thirteenth century. Between Gifford and Haddington lies *Lennoxlove* (open in summer) associated with Mary's adviser, Maitland of Lethington, and with Charles I's lady-love, La Belle Stuart.

BERWICK TO KELSO.

Between Kelso and Paxton, where the Liberties of the Borough and Town of Berwick come down to the river, the Tweed forms the Anglo-Scottish boundary for the greater part of the distance. There are good roads on each side of the river; that on the south side being the shorter.

Some 5 miles from Berwick, and on the Scottish bank, is the village of **Paxton,** supposed to have suggested the song of "Robin Adair." The neighbouring suspension bridge is of interest as the first of its kind to be built in Britain. Beyond Horncliffe is **Norham,** England, with the remains of a twelfth-century Castle celebrated as the opening scene of *Marmion.* (*The ruins are open daily; fee.*)

From its bold position, the Castle must have appeared as hardly less a fortress than a challenge, and it is not surprising that it changed hands incessantly. King John here concluded a treaty (1209) with William of Scotland which was so ambiguously worded that a year or so later Alexander of Scotland, the Papal legate and a representative of the English sovereign met at Berwick to define its meaning. Edward I was here during the Scottish interregnum, 1290–2, and here presided over the preliminaries for the Bruce-Balliol debates. In 1497 the celebrated Mons Meg was brought from Edinburgh Castle to assist in the unsuccessful assault and in 1513 James IV captured and partially wrecked the Castle on his way to Flodden.

Norham Church is interesting as a Norman building which has also seen warlike days, for in 1318 the Scots made it a strong-point during a siege of the Castle, and one of the numerous Anglo-Scottish treaties was signed within its walls.

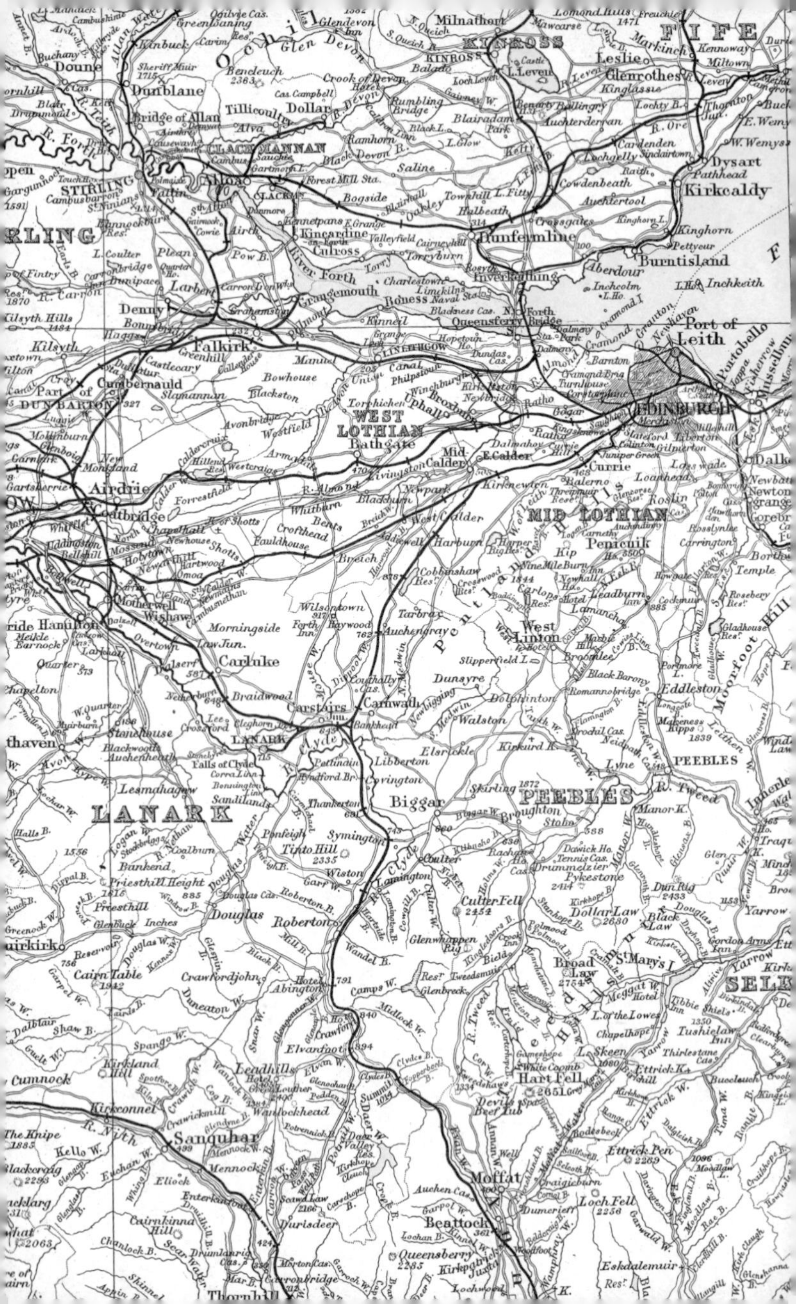

FIFE
KINROSS
Ochil
Doune
Dunblane
Bridge of Allan
Tillicoultry
Dollar
Alva
CLACKMANNAN
Alloa
STIRLING
Kinross
L. Leven
Leslie
Glenrothes
Markinch
Kennoway
Milnathort
Kinglassie
Thornton Jun.
Dysart
Kirkcaldy
Kinghorn
Burntisland
Aberdour
Cowdenbeath
Lochgelly
Dunfermline
Inverkeithing
Kincardine
Culross
Falkirk
Grangemouth
Bo'ness
Larbert
Denny
Queensferry
Forth Bridge
Port of Leith
Portobello
Musselburgh
EDINBURGH
LINLITHGOW
Cumbernauld
Kilsyth
Part of DUNBARTON
WEST LOTHIAN
Bathgate
Uphall
Broxburn
Mid Calder
E. Calder
West Calder
Airdrie
Coatbridge
Motherwell
Wishaw
Hamilton
Carluke
Carstairs
Carnwath
LANARK
Lanark
Lesmahagow
MID LOTHIAN
Penicuik
Pentland Hills
West Linton
Biggar
PEEBLES
Peebles
R. Tweed
Eddleston
Moorfoot Hills
Douglas
Abington
Crawfordjohn
Leadhills
Wanlockhead
Kirkconnel
Sanquhar
Durisdeer
Moffat
Beattock
Hart Fell
Broad Law
St. Mary's L.
Ettrick Pen
Eskdalemuir
Tinto Hill
Symington
Lamington
Culter Fell
Cumnock
Muirkirk
Cairn Table
Thornhill
Queensberry
SELK

BERWICK, EDINBURGH, STIRLING
English Miles
0
5
10
15
20
WARD LOCK & CO., LIMITED, LONDON.
© – John Bartholomew & Son Ltd. Edinburgh
Anstruther
Pittenweem
St. Monance
Elie
Earlsferry
Isle of May
OF FORTH
Bass Rock 350 ft.
Fidra
Craigleith
Canty Bay
Tantallon Cas.
North Berwick
Dirleton
Gullane
Tyninghame Ho.
Dunbar
Belhaven
E. Fortune
Drem Jun.
Athelstaneford
E. Linton
Longniddry
HADDINGTON
Stenton
Spott
Innerwick
Cockburnspath
Fast Castle
St. Abbs Hd.
St. Abbs
Coldingham
Eyemouth
Burnmouth
Ayton
Grantshouse
Oldhamstocks
Garvald
EAST LOTHIAN
Gifford
Lammermuir Hills
Abbey St. Bathans
Cranshaws
Longformacus
Chirnside
Marshall Meadows
BERWICK on Tweed
Tweedmouth
Spittal
Scremerston
DUNS
BERWICK
Lauder
Stow
Channelkirk
Oxton
Westruther
Polwarth
Marchmont
GREENLAW
Swinton
Ladykirk
Norham
Cheswick
Goswick
Ancroft
Lowick
Beal
Kyloe
Fenwick
Belford
Gordon
Hume
Eccles
Birgham
COLDSTREAM
Cornhill
Etal
Ford
Crookham
Flodden Field
Earlston
Smailholm
KELSO
Sprouston
Galashiels
Melrose
Newtown
St. Boswells
Abbotsford
SELKIRK
Lilliesleaf
Ancrum
JEDBURGH
Crailing
Yetholm
Morebattle
Wooler
Doddington
Chatton
The Cheviot 2676
Hedgehope Hill 2348
Windy Gyle
ROXBURGH
Denholm
Minto
HAWICK
Hobkirk
Carter Bar
Carter Fell 1815
Peel Fell 1964
Catcleugh Reservoir
Byrness
Rochester
Otterburn
Elsdon
NORTHUMBERLAND
Alwinton
Harbottle
Rothbury
Brinkburn
Whittingham
Ingram
Glanton
Riccarton Jun.
Hermitage
Cheviot Hills

Across the river from Norham is **Ladykirk,** owing its name to a vow of James IV, who when in danger while fording the river promised to build a church to the Virgin Mary if he came safely to land. *Upsettlington,* on the outskirts of Ladykirk, is historically important as the place where Edward I extracted from the candidates for the Scottish throne the promise of vassalship—a promise which was fraught with such momentous results for Scotland and hardly less for England (*see* p. 29).

A few miles above Norham the Tweed is joined by the Till, and finely placed in the angle formed by the two streams are the ruins of **Twizel Castle,** which, for all its Norman architecture, dates only from the eighteenth century. Near by are remnants of a small chapel in which the remains of St. Cuthbert rested when, tiring of Melrose Abbey—let us quote Scott :

> " In his stone coffin forth he rides,
> A ponderous bark for river tides ;
> Yet, light as gossamer it glides
> Downward to Tillmouth cell."

Scott's footnote is also interesting : " This boat is finely shaped, 10 feet long, 3½ feet in diameter and only 4 inches thick, so that with very little assistance it might certainly have swum. It lies, or at least did so a few years ago, beside the ruined chapel of Tillmouth." Twizel might have been a greater name in history had James IV been wise enough to prevent, or to try to prevent, the English from crossing the Till in 1513. As it was, they crossed unchallenged and so followed the **Battle of Flodden Field,** one of the most tragic of the many tragic encounters on the Border. The site of the Battle is 3½ miles south-east of Coldstream.

The object of James IV in crossing the Border was to cause Henry VIII to recall the forces with which he was warring against Louis XII in Flanders, and Pitscottie adds the information that the French Queen urged him to the invasion by sending him the ring from off her finger, fourteen thousand crowns to pay his expenses and inviting him to " come three feet on English ground for her sake." On the morning after the battle the chivalry of Scotland was no more, the King, his natural son, an archbishop, a bishop, two abbots, twelve earls, fourteen lords, many knights and gentlemen and about nine thousand men were slain ; on the English side few men of title were slain. A monument near Branxton Church is said to mark the spot where James IV fell.

Coldstream (*Newcastle Arms ; Crown*) is famous the world over by reason of the regiment of guards founded here in 1660 by General Monck. Overlooking the site of a ford (replaced by a picturesque bridge designed by Smeaton in 1763), Coldstream has always been of considerable importance, but most of the military crossings of the Border at this point seem to have been undisturbed, and the more exciting happenings in the history of the town have been provided by the runaway couples who came to be married at the bridge toll-house or elsewhere in this, the first burgh over the Border (*see also* Gretna Green, p. 83). It is a remarkable fact that no fewer than three Lord Chancellors of England were married thus—Lords Eldon, Erskine and Brougham.

Coldstream is the point at which the Border is crossed by motorists using the Morpeth-Wooler-Lauder-Edinburgh road, and as such is a very busy place in the season. For those going north the road leaves the Kelso road about 2 miles from Coldstream, almost opposite Wark Castle. Greenlaw is 10 miles and Lauder (p. 70) 22 miles from Coldstream.

West from Coldstream a mile or so, and on the English bank, is the site of **Wark Castle**, the traditional scene of the ball at which Edward III, retrieving the Countess of Salisbury's garter, uttered the words " Honi soit qui mal y pense," which became the motto of the most Noble Order of the Garter. Here as elsewhere, however, tradition and historical truth do not march side by side, and the whole episode is regarded as fiction.

Carham has little to show of historic interest, but it was the scene of a great battle in 1018. Here the Tweed ceases to mark the Border, which now runs south towards the Cheviot (2,676 ft. in Northumberland), the highest point in the range, which separates the two countries for the next 30 to 40 miles. **Kirk Yetholm** (*hotels: Youth hostel*), some 8 miles south-east of Kelso, was long the headquarters of the Scottish gipsies, the Faas.

KELSO.

Distances.—Berwick, 23 m.; London, 341 m.; Newcastle, 68 m.; Edinburgh 45 m.; Hawick, 21 m.
Early Closing.—Wednesday.
Hotels.—*Cross Keys* (30 rooms), *Ednam House* (33 rooms), *Queen's Head* (10 rooms), *Spread Eagle* (8 rooms), *Border* (*unl.*).
Races.—March, May and October.

Sports.—Golf (9-hole course); tennis; putting; swimming; fishing for trout in Tweed and Teviot, apply Kelso Angling Association; curling; ice rink.

Finely placed in a bend of the Tweed, where that river is joined by the Teviot about 25 miles above Berwick, Kelso is one of the most attractive of the Border towns, having a fine Rennie bridge, a wide picturesque market square, good shops and romantic surroundings. The chief monument of the town is the remains of **Kelso Abbey** (*Ministry hours*)—little more than the tower of the building founded by David I in the twelfth century. Standing so near the Border, the Abbey had a chequered history, and was finally besieged by the Earl of Hertford in 1545. Subsequently it was "restored," but happily the signs of restoration have been removed.

Kelso has claims to a place in the history of literature, for it was at the local Grammar School that Scott received part of his education and made friends with the then youthful Ballantynes, who later became his publishers.

On the western outskirts of Kelso are the grounds of **Floors Castle,** enclosed in a formidable wall pierced, at the point nearest the town, by good modern iron gates. A holly tree in Floors Park marks the spot where James II was killed by the bursting of a cannon during the siege of Roxburgh Castle in 1460. **Roxburgh,** now a mere village, was formerly more important than Kelso.

BERWICK TO LAUDER VIÂ DUNS.

Although not much used as a through route, this road is a very pleasant introduction to the southern slopes of the Lammermuirs, especially for those with time to explore some of the roads running up into the hills. The route leaves Berwick by the Scots Gate. Keep to the left after crossing the railway, soon passing on the right **Halidon Hill,** the site of a memorable battle in 1333, when the Scots endeavouring to relieve Berwick Castle were themselves severely beaten.

Chirnside is a favourite angling centre, as also is the historic town of **Duns.** From *Duns Law* (714 feet) there is a wide view over Lower Tweeddale. From Duns a wildly beautiful road runs across the hills to Haddington, following the Whiteadder almost to its source.

The Church at **Polwarth,** a few miles west of Duns, has several features of interest. Lauder (p. 70) is 18 miles from Duns, by Westruther, and 33 from Berwick.

FROM CARTER BAR TO EDINBURGH

BY JEDBURGH, MELROSE AND PEEBLES

OF the half-dozen points at which the Border is generally crossed, this is easily the most romantic. The road comes up from Corbridge or Newcastle and for many miles runs across fine but in no way remarkable moorland. Then, almost imperceptibly, one begins to climb the Cheviots. Signboards announce " the last hotel in England," Catcleugh reservoir is skirted—and suddenly at the top of a rise the whole landscape in front falls away to reveal a scene of great beauty, hills and valleys and woods, castles, churches, towns and villages innumerable being spread before one, and beside the road a simple board with dramatic touch reminds us that this is The Border (Carter Bar, 1,371 feet). As the road winds down the farther side there are further views of the wooded hills, and so to—

JEDBURGH.

Distances.—Melrose, 14 m.; Newcastle, 58 m.; Hawick, 11 m.; Kelso, 11 m. Edinburgh, 48 m.; London, 325 m.
Hotels.—*Royal, Spread Eagle, Jedforest.*

Though there is less suggestion of the Border town in Jedburgh than in, say, Hawick, yet few places have had a closer acquaintance with the perils which beset the nearest town to a disputed frontier, particularly when that town boasts a very fine abbey. The chief town in the middle marches, its castle (now no more) was alternately held by English and Scots and the place was almost from its foundation in the ninth century a scene of constant strife and bloodshed. Not only the town acquired fame in warlike circles: Jedburgh men were to be found on many a battlefield wielding the " Jeddart axe and staff " to such purpose that their war-cry " Jeddart's here " struck terror into many a heart—

Then rose the slogan, with a shout—
"To it, Tynedale, Jethart's here!"

There was also "Jeddart justice," that useful way of dealing with robbers and others which, like "Lydford law," consisted in hanging a man first and trying him afterwards.

The Act of Union deprived Jedburgh of much of its importance as a Border town, and it is now occupied with the manufacture of woollen goods and precision tools.

The remains of the **Abbey**—still the most distinguished among the Border Abbeys—are well seen from the road into the town from the south, though the best view is from the banks of the river to the left of the road. Founded by David I in the year 1118 for Canons Regular from Beauvais, the Abbey had a stormy history, being frequently involved in the incessant border frays. It was destroyed at Henry VIII's instigation when the Scots refused to betroth Mary Queen of Scots with Edward VI. A reformed church was built in the shell and used until 1875. (*Open* 9.30–7, 2–7 *Sundays*; *winter*, 10–4, 2–4. *Charge.*)

Only the Church of the Abbey remains, although in recent years excavations on the south side have disclosed remains of the cloistral buildings. The Church was a large cruciform building comprising nave, with side aisles, transepts and a choir with chapels. With the exception of the eastern end of the choir, the walls are fairly complete, and it is obvious that the building in its hey-day was of considerable beauty. The architectural styles range from the Norman piers in the choir to the Early English superstructure of the nave, but the architectural pride of the Abbey are the two late Norman doorways—that at the west end and that which led from the nave aisle to the cloisters. Unfortunately time has erased much of the finer detail work, but also in the south wall of the church a facsimile of the cloister doorway has been built. The cloister affords a splendid view of the south side of the church, with its fine unbroken ranges of windows. Note also the excellent tracery in the window in the north transept. Attached to the building is a small *Museum* with an important collection of early sculptured stones.

Reached by a lane leading off the main street is a large building known as **Mary, Queen of Scots House** (*open* 10–12, 1–8; *Sundays*, 1–5; *admission*, 10p.; *children*, 5p.). Within is an interesting collection of Mary, Queen of Scots' relics, etc. It was while the Queen was here, holding assizes, that news was brought to her of Bothwell, lying wounded in Hermitage Castle, 25 miles distant.

Characteristically she went to visit him, but the effort of riding there and back in a day brought on a fever to which she nearly succumbed.

To the south-west of the town, and easily reached by the Hawick road, *Dunion Hill* rises 1,092 feet and affords splendid views. The walk could be continued over *Black Law* (1,110 feet) and Watch Knowe. The Waterloo Monument, 3½ miles north at Penielheugh, is another good view-point. Those with time should explore the Jed valley for at least 3 miles up: that is to say, as far as **Ferniehirst Castle**, which as a stronghold of the Kerr family bore its share of border warfare. It is now a Youth Hostel. The original site of Jedburgh is at **Old Jedward**, some 3 miles farther up the valley.

Two miles north of Jedburgh the road forks: one branch running with the Teviot down to Kelso (p. 58), the other bearing westward for Hawick. The Lauder-Edinburgh road turns out of this in about a mile and crosses the river close to the hill crowned by the Waterloo Monument. This road follows the line of the Roman Dere Street and passes the battlefield of *Ancrum Moor* (1545), where the Scots defeated the English invaders. A few miles farther is **St. Boswells Green** (*Buccleuch Arms*), on the banks of the Tweed at the point where it bends to enclose the remains of Dryburgh Abbey, surely the most beautiful of Scotland's many lovely ruins.

DRYBURGH ABBEY.

Access.—A footbridge crosses the river to the Abbey from near St. Boswells Green. The nearest road bridge is a mile or so downstream. Leave the main road at St. Boswells Green, cross river to Clint Mains, where turn left, turning left at each subsequent choice of road. There is another road bridge at **Leaderfoot,** about 3 miles upstream, just below the lofty railway viaduct. After crossing this bridge turn immediately to the right, and to the right at each subsequent choice of road. This road gives good views across the river to the Eildon Hills, with the Bemersyde estate in the foreground.

Admission.—Daily all the year round. In summer 10 a.m. to 7 p.m. and 2–7 on Sundays; in winter the grounds are closed at 4 p.m. Admission, *fee.*

Hotels.—*Dryburgh Abbey* (licensed) at entrance to Abbey (34 rooms); *Buccleuch Arms*, St. Boswells Green; *Station, Dryburgh Arms* at Newton St. Boswells.

The remains comprise portions of the Abbey church, to the south of which lie the cloisters, refectory, chapter house, and other buildings, but the chief delight of the place is its lovely situation in a bend of the river, surrounded by the greenest of lawns from which rise gracious trees of all kinds. The ruins themselves can be quickly seen, but Dryburgh is a place in which to linger.

The Abbey was founded about 1150 for Praemonstratensian canons from Alnwick. In course of time the community became very rich and powerful, but the proximity of Dryburgh to the Border brought it the attention of successive invading armies and it was burnt and plundered four times in as many centuries. In 1919 Lord

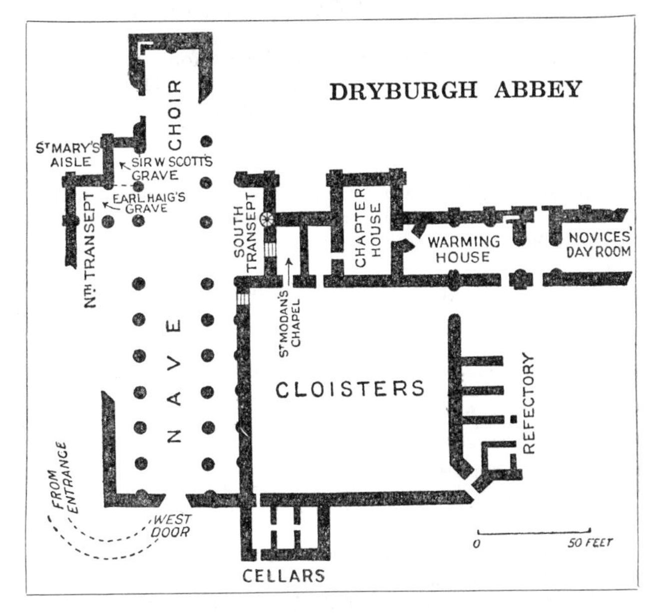

Glenconner presented the ruins to the nation, and the Department of the Environment now maintain it.

The remains need little description, though attention must be called to the richly moulded west doorway of the church ; the rose window at the west end of the refectory ; the Chapter House, adjoining which are the vault of the Biber Erskines and St. Modan's Chapel. St. Modan is said to have been abbot of a monastery which stood here in the sixth century. A peculiarity of the buildings on this side of the cloister is that they are on different levels.

Outside the Chapter House, and supported on props, is a very old juniper tree ; on the other side, at the boundary wall, is a yew said to be coeval with the Abbey.

For many the most important part of the Abbey is on the north side of the Church, where are the graves of Sir Walter Scott (d. Sept. 21, 1832) and of Earl Haig (d. Jan. 29, 1928), the latter generally strewn with Flanders poppies.

On the hillside behind the Abbey is a colossal statue of Wallace.

The road from Dryburgh to Leaderfoot passes the **Bemersyde** estate, the residence of the Haig family since the days of Thomas the Rhymer, who uttered the prophecy :

> " Tyde what may, whate'er betide,
> Haig shall be Haig of Bemersyde."

An ancient Border tower forms part of the mansion, which with the adjoining lands was presented after the 1914–18 War, by his friends and admirers, to Earl Haig of Bemersyde.

By Newstead (p. 70) one quickly reaches Melrose.

MELROSE.

Admission to Abbey: April to September, 9.30–7; Sundays, 2–7; October to March, 10–4 and 2–4. Admission, *fee*.
Car Park.—There is a car park close to the abbey ; cars may also be left in the Market Square, a short distance to the south.
Distances.—Edinburgh, 37 m. ; Jedburgh, 13 m. ; Dryburgh, 4 m. ; Galashiels, 4 m.
Early Closing.—Thursday.
Hotels.—*Burt's* (17 rooms), *King's Arms* (11 rooms), *Waverley Castle* (75 rooms), *Station*, *Bon Accord*, *George and Abbotsford* (26 rooms).
Sports.—Golf, fishing, bowls, tennis.

Melrose is a quiet little town on the southern bank of the Tweed which is much visited by those exploring the Scott Country. There are golf links and other amenities ; to rugby enthusiasts it is the birthplace of the " seven-a-side " form of the game ; but it is, of course, on account of its **Abbey** that the place is best known.

The Abbey was founded, like so many others, by David I early in the twelfth century and was occupied by Cistercians from Rievaulx Abbey in Yorkshire. Destroyed by Edward II, it was rebuilt from a grant made for the purpose by the Bruce and despite the hindrances caused by attacks from Richard II. A considerable part of the fabric belongs to the fifteenth–sixteenth centuries. From

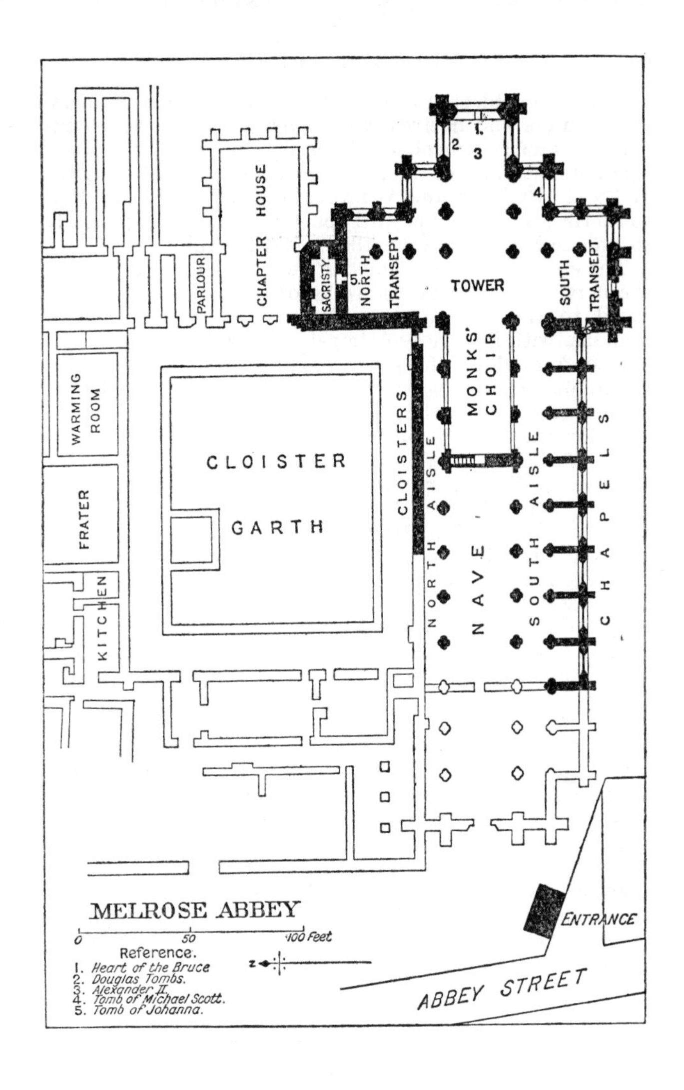
1.
2
3
4.
5.
CHAPTER HOUSE
PARLOUR
SACRISTY
NORTH TRANSEPT
TOWER
SOUTH TRANSEPT
MONKS' CHOIR
WARMING ROOM
CLOISTER GARTH
CLOISTERS
NORTH AISLE
SOUTH AISLE
NAVE
CHAPELS
FRATER
KITCHEN
ENTRANCE
ABBEY STREET
MELROSE ABBEY
0
50
100 Feet
Reference.
1. Heart of the Bruce
2. Douglas Tombs.
3. Alexander II.
4. Tomb of Michael Scott.
5. Tomb of Johanna.

1545 it was subjected to the tender mercies of Reformers, Covenanters and natives who regarded it as a very convenient quarry whenever building-stone was required. The remains are now under the protection of the Ministry of Public Building and Works, and much has been done to rid the grounds of unsightly encumbrances and generally to enhance and preserve this beautiful ruin.

The entrance lodge stands at the west end of the nave, the northern and western walls of which were long ago razed to the ground, though most of the south wall remains, with its series of chapels. Walking eastward we are confronted by the remains of the rood loft, passing which we are among high walls and can appreciate the former grandeur of the building. The Abbey is remarkable for the beauty and variety of its carved capitals: notice that over the clustered shaft adjoining the south-west pier of the tower. Notice, too, the splendid windows of the transepts and the great east window. In the vicinity of the High Altar, the heart of the Bruce was believed buried; a few yards westward lie the remains of Alexander II; to the north of them are tombs of the Douglases, and on the south, at the entrance to the sanctuary, is the tomb of Michael Scott, the Eildon wizard (*see* p. 70). North of the north transept was the sacristy, and in the doorway was buried Johanna, wife of Alexander II. From this point the extreme narrowness of the north aisle is well seen.

In recent years the Commendator's House and additional ground have been acquired and it has been possible to expose the foundations of an extensive range of domestic buildings to the north of the cloisters. The former magnificence of the place must be apparent even to the most hurried visitor; nevertheless, it is only to the leisurely examiner of its walls that the greatness of the Abbey is fully apparent.

In the churchyard are the graves of many of Scott's friends and retainers.

Melrose to Dryburgh.—Follow Abbey Street, past the entrance to the ruins, northward, shortly swinging to the right. Through Newstead to the bridge at Leaderfoot, where cross the river and turn immediately to the right, taking the right-hand road at each subsequent choice. For Dryburgh *see* page **62.**

Melrose to Abbotsford.—Take the main road westward out

of the town. In about a mile this crosses the river by a picturesque bridge: for Abbotsford do not cross the bridge, but keep to the left, and in about a mile the house will be seen below the road on the right.

ABBOTSFORD.

Access.—Abbotsford lies on the right bank of the Tweed about 3 miles to the west of Melrose from whence a good road runs as above. Cars can be hired at Melrose. On the other side of the river Galashiels is but 2 miles distant in a direct line, but vehicles must go upstream to Lindean or down towards Melrose in order to cross the river. About 4 miles south of Abbotsford is Selkirk, also with motor connections. Pedestrians can use the Galashiels–Melrose bus service to Abbotsford Toll, from whence it is a walk of 1½ miles. Various motor firms, notably in Edinburgh, organize "Scott Country" tours, including Abbotsford.

Admission.—Weekdays, 10–5. Admission, 20p., children 10p. Open from April to end October. Also Sunday afternoons 2–5.

Car Parking.—Cars, etc., are left beside the road at the entrance to the path leading down to the house.

Anything approaching a detailed description of Abbotsford would be impossible, even in a much more comprehensive volume than this. Strikingly beautiful in its situation, it is of greater interest as the creation of Sir Walter Scott, and of hardly less interest as a veritable museum of authentic relics of the Scotland which Scott loved, wrote about and, in fact, made known to the world at large, for until the publication of the Waverley novels the Highlands were generally regarded as far beyond the pale of civilization. Scott acquired the estate in 1811, and at first contented himself with enlarging the then existing Newharthaugh Farm (Clarty Hole). Subsequently, however, he built the present mansion, and planted many of the trees which now lend such charm to the countryside around, and at Abbotsford he died in 1832.

Abbotsford is distinguished among a host of houses associated with famous figures in that almost every yard of it bears the impress of its creator; here is no collection of "relics" scraped together with but little justification after Scott's death, but a wonderful assembly of arms, armour and the like, collected by himself during his lifetime and of which many pieces live eternally in his pages.

Attention will be attracted by the stone, half-way up the wall near the front door, inscribed:

"The Lord of armies is my Protector
Blessit ar thay that trust in the Lord. 1575."

This stone was the lintel of the old Edinburgh Tolbooth, the Heart of Midlothian (*see* p. 116), and is but one example of the manner in which historic relics have been incorporated into the house. The rooms shown include the Armoury and Entrance Hall, crammed with weapons and armour, and with some pictures which we leave the guides to describe ; Scott's Study, with its little " speak-a-bit " closet containing the " death mask " ; the Drawing-room, with its century-old Chinese wall-paper and furniture, perhaps the least picturesque of the Abbotsford apartments ; the Library, with Chantrey's bust of Scott, a case containing relics of Prince Charlie, Flora Macdonald, Rob Roy, etc. ; and dining-room with lovely views of the river recalling Lockhart's picture of the scene in this room in September, 1832 : " A beautiful day ; so warm that every window was wide open, and so perfectly still that the sound of all others most delicious to his ear, the gentle ripple of the Tweed over its pebbles, was distinctly audible as we knelt around the bed, and his eldest son kissed and closed his eyes."

Sir Walter Scott belongs to the numerous company of great Scotsmen whose careers ended in tragedy. Born in Edinburgh on August 15, 1771, he developed in infancy an incurable lameness ; and although this did not at any time daunt his spirit—his physical energy, for example, was prodigious, enabling him even in later life to walk 30 miles in a day or to ride a hundred without resting—the infirmity did undoubtedly help to intensify a natural love of reading. He would read everything that came his way, and in his early teens had probably read more (and, what is of greater importance, remembered more) than most men of three times his age.

In 1786 he was apprenticed to his father, a Writer to the Signet (a position more or less equivalent to that of an English attorney), but he seems never to have applied himself with much enthusiasm to the Law, although he was called to the Bar in 1792. In 1799 he became Sheriff-Deputy of Selkirkshire and in 1806 a Clerk of the Court of Session, both fairly lucrative posts, the latter especially making small claim upon his time. He wrote, but from the first he resolved to use literature " as a staff and not a crutch." His first publication, in 1799, was a translation of Goethe's *Götz von Berlichingen* ; in 1802 the *Border Minstrelsy* was printed and published by his old school friend Ballantyne, whom he had met at Kelso—where also he had come across the copy of Percy's *Reliques* which made such a profound impression upon his youthful imagination. The *Border Minstrelsy* made Scott famous so that publication of *The Lay of the Last Minstrel* created something of a sensation. His fame rose higher with *Marmion* and *The Lady of the Lake*, of which 20,000 copies sold in a few months. The *Lady*, however, marked the zenith of Scott's popularity as a poet, and the publication of several other poems confirmed the fact that his popularity as a poet was actually waning. Scott had, however, already issued *Waverley*, and its success (notwithstanding the anonymity of the author) encouraged him to confine his attentions to novels. In that vein he had no rival, and for years the novels poured from his pen with wonderful regularity and, all things considered, equally wonderful maintenance of standard.

In 1797 he had married Charlotte Margaret Carpenter. Their first home was at Lasswade; subsequently they moved to Ashiestiel, on the Tweed. With his rising success in the literary world Scott bought the farm of Clarty Hole, between Melrose and Galashiels, changed the name to the far more appropriate (since it referred to the home of the author of *Waverley*) Abbotsford and proceeded to rebuild the place in accordance with the same feudal spirit. Few men of the time could have conceived and carried out such a plan. He bought many historical relics, but a greater number were showered upon him by admiring readers, and when in 1820 he was knighted his future must have seemed assured.

But tragedy was impending. Scott had not only made the reputation of Ballantyne's and Constable's, the printers and publishers; he had also accepted partnerships in both the publishing and the printing businesses of these firms; and when in 1826 these firms became bankrupt Scott found himself liable, through no fault of his own except an excess of generosity towards those he regarded as his friends, for debts amounting to something like £117,000.

With a brave boast to his creditors ("Time and I against any two") he turned his pen and his intellect to the production of works which would not only pay the debts of his partners, but would enable him to regain all that he had lost. In six years he had repaid £70,000, but the task was greater than even his physique and will-power could perform. In February, 1830, symptoms of paralysis appeared. He continued his writing and in 1831 was induced to go abroad in the hope of restoring his health, but the hope was vain, and from Rome he made his way back to Scotland in the knowledge that the end was near. A tablet beside the road near Galashiels records his delight at again setting eyes on the country he loved so well. A few hours later he was back at Abbotsford and there it was that he died on September 21, 1832.

The **Eildon Hills**, to the south of Melrose, are best appreciated at a little distance—they are very well seen from the Bemersyde road to Dryburgh. Although there is but one hill, there are three peaks (of which the highest rises 1,400 feet above the sea), a subdivision popularly attributed (*vide The Lay of the Last Minstrel*) to that Michael Scott who lies buried at Melrose (*see* p. 66) and who, as a wizard, was condemned to find constant employment for a troublesome spirit. But alas ! the partition of the Eildons was accomplished in a night, so that to find occupation for the spirit, Scott was forced to fall back on the manufacture of ropes from sand.

Roman remains have been found on the hills, which are commonly identified with *Trimontium.* Each peak (the middle one has an indicator on its summit) is an excellent view-point, and it was Sir Walter Scott's boast that they commanded more than forty places " famous in war and verse." The ascent is quite easy : pass under the bridge beside the old Melrose station and climb the road to the golf links, beyond which are the three peaks. As for *Trimontium,* the site is marked with a large stone half a mile east of the village of Newstead, near Melrose. This was the largest Roman camp in the South of Scotland and several relics now in the National Museum of Antiquities, Edinburgh, were excavated there in 1908.

Melrose to Edinburgh viâ Lauder (40 *miles*).—Leave the town by Abbey Street, shortly turning to right for Newstead and the bridge at Leaderfoot, on the far side of which take the middle road (the road to the right goes to Dryburgh, *see* p. 66) and keep up the course of the Leader Water. Near **Earlston** are the remains of a residence of Sir Thomas Learmount, the prophetic poet of the thirteenth century, who is better known as Thomas the Rhymer, or Thomas of Ercildoune. Under the Eildon Tree (it was sited east of Melrose) he was wont to meet the Fairy Queen.

From Earlston it is 7 miles to **Lauder** (*Black Bull, Lauderdale*), a small royal burgh dating from the days of William the Lion. A portion of the old town walls existed until 1911. It was here that Archibald, 5th Earl of Angus, earned his title of " Bell-the-Cat " by declaring his readiness to carry out the sentence of his fellow conspirators against Cochrane and others of James III's favourites who were hanged, it is said, from Lauder Bridge (1482). Close by is *Thirlestane Castle*, the seat of the Earl of Lauderdale. A very interesting survival is the system of old burgess rights and customs still maintained in the ancient burgh.

From Lauder the road continues to climb over the Lammermuirs, the highest point (1,192 feet) being gained a mile or so short of **Soutra** (Soutra "aisle," to the left of the road, is the remnant of a hospice which formerly stood here). The hill is a grand view-point. As the road descends the northern flank of the range there is a fine prospect ahead, on a clear day, across the Forth to Fifeshire, the Forth Bridge showing up through the haze of "auld Reekie" and Inchkeith keeping its lonely watch more to the right.

MELROSE TO EDINBURGH VIÂ GALASHIELS.

Distance.—37 m.

Leave Melrose as for Abbotsford, but cross the river by the old bridge a short way beyond *Darnick*, with its old tower. The road now runs beside the Tweed, and then above the Gala Water. On the outskirts of Galashiels a wall-tablet records that "At this spot, on his pathetic journey from Italy home to Abbotsford and his beloved Borderland, Sir Walter Scott, gazing on this scene for the last time, 'sprang up with a cry of delight,' 11th July, 1832—Lockhart, chapter xxxviii."

Galashiels (*Douglas* (26 *rooms*), *Maxwell* (17), *Abbotsford Arms* (7), *King's* (9), *Royal* (19); *early closing, Wednesday*) is a busy industrial town mainly concerned with making tweed. The Scottish College of Textiles, the centre for higher education in textiles in Scotland, is situated in the town. A Braw Lads' Gathering, a local festival, is held annually in the town in June. The town is a very good centre for tours through the Scott Country and there are facilities for most sports. The War Memorial is a spirited piece of sculpture which many will like to compare with the representations of the old rievers at Selkirk, Hawick and other places on the Border.

From Galashiels the road traces the Gala Water towards its source in the hills, those on the east of the road being the Lammermuirs, the Moorfoots on the west. Pretty little Stow is passed, and still the road ascends, coming out finally on the high waste of Middleton Moor, from which it runs down to **Borthwick**, with a fine fifteenth-century Castle. Mary Queen of Scots and Bothwell made this their retreat in 1567, and were here nearly captured by Morton, Mary having to escape in the disguise of a page.

A mile to the north-east is the grand ruin of **Crichton**

Castle, well known to readers of *Marmion.* (*Open, except Fridays in winter,* 10–4, *or* 7 ; *Sundays, from* 2 ; *fee.*)

West of the road are the woods of Arniston Temple (its name recalling an early association with the Knights Templar) and the house from which Lord Rosebery takes his title. Also to the west of the road is **Cockpen,** a district which yields at least a title to Lady Nairne's humorous song " The Laird of Cockpen " ; with Dalhousie Castle (now a school) ; **Lasswade,** where Sir Walter Scott lived for some years after his marriage and which is supposed to be the original of " Gandercleuch " in the *Tales of my Landlord* ; and **Hawthornden,** a modern residence on the site of an old one associated with William Drummond, the poet, who was here visited by Ben Jonson. (*No longer open to the public.*) A mile or so south-west, and the goal of a delightful riverside walk from Lasswade or from Polton, is Roslin.

Roslin (or **Rosslyn**) **Chapel** (*open daily,* 10 *a.m. to* 5 *p.m. in summer, till dusk in winter ; admission, fee ; on Sundays open for Divine Service only, at* 10.15, 11.35 *and* 3.35), was founded in 1446 by William St. Clair, Earl of Orkney and Roslin, a descendant of one of the Norman companions of William I. The remains are extremely beautiful. The choir is a fine example of florid Gothic, there being thirteen different styles of arch. The exquisitely carved 'Prentice's Pillar is said to have been constructed by an apprentice in the absence of his master, who, on his return, burning with envy, ruthlessly slew the young artist. The Chapel sustained much injury at the Revolution of 1688, but was restored in 1862, and is now used as an Episcopal place of worship.

Roslin Castle was built by the founder of the Chapel. The more ancient parts are indicated by huge fragments. It must have been a place of great strength, moated, and only accessible by a drawbridge. It is finely situated on a steep promontory overhanging the river, which sweeps round two sides of it.

At Roslin, on February 23, 1302, took place the famous triple engagement with the army of Edward I, under Sir John de Seagrave—the Scots, under Sir Simon Fraser, defeating the three divisions of the English army as they came up in turn.

(For **Penicuik** *see* p. 75.)

Continuing from Borthwick towards Edinburgh the main road reaches **Newbattle Abbey,** which incorporates remains of a Cistercian abbey, founded by David I, the monks of which were the first to work coal seams in Scotland. Long the seat of the Kerrs, Marquesses of Lothian, it is now a College of Adult Education. Newbattle is on the outskirts of **Dalkeith,** with a place in Scots literature as the home of "Mansie Wauch." The town, however, retains few memorials of its historic past, apart from the ruins of the old Church on the north side of High Street. Dalkeith Palace, the seat of the Duke of Buccleuch, was designed by Vanbrugh for Anne, Duchess of Monmouth and Buccleuch, towards the end of the seventeenth century, but is no longer open to the public.

The more interesting way to Edinburgh passes **Craigmillar Castle,** now a lonely ruin, but in centuries past a place of some importance. It was an occasional residence of Mary Stewart, and here was planned the murder of Darnley, the "bond of blood" being dated from Craigmillar. (*Admission fee, daily from* 9.30, *Sundays* 10.)

GALASHIELS TO EDINBURGH VIÂ PEEBLES.

Along the breast of the hills westward of Galashiels runs the *Catrail*, a defensive work attributed to the Britons and originally consisting of a chain of forts connected by deep fosse and rampart. The terminal fort on Rink Hill commands lovely views over Tweeddale.

For the first few miles the road is occupied in swinging round the group of hills across which the Catrail runs. Then Tweeddale is entered at Caddonfoot, and across the valley is *Ashiestiel*, which was for some years the residence of Sir Walter Scott, prior to his removal to Abbotsford. It is charmingly situated against a background of hills—there are vivid descriptions of local scenery in the first four cantos of *Marmion*. The most interesting of the hills beyond Tweeddale is *Minchmoor* (1,856 feet): a short way north of the highest point is the Cheesewell, so called from the habit of travellers who dropped into its waters crumbs of cheese in order to propitiate the fairies reputed to haunt the spot.

By Walkerburn, busy with its woollen manufacture, we come to **Innerleithen** (*Traquair Arms*), an attractive little place boasting medicinal springs which are claimed as the prototype of Scott's "St. Ronan's Well." The town is a good centre for walks over the surrounding hills, and there is fishing in the Tweed and tributary streams. An excellent moorland road cuts through the Moorfoots by Glentress to join the Edinburgh–Galashiels road.

Across the Tweed from Innerleithen is *Traquair House*, the oldest inhabited in Scotland. Only the tower (reputed to be 1,000 years old) dates from prior to Charles I's time. Either side of the main gateway are the carved bears mentioned in *Waverley* as the Bears of Bradwardine. (Open 2–5.30 *except Fridays July–September, Sundays from early May. Admission fee to house and/or grounds.*) The house is rich in fascinating souvenirs and romantic history, but perhaps the most interesting legends attach to the main gates, which were locked after the visit from Prince Charlie in 1745, never to be opened until a Stuart king comes to the throne.

PEEBLES.

Distances.—Edinburgh, 23 m.; Galashiels, 19 m.; Selkirk, 21 m.; Moffat, 35 m.
Early Closing.—Wednesday.
Hotels.—*Hydropathic* (160 rooms), *Cross Keys* (12 rooms), *Park, Waverley, Venlaw Castle, County, Tontine* (30 rooms), *Green Tree*, etc.
Sports.—Golf. *Fishing* for trout and salmon in Tweed and tributaries, controlled by local angling association. Tennis, bowls, swimming, putting.

A royal burgh since the fourteenth century, Peebles is delightfully situated astride the Tweed. Screened on every side by hills, it has long enjoyed a reputation as a health and pleasure resort and is celebrated in the old Scots poem *Peblis to the Play*, ascribed to James I of Scotland. The *Cross Keys*, a quaint old hostelry, is the original of Cleikum Inn, and Miss Ritchie, who ran it in Scott's day, was the prototype of Meg Dods in *St. Ronan's Well*. On the north side of the town are the ruins of the thirteenth-century **Cross Church**, all that is left of a monastic establishment which derived fame from possession of a fragment of the true Cross and the relics of St. Nicholas of Peebles and to the patronage of James IV. The property is now under the care of the Department of the Environment (open).

Peebles was the birthplace (in 1800 and 1802) of William and Robert Chambers, the publishers, the former of whom presented to the town the Chambers Institution, a remarkable building once known as the Queensberry Lodging, where is said to have been born in 1725 the fourth Duke of Queensberry, " Old Q " of sporting fame—the " degenerate Douglas " denounced in Wordsworth's sonnet for laying low the fine woods around **Neidpath Castle,** a mile westward from the town. The Castle is finely situated at a bend in the Tweed and commands lovely views. Neidpath originally consisted of a plain peel tower. It belonged to the Frasers (cf. the carved strawberries over the courtyard gateway—French, *fraises*), who probably added the part which is now almost all that remains. In the eighteenth century the Castle was held by William Douglas, third Earl of March, who in 1778 succeeded as the Duke of Queensberry—" Old Q."

A mile or so beyond the Castle a road crosses the Tweed and runs up to the village of Manor, whence it is less than a mile to the *Black Dwarf's Cottage.* David Ritchie, from whom Scott obtained his character, was a brush-maker whose misshapen figure was matched by an equally unfortunate sourness of disposition, so that he was forced to become a recluse. As described by Scott, he built a cottage on this site, but his landlord rebuilt it a few years before his death (in 1811), since which the building has again been renewed. Ritchie was buried in Manor Churchyard. Strong walkers will find it a fine wild route up beside the Manor Water and over to St. Mary's Loch, though the walk should not be attempted by solitary strangers when mist is about. (*See also* p. 87.)

Hence to **Biggar,** *see* p. 88.

The first few miles of the road from Peebles to Edinburgh are alongside the Eddleston water, past Eddleston village (*Black Barony*) to the moors about **Leadburn** (*Leadburn Hotel*), a haunt of anglers : in addition to various streams, there are the Gladhouse and other reservoirs (*apply Edinburgh Waterworks Department*).

From Leadburn the road runs down to **Penicuik** (Pen-y-cook : the hill of the cuckoo), a paper-making place on the North Esk a few miles below that part of the river known as *Habbie's Howe* :

> " Gae far'er up the burn to Habbie's Howe,
> Where a' the sweets o' spring and summer grow.
> There, 'tween two birks out o'er a little linn,
> The water falls and makes a singing din ;
> A pool breast-deep, beneath as clear as glass,
> Kisses wi' easy whirls the bord'ring grass."

To reach Habbie's Howe and the neighbouring *Newhall House* (with its memories of Allan Ramsay's *Gentle Shepherd*) follow the Carlops road. For Habbie's Howe take the first opening on the left beyond Newhall gates.

Eastward from Penicuik is Roslin (p. 72). Hence to Edinburgh the road needs no description.

ROUTES VIÂ CARLISLE.

CARLISLE.

Car Parks.—Viaduct, The Sands, Drovers Lane, Devonshire Walk, etc.
Distances.—Edinburgh, 93 m.; Gretna Green, 9 m.; Glasgow, 95 m.; Berwick-on-Tweed, 90 m.; London, 300 m.; Scotch Corner (for A1), 68 m.; Keswick, 30 m.
Early Closing.—Thursday.
Hotels.—*County and Station* (100 rooms), *Crown and Mitre* (75 rooms), *Red Lion* (60 rooms), *Central* (75 rooms), and others.
Railway Station, one of the busiest in Britain, is on main London Midland Region route between England and Scotland. Connections also with Newcastle, Edinburgh and West Cumberland.

THOUGH Carlisle is in England, mention is here made of the city, as its geographical position makes it the key of the principal road and railway routes between England and Scotland.

Carlisle has a history that is surely just as eventful as that of any other city in Britain, but if (Macaulay notwithstanding) it is still as " merrie " as in the days of the Border balladists, it manages to conceal that fact from the casual observer. It is, in short, a busy industrial town.

The two chief sights are the Castle and the Cathedral, the former boasting one of the finest Norman keeps in the country. The **Castle** is open daily throughout the year, *admission fee*; and visitors who miss in the bustling streets of the town those relics which an acquaintance with history leads one to expect will find plenty to kindle the imagination behind these grim walls. Hardly less eventful has been the history of the **Cathedral.** Twice victim of fire, and in later years fiercely attacked by the Puritans and those who came after, there is little left of the original Norman nave. Fortunately there does remain much that is beautiful: note High Altar and lovely East Window.

Visitors from across the Atlantic generally seek out the Congregational Church in Lowther Street, the pastor of which a century ago was President Wilson's grandfather. President Wilson's mother was born at 83 Cavendish Place, Warwick Road. When President Wilson visited Carlisle in 1918 he was made a Freeman of the City, an honour also bestowed on Field Marshal Lord Montgomery in 1947.

CARLISLE TO EDINBURGH VIÂ HAWICK.

For the first few miles this route is identical with that *viâ* Beattock either to Edinburgh or Glasgow. At **Stanwix** (the Roman *Petriana*) the line of the Great Wall is crossed. Traces of the wall can be seen by digressing to the right, but the more impressive remains lie some way farther east, on the higher ground beyond Brampton and Castlesteads.

Two miles after crossing Carlisle's bridge over the Eden the Longtown and Hawick road keeps to the right at the fork. The Esk is crossed at Longtown, and beyond the railway level crossing go to the right. Ahead is seen the lofty Malcolm monument over Langholm ; to the left is *Solway Moss* where in 1542 the Scots suffered a severe defeat. The news of the battle reached James V at Falkland at the same moment as tidings of the birth of Mary at Linlithgow, an ill-omened conjunction which the King summed up in the oft-quoted remark, " It came wi' a lass, and it'll gang wi' a lass." The Border is crossed some 3 miles from Longtown at **Scotsdyke** : the point is marked by a small board bearing the word " Scotland "—a welcome contrast to the long stream of advertisements along the Gretna road (*see* p. 83).

A little above Scotsdyke the Liddel Water joins the Esk, and for some miles marks the Border. Beyond Newcastleton, in Liddesdale, the valley of the Hermitage leads to **Hermitage Castle**, about 20 miles from Scotsdyke. The Castle (*weekdays*, 10–4 or 7 ; *Sundays*, 2–4 or 7 ; *fee.*) is one of the largest and best preserved in the Borders. Founded in the thirteenth century, it came into the hands of the Douglases, who exchanged it with the Earl of Bothwell for Bothwell Castle. It was Bothwell's illness here which brought Mary riding over from Jedburgh (*see* pp. 61–2). From Hermitage a wild road across the Cheviots carries on to Hawick.

From Canonbie to Langholm the main road is at times very beautiful, running beside the tree-embowered Esk. In days past it was a favourite hunting-ground of Johnny Armstrong of Gilnockie, a notorious freebooter whose name was feared as far off as Newcastle, until James V took him at Carlenrig in Teviotdale and there hanged him and his company. The famous ballad suggests that the King acted dishonourably, but this is not so.

Langholm (*Crown*, *Eskdale*, *Ashley Bank*, *Buck*, *Ardill House* (bdg.)), is a pleasant little town near the confluence of the Ewes and Wauchope Waters with the Esk. It is a good angling centre (Esk and Liddel Fisheries Association issues tickets) and there are some good walks over the neighbouring hills. The monument on Whita Hill, east of the town, commemorates General Sir J. Malcolm (1769–1833), a governor of Bombay.

The Eskdale excursion is especially pleasing. At *Westerkirk* in 1757 was born Thomas Telford, the engineer, and thence onward there are ample evidences of even greater engineers, for Roman camps and castles, or remains of them, are sprinkled on either side of the valley all the way to *Eskdalemuir*. (The Church is 600 feet above the sea.) Hence a wild road leads up the valley to Foulbog summit (1,096 feet) and then down Ettrick-dale to *Tushielaw Inn* (*see* p. 81). Walkers can continue along a rough track to Tibbie Shiel's, on St. Mary's Loch (6 miles; *see* p. 81). Motorists reach St. Mary's Loch *viâ* the *Gordon Arms Hotel* on the Selkirk–Moffat road.

Another good excursion from Langholm is beside the Wauchope Water and on into the vale of the Kirtle Water and so to Ecclefechan (p. 83).

From Langholm to Hawick the main road at first follows the Ewes Water. Ewes hamlet is 4 miles out, and then the road begins the steep, relentless climb from pleasant Ewesdale to the grim uplands around **Mosspaul**, with *Wisp Hill* (1,950 feet) left of the summit. Beyond *Mosspaul Hotel* we cross the summit (853 feet) and enter Roxburghshire. Teviotdale is entered at the hamlet of **Teviothead**, with a pointed monument to Riddell, the poet (author of " Scotland Yet "), and a churchyard wall bearing a tablet recording the burial of Johnny Armstrong of Gilnockie (*see* p. 77) and his " galant companie."

The rest of the way to Hawick by Teviotdale is pleasant going through the wooded vale. **Branxholm Tower**, on the left as Hawick is approached, bravely bears the memory of the day when, as recorded in *The Lay of the Last Minstrel*—

> " Nine and twenty knights of fame
> Hung their shields in Branksome Hall;
> Nine and twenty squires of name
> Brought their steeds to bower from stall."

On the right is *Goldielands*, an old border peel; then on the left the Borthwick Water comes in, and so to **Hawick** (*Crown*, *Tower*, *Buccleuch*, *Kings*, *Teviotdale Lodge*, *Victoria*), which of all the Border towns seems best to retain that air of aloofness so often found along debated frontiers. The main street is dominated by the fine tower of the town buildings, and at the far end is a stirring sculpture to the "Callants" who in 1514 defeated an English force at Hornshole (*see below*) and captured their colours.

The Mote Hill, 450 feet high, is supposed to have been the meeting-place of the ancient Court of Justice. The *Tower Hotel* announces in its name that it incorporates a fragment of one of the fortified residences of Borderland. Hawick is a busy centre of mills for woollens, hosiery, etc., and is also a noted anglers' centre (Upper Teviotdale Fisheries Association). There are golf links and facilities for tennis, putting, etc., in a splendid public park.

Hawick to Jedburgh (11 miles)—a charming road beside the Teviot. *Hornshole Bridge* (2½ miles) was the site of the "Callants'" skirmish after Flodden; an encounter duly commemorated by a cross and the "Common Riding." **Denholm** was the birthplace of Leyden, the poet: a more celebrated "son" was Sir John Murray, whose fame lives in the New English Dictionary. Across the river, *Minto House* (Earl of Minto) is backed by the Minto Crags, where are the ruins of Fatlips Castle. Southward rises the shapely *Rubers Law* (1,392 feet), on the east side of which is the valley of the Rule Water, up which a wild road (summit level 1,250 feet) leads over to Liddesdale and Newcastleton: an easterly branch runs off to Carter Bar (p. 60) and Catcleugh. Ahead as the main road approaches Jedburgh (*see* p. 60) is the Waterloo Monument above Jedfoot.

Hawick to Selkirk (11 miles).—The road calls for no special mention, being characterized by far-spreading views over mountain and moorland. **Selkirk** is well placed above the south bank of the Ettrick, and is a favourite resort of those walking or riding in the Border country.

There is golf and plenty of fishing and all around are places of interest and beauty. The Common Riding and races in June attract large crowds. Hotels: *County* (11 *rooms*), *Woodburn* (6 *rooms*), *Heatherliehill* (11 *rooms*), *Glen* (12 *rooms*), *Fleece* (10 *rooms*).

At the east end of the High Street is another of the inspiriting Border monuments of which Hawick and Galashiels provide examples. "O Flodden Field" runs the inscription. It was erected in 1913 to mark the four-hundredth anniversary of the Battle of Flodden.

Selkirk is a very old town. It was incorporated as a Royal Burgh in 1535. A reminder of its antiquity is found on its coat-of-arms which portrays the Virgin and Child and the Royal Arms of Scotland with the Kirk of St. Mary's in the background. In the early years of the twelfth century, King David, before ascending the throne, brought monks from France and founded a monastery in Selkirk, but after a stay of several years the monastery was removed to Kelso.

The souters (i.e. shoemakers) of Selkirk were famed for their single-soled shoes, a fact enshrined in the lines beginning:

"Up wi' the souters of Selkirk,"

but shoemaking has given place to tweed manufacture as the predominating local industry.

In the Market Place behind a statue of Sir Walter Scott stands the old Sheriff Courthouse (*apply Town Clerk*) used by Scott when Shirra of Ettrick Forest. In the High Street another statue portrays Mungo Park, the explorer, who was born at Foulshiels near the town in 1771 (*see below*). A tablet in the Public Library brings a timely reminder that Selkirk was also the birthplace of Andrew Lang (d. 1912), and there is a good memorial bust of Tom Scott, R.S.A., the artist. Selkirk no longer has a train service; it is linked with Galashiels by bus.

SELKIRK TO MOFFAT.

Selkirk is at the eastern edge of the **Ettrick Forest**—a grand region of mountain and moor, loch and burn, through which runs the road to Moffat (34 miles; *bus but no railway*). From Selkirk Market Place go down the suggestively-named West Port, where stood the old Forest Inn, visited by Burns. Cross the bridge and keep to the left. On the right is *Philiphaugh*, where Leslie defeated Montrose in 1645, and on the left is soon seen the gaunt ruin of **Newark,** "renowned in Border story." Between Selkirk and Newark is the Duke of Buccleuch's estate, Bowhill. A cottage at Foulshiels, almost opposite the remains of a bridge leading across the river to Newark Castle, was the birthplace of Mungo Park. On Broadmeadows (now a Youth Hostel) came down the old drove road over Minchmoor (*see* p. 73).

On by **Yarrowford** the scenery is very lovely. Yarrow Church is passed, and the Yarrow Feus (feu = rent or lease), and then comes the intersection with the roads from Innerleithen (to the north: *see* p. 73) and Tushielaw and Ettrick (*see below*), 7 miles southward. This point is at the entrance to a neighbourhood celebrated in the history of Border minstrelsy. Mount Benger, half a mile north of the Gordon Arms, was for some time farmed by James Hogg, the "Ettrick Shepherd" (*see below*). **Dryhope Tower,** above the road on the right near the foot of St. Mary's Loch, was the home of Mary Scott, the "Flower of Yarrow." A little farther along is the ruin of 12th-century **St. Mary's Kirk,** with a quietly beautiful burying-ground, well known to lovers of Border ballads; and on the narrow isthmus separating St. Mary's Loch from the Loch of the Lowes is "**Tibbie Shiel's,**" which by the witchery of Scott, Christopher North (who made it the scene of so many *Noctes Ambrosianæ*), De Quincey, Aytoun, Lockhart, not forgetting James Hogg, arose from a humble cottage to a famous hostelry. "Tibbie Shiel" (Mrs. Richardson), the first hostess of the place, must be credited with at least as much of the transformation, for she was a "character" capable of holding her own with the great ones. She died in 1878 and lies buried near Hogg in Ettrick Churchyard.

A hilly road goes up the Meggat Water and over to Tweedsmuir by Talla Reservoir (*see* p. 87).

St. Mary's Loch is a beautiful sheet 3 miles long and about half a mile wide. In depth 80 to 90 feet it is 808 feet above sea-level, and is easily accessible by road. There is excellent fishing for trout, pike and perch (*Tibbie Shiel's*, the *Rodono* and *Gordon Arms Hotels* provide boats, etc.).

On the hill-side just above the isthmus dividing the two lochs is a monument to James Hogg, the Ettrick Shepherd.

A track crossing the isthmus climbs to 1,405 feet and joins the road from the *Gordon Arms* down to Ettrick Dale at **Tushielaw,** whence it is 3 miles up the valley to **Ettrick Church,** beside which Hogg was born and in the churchyard of which he was buried. Tushielaw (*inn*) is 15 miles from Selkirk by Ettrickbridge (*hotel*).

James Hogg (1770–1835), the "Ettrick Shepherd" of Wilson's *Noctes Ambrosianæ,* was the son of a farmer. His education appears to have been very slight, but at the age of about 25 he took to writing verse—"songs and ballads made up for the lassies to sing in chorus." His first poems were published anonymously, but subsequently he made the acquaintance of Sir Walter Scott, and as the result of encouragement from that kindly quarter he gave up shepherding and moved to Edinburgh to embark on a literary career. Although he has been acclaimed as "after Burns, the greatest poet that had ever sprung from the bosom of the common people," and the *Edinburgh Review* hailed him as "a poet in the highest acceptance of the term," he seems to have been beset by constant financial difficulties. He died in 1835 at the farm of Altrive, a couple of miles up the road from the *Gordon Arms* to Tushielaw, and, as already stated, was buried in Ettrick churchyard.

Beyond Tibbie Shiel's the Moffat road passes **Loch of the Lowes** and runs between steep hill-sides for some 3 miles. Then, on the right, a glimpse is caught of the **Grey Mare's Tail**, a magnificent cascade, one of the highest and finest in Scotland—now in the care of the National Trust. Although it can be seen from the road, a closer view amply repays the stroll of a few hundred yards to the mouth of the little glen into which it tumbles. The water comes from wild **Loch Skeen**, between White Coomb (2,695 feet) and Lochcraig Head (2,625 feet): a path strikes up the steep hill-side to the loch from a point about a mile below the road bridge near the Grey Mare's Tail (*see also* p. 86).

For the remainder of this route *see under* Moffat.

Selkirk to Galashiels (6 miles). The road runs along the eastern bank of the river for 2 miles. At Lindean it crosses the Ettrick Water (the road to the right at the entrance to the bridge leads prettily to Abbotsford in about 2 miles), and shortly after that it crosses the Tweed just above the point where that river joins the Ettrick Water. Near Abbotsford Ferry a glimpse will be caught of Abbotsford House, across the river, and then the road swings round Gala Hill to Galashiels. (For Galashiels and routes thence to Edinburgh, *see* pp. 71–5.)

CARLISLE TO EDINBURGH OR GLASGOW VIÂ BEATTOCK.

Railway.—For the greater part of the way the railway line keeps close company with the road.

Carlisle to Beattock, 40 m.; Edinburgh, 93 m.; Glasgow, 96 m.

This is the best known of the various routes over the Border, but in point of picturesqueness the first 20 miles north of Carlisle do not compare with similar stages on the Carter Bar or Coldstream crossings. Two miles beyond the bridge over the Eden, the road keeps to the left (that to the right leads to Longtown and Hawick, *see* p. 77). Four miles farther the Esk is crossed, and then the bridge over the little River Sark which here actually links the two countries. The road is devoid of romance to-day, if one may judge from appearances, but for centuries it has been famed as the way to **Gretna Green** (*Hall*), and many a fine race between runaway couples and thwarted parents has been decided along this straight and almost level stretch of road. Formerly hasty young couples could be married at a moment's notice by the smith at Gretna, since Scottish law recognized as man and wife a couple who had made a plain declaration before witnesses, but since 1940 it has been necessary for both parties to qualify by a residence of at least fifteen clear days in Scotland before giving notice of intention to marry. Marriages still take place at Gretna. Not only Gretna, but Coldstream and Lamberton (*see* pp. 57 and 49) also were noted for runaway marriages. Originally the Gretna "ceremonies" took place in the village, but with the erection of a new toll bridge over the Sark, business was attracted to the toll-house, since it lay only a few yards over the Border and often only a few yards spelt the difference between victory and defeat. Both the old "Smithies" are open to visitors at a fee and contain various relics of Gretna in its hey-day.

Disregarding the road westward to Annan and Dumfries (*see* p. 92) continue by Kirkpatrick and Kirtlebridge to **Ecclefechan** (*Ecclefechan*), where Thomas Carlyle was born in 1795 and in the churchyard of which he was buried. His birthplace, "The Arched House," contains a number of relics and is open on weekdays from 10 to 6 (National Trust). Readers of *Sartor Resartus* will have small difficulty in recognizing "Entephul."

Hoddam Castle, a few miles south-west of Ecclefechan by a lovely avenue which Carlyle named "the kindly beech rows," was the original castle of Scott's *Redgauntlet*. On the hills north-east of the village is *Burnswark*, worth visiting on account of the views over Solway and for its numerous remains of camps and forts indifferently ascribed to Hadrian and Agricola.

Six miles farther is **Lockerbie** (*King's Arms*, *Blue Bell*, etc.), a small market town whence a road runs westward to

Lochmaben, crossing the Annan just below its reception of the Dryfe. Here occurred in 1593 the last great contest between feudal houses on the border, the Johnstones defeating the Maxwells in a savage contest which is commemorated in the phrase "a Lockerbie lick."

The Castle of Lochmaben, now a shapeless ruin, claims to have been the birthplace of the Bruce (1278). The Castle loch is said to contain ten different kinds of fish, among them being the vendace, a small white fish somewhat resembling a dace (French: *vandoise*), which takes no bait and is only found in this and two adjacent lochs. The fish is netted in August.

From Lockerbie our route skirts the eastern side of Annandale, pregnant with memories of Border frays. At Beattock the road from Dumfries comes in on the left. That for Moffat also goes off on the left.

MOFFAT.

Distances.—Carlisle, 40 m.; Dumfries, 21 m.; Edinburgh, 53 m.
Early Closing.—Wednesday.
Hotels.—*Buccleuch Arms* (17 rooms), *Annandale Arms* (24 rooms), *Moffat House* (14 rooms), *Balmoral* (18 rooms), *Star* (12 rooms), *Auchen Castle* (26 rooms).
Sports.—Bowls, tennis, golf, fishing in numerous burns, in Loch Skene, St. Mary's Loch and the Loch of the Lowes.

Moffat is a very attractive little town near the head of Annandale and with good scenery on every hand. The discovery of mineral springs in the middle of the eighteenth century first attracted visitors, and although the place is now more generally known as a splendid centre for hill-walkers, anglers, golfers and motorists, it is still faintly reminiscent of Cheltenham in the gardened villas which augment the accommodation offered by the hotels.

At Moffat House, James Macpherson ("Ossian Macpherson") stayed during 1759, probably spending part of his time in working upon the poems which subsequently caused such controversy (*see* p. 326). Burns was also at Moffat, and is credited with writing on the window of the Black Bull Hotel the following comment aroused by the sight of two ladies who passed, the one small and dainty, the other more broadly built:

> "Ask why God made the gem so small,
> And why so huge the granite
> Because God meant mankind should set
> That higher value on it."

In the churchyard is the grave of **J. L. McAdam**, the road-maker, whose name is perpetuated, though now only in abbreviated form, in the second syllable of the word "tarmac."

Two miles south of Moffat is *Three Waters Meet*, where the Evan and Moffat Waters contribute their stream to the Annan. On the way are passed the Standing Stones, of which little seems to be known, and just beyond is Loch House Tower, an old square fortress with an echo from the high-road.

Westward from the Crawford road at Beattock the Garpol Water makes a pretty little glen with waterfalls (the ruin is that of Auchencat Castle, once held for the Bruce), and on the other side of the Moffat Water, near the Three Waters Meet, is Bell Craig Linn, another pretty spot; farther south is Wamphray with its pretty glen. But the prettiest thing of the kind in the neighbourhood is **Raehills Glen**, about 8 miles from Moffat on the Dumfries road.

The tapering hill of **Queensberry** (2,285 feet), 8–9 miles south-west of Moffat, commands a wide view, but the ascent in itself is less interesting than that to White Coomb and Hart Fell (*see* p. 86). The route is by a side road from Beattock Bridge to Earshaig and Kinnelhead, where cross the stream, turn left, and pass in front of a cottage. The mountain shortly comes into full view and further directions are unnecessary.

The left-hand road at the foot of Moffat Market Place runs out into **Moffat Dale**, down which the Moffat Water rushes through scenery that in the lower parts of the glen is very pretty. The upper parts are somewhat bare; forming a fitting prelude to the beauties of Yarrow, beyond **St. Mary's Loch** (*see* p. 81). Between 2 and 3 miles from Moffat the road crosses the picturesque *Craigie Burn* (*private*). Here lived Jean Lorimer, heroine of nearly a dozen of Burns's love songs. A house rather more than half a mile farther on occupies the site of an ale-house in which "Willie brew'd a peck o' maut" is supposed to have been written. As the road proceeds Saddle Yoke (2,412 feet) presents on the left a peaked appearance that is unusual in these parts.

From Bodesbeck Farm a walking route strikes up the eastern side of the valley into Ettrick Dale (about 10 miles to Ettrick Church; another 6 over the hills down to Tibbie Shiel's; longer by the road past Tushielaw).

Just under 10 miles from Moffat is the **Grey Mare's Tail,** for which and the route on to St. Mary's Loch and Selkirk *see* pages 80–2.

To White Coomb and Hart Fell.—This is the best hill excursion in the immediate neighbourhood of Moffat. A whole day should be allowed unless a lift can be arranged as far as Birkhill, on the Selkirk road, at the top of the rise beyond the Grey Mare's Tail. The footpath which leaves the road here soon vanishes, and one takes a westerly direction to the ridge, keeping the burn that drops into Dobs Gill considerably below on the left. The ridge gained, White Coomb appears in front and soon afterwards **Loch Skeen** shows itself below, amid wild scenery with screes descending steeply to its upper end. At the southern end are ancient moraines through which the Tail Burn makes its way to form the **Grey Mare's Tail** (p. 82). Make for this end of the loch and continue westward to a long green slope, beyond which is the almost level plateau of grass forming the top of **White Coomb** (2,695 feet). From White Coomb to Hart Fell is a walk of 1½–2 hours along the northern edge of the coombes that furrow the range from Moffat Dale. The views are good : especially that down the valley of the Blackhope Burn. Hart Fell (2,651 feet) is even more of a plateau than White Coomb ; its summit is distinguished by a cairn attached to which is a small stone enclosure. There is a fine prospect of the rich lowland country from this point. Westward the Devil's Beef Tub and the Edinburgh road are conspicuous, but those who descend that way will find a deep hollow to be crossed about half-way. The best way of prolonging the hill walk is to return to Moffat by a path (a couple of cairns mark the way) down the shoulder that has the Auchencat Burn on the left and passes above Hart Fell Spa.

MOFFAT TO EDINBURGH.

At the northern end of Moffat the Edinburgh road diverges to the left, crosses the Annan and begins the steep climb which does not cease for 7 miles and which carries it to 1,348 feet above sea-level. On the way up there are charming views back over Moffat, and at *Holehouse Linn* (2½ miles) a road on the left strikes over the hills to the main Glasgow road through **Evandale** (*see* p. 88). Two miles farther we look down into the **Devil's Beef Tub**, a remarkable green basin, 500 or 600 feet deep, with abrupt sides broken only by an outlet on the south, through which the infant Annan finds a way. In origin it recalls the corries of the Highlands, a terminal valley widened and deepened by glacial action. The name is said to have been derived from the fact that the Johnstones used the place as a pound for stolen cattle. In *Redgauntlet* the place is described as a " d . . . . ., deep, black, blackguard-looking abyss that goes straight down from the roadside as straight as it can do"; and pictures the Laird of Summertrees escaping from his captors by rolling from top to bottom "like a barrel down Chalmers' Close in Auld Reekie."

A mile beyond the Tub the road crosses the watershed at a height of 1,334 feet and shortly after passes to the left of *Tweed's Well*, the source of the Tweed. The road then follows the left bank of the Tweed and 15 miles from Moffat reaches **Tweedsmuir** (*Crook Inn*), south-east of which is the **Talla Reservoir** (Edinburgh water supply). At the head of the reservoir in 1682 took place the Covenanting conventicle at which Davie Deans was present, as described in *The Heart of Midlothian*. *Drumelzier*, to the right of the road, is often pointed out as the burial-place of Merlin, but the grave near the Kirk covers the remains of Merlin Caledonius and not Merlin Emrys, the great Welsh Bard.

The road through Drumelzier reaches Peebles (p. 74) in about a dozen miles, passing on the right the remains of Tennis Castle, the Church of Dawyck and on the left **Stobo**, with a church containing much Norman work. Then comes **Lyne**, with a tiny church containing some good Flemish woodwork and with some standing stones and the remains of a Roman Camp. On the hill south of the village over a footbridge across the Tweed is *Barns Tower*, a sixteenth-century stronghold now a youth hostel. The road from Barns to the south which joins the road along Manor Valley brings one in 2 miles to the Black Dwarf's Cottage (p. 75) and provides a good walk over the hills to St. Mary's Loch (*see* p. 81). For Peebles and the road on to Edinburgh, *see* pages 74–5.

The road beside the Lyne Water leads in about 3 miles to the ruins of *Drochil Castle*, a project of the Regent Morton's which was never completed owing to his death.

From Broughton the Edinburgh road strikes northward to Blyth Bridge (*Blyth Bridge Hotel*), on past the picturesque hamlet of Romanno Bridge, and so by Leadburn to Penicuik and Edinburgh as described on page 75.

CARLISLE TO EDINBURGH VIÂ BIGGAR.

As far as Beattock, the route from Carlisle is as described on pages 82–4, but instead of turning off to the east for Moffat it follows the Evan Water through the narrow valley. (Motorists who wish to include the Devil's Beef Tub in this route may do so at the cost of only slight extra mileage by going through Moffat to the "Tub" as described on page 86.) From the Tub retrace the route for a couple of miles to the road which turns off at Hole-house Linn and descends to the Evan valley about 5 miles short of the summit, which is 1,029 feet above the sea. Just beyond this point the infant Clyde is crossed, and a mile or so farther we definitely enter Clydesdale.

From Elvanfoot two fine mountain roads go westward to Nithsdale, the Clyde being crossed by a bridge about a mile below the village. That running south-west from the village goes through the Dalveen Pass (*see* p. 97) to Thornhill; the more westerly road, less suitable for motoring, goes to Sanquhar by Leadhills, Wanlockhead and the Mennock Pass (*see* p. 97).

Crawford (*Hillview, West End*) is a roadside village with numerous walks and excursions at hand.

Abington (*Hotels: Abington, Arbory*), 5 miles beyond Elvanfoot, is near an important parting of the ways: from the village a road on the left goes across to Hamilton (p. 90) and about 2 miles beyond it the main road forks, the Biggar–Edinburgh road crossing the river, the Tinto–Lanark road keeping to the western bank.

(*a*) The road which crosses the Clyde about 2 miles north of Abington follows the river downstream and then by Culter reaches **Biggar** (*Elphinstone, Hartree*), a small town spread out along one wide street. It was the birthplace of Dr. John Brown (1810–82), author of *Rab and His Friends* and other works popular reading in his time, and was also the home of early branches of the Gladstone family. Biggar is a clean, pleasant little place at which to stay, being a fair centre, among bracing surroundings, and with golf, fishing, bowling and other sports.

Half a mile beyond Biggar the road forks: that on the right goes by Skirling to Leadburn (*see* p. 75); straight ahead is the route by Dolphinton to West Linton and Carlops, on the eastern slopes of the Pentlands, and so to Edinburgh.

Abington to Glasgow by Hamilton.—A mile or so from Abington a good little road goes off on the left for Sanquhar (p. 97) by way of **Crawfordjohn,** of old noted for its curling stones. But the Glasgow road (A74) climbs north-westward to just on 1,000 feet and then drops to

Lamlash
Clauchlands Pt
Holy I.
1030
L.Ho.
Kingscross Pt
Whiting Bay
Largybeg
Dippin
Kilmory
Kildonan Cas.
Pladda I.
L.Ho.
F I R T H O F C
Troon
Barassie
Loans
Symington
Craigie
Lady I.
K y l e
Mauchline
Distinkhorn
1258
Monkton
Tarbolton
Sorn
R. Ayr
Prestwick
New Prestwick
Annbank
Catrine
Howford Br.
Airds Moss
Barskimming
Cronberry
599
AYR
R. Ayr
Stair
Auchinleck
Ochiltree
Lugar W.
Cumnock
R. Doon
Coylton
Drongan
Heads of Ayr
Burns Cot.
Alloway Kirk
L. Martnaham
Dunure Cas.
Dunure Sta.
Dalrymple
Hollybush
AYR
Rankinston
630
Culzean Cas.
Maybole
312
Cassillis
Barnshean
Shankston L.
Patna
550
533
Waterside
R. Nith
Dalleagles
Enoch Hill
1865
Kirkmichael
Baltersan Cas.
Crossraguel Abbey
Mont
L. Spallander
R. Doon
561
Dalmellington
Maidens
Turnberry Cas.
Light Ho.
Kirkoswald
Crosshill
Straiton
Bogton L.
Blairquhan
Kirk Hill
880
190
Kilkerran
Ness Glen
Killochan
Dailly
Tairlaw Br.
L. Muck
Loch Doon
Bow B.
Cairnsmore
Ailsa Craig
1097
Light Ho.
Girvan
Girvan W.
Bargany
C a r r i c k
L. Linfern
L. Bradan
L. Finlas
Craiglure
Stinchar R.
Carsphairn
Ardmillan Ho.
Barr
Alton Albany
Assel W.
Dularg
Starr
The G l e n k e n s
Lendalfoot
Pinmore
350
Polmaddie Hill
1852
Shalloch on Minnoch
2520
Carleton
Daljarroch
Muck W.
L. Shalloch
Rowantree
Kirriereoch Hill
2562
L. Enoch
Kells Range
L. Harrow
Bennane Hd.
Colmonell
142
L. Moan
Merrick
2764
Knockdolian
369
Craigneil Cas.
Ballochmorrie
Kildonan Ho.
L. Dow
L. Dungeon
L. Arron
L. Neldricken
Ballantrae
Tig W.
Barhill Sta.
449
Cross W.
Glenlee
Downan Pt.
Glenapp Ho.
Beneraird
1435
Corwar Ho.
L. Dee
New Galloway
Auchencrosh Hill
690
Chirmorie
L. Maberry
L. Dornal
L. Trool
Lamachan
2349
Black Laggan
Kenmure Cas.
Finnart Pt.
Carlock Hill
Altimeg Hill
Bargrennan
House-o'-Hill Inn
Larg Hill
2159
Clatteringshaws L.
Millfore
2146
KIRKC
Milleur Pt.
Finnart Ho.
Glenwhilly
L. Derry
L. Ochiltree
L. Cree
Murray Mont
Talnotry
Corsewall Pt.
L.Ho.
Kirkcolm
Loch Ryan
Shennas
G a l l o w a y
Penninghame
Cass Stewart
Challoch
Minnigaff
Glenamour
2331
Balsarroch
L. Connell
The
Cairnryan
Artfield Fell
The Moors
Balminnoch
Newton Stewart
Cree Bri.
Cairnsmore of Fleet
Bargaly
Palnure
Leswalt
New Luce
223
L. Heron
L. Ronald
Merton Hall
Lochnaw Castle
Inchlossan
Black L.
Auchmantle
WIGTOWN
Kirkcowan
Glasnick
Barrae
Bishop B.
Castramont
Creetown
Stranraer
Castle Kennedy
Carscreugh
Glenluce Abbey
Kirkchrist
WIGTOWN
Cassencary
Larg Hill
969
Gatehouse
Culhorn Ho.
Soulseat L.
Dunragit
Park
Glenluce
Barhapple L.
Mochrum L.
Clugston L.
Dunskey Ho.
Colfin
Garthland
Whitefield L.
Burnfoot
Carsluith
Anwoth
Kirkdale
Port Patrick
Castle L.
Malzie W.
Bladnoch
Stoneykirk
Dunskey Castle
Mochrum L.
Baldoon Cas.
Hattericks Cave
Kirkinner
Barnbarroch
Knockinaam
Auchenmalg B.
Eldrig L.
Elrig
Whauphill
Innerwell
Is. of Fleet
Sandhead Inn
Balgreggan
Craignarget
Mochrum
Sorbie
Garlieston
Wigtown
Kirkmadrine Ch.
Broughton Mains
Castle Stewart
Galloway Ho.
Bay
Ardwell Ho.
Ardwell Inn
Chapel Rossan
Port William
White L.
Castlewigg
Cas.
Logan Ho.
Monreith
Sea Fish Pond
Whithorn
Port Logan
Luce Bay
Monreith B.
Glasserton
Portyerrock
Carlton
Physgill Ho.
Isle of Whithorn
Kirkmaiden
Drummore Inns
St Ninian's Cave
Burrow Head
Dunman
522
Portankill
St Medan's Cave
Lighthouse
Mull of Galloway
to Glasgow 110 m.
to Heysham 192 miles

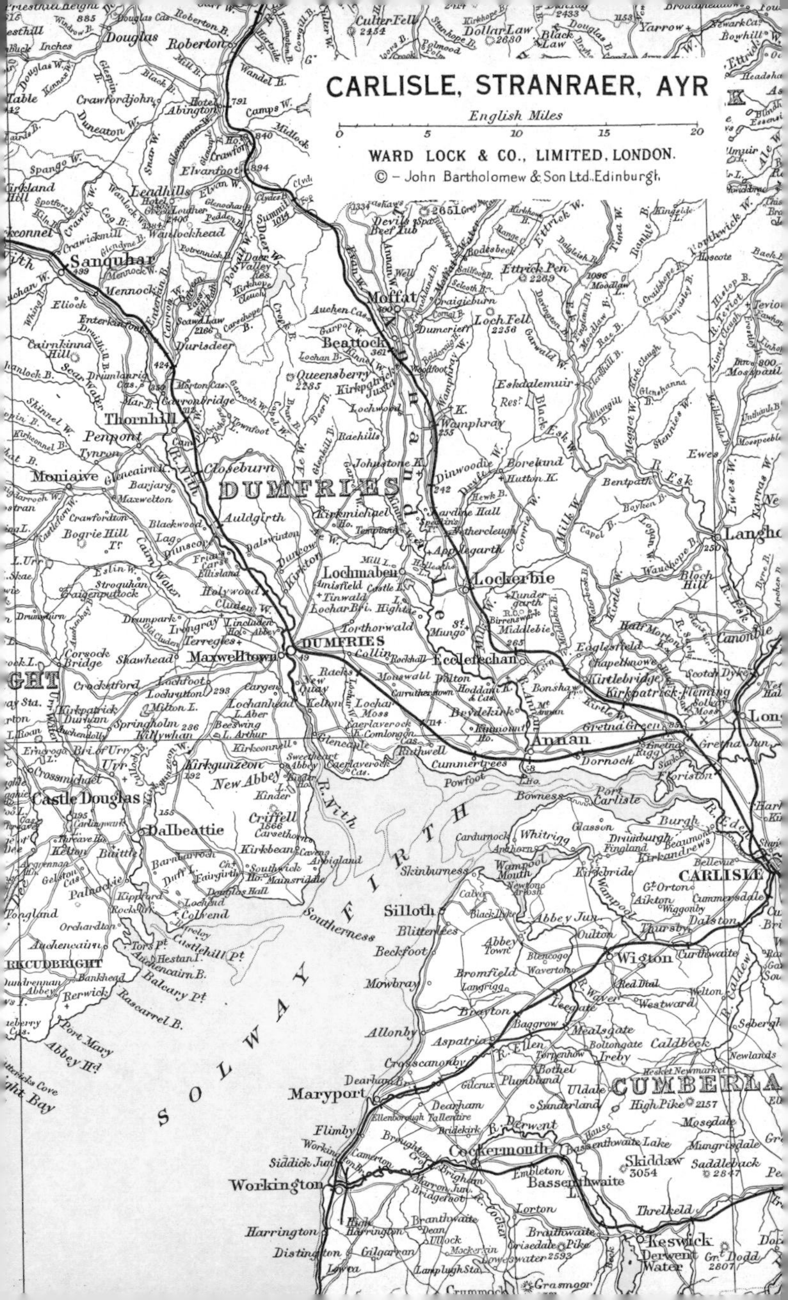
CARLISLE, STRANRAER, AYR
English Miles
0 5 10 15 20
WARD LOCK & CO., LIMITED, LONDON.
© – John Bartholomew & Son Ltd. Edinburgh
Douglas
Robertson
Crawfordjohn
Abington
Leadhills
Wanlockhead
Elvanfoot
Sanquhar
Mennock
Durisdeer
Carronbridge
Thornhill
Penpont
Tynron
Moniaive
Closeburn
DUMFRIES
Auldgirth
Moffat
Beattock
Queensberry 2285
Kirkpatrick Juxta
Wamphray
Dinwoodie
Boreland
Eskdalemuir
Ettrick Pen 2269
Loch Fell 2256
Kirkmichael
Lochmaben
Lockerbie
Holywood
Dumfries
Maxwelltown
Ecclefechan
Annan
Kirtlebridge
Kirkpatrick-Fleming
Gretna Green
Gretna
Canonbie
Langholm
Bentpath
Ewes
Castle Douglas
Dalbeattie
Kirkgunzeon
New Abbey
Criffell 1866
Kirkbean
Southerness
Caerlaverock
Ruthwell
Cummertrees
Powfoot
Bowness
Port Carlisle
Burgh
CARLISLE
Silloth
Abbey Town
Wigton
Aspatria
Allonby
Maryport
Flimby
Workington
Harrington
Cockermouth
Bassenthwaite
Skiddaw 3054
Saddleback 2847
Keswick
Derwent Water
Caldbeck
High Pike 2157
SOLWAY FIRTH
CUMBERLA
R. Nith
R. Esk
R. Eden
R. Derwent
Kirkcudbright
Balcary Pt.
Hestan I.

Douglasdale, a valley extending from the foot of Caintable to the confluence of *Douglas Water* with the Clyde. The valley was the cradle of the great Douglas race, who played such a prominent part in the history of Scotland and were at once the glory and the scourge of their country.

Sir Walter Scott made his last pilgrimage in Scotland to this locality, while preparing for his last novel, *Castle Dangerous*, and he has described with a master hand the ruins of the famous old castle, and the choir of the ancient Church of St. Bride, under which the chiefs of the princely race of Douglas were buried for centuries. From Douglasdale the road climbs north-westward again, and then by Lesmahagow descends finally to the increasingly industrial vale of the Clyde and so by Hamilton (p. 90) to **Glasgow.**

(*b*) The road which keeps to the west side of the Clyde below Abington soon comes in sight of **Tinto,** " the hill of Fire," celebrated through Lanarkshire for its conspicuous height (2,335 feet). The easiest ascent of the hill is up the north-east slope by an obvious path commencing about half a mile west of Thankerton. There is an excellent view-indicator on the summit. The name recalls the Beltane fire of the Druids, whose altars crowned its summit, and the beacon fires of later ages. A hole in a large stone on the summit is said to be the impress of Wallace's thumb ! *Fatlips Castle*, on the eastern flank of the hill, is likewise said to be the haunt of a brownie.

LANARK.

Distances.—Edinburgh, 33 m. ; Glasgow, 24 m. ; Moffat, 35 m. ; Carlisle, 77 m.
Early Closing.—Thursday.
Hotels.—*Clydesdale* (12 rooms), *Caledonian* (7 rooms), *Royal Oak* (13 rooms).
Railway Station at end of short branch from the line between Carluke and Carstairs (5 m.).
Sport.—Golf, bowls, fishing, tennis. Races under Jockey Club Rules annually at two meetings.

Lanark, county town of Lanarkshire, is a Royal Burgh of some antiquity and had a prominent place in Scottish history. It was the scene of many of Wallace's exploits ; and in the twelfth-century St. Kentigern's Church he is believed to have been married to Marion Bradfute. One of the church bells, now hanging in the Town Steeple, is reputed to be the oldest in Europe : it is inscribed Anno 1100.

Lanimer Day, in June, is for many the most popular festival of the year at Lanark. The custom originated in the riding of the Marches ; but it has been so embellished with processions, the crowning of a local schoolgirl as Lanimer Queen, and a variety of racing and other sports, that it now attracts attention over a wide neighbourhood.

Braxfield was the seat of Lord Braxfield, the judge whom R. L. Stevenson portrayed in *Weir of Hermiston.*

Formerly Lanark was visited for its proximity to Corra Linn, Bonnington Linn and Stonebyres Linn—the Falls of Clyde—but hydro-electric installations have to some extent interfered with this lovely river scenery.

At the west end of Lanark the road forks. The right-hand branch is the direct road to Stirling and the North. It passes through **Carluke** to the east of Coatbridge and Airdrie, joins the busy Glasgow–Stirling road at Cumbernauld, crosses the Forth and Clyde Canal, and then passes through Denny and on to Stirling.

The left-hand branch descends to the Clyde, which is crossed at Kirkfieldbank, and then follows the west side of the river for three miles to Crossford, half a mile to the west of which are the extensive ruins of **Craignethan Castle,** the original of Tillietudlem in Scott's *Old Mortality.* Tradition says that Queen Mary sheltered here after her escape from Loch Leven. In the neighbourhood is *Lee Castle*, where was kept the Lee Penny, which figures so prominently in *The Talisman.* The ancient Pease Tree at Lee even in Cromwell's time was hollowed with age and capacious enough to permit him to dine with a party of friends.

Opposite Motherwell, on the west side of the Clyde, is **Hamilton** (*Hotels: Commercial, Grange, Glen, Royal, Chantinghall; Y.W.C.A.*, High Patrick Street). Hamilton lies some eleven miles south-east of Glasgow. On its eastern side are extensive parks. The town is built at the junction of two important thoroughfares. One is the main highway between Glasgow and London and the other the route through Strathaven to Ayr and Stranraer. The main road north from the town, Bothwell Road, runs alongside the Low Parks, part of which is the well-known Hamilton Park Racecourse. In the parks also is the Hamilton Mausoleum (1850) designed by David Bryce. Hamilton Parish Church was designed by William Adam in 1732. On the Barncluith road the sixteenth-century house of *Barncluith* has fine terraced gardens.

To the south are the High Parks with the ruins of **Cadzow Castle,** once the ancient residence of the

Hamiltons ; it was dismantled by the Regent Murray after Langside. The White Cattle which are found in the park are regarded as survivors of the native wild cattle of Scotland. On the other side of the Avon from Cadzow is *Chatelherault*, designed by the elder Adam in imitation of the Château Herault in Poitou (the Duke of Hamilton is Duke of Chatelherault).

A mile or so downstream from Hamilton is **Bothwell Brig,** where the Covenanters were defeated on June 21, 1679, after a fierce struggle, by the royal forces under the Duke of Monmouth and Graham of Claverhouse. There is a graphic account of the conflict in Scott's *Old Mortality*. The bridge was rebuilt in 1826, but portions of the old structure were retained. **Bothwell Castle** (open standard Ministry hours) lies a mile west of the bridge. The castle was built in the thirteenth century by the family of de Moravia, and played an important part in the Wars of Independence. It was one of the largest in Scotland. The walls are upwards of 15 feet thick in many parts, and 60 feet high at the rampart facing the river.

The village of **Bothwell** is a favourite residential resort. Dr. James Baillie, afterwards Professor of Theology in Glasgow University, was at one time minister of the parish, and his famous daughter Joanna, the friend and correspondent of Sir Walter Scott, and herself an authoress of distinction, was born (1762) in the manse here.

On the opposite side of the Clyde from Bothwell are the ruins of **Blantyre Priory,** founded by Alexander II towards the end of the thirteenth century. The village of **Blantyre** has a number of light engineering firms. Here David Livingstone, the great African missionary-explorer, was born in 1813. His birth house, a tenement building, is now the *Livingstone National Memorial*, in which are preserved a unique collection of personal relics, murals and tableaux (*charge ; tearoom and gardens*).

So by Cambuslang and Rutherglen to Glasgow (p. 135).

CARLISLE TO GLASGOW VIÂ DUMFRIES AND KILMARNOCK (114 miles).

Railway.—Road and rail maintain close company throughout.

This route, slightly longer than others, passes through the heart of the Burns Country. It has already been described on pages 82–3 as far as Gretna, where the left-hand turning is taken. As the road runs westward along the shores of the Solway Firth, there are distant views of Criffel (1,866 feet), far away in the west, and of the Lakeland mountains to the south. Nine miles from Gretna is the busy town of **Annan** (*Central, Queensberry, etc.*), offering golf and fishing and a number of interesting trips into the hinterland, no fewer than half a dozen roads radiating from the vicinity. Annan was the birth-place of the celebrated preacher Edward Irving (1792), and it was here also that he was deposed by the local presbytery for his heretical opinions. Thomas Carlyle was a student and later teacher at Annan Grammar School.

The more interesting route from Annan to Dumfries is that *viâ* **Ruthwell**, in the parish church of which is a cross that is said to be the most ancient, as it is certainly the most graceful, of Runic monuments. From Ruthwell a devious road leads to **Caerlaverock Castle** (*open*), on the shores of the Firth. Of Edwardian type, the castle is triangular in plan, with two towers at the gatehouse and one at each of the other two angles. Parts of the screen walls are original; others represent successive rebuildings. Over the gateway are the Maxwell arms and the motto "I bid ye fair." Caerlaverock Church contains the grave of R. Paterson, the original of *Old Mortality* (*see* p. 100). From Caerlaverock Dumfries may be reached by a road skirting the pleasant estuary of the Nith and passing through the little resort of Glencaple (*Nith Hotel*).

DUMFRIES.

Distances.—Edinburgh, 74 m.; Glasgow, 75 m.; Carlisle, 32 m.; Stranraer, 75 m.
Early Closing.—Thursday.
Hotels.—*Station, King's Arms, Balmoral, County, Newton, Nithsdale, Waverley, Queensberry, Eden, Cairndale, etc.*
Railway Station on Carlisle–Kilmarnock–Glasgow main line.

Dumfries is a busy town in a wide loop of the Nith, about 5 miles above the point where that river empties itself into the Solway Firth. Its interests for some visitors are bound up with Burns, who is buried in St. Michael's Churchyard; but it is also a good holiday centre, and offers golf (2 courses), boating, river and loch fishing and a fine indoor swimming pool. Those who approach Dumfries by the road from Caerlaverock enter the town by St.

Michael Street, at the eastern end of which is the Churchyard. The Burns mausoleum is at the farthest corner from the entrance, while his original grave, marked with a wooden sign, is at the north-east corner of the churchyard. The monument within (restored 1935) represents "the genius of Coila finding her favourite son at the plough." Jean Armour and other members of the poet's family are also buried here.

A hundred yards westward of the Church, Burns

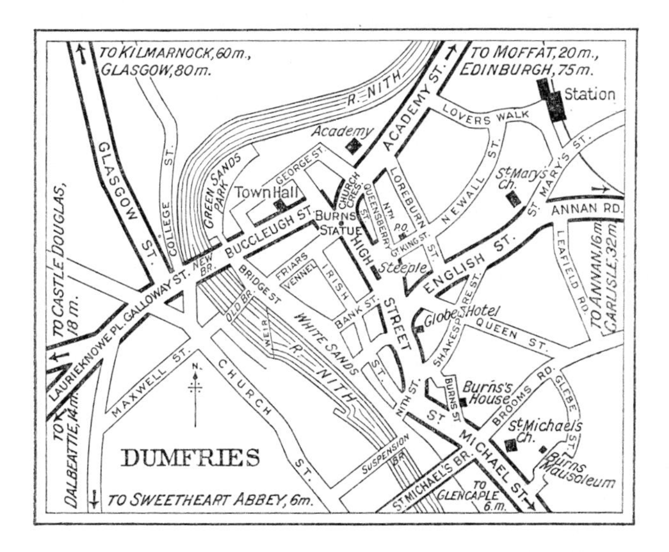

Street branches off to the right from St. Michael Street, on the right of it is **Burns's House**, the poet's home from 1793 until his death in July, 1796. The House (*Admission fee*) has been renovated and fitted up as a Museum of books and relics. Turn to the left at the far end of Burns Street and then to the right, and on the right will be seen the *Globe Inn*, Burns's "Howff," where he often forgathered with his friends. Here are shown his chair, a windowpane with verses traced by his hand, and other interesting relics.

Those entering Dumfries by the direct Annan road

pass on right the County Buildings, in front of which is a monument to the Duke of Queensberry (d. 1778), and will find the *Globe* and Burns Street by bearing left at the fountain at the end of English Street.

From this fountain High Street goes on past the lofty Midsteeple (erected 1704). Near the end of High Street, marked by a statue of Burns, stood the old Greyfriars Monastery in which Bruce slew the Red Comyn for his adherence to the English. A tablet on the wall in Castle Street records the event. The continuation of High Street is named after the Academy, standing a little to the north and numbering among its " old boys " Sir J. M. Barrie, O.M.

Our road bears left at this point, and by Buccleuch Street reaches the New Bridge (1794). The Old Bridge (15th century) succeeds one of Devorgilla's day (*see* below).

Across the river, and since 1929 amalgamated with Dumfries, is **Maxwelltown,** with the old windmill, once an observatory, and now part of the large Burgh Museum (*free, camera obscura, fee*), and which includes an interesting Burns collection and some archæological exhibits.

The road turning left beyond the Bridge over the Nith leads southward in about 6 miles to the remains of **Sweetheart Abbey** (*weekdays,* 10–7*; Sundays,* 2–7*; winter,* 4 *p.m.; admission, fee*), a beautiful Cistercian foundation of the thirteenth century which derives its name from the fact that the foundress, Devorgilla, ordered the heart of her husband, John Balliol, which she had cherished in a casket, to be buried in her tomb. John Balliol was the father of the puppet-king Balliol and the founder of Balliol College, Oxford. The arches of the nave and the massive central tower are in good preservation, and there are considerable remains of the transepts and chancel; the only part roofed over is part of the south transept. The style is Early English and Decorated. In a westerly direction is the Waterloo Monument on a northern spur of Criffel.

Southward of the village of New Abbey is Loch Kindar, and beyond that is the lane which forms the beginning of the ascent of **Criffel** (1,866 ft.), which, for its height and the comparative ease of the climb, gives a greater width of view than any other eminence, though it is even more noted as a feature of views from distant points, such as the Lakeland mountains, the Isle of Man, the Cheviots, etc. At the south-eastern foot of the mountain are the ruins of *Wreaths Castle*, once the property of the Regent Morton. The slopes of Criffel are a good point from which to observe the extraordinary tidal range of the Solway : from the shore southward of the mountain the waters ebb and flow over at least 4 miles of sands.

For Castle Douglas and the route to Wigtown, *see* pp. 99–104.

The Kilmarnock road is the first turning to the right beyond the New Bridge at Dumfries. **Lincluden College** can be reached by car by that road, turning off Jock's Loaning. Alternatively there is a way by cutting through the Lincluden housing estate. The ruins (*weekdays*, 10–4, *summer*, 7 ; *Sundays*, from 2 p.m. ; *admission, fee*) stand where the Cairn flows into the Nith, and comprise a small portion of the twelfth-century Benedictine Nunnery and more considerable remains of buildings erected in the fourteenth–sixteenth centuries when the Abbey had become a College. They are seen from the main road about 2 miles from Dumfries. In the transept of the little church note the tomb of the Provost, with the inscription, " You who tread on me with your feet remember me in your prayers." The chief feature in the chancel is the canopied tomb of Margaret, Countess of Douglas.

The Moniaive Valley.—Less than 3 miles from Dumfries the Glasgow road crosses the Cairn, and a road goes off on the left for Moniaive, passing almost immediately on the right a circle of standing stones known as the *Twelve Apostles*, though only eleven are present. A mile or so farther along this road a divergence to the left runs to **Irongray**, where, near the south-east corner of the Church, is buried the original of " Jeanie Deans," the gravestone bearing an inscription written by Sir Walter Scott. A little farther west is a Covenanters' Stone, the last object of the renovating care of " Old Mortality " : as with so many of these stones, the inscription is uncompromisingly blunt.

The main road next comes to Dunscore, about 6 miles to the west of which, and reached by a rough road, is the farm of **Craigenputtock**, " Cacophonious Craigenputtock," the abode of Thomas Carlyle from 1828 to 1834. Here he entertained Emerson and wrote *Sartor Resartus* and several of his essays. Four miles above Dunscore the Moniaive road passes *Maxwellton House*, the birthplace of Annie Laurie, the subject of the famous song, who is said to have been buried in the neighbouring churchyard of Glencairn.

Moniaive (16 miles from Dumfries) is a pleasant little place with a seventeenth-century market cross and a monument to the Rev. J. Renwick, the last of the Covenanting martyrs, who was executed at Edinburgh, 1688. The road between Moniaive and Thornhill passes the hill of *Tynron*, where the Bruce is said to have taken refuge after the murder of the Comyn at Dumfries.

A little more than 3 miles beyond the bridge over the Cairn, the Dumfries–Kilmarnock road passes the farm of **Ellisland,** where Burns lived for three years and where he wrote " Tam O'Shanter," " Ye Banks and Braes " and other poems. The farm is now a national possession in the care of the town of Dumfries ; there is admission to the display rooms in the farm, and through the stackyard and beside the river. Beyond Ellisland is Friar's Carse, the scene of the bout described in " The Whistle " : it is now a convalescent and holiday home.

On the other side of the river is *Dalswinton,* with a small loch on which, in October, 1788, was launched " the first really satisfactory attempt at steam navigation in the world." William Symington was the engineer and Robert Burns one of the passengers. The bridge over the Nith at Auldgirth was built by Thomas Telford.

Thornhill (*Buccleuch & Queensberry*), an attractive little place spread out along the main road, has a seventeenth-century cross, and a tall column (1714) topped by the winged horse emblem of the Queensberrys. Across the river slightly north of the village is Drumlanrig Castle (Duke of Buccleuch) : there is a pleasant walk or drive through the policies. In the park are the ruins of *Tibber's Castle,* well worth visiting.

The road under the railway (station closed) leads, in a series of turns, to *Crichope Linn* in about 3 miles—a secluded little spot well worth visiting. Half a mile upstream from the Linn is a fall known as the *Grey Mare's Tail,* not to be confused with the much finer fall of that name above Moffat. By turning to the left after passing under the railway one can reach in 2 miles the ruin of *Morton Castle,* of thirteenth-century date.

At **Carronbridge,** 1¾ miles beyond Thornhill, there goes off on the right the 20-mile road to Elvanfoot and Crawford, in Clydesdale, by way of the Dalveen Pass, a fine run through striking scenery which also provides part of the most direct route from Thornhill to Edinburgh. Three miles from the fork a road goes off on the right to **Durisdeer**, with a church containing memorials of the Queensberry family ; the village has a strange, out-of-the world appearance. Beyond it the Well Path ascends the hills and rejoins the main road at the far end of the Dalveen Pass.

Some 6 miles from Carronbridge the road swings sharply to the right and enters the Dalveen Pass. A farm road strikes off on the left at this point for Nether Dalveen Farm, where is a monument to Daniel McMichael, the Covenanter, from which it is less than a mile over the dip in the hill to the **Enterkin Pass**, whence the way is clear to Leadhills. The pass is a long V-shaped defile seen at its most striking aspect from the Leadhills end (*see below*).

Through the **Dalveen Pass** the road winds between steep, treeless hillsides which rise to nearly 1,000 feet above it and seem to close it on every side. The summit, where the road passes into Lanarkshire and enters the Clyde basin, is 1,140 feet above the sea, a rise of 930 feet from Carronbridge. Hence to **Elvanfoot** the road bears company with the Potrail Water and, later, the Daer Water, the two chief tributaries of the Clyde, and very "fishful" streams. It should be noted that the road bridge across the railway is some distance north of Elvanfoot village ; motorists should be on guard against a premature turning out of the road opposite the station (*closed*). For Elvanfoot and routes hence, *see* page 88.

The main Kilmarnock road keeps to the left at the Carronbridge fork, and with views of Drumlanrig Castle (Duke of Buccleuch) on the left it descends to the Nith, which bears it close company for several miles. Then the valley opens out and we come to **Sanquhar** (pronounced *Sanker*), a name well known to students of history.

A monument in the main street bears an inscription recording the "Declarations of Sanquhar," wherein Richard Cameron (1680) renounced allegiance to Charles II and James Renwick repudiated James II. Sanquhar Castle, a fine ruin to the south of the town, was once the seat of the Queensberry family ; it now belongs to the Marquis of Bute, one of whose titles is Earl of Sanquhar.

By the Mennock Pass to Leadhills (10 miles from Sanquhar).—The route leaves the Thornhill road about 2½ miles south of Sanquhar and for a while winds up a beautifully wooded glen, which is succeeded by a deep hill-gorge. For several miles the narrow valley is level and presents a charming scene of simple beauty. Then comes the ascent to **Wanlockhead** (*Youth Hostel*) and **Leadhills** (*Hopetoun Arms*), two villages which owed their existence to the former nearby lead mines. Lying as they do some 1,300 feet above sea-level, they yield only to Flash, near Buxton, Princetown on Dartmoor, and Nenthead in Cumberland on the score of altitude. Leadhills was the birthplace of Allan Ramsay (1686–1785), author of *The Gentle Shepherd.* A stone in the churchyard marking the death of one Taylor, who died at the age of 137, suggests that the situation of the village is healthy enough. Near the churchyard is a monument to William Symington, the pioneer of steam navigation.

Near Elvanfoot (*see* p. 88) on Clydeside is the farm of *Hole*, near which was found the gold from which James V coined his "bonnet-pieces," so called from the fact that they were impressed on one side with a portrait of His Majesty wearing a bonnet.

From Sanquhar a road runs up beside the Crawick Water for 14 miles to **Crawfordjohn** (p. 88). On the west side of the Nith is the Euchan Glen, with a chalybeate well and a rocky gorge called the Deil's Dungeon.

Above Sanquhar the Kilmarnock road runs pleasantly beside the Nith, by Kirkconnel, to **New Cumnock** (*Crown, Threave*), where Burns's "Sweet Afton" comes down on the south from the slopes of Blacklorg Hill (2,231 feet). Just beyond the bridge over the Afton Water a cross-country road goes off left, to Dalmellington (p. 102); our road turns right through the town and at the north end turns left, in 5 miles reaching **Cumnock**, with many memories of "The Killing Time." Hence a road on the right goes up beside the Lugar Water to Muirkirk, near the head waters of the Ayr river, and thence past the Glenbuck reservoirs to Douglas (p. 89). Westward is the road *viâ* Ochiltree to Ayr. A mile or so beyond Cumnock the road passes the house of *Auchinleck* (pronounced *Affleck*), a mile or so to the west. This was the residence of Boswell's family, and as such was visited by Dr. Johnson on his return from the Hebrides. Thence by wooded country to Mauchline (p. 162), and so to **Kilmarnock** (p. 155).

From Kilmarnock Cross, Portland Street and Wellington Street lead out and on to Fenwick, and so over the hills to **Glasgow** by a road which climbs to over 700 feet and commands grand views across the Lower Clyde to the distant mountains around Loch Lomond. Glasgow is entered by way of Giffnock.

CARLISLE TO STRANRAER AND GLASGOW BY THE COAST.

Distances.—Carlisle to Stranraer, 110 m.; thence to Ayr, 50 m.; thence to Glasgow (direct), 32 m.; (by coast) 70 m.

As far as Dumfries this route has been described on pages 91–2. From Dumfries to Castle Douglas (18 miles south-west) there are three routes: the main road by Crocketford (whence a branch crosses the hills by Balmaclellan to New Galloway, p. 100); the more interesting route *viâ* Dalbeattie, and that which comes to Dalbeattie by way of a wide sweep around the base of Criffel. All three routes start from the western end of the New Bridge of Dumfries; the Criffel road going off on the left in about 400 yards and the Crocketford road to right at the fork 400 yards farther along the Dalbeattie road.

The Criffel road is the most picturesque of the three, running near Sweetheart Abbey (p. 94) and then round the base of Criffel (p. 94) and by Kirkbean. *Arbigland*, on the shore near Kirkbean, was the birthplace (1747) of the notorious Paul Jones. Thence by a succession of picturesque and popular villages including **Rockcliffe** (*Baron's Craig*), and **Kippford to Dalbeattie** (*Galloway Arms*), where the stream known as the Kirkgunzeon Lane runs into the Urr Water, which a mile or so lower down forms what is known as the Rough Firth. Dalbeattie is a clean and attractive little place built of grey granite from its own quarries and situated among very pleasant scenery. About 3 miles north of Dalbeattie is the **Moat of Urr**, one of the most perfect relics of its kind in Britain. A resemblance has been traced to the Tynwald Hill in the Isle of Man, and it has been conjectured that it formed an open-air seat of justice when Galloway was an independent kingdom. It consists of three distinct terraces surrounded by a fosse.

Castle Douglas (*Douglas Arms, King's Arms, Royal, Crown, Commercial, Imperial*) is a modern town owing its foundation to the marl in Carlingwark Loch, which was formerly used as a fertilizer. It is a busy little place at the north end of the loch. Not far distant, on an island in the river Dee, is the ruin of **Threave Castle** (*open in summer, 10–7 weekdays except Thursdays, Sundays, 2–7; admission, fee*), a fourteenth-century keep built by

Archibald the Grim, 3rd Earl of Douglas, whose character as a host may be inferred from an inspection of the granite knob projecting from the front of the Castle and known as " Gallows Knob," which, the founder was wont to boast, " never wanted a tassel." The castle (NT) is in the care of the Department of the Environment. The gardens at *Threave House* (NT), now a gardening school, are open to the public (*charge*).

Castle Douglas to Ayr (50 miles), a splendid run comprising some of the best scenery in South-West Scotland. As the road leaves Castle Douglas the monument to Neilson, inventor of the hot-blast, is conspicuous on a hill to the left. Along by Crossmichael the Dee widens to several loch-like reaches and beyond Parton forms the long *Loch Ken*. Near the head of the loch is Kenmure Castle, a modified fifteenth-century house in which Burns stayed.

Beyond the loch is **New Galloway** (*Kenmure Arms, Cross Keys*), a neat little burgh which is the centre for some pleasant excursions among the hills. There is good fishing. The burgh is in the parish of Kells and the church is half a mile away on the brow of a hill. There are some curious gravestones in the burying ground, notably one to a sportsman named John Murray (d. 1777).

One cannot travel far in this neighbourhood without being aware of the **Galloway Hydro-Electric Scheme**, a huge undertaking comprising five power stations, seven reservoirs and the necessary dams, tunnels, aqueducts and pipelines to impound and convey the water. One of the reservoirs—an enlargement of Loch Doon—would normally discharge down the River Doon to the Ayrshire coast, but by means of a dam and tunnel 6,600 feet long its waters are diverted to the Deugh watershed to pass in turn through the power stations at Kendoon, Carsfad, Earlstoun and Tongland.

These four power stations are in series, Kendoon, Carsfad and Earlstoun being in the hills between the villages of Carsphairn and Dalry, and Tongland at the head of the estuary near Kirkcudbright, the capital of the Stewartry. The fifth station, Glenlee, is supplied (by means of a tunnel 19,000 feet long by 11 feet 6 inches in diameter) from an artificial loch, Clatteringshaws, on the upper reaches of the Blackwater of Dee, the water afterwards discharging into the Ken and flowing to Tongland along with the water from the other three stations. The storage represents an aggregate capacity equivalent to about 35,650,000 units of electricity, which is one-fifth of the estimated annual output of the whole scheme.

From New Galloway there is a pleasant route over the hills westward to Newton Stewart (p. 103). The road eastward to Dumfries passes **Balmaclellan,** charmingly situated. Here is a monument to " Old Mortality " (*see*

p. 92) who devoted so much time to furbishing up the inscriptions on the tombs of the Galloway Covenanting martyrs and who provided the title for Scott's novel. His real name was Robert Paterson and he died in 1800, aged 88. The Covenanters' Stone found near the south side of the church is remarkable for the bluntness of its inscription. From near the Church a path leads northward to the road from Dalry to Moniaive, passing the ruins of Barscobe Castle.

Dalry (*Lochinvar, Milton Park, Commercial*) on the *Ken*, is a very popular little centre with anglers and walkers. It slopes steeply up from the riverside in one street. In the kirkyard are some Covenanters' tombs with the customarily blunt inscriptions, but more notable examples of these outpourings are at Balmaclellan (*see above*) reached by a path or a road over the hills south-eastward.

From Dalry to Carsphairn there are two roads—the old one, hilly, but commanding the best views, and the new one, which passes through the best valley scenery. About 2 miles from Dalry, Earlstoun Tower will be seen in the valley. Some miles farther a mountain route from Moniaive comes in on the right. **Carsphairn** (*Salutation*) is a small village of one street, on a tableland 600 feet above the sea and flanked by lofty green mountains, all easy of access and affording views that are wide rather than striking. From the north end of the village a track goes westward across the meadows beyond the river, and some 2 miles farther passes the abandoned Woodhead Lead Mines, the ridge beyond which commands a good view of *Loch Doon* (now a reservoir under the Galloway Scheme: *see* p. 100). The loch is some 5 miles long by half a mile wide; fishing is free. A remarkable early castle, which would have been submerged by the artificial raising of the loch, has now been removed from its island site to the shore of the loch. The actual work of transference, stone by stone, was carried out by the Ancient Monuments Department of the Ministry of Public Building and Works. At the foot of the loch, which is more easily reached from the road near Dalmellington, is little *Ness Glen*. The path from Carsphairn descends to the head of the loch, but the walk down the western side to the glen is monotonous.

It is some 6 miles on from Carsphairn to *Loch Muck*,

from which a track runs up to the foot of the Ness Glen. From **Dalmellington** (*Eglinton, Ladywell House*), 6 miles farther, roads run eastward to New Cumnock (*see* p. 98) and westward to Maybole (p. 160) and Girvan, but we follow the Doon through the hills to beyond Patna, whence the river sweeps away on the left and the road goes straight ahead towards **Ayr** (p. 156).

The main Wigtown road from Castle Douglas keeps on the north-western shore of Carlingwark Loch, but those with time to spare may be recommended to take the road down the eastern side of the loch and join the road from Dalbeattie near Palnackie. Above the road hereabout is a picturesque rock known as the *Lion's Head*, and a mile southward is *Orchardton Tower*, the last remaining Round Tower in Galloway. The best view-point in the neighbourhood is *Ben Gairn* (1,250 feet), to the west of the road from Castle Douglas, and forming with the neighbouring height of Screel a very attractive walk. From Auchencairn the road goes towards Kirkcudbright *viâ* **Dundrennan,** with the picturesque ruins of the Abbey, where in 1568 Mary spent her last night on Scottish soil after the defeat at Langside had dashed hopes raised by the escape from Loch Leven. The Abbey was founded in 1142 by David I or his friend Fergus, Lord of Galloway, for Cistercians from Rievaulx in Yorkshire. (*Weekdays,* 10–7 ; *Sundays,* 2–7. *Winter,* 10–4 *and* 2–4. *Admission, fee*) Port Mary, on the coast southward of the Abbey, is said to be the spot from which the hapless Mary took boat for England.

KIRKCUDBRIGHT

(pronounced *Kirkoobrie*) (*Hotels : Royal* (22 *rooms*), *Mayfield* (30 *rooms*), *Selkirk Arms* (16 *rooms*)) is the capital of Galloway, the patron saint being St. Cuthbert, hence the name of the town. It is one of the most ancient towns in Scotland, and is beautifully situated on the river Dee, near the head of Kirkcudbright Bay. In mediæval days the port was among the first six in Scotland, but it greatly decayed during the seventeenth century. The royal castle, situated at the Castledykes, was one of the national fortresses which figured in the War of Independence. Among the remains are the Tolbooth, with its beautiful spire, built from stones taken from Dundrennan Abbey, and the castle of the McLellans, Lords Kirkcudbright (*weekdays*, 10–4 or 7 ; *Sundays*, 2–4 or 7 ; *charge*). Among the public buildings are the Town Hall and the interesting Stewartry Museum, while Broughton House (*Mon.–Fri.* 11–1, 2–4 ; *April* 2–4 *only* ; *Winter*, *Tues. and Thurs.*, 2–4 *only*) is a delightful Georgian House with large library and art collection. The river, which is tidal for about two miles above the town, is spanned by a bridge affording easy access to western Galloway.

The district has many literary associations, particularly with Burns. In Borgue parish, on the western side of the bay, is laid the scene of Stevenson's *Master of Ballantrae*, and the shores of the bay were the haunt of Dirk Hatteraick and his smugglers in Sir Walter Scott's great romance, *Guy Mannering*. Paul Jones, the "Father of the American navy," was a native of the district, and commanded ships belonging to the port. Kirkcudbright Bay was one of the places selected for the landing of the Spanish Armada and also for French invasions in aid of the Stewart dynasty. At **Tongland,** about 2 miles north of Kirkcudbright, is a very large hydro-electric power station (*see* p. 100).

From Kirkcudbright we continue westward to Gatehouse, which soon comes into view in the valley below, and to the left the Water of Fleet is seen widening to form Fleet Bay. **Gatehouse of Fleet** (*Cally*, *Angel*, *Anwoth*, *Murray Arms*) is a very pretty town nestling in a wooded valley amid green hills that rise on the west almost to the dignity of mountains. A mile south of the town is a conspicuous Monument to Samuel Rutherford (1600–61), one of the great preachers of the Covenant. Near the foot of the monument is **Cardoness Castle,** and to the northwest is the old Kirk of Anwoth (built 1626), with a picturesque graveyard containing a Covenanter's tomb with characteristic inscription. From the Kirk an old Military Road provides a good walk over the hills to Creetown, 7½ miles west of Gatehouse of Fleet in a direct line, but 12 miles by the pretty road past Anwoth and along the coast. Six miles from Gatehouse the shore shows a rocky ridge, beneath which is Dirk Hatteraick's Cave, one of several in the vicinity. Barholm Tower, among woods on the right, is one of the places reputed to be the "Ellangowan" of *Guy Mannering*—another is Caerlaverock Castle (p. 92). This, too, is the country of *Redgauntlet.*

Above **Creetown** (*Barholm Arms, Ellangowan*) the bay contracts to the estuary of the Cree. **Newton Stewart** can vie in situation with any town of its size in Scotland (*Hotels : Belhotel* (*17 rooms*), *Black Horse, Galloway Arms* (*24 rooms*), *Kirroughtree House, Grapes, Crown, Creebridge*). *Fishing, bowls, tennis.* Its one irregular street runs for nearly a mile alongside the river ; on the west the ground rises gently, but on the east the loftiest range of hills in the south of Scotland begins with *Cairnsmore of Fleet* (2,329 feet), whose summit is not more than 6 miles from the town. Across the river is **Minnigaff,** the town's more ancient suburb.

From Newton Stewart a hilly but wildly beautiful road runs over the hills to **New Galloway** (18 miles). Eight miles out is a granite monument to Alexander Murray (1775–1813), who from a shepherd boy on these hills rose to be Professor of Oriental Languages at Edinburgh University. Beside the Upper Bridge of Dee, some 12 miles from Newton Stewart, is the dam of the Clatteringshaws Reservoir of the Galloway scheme (*see* p. 100). From the Bridge a track goes off on the left to **Loch Dee,** which is also approached on foot from Newton Stewart by a path beside the Penkill Burn at Minnigaff.

There is also a road north-westward to **Girvan** (p. 16), 30 miles away on the west coast, passing the entrance to Glen Trool, where lie **Loch Trool,** a gem and a National Forest Park (*Youth Hostel*). A road leaves the Girvan highway at Bargrennan (*Inn* ; 9 miles from Newton Stewart). In about a mile and just beyond the village of Glentrool, a right turn leads through woods to beautiful Glen Trool. Loch Trool lies to the right of the road, but neither the glen nor the loch is fairly seen until one is close to them. Three miles to the north of the head of Loch Trool stands **Merrick** (2,764 feet), the highest mountain in the south of Scotland. It may be ascended by the path from Buchan Farm to Culsharg and thence over the lower top of Benyellary (2,360 feet) to the highest point.

From Bargrennan Bridge the Girvan road climbs to some 500 feet above the sea, crosses the headwaters of the Cree and enters Ayrshire, still climbing until the highest point (558 feet) is reached, 1½ miles farther. Beyond Barrhill (whence the railway from Stranraer keeps company with the road) a very pretty valley is entered. **Pinwherry Castle,** the ruins of which are seen on the right, was a stronghold of the Kennedies, and from Pinwherry station there is a good view down the strath of the Stinchar stream to the peaked hill of Knockdolian, near Ballantrae. Then the descent to **Girvan** (p. 162) begins.

Southward from Newton Stewart the promontory of the **Machars** extends for some 25 miles to Whithorn and Isle of Whithorn. **Wigtown** (*Galloway*) is a quiet little town with a ruined old Church, in the burying ground of which are the graves of Margaret MacLachlan and Margaret Wilson, the Wigtown Martyrs. In striking contrast to the sad suggestiveness of this monument is the in-

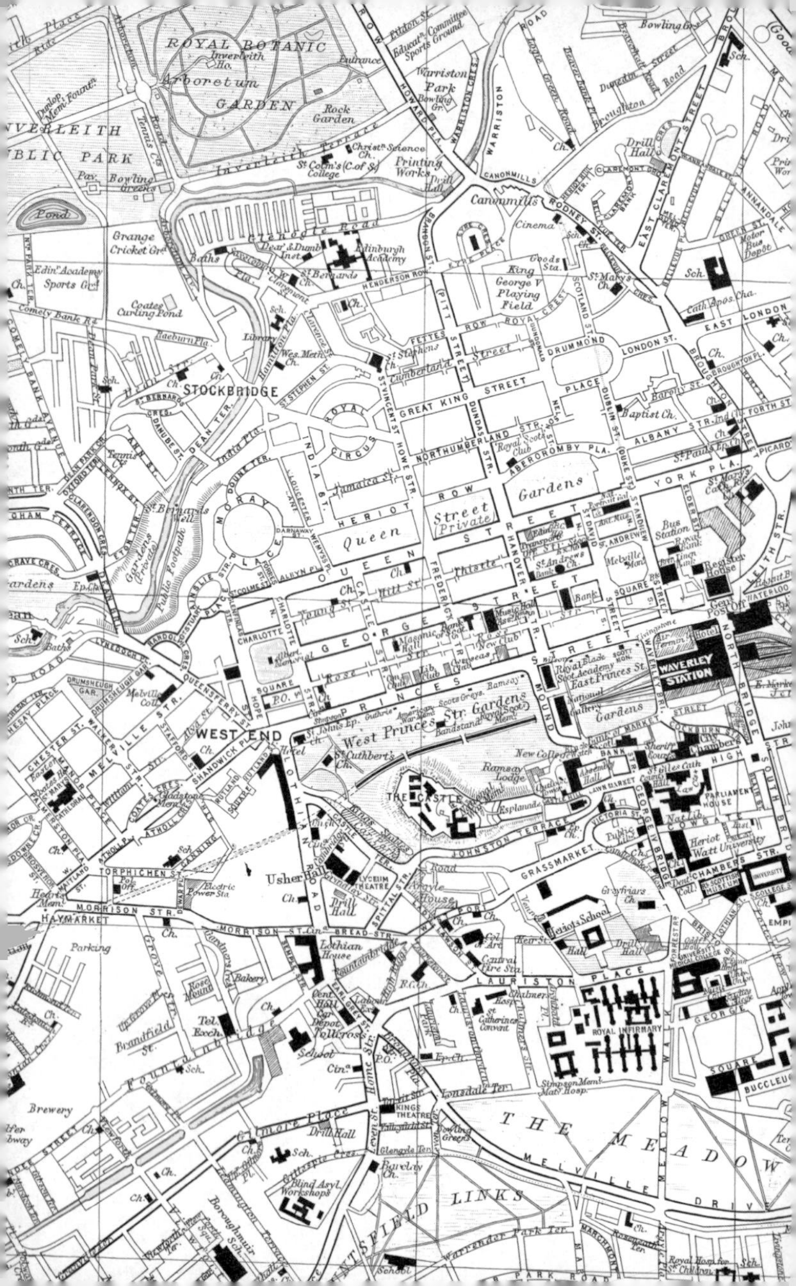

ROYAL BOTANIC GARDEN
Inverleith Ho.
Arboretum
Rock Garden
Entrance
Inverleith Terrace
INVERLEITH PUBLIC PARK
Pond
Bowling Greens
Pav.
Tennis Cts
Dunlop Mem! Fount.
Christn Science Ch.
St Colm's (C. of S.) College
Printing Works
Drill Hall
Warriston Park Bowling Gr.
Educatn Committee Sports Ground
HOWARD PLA.
WARRISTON CRES.
WARRISTON
CANONMILLS
Canonmills
Cinema
Inverleith Row
Logie Green Road
Broughton Road
Dunedin Street
Bowling Gr.
Drill Hall
EAST CLAREMONT STREET
BELLEVUE
ANNANDALE
Motor Bus Depot
Sch.
Grange Cricket Grd
Edinr Academy Sports Grd
Coates Curling Pond
Comely Bank Rd
COMELY BANK AVENUE
Raeburn Pla.
Baths
Deaf & Dumb Inst.
Edinburgh Academy
St Bernards
Henderson Row
Goods Sta.
King George V Playing Field
St Mary's Ch.
Cath. Apos. Cha.
EAST LONDON
Library
Wes. Meth. Ch.
STOCKBRIDGE
St Stephens Ch.
FETTES ROW
ROYAL CREST
DRUMMOND
LONDON ST.
Cumberland Street
GREAT KING STREET
PLACE
Barony St.
ROYAL CIRCUS
Baptist Ch.
NORTHUMBERLAND STR.
ALBANY STR.
FORTH ST.
Royal Scots Club
ABERCROMBY PLA.
St Paul's Ep. Ch.
YORK PLA.
St Mary's Cath. R.C.
DUNDAS STR.
HOWE STR.
St VINCENT ST.
INDIA ST.
Jamaica St.
HERIOT ROW
Street (Private)
Gardens
Queen
QUEEN STREET
MORAY PLACE
St Bernards Well
Public Footpath
Gardens (Private)
ETON TER.
DEAN TER.
India Pla.
Bus Station
Royal Bank
Register House
Melville Mon.
St Andrews Ch.
ST. ANDREW SQUARE
Thistle
Hill St.
Young St.
HANOVER STR.
FREDERICK STR.
CASTLE STR.
CHARLOTTE
GEORGE STREET
Music Hall
Assembly Rooms
Masonic Hall
New Club
Rose
Albert Memorial
CHARLOTTE SQUARE
P.O.
PRINCES STREET
Gen! Post Off.
WATERLOO
Hotel
Air Terminal
WAVERLEY STATION
NORTH BRIDGE
Royal Scot. Academy
Royal Black
Scott Mon.
East Princes St.
National Gallery
Gardens
MOUND
Lynedoch Pl.
DRUMSHEUGH GAR.
Melville Coll.
QUEENSFERRY ST.
WEST END
MELVILLE STR.
CHESTER ST.
Ch.
SHANDWICK PL.
West Princes Str. Gardens
Bandstand
Royal Scots Mem.
Scots Greys
Ramsay
St Johns Ep.
Guthrie
American War Mem!
St Cuthbert's Ch.
THE CASTLE
Esplanade
Ramsay Lodge
New College
Assembly Hall
BANK STR.
LAWN MARKET
HIGH
St Giles Cath.
Sheriff Court
Chambers
PARLIAMENT HOUSE
COCKBURN ST.
MARKET STREET
COWGATE
Nat. Lib.
Heriot Watt University
CHAMBERS STR.
ROYAL SCOTTISH MUSEUM
UNIVERSITY
SOUTH BRIDGE
Dent. Coll.
GEORGE IV BRIDGE
VICTORIA ST.
JOHNSTON TERRACE
GRASSMARKET
Greyfriars Ch.
LOTHIAN ROAD
Usher Hall
LYCEUM THEATRE
Drill Hall
Argyle House
TORPHICHEN ST.
Electric Power Sta.
Post Off.
MORRISON STR.
HAYMARKET
Hearts Mem.
Gladstone Memorial
ATHOLL CRES.
Coates Cres.
PALMERSTON PLA.
Easter Coates Ho.
St Mary's Cathedral
William St.
MANOR PLACE
Parking
BREAD STR.
Lothian House
Fountainbridge
Bakery
Rose Mount
Grove St.
Tel. Exch.
Brandfield St.
Fountainbridge
Cent. Hall
Car Depot
Tollcross
School
EARL GREY ST.
Home St.
P.O.
Cin.
Coll. of Art
Central Fire Sta.
Heriots School
Drill Hall
LAURISTON PLACE
Chalmers Hosp.
St Catherines Convent
ROYAL INFIRMARY
FORREST RD.
BRISTO
MEDICAL COLLEGE
UNIVERSITY
GEORGE SQUARE
BUCCLEUCH
Simpson Mem! Mat! Hosp.
Lonsdale Ter.
THE MEADOWS
MELVILLE DRIVE
KINGS THEATRE
Bowling Greens
Glengyle Ter.
Barclay Ch.
Leven St.
Brewery
Gilmore Place
Drill Hall
Sch.
Blind Asyl. Workshops
Boroughmuir Sch.
BRUNTSFIELD LINKS
Warrender Park Ter.
MARCHMONT
Rosneath Ter.
Royal Hosp. for Sick Children
PARK ROAD
School
Ch.

CENTRAL EDINBURGH
SCALE OF HALF A MILE
0
1/4
1/2
WARD LOCK & CO., LIMITED. LONDON.
© – John Bartholomew & Son Ltd. Edinburgh
PILRIG
LEITH WALK
Goods Sta.
LONDON ROAD
ROYAL TERRACE
Gardens
REGENT ROAD
CALTON ROAD
CANONGATE
HOLYROOD ROAD
PALACE OF HOLYROOD
Parade Ground
THE QUEEN'S DRIVE
St. Margarets Loch
Whinny Hill
Crow Hill
HOLYROOD PARK
SALISBURY CRAGS
HUNTERS BOG
Radical Road
ARTHURS SEAT 822 ft.
Nether Hill
Lions Haunch
Dunsapie Loch
Dunsapie Rock
Ancient Cultivation Terraces
Samsons Ribs
Bird Sanctuary
Lochend Loch
Meadowbank Stadium
Brewery
Goods Line
Elsie Inglis Memorial Maternity Hosp.
Bowling Rink
Bus Garage
Huntly Ho. (Museum)
Moray Ho.
Lochview Court
Holyrood Court
Pleasance Trust
Deaconess Hosp.
Royal Commonwealth Pool
Pollock Halls of Residence
Albert Gate
ST. LEONARDS STREET
E. PRESTON STR.
WEST PRESTON STR.

scription on a stone opposite the south-west transept of the old kirk:

> "And his son John of honest fame,
> Of stature small and a leg lame,
> Content he was with portions small,
> Keep'd shop in Wigtown and that's all."

The *Martyrs' Monument* perpetuates the memory of the two women already named, who were tied to a stake and drowned by the tide in the never-to-be-forgotten 1685, and of three men who were hanged without trial. The inscription is more remarkable for simple fervour than for grammatical flourishes.

The *Torhouse Stones*, 3 miles west of Wigtown, comprise a circle of 19 monoliths, each about 5 feet high, enclosing three central blocks. South of Wigtown is **Baldoon Castle**, the parental home of David Dunbar, the Bucklaw of *The Bride of Lammermuir*. From Sorbie, with a square old tower, a road goes eastward to **Garliestown**, busy with the milling and timber trade. At **Whithorn** (*Grapes, Castlewigg*) the main feature of interest is the ruin of the Priory Church, supposed to occupy the site of St. Ninian's Chapel, the first Christian Church in Scotland. An interesting collection of early sculptured monuments is housed in the adjacent museum (*admission, fee*) (*open weekdays only*, 10–7 *or* 4). South-east from the village is the so-called *Isle of Whithorn*, actually a peninsula. Near the south end of the harbour are the ruins of St. Ninian's Kirk, which disputes with the Priory Church the honour of standing upon the site of St. Ninian's Chapel (early fifth century).

On the west coast of the promontory, some 4 miles from Whithorn, is **St. Ninian's Cave**, with crosses cut in the rock by pilgrims.

Glenluce (*King's Arms, Judge's Keep*) is prettily placed near the head of Luce Bay. A mile to the north is the twelfth-century Abbey (*open standard hours*) in a beautiful situation, and of much architectural interest.

Five miles westward the road skirts the extensive grounds of Lochinch and the gardens of **Castle Kennedy** (*gardens daily, April to September*, 9 *a.m. to* 5 *p.m. Admission fee. Free car park.*)

Three miles farther is **Stranraer** (*Buck's Head* (20 rooms), *George* (31 rooms), *North West Castle* (35 rooms); *Youth Hostel, caravan sites*), which, from a commercial point of view, is the chief town in south-west Scotland west of Dumfries. It stands at the head of **Loch Ryan**, which is 8 miles long and nearly 3 miles wide, and provides a sheltered harbour for the car ferry making the short sea trip across to the Irish coast at Larne, 30 miles away. In addition to the inevitable interests of the waterside, there is golf, boating, bathing, fishing, tennis, etc., and the town is a good centre for the exploration of the peninsula terminating southward in the Mull of Galloway.

From Stranraer the road strikes southward to Luce Bay near **Sandhead.** At Kirkmadrine, near Stoneykirk, are three of the earliest Christian monuments in Britain (fifth or sixth century). From **Drummore** (*Queen's*), prettily situated in front of a little bay, the chief excursion is to the lighthouse at the Mull (5 miles). There is a motor road, but the best walking route is along the coast by Portankill, where are the ruins of **Kirkmaiden Old Church,** the most southerly parish in Scotland, the greatest north-south measurement of the country being popularly " Frae Maiden Kirk to John o' Groats." The path then climbs the cliff past *St. Medan's Chapel* (a cave with remains of walls) and joins the road across the Tarbet (*see* p. 195) to the Lighthouse.

Port Logan, on the western coast, is at the head of a pretty bay and has a tidal fish-pond inhabited by remarkably tame fish.

The most important place on the west coast is **Portpatrick,** 7 miles from Stranraer by road. (*Cross Keys, Fernhill, Portpatrick, Melvin Lodge, Roslin ; several boarding-houses ; golf.*) It is picturesquely situated overlooking the remains of a harbour built by Rennie.

Stranraer to Girvan by the Coast.—The first few miles are along the southern and eastern shores of Loch Ryan past Cairnryan (*Lochryan Hall*). Near the mouth of the Loch the road turns inland up **Glen App. Ballantrae** (*Royal, King's Arms*) is a fishing village with golf links and other attractions for those who like unsophisticated holiday resorts. When R. L. Stevenson visited the village in 1878, his eccentricity of costume caused the people to stone him. *The Master of Ballantrae* was laid at Borgue (p. 101) and not here.

Some 5 miles beyond Ballantrae is the ruined tower of **Carleton Castle,** where May Cullean, the eighth wife of a wicked baron who had disposed of seven wives by pushing them over the cliff, turned the tables on her liege lord and threw him instead—a feat not undeservedly commemorated in a well-known ballad.

Girvan and the coast northward to Glasgow are described on pages 148–62.

EDINBURGH.

Access from the South.—*Rail.* From London (King's Cross) *viâ* Berwick to Waverley Station. Journey from London by the best trains is now made in between six and six and a half hours.

Road. *See* foregoing pages. Motor coaches from London and other centres.

Air. *See* p. 17.

Banks.—Bank of Scotland, Royal Bank of Scotland, Clydesdale Bank.

Car Parking Places.—Limited accommodation on south side of Princes Street (e.g. at foot of Mound). Also: Charlotte Square, St. Andrew Square, George Street—all with parking meters; Castle Terrace (charge); Rutland Square, Queen Street (between Hanover Street and Frederick Street), Abercromby Place, Heriot Row, Atholl Crescent, Coates Crescent, Johnston Terrace, Chambers Street, etc.

Churches, etc.: (The services are usually at 11 a.m. and 6.30 p.m.)

Church of Scotland: St. Giles, High Street. *See* p. 117. St. George's West (11 and 7); St. Cuthbert's, Lothian Road; St. Andrew's and St. George's, George Street; Greyfriars; Canongate Kirk.

Congregational: George IV Bridge. Morningside, Morningside Road.

Methodist: Nicolson Square and Central Hall, Earl Grey Street.

Baptist: Dublin Street, West Rose Street and Queensferry Road.

Scottish Episcopal: St. Mary's Cathedral (Palmerston Place), 8, 11, 3.30, 6.30; St. John's, Princes Street, 8, 11.15, 6.30; St. Paul's and St. George's, York Place, 11 and 6.30.

Roman Catholic: St. Mary's Cathedral (Broughton Street), 7.30, 8.30, 10, 11 (or 11.30), 6.30. Sacred Heart, Lauriston Street, 11, 6.30.

Synagogue in Salisbury Road.

Early Closing.—On Monday, fishmongers; on Tuesday, drapers and jewellers; Wednesday, bakers, butchers, grocers, chemists, hairdressers, stationers. Shops of the kind in Princes Street and other fashionable quarters, however, usually close instead at 1 p.m. on Saturday.

Festival.—The Edinburgh International Festival occupies three weeks between mid-August and mid-September. It is a cultural occasion of the first rank. Festival Office: 21 Market Street.

Golf.—Golf was played in Edinburgh as long ago as 1457. To-day there are some fifty courses within easy reach of the city, and many within the municipal boundaries. The charges, especially on the municipal courses, are moderate. Sunday play on some public courses.

Information Centre and Service. City Information and Accommodation Service, 1 Cockburn Street, EH1 1BP (Tel.: 031-226 6591).

Hotels.—*North British* (202 rooms), Princes Street; *Caledonian* (171 rooms), Princes Street; *Mount Royal* (132 rooms), Princes Street; *Royal British* (78 rooms), Princes Street; *Carlton* (87 rooms), North Bridge; *George* (86 rooms), 21 George Street; *Roxburghe* (75 rooms), Charlotte Square; *Grosvenor Centre* (163 rooms), Grosvenor Street; *Esso Motor* (120 rooms), Queensferry Road; *St. Andrew* (40 rooms), South St. Andrew Street; *Learmonth* (196 rooms), Learmonth Terrace; *Bruntsfield* (50 rooms), Bruntsfield Place; *Braid Hills* (56 rooms), Braid Road; *Old Waverley* (70 rooms), Princes Street. Unlicensed hotels include: *Shelbourne* (122 rooms), Hart Street; and many others.

Population.—465,421.

Post Office.—Head Office at east end of Princes Street (Waterloo Place). Open weekdays, 8 a.m. to 6.30 p.m. Saturdays, 8.30-6. (Sundays, 9-10, letters and telegraph only.)

SIGHTSEEING.—Not even London is more crowded with interest than the Scottish Capital. For the visitor with a limited period of time at his disposal the following itinerary comprises all the more important sights of the city, and if the suburbs of Leith, Newhaven and Granton are omitted the tour can be made in a single day, if full use is made of a private car or Corporation buses. That part of Edinburgh which most interests visitors is almost entirely included in a parallelogram having George Street and the Calton Hill for its northern boundary and the Castle and the line of thoroughfare eastward to Holyrood on the south. Princes Street bisects this parallelogram into the modern section and the historic "Old Town." Our itinerary begins with the latter, so that if there is insufficient time for the completion of the tour, at least the most significant places will have been seen.

In connection with the Corporation Transport system are sightseeing tours by motor coach, starting from Waverley Bridge and of varying extent and period. Visitors with some time at their disposal should see our *Guide to Edinburgh*, which contains much that has to be omitted from this volume.

TIMES OF ADMISSION TO PLACES OF INTEREST.

Botanic Garden and Arboretum, Inverleith Row. Free, from 9 a.m. (Sunday, 11 a.m.) till sundown. Hothouses, 10 a.m. (Sunday, 11) till 5 p.m.

Canongate Tolbooth. Weekdays, 10–5. Charge.

Castle. *Admission fee.* Open weekdays, 9.30–6 p.m. all apartments; 6–9 p.m. precincts only. These hours apply May to October inclusive—hours slightly shorter in winter and during Tattoo period. Sundays from 11 a.m.

City Museum, Huntly House, Canongate. Weekdays, 10–5; also (in summer) Wednesdays, 6–9; closed Sundays except during Festival when it is open 2–5. Admission *fee*.

Holyroodhouse, Palace of, and Chapel Royal. *Historical and State Apartments:* Open daily. Admission *charge*. *Hours:* 9.30 (Sunday, 11) till 6; in winter, 9.30 (Sunday, 12.30) till 4.30. During Royal Visits and at General Assembly time (mid-May–mid-June) the Palace is closed to the public.

John Knox's House, High Street. Weekdays, 10–5, *fee*.

Lady Stair's House, Lawnmarket. Weekdays, 10–4; Saturday, 10–1; 10–5 daily during Festival; closed Sundays except during Festival when it is open 2–5. Admission, *fee*.

Museum of Childhood, Hyndford's Close, High Street. Weekdays, 10–5 and Sundays during Festival, 2–5. Charge.

National Gallery, The Mound. Free. Weekdays, 10–5; Sunday, 2–5. During Festival, 10–8.

National Library of Scotland, George IV Bridge. Free. Reading Rooms for purposes of reference and research open daily, 9.30–8.30; Saturday, 9.30–1. Exhibition open daily, 9.30–5; Saturday, 9.30–1; Sunday, 2–5; and during the Festival in addition, every day (except Sunday) till 8.30.

National Museum of Antiquities of Scotland, Queen Street. Free. Weekdays, 10–5; Sunday, 2–5 (later during Festival). **Museum Gallery,** 18 Shandwick Place. Weekdays, 10–5.

Nelson Monument, Calton Hill. Open daily, 10–7: October–March, 10–3: closed Sundays. Admission, *fee*.

Outlook Tower, Castle Hill. Open April–October, 10–6. Sunday, 12.30–6. Admission, *fee*. Café.

Parliament House, Parliament Square. Daily (during the sitting of the Courts), 10–4.30; Saturdays, 10–12.30. Free.

Register House. Daily, 9.30–4.30. Saturday, 9.30–12.30. Free.

Royal College of Surgeons Museum, Nicolson Street. Free. Open to the Medical Profession daily, 9–5, Saturday, 9–12. Public admitted by special permission only

Royal Scottish Academy, Mound. Annual Exhibition held from late April until early August. Reopens later in August for special Festival Exhibition. Weekdays, 10 a.m.–9 p.m., Sundays, 2–5 p.m. Admission charge.

Royal Scottish Museum, Chambers Street. Free. Daily, from 10 till 5; Sunday, 2–5 p.m. Tea room except Sundays.

St. Giles Cathedral, High Street. Daily, 10–5. Free. Thistle Chapel, *fee*. Sunday services at 11 and 6.30.

Scottish National Gallery of Modern Art (Royal Botanic Gardens). Open 10–6, Sundays 2–5. Free.

Scottish National Portrait Gallery, Queen Street. Free. Open weekdays, 10–5; Sunday, 2–5.

Scottish National War Memorial. *See* under Castle.

Scott Monument, Princes Street. Open daily, April 1–September 30, from 10 till 7, Sunday, 1–7; October 1–March 31, from 10 till 3; closed Sundays. Admission, *fee*.

Signet Library, Parliament Square. Open on weekdays from 10–4; Saturday, 10–12.

Sports Centres.—Meadowbank Sports Centre, London Road, daily 9 a.m.–11 p.m.; Royal Commonwealth Pool, Dalkeith Road, daily; Hillend Ski Centre, daily.

University, South Bridge. Open free daily. *Library:* admission on written application.

Zoological Park, Corstorphine. Open 9–7 in season (Sunday, 12–7); other months 9 (Sunday, 12) till sundown. Admission charge. Aquarium, charge. Restaurants. Car Park.

THE HISTORY OF EDINBURGH.

The early history of Edinburgh is hard to discover. The commanding position of the Castle Rock would certainly make it a desirable fortress for the people who were in Scotland before the Romans came, but it seems to have played no particular part in the Roman system of defence. When the Angles of Northumbria over-ran the Lothian the place was of importance and it is said to take its name from Edwin, King of Northumbria (617–33). It was conquered by the Scoto-Pictish kings as they pressed south; the date of this re-conquest is usually assigned to the reign of Indulf (954–62).

It was long before the town became the recognized Capital. Malcolm Canmore (1057–93) had a fort on the Castle-hill; his wife built a chapel there, and his son David (1124–53) granted a church upon the hill to the Regular Canons whom he afterwards established at Holyrood House. His successors used the stronghold as a repository for their treasures and muniments. Alexander II (1214–59) lived much at his foundation of the Blackfriars, and Alexander III at the Castle. Robert the Bruce granted Edinburgh a Charter in 1329, conveying to it the Port of Leith.

Meanwhile a burgh had sprung up, a huddle of houses clustering along the eastern slope of the Castle Hill, up the centre of which ran one long road, called by various names, from the Castle down to the city boundary, whence it continued as the Canongate to Holyroodhouse. The Canongate, however, was a separate burgh dependent upon the Abbey of Holyrood. As the centuries passed this burgh progressed; its rights were fortified by royal charters; it developed in gild and craft the machinery of civil governments, and became a great centre of trade and industry. By the end of the fifteenth century, after the loss of Berwick (1482), Edinburgh was the chief town of Scotland, and though the kings still might hold their parliaments at Stirling or Perth, and might often reside in their palaces of Stirling, Linlithgow, Dunfermline ard Falkland, Edinburgh, during the sixteenth century, was definitely the capital. When James VI, angered by a riot on December 17, 1596, threatened to remove the machinery of government to Linlithgow, the citizens made a complete surrender. They realized the importance of being a capital city. After the Union of the Crowns (1603) a great deal of the glamour departed, but the parliament still met (as a rule) in Edinburgh, and Edinburgh was the seat of government. When the Scottish Parliament came to an end in 1707, the city's political importance dwindled; but it remained the centre of a great judicial system, and amongst the lawyers of Parliament House were to be numbered many men of exquisite wit and deep learning. Literature and philosophy flourished, and the coteries to which first Burns and then Scott were introduced were of European reputation. This gay and cultured society lived for the most part in the tall houses which lined the central street, and the numerous "closes" which branch off from it. The Cowgate itself was once a fashionable street. What suburbs there were lay mainly to the south, for north of the Castle hill was the marshy Nor' Loch. But towards the end of the eighteenth century, society began to move northwards, and in the first decade of the nineteenth century the stately and harmonious "New Town" came into being. The Nor' Loch remained as a fœtid marshy rubbish heap until the early nineteenth century, when it was drained and its bed converted into beautiful Gardens, through which (though partly hidden in the hollow) the railway draws a disfiguring line. Even so, Princes Street is still reckoned one of the three great streets of the world.

EDINBURGH CASTLE.

(Admission, *see* p. 108.)

Both to look at and to look from, the Castle is the most satisfying thing in Edinburgh—by night, on festive occasions, floodlighting lends peculiar enchantment to the view of it from Princes Street; and whatever else is omitted from even the briefest sightseeing tour of the city the Castle should be visited. The rugged hill rises precipitously from West Princes Street Gardens and King's Stables Road, on its western sides, but on the east it is easily ascended from the Lawnmarket. The main gateway

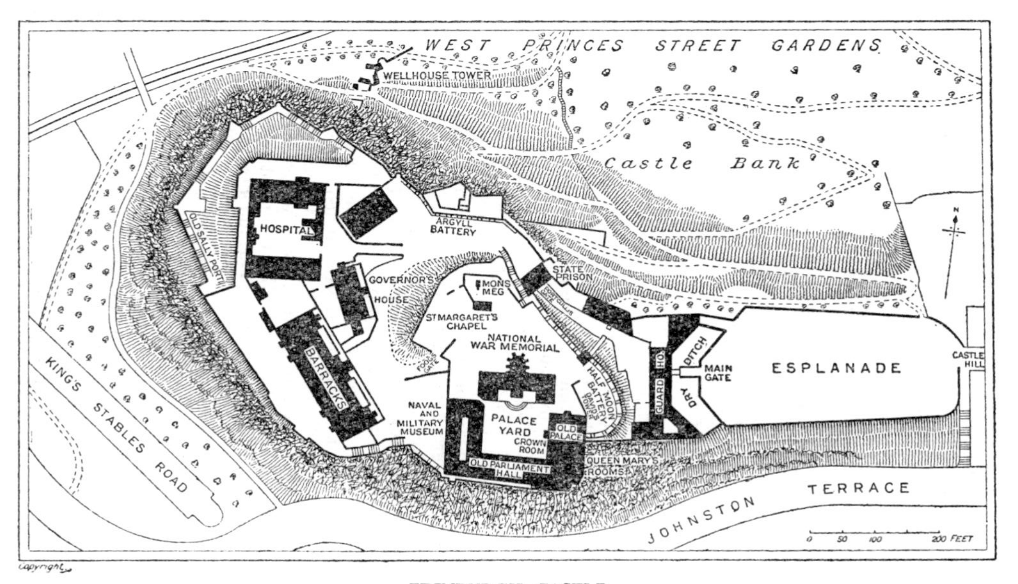

EDINBURGH CASTLE

is approached by a wide **Esplanade,** for centuries the scene of executions by axe and stake and in modern times of regimental drill. In Festival time the Esplanade provides an incomparable stage for a military tattoo.

During the reign of Charles I the Esplanade—part of the Castle Hill—was declared to be an integral part of Nova Scotia, in order that the Nova Scotian baronets created under Commission of William Alexander, Earl of Stirling, might "take seisin" of their new possessions. This decree has never been annulled and it has been contended that the parade ground is legally a part of Nova Scotia (or New Scotland).

The Castle Rock is interesting geologically, for although definite proof is wanting, it resembles the core of basalt plugging up a volcanic vent. It is a perfect example of Crag-and-Tail formation resulting from glacial action. Advancing from the west, the ice split against the Crag, excavating a deep hollow on each side, the Grassmarket and the old Nor' Loch, now the site of Princes Street Gardens, while the "tail" is seen in the gentle slope of the Esplanade and the Royal Mile.

The Castle is entered by the **Drawbridge** over the dry moat. In niches on either side of the gateway stand bronze statues of *Bruce* and *Wallace*, the national heroes of Scottish independence, which were unveiled in 1929 by T.R.H. the Duke and Duchess of York (afterwards King George VI and Queen Elizabeth). From the Ticket Office the steep narrow path leads to the **Portcullis Gate,** beneath the **State Prison,** otherwise known as **Argyll's Tower** on the site of the **Constable's Tower,** destroyed in the great siege of 1573, when Mary's garrison, under the brave Kirkcaldy of Grange, was compelled to capitulate. The walls are of enormous thickness—10 to 15 feet. The tower took its name from the two Argylls, father and son, Marquis and Earl, who were in turn imprisoned in the Castle preparatory to their execution, owing to their staunch adherence to the Covenant. The cell immediately over the archway, reached from above by a descending stair, was the scene of "Argyll's Last Sleep," a picture that embodies the most touching of the legends that gather about the human and heroic figure of the 9th Earl.

Beyond the Portcullis Gateway, on the right, is the **Argyll Battery,** on the edge of the cliff overlooking West Princes Street Gardens.

Behind, and on the brink of the precipice, is the old **Sally Port,** built on the site on which, it is said, the body of Queen Margaret was in 1093 carried off for sepulture in Dunfermline by her confessor, Turgot, despite the watchfulness of Donalbain. Here, too, Claverhouse held his famous interview with the governor of the Castle (1689) before he rode off to raise the Highlands.

The highest summit of the Castle Rock is 443 feet above the sea, and is variously known as the Citadel, **King's Bastion** and the Bomb Battery. Here is the famous gun nicknamed Mons Meg, and from this point there are fine views over the city. The site of Malcolm Canmore's Palace or hunting seat must have been hereabouts.

Adjoining the Battery is **St. Margaret's Chapel,** erected (*c.* 1090) at the instance of the queen of Malcolm Canmore. The interior of the Chapel is only about 17 feet by 11. It was restored in 1853, by command of Queen Victoria. It is an interesting example of Early Norman work.

On the **Half-Moon Battery,** the eastern front of the citadel, are the **Well** and the **Time Gun.** The gun is fired at 1 p.m. (Civil Time) daily, except Sundays; the associated clock is electrically controlled from the Royal Observatory on Blackford Hill. This battery was built by the Regent Morton after the siege of 1573. It forms a curtain round the ruins of **David's Tower,** built by David II, 1367, and destroyed in the siege. The ruins were found only in 1913, after being hidden for three hundred years. Excavation also revealed here the vaulted reservoirs that contained the Castle's water-supply.

The apex of the Castle rock is now crowned by—

THE SCOTTISH NATIONAL WAR MEMORIAL,

a building which has been well called "a coronach in stone." Designed by Sir Robert Lorimer, A.R.A., R.S.A., and inaugurated in 1927 by the Prince of Wales (now the Duke of Windsor), it stands on the site of barrack buildings which in turn succeeded the Chapel of St. Mary, founded by David I, rebuilt by David II in the fourteenth century, and finally demolished to make room for the barracks (1751).

The Memorial consists of a Gallery of Honour with projecting bays and entered by a noble porch, on each side of which wreaths are laid and over which is a figure representing the Survival of the Spirit. The slightly severe aspect of the exterior, with its walls of ashlar, gives no hint of the rare beauty of the interior, and the visitor can hardly fail to experience a feeling of awed surprise on entering. Straight in front is the archway of the Shrine, guarded by exquisitely designed gates.

To right and left stretches the nobly proportioned **Hall of Honour,** its walls occupied by regimental and other memorials, while the frieze bears the names of battle honours. Each Scottish regiment, whether raised in the Home Country or in the Overseas Dominions, has its own memorial, and visitors can read, on the walls and in the Rolls of Honour, the numbers and names of these who served and fell in the world wars.

The **Shrine,** in the words of the late Sir Lawrence Weaver, "bears much the same relation to the Hall of Honour as the sanctuary of a church to its nave. The Hall is for record and remembrance ; the Shrine for those deep emotions that transcend individual sorrows and swell into a *sursum corda* for those who see what the sacrifice has won for mankind." To this end the stained-glass windows and other decorations were designed, in every case by Scottish craftsmen. On either side is a fine bronze frieze in which are depicted Scots men and women in all their varied wartime uniforms, and in the centre, below the hovering figure of St. Michael, is the beautiful **Casket**, given by King George V and Queen Mary and containing the hundred thousand names of the fallen. Through the floor of the Shrine the rugged rock of the hill has been allowed to project, as if to prove on what a sure foundation is based this symbol of a nation's grief and gratitude.

The Memorial is extraordinarily comprehensive ; even man's humble yet helpful animal friends that played a rôle in the first World War are not forgotten.

The **Palace Yard,** or *Crown Square*, overlooked by the Memorial, contains nearly all the historic apartments of the Castle. **Queen Mary's Bedroom,** at the south-east corner, was the birthplace, on June 19, 1566, of James the Sixth of Scotland and First of England. In these confined **Royal Apartments** are a number of portraits, plans, and other early relics.

The vaulted **Crown Room** adjoins the Royal apartments. Here, secured in a strong iron cage, are to be seen the **Scottish Regalia,** or the " Honours of Scotland," a crown, sceptre, sword of state, and other jewels. With them are exhibited the golden collar of the Garter, conferred by Queen Elizabeth on James VI, with the George and Dragon, the badge of the Order bequeathed by Cardinal York, the brother of Prince Charles Edward, to George IV, and sent to Edinburgh Castle in 1830. Here, too, is the oak chest in which the regalia were deposited at the Union, and in which they lay concealed for over a century until they were " officially " discovered in 1817 by a Commission, among the members of which was Sir Walter Scott. They had been " lost " previously at the time of the Commonwealth, having first been hidden under the pulpit of the Church of Kinneff in Kincardineshire (*see* p. 353).

In the **Old Parliament Hall, or Banqueting Hall,** on the southern side of the quadrangle, the earlier meetings of the Scots Estates, or Parliament, are believed to have been held ; among others the first Parliament of James II, March 20, 1437. The hall was rebuilt early in the sixteenth century by James IV. Here also many banquets were held, including those given to Charles I in 1633 on his first visit to Scotland, and, exactly fifteen years later, by the Earl of Leven to Cromwell and Heselrige. The Hall is now a museum of armour.

On either side of the Square is the **Scottish United Services Museum** (opened 1933), which contains a number of interesting historical exhibits such as uniforms, medals, prints, etc., relating mostly to Scottish Regiments, and contains also some exhibits of interest in connection with Scottish Naval and Air Force history.

From the Esplanade, Castle Hill leads to the Lawnmarket and the High Street. As may be imagined, the houses on either hand have sheltered many famous personages and seen many a twist given to history, but one by one the old buildings are vanishing, and few of them, new or old, have any appearance of grandeur. Boswell's Court was the residence of Dr. Boswell, uncle of the biographer of Dr. Johnson. At the junction with Johnston Terrace stands the *Tolbooth Parish Church* ; here the chair of John Knox is preserved.

On the north side of the street is the **Outlook Tower** (*see* p. 108), with camera obscura and some very interesting features connected with geography, history, art and sociology.

The **Lawnmarket** is said to derive its name from the fact that the lawn or cloth sellers of the city had their booths in it.

Opposite the south entrance of the General Assembly Hall of the Church of Scotland (which stands on a site once occupied (*c.* 1544) by Mary of Guise, Regent of Scotland) is all that remains of the **West Bow**, of old one of the principal approaches to the city. Neighbouring the Hall is **Milne's Court**, erected in 1690 by the King's Master Mason for Scotland, Robert Mylne, who enjoyed the distinction of being the seventh (and last) of his race who in succession had held that honour. Just beyond Milne's Court is **James's Court.** David Hume lived in the house in the eastern corner. When he left it to go to the New Town the flat was purchased by Boswell, the biographer of Johnson, who came here in the year 1773.

Lady Stair's Close takes its name from Elizabeth, Countess Dowager of Stair, in her day a leader of fashion. Her house was the scene of the remarkable incident recorded in Scott's story of *My Aunt Margaret's Mirror.* The house is now a **Museum** containing relics of Robert Burns, Sir Walter Scott and R. L. Stevenson.

Over the Lawnmarket entrance to Lady Stair's Close is a tablet stating : " In a house on the east side of this close Robert Burns lived during his first visit to Edinburgh, 1786."

On the opposite side of the Lawnmarket, the picturesque **Riddle's Court** (with its houses of Bailie Macmorran and David Hume, the philosopher) repays a visit. Lower down the street we come to **Brodie's Close,** where lived Deacon William Brodie, who was a member of the Town Council.

In an evil hour he gave way to gambling and dissipated habits, and finally became the secret leader and director of a gang of housebreakers. After long escaping detection he was arrested and hanged in 1786–7. The turnpike stair on the right leads to the house (with fine ceilings of 1645 and 1646); the door with its massive lock is said to have been made by the Deacon's own hands. The story is the foundation of the play by R. L. Stevenson and W. E. Henley.

Before entering the High Street we see on the left Bank Street, which leads down to the *Bank of Scotland* (founded 1695) and the Mound, and on the right George IV Bridge, where now stands the new building of the—

National Library

(**Admission,** *see* p. 108)

opened by H.M. the Queen in 1956. The Library was formerly the Advocate's Library, founded in 1682 by Sir George Mackenzie and made over to the nation in 1925 by the Faculty of Advocates. It contains the largest and most valuable collection of books and manuscripts in Scotland (nearly two million) and is one of the libraries entitled to claim a copy of every new work published in Great Britain. In the hall devoted to the permanent exhibition (*open free*) are illuminated manuscripts, early printed books, notable examples of Scottish painting and bookbinding, and manuscripts of well-known Scottish personages—for example, Mary, Queen of Scots, Burns, Scott, Carlyle, and R. L. S. A smaller hall is used for temporary exhibitions of books and manuscripts.

High Street.

Returning to the High Street we pass, on the left at the corner of Bank Street, the buildings of the Sheriff Court. Opposite, on the right, is a quadrangular space bounded by St. Giles Cathedral, the Signet Library, and the Midlothian County Buildings. A few steps farther in the direction of the Cathedral a **Heart** will be seen figured on the causeway in parti-coloured stones. This marks the spot where stood the portal of the **Old Tolbooth,** in which the opening incidents of

Scott's great novel, *The Heart of Midlothian*, took place. The Tolbooth—whose site as a whole is likewise indicated by special paving-blocks—was finally demolished in 1817, the entrance gate being presented to Sir Walter Scott and by him taken to Abbotsford (*see* p. 67). **Advocate's Close**, an alley which comes up from Cockburn Street on the left almost opposite the Cathedral, is a good example of a typical Edinburgh feature. On the right-hand side of the Close (as you descend) and also on the house of Bishop Adam Bothwell (who married Mary, Queen of Scots, to Bothwell), which looks down on it from the left, are examples of the pious mottoes wherewith citizens adorned their lintels and dormers.

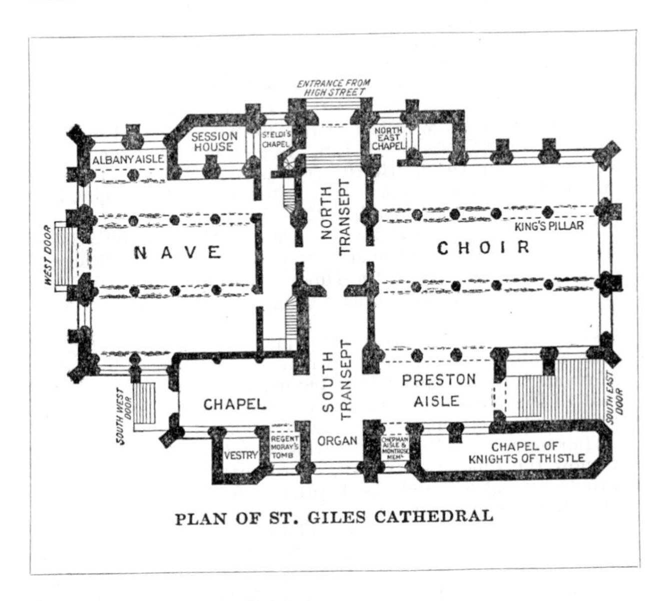

PLAN OF ST. GILES CATHEDRAL

St. Giles Cathedral
(High Kirk of Edinburgh)

(Admission, *see* p. 109.)

The Church is a beautiful Gothic edifice, 206 feet long and 129 feet in breadth across the transepts, 110 at the west end, and 76

across the choir. The spire, or " Crown of St. Giles," is 161 feet high, and terminates in the representation of an imperial crown; from its form and the elevation of the spot it is seen with fine effect from most parts of the city.

Enter by the west or north door from the High Street. In the far (north-eastern) corner is the **Chapel of the Most Ancient and Most Noble Order of the Thistle.** Opened in 1911, it is a small but beautiful example of modern Gothic, and was designed, like the National War Memorial, by Sir R. S. Lorimer, R.S.A. The Royal stalls are at the west end, and there are fourteen others for the rest of the knights.

To the west of the Chapel is the **Preston Aisle,** in which is the **Royal Pew,** occupied during Assembly time by the representative of the Sovereign, the Royal High Commissioner. Opening off the Preston Aisle is the **Chepman Aisle** (Walter Chepman was the first Scottish printer: d. 1532), which contains a monument to the Marquis of Montrose, whose body was interred in the vaults beneath in 1661, some years after his execution.

At the end of the South Transept is a fine modern organ. To the west is the Moray Aisle, once three chapels. In its west wall is a bronze *Memorial to Robert Louis Stevenson*, by St. Gaudens, a tribute from admirers of " R.L.S." in all quarters of the world.

Near at hand, in the South Aisle, is the **Vesper Bell,** a survival of pre-Reformation times. The Latin inscription signifies: " O Mother of God, Remember Me. 1452."

Off the west end of the **North Aisle** is the **Albany Aisle,** said to have been built by Robert, Duke of Albany, in expiation of the murder of his nephew, the Duke of Rothesay, in 1402. In 1951 the Aisle was furnished as a congregational War Memorial Chapel.

Just west of the High Street entrance is **St. Eloi's Chapel** (or the Hammermen's Chapel), where the craftsmen dedicated the famous " Blue Blanket," or banner of the trades.

East of the High Street entrance is an ancient Chapel which was restored as a memorial to Dr. William Chambers (1800–1883) in recognition of his great work in renovating the Cathedral. It is now the Chapel of Youth, containing Colours of various Youth Organizations and the baptismal font.

The Church contains many other memorials of famous Scottish churchmen, statesmen, soldiers and philanthropists.

The four octagonal pillars supporting the Tower of the Cathedral are said to be part of the Norman building erected in 1120. Stretching eastward from these pillars is the **Choir,** with the Pulpit, beautifully carved in Caen stone by John Rhind and illustrative of the six acts of mercy.

History.—The exact date of foundation is unknown, but from very early times a church stood on or near the spot. Alexander I, " the Fierce," is said to have built the Church which, when Richard II of England invaded Scotland in 1385 and burnt Edinburgh, nearly shared the fate of most other buildings in the city. The entrance porch, a portion of the choir and nave, and the base of the spire were all that escaped destruction. The Church lay in ruin for two years; then the civic authorities set about rebuilding it and added five chapels on the south-west of the nave. The side aisles—the most beautiful of which is the Albany Aisle—were built by private individuals. About fifty years later, transepts were added, completing the cruciform character of the edifice, and the chancel was extended eastward. In 1466, James III made the Church collegiate. Thirty-six altars were set up, and the ecclesiastics connected with St. Giles formed a wealthy and influential corporation.

About a century later the Church was partitioned off, to form two separate "kirks"—the High or Parish Church and the Tolbooth Church (in the latter of which John Knox preached). Other portions were fitted as a grammar school, court of justice, a town clerk's office, a prison, and a weaver's workshop, and an odd corner was even found in which to stow away the gallows. As the population of Edinburgh increased, new churches were needed; and these were presently provided by purging the edifice of most of its "secular and profane uses," and dividing it into four churches. The choir was the High Church; the Tolbooth Church was in the south-west corner; Haddo's Hole or the Little Kirk in the north-west; and the Old Kirk in the middle and part of the south side. The Preston Aisle was still used for meetings of a public nature; and eventually the dark central space under the spire, with the north transept, was fitted up as a police office.

In the Cathedral on Sunday, July 23, 1637, took place a famous incident, handed down by "constant oral tradition." Charles I had ordered the English Church service to be read in every parish church in Scotland, and as Dean Hannay in St. Giles began the new service in the reading-desk, an organized protest was made which soon became a riot. It is said that a kail-wife, Jenny Geddes by name, whose stance was at the Tron, flung her stool at his head, with the result that a riot ensued. A tablet commemorates the Dean.

After the restoration of Charles II, the Church was once more made a cathedral, and episcopacy re-established; but the last of the State bishops was ejected at the Revolution of 1688, and since then, although still popularly designated St. Giles Cathedral, the Church has had no ecclesiastical claim to the title.

The building was ruthlessly "restored" in 1829; and in 1832 the four churches of which it consisted were reduced to three, viz. the High, West St. Giles and Trinity College, and the police office was removed. In this maimed condition it remained until 1871, when the restoration was begun. These alterations resulted in the removal of two of the congregations and the opening of the building from end to end, so that it now forms one grand church, nearly cruciform in shape, such as it was before the time of Knox. The building was reopened in 1883.

The open space south of St. Giles, formerly the graveyard, is known now as **Parliament Square**. In it *John Knox* was buried in 1572. In the square is an equestrian statue of Charles II, erected 1685, and probably the oldest lead statue of its kind in Britain.

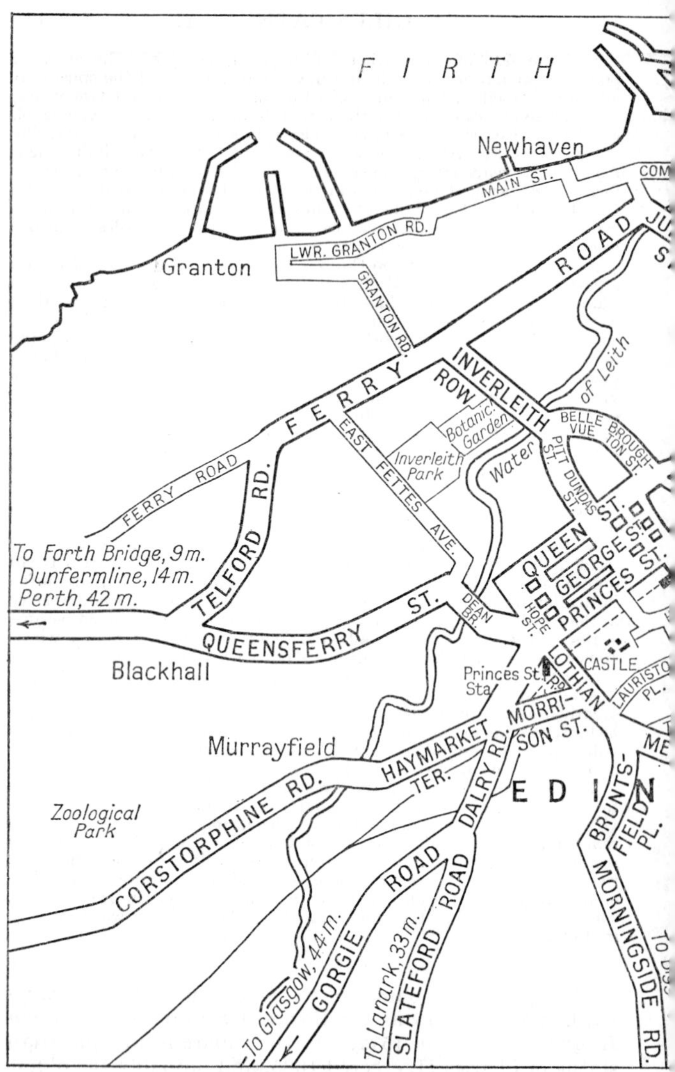
FIRTH
Newhaven
MAIN ST.
COM
LWR. GRANTON RD.
Granton
GRANTON RD.
ROAD
FERRY
INVERLEITH
ROW
of Leith
Botanic Garden
Inverleith Park
Water
BELLE VUE
BROUGHTON ST.
PITT ST.
DUNDAS ST.
FERRY ROAD
TELFORD RD.
EAST FETTES AVE.
QUEEN ST.
GEORGE ST.
PRINCES ST.
HOPE ST.
To Forth Bridge, 9 m.
Dunfermline, 14 m.
Perth, 42 m.
QUEENSFERRY ST.
DEAN BR.
Blackhall
CASTLE
LOTHIAN RD.
Princes St. Sta
MORRISON ST.
LAURISTON PL.
Murrayfield
HAYMARKET TER.
DALRY RD.
CORSTORPHINE RD.
EDIN
BRUNTSFIELD PL.
Zoological Park
ROAD
GORGIE
ROAD
SLATEFORD
To Glasgow, 44 m.
To Lanark, 33 m.
MORNINGSIDE RD.

Main Roads

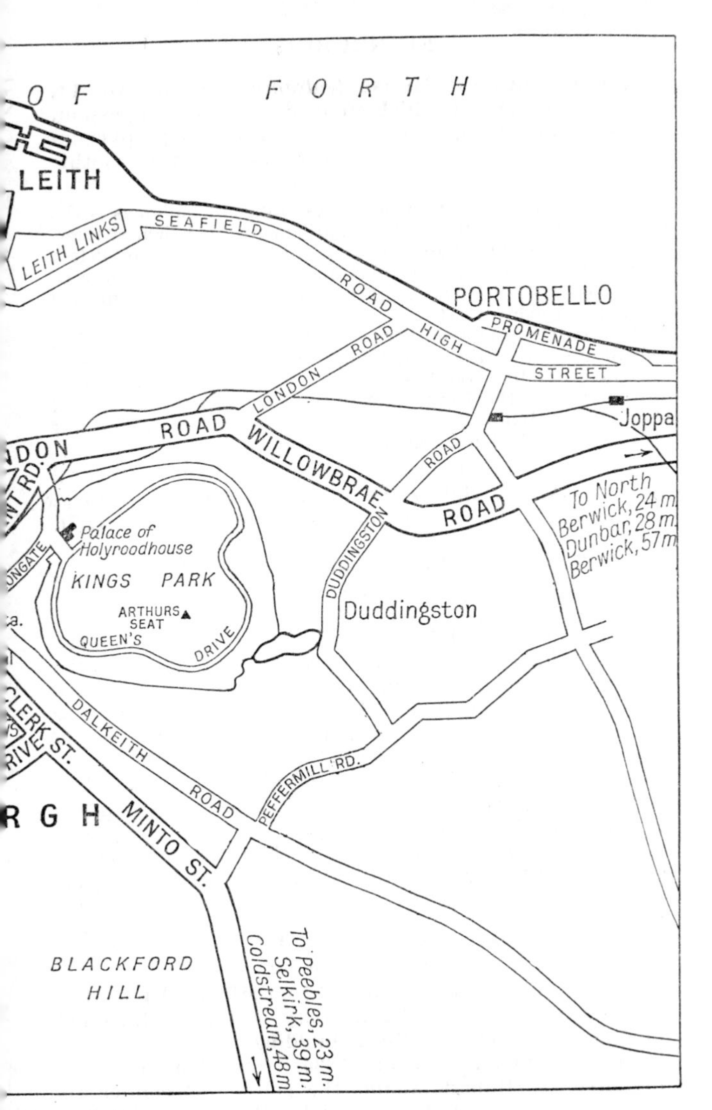
O F
F O R T H
LEITH
LEITH LINKS
SEAFIELD
ROAD
PORTOBELLO
HIGH
PROMENADE
STREET
ROAD
LONDON
Joppa
DON
ROAD
WILLOWBRAE
ROAD
ROAD
To North
Berwick, 24 m
Dunbar, 28 m.
Berwick, 57 m
Palace of
Holyroodhouse
KINGS PARK
ARTHURS
SEAT
QUEEN'S
DRIVE
DUDDINGSTON
Duddingston
DALKEITH
ROAD
PEFFERMILL RD.
ST.
MINTO ST.
R G H
BLACKFORD
HILL
To Peebles, 23 m.
Selkirk, 39 m.
Coldstream, 48 m

EDINBURGH.

The **Parliament House** (*entrance—free—at No.* 11, *south-west corner*), in which are held the Courts of Session, dates from 1632–40, although in 1808 a Grecian propylæum and colonnade were erected in place of the former Gothic front.

The most interesting portion of the range of buildings is the great hall in which the Scottish Parliaments held their sittings. It is called the **Parliament Hall**, and is 122 feet long by 49 feet in breadth, with a fine oak roof and floor, similar to those of Westminster Hall. The Scots Parliament met here from 1639 until the Union in 1707.

Beneath the ornate southern window one passes to the corridor, where are five of the eight Courts of the **Outer House**, each presided over by a Lord Ordinary. Farther along the corridor, to the left, is the **Inner House**, divided into the **First** and **Second Divisions**. It was in the First Division that Sir Walter Scott had his seat as Principal Clerk.

The range of buildings extending between the Cathedral and the County Hall is the **Signet Library** (*admission, see* p. 109), belonging to the Society of Writers to H.M. Signet.

At **The Cross**, also once known as the *Mercat Cross*, Royal proclamations are read by the Heralds—a picturesque proceeding.

We have returned to the **High Street**, and note on the opposite side the **City Chambers**, for long known as the Royal Exchange (built in 1753 and extended in 1933). Under the Central Arch is the city's simple **Cenotaph** or Stone of Remembrance, in honour of those who died in the two World Wars. Behind is the entrance to the headquarters of the Edinburgh Municipality, now ruling over an area of 34,781 acres, containing a population approaching half a million people.

A short way from this block of civic buildings, as one goes southward along South Bridge, beyond Chambers Street, is the—

University of Edinburgh.

(Admission, *see* p. 109.)

Though youngest (founded 1583) of the four older Scottish Universities, Edinburgh University is not the least important. The **Old College** buildings were erected at intervals between 1789 and 1834, from plans originally prepared by Robert Adam, the celebrated eighteenth-century architect, and modified by Playfair. The form is a regular parallelogram, 356 feet long by 225 wide, partly Palladian, partly Grecian. The portico of the principal front has six Doric pillars, and is surmounted by a graceful dome of three stages, 153 feet high, terminating in a figure of "Youth holding aloft the Torch of Knowledge."

The teaching staff of the University consists of some 140 professors and 1,400 non-professional members allocated among the faculties of Divinity, Law, Medicine, Veterinary Medicine, Arts, Science, Social Science, and Music. The students generally number about 10,500, over one-third being women.

On the north side of Chambers Street is Old College Wynd, now Guthrie Street, where (in a house no longer standing) Sir Walter Scott was born (August 15, 1771). Farther west is the Heriot Watt University; on the south the **Royal Scottish Museum** (*admission, see* p. 109), one of the most important institutions of its kind in the kingdom. There are four departments: art and archæology, natural history, geology and technology. The art department is concerned with the decorative arts of the world at all periods, among them the arts of primitive peoples, and includes such masterpieces as the Lennoxlove toilet-service and an unrivalled collection of Chinese carved lacquer. The natural history department has representative collections of all British and foreign fauna. The technology department is celebrated for its series of working models, many of them made in the museum workshops. Free lectures and film-shows are presented in the lecture-theatre.

Beyond the western end of Chambers Street is the **Greyfriars Churchyard**, anciently the garden of the Franciscan monastery which stood in the Grassmarket. The site was granted by Mary, Queen of Scots, after the Reformation, as a burying-ground for the town. It contains the flat tomb on which, says tradition, the National Covenant was signed, on March 1, 1638, by an excited multitude, some of whom drew blood from their arms and inscribed their names with it in lieu of ink. The evidence goes to show that the "signing" was all done inside the Church. The **South Ground**, in the south-west angle of the churchyard, bears above the entrance the label "Covenanters' Prison." Here, in June, 1679, about 1,200 Covenanters, taken at Bothwell Bridge, were confined five months, unhoused, and almost unfed. Besides the Martyrs' Memorial, the churchyard contains the graves of George Buchanan, Allan Ramsay, William Adam, and many another famous Scot.

Adjoining Greyfriars (pass through Commemoration Gates) is **George Heriot's School**, founded and endowed by George Heriot (*c.* 1563–1624), goldsmith to James VI.

Meadow Walk leads southward between the University Medical school and the Royal Infirmary and gives access, on the left, to **George Square.** At No. 25 Sir Walter Scott spent his early years. A pioneer suburb (1766), this Square is now being transformed by the University. New University buildings on the east and south sides of George Square include the Appleton and David Hume Towers, and the **University Library.** The library, formerly in the Old College, is believed the largest single University library building in Europe. Near the east end in Buccleuch Street is the Archers' Hall, the headquarters of the **Royal Company of Archers** (formed about 1676), who constitute the Sovereign's Bodyguard for Scotland.

Near the western end of the Meadows (which lie just beyond George Square on the south) is Tollcross, southward from which one passes, on the left, the *Bruntsfield Links*, a stretch of grassland which for generations has been devoted to golf. In Colinton Road, off Morningside Road, are the huge Napier Technical College and George Watson's College, a famous school for boys. The wall of Morningside Parish Church contains the *Bore Stone*, in which was planted the royal standard when the Scottish army which mustered on the Boroughmuir assembled here prior to marching to Flodden; and so to the **Braid Hills.** Here are highly popular municipal golf courses, on which many a well-known player has learnt the game. From the Braid Hills hotel a motor road skirts the north side of the hills, with grand views over the city, and from this road paths descend to the Braid Burn, from which one can climb **Blackford Hill,** with another golf course and the *Royal Observatory* (*Weds., 3 p.m.*) or follow the stream up through the charming woods of *Hermitage Park* or down to Liberton Dams.

A short way eastward of St. Giles is the former **Tron Church,** so named from the public weighing beam—the salt *tron*—which stood within a few yards of it. We now cross the junction with North Bridge, and two hundred yards farther down the High Street, on the left, is **John Knox's House** (*admission, see* p. 108), which, with neighbouring Mowbray House, has been saved from impending demolition and restored. Although doubt has been expressed whether the Reformer really had this house as his "manse," there is good reason for believing that he inhabited it for some time while his own was repairing. The possessor with whom it is most clearly identified is James Mossman, an Edinburgh jeweller, whose initials and arms, with those of his wife, are carved on one of the panels. Extending over part of the front above the ground floor are large Roman letters—"Lufe God abufe al, and thi nychtbour as thiself." The interior is well worth a visit, many relics of Knox being stored here.

The **Canongate** extends for about a third of a mile from St. Mary's Street to Holyrood. Even more than the High Street of Edinburgh, the Canongate was formerly the fashionable residential quarter. "As the main avenue from the palace to the city," says Chambers, "it has borne upon its pavement the burden of all that was beautiful, all that was gallant, all that has become historically interesting in Scotland for the last six or seven hundred years." It became very shabby, though municipal rebuilding is ridding it of much of its squalor, and it is a most fascinating portion of the city.

A little farther on is **St. John Street**, entered under an archway. In the house over the archway Tobias Smollett resided in 1756 with his sister, Mrs. Telfer, of Scotstoun. The **Canongate Kilwinning Lodge of Freemasons**, of which Burns was a member, meets in the building on the right immediately beyond the archway. The Lodge has many quaint and curious records. On application to the Lodge secretary, visitors—masonic and otherwise—are permitted to look over St. John's Chapel (1736), charter granted 1677, and one of the oldest masonic chapels in the world.

Immediately below St. John Street is **Moray House** (*open free on application*), now a training college, but retaining elaborate ceilings and other relics of once stately days. In the garden behind is the summerhouse where the Commissioners met to sign the Treaty of Union (*see* p. 35).

Farther down is the **Canongate Tolbooth** (1591). It is in the French style of architecture, with turrets and projecting clock. The building formerly contained a jail and court rooms, but now houses the Telfer Dunbar Tartan Collection and exhibitions are held from time to time in its finely panelled hall.

Adjoining the Tolbooth is the **Canongate Kirk** (1688), the Kirk of Holyroodhouse. Its churchyard contains the graves of Adam Smith, author of *The Wealth of Nations*; of Dugald Stewart, Professor of Moral Philosophy; of the poet Robert Fergusson; of Mrs. Maclehose, Burns's "Clarinda." Nearly opposite is **Huntly House**, a quaint old timber-fronted mansion, now, in its reconditioned state, the home of the *City Museum* (*admission, see* p. 108). At the foot of the *Royal Mile*, which we have covered in our descent from the Castle, is—

THE PALACE OF HOLYROODHOUSE.

(**Admission,** *see* p. 108.)

Historical Note.—The Palace was at first intimately connected with the Abbey built by David I and dedicated to the Holy Rood, the

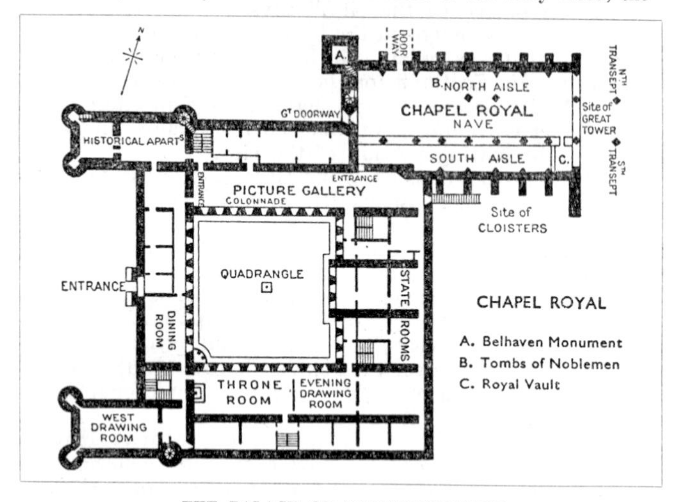

THE PALACE OF HOLYROODHOUSE.

Virgin and All Saints, in gratitude, it is said, for deliverance from danger while hunting.

The Abbey was richly endowed, and it gradually became a royal residence. It is certain, however, that James IV lived here and began building the Palace ; the tower commonly attributed to James V was built by him, and it appears from the accounts that the work done by James V was largely alteration and renovation. In 1544 the Palace and Abbey were burnt during the English invasion, only the church and north-west tower escaping. The Palace was the principal residence of Mary, and of her son, James VI, to the time when he ascended the English throne. During that stirring period it was the scene of many important events. In 1650 a fire destroyed the greater portion, the structure built by James IV again escaping. Cromwell ordered the Palace to be restored ; but all his work was pulled down in 1671, when Charles II decided on the erection of a new palace, from the plans of Sir William Bruce of Kinross, who held the office of King's Surveyor in Scotland. Bonnie Prince Charlie held Court at Holyrood in September–October, 1745, ere setting off on his ill-fated march on London. In 1830–2 Charles X of France lived here in exile. Nowadays the Palace is frequently and regularly used as a royal residence. Since 1929 its official designation has been, as in bygone days, the Palace of Holyroodhouse.

The general style of architecture is French, of the time of Louis XIV. The old tower remains at the northern end of the western front, and that at the southern end, built by Bruce, is a copy of it. The grand entrance is surmounted by the royal arms of Scotland ; above is a small octagonal tower, terminating in an imperial crown. The building surrounds a quadrangle, the northern side containing the Picture Gallery, the southern side the State Apartments.

On entering, turn to the left, to—

The Historical Apartments,

of which the first is the **Picture Gallery,** the largest apartment in the Palace, measuring 150 feet long, 24 feet wide, and 20 feet high. Here the Young Pretender, Charles Edward, held levees and balls during his brief stay in the Scottish capital in 1745 ; and since the Union the gallery has been used for the election of the representative Peers of Scotland, and the levees of the Lord High Commissioner to the General Assembly of the Church of Scotland. The portraits of the ancient Scottish Kings, real or imaginary, were executed in 1684–6 by a Fleming, James de Witt or Jakob de Wet, who completed the 110 works, from " originalls " supplied by the Government, in two years, receiving the princely sum of £120 sterling yearly, and having to find his own colours and canvas.

From the Picture Gallery we pass to the **Duchess of Hamilton's Drawing-room,** and thence to **Lord Darnley's Apartments,** in the old tower of the Palace. Mary was married to Henry Stewart, Lord Darnley, eldest son of Matthew, Earl of Lennox, on July 29, 1565, and thus were united two lines of succession to the English throne. Darnley's rooms consisted of an **Audience Chamber,** the room called **Lord Darnley's Bedroom,** and his **Dressing-room.** In these rooms are good specimens of ancient tapestry, and many portraits.

A door in the Audience Chamber leads to a staircase by

which **Queen Mary's Apartments** are reached. There is also a small private staircase, closed to the public, by which the murderers of Rizzio gained access to the Queen's rooms. The first room of the suite is **Mary's Audience Chamber,** 24 feet long and 22 feet wide.

We next see **Mary's Bedroom,** a little smaller than the other. Above the fireplace are examples of Queen Mary's embroidery. The bed is of a more recent period, all the ancient royal furniture at the Palace having been plundered or destroyed by Cromwell's troopers. The small **Dressing-room** occupies the Southern Tower. A little to the west of it is a door, half hidden by tapestry, communicating with a secret staircase on the north side of the room; and near the head of this staircase is another door leading to the most interesting of all Queen Mary's apartments, the **Supper-Room,** in the North Tower. Here Rizzio was attacked by Ruthven and the other conspirators, the craven Darnley being also present, and dragged through the bedroom and the Audience Chamber to the head of the principal staircase, where his body was left with fifty-six wounds. A brass tablet is inscribed: "The body of David Rizzio was left here after his murder in Queen Mary's Supper Room; 9th March, 1566."

The **State Apartments** are entered from the east end of the Picture Gallery. Redecorated during the reign of George V, under Queen Mary's direction, they contain interesting portraits, tapestry and furniture, besides fine ceilings and panelling.

The ruins of the **Chapel Royal** are entered from the north-west corner of the quadrangle. Here were married many of the Scottish monarchs, among them James II, James III, James IV, James V and Mary, and Anne of Denmark, bride of James VI. Charles I was crowned here (1633). The walls of the Chapel Royal, the nave, are the only portion of the old Abbey Church still standing, and its ruined condition is largely the work of an angry Revolution mob (1688). The Church was twice devastated by the English (1544 and 1547) and after the Reformation the choir and transepts fell into complete ruin, though the present east end was erected largely from the debris. The foundations of the demolished parts of the Church, including those of the Chapter-house, have been uncovered, and along with these were discovered a number of ancient graves. On a tablet above the doorway is an inscription placed by Charles I: "*Basilicam hanc, semi rutam, Carolus Rex optimus instauravit, M.D.cxxxiii.* (1633). He shall build ane house for my name, and I will stablish the throne of his kingdom for ever." The floor of the nave is paved with gravestones, and there are several interesting tombs in the Chapel.

The inscription on the **Royal Vault**, in the south-east corner, restored by Queen Victoria in 1898, records that it contains "the remains of David II; of James II and his Queen, Mary of Gueldres; of Arthur, third son of James IV; of James V and his Queen, Magdalen, and second son Arthur, Duke of Albany; and of Henry, Lord Darnley, consort of Mary, Queen of Scots."

In the garden on the north side of the Palace is a sun-dial, which has a separate gnomon on each of the twenty sides of the apex of the pedestal. It is of seventeenth-century date, having the cypher of Charles I and his wife Henrietta Maria.

In a small enclosure of grass and trees at the foot of Abbeyhill is a quaint old building, with pyramidal or conical roof, and dormer windows. This structure, which was repaired in 1852, is known as **Queen Mary's Bath**, where, says tradition, the beautiful Queen was wont to bathe in white wine to increase her charms.

Adjoining Holyrood is **Holyrood Park**, which includes **Arthur's Seat**, a rugged, double-coned extinct volcano, from which there are fine views over the city; and the **Salisbury Crags**, which present a precipitous front of solid rock rising to 550 feet above the sea. The highest and most romantic point is the *Lion's Head* (823 feet: view indicator on summit) of Arthur's Seat, to which a path mounts from St. Margaret's Well. A splendid drive, the *Queen's Drive*, about 3½ miles long, encircles the base of Arthur's Seat and the Salisbury Crags, passing beside St. Margaret's Loch and Dunsappie Loch, and overlooking (to the south-west) *Craigmillar*, with its ruined castle and numerous breweries, and *Duddingston*, with its old church and reed-skirted loch (a bird-sanctuary).

THE NEW TOWN.

Having inspected typical parts of Old Edinburgh, we may now turn our attention to the "New Town," to which we cross he railway-traversed valley by the North

Bridge, most striking of the City's many viaducts, by the humbler Waverley Bridge farther west, or by the curving, plunging Mound. Of modern Edinburgh the principal sight and symbol is—

Princes Street.

Nearly a mile in length and bordered on one side by gardens, the street might more appropriately be known as Princes Terrace; but Princes Street owes a great debt to the Castle Hill, which, as elsewhere in the city, lifts the view to a very high standard of beauty. Here are many of the chief shops of Edinburgh, with hotels and restaurants, and at the east end the *Waverley Station* fills the valley. In the foreground the graceful **Scott Monument** (1844; designed by George Meikle Kemp) rises from the gardens, an open Gothic tower 200 feet high (*admission, see* p. 109) with a statue of Sir Walter by Sir John Steell, R.S.A., and figures of characters in Scott's works.

Just west of the monument an embankment known as **The Mound** crosses the valley and supports two imposing public buildings designed in classical style by W. H. Playfair and housing the **Royal Scottish Academy** and the National Gallery. In the former (adjoining Princes Street) periodical exhibitions of the works of living artists are held, and there is a permanent Diploma Collection of Academicians (*admission, see* p. 109).

The **National Gallery** (*admission, see* p. 108) contains a small European collection of very high quality, including pictures by Rubens, Velasquez, El Greco, Rembrandt, Watteau, Gainsborough, Constable, etc. There is an outstanding room of French Impressionism, including pictures by Degas, Gauguin, Cézanne, van Gogh, and a fairly full representation of Scottish painting up to 1900, including a good representation of Raeburn.

Beyond the Mound the **West Princes Street Gardens** occupy what was formerly the bed of the Nor' Loch. At the eastern entrance, beside the Statue of Allan Ramsay, the poet, is a fascinating *Floral Clock*, and down below is the *Royal Scots Monument* (1952). In the summer season there are open-air performances in the afternoon and evening by military and other bands, concert parties, etc., and dancing is provided for. On the Garden Walk, facing the Castle Rock, has been placed the impressive **American Memorial** to Scots who laid down their lives in the 1914–18 War, presented by subscribers in the United States of Scottish blood or sympathies. It was the work (1924–7) of Professor R. Tait McKenzie.

In the Gardens, across the railway, at the foot of the

Castle Rock, are the ruins of the **Well-house Tower,** built in the reign of David II to protect what is thought to have been the only water supply the garrison then had, and enlarged in the reign of James II. At the west end of Princes Street is **St. John's Episcopal Church,** a fine Later Gothic structure, some of the details of which are copied from Westminster Abbey and St. George's Chapel, Windsor. At the rear is a Celtic cross in memory of *Dean Ramsay* (1793–1872 ; author of *Reminiscences of Scottish Life and Character*, a classic of humorous literature), who was for many years incumbent here. Scott's mother and *Sir Henry Raeburn* (1756–1823), the portrait painter, are buried in the Dormitory at the east-end.

Also at the west end of Princes Street is the **West Kirk,** or St. Cuthbert's Church, the history of which goes further back than that of any other religious institution in Edinburgh. As early as the eighth century the site was occupied by a church dedicated to Cuthbert, Bishop of Durham, who died in 687. There have been seven buildings on this same site, the present church having been built in 1892–3. The tower, built in 1787–90, is the only remaining part of an eighteenth-century edifice. In the burial-ground are interred Napier, the inventor of logarithms, and De Quincey, of " Opium Eater " fame. At the foot of Lothian Road are Princes Street Station (closed) and the *Caledonian Hotel.* Halfway up Lothian Road is the **Usher Hall,** the City's main hall.

At the eastern end of Princes Street are the **Waverley Steps,** one of the windiest spots in Britain. The steps lead down to the **Waverley Station.** On their west side is the *Waverley Market* (exhibition hall), and on the other side the towering *North British Hotel* (British Transport). On the far side of the Hotel is the **Post Office,** and opposite that, across Princes Street, the **Register House,** a very pleasing Adam building, in which are preserved the public records of Scotland, both legal and historical. Among the historical documents permanently exhibited are the Treaty of Northampton (1328), an example of the National Covenant (1638), and the original Articles of the Treaty of Union (1707). Eastward, Princes Street is continued by Waterloo Place past the base of **Calton Hill,** where the chief feature is **St. Andrew's House,** home since 1939 of Scottish Government Departments, on the site of old Calton Gaol, its fresh stones looking particularly fresh in Auld Reekie. Here, too, is the **Royal High School,** a thirteenth-century foundation. Sir Walter Scott was among its many brilliant pupils. Opposite is the **Burns Monument,** and high above it the **National Monument,** modelled on the Parthenon in 1822 to commemorate gallant achievements during the Peninsular War. It was never finished, owing to lack of funds, but is probably no less picturesque on that account. Nearer the road is the **Nelson Monument,** shaped something like a telescope and with a small museum of relics (*admission, see* p. 108). The time ball at the top falls daily exactly at 1 p.m., Greenwich time. Westward of the National Monument is the **Observatory** of the Astronomical Society of Edinburgh (*admission on written application to Director*) and founded in 1776.

On the south side of Waterloo Place are the Old Calton Burying Ground, in which are, besides the graves of many historic figures, a tall *Obelisk* in memory of five " Chartist Martyrs," sentenced (1793–4) to transportation; the circular, temple-like *Tomb of Hume*, the philosopher; and a monument, with a statue of President Lincoln, which forms a memorial of the Scots-American soldiers who fell in the American Civil War. Beyond the Old Royal High School Regent Road leads down towards Portobello (*see* p. 56).

North of Princes Street and parallel with it is **George Street**—the pride and starting point of Georgian Edinburgh—extending from St. Andrew Square to Charlotte Square. From **St. Andrew Square** (off whose north-east corner is the bus station of Scottish Omnibuses, Ltd.) the New Town spread (1770–1825) northwards and westwards in graceful stone terraces, squares and crescents, rich in literary and other interest—to Queen Street, Heriot Row (R. L. S. lived at No. 17), Moray Place (Edinburgh's finest circus) and Randolph Crescent, among others. At the east end of Queen Street are the **Scottish National Portrait Gallery** and the **National Museum of Antiquities of Scotland** (*admission, see* p. 109).

The Gallery contains portraits of most of the major figures in Scottish history from the end of the sixteenth century to the present day. There are examples of the works of Dobson, Lely, Kneller, Reynolds, Gainsborough and Raeburn.

The Museum has very rich collections illustrating life and art in Scotland from he Stone Age to historical times. They include the Roman silver treasure from Traprain (*see* p. 52), sculptured stones and reliquaries of the Celtic Church, jewellery of Mary Queen of Scots, the " Maiden "—a sixteenth-century guillotine, Jacobite relics, Highland harps and weapons. Parts of the rapidly growing collections illustrating domestic life, costumes and agriculture in the recent past are shown at a branch, The Museum Gallery.

St. Andrew's Church, near the eastern end of George Street, was the scene of the Disruption of the Church of Scotland in 1843; and at 108 Scott lived for a short time after his marriage, while at 39 Castle Street, off George Street, the Waverley Novels were in large part written.

Charlotte Square, one of the finest examples of the work of the Adam brothers, has, in the gardens, the *Albert Memorial* (1876) by Sir John Steell; in the south-west corner, the birthplace of Earl Haig; and on the west side, St. George's Church, with a dome modelled on that of St. Paul's Cathedral. Hope Street enters Princes Street at the West End, whence Queensferry Street leads by way of the **Dean Bridge** to the Queensferry Road (*see* p. 256). The Dean Bridge (1832: one of Telford's best works) boldly spans the deep and lovely valley of the *Water of Leith*. By Bell's Brae one can descend to the old Dean Village, near the **Dean Cemetery**, which contains the graves of many distinguished men. From Queensferry Street, going by Melville Street, one reaches **St. Mary's Episcopal Cathedral**, one of the most beautiful ecclesiastical buildings erected in Scotland since the Reformation. It is in the Early Pointed Style, from the designs of Sir Gilbert Scott, and was built in 1874–9. Palmerston Place leads from the west end of the Cathedral to Haymarket Station, whence the Glasgow road (A8) runs past palatial Donaldson's School for the Deaf (1851) to **Murrayfield**, where is the ground of the Scottish Rugby Football Union, and so to Corstorphine, passing the **Scottish Zoological Park**, one of the finest in Europe. The grounds include refreshment rooms, a Children's Farm, an Aquarium and a unique collection of animals. A little beyond Corstorphine, which cherishes a fifteenth-century Church, are **Turnhouse** (Edinburgh's aerodrome) and the Royal Highland and Agricultural Society's *Showground* at Ingliston.

The **Royal Botanic Garden** lies on the northern side of the city and is most directly reached from Princes Street by Hanover Street and its continuations, starting opposite The Mound. The garden consists of about 65 acres and contains new Plant Houses, a Plant Exhibition Hall and science research facilities including a library and herbarium. There is an extensive Arboretum and world-famous Rock Garden and a Demonstration Garden. In Inverleith House is Scotland's new **National Gallery of Modern Art.** West of the Botanic Garden are the grounds and the striking building of *Fettes College*, an important public school for boys. At 8 Howard Place, near the eastern gate of the Garden, was born Robert Louis Stevenson.

At the Botanic Garden we are within a mile of Edinburgh's maritime suburbs, of which the principal is **Leith**, or—

Leith, Port of Edinburgh.

Leith, Port of Edinburgh, is situated in the sheltered waters of the Firth of Forth approximately 30 miles from the open sea. It has many natural advantages, a safe anchorage and good road connections. The Harbour was conveyed to Edinburgh by Royal Charter in 1329, and during its long history it has seen many thrilling events.

Since 1838 the control of the Harbour and Docks have been vested in a statutory body, the Leith Dock Commission, and during this period constant expansion and improvement of facilities have taken place. In recent years it has become a major bulk grain importing port, and the high elevators at the Edinburgh and Imperial Dock and the Western Harbour dominate its skyline.

The **Trinity House of Leith** is a venerable institution which originated as a charitable society to relieve distressed seamen, but which since 1797 has been by charter a corporate body to examine and under seal to license persons to be pilots. Almost opposite is *St. Mary's Church*, renovated in 1848 and retaining few traces of age.

A mammoth development scheme for Leith Docks has been approved by the Government.

Westward of Leith is **Newhaven,** a quaint little place with harbour and busy fish market. Westward again is **Granton,** with a spacious harbour largely used by trawlers and other fishing craft. Out at sea the rocky isle of **Inchkeith** has a lighthouse to guide Forth shipping ; and in time of war it defends the upper reaches of the Firth. A marine promenade has been constructed between Granton and Cramond (*see* p. 256) and a municipal golf course and caravan site at Silverknowes add to the attractions of this seaside pleasure ground.

GLASGOW.

Access.—By *Road* (*see* pp. 11–15).
By Rail. To Central Station (trains from Euston Station, London; also those from St. Pancras Station, London); Queen Street Stations (trains from King's Cross Station, London). The journey from London (Euston) by the best trains takes six hours.
By *Steamer.* *See* p. 15.
By *Air* (Glasgow airport). Current arrangements may be learned at any tourist office, or from British European Airways, 122 St. Vincent Street.

Churches, etc.—*Presbyterian:* The Cathedral (p. 138); University Chapel; Barony Parish Church, Cathedral Square; Andrew's Parish Church, St. Andrew's Square.
Episcopalian: St. Mary's Cathedral, Gt. Western Road; St. Andrew's, Turnbull Street.
Roman Catholic: St. Andrew's Cathedral, Clyde Street; St. Aloysius, Hill Street; St. Francis, Cumberland Street; St. Mungo's, Parson Street, Townhead.
Congregational: Trinity, Claremont Street.
Baptist: Bath Street and Pitt Street; Creswell Street, Hillhead.
Methodist: St. John's, 20 Sauchiehall Street.
Friends: 16 Newton Terrace, Sauchiehall Street.
Greek Church: 27 Dundonald Road, W.2.
Synagogues: South Portland Street and Garnet Hill, Garnet Street.

Golf.—Numerous links on every hand, including the famous links at Prestwick and Troon, easily reached by road or rail.

Hotels.—*Central* (240 rooms; adjoining Central Station); *St. Enoch* (155 rooms); *Lorne* (46 rooms), Sauchiehall Street; *North British* (84 rooms); *Adelphi*, Howard Street (50 rooms); *Bath*, Bath Street; *Royal*, Sauchiehall Street; *Ivanhoe*, Buchanan Street; *George*, Buchanan Street (76 rooms); *Blythwood*, 320 Argyle Street (75 rooms); *Royal Stuart*, Jamaica Street (115 rooms); *More's*, India Street (64 rooms).
Unlicensed Hotels: *Duncan's*, Union Street (40 rooms); and others.

Population.—927,948.

Post Office.—George Square.

Underground.—This is an underground electric railway, 6½ miles long, running round the city and its western suburbs. Three-minute service from 6 a.m. until 11 p.m.

Youth Hostel.—11 Woodlands Terrace, Charing Cross.

FOR a city of its size and antiquity Glasgow is not very rich in objects of architectural or historical interest —the Cathedral, Provand's Lordship and the Corporation Art Gallery and Museum with the neighbouring University nearly exhaust the list in that direction. Any lack of archæological showplaces is, however, amply compensated by the industrial and human interest of the city. Clyde shipbuilding yards have led the world since the momentous day when Henry Bell's *Comet* introduced steam propulsion; Clydeside engineers are to be found wherever there are engines to be nursed, and if in less prosperous years the achievements of Clydeside shipyards have been less spectacular than in the flourishing days just before the 1914–18 War, the influence of other great Glasgow industries has been potent in many directions.

The stranger who wanders along the quays and wharves of the Broomielaw will realize, if he has not done so before, how great is the interdependence between this, the third most populous city in Britain, and the wild country stretching almost from the municipal boundaries to Cape Wrath and the farthest Hebrides. Flocks and herds and the abundant produce of the seas are poured into Glasgow daily, and in return almost every artificial requirement of life is sent to every hamlet in the western Highlands accessible by steamer—for notwithstanding the railway and the development of the motor, boats still play an important part in the transport system of western Scotland : a fact which tourists, unless they are motoring, will quickly realize.

The city is well equipped with public transport, and all the major places of interest may be reached by this means with no difficulty.

For places on the river and Firth of Clyde, see page 148.

The focal point of Glasgow's business life is **George Square.** The two main railway termini are close at hand ; here are the **Bank of Scotland, the Merchants' House** (the meeting-place of the Chamber of Commerce), the head **Post Office.** The eastern side of the Square is filled by the frontage of the **Municipal Buildings** (the elaborately decorated Banqueting Hall and other apartments may be seen Monday, Tuesday, Wednesday and Friday). Glasgow has a well-merited celebrity for its municipal administration, and a hint of the complexity of the task may be caught by walking eastward from George Square and noting how far back this immense block of buildings extends. The Municipal Information Bureau is in the Square.

Of the monuments in the Square the two most notable are the *War Memorial*, at the eastern end, and the lofty monument to *Sir Walter Scott*. In connection with Chantrey's statue of *James Watt*, we may recall the tradition that Watt, a native of Greenock, solved the practical application of the steam-engine during a Sunday afternoon walk on Glasgow Green in 1765.

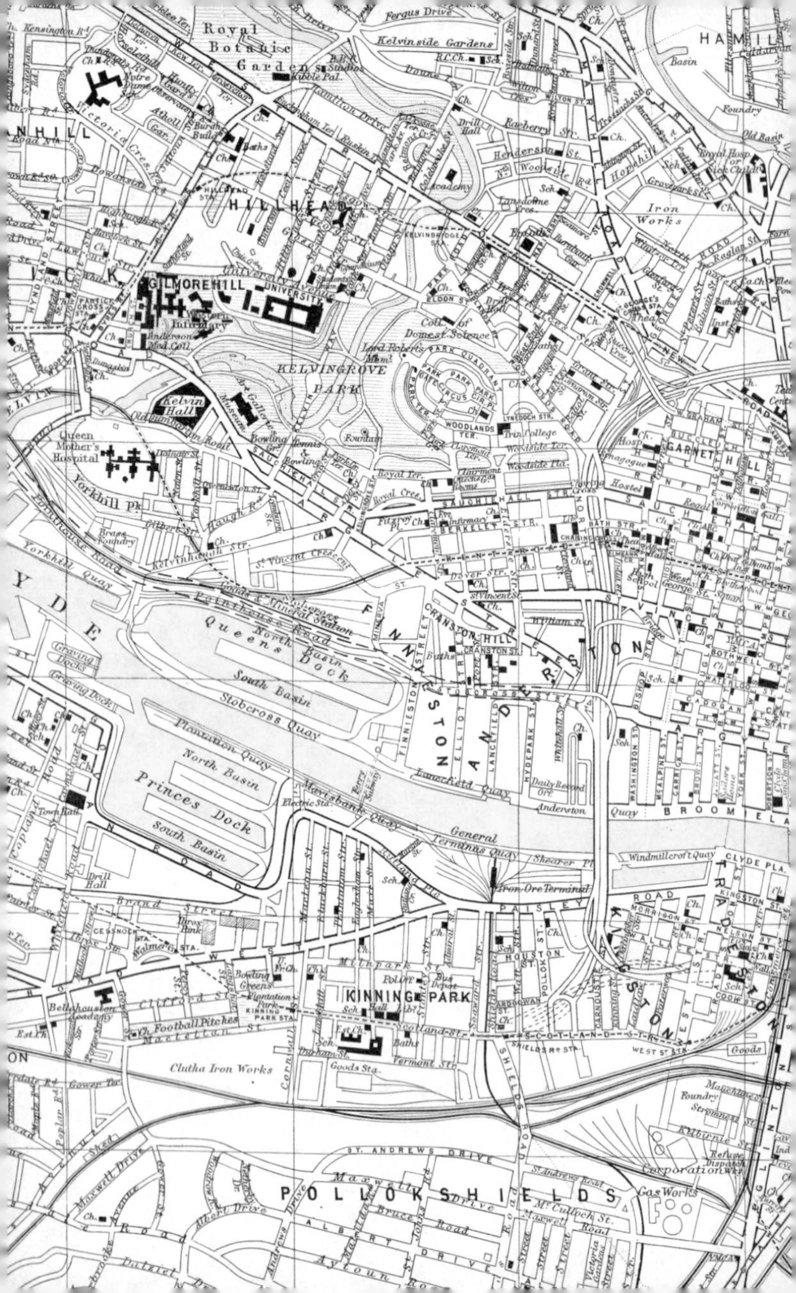

Royal Botanic Gardens
Kibble Pal.
Fergus Drive
Kelvinside Gardens
HAMIL
Basin
Foundry
Old Basin
Hamilton Drive
Great George St.
Raeberry St.
Henderson St.
Woodside Rd.
Academy
Royal Hosp. for Sick Child.
Iron Works
HILLHEAD
Hillhead St.
Gibson St.
University Avenue
UNIVERSITY
GILMOREHILL
Western Infirmary
Anderson Med. Coll.
Coll. of Domest. Science
Lord Roberts' Mem.
KELVINGROVE PARK
PARK CIRCUS
PARK QUADRANT
Kelvin Hall
Art Galleries & Museum
Queen Mother's Hospital
Yorkhill Pk.
Sauchiehall St.
Fountain
Bowling Gr.
Tennis & Bowling
Woodlands Rd.
Woodside Ter.
Woodside Pla.
Trin. College
Charing Cross
GARNET HILL
Synagogue
Hostel
Bath Str.
Berkeley Str.
St. Vincent Crescent
Kelvinhaugh St.
Yorkhill Quay
Brass Foundry
Pointhouse Road
Goods & Mineral Station
Queens Dock
North Basin
South Basin
Stobcross Quay
FINNIESTON
ANDERSTON
Cranston Hill
Baths
Elliot St.
Lancefield St.
Hydepark St.
Argyle St.
Broomielaw
Washington St.
McAlpine St.
Robertson St.
York St.
Plantation Quay
Princes Dock
Lancefield Quay
Anderston Quay
Daily Record Off.
Graving Docks
Clyde
Mavisbank Quay
General Terminus Quay
Shearer Pl.
Windmillcroft Quay
Iron Ore Terminal
Paisley Road
Kingston
Tradeston
Clyde Pla.
Kingston St.
Morrison St.
Nelson St.
Wallace St.
Town Hall
Drill Hall
Brand Street
Ibrox Park
Cessnock Sta.
Bellahouston Academy
Football Pitches
Clifford St.
Bowling Greens
Plantation Park
Kinning Park Sta.
KINNING PARK
Scotland St.
Durham St.
Vermont St.
Goods Sta.
Shields Rd. Sta.
Shields Road
West St. Sta.
Goods
Clutha Iron Works
Foundry
Stromness St.
Kilbirnie St.
Refuse Dispatch
Corporation Wks.
Gas Works
St. Andrews Drive
Maxwell Drive
POLLOKSHIELDS
Albert Drive
Bruce Road
Aytoun Road
McCulloch St.
Maxwell Road
Victoria Gardens
Eglinton St.

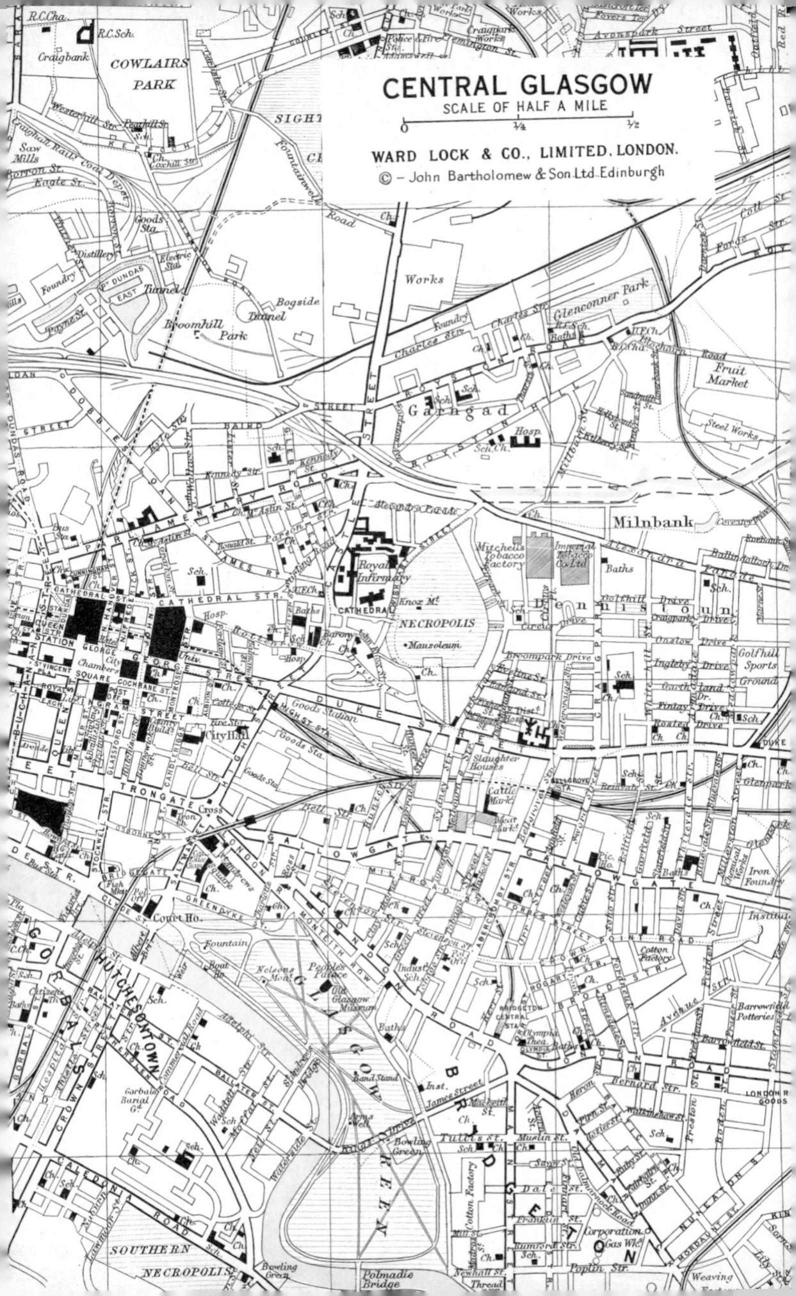
CENTRAL GLASGOW
SCALE OF HALF A MILE
0
1/4
1/2
WARD LOCK & CO., LIMITED, LONDON.
© - John Bartholomew & Son Ltd. Edinburgh
COWLAIRS PARK
Craigbank
Saw Mills
Eagle St.
Goods Sta.
Distillery
Foundry
Tunnel
Broomhill Park
Bogside
Works
Glenconner Park
Fruit Market
Steel Works
Garngad
Milnbank
Royal Infirmary
CATHEDRAL
NECROPOLIS
Mausoleum
Knox Mt.
Mitchells Tobacco Factory
Imperial Tobacco Co. Ltd.
Dennistoun
Golfhill Sports Ground
QUEEN STR. STATION
GEORGE SQUARE
City Chambers
City Hall
TRONGATE
GALLOWGATE
Slaughter Houses
Cattle Mark.
Meat Mark.
Iron Foundry
Court Ho.
Fountain
Peoples Palace
Old Glasgow Museum
Nelsons Mont.
GLASGOW GREEN
BRIDGETON
Olympia Thea.
Cotton Factory
Barrowfield Potteries
GORBALS
HUTCHESONTOWN
Gorbals Burial Gd.
CALEDONIA ROAD
SOUTHERN NECROPOLIS
Bowling Green
Polmadie Bridge
Corporation Gas Wks.
Weaving Factory
LONDON RD. GOODS

From the south-west corner of George Square busy Queen Street leads to Argyle Street, passing on the right the **Royal Exchange,** a Grecian building designed by Hamilton, now housing Stirling's Library and the Commercial Library.

Ingram Street, on the left, leads to **Hutcheson's Hospital,** a wealthy foundation which originated in the bequests of two brothers Hutcheson in the seventeenth century. Of the net annual income, which is a substantial amount, three-fifths are devoted to pensions and two-fifths to education. The hospital buildings are now occupied by the Glasgow Educational Trusts.

Queen Street terminates in **Argyle Street,** which to the left leads into **Trongate,** a bustling thoroughfare which has changed considerably since the days when it was haunted by Burns, Sir Walter Scott, Adam Smith, David Hume and other great men of the day. Not long since, however, something of its historic appearance has been recaptured by the successful reproduction of the old Cross, standing at the junction of the Trongate, High Street, Saltmarket and Gallowgate. The **Tron Steeple** straddling the pavement a little west of the Cross is all that remains of St. Mary's Church—the Tron Church was burnt down in 1793.

High Street, on the left, leads up past the Tolbooth Steeple (1627) to the Cathedral; but those with time should pass down the **Saltmarket**—its glories sadly departed since the days when Bailie Nicol Jarvie and other douce Glasgow merchants of olden time here won their crowns, kept their crowns and counted their crowns and flavoured their punch with limes grown on their own little farms " yonder awa' " in the West Indies. At the lower end of Saltmarket is an entrance to **Glasgow Green,** dating back to 1662. It has an area of 136 acres and the drive round it describes a circuit of 2½ miles. Provision has been made for most games. In the *People's Palace* is the **Old Glasgow Museum** with exhibits and pictures of the history and life of Glasgow.

From the foot of Saltmarket, buses run up past the Trongate and by **High Street** to the Cathedral. It is difficult to believe that at one time the High Street was quite monastic in character; two plaques near the gates of the railway goods station are the only evidence of the former old College on the site which housed the original

Glasgow University. Adam Smith laid the foundations of modern economic science while Professor of Moral Philosophy at this College; while James Watt was attached to it as philosophical instrument-maker he made his experiments which led to the steam-engine; and in the College gardens Francis and Rashleigh Osbaldistone fought (*Rob Roy*).

High Street climbs steadily to Cathedral Square, the final few hundred yards being known as the "Bell o' the Brae."

The Cathedral.

The Cathedral is open every weekday, April to October, 10–7; October to March, 10–5; Sundays, 10.30–8 except during service hours.

Sunday services at 11 a.m. and 6.30 p.m.

Permission to photograph the interior can be obtained from the local office of the Department of the Environment, Argyle House, Lady Lawson Street, Edinburgh, EH3 9SD.

This, the Parish Church of Glasgow, is a perfect specimen of Early English Gothic architecture. It and the Cathedral of Kirkwall are the only churches in Scotland in the condition in which they were before the Reformation, except that, in 1846 and 1848, two western towers of Glasgow were pulled down, a sadly misguided action.

About the year 543 St. Kentigern, better known as St. Mungo, now the patron saint of the City, built a simple Church on the present site. It is a forgotten but noteworthy fact that he brought Christianity to Glasgow twenty years before Columba brought it to Iona. On the holy site the Cathedral was founded in the days of Bishop John and dedicated 1136. Of this Norman church a few stones remain. A second Cathedral was dedicated in 1197. Of course the Cathedral was not built at one period, but spread over centuries, and owes its completion to many builders and the generosities of many churchmen.

After the Reformation the beautiful building suffered much through sheer neglect, being divided up into no fewer than three distinct Parish Churches; but in the first quarter of the nineteenth century a restoration was completed. The Munich painted glass has been replaced by modern stained glass, and there is some sixteenth-century Flemish and seventeenth-century Swiss glass. The

Cathedral is now maintained by the Department of the Environment as property of the Crown.

The **Nave** has a peculiar charm of simple majesty, folded in stillness. The very fine rood screen is one of the few solid stone screens remaining in Scotland, and bears a close resemblance to the one in Canterbury Cathedral. The sculptured figures upon it represent the Seven Ages of Man.

Behind the Altar is the fine **East Chapel**—in mediæval times four separate chapels; in one of which is to be seen an ornamental tombstone of 1633.

Near the Sacristy door, in glass case, note the old Bible of the Reader's Lectern, of date 1617: it disappeared in 1745, but was restored to the Cathedral in 1849. It is bound in oak boards, covered with native sealskin. The preacher's hour glass—an object once common to all pulpits—stands on the pulpit. The sand takes thirty-eight minutes to run out, suggesting a longer sermon than is commonly acceptable to-day!

In the **Sacristy** may be seen the chair said to have been occupied by Oliver Cromwell during Divine Service.

The **Crypt**, acknowledged to be one of the finest Gothic vaulted crypts in Europe, is entered by steps beside the Rood Screen. Here is the Shrine of St. Mungo, where the saint was buried on January 13, 603. Here, also, is an ancient well. At its source on the hillside St. Mungo is said to have baptized his converts when all around was wild forest and moorland. The well is closed, but the water of the spring is still quite fresh. In the Chapel of St. Andrew is the effigy of Bishop Wishart—the friend and supporter of Wallace and Bruce—a great Scottish patriot whose help was valued highly by those leaders, and whose influence was acknowledged fully by the English enemy of the time. Also in the crypt is a tombstone of some Covenanters of the seventeenth century—"The Killing Time" (*see* p. 34)—who were put to death for the faith, at the corner of the Cathedral.

Opening from the Crypt at its north-east corner is the **Chapter House**, recently restored and furnished.

Until the beginning of the nineteenth century the Crypt was used by the congregation of the Barony Kirk. It is described in Chapters 19 and 20 of Scott's *Rob Roy*, and one of the pillars is known as Rob Roy's pillar, from the assignation there between him and Francis Osbaldistone.

Another vaulted crypt, known as Blacader or **Fergus's Aisle,** is the last piece of building before the Reformation. The grave of the holy man was there, surrounded by a grove ; and a quaint carving on the arch near the entrance, just above the stair, shows the body of Fergus on a cart —the legend being that he was so conveyed, by a yoke of wild oxen to the place where, when they stopped of their own accord, he was buried.

Eastward of the Cathedral lies the **Necropolis,** most conspicuous among its memorials being that of John Knox.

On the western side of Cathedral Square is—

Provand's Lordship.

Admission, *fee.* Open every day except Sunday; April to September, 10 a.m. to 12.45 and 2 to 5 p.m.; October to March, 11 a.m. to 12.45 p.m. and 2 to 4 p.m.

Now the only surviving mediæval domestic building in Glasgow, Provand's Lordship dates from about 1471.

The building was probably the residence of the master or Preceptor of the almshouse for twelve aged men founded by Bishop Andrew Muirhead (1455–73) and known as St. Nicholas Hospital. The remainder of the buildings have vanished, for the hospital shared the common fate of such establishments at the Reformation ; but it is interesting to note that the Lord Provost of Glasgow is still *ex officio* Preceptor of St. Nicholas Hospital.

At all events the building came to be, or contained, the town house or " manse " of one of the canons of Glasgow Cathedral, whose *prebend* (or living) lay outwith the boundary of the city, in Lanarkshire near the present Baillieston. The lands in question came to be called " Provan " or " Provand "—" Provand " may just be " *prebend* " in another form.

Like other lands they were secularized at the time of the Reformation; the "canon " of the day whose name was William Baillie, obtained a charter from Queen Mary in 1562, became a lay laird, and ultimately a person of consequence.

In pre-Reformation days both James II and James IV became honorary canons, but there is no evidence that James IV ever stayed in the house now called Provand's Lordship.

For another legend, namely, that Queen Mary once lived there, some sort of case can be made. When she came to visit the ailing Darnley for a few days in January 1567 there was no obvious house to receive her. Darnley's father Lennox, pleading illness, stayed in Crookston Castle and, in any case, the Hamiltons who escorted her were at deadly feud with the Lennox Stewarts. Mary did not stay with Lennox and obviously she did not stay in the infected house wherein her husband lay.

Many of the ecclesiastical buildings had been damaged or lost in the troubles of the Reformation, but there was no reason why the prosperous William Baillie, to whom the Queen had already given a charter, should not have preserved his house in order good enough to house the Queen.

After Baillie's death the fortunes of the house declined. Its situation, which had been very near the centre of the old city, became less desirable; ownership passed from hand to hand and the building was in a poor state when it was taken over by the Glasgow Corporation.

In 1906 a body of Glasgow Citizens formed a little society to take over the feu, for which they paid themselves and in succeeding decades generous gifts from members and from fellow citizens have enabled the Society to acquire ownership of the house and to enrich it with furniture, Scottish domestic appurtenances and pictures, which illustrate Scottish domestic life for about four centuries.

The collection, which includes a very charming portrait of Mary Queen of Scots as a girl (attributed by some to Holbein) and a portrait of James VI and I by George Jamesone (1586–1644), is well worth a visit.

On the same side of the Square is the Barony Parish Church, a successor to the building so long associated with Dr. Norman Macleod. An old cottage which stood just to the west of the church was rather doubtfully connected with Darnley's visit to Glasgow, referred to above. The name of Rotten Row invites comparisons between this drab thoroughfare and the tree-shaded lane in London. Yet odd fragments of buildings hint at times that were very different, and indeed one need go no farther than the pages of Scott for reminders that Glasgow has a history, however carefully it may conceal evidences of it. George Street leads back to George Square, passing on the right the former Royal College of Science and Technology, now **Strathclyde University**. This was founded by Professor Anderson as a true "People's College"; the medical schools were in 1889 removed to Dumbarton Road, and are now incorporated in the University.

An exploration of the western half of central Glasgow might begin with a bus ride from the north side of George Square, by St. Vincent Street and Argyle Street to Kelvingrove Park and the—

Art Gallery and Museum.

Open free daily: Mondays to Saturdays, 10–5; Sundays, 2–5.

The collections are housed in a striking French Renaissance building, which is, however, best appreciated when viewed from the vicinity of the University, on the northern side of the Park. The block was built in 1901 from the plans of John W. Simpson and Milner Allen, of London, with money from the Glasgow International Exhibitions, 1888 and 1901, and by public subscription. Twin central towers, rising to 172 feet, form the principal feature of the exterior. The building, of red sandstone, is 448 feet long and 256 feet wide, and is two storeys in height. On entering, the visitor finds himself in a great central hall, extending upwards through the two storeys. On each side is a court 106 feet long and 64 feet wide. These give access to the galleries, about twenty in number, those on the ground floor containing the **Museum.**

The East Court contains natural habitat groups of the mammals and birds from Africa, Australia, India, Scotland and the Polar Regions. The West Court houses a collection of ship models illustrating the history of shipping. The rooms round these are devoted to various sections, illustrating Arms and Armour, Engineering, Archæology, Ethnography, Geology and Birds in their natural habitat. A section of Egyptology is included which contains many important exhibits. There is also a fine collection of metal-work, pottery and glass.

The *Art Collections.* The upper galleries contain the collection of pictures belonging to the city. The Venetian, Roman, Florentine and other Italian Schools are represented by the works of Titian, Giorgione, Giovanni Bellini, Botticelli, Canaletto, etc., while included with the collections relating to other great Schools are creations of such men as Mabuse, The Master of Moulins, Rubens, Vandyck, Velasquez, and others too numerous to mention. These galleries are specially rich in choice pictures of the Dutch School. There are some fine examples of Rembrandt, particularly the " Man in Armour " ; and characteristic pictures by Ruysdael, Hobbema, Ostade, Jan Steen, Wouverman, and Cuyp. Among many notable modern British works of art, Whistler's portrait of Carlyle will attract special attention, as will also certain outstanding canvases of Reynolds, Raeburn, Allan Ramsay and other portraitists of that period. Richard Wilson and Morland, with their illustrious contemporaries, Sir David Wilkie and J. M. W. Turner, are also in evidence, the latter particularly by his renowned work, " Modern Italy—The Pifferari." There is also the well-known painting, " Christ of St. John of the Cross," by Salvador Dali.

The galleries were, a few years ago, enriched by a gift from Sir William and Lady Burrell. It included items of outstanding importance among tapestries, pictures, porcelain, stained glass, furniture and silver, etc. Glasgow is recognized as one of the most important and progressive art centres in Britain.

Kelvingrove Park is in two sections, which slope more or less steeply to the Kelvin River as it hurries down to lose itself in the busy Clyde. Facing the Art Gallery and Museum across the valley is—

THE UNIVERSITY OF GLASGOW,

an excellent example of Sir George Gilbert Scott's Early English work, to which have been added various features in Scottish baronial Gothic, notably the splendid gateway, surmounted by a crocketed spire, of which the top is 300 feet above the ground.

The University was founded in 1451, and a Pedagogy was soon in use. In the middle of the seventeenth century, the College in the High Street (*see* p. 137) was built, and this was its home until 1870, when classes were held for the first time in the building before which we stand. The entrance lodge on University Avenue was built from the stones of the High Street college gateway. The balustrade of the Lion and Unicorn Staircase, facing the Principal's House, also came from the College in the High Street.

The University includes faculties of Arts, Divinity, Law, Medicine, Science, Engineering and Veterinary Medicine ; there is a teaching staff of a thousand, and the average number of students on the rolls is about nine thousand, of whom nearly a third are women. Many extensions to the buildings have been made and several large new buildings added including a striking new library.

On application to the porter in the gateway tower one can usually (except Saturday afternoons and Sundays) be shown over the *Randolph Hall* and the *Bute Hall*, in which the principal University functions are held, and the impressive War Memorial Chapel.

The University *Library* contains well over 600,000 volumes and is especially rich in theological and philosophical literature.

The **Hunterian Museum** (*open free daily*, 9–5 ; Saturday, 9–12) originated in a valuable collection of anatomical specimens, paintings, manuscripts, etc., bequeathed by William Hunter, M.D., brother of the more celebrated John Hunter. The museum is strong in Zoology, Geology and Archæology and contains many valuable prehistoric and Roman remains.

The medical work of the University is fostered by association with the **Western Infirmary**, the Royal Infirmary and other large hospitals in Glasgow.

West of the University, easily reached by public transport, is **Whiteinch**, famous for the *Fossil Grove* in its Victoria Park. All who visit the West of Scotland should make a point of seeing this unique series of the bases of fossilized trees *in situ*. (*Admission free.*)

A short walk northward from the University leads to

the Great Western Road in the vicinity of the well-kept **Botanic Gardens** (*open free daily until dusk*). There are to be seen a large variety of trees and shrubs, both native and foreign. There is an extensive range of glasshouses, and in its Kibble Palace a unique collection of tree ferns. Beyond the Gardens stretches suburbia, so we return along Great Western Road, which presently crosses the Kelvin by a bridge just short of Woodlands Road, on the right, by which one can reach **Sauchiehall Street.** Those who do not visit the Botanic Gardens will find Sauchiehall Street at the south-east side of Kelvingrove Park. Sauchiehall Street is a busy and popular thoroughfare for shopping and promenading, and its air of alert prosperity is a refreshing antidote to the atmosphere of some of the poorer parts of the city. Here or near at hand are the principal shops, cinemas and theatres, and near the eastern end are Queen Street station, and George Square, from which we started the tour. In North Street, a few yards south of the important cross-roads known as Charing Cross, is the **Mitchell Library,** the largest public reference library in Scotland. The library, which originated in a bequest by Stephen Mitchell, a wealthy tobacco manufacturer (*d.* 1874) was opened in 1877 and moved to its present site in 1911. The stock of the library, which is now approaching 900,000 volumes, includes special collections of music, Glasgow local histories, and Scottish poetry, particularly the poetry of Robert Burns.

GLASGOW TO ABERFOYLE AND THE TROSSACHS.

NORTH and west of Glasgow are the **Campsie Fells** and the Kilpatrick Hills, and between these various roads pass northward by Killearn to Stirling and to Aberfoyle. The road between Aberfoyle and the Trossachs is a very popular route, affording direct access to the heart of the Trossachs and also permitting a good circular road tour from Glasgow *viâ* Callander–Trossachs–Aberfoyle.

Campsie, on the southern slopes of its fells, has a pretty glen, and a mile or so westward and also at the foot of the fells is ever popular **Strathblane,** with several interesting short excursions at hand. In the neighbourhood of Killearn the aqueduct which brings Glasgow's water from Loch Katrine is encountered, and then comes the flat strath in which the river Forth is born—country so graphically described in *Rob Roy*.

Aberfoyle is an excellent and beautiful centre for tourism, having a motel, restaurant facilities and several hotels. Notable among the hotels is the *Bailie Nicol Jarvie* with its close association with Rob Roy. It is situated at the southern entrance to the Queen Elizabeth Forest Park. The district around the village is particularly suitable for such activities as walking, pony-trekking, hill climbing and fishing. In nearby Loch Achray (p. 289) dinghy sailing and water ski-ing are increasing in popularity. The Forestry Commission have opened up attractive walks and viewpoints with picnic places throughout the forest. For peace and quiet these roads, free of vehicular traffic, must increasingly become attractive to tourists and others.

Westward from Aberfoyle a beautiful road passes Loch Ard and Loch Chon and then descends to **Glen Arklet,** which connects Loch Katrine (at Stronachlachar) with Loch Lomond at Inversnaid (*see* p. 194). The route is not, however, a through route for vehicles and the only outlet for pedestrians is by the steamer services on Loch Lomond and Loch Katrine. The alternative is for them to follow the rough but beautiful track along the east shore of Loch Lomond to Ardlui or walk round the head of Loch Katrine by Glengyle to the Trossachs Pier.

There is a very good walk over Ben Lomond to **Rowardennan** (p. 195) from the western end of Loch Ard. Go down the road which crosses the stream connecting Lochs Ard and Chon, and a short way farther, by a farmhouse called Blairhullichan, leave the road by a track which crosses the ridge in front to the Duchray Water, which is crossed by a wooden bridge. For **Ben Lomond**, however, turn to the right on the near side of the river and follow a rough track which goes some way up Glen Dubh, whence a steep climb leads to the summit, the Rowardennan route (*see* p. 193) being joined a little way below the top. For Rowardennan, after crossing the Duchray, follow the stream running down from the col between Ben Lomond and Beinn Uird; on reaching the top of the ridge Rowardennan is seen below, on the shores of Loch Lomond.

About 3 miles east of Aberfoyle, and skirting the road to Stirling and Callander, is the **Lake of Menteith** (" Moor of the Teith "), from 1 to 1½ miles across in every direction. This is Scotland's only *lake.* On *Inch-mahome*, the " Isle of Rest " (R. B. Cunninghame Graham, author and traveller, was buried here in 1936), are the ruins of a priory of Early English date (*admission charge, including boat. Open weekdays* 10–4 *winter*, 7 *in summer ; Sundays from* 2 *p.m.*). Here David II was married to his second wife in 1363, and here, when five years old (1547), Mary Queen of Scots was taken for safety. *Queen Mary's Bower* is still visible on the south-east shore. Port of Menteith, the village situated on the lochside, has an excellent hotel where fishing, boating, water ski-ing, and curling in winter may be enjoyed. There is also a private caravan site on the shore of the loch.

A second and much smaller island, called *Talla*, contains the ruins of a fortress once occupied by the Earls of Menteith.

Aberfoyle to the Trossachs, direct, 7 miles.—The Duke's Road which connects Aberfoyle with the Trossachs was built by the Duke of Montrose as a rough toll road for horse-drawn vehicles and pedestrians. It is now a well engineered and popular route into the Trossachs, ascending steeply from Aberfoyle in a series of loops which provide magnificent views to the south and west. The road passes through the Forestry Park, but clearances have been provided for picnics. Two viewing points with mountain indicators have been provided and the Marshall Pavilion at one of these caters for indoor picnicking and from here magnificent views are obtained to the south and the west. Descending, we get a glimpse of Loch Vennachar, but the prettiest object is little **Loch Drunkie**, lying in a deep wooded basin on the right. Then, as we bend sharp to the left, the prospect opens up over the Trossachs. A strip of the middle of Loch Katrine is seen with Ben Venue (2,393 feet) to the left and a mountain background in which the chief heights are Ben Lui, beyond the loch, and the twin pyramids of Stobinian and Ben More to the north.

The final mile or so lies between Loch Achray's wooded shores and the glossy slopes of Ben Venue, passing, after the main valley is reached, the *Achray Hotel* (30 *rooms*). For the Trossachs, *see* page 289.

GLASGOW TO STIRLING AND EDINBURGH.

Only 25 miles separate western Scotland at the Broomielaw from the waters of the Firth of Forth at Grangemouth, and roads, railways, the Forth and Clyde Canal and the rivers Kelvin and Bonny all crowd through the mile-wide "pass" below the Kilsyth Hills. The pass ends at Dennyloanhead, and here is a parting of the ways. Northward the main routes to the Highlands travel up between the hills and the Forth—another "pass," at the north end of which Stirling occupies a fine strategic position ; eastward roads and railways follow the Forth to Edinburgh, passing through Falkirk and Linlithgow and giving good views of the Forth Bridges.

The Forth and Clyde Canal (closed) ran from Bowling, on the Clyde, to Grangemouth (p. 259), a distance of 38 miles. The summit point is 156 feet above sea-level, necessitating 39 locks. The Canal closely follows the line of the **Antonine Wall,** a Roman rampart erected about A.D. 142 to restrict the raids of the northern tribes. Some 40 miles long, it consisted of a ditch 20 feet deep and 40 wide and a sod-and-stone rampart 10 feet high, and along the southern side ran a paved road, with forts at intervals. Extensive remains are to be seen near Castlecary, and in recent years the remains of a fort have been laid bare at Cadder, near Bishopbriggs. The local name for the earthworks is "Grim's Dyke."

Road routes between Glasgow and Edinburgh:

1. Leave Glasgow by Argyle Street, Trongate, Gallowgate and Tollcross Road. Bellshill is 9 miles from Glasgow, **Whitburn** 23 miles, and **Edinburgh** 44 miles.

2. Leave Glasgow by Queen Street, George Street, Duke Street and Shettleston Road. Thence *viâ* **Coatbridge** (9 miles), Airdrie (12 miles), **Bathgate** (25 miles), Broxburn (33 miles) and **Corstorphine** to **Edinburgh** (44 miles).

3. The A8 road via Newhouse and Harthill is fast and avoids the towns, but is scenically uninteresting.

THE RIVER AND FIRTH OF CLYDE.

(Glasgow to Ayr by the Coast.)

Railways.—Except for the short break between Wemyss Bay and Largs the railway hugs the coast all the way.

HAMILTON, Lanark and other places on the Upper Clyde are described on pages 89–91. Here we go "doon the watter" from Glasgow to where the river merges into the Firth, the Firth into the sea.

Western Scotland, more than any other part of Britain, depends for its intercommunication upon the boat, and the Clyde is starting off point for many of the passenger steamer trips to the coast and off-shore islands. From Glasgow it is necessary to travel by rail or bus to Gourock, Wemyss Bay, or Craigendoran on the north, to join the steamers.

The Clyde below Glasgow is under the control of the *Clyde Port Authority*, who have jurisdiction over Clydeport, comprising the ports of Glasgow, Greenock and Arbrossan, and an area of some 450 square miles extending 55 miles down river from the heart of Glasgow to a line drawn from Gailes on the Ayreshire coast to Corrygills Point in Arran. Almost two-thirds of Scotland's foreign sea-borne trade passes through Clydeport. The many docks and wharves of Glasgow are busy with the import of crude oil, iron ore, grain and other raw materials, and the export of iron and steel, machinery, vehicles, whisky and many manufactured goods.

Govan, on the south, has an old burying-ground containing early Christian monuments said by some to be coeval with the better-known monuments at Iona. At Yoker, on the north, is the site of an electricity station of great importance to the Scottish "grid" system.

Renfrew, on the south bank, is very active, while a notable feature of the town is the fine old Steeple, a mile inland. Renfrew is interesting from its connection with the Royal House of Stewart. In 1157 Malcolm IV, confirming an earlier grant by David I, gave Renfrew

Castle and adjoining lands to Walter Fitzalan, whom he appointed King's High Steward. This office remained hereditary in the family, who now assumed the name of Stewart. A descendant of Fitzalan, also named Walter, married the Bruce's daughter Marjory, whose son, the first of the Stewart line, ascended the Scottish Royal Throne in 1370. From the fifteenth century Renfrew has given the title of Baron to the Heir-Apparent to the Scottish Throne. Nothing now remains of Renfrew Castle.

Paisley,

a few miles south of Renfrew, is known the world over as a busy centre of the thread manufacture, being especially associated with the Coats and Clarks concerns. It is a by no means uninteresting blend of old and new: on the one hand such modern work as the Coats Memorial Church, and new housing estates with their 15-storey blocks of flats, on the other the remains of the twelfth-century Abbey, parts of which have been restored to form the Parish Church. The Abbey was founded by that Walter Fitzalan who became first Lord High Steward, but the original building was destroyed by Edward I, and the present Abbey dates from the fifteenth century, though much of it is in an earlier style of architecture. The chief external feature is the fine west front, with deeply recessed doorway and graceful windows. Within the building attention is caught by the triforium of rounded arches and the clerestory passage, carried outside alternate pillars on corbels. Off the south transept is the St. Mirin Chapel, founded in 1498.

In the choir is an effigy of Marjory Bruce, whose son was the first monarch of the Stewart line; and in 1888 a memorial was placed in the choir " to the members of the Royal House of Stewart who are buried in Paisley Abbey, by their descendant, Queen Victoria."

In High Street is a *Museum and Art Gallery* (*open from* 10 *to dusk; free*) with collections of shawls, pictures, and relics of local literary figures. Accessible from the museum is the *Coats Observatory*, housing two medium-diameter telescopes. Also in High Street is the public library.

Elderslie, near Paisley, is the reputed birthplace of

William Wallace; but the so-called "Wallace's House" is more modern than that.

The Braes of Gleniffer, a mile or so south-west of the town, above the Johnstone Road, command magnificent views across the Clyde to the hills beyond. A little to the south-east of Paisley, and on the banks of the White Cart River, are the ruins of **Crookston Castle,** where, according to tradition, Mary Queen of Scots and Darnley were betrothed: it is certain that they stayed here after their marriage.

On the north side of the river from Renfrew is **Clydebank,** famous for the great ships built here including the liners *Queen Mary* and *Queen Elizabeth* and the more recent *Queen Elizabeth II.*

Erskine Bridge, opened in 1971, is useful for motorists travelling north or south and desiring to cross the Clyde without going through the traffic-laden streets of Glasgow. The bridge supersedes a ferry named after Erskine House, formerly the residence of the Lords Blantyre, but now a hospital for limbless sailors and soldiers. The obelisk on the hill beyond commemorates the eleventh Lord Blantyre, who passed unscathed through the Peninsular War, but was shot accidentally in Brussels in 1830.

On Dunglass Point, about half a mile farther down on the same side, is **Dunglass Castle,** an ancient seat of the Colquhouns of Colquhoun and Luss. The Roman wall of Antoninus, erected in A.D. 140, and extending from the Forth to the Clyde, terminated here (*see* p. 147). A conspicuous obelisk commemorates Henry Bell, who was the first in Europe to apply steam-power to marine purposes. His little steamer, the *Comet*, built at Port Glasgow, was launched in 1812. As was duly set forth in the newspaper advertisements of the time, it traded between Glasgow, Greenock and Helensburgh by the power of wind, air and steam.

On the right, at **Bowling,** are the western terminal locks of the Forth and Clyde Canal (*see* p. 147), and then the rugged rock of Dumbarton comes into view on the right. **Dumbarton** is industrial, but has its place in history. The rock is supposed to have been fortified in prehistoric times and has been identified with the

Theodosia of the Romans. Its name is a corruption of Dun-Breton: "the hill of the Bretons," and for county purposes the name is still spelt Du*n*barton. Dumbarton is held to have been the birthplace of St. Patrick (the claim is disputed by Old Kilpatrick).

According to tradition, Wallace was confined in the Castle for some time; certainly it was from Dumbarton Castle that Mary, Queen of Scots, when a child was conveyed to France for safety, and it was while on her way to Dumbarton Castle that she met her final defeat at Langside. (*Castle open, charge, weekdays* 10–7; *Sundays* 2–7; *winter*, 10–4 *and* 2–4.)

Northward from Dumbarton to Loch Lomond stretches the Vale of Leven, now built on, associated with Tobias Smollett, who was born at Dalquhurn, and is commemorated by a statue in Renton schoolyard; and Thomas Campbell, the poet, who for a time acted as tutor in the district. For Balloch and Loch Lomond *see* page 191.

Almost opposite Dumbarton Rock, across the Clyde, is *Finlayston House*, wherein Knox first dispensed the sacrament according to the rites of the Reformed Church, in 1556. A little farther west are the round towers and battlements of *Newark Castle* (*open weekdays*), an old stronghold of the Maxwells, and then comes **Port Glasgow.** This busy place originated in the determination of seventeenth-century Glasgow merchants to overcome the disadvantages of the shallow river. Boats could not then come up to the city, so a new port was founded where there was deep water, and although its original purpose has long lapsed, Port Glasgow is still of considerable consequence on Clydeside. From the hills above Port Glasgow there are grand views across the Clyde to Ben Lomond and neighbouring heights: these are enjoyed by those who come over by road from Paisley by **Bridge of Weir** and **Kilmacolm**—favourite residential suburbs for Glasgow folk.

Greenock is a busy port and industrial town which is important to tourists as a kind of distributing centre for numerous steamer routes, a popular practice being to travel from Glasgow to Greenock or Gourock by rail or road and at Gourock join the boat. It was the birthplace of James Watt and of Captain Kidd, and in the cemetery is the grave to which the remains of Burns's Highland Mary (*see* p. 159) were removed in 1920 when the West Kirk Burying Ground was acquired for a shipyard extension. The **Kirk** itself has been re-erected on the esplanade to west of the Container Terminal: it was the first to be built after the Reformation and the first Presbyterian church confirmed by National Parliament. It has some good modern stained glass. On Lyle Hill is a striking memorial to Free French sailors.

Gourock.

Car ferry to Dunoon.
Distances.—Ardrossan, 26 m.; Glasgow, 26 m. Wemyss Bay, 8 m.
Early Closing.—Wednesday.
Hotels.—*Queen's, Bay, Cloch, Firth, Fairlight*; numerous boarding-houses.
Sports.—Bathing, bowls, golf, tennis, steamer trips, yachting.

Greenock merges into Gourock, built on and around Kempock Point. The sheltered bay is a great place for yachtsmen, and the town itself is a very popular resort, with bathing, boating of all kinds and splendid views of the unceasing traffic of the Clyde, with the cloud-capped hills beyond. For Dunoon *see* page 185; for Rothesay and Bute *see* page 163.

Onward from Gourock to Ardrossan and Ayr by the coast is a magnificent run, taken in either direction, the road running within a few yards of the shore for nearly the whole 26 miles to Ardrossan and within sight of the sea for the remaining 25 miles. The railway also skirts the shore for some way north of Wemyss Bay and south of Largs, but between those places there is no direct rail communication. **Cloch Point**, with its lighthouse, is opposite Dunoon (p. 185); thence, skirting the grounds of Ardgowan House and by pretty Inverkip, to **Wemyss Bay** (*Wemyss Bay*), an attractive resort with a large railway station, designed to cope with the rail-steamer excursion traffic (car ferry to Rothesay), and a really magnificent outlook across the Firth. Castle Wemyss (nineteenth century) lies on the north side of the bay; to the south the rocky foreshore runs along by **Skelmorlie**, now almost one with Wemyss Bay. Skelmorlie Castle is well placed, and the ruins of Knock Castle also attracts attention. Hence to Largs interest is principally in the views over the water to Cowal, Bute and Arran.

AYR, GLASGOW, INVERARY
English Miles
0 5 10 15 20
WARD LOCK & CO., LIMITED, LONDON.
© – John Bartholomew & Son Ltd. Edinburgh
Lunga I.
Scarba I.
1470
Shuna I.
Craignish Cas.
Ardfern
Kintraw
Ford
Strait of Corrievreckan
Maol na Cala
Killoran B.
Carn nan Eun 493
L. Sgoltaire
Kilchattan
Colonsay Ho.
Colonsay
L. Fada
Scalasaig
Inn
L. Staosnaig
Dungallan
Ardskinish Pt.
Balaruminmore
Oronsay
Kinachdrach
Glengarrisdale B.
Clachbheinn
912
Glendebadel B.
1210
Ben Garrisdale
Ben Breac
1527
Rainberg
1495
Sian B.
Ardlussa
JURA
Loch Tarbert
Tarbert B.
Lagg
1660
Paps of Jura
2571
2407
Glas Beinn 1839
Dubh Beinn 1737
Feolin Ferry
Small Isles K.
Small Isles Bay
Craighouse
Jura Ho.
Ardfin
Ardmenish
Lowlandman B.
Brosdile I.
Fraoch I.
Sound of Jura
L. Crinan
Crinan
Crinan Canal
Kilmartin
Bellanoch
Charsaig
Tayvallich
Ardrishaig
Loch Sween
Cruach Lusach
Kilmichael Inverlussa
Tayinish
Keills
Dana
Ellery
Achoish
Corr I.
Mór I.
Kilmory
Knap Pt.
Loch Killisport
Ormsary
Stonefield
Mounterins
1840
1574
Barmore
Balhaire
Cretshengan
Kilberry
Dunmore Ho.
Kilcalmonell Ch.
Inn
Redhouse
Whitehouse
West L. Tarbert
L. Stornoway
Ardpatrick Ho.
Clachan
Ballinakill
Claonaig
Bonachan
Port Mór
Ballochroy
W. Tarbert B.
Gigha I.
Gigha K.
Auchamore
Gigalum
Cara I.
Killean K.
Rhunahaorine
Gortinanane
Largie Cas.
Tayinloan
Killean
Crossaig
Cour
Sunadale
Grogport
Whitehouse
Clachaig W.
Barr W.
Bellochantuy
Carradale K.
Airds
Carradale
Ben Tuirc
1491
Torrisdale
Glenbarr
Abbey
Cleongart
Saddell
Saddell Ho.
Saddell Cas.
Sgreadan Hill
1293
Ugadale
Blackwaterfoot
Glen Lussa
Kilkenzie
Power Sta.
Ardnacross B.
Machrihanish Bay
Machrihanish
Campbeltown
Campbeltown L.
Losset Park
Davarr I.
Drumlemble
Kildalloig
Ben Ghaoilean
1154
Achinhoan Hd.
Earadale Pt.
Killellan Ho.
Conie Glen
Dun Ban
Glen Breackerie
Glenadale
Strone Glen
Gl. Kerran
Polliwilline B.
Macharioch
Carskey
Southend
Keil
L. Ho.
1309
Mull of Kintyre
Sheep I.
Sanda I.
L. Ho.
KILBRANNAN SOUND
KINTYRE
KNAPDALE
Rubha Mhail
L. Ho.
Sound of Islay
Sgarbh Breac
1192
Nave I.
Ardnave
Tòn Mhór Pt.
Sanaigmore
L. Corr
Gruinart
L. Gruinart
Kilnave
Garbhheinn
Kilanailean
Distillery
Port Askaig
Inn
Finlaggan
Ballygrant
Dun Bhoraraic
L. Gorm
Drolsay
R. Drolsay
L. Skerrols
Islay Ho.
R. Sorn
Kilchoman
Bruichladdich
Pier
Bridgend
Inn
Barr
ISLAY
Kilchiaran
Port Charlotte
Loch Indaal
Bowmore
Inn
The Rhinns
Laggan R.
Dulch R.
Octofad
Portnahaven
Laggan Bay
Big Strand
Mc Arthurs Hd.
L. Ho.
Proaig B.
Ben Bhan
1544
Beallach a Gaoch Pt.
Ardtalla
Claggain Bay
Kintour B.
Kintour
Ardmore Pt.
Kinnabus
Ardbeg
Kildalton Ho.
Sloch Mhaol Doraidh
Glen Astle
Port Ellen
Imirsi I.
The Oa
Laphroaig
Lagavoulin
Texa I.
Mull of Oa
Dun Aidh
Ballychatrigan
Otter Rk.
Rathlin I.
L. Ho.
Bengore Hd.
Sheep I.
Portrush, Londonderry, Sligo, etc.

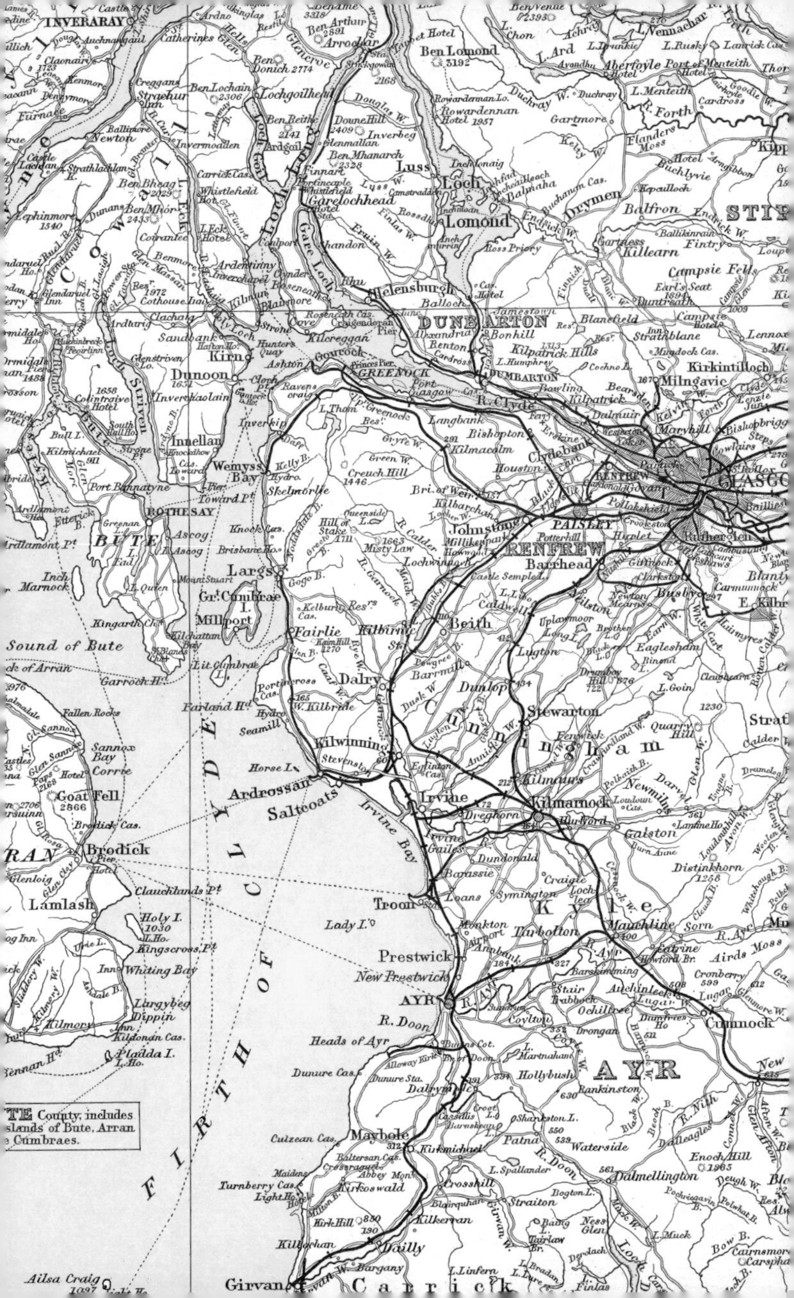

INVERARAY
Ben Arthur 2891
Arrochar
Ben Lomond 3192
Ben Venue 2393
L. Chon
L. Ard
Aberfoyle
Port of Menteith
L. Menteith
R. Forth
Flanders Moss
Buchlyvie
Balfron
Drymen
Killearn
Fintry
Campsie Fells
Earl's Seat 1894
Strathblane
Lennox
Milngavie
Kirkintilloch
Lochgoilhead
Strachur
Newton
Strathlachlan
Ben Lochain 2306
Loch Goil
Loch Long
Douglas W.
Ardgoil
Inverbeg
Ben Mhanarch 2328
Luss
Loch Lomond
Balmaha
Garelochhead
Gare Loch
Shandon
Helensburgh
Rhu
Balloch
Kilcreggan
Gourock
Cowal
Dunoon
Kirn
Hunters Quay
Innellan
Loch Striven
Glendaruel
Colintraive Hotel
Kyles of Bute
DUNBARTON
Dumbarton
Bonhill
Alexandria
Kilpatrick Hills
GREENOCK
Port Glasgow
Langbank
Bishopton
R. Clyde
Bowling
Clydebank
Dalmuir
Bearsden
Maryhill
Bishopbriggs
Kilmacolm
Houston
RENFREW
Govan
Partick
GLASGOW
Paisley
Johnstone
Pollokshields
Crookston
Rutherglen
Cathcart
Busby
Barrhead
RENFREW
Bri. of Weir
Kilbarchan
Lochwinnoch
Inverkip
Wemyss Bay
Skelmorlie
Largs
Gr.t Cumbrae
Millport
Lit. Cumbrae I.
Fairlie
Kilbirnie
Beith
Dalry
W. Kilbride
Seamill
Kilwinning
Stevenston
Ardrossan
Saltcoats
Irvine
Irvine Bay
Dreghorn
Kilmarnock
Hurlford
Galston
Newmilns
Kilmaurs
Stewarton
Dunlop
Lugton
Eaglesham
Cunninghame
Kyle
Dundonald
Troon
Symington
Tarbolton
Mauchline
Sorn
Catrine
Prestwick
New Prestwick
AYR
R. Ayr
Auchinleck
Ochiltree
Cumnock
Coylton
Drongan
R. Doon
Heads of Ayr
Dunure Cas.
Alloway Kirk
Dalrymple
Maybole
Kirkmichael
Kirkoswald
Culzean Cas.
Maidens
Turnberry Cas.
Crosshill
Straiton
Patna
Dalmellington
Waterside
Hollybush
Rankinston
AYR
Kilkerran
Dailly
Girvan
Carrick
Ailsa Craig
BOTHESAY
Rothesay
Port Bannatyne
BUTE
Kingarth Ch.
Sound of Bute
Inch Marnock
Garroch Hd.
Farland Hd.
FIRTH OF CLYDE
Horse I.
Lady I.
Brodick
Brodick Cas.
Goat Fell 2866
Corrie
Sannox Bay
Lamlash
Holy I. 1030
Kingscross Pt.
Whiting Bay
Dippin
Kildonan Cas.
Pladda I.
Kilmory
ARRAN
BUTE County includes islands of Bute, Arran & Cumbraes.

Largs.

Distances.—Glasgow, 30 m.; Gourock, 14 m. Ardrossan, 10 m.
Early Closing.—Wednesday.
Hotels.—*Marine and Curlinghall* (90 rooms), *Victoria, Elderslie, Castle, Largs, Springfield*; (*unl.*) *Mackerston, Burnlea, Haylie,* etc. Many boarding-houses.
Sports.—Two golf courses, tennis, bowls, yachting and steamer trips, bathing, sea-fishing.

Largs is a popular and progressive resort with bathing station, golf courses and a pavilion for dances, cinemas, etc. Like several other such places along this coast, it is separated from the shore by a broad strip of turf which imparts a sense of spaciousness that accords well with the ever-interesting views westward.

It was at Largs that in 1263 King Haakon of Norway was surprised and routed by Alexander III before he had time to get his troops into battle array after their landing. The king himself managed to escape to Orkney, where however he died and was buried (*see* p. 433). His defeat caused the cession of the Isle of Man and the Hebrides to Scotland on condition of an annual tribute, which was paid until the days of James I.

Just off Largs is the north end of **Great Cumbrae Island.**

The only town is **Millport** (population about 2,000) at the southern end of the island. It is an attractive little place with good bathing, boating, and golf. (*Hotels : Royal George, Millerston* and several guest houses.)

The Cathedral of the Isles, a part of the Scottish Episcopal Church, was built in 1849 from designs by Butterfield. In the older, parish, churchyard is the tomb of the Rev. James Adams, minister of the parish of the Established Church from 1799 to 1831, and ever remembered for his habit of praying for " The Greater and Lesser Cumbrae, Bute and Arran, and the adjacent islands of Great Britain and Ireland."

At Keppel on the outskirts of Millport is a most interesting *Marine Biological Station,* with a modern aquarium and a museum.

Great Cumbrae is encircled by a coast road (about 10 miles) and an inner hill road which command grand views. The lighthouse on Little Cumbrae, the companion island to the south, is of interest.

Fairlie, on the mainland opposite the Great Cumbrae,

has been well known for its yacht-building. In the charming little glen are the ruins of the sixteenth-century Fairlie Castle. From Fairlie steamers run to Millport and also convey cars to Brodick in Arran (*see* p. 165).

South of Fairlie are the huge towers of the Hunterston Nuclear power stations and charming **West Kilbride** and **Seamill** (*Hydro*), on the coast. Then comes **Ardrossan,** with steamer services to and from Arran and the north of Ireland (*Kilmeny, Eglinton Arms, Ingledene*). Ardrossan and **Saltcoats** (*Westfield, Vernon*) together form a very popular resort. There is a yacht pond, bathing pool, putting, tennis, and a very fine sandy bay. Ardrossan Castle, captured from the English by Wallace, was finally put into ruin by Cromwell.

Kilwinning, a few miles inland from Ardrossan by way of busy Stevenston, is notable as the home of freemasonry in Scotland, Mother Lodge Kilwinning (No. 0) having been founded in 1107, at the same time as the Abbey, of which the few remains have been incorporated into the present Parish Church.

Between Kilwinning and the sea is a somewhat desolate area of sandhills in which are large explosive works. Through this the River Garnock winds to the sea, and the Irvine, after making an extraordinary loop, joins it just below the town of **Irvine** (*Eglinton Arms, Grange, Redburn*), one of the most ancient royal burghs in Scotland. At Irvine Robert Burns spent some time (1781–3) as a flax-dresser ; both his shop and the house in which he stayed have been burned down. Lesser links with literature were the Scottish novelist John Galt, who was born here in 1779, and James Montgomery, the poet.

A few miles inland from Irvine is—

Kilmarnock,

Hotels.—*Broomhill, Foxbar, Golden Sheaf, Market, Ross, Station.*
Early Closing.—Wednesday.
Sports.—Golf, bowls, pitch and putt, tennis and indoor swimming-pool.

a busy industrial town that is of interest to Burns lovers as the place where " Wee Johnny " Wilson had his printing press, by the agency of which the first edition of Burns's poems was printed (1786). In the graveyard of the Laigh Kirk lie the remains of Tam Samson, on whose grave Burns wrote :

"Tam Samson's weel-worn clay lies here,
Ye canting zealots spare him!
If honest worth to heaven rise,
Ye'll mend, or ye win near him."

But the principal place of Burns pilgrimage in Kilmarnock is the **Burns Monument** in Kay Park, which contains a museum with many relics of the poet. From the monument there are splendid views, by far the most striking feature being the peaks of Arran, seen to perfection across the low land lying between Kilmarnock and the coast.

For Mauchline, Tarbolton, and other haunts of Burns *see* page 162.

At **Riccarton**, now part of Kilmarnock, Wallace is reputed to have passed his youthful days; and the road eastward to Strathaven (20 miles) and Hamilton (27 miles) passes **Loudoun Hill**, where Wallace defeated the English and where in 1306 Bruce with 600 men gained a striking victory over the Earl of Pembroke and his army of 6,000. At **Drumclog**, farther east, Claverhouse was defeated by a Covenanting force in 1679.

Troon.

Distances.—Ayr, 8 m.; Glasgow, 30 m.; Kilmarnock, 10 m.
Early Closing.—Wednesday.
Hotels.—*Marine* (72 rooms), *Craiglea* (21 rooms), *South Beach* (27 rooms), *Welbeck* (14 rooms), *Ardneil*, *Knowe*, *Sun Court*, *Portland Arms*, etc.
Golf.—There are five courses. The three municipally controlled courses are Darley, Lochgreen and Fullerton, and the others Troon Old Course and the Portland Course.

Approaching Troon, on the coast, one is made aware of the local importance of Golf. There are five first-class courses around the town, but Troon has other attractions and is in fact a very popular holiday resort. There are fine sands, with good bathing (there is an excellent open-air swimming pool), boating, tennis and other sports, together with a concert hall and other places of indoor amusement. Here again the sea-front is bordered by a wide strip of turf which adds considerably to the pleasures of the sands. On the north side of the little promontory which forms the southern horn of Irvine Bay is Troon Harbour, carrying on shipbuilding and breaking. The rocky islet (a bird sanctuary) with beacon and white lighthouse seen a few miles to seaward is **Lady Isle**; far away in the westward is Ailsa Craig (*see* p. 162). The prominent building at the back of the town is *Marr College*, a senior secondary school.

Prestwick.

Early Closing.—Wednesday.
Hotels.—*Auchencoyle* (7 rooms), *Carlton* (9), *Golden Eagle* (6), *Links* (13), *North Beach* (13), *Parkstone* (32), *Queen's* (39), *St. Nicholas* (16), *St. Ninians'* (17), *Towans* (57), *Earlston* (12) and many others.
Sports.—Golf, bowls, tennis, bathing-lake, sea-bathing and boating.

Four miles south of Troon is the ancient burgh of **Prestwick,** another great centre for golfers. Its international Airport is noted for its freedom from fog. Prestwick has also come to the fore as a general holiday resort. The sea-water bathing lake, which is 100 yards long, is one of the largest in the country. There are three 18-hole courses; the links of the Prestwick Club are one of the Championship courses. The town is pleasing, and boasts a market cross and a well at which Robert Burns is reputed to have been cured of leprosy. Four miles south of Prestwick is Ayr.

AYR.

Distances.—Burns's Cottage, 2½ m.; Alloway Kirk, 2¾ m.; Ardrossan, 20 m.; Dumfries, 59 m.; Edinburgh, 72 m.; Glasgow, 33 m.; Kilmarnock, 12 m.
Early Closing.—Wednesday.
Hotels.—*Station, County, Eldon House, Ayrshire and Galloway, Berkeley, Marine Court,* etc. *Butlin's Holiday Camp. Youth Hostel.*
Parks.—Belleisle, Craigie.
Population.—48,000.
Sports.—Golf (3 municipal courses), tennis, bowls, bathing, boating, sea-fishing. Race meetings in April, May, June, July and September (flat), and in January March, April, May, October, November, December (jumping).

Ayr is a busy and attractive town which owes something at least of its prosperity to its connection with Robert Burns. The town stands on the banks of the Ayr at the point where that river enters the Firth of Clyde, so that it can also offer the attractions of a seaside resort. The sandy beach is bordered by a wide expanse of turf, with a dance pavilion, amusements, etc. At the north end of the beach is the **Harbour** and swimming pool, and near the south end are two golf courses. Overlooking the beach are the County Buildings, but the town is dominated by the **Town Steeple,** a very fine piece of work which is perhaps best appreciated from a viewpoint at the far end of the **New Bridge,** by which the main road crosses the river. From this bridge also is a good view of the **Auld Brig** immortalized by Burns in his poem *The Brigs of Ayr.* Its antiquity is undoubted, and it still stands a champion of the soundness of thirteenth-century workmanship. The New Bridge against which Burns imagined it inveighing was a predecessor of the present New Bridge.

From the Steeple, **High Street** leads up to the Station, passing on the way the former *Tam o' Shanter Inn*, now a museum, though still with its thatched roof and primitive fittings, and boasting on its front a large picture showing Tam, mounted on his " grey meare Meg," setting off for Alloway and the exciting incidents related by Burns.

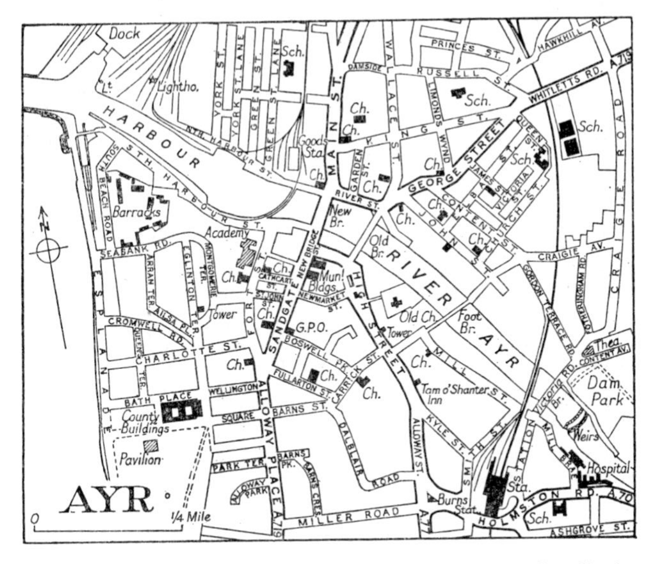

Just outside the station yard is a Burns statue by G. A. Lawson, and the road to the south at this point leads in about two miles to Burns Birthplace and Alloway (*see next page*).

With Burns, Ayr honours Wallace : there is a Wallace Tower (reconstructed on the site of a tower in which he was confined) just below the *Tam o' Shanter* in High Street; on Barnweil Hill, about 6 miles north-east of the town, a prominent monument commemorates the patriot, while closer at hand in the same direction is the cairn at **Auchincruive** to the joint memory of Burns and Wallace. The

Auchincruive estate now belongs to the West of Scotland Agricultural College. On this side of the town also is Ayr's very popular Racecourse.

Ayr's **Parish Kirk** is entered by a narrow way a little below the Wallace Tower in High Street: in the lych-gate are some of the heavy iron grave-covers which were common in the days of the body-snatchers. The graveyard will interest epitaph hunters; the Martyrs' Tomb is near the river on the east side of the church—its inscription concluding:

> "Boots, thumbkins, gibbets were in fashion then,
> Lord, let us never see such days again."

The building was erected in 1654 and still retains its original canopied pulpit and three galleries.

Ayr is said to have been the site of a Roman station, but there is little evidence as to this. William the Lion, who built a castle at the mouth of the River Ayr, granted the town a charter in 1202, raising it to the dignity of a Royal Burgh. It was here that Wallace first openly organized resistance against the English forces, and the town was the scene of one of his notable exploits, "the burning of the Barns of Ayr." A parliament convened by Robert the Bruce for the purpose of settling the succession to the Scottish throne met here, and it was from the port of Ayr that Edward Bruce embarked in 1315 with a small army for the purpose of invading Ireland. In 1652 the English Commonwealth built the fort of Ayr, of which traces remain on the height to the west of the harbour. The ancient church of St. John, founded in the twelfth century, which stood here, was converted into an armoury. By way of compensation, the Protector gave a donation of 2,000 merks to assist in building the Church already referred to.

Excursions from Ayr include walks beside the river and to the Wallace and Burns memorials mentioned above, and visits by rail or road to various spots associated with Burns, pre-eminent being that to—

Burns Birthplace.

Admission charge to Cottage and Museum. Catalogues. Open every weekday and on Sundays in summer, 2–7 p.m. July–Aug. Sundays from 10. Free car park.

The "Auld Clay Biggin" built by Burns's father stands beside the road to Alloway, about 2½ miles south of Ayr steeple. On the way from Ayr one passes various points associated with the wild ride of Tam o' Shanter. About a mile from the steeple, the Alloway road crosses the Slaphouse Burn about 200 yards east of—

"the ford
Whare in the snaw the chapman smoor'd,"

and a short distance beyond the ford in the garden of a wayside cottage may be found the—

"meikle stane
Whare drunken Charlie brak's neck-bane."

A little farther on an ash-tree surrounded by a paling marks—

"the cairn
Whare hunters fand the murder'd bairn."

Burns Birthplace is a low thatched cottage abutting on to the pavement and with little external suggestion of its value and importance in the world of literature. The inner rooms contain various articles of simple furniture, and there is a "set-in" bed similar to that in which Burns was born on January 25, 1759.

Adjoining the birthplace is a museum of manuscripts, letters and other relics of the poet, and the gardens are pleasantly laid out.

Robert Burns was born at Alloway, January 25, 1759, and died at Dumfries (p. 93), July 21, 1796. The first seven years of his life were spent here; in 1766 the family moved to Mount Oliphant, 2 miles from Alloway. His father was a peasant farmer who gave his son the best available education, and this education inclined to the literary side. His youth was spent working on the farm, with a brief interlude at Irvine (p. 154), where he tried his fortunes as a flax-dresser. When William Burns died in 1784 Robert and his brother took on the farm at Mossgiel (p. 162) and shouldered the maintenance of the widow and several younger children. It was, however, an unfortunate venture, and Robert's interest in the farm was lessened by his affair with Jean Armour—an affair which so incensed the Armour family that Burns thought it best to seek his fortunes abroad. Meanwhile, Jean Armour and he parted with some show of recrimination, and Burns turned to "Highland Mary"—Mary Campbell, dairymaid at Montgomery Castle near Mossgiel—who, however, died shortly afterwards. Burns decided to go to Jamaica, and had indeed composed his farewell song ("The Gloomy Night is Gathering Fast") when the success of his first book of poems introduced him to literary circles in Edinburgh, and brought in a sum of money that was welcome, if small, and sufficed to banish ideas of emigration.

After a tour of the Border, he returned to Mossgiel, this time to be received with open arms by the Armours—a welcome not without embarrassment, one imagines, for by now the correspondence with Clarinda (Mrs. Maclehose) was flourishing. However, in 1788 he rented the farm of Ellisland (p. 96) near Dumfries and married his Jean. Farming was no more prosperous at Ellisland than at Mossgiel, and ere long he applied for the post of excise officer, which brought him in an additional £50 per annum. Once again, too, farming was subjugated to other interests, and in 1791 he sold the farm, moved to a small house in Dumfries, and turned from poems to political squibs which, as the work of an excise officer, were looked at askance by some of his strictly loyal and carefully-spoken superiors. Then came that almost quixotic period when, notwithstanding his poverty and that of his family, he refused to accept payment for the grand series of songs he contributed to Thomson's *Collection*; refused, too, an annuity of £50 offered in return for poetical articles for the *Morning Chronicle*. Scotland has been much blamed for the poverty of his final days, but the blame can hardly go undivided.

Following the main road southward from Burns Birthplace for a quarter mile, one comes on the right to the old **Church of Alloway**, where Tam o' Shanter—

> "saw an unco sight!
> Warlocks and witches in a dance . . ."

and from the winnock-bunker in the east wall "Auld Nick"—

> "Screwed the pipes and gart them skirl
> Till roof and rafters a' did dirl."

Another side of the poet's genius is displayed in the inscription on his father's tombstone—

> "O ye whose cheek the tear of pity stains."

Across the road from the Church is the **Burns Monument** (*admission, fee; open weekdays all day, Sundays in summer,* 2–7)—a Grecian temple copied from the monument of Lysicrates at Athens. It contains various relics, including Jean Armour's wedding ring, and two Bibles said to have been exchanged between Burns and Highland Mary. Many admirers of Burns will consider that a more fitting memorial than the Grecian temple is the summer-house in the garden containing Thom's clever sculptures, representing Tam o' Shanter and Souter Johnie. The gardens are pretty and give nice views of the Auld Brig o' Doon, and the riverside grounds of the adjoining Burns Monument Hotel are also open for a small fee.

The farm of **Mount Oliphant**, to which the Burns family removed in 1766, is on rising ground about 2 miles east of the Auld Brig. It was here that Burns composed his first song, "My Handsome Nell."

The road crossing the New Brig o' Doon climbs to give good views eastward and in about 5 miles reaches **Maybole** (*King's Arms, Carrick*), a sleepy old town with a reputation for the manufacture of footwear and agricultural implements, and of interest to Burns students as the place where the poet's father and mother first met.

From Maybole our road to Turnberry is across the hills, passing the ruins of **Crossraguel Abbey** on the left a few miles out. The ruins (*weekdays* 10–7 *in summer*, 10–4 *in winter. Sundays* 2–7 *or* 4 ; *admission, fee*) comprise nave and chancel of the Abbey Church, the chapter house, south of the chancel, remains of the cloisters, dovecot, and the gatehouse at the south-west, still imposing.

Kirkoswald is a neat village notable as the burial-place of Burns's Tam o' Shanter. (The gravestone is at the west end of the Church, Tam's real name being Grahame.) In the centre of the village is Soutar Johnie's Cottage, preserved as nearly as possible as it was in Burns' day.

Kirkoswald is not far from the coast, along which a road has come from Ayr by way of **Dunure,** where is a ruined cliff castle. It was in the black vault of this grim keep that the fourth Earl of Cassillis, anxious to enrich himself at the expense of the Church, in 1570 " roasted in sope " a commendator (= lay abbot) of the neighbouring Abbey of Crossraguel in an attempt to secure a share of the ecclesiastical revenue. The dignitary, however, remained obdurate, and, escaping, appealed to the Privy Council, with but little satisfaction. The Kennedys of Dunure are now represented by the Marquis of Ailsa, who has given his former seat, **Culzean Castle,** the next notable building passed, to the National Trust for Scotland. The policies and castle are open to the public (10–dusk, *charge*). The castle was built as a residence towards the end of the eighteenth century and contains a National Guest Flat placed at the disposal of General Eisenhower after the Second World War.

Turnberry of to-day is manifestly Turnberry Hotel (120 rooms) and a hamlet. The famous resort hotel surmounts the scene of its two 18-hole golf courses—the championship Ailsa and the newer Arran, on which non-resident visitors may play. On the neighbouring " Bogle's Brae " was kindled the mysterious beacon fire which summoned Bruce and his followers from Arran : an incident familiar to readers of Scott's *Lord of the Isles.*

Girvan, 5 miles south of Turnberry, is a small seaport and holiday resort. (*King's Arms, Haven, Queen's, Hamilton Arms, Ailsa ; many boarding-houses.*) There is good bathing, golf and fishing, tennis courts and bowling greens, indoor pool, and trips to the lonely rock of **Ailsa Craig,** 10 miles out at sea, are popular, although the rock is uninhabited except for the keepers of its lighthouse and the myriads of seabirds.

For the coast southward to Stranraer and the Mull of Galloway *see* page 106.

Ten miles north-east of Ayr by road is **Mauchline** (*Poosie Nansie's Inn, Loudoun Arms*), "the Mecca of Burns pilgrims." Most of the buildings associated with the poems have gone, but Poosie Nansie's hostelry remains. The churchyard was the scene of "The Holy Fair," and here are the graves of Daddy Auld, Mary Morison, Holy Willie and many others mentioned by Burns. Close by the churchyard and the ruins of Mauchline Castle is the house where Gavin Hamilton lived and where Burns and Jean Armour were married. Also close at hand is the small house in which they lived until the house at Ellisland was ready.

Chief interest of the neighbourhood centres in the farm of **Mossgiel,** where Burns lived for seven years. It is 1½ miles north-west of Mauchline, on the Tarbolton road. Burns and his brother, Gilbert, rented this farm for four years from the time of their father's death, in 1784, and here were written *The Cottar's Saturday Night* and many other of his best poems. Here is the field where he ploughed up the daisy and turned up the mouse's nest—simple events which his muse has immortalized. The house has been rebuilt. Some way farther along the Tarbolton road is a turning leading to the farmstead of **Lochlea,** which was Burns's home from his seventeenth to his twenty-fourth year, his father having moved here from Mount Oliphant. It was at Lochlea that the elder Burns died.

At **Tarbolton** Burns became a freemason. Here he founded his first debating society—the Bachelor's Club—in an old house (National Trust : museum). At Coilsfield House (now Montgomerie Castle) near by, "Highland Mary" was a dairymaid. Still pointed out is the spot near the old thorn tree, at the junction of the Fail with the River Ayr near the main road 2½ miles west of Mauchline, where Burns and Mary last met "to live one day of parting love." (Mary, it will be remembered, went to visit relatives in Argyllshire, and fell sick and died at Greenock, on her return journey.)

ROTHESAY AND BUTE.

Rothesay is the chief—in fact the only—town on the **Island of Bute**, which (about 15 miles long by 6 across at the widest part) lies to the south of the Cowal Peninsula and about 7 miles across the Firth of Clyde from Wemyss Bay. It is immensely popular with Glasgow and Clydeside folk. The island contains considerable archæological remains including burial urns, stone circles, cists, at least a dozen forts and strongholds of various periods, and Celtic chapels.

ROTHESAY.

Access.—From Glasgow and the mainland either *viâ* Wemyss Bay—the quickest route—*viâ* Gourock *viâ* Greenock, or *viâ* Craigendoran. Car ferry from Wemyss Bay.
Early Closing.—Wednesday, except during the season.
Golf.—Municipal 18-hole course, 30p. round. 13-hole course at Port Bannantye. 9-hole course at Kilchattan. Putting greens on Esplanade.
Hotels.—*Grand Marine*, *Victoria*, *Glenburn* (113 rooms), *Lorne*, *George*, *Craigmore*, *Marine House*, etc., and numerous private hotels and boarding houses.
Population.—6,225.
Sports.—Boating of all kinds in the Bay ; bathing, bowls, tennis, golf (*see above*), dancing and other amusements ; and there is good fishing, special " fishing cruises " being organized. Indoor swimming-pool.
Yachting.—The Isle of Bute Sailing Club welcomes visiting yachtsmen who may participate in their races, which are held twice weekly.

The rousing resort of Rothesay is probably the most popular watering-place on the Clyde. In addition to the natural beauty of its situation, the mild and equable climate of the island of Bute is an attraction of great importance to invalids. The range of temperature is about 18 degrees less than the average of Scotland, being 13 degrees warmer in winter and 5 degrees cooler in summer.

The **Pier**, the focus of Rothesay life, is seldom without one or more steamers landing or embarking passengers, and in the variety of trips it offers it rivals many a railway station.

Rothesay Castle is first recorded in 1230 when besieged and captured by the Norsemen. The fortress was captured by King Haakon in 1263, but his defeat at Largs restored the stronghold to Scottish hands. The castle played a minor part in the wars of Wallace and Bruce, and was a favourite residence of Robert II, the first of the Stewarts. The main part of the castle dates from the thirteenth century and consists of a circular curtain wall with four huge round towers. The newer portion, completed by James V, is at the north entrance, while within the inner courtyard is the chapel. The castle and grounds are in the care of the Department of the Environment and are open to the public at the usual hours, *charge.*

The **Norman Stewart Institute** was erected from funds provided by the late Norman Stewart, of Richmond Virginia, and his nephews, John, Daniel, and Bryce Stewart—all natives of Rothesay. The second floor houses the headquarters of Bute County Library.

The **Museum** of the Natural History Society is in Stuart Street.

The shore road by Craigmore and Ascog to Mount Stuart, the seat of the Marquis of Bute (about 5 miles), affords a variety of views. The model village of **Kerrycroy,** which was designed by a former Marchioness of Bute, is 3½ miles from Rothesay. Here the splendid avenue leading up to *Mount Stuart* begins. In the extensive grounds are some very fine beech and lime avenues.

The village of **Kilchattan Bay,** a favourite resort of summer visitors, is connected with Rothesay by a regular service of buses. It has a fine, sandy beach.

Near Kilchattan Bay, at the south end of the island, are the ruins of the ancient **Chapel of St. Blane,** amid most attractive scenery and commanding a fine view of the Arran hills. St. Blane had two cemeteries attached to the Church, one for men, the other for women. This arrangement is accounted for by the following tradition:

At the time the Church was built, St. Blane brought some consecrated earth from Rome. This earth was taken from the ship at Kilchattan Bay, placed in two creels, and slung over horses' backs to be carried to the burying-ground. Before it had been carried far the back-band broke, and the priest in attendance asked a woman who was gathering shell-fish to lend him her belt to supply the place of the broken back-band. She refused, and the priest declared that no women should ever lie in the holy earth. The consecrated earth was therefore placed in the upper ground alone, and women were buried in the lower ground.

In the neighbourhood is a circular enclosure of ancient masonry known locally as the *Devil's Cauldron* ; it may have been used as a place of penance in the Middle Ages. About a mile from it is *Dunagoil,* a vitrified fort and the site of a very early British village.

Port Bannatyne (*East Neuk*) nestles down among the trees on the eastern shores of Kames Bay. **Kames Castle**, with its woods and lawns, is at the head of the bay. The oldest part of the Castle, a large tower, dates from the fourteenth century. Kames was the birthplace of John Sterling, the friend of Carlyle. **Ettrick Bay**, on the western side of the island, is a lovely beach of white sand and shells, a real summer playground, in the best sense of the term. In the neighbourhood are remains of a hill fort, and traces of a circle of standing stones.

A charming short trip is that by boat to **Ormidale**, on Loch Riddon; thence by road to *Glendaruel* (*see* p. 172). The return may be made by the road along the eastern shore of Loch Riddon to **Colintraive**, where the car ferry for Rhubodach can be joined.

ARRAN.

Access.—The most direct route to Arran is from Ardrossan by steamer (summer) and from Fairlie (winter). The Campbeltown steamers call at Loch Ranza (summer only).

Buses.—There is a good bus service on the island running in connection with steamer calls, and various and numerous motor tours are arranged around the island.

Arran is the largest and most picturesque of the islands in the Firth of Clyde. For the antiquary there are tumuli and monoliths of considerable interest; the flora embraces some rare mountain plants; and for the geologist the island displays a greater succession of strata than any other part of the British Isles of equal extent. The standard work on the subject is Bryce's *Geology of Arran*. The island is about 12 miles distant from the Ayrshire coast, and is 20 miles long, 11 broad, and about 56 in circumference. There is a good road all the way round the island.

Arran, from the Ayrshire coast, seems a mass of bold, rugged mountains rising from the sea, but on nearer approach this effect is softened by cultivated fields and stretches of woodland. The first place of call for the car ferries from Ardrossan is **Brodick** (*Douglas*, *Altana*), on the bay of the same name. The view on entering is exceedingly pleasing. **Brodick Castle** is mainly modern, but incorporates part of an old stronghold supposed to date from the time of the Norse occupation of the island.

It has a very fine garden and is open Easter week-end and May–September 10–5 (NT); *admission fee.* The old castle is associated with the adventures of King Robert Bruce, as is duly recorded by Barbour, and by Sir Walter Scott in the *Lord of the Isles.* The village has some modern hotels, tennis courts and an 18-hole golf course. The beach affords good bathing. *Youth Hostel.*

Every visitor to Arran will, of course, climb—

GOAT FELL

(2,866 feet), weather permitting, to enjoy the magnificent prospect from its summit. The ascent commences at the south entrance to the grounds of Brodick Castle, and is not difficult. Five hours should be allowed for the ascent and descent.

Two hundred yards north of the bronze statue to the Duke of Hamilton in front of the schoolhouse a path leads across a bridge over the Rosa Burn, and thus cutting off a corner comes out into the road again opposite the park of Brodick Castle. Turning to the right, the path for Goat Fell (finger-post) is soon reached on the left, leading through a little wood to the open moor. Hence to the top of the eastern ridge of Goat Fell the track cannot be mistaken. From the top of the ridge the route to the summit of the mountain is over rough granite boulders, and in places is steep, though nowhere difficult. When the boulders appear insuperable in front, " fetch a compass " slightly to the left.

The *summit* of **Goat Fell** (*Ben Gobhar*) consists of a confused group of boulders, whose perpendicular sides afford shelter from every wind that blows. The broad belt of sea which surrounds the island gives a wonderful extent and variety to the prospect. Only on the western side, where the jagged ridges on the other side of Glen Rosa rise to an almost equal height, is the view at all curtailed. Northwards Loch Fyne stretches far away to Lochgilphead and the low hills of Argyllshire, over which, in a north-westerly direction, the Paps of Jura are visible. Ben Cruachan is in the remote distance, a little to the right of Loch Fyne, in which direction the western arm of the Kyles of Bute extends. Then, farther east, come the mountains grouped round the heads of Loch Long and Loch Lomond. Ben Lomond rises almost in a line with the Firth of Clyde, at the entrance to which the Great and Little Cumbrae Islands are visible, the white houses of Millport gracefully fringing the snug little bay at the southern end of the former. Due east is Ardrossan, with its neighbouring chimneys and other signs of commercial activity, and farther south Ayr is recognizable by its lofty spire. Then over the southern extremity of the island we note Ailsa Craig, backed by the peninsula on which stand Stranraer and Portpatrick; while south-west we look over Campbeltown and the Mull of Kintyre to the Antrim coast. The Isle of Man is sometimes to be seen. The most striking object close at hand is Glen Rosa, some 2,000 feet below—an emeraldine vale intersected by a silver thread.

Besides the way by which we have ascended, and that which we are about to describe, there are two practicable **routes down** the mountain—the first to **Corrie** by the Whitewater Glen, the second by the southern spur of the mountain, inclining left towards the end of the ridge and rejoining the line of ascent.

Glen Rosa may be included by a detour of 4 miles (there and back). From the foot of the String Road, take the first road on the right, and cross the Shirag burn at a very pretty spot and then, bending to the right again, reach the *Glenrosa Farm*, beyond which a plain track threads the green pastures of *Glen Shant*—as this lower part of the valley is called. The great point of the walk is the marvellously quick change afforded by it into the wildest possible mountain scenery. In twenty minutes the turn of the glen is reached at the foot of a little torrent, the Garbh Allt, and, unless you are going on over the *col* between Cir Mhor and Goat Fell—the "Saddle"—into Glen Sannox, you can fully comprehend Glen Rosa from the little humps just beyond the crossing. The view is one of the finest of its kind.

A fine expedition may be made from Glen Rosa up the Garbh Allt over Ben Nuis (Noosh) and Ben Tarsuinn, and then along the ridge to the foot of A'Chir. Skirt A'Chir low down on the Glen Iorsa side (A'Chir itself is only for experienced rock climbers) until you reach the A'Chir-Cir Mhor *col*, from which point a short scramble takes you to the summit of Cir Mhor itself. Continue along the ridge over the Castle to Fergus' Seat, and descend westwards to the main road at Sannox. There is a precipitous gap in the ridge between the Castle and Fergus' Seat, known as the Carlin's Leap or the Witch's Step. This must be avoided by descending a little to the *left*, or north side, at that point. Note, this whole expedition involves a good deal of scrambling, and should only be attempted by strong walkers in fine and clear weather. The views are magnificent. Time, about 12 hours.

The descent to the *col* or saddle between Glen Rosa and Glen Sannox should be attempted only in good weather. From the summit of Goat Fell a track amongst boulders descends to the ridge leading to North Goat Fell. Some granite tors block the way, and these should be passed by sheep tracks on the Whitewater Glen side. Reaching North Goat Fell summit, an arm of the mountain stretching in a north-easterly direction must be avoided, and a rapid descent made along the top of the ridge in a north-westerly direction to the *col*, which is plainly visible below, backed by the precipitous crags of *Cir Mhor*. Hands as well as feet may be called into requisition during this part of the descent, but there is no real danger. From the *col* there may be some difficulty in finding a route down into Glen Sannox. Do not attempt to descend directly from the *col*. Proceed along the ridge west for some 150 yards, then descend sharply to your right over turf and stones. After descending some 50 feet you will see on your left a wall of rock, at the base of which runs a dyke with the usual stair-like rock steps. Go down this dyke, and then the bed of a burn and the path intertwine and charge into each other amid heather and rock till the main burn in Glen Sannox is reached.

In descending the glen this burn should be crossed (to the north side) if the water permits, and a rough track followed down the left bank to about ½ mile from the coast road. Cross this near a barytes mine and, passing a graveyard, join the main road, 1½ miles north from Corrie Hotel.

Five miles south from Brodick is **Holy Isle** (*St. Molaise*), more than a mile in length, rising to an altitude of 1,030 feet, and acting as a natural breakwater to Lamlash Bay. Here, before his defeat at the battle of Largs in 1263, Haakon mustered his fleet. Holy Isle has a most picturesque appearance, with its grassy slopes, heath-clad acclivities, and, higher, its rugged columnar masses. The view from the summit is fine, but the ascent is difficult. The island takes its name from a tradition that St. Molaise, a disciple of St. Columba, resided on it. The **Saint's Cave** is a water-worn recess in the sandstone rock, about 30 feet above the level of the sea. The roof and sides of the cave are covered with rude marks and inscriptions of different periods, including a short Runic inscription cut in the roof in characters about 1½ inches in length. On the shore below the cave a circular well is pointed out as the bath of St. Molaise, and a large block of sandstone, surrounded by a number of artificial recesses, is called the Saint's Chair. The well had for centuries a great repute for curing all kinds of disease.

LAMLASH,

second largest village in the island, has a picturesque appearance from the sea. The Parish Church of Kilbride, erected by the late Duke of Hamilton in 1885, is the most prominent building. Hotels (*Lamlash, White House, etc.*) and boarding-houses. Golf course.

At the southern extremity of the bay is **King's Cross Point**, where, according to tradition, King Robert Bruce embarked for the mainland when he received the assumed signal from Turnberry (*see* p. 161), and beyond the point is the pleasant village of **Whiting Bay** (*golf course : Youth Hostel*).

Southward by road from Whiting Bay is **Glen Ashdale**, with its two waterfalls. The second fall, at the head of the glen, known as *Eas a Chranaig*, is the highest waterfall in Arran.

Southward again the road, which is now a rather stiff climb, passes Dippin Head, near which are some interesting basaltic pillars. Beyond Dippin Lodge the direct road passes a charming little glen, which is seen at its best on a bright summer day after heavy rain, when the burn brawls over its many cascades.

It is well to make a circuit and visit **Kildonan Castle**, an old ruin on an elevated site overlooking the sea. It was used as a hunting-seat by the Scottish kings when Arran was Crown property. A little farther, near the shore, is *Kildonan Hotel*, from which a fine view is obtained of the small island of **Pladda**, immediately south of Arran. Away in the distance Ailsa Craig is seen. Shortly after leaving the inn we may rejoin the main road round the south of the island. On the coast **Struey Rocks**, at Bennan Head, will repay inspection. Here is the famous *Black Cave*, which runs into the cliffs for about 50 yards and is 80 feet high. A detour may be made northward to visit the pretty waterfall called **Essiemore** (" Great Fall "), under the shadow of Auchenhew Hill.

Beyond Bennan there is a fine view of the Mull of Kintyre in front, across Kilbrannan Sound, Campbeltown being almost due west. Thence through a pleasantly wooded country to the village of **Lagg** (hotel), " the hollow," a charming resort for a quiet holiday. The *Torrylin Water*, which runs through the glen, affords fishing.

A mile beyond Lagg the high-road is joined by the hill-road from Lamlash, which passes through Scorrodale and **Glen Monamore**, affording a series of charmingly varied views of hill and vale. The descent to *Sliddery Water* brings us to the west side of the island, and after crossing the stream the road turns northward, keeping pretty close to the shore. On the shore at **Sliddery** is a green mound, known as *Castle Hill*, on which are remains of a keep, supposed to have been built by the Norsemen.

We now journey along the west coast of the island, and a walk of fully 5 miles along a picturesque road brings us to the pleasant village of **Blackwaterfoot** (*Blackwaterfoot, Rock, Kinloch, Greannan*), on Drumadoon Bay. A 12-hole golf course skirts the shore.

At the northern extremity of Drumadoon Bay is **Drumadoon Point,** which has interesting basaltic columns. At the top are the remains of an old fort, and near them is a standing stone, which, according to popular tradition, marks the grave of Fingal's daughter. Farther north is the **King's Hill,** with a number of caves in which King Robert Bruce, Sir James Douglas, and their followers are said to have lain in hiding for months. The largest is known as the **King's Cave,** and the others as his Kitchen, Cellar, and Stable. There is also a tradition that these caves were used by Fingal, of Ossianic legendary repute.

At **Tormore,** about two and a half miles north of Blackwaterfoot, it is worth walking about a mile east from the road, where, on a moor close to Machrie Water, are the **Standing Stones of Tormore,** the most important prehistoric remains in Arran.

Resuming our journey northward, we skirt the shores of **Machrie Bay,** and passing the village of **Auchencar,** on the slope of Beinn Lochain, reach *Iorsa Water*, which rushes down a wild glen overshadowed by lofty, boulder-strewn mountains. About 4 miles beyond **Pirnmill** is the village of **Catacol,** at the foot of a glen of the same name. From Catacol, a walk of about 2 miles round the White Point, and eastward along the romantic shores of **Lochranza,** brings us to the picturesque village (*hotel : Youth Hostel*). Lochranza Castle, of which the ruins remain, dates from the seventeenth century. The scenery in the neighbourhood of Lochranza, with its background of greensward, wild ravines, and cloud-reaching mountains, is justly reckoned among the finest in Scotland.

From Lochranza to Corrie is 10 miles in a south-easterly direction. Towards the north Torr Meadhonach hill (1,083 feet) shuts out the view of the sea. About 3 miles from Lochranza the head of **Glen Chalmadale** is reached, and through this lonely valley the road descends towards the east side of the island. Approaching the coast at Sannox Bay, we get a good view up **Glen Sannox,** the wildest of the Arran glens. From this point a walk northwards along the coast for about a couple of miles would bring us to the *Fallen Rocks*, huge sandstone blocks of all shapes and sizes that have fallen from the top of the cliffs.

At the southern end of **Sannox Bay** lies the village of **Corrie**, and 6 miles farther is **Brodick**. The scenery all the way is most attractive.

GLASGOW TO ARDRISHAIG AND OBAN.

Steamer to Ardrishaig, thence to Oban by road.

This is one of the most popular cruises from Clyde resorts. Trains leave Glasgow (Glasgow Central Station) and connect with the steamer starting from Gourock.

The Clyde as far as Gourock has been described on pages 148–52.

Steaming across from **Gourock** to **Dunoon**, a distance of about 4 miles, we enjoy on a fine day a prospect scarcely equalled and certainly not surpassed in Britain. In front is the Argyllshire shore, with its magnificent background of hills. On our right we have a fine view of **Loch Long**, stretching away northwards, with the pleasant summer resorts of **Kilcreggan** and **Cove** on one side, and **Strone** and **Blairmore** on the other. The shorter and smaller inlet to the south of Loch Long is the **Holy Loch**. The prominent mansion on the height at **Strone Point**, between Loch Long and the Holy Loch, is Dunselma, for long the residence of one of the Coats family, of the famous Paisley thread company, and now a Youth Hostel. It is at the southern extremity of the Argyll National Forest Park.

On the left, when **Cloch Point** with its lighthouse is passed, a far-reaching stretch of the Renfrewshire and Ayrshire coast is disclosed. Away to the south, over the extensive waters, Bute and the Islands of Cumbrae are seen.

Dunoon (*see* p. 185) is one of the most popular and central seaside resorts on the Firth of Clyde. Here passengers who have travelled *viâ* Craigendoran are taken on board.

Innellan (p. 186) is the next place of call.

Nearly opposite Innellan is **Wemyss Bay**, beyond which Skelmorlie and Largs are visible on the Ayrshire side, and towards the south-west a glimpse may be had of the peaks of Arran.

Beyond Innellan is **Toward Point**, the southern extremity of the Cowal district of Argyllshire (*see* p. 187).

Here is a lighthouse. We now head to westward, making for Rothesay Bay, and with grand views of **Loch Striven**, which stretches northward for 9 miles amid lonely hills. It affords a most pleasant prospect when the sun shines brightly, but in stormy weather has a dark and gloomy aspect. It is known as the "Rothesay weatherglass," and it is said that it is sure to rain in Rothesay whenever a mist hangs over this loch.

From **Rothesay** (*see* p. 163) we head northward and pass **Kames Bay**, on the south side of which the village of **Port Bannatyne**, practically a continuation of Rothesay, ranges itself in crescent form. Behind the bay is the green hill of Kames (875 feet).

Continuing our north-west course, we enter the **Kyles of Bute**, and are amid the most enchanting scenery of the Firth of Clyde. The word Kyle, of Gaelic origin, means a narrow passage or strait. These particular Kyles are from half a mile to a mile in width. The northern end is the more picturesque. After clearing the mouth of Loch Striven, we notice on the Cowal shore, on the right, *South Hall*. The extensive woods with which it is surrounded were planted to represent the position of the British and French armies at the Battle of Waterloo.

Shortly before reaching the mouth of Loch Riddon, we touch at **Colintraive**. This is a favourite place for picnics, as there are many delightful walks in the neighbourhood. The Bute graziers used to swim their cattle across the Kyles here from the mainland, on their return from the Argyllshire markets, and hence arose the name of Colintraive, which means the "swimming narrows." From Colintraive there is a car ferry to Rhubodach in the Isle of Bute.

Beyond Colintraive the small Burnt Islands that dot the surface of the water, as well as the hills on the Bute and Cowal shores, seem every few minutes as if they would bar all further progress.

Eilean Dearg, or Red Island, is the small island on the east side of Loch Riddon about a mile from the entrance. It was selected as his chief place of arms by Archibald, ninth Earl of Argyll, in his unfortunate rising in conjunction with the Duke of Monmouth, in 1685. The place was so protected by rocks and the water so shallow that it was believed, falsely, as the event proved, to be secure from attack by the King's frigates.

Soon after rounding the north end of Bute, we touch at **Tighnabruaich**, which signifies in Gaelic, " the house on the brae," and was so called from an inn that was formerly the only dwelling on the spot. It is a delightful seaside retreat with hotels and youth hostel.

Having passed **Kames Pier**, we skirt the west, or Cowal, shore for about 5 miles, till abreast of **Ardlamont Point**, nearly opposite which is Ettrick Bay, in Bute.

Rounding Ardlamont Point we enter **Loch Fyne**, the longest of the many arms of the Firth of Clyde. Stretching far up into the heart of Argyllshire, this loch affords a clear run of 36 miles to Inveraray, or of 42 to its northern extremity. Loch Fyne is famous for the size and superior quality of its herrings.

After calling at **Tarbert** (*see* p. 187), we enter **Loch Gilp**, an inlet of Loch Fyne, with its port, Ardrishaig, and Lochgilphead, which are about a mile apart. At **Ardrishaig** (the " height full of briars ") (*see* p. 181) the outward voyage of the steamer ends, and passengers for Oban and the north land and proceed to the motor-coach which is waiting to convey them to Oban (*see* p. 182).

The boat leaves Ardrishaig on the return journey about 1 p.m. The distance from Glasgow to Ardrishaig and back is about 180 miles, and for anyone who has only a day to spare the trip is most enjoyable and gives an excellent impression of the picturesque scenery of Scotland's indented western coast.

Glasgow to Inveraray. (For the **Loch Eck Route** from Dunoon to Strachur, a very fine motor run of about 24 miles, *see* pp. 183–4.) The trip to Inveraray is second to none of the cruises on the Firth of Clyde in beauty and variety. The route is the same as that described on foregoing pages as far as the middle of Loch Fyne, but instead of calling at Tarbert and Ardrishaig the steamer pursues its way through the charming scenery of the upper reaches of Loch Fyne to Inveraray. As steamer services are subject to change, full inquiry should be made at agents' offices. This part of the loch is described on pages 180–1.

GLASGOW TO OBAN VIÂ LOCH LONG AND INVERARAY.

This is a motor route. Railway as far as Arrochar only.

THE especial feature of this route (about 115 miles) is the succession of views in which tree, rock and water are combined with varying but ever-charming effect.

From Glasgow to **Dumbarton** (p. 151) the road is almost entirely industrial, but onwards to Helensburgh it improves and the views across the Clyde are good.

The importance of **Craigendoran** as a junction between the steamer services and the railway has tended to overshadow the attraction of the village itself—which is perhaps as well, for it is quite a small place with none of the blatant allurements usually associated with the vicinity of such busy and popular railway stations and steamer piers.

Helensburgh (*Queen's, Imperial, Cairndhu, Commodore*) is a modern town of wide, straight streets and with a busy pier, golf course and sports grounds and a bathing pool. The name was given in compliment to the lady of Sir James Colquhoun, the owner of the land on which the town is built. The streets running inland climb the rising hill behind and open up glorious views across the Clyde and the Gareloch, while from the crest of the ridge there are views eastward to Ben Lomond and the Campsie Fells. A granite obelisk commemorates Henry Bell, who was Provost of the town, and whose *Comet* (1812) was the first vessel to be propelled by steam. The pier from which he conducted his experiments was in front of his residence, now the Queen's Hotel.

A little east of the rebuilt Fruin Bridge, on the Luss road, are the ruins of Bannachra Castle. Four miles from Helensburgh this road joins the lovely highway bordering the western shores of **Loch Lomond** (*see* p. 191). **Glen Fruin** was the scene of a terrific clan battle in which the MacGregors massacred the Colquhouns (see the appendix to *Rob Roy*).

Helensburgh is at the mouth of the **Gareloch,** an arm of the sea about 6 miles long and with an average width of three-quarters of a mile, the upper part of which has virtually become one vast ship-breaking yard. A good road runs within a few yards of the shore all the way round.

Two miles from Helensburgh, on the loch side, is the pretty little village of **Rhu,** in the churchyard of which is the grave of Henry Bell, over which is a statue of the pioneer of steam navigation, erected by the late Robert Napier, the shipbuilder. To the north of the village is the romantic **Whistler's Glen,** which figures in *The Heart of Midlothian.*

The village of **Garelochhead** (*Garelochhead, Woodlea*) is well placed, with good views down the loch and with boating, fishing and other attractions. Numerous tea-rooms and apartment houses cater for visitors, and the village is very popular with Glasgow folk. There is a pleasant recreation ground with games facilities. The best short excursion is to the top of the hill on the Arrochar road, near **Whistlefield.** This is a grand view-point, commanding nearly the whole of the Gareloch, a section of Loch Long and part of Loch Goil. Near here, on Loch Long, is **Finnart,** where giant tankers discharge oil, which is piped to Grangemouth refineries.

Another excursion from Garelochhead is across the hills to the head of **Glen Fruin** (p. 174) and on to Fruin Bridge, on the Luss–Helensburgh road.

From Garelochhead a good road runs southward down the eastern side of the Roseneath peninsula, passing Mambeg, Rahane and Clynder, on the Gareloch, which are favourite holiday quarters for those lucky enough to secure accommodation. The village of **Roseneath** is beautifully placed against a background of trees, a quarter mile from its pier. The ruins of the old church are of interest from the charm which Sir Walter Scott has thrown over the locality in *The Heart of Midlothian.* It is easy to associate the old building with the labours of Reuben Butler, the husband of Jeanie Deans. The hill behind the village is well worth climbing for the sake of the view from the top. The former castle, once the seat of the Argyll family, which was situated a little over a mile south-east of the village, has been demolished and the site is now developed as a modern caravan park.

The precipitous rock to the north, known as **Wallace's Leap,** has the tradition of being the point from which Wallace leapt on horseback to make his escape across the loch to Cairndhu Point.

The road from Roseneath cuts across the peninsula to **Kilcreggan** and **Cove,** attractive little places looking across the Clyde to Gourock. Thence the road runs up the eastern shore of Loch Long as far as

Coulport, where it ends. Motorists and others who do not care to face the rather rough road which crosses the peninsula from near Coulport must return to Garelochhead by the same road.

From Garelochhead the road climbs to Whistlefield (*see above*) and then follows a fine run down to the shores of **Loch Long**, a narrow and highly picturesque arm of the sea penetrating 16½ miles inland to Arrochar. Across the water is seen the **Ardgoil Estate**, ironically known as *Argyll's Bowling Green.* It was generously presented to the citizens of Glasgow in 1906 by the then Lord Rowallan, "As it seems to me desirable that our fellow-citizens should have a mountain territory which will be their own for all time." The estate, which fills the triangular area between Lochs Long and Goil, forms part of the **Argyll National Forest Park.** The Park has a total area of 54,000 acres, of which 19,000 are reserved for afforestation and the remainder set aside as a National Park, in which use it has been a popular success. There are several youth hostels, camping grounds, car parks, etc., in the parts open to the public.

Arrochar, at the head of Loch Long, is an attractive little village which enjoys a high reputation as a holiday resort. Although situated on Loch Long, it is within 2 miles of Loch Lomond at Tarbet (*see* p. 195), and in the midst of richly varied scenery. There is good fishing available in the lochs, and in addition to the hotels (*Arrochar* (26 *rooms*) ; *Loch Long* (45 *rooms*) ; *Arrochar House* (*private*), *several private hotels ; caravan site at Glen Loin House*) most of the cottages seem to offer apartments. The railway station is along the Tarbet road.

The most obvious mountain excursion from Arrochar is the ascent of **The Cobbler,** as **Ben Arthur** (2,891 feet) is called from a fanciful reading of the profile made by the rocky summit.

The easiest route to the Cobbler is by following, from the Torpedo Station, the south bank of the Buttermilk burn right up into the Cobbler Corrie. There is then a steep rise to the dip between the centre and north peaks, from which either top is easily reached. The south peak is for rock climbers only. **Ben Ime** (3,318 feet), 1½ miles north of the Cobbler, is the highest peak in the district and is a magnificent view-point. Its ascent requires very little additional exertion and should be made if the weather is clear.

From Arrochar the Inveraray road rounds the head of the loch, passing the caravan ground at Ardgarten, and then turns away from the soft beauty of Loch Long into wild and rugged **Glen Croe**, over which The Cobbler frowns on the right. Glen Croe is less bold and rugged than Glencoe, but it has much of the sterile grandeur which characterizes the more famous pass. Beside the road at the top of Glen Croe is a stone appropriately called "*Rest and be Thankful*," and although a good road has been made which minimizes the need for rest, the view is such that few who pause are unlikely to echo Wordsworth's "who would rest and *not* be thankful?" Another stone by the roadside at this point is inscribed, "Military Road repaired by 93^d Regt. 1768. Transferred to Commissioners for H.R. & B. in the year 1814." From this point a rough hill road goes south-west to **Hell's Glen** and so to either **Lochgoilhead** or St. Catherine's. The main road descends beside Loch Restil and the series of falls below it to the bridge at the head of **Glen Kinglas**, and to Cairndow, on the shore of Loch Fyne. It is worth looking back along Glen Kinglas for the fine views of **Ben Ime**, raising its 3,318 feet like a tremendous wall at the eastern end of the valley. As we approach the end of the valley, a road (*see* p. 183) doubles down to the left for St. Catherine's, Strachur and Dunoon (*see* p. 185).

Our road, however, bears off to the right, passing above **Cairndow**, which consists of little more than an hotel, a church and a cottage or two (it is reached by keeping along the *old* road). Hence the route proceeds to round the head of **Loch Fyne**, one of the longest (42 miles) of the narrow arms of the sea which penetrate this western coast and add charm as well as miles to road routes. The turreted tower of *Dundarave Castle*, close to the shore about 6 miles along the road, is a prominent feature. All around is much evidence of hydro-electric development in connection with the Glen Shira scheme.

The crinkled mountain-top seen eastward from this point is **Beinn an Lochain** (2,992 feet), above *Rest and be Thankful*, and not The Cobbler as might easily be supposed. A mile or two beyond Dundarave the road rounds Strone Point, and suddenly Inveraray springs into view across the water; but to reach it the road has first to round the inlet from Loch Fyne known as **Loch Shira** (the saddleback bridge at this point has been scheduled as a National Monument). North of the town is the wooded hill of Duniquaich, a favourite viewpoint, and then, on the west bank of the Aray River, **Inveraray Castle,** the seat of the Duke of Argyll. Although the family have been settled here since the fifteenth century the present castle dates only from 1745. With its background of trees, it makes a very charming picture. It was designed by Roger Morris, with the elder Adam. Completed by John Adam and Robert Milne, it is of blue-green chlorite slate, quarried on both sides of Loch Fyne. The Castle is open, *charge*, from early April to mid-October.

Inveraray.

Distances.—Arrochar (by Cairndow), 22 m.; Ardrishaig, 26 m.; Dalmally, 15 m.; Dunoon (by road, 40 m.).
Hotels.—*Argyll Arms, George, Loch Fyne: Youth Hostel.*
Sports.—Fishing (salmon, sea and brown trout) in Aray, Douglas and Garron Rivers and Loch Dubh; good sea-fishing. Tennis, boating and bathing.

Inveraray was originally a burgh of barony, under the Argyll family, but became a royal burgh early in the seventeenth century. It was the centre of the great power of the Campbells (*see* the *Legend of Montrose* and *Catriona*). When the fourteenth-century castle was rebuilt in 1745 the then Duke of Argyll also rebuilt the town, which, according to Pennant, was composed of wretched hovels. It now consists almost entirely of frontage, and most visitors are surprised to find that the population is hardly more than 500, although Inveraray is the county town of Argyll, which in point of area yields precedence in Britain only to Yorkshire and Inverness-shire.

With its background of green wooded hills and in front the clear waters of the loch, Inveraray has a very attractive appearance—a feature which has been enhanced by the colour-washing of the houses facing the water. The large gateway beside the hotel guards a fine Avenue, more than a mile long and leading to the pretty *Essachosan Glen*, or Lovers' Glen. Also reached by the avenue is All Saints' Episcopal Church, visited for its bells, hung in a lofty square tower.

The Parish Church, at the head of the short main street, used to comprise two churches under a single roof, for separate services in Gaelic and English. The Gaelic church end has been converted into a fine church hall, both Gaelic and English services being now held in the church proper. A monument in a nearby garden is a grim reminder of local participation in the Monmouth Rising (1685). At the foot of the street, on the quay, is a fine Iona cross inscribed (translation), " This is the cross of the noble men, namely Duncan MacComyn, Patrick his son and Ludovick the son of Patrick who caused this cross to be erected."

Although as we see it Inveraray is less than two centuries old, the little town has an air of history, as though the very stones remembered the bitter, relentless days of clan warfare, the Monmouth Rising and other occasions of fire and slaughter, and it is not surprising that it has figured in several historical romances, foremost among them Neil Munro's *John Splendid* and *Gillian the Dreamer*.

Private roads run up **Glen Shira**, north-east of Inveraray, to a ruin (7 miles) known as **Rob Roy's House.** The *Shira* (literally, "the silent river") rises on **Beinn Bhuidhe**, a mountain 3,106 feet high, about 11 miles north-east of Inveraray. The river flows through a beautiful glen, and is well stocked with trout. Close to its mouth the river widens out as **Dubh Loch** and flows into **Loch Shira**, as the inlet on which Inveraray stands is called, about a mile north of the town.

INVERARAY TO CLADICH AND DALMALLY BY GLEN ARAY.

Glen Aray is delightful: it is worth going a mile or so up for the sake of the view of Duniquaich through the trees. The *Aray* has several fine cascades, and the glen itself, about a mile wide, is well wooded and is clothed with purple heath and golden broom. The best of the waterfalls is at **Linaghluten** (or Linneghlutton), between 3 and 4 miles from Inveraray (permission must be obtained to pass through the Castle estate); and opposite, behind some trees, is the site of one of **St. Mungo's** churches, where is now Kilmun farm. A short distance farther is **Tullich**, where a knoll is pointed out as the site of one of the ancient open-air courts, where rough and ready justice was dispensed. The hamlet of **Carnus**, on the opposite side of the glen, was traditionally a place of sanctuary under the protection of the Church ; but it was pillaged by the Athole men in the raid of 1685.

At **Tighnafead** (just beyond is a granite memorial cairn to Neil Munro) we leave the domain of the Argylls and the richly wooded Glen Aray. In Gaelic, Tighnafead signifies " the house of the whistle," the name being derived from a wayside inn. From this point a climb of 2 miles brings us to the summit (675 feet above the sea) of the pass connecting Glen Aray with the basin of Loch Awe. Here the devout used to kneel on first coming in sight of the sacred island of Inishail. From now on there are delightful views of **Loch Awe.** Two miles farther is the picturesque hamlet of **Cladich** close to Loch Awe.

The road to Dalmally proceeds northward along the eastern side of the loch. On the right is a monument in memory of Duncan Ban Macintyre (d. 1812), a famous Gaelic bard, who was born in this district. **Kilchurn Castle** (p. 210), on a peninsula near the top of the loch, is one of the grandest baronial ruins in Scotland. For Dalmally and the route from Loch Awe to Oban, *see* pages 197–9.

The 25-mile run from Inveraray to Lochgilphead is beside Loch Fyne for all but the last mile or two and with the exception of the inland detour beginning about 2 miles out, and rejoining the lochside at Furnace. On this detour the road passes from the valley of the Douglas Water (a " Roman " bridge is 200 yards downstream from the present bridge) to that of the Leacann Water, and as it climbs above the woods there are splendid mountain and loch views. Across the water from **Furnace, Strachur** (*see* p. 183) lies slightly to the north-east, while south-eastward from **Crarae,** where is a granite quarry, a glimpse may be caught of the picturesque ruins of *Castle Lachlan*, at the mouth of Strathlachlan. The address of the Laird of Strathlachlan, by the way, affords excellent practice for those anxious to acquire the Scottish guttural " ach "—it is " Lachlan Maclachlan of Stra'lachlan, Castle Lachlan, Stra'lachlan, Loch Fyne."

Beyond **Minard,** a hamlet spread at the water's edge, comes **Lochgair** (*Lochgair Hotel*, 24 *rooms*), another quiet little place at the head of the inlet known as Loch Gair : the " short loch." Beyond, the road rounds the promontory enclosing Loch Gilp, on the far side of which is seen Ardrishaig. **Loch Gilp** is only a couple of miles long, but **Lochgilphead** is an administrative centre of Argyll, with hotels (*Stag* (28 *rooms*) *Argyll* (12 *rooms*)), and pleasant views down the loch. **Ardrishaig** (*Royal* (13 *rooms*), *Auchendarroch*, *Anchor*, *Argyll Arms*) is perhaps equally situated in this respect. It is on the route of the Glasgow–Oban tour by steamer and coach; it is also the gateway, so far as road traffic is concerned, to the 50-mile long and little known Kintyre peninsula, and it offers endless sport for anglers in the fishing lochs and streams. There is a fine bowling green and tennis courts.

The **Crinan Canal**, which enters the loch at Ardrishaig, was cut to afford expeditious and safe communication between the West Coast and Isles on the one hand and Loch Fyne and the Firth of Clyde on the other, and to avoid the circuitous and often rough passage of 70 miles round the Mull of Kintyre. Its formation was begun in 1793; but owing to unforeseen obstacles it was not opened until 1801, and then only in an incomplete state. It was finished in 1817, under the direction of Telford. It is 9 miles in length, and has fifteen locks. Like the Caledonian Canal, the Crinan Canal is a State undertaking and is under Government control.

At one time the swift passenger traffic was conducted by means of a track-boat, drawn by horses ridden by postilions in bright scarlet uniforms.

For many years the Canal formed a link in the tour from Glasgow to Oban by carrying passengers from the pier at Ardrishaig to that at Crinan, but the latter part of the tour is now done by coach, and the Canal is left to coasting steamers, pleasure yachts and other craft. A disadvantage of the Canal for fast traffic is the number of locks which have to be passed. Queen Victoria passed through the canal in 1847, hence the reason why it is now referred to as the "Royal Route." The scenery is quiet and unassuming. At the north-west end of the Canal is the small village of **Crinan**, with a good hotel, post office and a few houses in which apartments may be obtained. Crinan is an excellent centre for fishermen or those boating in the neighbouring loch and the Sound of Jura. A road runs beside the Canal all the way from Ardrishaig.

For the road from Ardrishaig to Campbeltown and Kintyre *see* pages 187–9.

ARDRISHAIG TO OBAN (38 miles).

The first few miles of this route are very different from most roads in this rugged part of Scotland, skirting as they do the great marsh, Moine Mhor. At Cairnbaan the Crinan Canal and its accompanying road go off on the left. (The Canal may be seen and Crinan visited in the course of a detour, the main road being rejoined by the straight road crossing the marsh from Bellanoch, on the Canal, to near Kilmartin village in a region rich with relics—hill forts, cairns, cup and ring rock markings, etc.—of *Dalriada* (c. 500), nucleus of the kingdom of the Scots, whose primitive capital was Dunadd. Beyond **Kilmartin** the scenery begins to brighten up. On the right is the road to Loch Awe and Dalmally (*see* p. 197); on the left are the ruins of **Carnassarie Castle** (*see* p. 207), and then the road passes round the end of Loch Craignish, with distant glimpses of Jura. Prettier sea views are those from Asknish Bay, farther north; opposite are Shuna and Luing and in the foreground are numerous smaller islands. Now the road skirts Loch Melfort to **Kilmelfort** (or Kilmelford) (*Cuilfail Hotel*), a hamlet that forms good headquarters for fishermen and others whose joy is in the waters. There is good sea-bathing.

From the *Cuilfail Hotel* the road climbs past Loch nan Druimnean to the **Pass of Melfort**, one of the most picturesque bits of country in the Western Highlands. The rocks on each side are several hundred feet in height, and in many places overhang the old road, cut out of the side of the steep acclivity, while the river flows through a beautiful ravine much lower down. The new road does not go through the Pass of Melfort (now closed owing to falls of rock), but runs over a hill above it, commanding a magnificent view of Loch Melfort. Thence by Glen Gallain the road descends to **Kilninver**, charmingly placed opposite the entrance to the nearly landlocked **Loch Feochan** (boating and fishing).

Hence a road runs out *viâ* Loch Seil and Clachan to Easdale and Luing. **Clachan Bridge** spans Clachan Sound, an arm of the sea, and leads to the island of **Seil** (*Inshaig Park Hotel*). The road goes southward through Seil, till, near Kilbrandon Church, it forks—the sharp turn to the right leading to **Easdale**, 2 miles; and the way right ahead on to **Cuanferry**, 1¼ miles, for the island of **Luing**. Much of the area is dotted with slate quarries. The scenery is greatly varied.

The next few miles are alongside the loch, then comes a short climb past Kilmore, and suddenly between the rocks on the right there are views of McCaig's Tower above **Oban** (*see* p. 200).

ARROCHAR TO STRACHUR, DUNOON AND INNELLAN.

Although the steamer route from Helensburgh to Dunoon is a matter of less than 10 miles, by road it is a journey of nearly 70 miles, owing to the fact that Loch Long and Loch Goil have to be skirted, to say nothing of the mountainous region to the west of those lochs. The road as far as **Glen Kinglas** has already been described (*see* pp. 175–7). About a mile from the western end of the glen, where it runs down to Loch Fyne, the Strachur road doubles off on the left and soon reaches the shore of Loch Fyne at **St. Catherine's,** an attractive hamlet with hotel, post office and one or two cottages. Inveraray is seen across the loch. (Between Glen Kinglas and St. Catherine's a road goes off on the east into Hell's Glen and so to **Lochgoilhead.**)

Strachur is a pleasant village spread out along the loch-side with hotel, post office, shops, garage and houses where apartments may be secured. There are tennis courts, and fishing and boating on the loch, and walking and driving in the attractive country around provide plenty of activity and entertainment for visitors.

At Strachur the Dunoon road turns inland, shortly entering the long and picturesque glen in which lies **Loch Eck,** the narrowest loch, in proportion to its length, in Scotland. As the loch is approached attention is claimed by a hillock on the left which bears a monument to Captain John Lauder, killed in the 1914–18 War, and also the grave of the wife of Sir Harry Lauder.

Though so near to bustling Dunoon and industrial Clydeside, the glen remains absolutely unspoilt, and thanks to extensive afforestation schemes it is likely to evade the builder's clutches for years to come. The mountains on both sides are high, green and steep, sinking directly into the lake with but little intervening space for pasture land or road. From *Whistlefield Hotel*, 2½ miles from the northern end of the loch, a roughish but interesting road climbs over the hills to **Ardentinny**, on Loch Long (*see* p. 176). At the southern end of Loch Eck is the estate of **Benmore**, part of which was given in 1925 to the nation by the late Mr. Harry Younger, for afforestation. (*The policies and gardens are open daily from 9 a.m.; small admission charge*). All round we see—and smell—the scented bog myrtle, the badge of the Campbell clan. In the lovely gorge known as *Puck's Glen* is a rest-hut, panelled with wood representing every variety of tree on the estate, to the memory of Sir I. Bayley Balfour, formerly King's Botanist for Scotland.

Beyond Benmore we reach **Holy Loch**, notorious as a *Polaris* base but which gained its name from the wreck of a vessel bringing soil from the Holy Land to Glasgow for St. Mungo, who proposed to lay on it the foundations of his cathedral there. A portion only of the precious cargo was saved, and on the spot where it was landed there was built the church of **Kilmun**, says tradition.

An old tower in Kilmun belonged to a collegiate church founded in 1441 by Duncan the Prosperous, the first Lord Campbell, from whom the Duke of Argyll traces his descent. Duncan was buried here, his tomb bearing the inscription, "*Hic jacet Dominus Duncanus, Dominus de Campbell, Miles de Lochow*, 1453." Kilmun has been the burial-place of the Argyll family ever since, a square, plain, pavilion-roofed mausoleum covering their remains. Kilmun village is a popular summer resort, sheltered from north winds by Kilmun Hill, and with interesting views over the Holy Loch, with its boats of all kinds, to Dunoon.

The road to Dunoon, however, goes down the western side of the loch. From near the bridge over the Eachaig a good road goes off on the right across the hills to **Loch Striven** and on to **Glendaruel**, at the head of Loch Riddon, by which one can get up to Strachur on Loch Fyne (*see* p. 183) or to Colintraive in the Kyles of Bute (*see* p. 172).

At **Sandbank** there is a choice of roads: the direct road to Dunoon keeps straight ahead, inland; the more interesting way is by the road skirting the Holy Loch by Ardnadam and **Hunter's Quay**, suburbs of Dunoon, from which ferries cross to Kilmun and Strone; and **Kirn**, which is so joined with Dunoon as to be practically indistinguishable from it.

DUNOON.

Access.—Dunoon is most directly reached by steamer, being only **4** miles from Gourock and 9 miles from Craigendoran. Car ferry to Gourock.
Bathing.—Good sea bathing and modern pool.
Bowls.—Municipal Greens, Argyll Street; Dunoon Bowling Club, **Mary Street Kirn and Hunter's Quay Club, Ardenslate Road.**
Early Closing.—Wednesday.
Entertainments.—Summer show in Queen's Hall; bingo in Burgh Hall; amusements in Castle Gardens Pavillion; barbecues; Highland games; Pipe bands in Argyll Gardens; ceilidhs in Masonic Hall.
Golf.—18 holes (Cowal Golf Course).
Hotels.—*Argyll, McColl's, Esplanade, Glenmorag, Selbourne, Tor-na-Dee, Wellington, Blarevhin, Caledonian* and many others. Numerous boarding houses.
Population.—9,122.
Putting Greens in Castle Gardens and West Bay.
Steamer Trips on the Firth of Clyde.
Tennis.—Hard courts at Castle Gardens.

Dunoon disputes with Rothesay the honour of being the most popular resort on the Clyde. It is a merry little place, built on either side of a slight promontory looking across the Firth to Cloch Point, with its lighthouse. To those fresh from the quiescent beauties of Loch Eck the bustling streets and promenades of Dunoon are almost bewildering; but the majority of Dunoon's clientèle reach it by steamer, and the pier is certainly the most interesting point in the town and probably the most important. All day long in summer steamers call at the pier, embark or disembark passengers and promptly put off for the next stopping-place; and the brisk and efficient manner in which the Clyde steamers are handled is something to behold. The business portion of the town lies north and east of the pierhead; holiday joys are grouped around the **East and West Bays**, with paddling pools, bathing facilities, boating, putting, tennis courts and other attractions. Hunter's Quay is a centre for yachting and Kirn has a pleasant Lido on the foreshore.

The **Castle Hill**, a well-wooded knoll between the bays, overlooking the pier, is laid out as a recreation ground. On a knoll on the front is a bronze *Statue of Highland Mary*, who was born at the farm-house of Auchamore, a mile distant. Adjoining the Gardens is the Queen's Hall, where summer shows are held.

For all its modernity, Dunoon has a considerable history. It is supposed that there was a stronghold here on Castle Hill, overlooking the pier, shortly after the settlement of a Dalriadic colony in Cowal in the sixth century. It is claimed that the place had an association with the office of High Steward, or its equivalent, under Malcolm Canmore, and certainly it was held by later Stewarts. On the accession of the Stewarts to the Scottish throne Dunoon Castle became Crown property. Its hereditary keepership was bestowed upon Sir Colin Campbell, of Lochow, an ancestor of the Duke of Argyll. In 1563, Mary, Queen of Scots paid a visit to Dunoon to see her favourite sister, Lady Jane Stewart, natural daughter of James V, and the first wife of Archibald, Earl of Argyll.

In 1646, Dunoon was the scene of the massacre of the Lamonts by the Campbells. There had long been enmity between the two clans, and it culminated in a raid by the Campbells on the territories of the Lamonts in Cowal and Bute, when Toward Castle and other residences were burnt and several hundred prisoners taken. The victors promised to spare the lives of their prisoners, but, forgetful of this pledge, they murdered a few of them and conveyed the rest to Dunoon, where thirty-six were hanged on one tree, and others were murdered with dirks, swords and pistols. Shortly afterwards the seat of the Earls of Argyll was removed from Dunoon to Inveraray, and Dunoon Castle was allowed to fall into ruin. The town rapidly sank to insignificance, and in 1822 was simply a small Highland clachan, with a church, a manse, three or four slated cottages, and a few thatched cottages and huts. The introduction of steam navigation brought Dunoon within easy reach of Glasgow, and it gradually became a popular seaside resort.

By reason of its geographical situation, the principal excursions from Dunoon are made by steamer; of the land excursions the most popular is by Loch Eck (*see* p. 183) to Loch Fyne and thence by steamer down Loch Fyne and through the Kyles of Bute back to Dunoon (through tickets are issued for the round, which may be done in either direction). There is also the very enjoyable road along the shore past Innellan and up Loch Striven, and behind the town is the height known as the *Bishop's Seat*, which gives as fine a view as any elevation of 1,651 feet. There are various routes up: one of the most pleasant is to follow the Loch Eck road to where it turns to the right to cross the Eachaig river. Here turn left along the Glen Lean road for a mile, then turn off by a path on the left which runs up through Glen Kirn to the Giant's Know and the Bishop's Seat. The path from Glen Kirn continues to Inverchaolain, on Loch Striven, whence a lift may be obtained on a conveyance going round the peninsula to Dunoon.

Innellan (*Royal*, etc.), 4 miles south of Dunoon, is laid out on a hill-side sloping steeply down to the shore, so that practically every house has an uninterrupted view across the Firth of Clyde to the wooded eastern shore about Wemyss Bay. The ruins of *Knockamillie Castle* are on the hill-side near the Royal Hotel, and there are remains of a seventeenth-century mansion of the Argyll family.

South from Innellan the hills fall back from the coast, and the flattish land at the end of the promontory terminates in **Toward Point**, with its lighthouse. Among the woods west of the lighthouse is *Toward Castle*, dating only from 1821. The Castle of the Lamonts, Lords of Cowal, was burnt by the Campbells in 1646 at the time of the massacre of the Lamonts at Dunoon (*see* p. 186). The ruins are near the road in the vicinity of the quay. The road up the eastern shore of **Loch Striven** goes only as far as the point known as The Craig, 3 miles beyond Inverchaolain; but a path goes from Inverchaolain to Glen Kirn and the head of the Holy Loch, and another runs along the shore from the Craig to the head of the loch and there connects with the Glen Lean road (*see* p. 186).

For steamer Dunoon to Rothesay, etc., *see* page 172.

ARDRISHAIG TO CAMPBELTOWN AND THE MULL OF KINTYRE.

Scottish roads are kind to those who like the sea but prefer not to be on it, and the trip from Ardrishaig to Campbeltown and back enables one to travel within a few yards of salt water for at least 70 miles.

The first stage is down the shore of Loch Fyne to **Tarbert** (*Tarbert* (*24 rooms*), *Columba* (*14 rooms*), *Castle, West Loch, etc.*), an interesting little holiday resort at the foot of the hills enclosing its harbour, a herring fishery port. The name *Tarbert* denotes an isthmus across which boats could be dragged (cf. Tarbet, on Loch Lomond), and by crossing the narrow slip of land which here links Kintyre to Knapdale one has a complete change of scenery from the breezy waters of Loch Fyne to the sheltered surface of **West Loch Tarbert**, on which swans float and where are facilities for boating, etc. An hotel and a few houses at the head of the loch are distinguished from the more important settlement by the name of **West Tarbert**. The road follows the southern shore of the loch, and as the sea is approached the island of **Gigha** appears in front, and then, from Clachan, Islay and Jura rise magnificently from the waters, away to the west. From West Tarbert steamers run on weekdays to Islay in connection with the Glasgow–Ardrishaig boats (motor-coach from East Tarbert) and call on certain days at Gigha or Jura. *The Road to the Isles* was written during the first world war by the Rev. Dr. MacLeod, a former parish minister of Gigha. The island boasts an ogham stone.

At **Tayinloan** Gigha is less than 3 miles distant, and a ferry crosses. Thence to Campbeltown the road passes through a number of small clachans, but chief interest lies in the succession of grand sea-views: on a reasonably clear day Rathlin and Fair Head, in Ireland, are well in sight. Four miles beyond Bellochantuy the road turns inland to skirt a wide, flat expanse which extends from east shore to west shore and is only just high enough above sea-level to prevent the southernmost portion of Kintyre from being an island. The dunes along the western edge of this Moss bear the famous golf links of **Machrihanish** (*Ugadale Arms, The Warren: Airport*), a small village linked by road with **Campbeltown** (*Hotels: Argyll, White Hart, Royal, etc.*), at the head of a loch penetrating the eastern shore of Kintyre. The town is a good centre for the exploration of this little-visited corner. There is a well-carved Iona Cross at the Quay head. The road continues to **Southend,** the most southerly village in Kintyre, with hotels. A single track road, with periodic passing places climbs over 1,000 feet and down to the **Mull of Kintyre**, with a lighthouse and very fine views across the North Channel to Ireland. Opposite Southend is the lonely island of *Sanda*, with Sheep Island and one or two rocks at the eastern end. The south-east coast of Kintyre is skirted by a narrow road from Southend to Campbeltown which in its later stages affords fine distant views of Arran.

From Campbeltown a reasonable road leads up the west shore of the Kilbrannan Sound; but it is hilly and has some bad bends. On the other hand it commands magnificent views of Arran. *Saddell*, nearly 10 miles from Campbeltown, has the ruins of a small twelfth-century monastery. From a point about 4 miles north of Saddell a short road runs east to **Carradale,** which offers good fishing, and the hills behind it are worth exploration. On the shores of the bay is a vitrified fort, and the ruins of Airds Castle overlook Kilbrannan Sound. Next, as we go northward, comes the suggestively named **Grogport**, and then, at Claonaig, our road turns inland across the peninsula to the shores of West Loch Tarbert. (A little farther up the coast is **Skipness**, with ruins of a castle with a massive tower, and walls 7 feet thick.)

From Tarbert to Ardrishaig the most direct road follows the eastern shore of Knapdale ; from West Tarbert a lonely road follows the northern shore of West Loch Tarbert and then strikes northward along the coast to Loch Killisport and so to Inverniel, a few miles south of Ardrishaig. Walkers who like to get off the beaten track can go west from Achahoish, at the head of Loch Killisport, by a rough and wild road which approaches the coast at Kilmory, whence another lonely road runs up the eastern shore of Loch Sween to Bellanoch, on the Crinan Canal.

Near the mouth of the loch is **Castle Sween**, one of the earliest stone castles in Scotland.

Islay and Jura.

Separated only by the Sound of Islay, half a mile wide (car ferry between Port Askaig and Feolin in Jura), these two islands may well be regarded as one by tourists. Islay is fairly well provided with hotels and houses which "let," while there is an hotel (*Jura*) at Craighouse) and some recent housing development. Islay is the larger of the two, being nearly 25 miles from north to south and almost 20 across at the widest part. Access is by car ferry from West Tarbert with calls at Gigha and Jura at certain times. There is also an air service from Glasgow. **Port Ellen** is the commercial capital of Islay. It has hotels (*White Hart*, *Islay*, *Ardview*) and there is good golf at **Machrie** where also is an hotel. Southward from the village the coast rises to The Oa, terminating in the *Mull of Oa*, a grand viewpoint. Inland from Port Ellen a bus service runs to **Bowmore** (*Bowmore*, *Lochside*, *Imperial*), a small village on the shore of Loch Indaal, which penetrates far into the south coast of the island. Thence the road continues round the loch past Bridgend and Uiskentuie beyond which a turning on the right leads to Kilchoman Church with a fine cross and a reminder of wartime in the memorial to those who perished in the *Otranto* collision in October, 1918. Islay has another such memory : near **Port Charlotte** (*hotel*) on the western shore of Loch Indaal, were buried troops from the U.S.A. drowned when the *Tuscania* was torpedoed in February,

1918. The most southwesterly village on Islay is the little hamlet of **Portnahaven** west of Rhinns Point, whence a road runs up the west coast to Kilchoman. From Bridgend (*hotel*) the road to **Port Askaig** (*hotel*) goes off northward. The village is principally of importance as one of the links between Islay and the mainland and the termination of the ferry to Jura. At different points of the island remarkable examples of ancient Celtic gravestone sculpture can be seen.

Islay is a noted whisky distilling area and there is a busy cheese-making industry.

The wild, inhospitable shore of **Jura** is well known to those sailing through the Sound of Jura. The island is nearly 30 miles long and in places nearly 9 miles across. But for a neck of low-lying ground about midway, Jura would be two islands, for Loch Tarbert penetrates the west coast to within a mile of the eastern shore. A road from Feolin ferry runs round the southern end of the island and as far up the east coast as this; otherwise the island is almost trackless. The most distinctive features are, of course, the "Paps," rising some 2,571 feet and accessible from Feolin. On the Atlantic side lie remarkable "raised beaches" and numerous caves.

Westward from Jura is another pair of islands separated only by a narrow gulf—**Colonsay** and **Oronsay**, renowned at one time for cheese-making. In this case it is the northern island which is the more populated, and there is a small hotel at **Scalasaig** (mail steamer to and from Port Askaig several days each week). The coast of both islands is deeply indented: here indeed one feels oneself "at the edge of beyond." On Oronsay, to which one can cross dryshod at low tide, are the ruins of a fourteenth-century Priory with a finely sculptured sixteenth-century cross and here in 1882 was found the grave of a Viking, buried in his ship and with his horse beside him. Oronsay is known to botanists as the haunt of the extremely rare lady's tresses orchis. The sandy beach of Kiloran Bay affords wonderful bathing when the weather is propitious.

At the north end of Jura is the whirlpool of **Corrievreckan**, through which the waters swirl and boil as they pass between **Jura** and **Scarba.**

GLASGOW TO OBAN VIÂ LOCH LOMOND AND CRIANLARICH.

THE best way to make this journey is by a combination of rail or road and steamer, for the full beauties of the "bonnie banks of Loch Lomond" can only be appreciated from the water. The grand road along the western shore of the loch (*see* p. 195) presents wonderful views of Ben Lomond and the eastern shore, but nothing is seen of the beauties of the mountains bordering the loch on the west. The all-rail route, on the other hand, gives lovely glimpses of the Gareloch and of Loch Long, but from the train only the northern and less characteristic part of Loch Lomond is seen.

Steamers run from Balloch, at the south end of the loch, to Ardlui at its northern end, a distance of some 25 miles of cruising, and at both these points are railway stations and main roads. Certain trains run in connection with the boats and there are through bookings.

The eastern shore is closed ground to motorists except for a few miles at the southern end from Drymen to Rowardennan, and at Inversnaid, the terminus of the road from Stronachlachar and Aberfoyle (*see* p. 146).

A delightful way to see the beauties of Loch Long and Loch Lomond is by steamer from Craigendoran to Arrochar, across to Tarbet by motor, and down Loch Lomond by steamer to Balloch, with rail connections to Craigendoran and Glasgow.

LOCH LOMOND.

Fishing.—There is excellent fishing for trout, sea trout, salmon, perch and pike. The waters are stocked and cared for by the Loch Lomond Angling Improvement Association. (*Secretary* : 86 St. Vincent Street, Glasgow.)

In individual features Loch Lomond is surpassed by other Scottish lochs : it has neither the matchless depth and delicacy of colouring which characterizes the foot of Loch Katrine, nor the wild grandeur of Loch Coruisk, nor the wild dignity of Loch Maree. Taken as a whole, however, it blends together in one scene a greater variety of the elements which we admire in lake scenery than any other Scottish loch. In one feature it stands unrivalled : that peculiarly British enchantment of scenery which is imparted by islands rising from the mid-waters is nowhere better exemplified than on Loch Lomond. The length of the loch is 22½ miles ; greatest depth, 623 feet ; its greatest width is 5 miles, but north of Rowardennan it is seldom wider than three-quarters of a mile.

There are two roads from Glasgow as far as **Dumbarton** (p. 151), then road and rail strike northward through the busy town and by Renton (p. 151), with its memories of

Tobias Smollett, to **Balloch,** the principal port of Loch Lomond. Here is a great variety of boats, from steamers to canoes, and there are tea gardens, hotels, car parks and other facilities, for Balloch is very well organized—and has need to be in the season, when it is besieged by visitors (*Youth Hostel*, 2 miles). Balloch Castle and its domain were bought in 1915 by the Corporation of Glasgow, and one may wander at will in the lovely grounds; some traces are to be seen of the Castle, once one of the principal seats of the Earls of Lennox. Among the trees on the western shore is Cameron House, the home of the Smolletts of Bonhill.

By Steamer from Balloch to Inversnaid.[1]

(25 miles of cruising; time occupied, about two hours; piers at Balmaha, Rowardennan, Tarbet and Inversnaid.)

For Road Route, *see* p. 194.

From Balloch a course is threaded among the lovely islands which characterize this southern end of the loch. The first of the islands is **Inchmurrin** (the grassy island), the most considerable of the group. It is used as a deer park by the Duke of Montrose; at the south-west point are the ruins of an old castle of the Earls of Lennox. To the westward of the island is the entrance to **Glen Fruin,** the scene of the massacre of the Colquhouns by the MacGregors (see the appendix to *Rob Roy*). We pass the islets of Creinch and Torrinch, and see on the eastern shore on a headland, **Ross Priory,** where Sir Walter Scott was a welcome guest when getting local information for *Rob Roy*. Farther east is **Buchanan Castle,** formerly a ducal seat but now an hotel. The next large island is **Inchcailloch,** or "Women's Island," so named because a nunnery once existed there. The cemetery was the burial-place of the MacGregors, and it will be remembered that Rob Roy swore to Bailie Nicol Jarvie "Upon the halidome of him that sleeps beneath the grey stane of Inch-cailliach!" The steamer, passing between this island and the mainland, touches at **Balmaha,** the pass of which (road from Drymen) guarded the entrance to the Highlands. Near Balmaha the *Endrick Water* flows into the loch. About 6 miles up the river, beyond the hamlet of Drymen, is the pretty village of **Killearn,** where George Buchanan, the historian, was born. Between Balmaha and Luss, on the other side

[1] See footnote, p. 16.

of the loch, is a cluster of islands of all shapes and sizes. The chief of these are *Inch Fad*, "the long island," partly under cultivation; *Inch Moan*, the peat island, very low-lying; *Inch Tavannach*, or monks' island; *Inch Connachan*, or Colquhoun's Island; *Inch Cruin*, arable and cultivated; and *Inch Lonaig*, remarkable for its fine yew trees. On *Inch Galbraith*, a small island a little south of Inch Tavannach, are the ruins of an old castle. The village of **Luss** is delightfully situated in the shelter of wooded hills at the entrance to Glen Luss (*see* p. 195).

Steering north, the steamer enters the upper region of the loch, which contracts in breadth and derives a new character from its mountainous boundaries. **At Rowardennan** (*Rowardennan; Youth Hostel*), passengers land who plan an ascent of **Ben Lomond.**

This is the easiest route. The distance to the top (3,192 feet) is 4 miles; time about two and a half to three hours. The view (indicator on summit) is magnificent. The Grampian mountains and the Argyllshire hills are seen towering aloft, and in the loch below are—

> Those emerald isles, which calmly sleep
> On the blue bosom of the deep."

Rowardennan to Aberfoyle (good walkers take four to five hours).—About midway between Rowardennan and the summit of Ben Lomond a path strikes off eastward from the dip between Ben Lomond and Beinn Uird and follows the right bank of a stream to the Duchray Water, which is crossed by a bridge. Ascend ridge beyond the river, then take path to left of Loch Ard, crossing Glasgow Waterworks Aqueduct. The Inversnaid–Aberfoyle road is joined 5 miles west of Aberfoyle (*see* p. 145).

A grand walk along the steep sides of the loch leads through **Craig Royston** from Rowardennan to Inversnaid (*see* p. 194).

From Rowardennan a ferry crosses the loch to Inverbeg (*see* p. 195). On the eastern side is the *Craig Royston* of Sir Walter Scott, which two centuries ago echoed back the vengeance cry of the MacGregors:

> "Through the depths of Loch Katrine the steed shall career
> O'er the heights of Ben Lomond the galley shall steer,
> And the rocks of Craig Royston like icicles melt,
> Ere our wrongs be forgot or our vengeance unfelt."

A little short of Tarbet (but on the east side) is a cavity on the crag-side called *Rob Roy's Prison*.

From **Tarbet** (*see* p. 195) one can drive or walk across to **Arrochar** and sail down **Loch Long**, or proceed either north or south from the Arrochar and Tarbet station of the West Highland branch of the railway.

The steamer next proceeds to **Inversnaid** (*see* also p. 293) on the eastern side of the loch.

To the right of the large hotel the Arklet stream, cascading down from Loch Arklet, makes the fall which was the scene of Wordsworth's well-known poem beginning—

"Sweet Highland girl, a very shower
Of beauty is thy earthly dower."

But those who hope to find at Inversnaid nothing but

"The cabin small,
The lake, the bay, the waterfall . ."

will be disappointed, particularly if they arrive on a busy afternoon.

Among short walks from Inversnaid is that northward along the wooded lochside, past **Rob Roy's Cave,** where the outlaw often took refuge from his enemies. There is a tradition that Bruce found a hiding-place in this district after his defeat by McDougall of Lorne. The rough track may—with some difficulty—be followed all the way to the head of Loch Lomond.

In the opposite direction, a fine route for good walkers begins by the bridge over the Arklet close to the point where the Snaid Burn comes in from the north, about a mile above *Inversnaid Hotel* and a quarter of a mile above the Church. The walk passes high above the eastern banks of Loch Lomond, through Craig Royston (*see* p. 193) to Rowardennan.

Approaching the head of Loch Lomond, the steamer passes **Inveruglas Isle,** with the ruins of a Highland keep. Near where the loch narrows still farther is **Island Vow,** with the ruins of a stronghold of the Macfarlanes. Close to the railway is an immense boulder known as the **Pulpit Rock,** because religious services were once conducted from it. A mile beyond this is the pier at **Ardlui,** at the head of the loch (*see* p. 195).

BALLOCH TO ARDLUI BY ROAD.

The road alongside Loch Lomond is one of the most beautiful in Britain. For practically the whole distance of nearly 30 miles it runs within a few yards of the lapping waters, and as it follows the winding shore it opens up through the trees magnificent and ever-changing views across the loch to the richly coloured slopes on the other side culminating in Ben Lomond and other no less lovely mountains. During the first 10 miles from Balloch interest centres in the numerous islands which gem the southern end of the loch and which have already been enumerated. The road emerges from the trees opposite Inch Tavannach (or Monks' Island), and then **Luss** (*Colquhoun Arms, Inverbeg, The Strone*) is reached—a delightfully situated little village which every July is the scene of one of the most popular of the smaller Highland Gatherings. As may be imagined, it draws considerable crowds from Glasgow.

On the shores of the loch beyond Luss is a favourite camping-ground. Now the loch begins to narrow, and from the little promontory near **Inverbeg** (*hotel*) a ferry crosses to **Rowardennan** (*hotel*), from which a path (4 miles) climbs to the summit of **Ben Lomond** (3,192 feet; *see* p. 193). From the western shore of the loch are enchanting glimpses of the mountain, which changes its appearance with every mile of the road and every shifting of cloud or sun. A little under 10 miles from Luss is **Tarbet** (not to be confused with Tarbert on Loch Fyne or Tarbert in Harris; all these names signify narrow strips of land across which boats could be hauled). Tarbet consists of a palatial hotel (50 *rooms*) and one or two houses and cottages where accommodation of a humbler sort can be obtained. It marks the half-way point in the trip along Loch Lomond and is busy with road traffic also, for here comes in the road which runs over the narrow ridge (1½ miles) separating Loch Lomond from Loch Long, a sea loch at the head of which is **Arrochar** (*see* p. 176). The motor run from Glasgow to Tarbet, Arrochar and back *viâ* the Gare Loch and Helensburgh is deservedly popular. Glasgow folk are to be envied for their proximity to such magnificent scenery.

A mile or two beyond Tarbet the Inveruglas Water comes in on the left, down a wide valley which gives grand views of Ben Vorlich, Ben Ime and Ben Vane. On the shore of Loch Lomond is a generating station whose motive power is derived from water piped down to it from Loch Sloy. Across the water (*ferry*) is Inversnaid, an important point on the Trossachs–Loch Lomond tour (*see* pp. 194 and 145). As the road rounds the eastern foot of Ben Vorlich, the *Pulpit Rock* is seen to the left of the road and the head of the loch comes into view. **Ardlui** is a small village to which a pier and a railway station have given considerable importance to tourists. There is an hotel (*Ardlui*), and accommodation can be obtained elsewhere in and around the village. Good fishing for trout, sea trout and salmon.

From Ardlui to Crianlarich, road and rail ascend **Glen Falloch,** rising about 600 feet in 9 miles. The lower part of the glen is well wooded, and the river, which has a somewhat sluggish course for some little distance before entering Loch Lomond, runs swiftly over a rocky bed in its higher parts, forming about 2½ miles above Inverarnan the *Falls of Falloch.* The view, looking back, as we ascend is very fine, the combination of wood, loch, stream and mountain grouping itself most effectively. Before reaching **Crianlarich** the nearer hills on the right drop down to Glen Dochart, and disclose the huge mass of **Ben More** (3,843 feet ; *see* p. 297) on the right. Crianlarich, with good hotel (*Crianlarich Hotel,* 28 *rooms ; Youth Hostel*) and other accommodation, is a splendid centre, having easy access to Loch Lomond, to Killin and Loch Tay, and to Oban (from the " lower " station, if by rail) and the west ; while the Glencoe road or the West Highland line (" upper " station) affords a fine run to Fort William. There is excellent fishing near the village.

From Crianlarich the course is westward up Strath Fillan to **Tyndrum** (*Gaelic = house on the ridge* : Hotel *Royal* (79 rooms) and other accommodation), about 800 feet above sea-level and a splendid centre for walkers, motorists and others. There are remains of lead mines west of the village and other minerals have been found. Once an important coaching centre, Tyndrum looks like regaining its importance to road-travellers, for here the main Lochearnhead–Oban road is met by the magnificent highway (*see* p. 229) from Fort William by Glencoe and Bridge of Orchy.

From Tyndrum we pass to **Glen Lochy**—the " wearisome glen " some call it : a name to be remembered by walkers going eastward. Travellers westward have before them a grand and ever-changing view over the green strath below, the dark, blue-shadowed Cruachan beyond Dalmally contrasting well with the smoother hills to the left. Farther down, **Glen Orchy** comes in on the right (*see* p. 229). Far ahead the monument (to Duncan Ban McIntyre, the Gaelic poet) near Dalmally marks the northern end of Loch Awe.

Dalmally consists of a church, an hotel (with salmon fishing), a scattered handful of houses, and a post office. A much-worn stone in the roadway before the hotel is locally known as "Bruce's Chair." From Dalmally there are fine views of the deep, hollowed eastern flank of lofty Cruachan. Then we get a sudden view of **Loch Awe** with Kilchurn Castle ruins (p. 210) close at hand.

Beside the northern end of Loch Awe a small hamlet has gathered. (For Loch Awe, *see* p. 207.) For several miles the Oban road winds along the steep, wooded southern bank of Cruachan, the waters of the loch below on the left and on the right a succession of rills and falls tumbling down to the loch from the slopes above. The best of these are the **Falls of Cruachan,** seen framed through the railway arch about 4 miles west of Loch Awe Hotel. A mile or so farther west are the **Falls of Brander.** By this time the road has left the open loch-side and entered the narrowing steep-sided gorge, a fjord-like arm of the loch, known as the **Pass of Brander.** Where the loch ends the **Pass of Awe** begins, the River Awe rushing down the widening valley and providing good salmon fishing. The Pass of Awe was the scene of many a fierce fight between the MacNaughtons, the MacGregors and other rival clans, as numerous burial cairns attest. Robert Bruce and Sir James Douglas forced their way through the pass in 1308 after laying low their MacDougall opponents. Some way down, the road crosses the river by the Bridge of Awe.

The vast Loch Awe Hydro-electric Scheme includes a barrage in the Pass of Awe, a reservoir high up the Allt Cruachan and underground power station.

Cruachan is most easily ascended from the Bridge of Awe. From the east end of the bridge a track leads past the railway and then bears left, following the right bank of the Awe downstream. A short way beyond the railway, however, a path doubles back on the right and follows a fairly steep but obvious path eastward to the summit. Cruachan is one of the highest mountains in Argyllshire. It has two crests: the eastern (or Dalmally: *Cruachan Beann*) is 3,689 feet, the western, *Stob Dearg*, 3,611 feet. The connecting ridge is about three-quarters of a mile long and 3,400 feet above sea-level.

A more direct route to the eastern peak is from beside the Falls of Cruachan starting by the western bank of the Cruachan stream until a branch of the stream shows the way to a ridge on the left connecting a prominent shoulder with the main peak. When the ridge is scaled the main route lies to the right.

The two routes given above may be combined, of course; good walkers may strike eastward from the main summit along the main ridge by Drochaid Glas (3,312 feet) and Stob Diamh (3,272 feet), which is the middle peak of the three forming the "horseshoe," and descend by either of the other two peaks to the main road near the head of the loch. (*Youth Hostel*, ¼ mile west of Loch Awe *village*.)

The View.—From its position, no less than its altitude, Cruachan presents some of the finest and most extensive mountain views in Scotland. Compared with Ben Lomond it is a giant, and its outlook is correspondingly great. From the bold granite precipices of its sharp and rugged summit, which is pointed, we look down upon its red and furrowed sides into the upper part of Loch Etive, and over the magnificent group of mountains which, extending north and east, form one of the finest landscapes in the Highlands.

Westward the view includes the lower portion of Loch Etive, Dunstaffnage, and the mountains of Mull and Morvern; southward, a great portion of Loch Awe; toward the south-west, Lochs Nell and Feochan and the Paps of Jura. From the summit of the Taynuilt peak one may see, eastward, the Dalmally peak, Ben Lui, Ben Buie, Ben Ime, and Ben Lomond; towards the north-east, the upper portion of Loch Etive, the Glencoe heights, and Ben Nevis; southward, Loch Fyne and the heights in the Isle of Arran.

Below the Bridge of Awe the scenery becomes softer and the views widen, embracing Loch Etive and the "Braes abune Bonawe." On the far side of the river is Inverawe House, whence Argyll set out to plunder the "bonnie house of Airlie," and where, about 1756, Major Duncan Campbell had the tragic Ticonderoga Vision, which forms the subject of one of Sir Thomas Dick Lauder's *Tales of the Highlands*. **Taynuilt**, with hotels (*Taynuilt*, *Selma*, and others), church and a handful of cottages, is a good centre for walks and rides, and across the open strath is **Bonawe**, a quarrying hamlet at the mouth of the Awe.

The woody hillside behind the village is celebrated in the well-known song, ***The Braes abune Bonawe*:**

"When simmer days clead a' the braes
Wi' blossomed broom sae fine, lassie
At milkin' shiel we'll join the reel—
My flocks shall be a' thine, lassie.

Wilt thou go, my bonnie lassie?
Wilt thou go, my braw lassie?
Wilt thou go? say Aye or No!
To the braes abune Bonawe, lassie?"

Looking up the loch from Bonawe, on the right one sees lofty **Ben Cruachan** (p. 197). Far ahead rises the twin mountain **Buachaille Etive**, the "Shepherds of Etive." On the east shore of the loch, at its head, is **Ben Starav** (3,541 feet), while **Ben Trilleachan** (2,752 feet) is on the west.

Taynuilt is at the northern end of **Glen Nant** (p. 209), a popular route to Loch Awe at **Taychreggan.**

A few miles westward, at the hamlet of ***Ach-na-Cloich*,**

the Oban road approaches the shores of **Loch Etive** ; then as it rounds a bend there springs into view the iron bridge at Connel. Beyond the bridge are lovely distant views of the mountains of Morvern and Mull. **Connel** is an attractive little village with hotels (*Falls of Lora, Dunstaffnage*) and other accommodation for visitors, grand views, boating, fishing and limitless walks and excursions. A small boat runs up and down Loch Etive from Ach-na-Cloich, and the many grand steamer trips from Oban are easily joined. The former railway bridge across Loch Etire has been adapted for cars and walkers thus opening up the route to Ballachulish. St. Oran's church is built after the style of Iona Cathedral.

Just below the bridge are the **Falls of Lora,** less fall than rapids, for it is only at low tide that the water falls over the reef of rocks which here impedes the stream ; at low spring tide, however, the sight is impressive enough. The falls are frequently mentioned in the Ossianic poems—"The murmur of thy streams, O Lora ! brings back the memory of the past ; the sound of thy woods, Garmallar, is lovely in mine ear."

From Connel the road continues to skirt the winding loch, with grand views across the water ; it passes the village of Dunbeg and then bears inland at Dunstaffnage Bay (*see* p. 205). Shortly **Oban** is suddenly seen lying below on the left, with the beautiful Kerrera Sound and island beyond.

An alternative route to Oban, now re-surfaced, leaves the main road at Connel at the *Dunstaffnage Arms* and winds through Glencruitten Hills passing Loch Nell and Glencruitten golf course, entering Oban at the south end of the town.

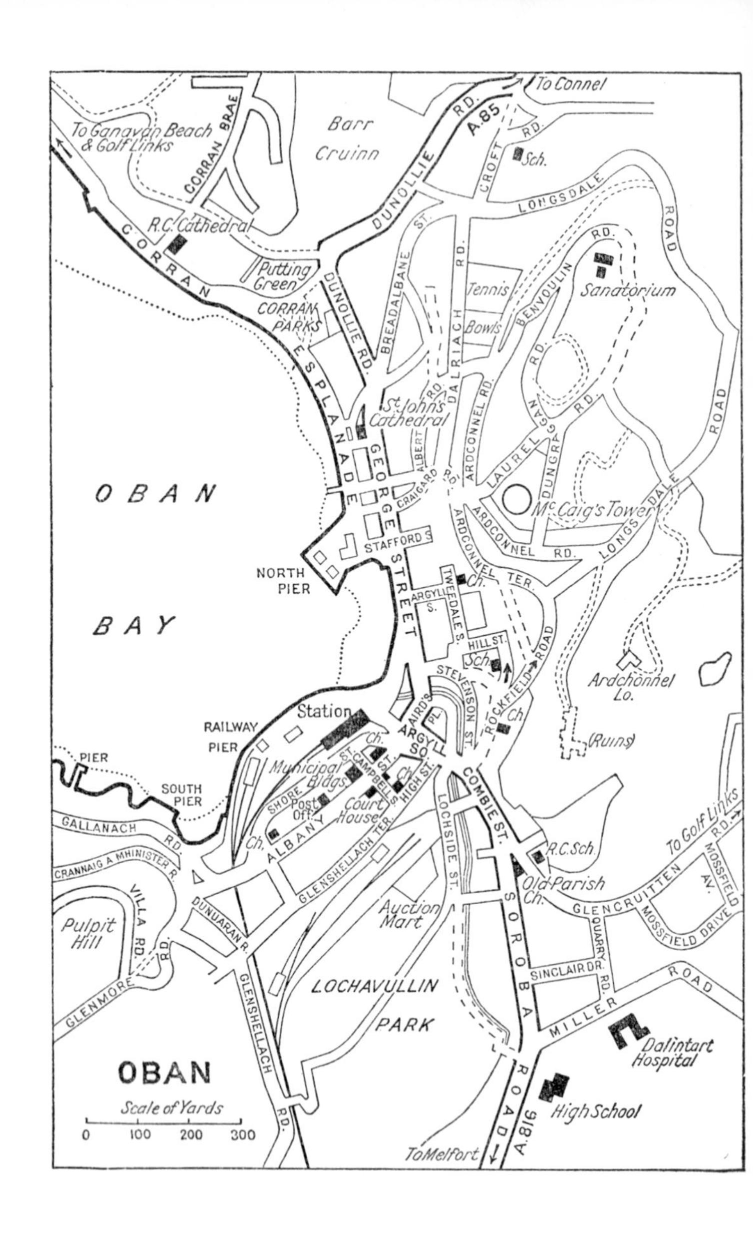
OBAN
Scale of Yards
0
100
200
300
OBAN BAY
To Ganavan Beach & Golf Links
CORRAN BRAE
Barr Cruinn
To Connel
DUNOLLIE RD.
A.85
CROFT RD.
Sch.
LONGSDALE ROAD
R.C. Cathedral
CORRAN
Putting Green
DUNOLLIE RD.
CORRAN PARKS
ESPLANADE
BREADALBANE ST.
DALRIACH RD.
Tennis
Bowls
BENVOULIN RD.
Sanatorium
St. John's Cathedral
ALBERT RD.
ARDCONNEL RD.
LAUREL RD.
DUNGALLAN RD.
GEORGE STREET
CRAIGARD RD.
Mc Caig's Tower
LONGSDALE
ARDCONNEL RD.
STAFFORD S.
NORTH PIER
ARDCONNEL TER.
TWEEDALE S.
Ch.
ARGYLL S.
HILL ST.
Sch.
ROCKFIELD ROAD
Ardchonnel Lo.
STEVENSON ST.
AIRD'S PL.
Station
RAILWAY PIER
ARGYLL SQ.
Ch
(Ruins)
PIER
Ch.
ST.
Municipal Bldgs
CAMPBELL S.
Ch.
SOUTH PIER
SHORE ST.
Post Off.
Court House
HIGH ST.
COMBIE ST.
LOCHSIDE ST.
GALLANACH RD.
Ch.
ALBANY ST.
GLENSHELLACH TER.
R.C. Sch.
To Golf Links
MOSSFIELD RD.
CRANNAIG A MHINISTER R.
Old Parish Ch.
GLENCRUITTEN
MOSSFIELD AV.
VILLA RD.
DUNUARAN R.
Auction Mart
SOROBA
MOSSFIELD DRIVE
Pulpit Hill
QUARRY RD.
RD.
SINCLAIR DR.
ROAD
GLENMORE
GLENSHELLACH RD.
LOCHAVULLIN PARK
MILLER
Dalintart Hospital
ROAD
High School
A.816
To Melfort

OBAN.

Access.—From Glasgow *viâ* Loch Lomond, *see* p. 191; *viâ* Inveraray, p. 174; from Perth and Killin, *see* pp. 280–4, etc.

By Rail: Oban is the western terminus of the line from Glasgow *viâ* Helensburgh and Crianlarich. In summer observation cars are attached to certain trains, (supplementary fares).

Distances.—*By Road.*—Ardrishaig, 39 m.; Ballachulish, 36 m.; Edinburgh (*viâ* Callander and Crianlarich), 124 m.; Fort William, *viâ* coast and Ballachulish Ferry, 48 m., *viâ* Kinlochleven 68 m., *viâ* Dalmally, Bridge of Orchy and Glencoe, 80 m.; Glasgow, *viâ* Tarbet, Arrochar and Inveraray, 100 m., *viâ* Tarbet and Crianlarich, 93½ m.; Loch Awe Pier, 22 m.; Taychreggan, 20 m.

Early Closing.—Thursday.

Fishing.—Good salmon and sea-fishing and trout abound in neighbouring hill lochs.

Golf.—Pitch and putt at Ganavan, adjoining Bathing Beach, and small 6-hole course.

Glencruitten course, half-mile from Oban Railway Station. 18 holes. Excellent club-house.

Hotels.—*Park* (85 rooms), *Alexandra* (59 rooms), *Great Western* (75 rooms), *Caledonian* (70 rooms), *King's Arms* (32 rooms), *Atholl* (10 rooms), *Columba* (39 rooms), *Achnamara* (12 rooms), *Argyll* (37 rooms), *Regent* (38 rooms *Royal* (131 rooms), *Crown*, *Marine* (39 rooms), and many others.

Population.—7,000.

Post Office.—Albany Street. Sub-offices on Esplanade and Soroba Road.

Sports.—Bathing, boating (for yachting, *see* p. 201), bowls, fishing, golf, tennis Indoor entertainments include cinema and regular concerts ,dances, etc.

Youth Hostel.—Silver Jubilee Hostel ,Esplanade.

OBAN occupies a natural amphitheatre facing a sheltered bay across the mouth of which is stretched the island of Kerrera. It is little more than a century old—a not unpleasing medley of large modern buildings of no particular style jostling smaller shops and houses which contrive to suggest a greater antiquity than is strictly justifiable. On the slopes behind the town are some splendidly situated residences; the skyline is broken by an immense circular stone tower which a local banker, McCaig, erected to his own memory late last century. Towards the southern end of the town are the station and the Railway Pier, the Post Office, the Municipal Buildings and the banks; running northwards through the town is **George Street**, the principal business thoroughfare, and parallel to that the **Esplanade** curves round the bay and is continued past Dunollie Castle to **Ganavan,** where is Oban's bathing beach.

The climate is mild, equable and healthy.

Oban is very well provided with hotels and boarding-houses of all kinds, has golf links, tennis courts, bowling and putting greens, etc., and it is a splendid centre from which to tour the Western Highlands, but its interests on the water are even greater. Standing on the Pier, one has a rare sense of being at the edge of beyond, and even those unable to indulge in any of the steamer trips can derive endless enjoyment from the contemplation of the arrival and departure of the steamers which, on weekdays, maintain communication with the islands whose shadowy forms can be discerned far to the westward. Business-like boats most of them are, carrying mails, fish, vegetables and other stores as well as passengers and their cars and bicycles ; and the manner in which the cargo is swung ashore and dealt with must always appeal to town-folk to whom the handling of steamers often appears a somewhat tedious affair. The steamer services start from the North Pier, whilst the South Pier is used principally by fishing vessels. Fish auction sales take place at the South Pier. Farther west is the Lighthouse Pier.

The **Scottish Episcopal Cathedral of St. John the Divine** is in George Street. An appeal fund is seeking money to enable the building to be completed. The Free High Church, in Rockfield Road, behind Argyll Square, was designed by Augustus Pugin and won Ruskin's praise.

On the Esplanade is the **Roman Catholic Cathedral,** a noteworthy granite building designed by Sir Giles Scott.

Oban Bay, being remarkably safe through the protection afforded by the Island of Kerrera, is a favourite yachting station, and there is a Sub-Aqua club.

It is during the Yachting Week early in August that the bay presents its busiest and gayest aspect, while in late August is held the Argyllshire Highland Gathering, to which thousands flock. Throughout the season, however, Oban is never dull and between excursions delightful hours can be spent in many satisfying pursuits.

The best short excursion from Oban is along the **Corran Esplanade,** with its charmingly placed hotels and boarding-houses, and the continuing road to Ganavan Sands and the Golf Links, 2 miles of continual interest, either ashore or across the water: the sea-views at sunset are especially fine. On the outskirts of the town the road comes in sight of **Dunollie Castle,** picturesquely surmounting a little headland; and on the right is a huge upright pillar of conglomerate known as the **Dog Stone,** or *clach-a-choin*, from the tradition that Fingal (*see* p. 213), the great hero of Gaelic mythology, used it as a stake to which he tied his great dog Bran. Geologists attribute the stone and its abrasions to the action of the sea in remote ages when the coast was exposed to the open ocean.

Dunollie Castle (*not now open to the public*).—The principal part is the donjon or keep; but fragments of other buildings, overgrown with ivy, attest that it has been a place of importance. The keep probably formed one side of a courtyard, the entrance being by a steep ascent from the neck of the isthmus, formerly cut across by a moat, and defended, doubtless, by outworks and a drawbridge. Beneath the Castle stands the modern mansion of the Chief of the Clan MacDougall.

There is no authentic record of the foundation of Dunollie Castle. The north curtain wall probably dates as far back as the twelfth century, the traditional date being *circa* 1150. The castle was the principal seat of the MacDougalls, Lords of Lorn. Their descendant, MacDougall of MacDougall, Chief of the Clan MacDougall, is still in possession. The estate was forfeited in 1715, as its possessor had joined the Old Chevalier, James Francis Stuart, but it was restored to the family for their loyalty in 1745. The word Lorn (or Lorne), by the way, is said to be derived from Loarn Mor, the name of one of the leaders of the Scots when they passed from Ireland to Argyll. The territory to which his name became attached was his share of the spoil.

The MacDougall of Bruce's time married a daughter of the Red Comyn, whom Bruce slew in the precincts of St. Michael's Church at Dumfries. As readers of the *Lord of the Isles* know, he was Bruce's mortal enemy, and sought by every means vengeance for the death of his father-in-law. In 1306 he defeated Bruce at Dalree (near Tyndrum), and there secured—

> "The brooch of burning gold
> That clasps the chieftain's mantle-fold,
> Wrought and chased with rare device,
> Studded fair with gems of price."

For generations the brooch was an heirloom of the family. It fell into the hands of Campbell of Bragleen when Gylen Castle, on the Island of Kerrera, was sacked and burnt in 1647, and it was not restored to the MacDougalls till 1826. It is *not* on view to the public.

At **Ganavan** (1½ miles farther) are putting greens and a bathing beach, and a very popular caravan ground, a pavilion with tea-room, etc. There is a bus service between Ganavan and Oban.

Other short walks from Oban include **Glencruitten**, east of the town and reached by a road bearing to the left at the end of Combie Street, which starts at Argyll Square; **Glenshellach**, to the south-west, with grand views and preserving in Soroba Lodge associations with Robert Buchanan (1841–1901), poet and novelist; and **Pulpit Hill**, also to the south-west, the finest of Oban viewpoints (*indicator*). The direct route from Argyll Square is along Albany Street; cross the railway and take footpath in front of Alma Crescent. Another pleasant walk, especially at evening, is along the Gallanach road, looking over the water to Kerrera, to which ferries cross from beyond Kilbowie, as well as from Oban Harbour.

The Island of **Kerrera** (the accent is on the first syllable) is about 4 miles long and 2 broad. From its uplands there are grand views of sea and mountain.

Near the south end of the island is the remnant of **Gylen Castle**, erected in 1587 as a stronghold of the MacDougalls of Lorn, who kept here the brooch taken from Bruce at Dalree (*see* p. 202). The MacDougalls holding the castle for the King in the civil wars of the seventeenth century, it was destroyed by a detachment of Leslie's army.

The island possesses historical interest from the fact that Alexander II died on it in 1249, while advancing against the Western Islanders who still acknowledged the King of Norway as their master. A hut was prepared for him in a field on Horseshoe Bay still known as Dalrigh (the king's field), and his body was removed thence to Melrose Abbey for burial. In "The King's Field" is a spring bearing the name of the **King's Well**. Tradition says that Alexander drank of its waters.

In Horseshoe Bay King Haakon of Norway, with his fleet of galleys, took shelter on his way to overwhelming defeat at Largs (1263), at the hands of the Scottish King, Alexander III, who thereby added to his kingdom the Western Isles, held for centuries by the Norsemen.

At the north end of the island is an obelisk in memory of David Hutcheson, MacBrayne's predecessor.

Dunstaffnage Castle (*at present closed for restoration*) is reached by road *viâ* the new village of Dunbeg on Dunstaffnage Bay, 3 or 4 miles from Oban on the road to Connel. Bus service to the point where a track leads to the Castle.

The ruin stands on a promontory, almost an island, at the entrance from Loch Linnhe into Loch Etive. It was built in the thirteenth century on a natural platform of rock. The entrance is at the south-east corner, the restored gatehouse being reached by a comparatively modern stone staircase. The walls in parts are 9 feet thick. Not far from the Castle are the remains of a small chapel where some of the early Scottish kings are said to have been buried. It is now the burial-place of the Campbells of Dunstaffnage (hereditary Captains of the Castle).

Dunstaffnage was a strong place of the Dalriadic Scots during part of the period from the fifth till the middle of the ninth century, when Scone became the capital of the united Picts and Scots.

Its claim to have been their capital is very doubtful, but it boasts that it was one of the places which has held the famous *Stone of Destiny*, on which for centuries the Kings of Scots were crowned. The fabled stone is said to have been Jacob's pillow on the plains of Luz (Genesis xxviii. 11). It was brought from Ireland first to Iona and then to Dunstaffnage, where it served as Coronation Stone of the Scottish kings until taken to Scone about 850. It was in 1296 removed by Edward I to Westminster Abbey, which led later, on the accession (1603) of James VI of Scotland as James I of England, to the fulfilment of the ancient prophecy:

> "If Fates go right, where'er this stone is found,
> The Scots shall monarchs of that realm be crowned."

About the twelfth century Dunstaffnage fell into the hands of the Lords of Lorn, on whom Bruce had his revenge (for the loss of his brooch at the battle of Dalree, *see* p. 202), when he captured the Castle after smiting the MacDougall clan in the Pass of Brander (1308). The Campbells were then put in charge of it, and to this day the Castle is Crown property, the Duke of Argyll, as Chief of the Clan Campbell, being its "Hereditary Keeper" and the Campbells of Dunstaffnage "Hereditary Captains."

The Castle was garrisoned by Hanoverians during the rebellions of 1715 and 1745. In 1746 it held for ten days Flora Macdonald, while on her way to London as a State prisoner for having, after the battle of Culloden, planned and aided the escape of Prince Charles, whom she conducted to Skye disguised as her tall Irish maid, Betty Burke. Dunstaffnage has not been used as a residence since 1810, when a great fire made it a ruin.

EXCURSIONS FROM OBAN.

OBAN is the principal port on the West Coast of the Highlands and offers unrivalled facilities for steamer trips. It is also a good centre for rail and road excursions.

LOCH AWE.

Access.—A good road runs from end to end of Loch Awe, and the ends of the loch are also in touch with the two main routes between Oban and south and east Scotland; the loch can therefore be visited *en route* to or from Oban, Fort William, etc., or it may form part of a circular trip either from Oban or elsewhere.

The route from Glasgow *viâ* Ardrishaig to Ford, at the south end of the loch, has been described on pp. 171–82.

Hotels along the Loch.—*Loch Awe* (70 rooms), near the pier at the northern end of the loch.

Portsonachan (23 rooms), on the east side, about one-fourth of the way down.

Taychreggan (22 rooms) on the west side, opposite Portsonachan.

Ford Hotel (15 rooms), quarter of a mile from Ford Pier, at the southern end.

Dalmally Hotel, about a mile from north-east end of the loch.

Fishing.—The loch abounds in salmon, trout, perch and pike; the sport is good and the landlords of the hotels on the Loch shores have boats available for their guests. The Loche Awe Hotel has salmon fishing in River Awe. The River Orchy provides excellent salmon fishing. The Dalmally, Tyndrum, Bridge at Orchy and Inveroran hotels all have preserves for the use of guests.

Oban to Loch Awe by the Melfort Route.

The Oban–Ardrishaig motors pass to the west of Ford, near the south end of Loch Awe.

The road route leaves Oban by Combie Street and Soroba Road, with a view of Pulpit Hill on the right; then it climbs in among broken little green hills.

The highest point is reached about 2½ miles from Oban. On the right a branch road turns off to **Kilbride**, a mile to the south-west, with a ruined church, an old burial-ground, and a finely carved Celtic cross dating from 1516.

From just beyond the third milestone, Ben Lui may be seen through the trees. Then comes a view of a portion of **Loch Feochan**, an arm of the sea terminating in a lovely glen, watered by a boisterous mountain stream.

Just beyond the new church of Kilmore and Kilbride a road on the left leads back to **Loch Nell** (*Loch of the Swans*). It is a picturesque sheet of fresh water, 2 miles long and about half a mile wide. The best view is obtained from the **Serpent Mound**, on the western side, about a quarter of a mile from the spot at which the lake is reached, the panorama from this point including the double-peaked Cruachan. The mound is formed of boulders and is supposed to be a relic of serpent worship. It is about 80 yards in length, and in the form of an elongated letter S. An exploration of the head of the " serpent " yielded a flint instrument and charcoal.

About a hundred yards south of the mound is a cromlech, of which only the top stone is visible from a distance. According to local tradition, it marks the grave of the Ossianic hero, Cuchullin.

The walk back to Oban can be varied, without being lengthened, by continuing up the road past the loch for a couple of miles to the Glencruitten road.

Hence to the turning for Ford, opposite the ruins of Carnassarie, 28 miles from Oban, the route is described on page 182.

Carnassarie Castle was built about the middle of the sixteenth century, and burned as a Campbell possession during the Earl of Argyll's rebellion in 1685. It was the seat of John Carswell, last Bishop of the Isles and Abbot of Iona, and is now cared for by the Department of the Environment (*always open*).

Carswell received his preferment that he might transfer the temporalities of the bishopric to the Earl of Argyll, whose chaplain he had been. He is remembered yet in Gaelic satires and proverbs as a type of niggardliness and rapacity. But it must also be recorded that he was the author of the first book printed in Gaelic, a translation of Knox's " Liturgy " in 1567.

Here the road to Loch Awe leaves the Oban–Ardrishaig highway and enters the **Pass of Craigenterive.**

Dog's Head Loch, a small sheet of water about 2 miles on, is held to justify its name by its appearance when seen from the neighbouring hills. Then we come to a pretty reed-fringed lake known as **Loch Ederline,** and shortly afterwards to **Ford.** For the road up the eastern side of Loch Awe cross the bridge opposite the hotel ; for the Pier keep straight on for another three-quarters of a mile. The road continues along the western shore of the loch to join the Taynuilt road at Kilchrenan.

LOCH AWE,

one of the largest and most beautiful lochs of Scotland, is 23 miles in length, with a maximum depth of 307 feet and a breadth not exceeding $\frac{3}{4}$ mile. It is surrounded by wooded mountains, and, like so many of the Scottish lochs, is studded with islands, generally beautifully tufted with trees, and some large enough to be pastured.

Unlike most lochs, its tamest part is at the head, a peculiarity geologists attribute to the fact that originally its outflow was at the south, its surplus waters being conveyed into the Sound of Jura, instead of reaching Loch Etive by means of the Awe river, as they do at present.

The district around the north end of the loch originally formed part of the extensive tract possessed by the numerous and powerful clan, Gregor; but in the fifteenth century the Campbells obtained a footing, and the shores and islands of the loch, and the recesses of the surrounding mountains and glens, were for generations their retreat in time of danger.

Kilneuair Church, near Ford, is mentioned in the Argyll charters as far back as 1394. After it ceased to be used as a place of worship, tradition says it was the haunt, at night, of spirits undergoing the torments of purgatory; and it is related that—

> "A tailor who was sceptical on the subject of apparitions ventured to bet that he would make a pair of trews within the walls of the church during the midnight hours. He went with his torch bravely to redeem his pledge; but he had not sewn much when a sepulchral voice directed his attention to a hand of gigantic size arising from one of the graves in the area of the church, and he heard the words, 'Seest thou this huge, hoary hand, tailor?' 'I see that, but will sew this,' said the tailor. The voice again uttered, 'Seest thou this large, grey head, tailor?' 'I see that, but will sew this,' said the tailor. Thus the conversation proceeded until all the members of the skeleton appeared. Then the tailor fled; and it was time, for the bony hand that was stretched out to seize him struck and left its impression on the wall."

Fincharn Castle, near the church, was once a stronghold of the Macdonalds. Passing pretty islets we come, 8 miles from Ford, to **Portinisherrich**, on the eastern shore. Visitors from across the Atlantic will be interested in "New York," on the western shore opposite Portinisherrich. About half a mile north are Dalavich Church, on the western shore, and, near the eastern bank, the islet of **Innis Chonnel**, on which are the ivy-coloured ruins of the **Castle of Ardchonnell**, once the chief seat of the Campbells. Their slogan, or war-cry—"It's a far cry to Lochow," i.e. Loch Awe—with which they derided their foes, is said to have indicated the impossibility of reaching them in their distant fastnesses. A legend connects it with a remark of Campbell of Inverliver, on carrying away (1499) the red-haired little Muriel, heiress of Cawdor, in distant Nairnshire, to the protection of his chief here. "Suppose she should die ?" said one of his men. Inverliver laughed and replied, "Muriel of Cawdor will never die as long as there is a red-haired lassie on the shores of Lochow."

The **Falls of Blairgour,** about 2 miles north of Portinnisherrich, are about 90 feet in height.

On the west side of the loch a good road from Ford continues through Dalavich, a forestry village, to Avich and thence to Kilchrenan. For the first 9 miles it is bordered on the west by the **Inverliever Estate,** maintained by the Government as a State Forest. Beyond it the little river *Avich* comes down to the loch from **Loch Avich,** Ossian's Loch Launa, a picturesque sheet (over 3 miles long) surrounded by scenes of Highland grandeur, and with a level 200 feet above that of Loch Awe. Immediately by the Avich is a hill road leading off to the west and running along the northern shore of Loch Avich and on to Kilmelfort (p. 182).

North of Avich the loch side road passes through Inverinan and then comes **Taychreggan,** facing, on the opposite bank, **Portsonachan.** The meaning of these formidable names is respectively "the house on a little rock," and "the port by the mound in the little field."

Taychreggan is near the head of **Glen Nant,** a favourite route over from Taynuilt (p. 199).

A little over a mile from the hotel at Taychreggan is the old graveyard of **Kilchrenan** ("the church on the little craig"), containing a massive granite monument erected by a Duke of Argyll in memory of his ancestor, Cailean Mor ("Great Colin")—whose descendants were the Macallum Mores of Sir Walter Scott—to whom the Campbells owe the foundation of their greatness. He was the hero of many of the clan's forays; and it was while returning from one in 1294 that he was slain by an arrow shot by an enemy lying in ambush on the Streng of Lorn, 8 miles from Kilchrenan, the exact spot where the chief fell being marked by a large cairn.

Beyond Portsonachan (*hotel*) and Ardbrecknish the loch widens. Soon we pass the **Priests' Isle,** so called from a tradition that it was the residence of a colony of priests. Two miles farther the loch attains its greatest width, and the view becomes magnificent.

From Cladich, on the eastern shore, a road runs through Glen Aray to Inveraray (*see* p. 180).

Inishail, "the isle of repose," a green spot, and one of the most interesting of the many islands on the loch, was at one time the site of a Cistercian nunnery, and was for ages the burial-ground of the various clans who held sway in this part of Argyllshire. On the southern part of the island is the ruin of a chapel. From near this point there are good views on the left of the **Pass of Brander** (*see* p. 197), which stretches between the high hills, and encloses a narrow arm of the loch leading to its outlet into the River Awe.

North of Inishail are a number of smaller islands, of which the first is **Eilean Fraoch**, named, according to a Celtic tradition, after a gallant knight, the lover of the fair Gealchean.

Fraoch means simply "heath," but here is the story. The girl's mother, Mai, also loved the hero, and that she might be the successful rival of her daughter she bade Fraoch fetch from the island the apples of immortal youth which were under the protection of a dragon. Desirous of pleasing her for her daughter's sake, Fraoch undertook the quest. He slew the dragon but died of the wounds he received, while Mai was poisoned by eating the fruit. In 1267 Alexander III gave the island to Sir Gilbert MacNaughton, on condition that he would entertain the king of Scotland should he ever visit that part of the country; and the head of the family in 1745 accordingly made preparations for receiving Prince Charles Edward in case he passed that way when he landed at Glenfinnan. Only fragments of the castle walls remain.

The monument prominent on a height on the right commemorates Duncan Ban McIntyre (1724–1812), the Highland bard.

On a peninsula at the foot of the loch, near Loch Awe village, is the ruin of **Kilchurn** (*kil-hoorn*) **Castle**.

The oldest portion is the tower, built in 1440 by Sir Colin Campbell, ancestor of the Breadalbane family. Sir Colin soon after left for a crusade in the Holy Land. When he had been seven years from home and his lady had heard nothing of him, a report reached the castle that he was slain in battle; and his supposed widow in due time accepted another suitor, MacCorquodale. The wedding-day was fixed, but on its morning the missing lord entered the castle in disguise. Amid the festivities preceding the celebration of the nuptials, he disclosed himself, to the great delight of his lady and his followers. (A similar story is told in Scott's *The Betrothed*, and as there were no crusaders about the year 1440 the story must be regarded as apocryphal.) The castle was greatly enlarged in 1693, and it continued to be a residence of the family till 1740. It owes its ruinous condition to an economical steward who took out the roof timber for use in the castle that was being built at Balloch, or at Taymouth. The ruin shows a square tower surrounded by high walls, with battlements and round turrets at the angles.

TO STAFFA AND IONA.

Steamer leaves about 9 a.m. and is due at Oban again about 6 p.m.

The boats for landing at Iona are large, each capable of carrying from forty to seventy passengers. At Iona is a concrete jetty for the landing of passengers. The steamers go close inshore at Staffa to give passengers a good view of Fingal's Cave.

The voyage covers about 120 miles.

This excursion, the most popular sea trip from Oban, includes the circuit of the Island of Mull. The service runs each weekday during summer.

For those not wishing to make the full steamer round, a boat (car ferry) leaves Oban daily for Craignure. Bus is then taken to Fionphort for the western end of Ross of Mull and then ferry to Iona.

Crossing Loch Linnhe towards the east shore of **Mull**, the steamer makes for **Lismore Lighthouse**. "Lismore" is generally translated the "Great Garden," but in ancient Gaelic *lis* meant "a fort," not (as now) a "garden"; and it is argued that the island took its name, not from its fertile soil, but from the fortified monastery of Moluag, a Pictish saint, who, about the year 560, established his chief cell here. His staff was held to be the Duke of Argyll's title for the possession of certain lands. Before reaching the island the summit of Ben Nevis may be seen far up Loch Linnhe. Nearly opposite the lighthouse is the **Lady Rock**, covered by the sea at high tide.

The rock owes its name to the tradition that one of the Macleans of Duart placed upon it his wife, a daughter of the Earl of Argyll. She was rescued from her perilous situation by fishermen whom her cries attracted, and then proceeded to her father's castle at Inveraray. Some days later she was followed by her husband, in deep mourning. Having sorrowfully told his father-in-law of the mysterious disappearance of his wife, he was surprised to see the door open and the lady present herself before him. He was allowed to leave the castle in safety, but some years afterwards he was slain in Edinburgh by his brother-in-law, Campbell of Calder.

Duart Castle, the seat of the chief of the Macleans, may be seen on the nearest prominent point of Mull.

A castellated tower near the point is a memorial of William Black the novelist (1841–98). The site is singularly appropriate, being in the vicinity of the closing scene of one of his most powerful stories, *Macleod of Dare*.

The view from the steamer at this point is one of the finest imaginable. In front are the hills of Kingairloch, Morvern, Ardnamurchan and Mull. On looking backward, Cruachan can be seen towering above the Argyllshire hills. Eastward are Ben Nevis, the Peaks of Glencoe, and Loch

Linnhe, and southward are the Paps of Jura and the Isle of Colonsay.

Having passed Duart Castle, we are in **The Sound of Mull,** a strait 2 miles wide and nearly 20 miles long, separating the island of Mull from Morvern on the mainland. From **Craignure,** the steamer passes over to the Morvern shore, where, on a projecting rocky site, is the shell of the feudal keep of **Ardtornish,** one of the principal strongholds of the Lords of the Isles—a line of independent or semi-independent chiefs who governed the Western Isles (*see* p. 30).

Westward of Ardtornish the steamer passes the mouth of **Loch Aline,** "the beautiful loch," its steep sides picturesquely wooded. At its head is **Kinlochaline Tower,** which tradition says was built by an Amazon of the Clan McInnes, who paid the architect with its bulk in butter. It is national property and is open to inspection (key at neighbouring cottage).

Some 5 miles west from Lochaline Pier is the Manse of *Fiunary*, the home of three generations of clerical Macleods. It was the original of Norman Macleod's *Manse in the Highlands*, and forms the subject of one of the finest of Gaelic songs, *Farewell to Fiunary*, composed by the father of Norman Macleod on becoming parish minister of Campbeltown.

Across the Sound is **Salen** (p.220). We next pass the ruin of **Aros Castle,** once a residence of the Lords of the Isles, and get a fine view of the saddle-shaped mountains, Ben Talaidh (or Talla) and Ben More (3,169 feet), the highest point of Mull. Steaming by Drimnin, we glide into the harbour of **Tobermory** (p. 221), the chief town in the island.

Beyond Tobermory **Loch Sunart,** striking off from the north end of the Sound of Mull, pierces into North Argyll for a distance of 20 miles and separates classic Morvern from the district to the north of Loch Sunart which is called **Ardnamurchan** from the name given to its extremity ("the cape of the great seas"), the most westerly point on the mainland of Britain—being, indeed, 20 miles west of the meridian of Land's End.

After leaving Tobermory we pass on the Mull side *Bloody Bay*, the scene of a sea-fight between the Macleods and the Macleans in the fifteenth century. On the Ardnamurchan shore just opposite is **Kilchoan** (*hotel*) and on its right on the coast the ruins of **Mingary Castle**, where James IV held a court in 1495 and received the submission of the island chiefs. Then, rounding **Ardmore Point**, we are on the open waters of the Atlantic.

Far away to the north are visible the islands of **Canna, Rhum, Eigg** (*egg*), and **Muck** (*see* pp. 236–7), and westward are **Coll and Tiree.** Coll and Tiree are paradises of the wild-fowler. Both are included in the " Inner Islands " service from Oban ; Tiree can be reached by air from Glasgow. They repay a visit (*hotels*).

Turning southward, we pass near the **Treshnish Isles**, a rocky ridge extending for 5 miles in a north-easterly direction. The best known is the Dutchman's Cap, at the south of the group. On the left we pass the supposed scene of Campbell's poem, *Lord Ullin's Daughter*, for Loch na Keal in Mull is the " dark Loch Gyle " and at its entrance is " Ulva's Isle."

> " Now who be ye would cross Loch Gyle,
> This dark and stormy water ?
> Oh, I'm the chief of Ulva's Isle,
> And this Lord Ullin's daughter."

Loch Tuath separates Ulva from Mull and is connected with **Loch na Keal**, which nearly bisects the island of Mull, there being only 4 miles between its head and Salen Pier. Lying so close to Ulva as to appear part of it when viewed from the deck of the steamer, is the smaller and less lofty island of **Gometra.**

Ulva and Gometra rise respectively to a height of 1,025 and 503 feet, and by some are considered as much worthy of admiration as the Giant's Causeway in Ireland.

Southward of Ulva and Gometra, **Little Colonsay** is passed. Beyond it and nearer Mull is **Inch Kenneth**, a small green islet on which Dr. Johnson and Boswell spent what the Doctor called the most agreeable Sunday he ever passed, at the cottage of Sir Allan MacLean and his two daughters.

Due west of Inch Kenneth, 6 or 7 miles, is—

STAFFA,

" the isle of staves or columns." It is roughly oval in shape and about 2 miles in circumference and uninhabited. Its length is a mile ; its breadth a quarter of a mile. On the south its cliffs rise to a height of 135 feet.

The chief object of interest is **Fingal's Cave**, so named from

Fion-na-Gael (Fingal), the great Gaelic hero, whose achievements have been made familiar by the *Fingal* of Macpherson. It is entered by a majestic arch, domed over, and resting on basaltic pillars. The roof rises 60 feet above high-water mark, and the cave penetrates 227 feet into the isle, its width gradually decreasing from 42 feet at the mouth to about 20 feet at its far end. It is very remarkable that this stupendous basaltic grotto remained unknown to the outer world until 1772, when it was visited by Sir Joseph Banks, who, on his way to Iceland, was driven into the Sound of Mull, and there heard from the inhabitants of the great natural wonder.

The Gaelic name of Fingal's cave—Uaimh Binn—means the "musical cave," and has reference to the harmonies called forth by the billows.

Under suitable conditions of wind and tide boats have been rowed to the extremity of the cave. The end of the cave can be reached by walking along the tops of the broken columns, though the way is now very dangerous for pedestrians.

Terminating in a long projecting point at the eastern side of the great cave is the **Causeway**, also formed of columns. The pillars are for the most part hexagonal, some few are pentagonal, and others have seven, eight, and even nine sides. There is said to be only one square stone on the island—the Corner Stone, as it is called.

The Causeway affords a fine view of the **Bending Pillars**, which present the appearance of being made crooked by the immense weight they support. Half-way along the Causeway is **Fingal's Chair**, a rocky throne in which one has only to sit and form three wishes to have them fulfilled!

Separated from the Causeway by a narrow channel is **Buachaille**, or the Herdsman, a conical pile of columns rising to the height of 30 feet and forming the first of the series of pillars known as the **Colonnade.**

A staircase at the end of the Causeway gives access to the top of the cliffs, from which is obtained the best view of the **Clam Shell or Scallop Cave.** This cannot be entered either by boat or on foot. It is 130 feet long by 8 broad and 30 high. On one side are basaltic pillars bent like the ribs of a ship; on the other are ends of columns protruding and honeycombed.

A little to the west of Fingal's Cave is the **Boat Cave,** which can be entered only by sea—hence its name. It is a long opening resembling the gallery of a mine, about 16 feet in height, 12 in breadth, and 150 in length. The columns which overhang it, and those in its neighbourhood, are the longest in the island.

The most notable of the many other caves in the island is the **Cormorants' or Scarts' Cave,** also called **Mackinnon's Cave,** the westernmost of three opening into the south-western face of the cliffs. It is easy of access by a small boat. From the entrance nearly to the end the height is 50 feet and the breadth 48. The cave is 224 feet long, and terminates in a gravelly beach, where a boat may be drawn up. As it is excavated in the lowest stratum, the interior is without ornament. The gloom is so deep in some of its recesses that the movement of the oar excites the phosphorescent gleam of the floating medusæ.

There are the remains of what is believed to have been an ancient Chapel on the island, which for over a century has been uninhabited, the only sounds heard in its solitudes being the cries of the sea-birds.

South of Loch Scridain is the long promontory known as the **Ross of Mull,** introduced in Stevenson's *Kidnapped.* It is separated from Iona by the Sound of Iona, less than a mile wide (ferry from Fionphort).

After a voyage of 6 miles from Staffa, lasting a little over half an hour, we reach the sacred island of—

IONA.

Access.—*See* p. 211.
Hotels.—*St. Columba* (*unl.*) (27 rooms); *Argyll* (*unl.*) (8 rooms); *Traighmhor* (4 rooms).

Iona was anciently known as I-Chaluim-Chille (that is to say, "the island of the cell of Columba"). The early name was simply Hy. "Iona" is an adjective form of this. *Iona Insula* means "The island of Hy." But the earliest spelling is Ioua, or simply I, the "island."

Iona, which belongs to the Duke of Argyll, is 3 miles long by one and a half wide. Its shores are marked by low headlands and small bays; the only landing-place is a concrete jetty. Wordsworth, who wrote three sonnets on Iona, thus alludes to the children's share in a traffic originating in the practice of pilgrims carrying away relics or charms:

> "How sad a welcome! to each voyager
> Some ragged child holds up for sale a store
> Of wave-worn pebbles; pleading on the shore
> Where once came Monk and Nun with gentle stir,
> Blessings to give, news ask or suit prefer."

The island first became celebrated through St. Columba crossing over to it from Ireland with twelve companions in the year 563, and founding a monastery from which missionaries went forth to spread the doctrines of Christianity over the adjacent mainland. Iona was afterwards famous as the burial-place of the kings and princes of Scotland, who were influenced in their choice not only by its supposed sanctity, but also by a desire of preserving their remains from the fate awaiting those buried in less favoured spots; for it was foretold that—

"Seven years before that awful day,
When time shall be no more,
A watery deluge will o'er-sweep
Hibernia's mossy shore;
The green-clad Islay, too, shall sink,
While, with the great and good,
Columba's happy isle shall rear
Her towers above the flood."

While all this has yet to be accomplished, most literally and completely has been fulfilled the prophecy of Columba: "This place (Iona), small and mean as it appears, shall be honoured not only by the kings of the Scots and their people, but by the rulers of strange nations, and those subject to them. By the holy men also of other churches it shall be held in reverence."

The monastery erected by Columba was repeatedly destroyed by Norse invaders, and restored again (as by Queen Margaret, late in the eleventh century). About 1200 it became a Benedictine house. Of a nunnery founded at the same time there remain the chancel, nave, and portions of the vaulted roof of the Chapel, a building of Norman architecture, supposed to have been built in the early part of the thirteenth century. The charter of the nunnery is one of the treasures of the Vatican. The ruin measures 60 feet by 20, and contains many tombs, the most notable being that of the last prioress, Anna, who died in 1543. West of the nunnery is the Street of the Dead, leading from the Martyrs' Bay to Reilig Oran (St. Oran's Cemetery), passing the Parish Church, and Manse, and **McLean's Cross**, 11 feet high. It dates from the fifteenth century.

Reilig Oran, "the Westminster Abbey of Scotland," has claims to be the oldest Christian burial-place in Scotland. In it is "gathered together perhaps the most extensive holy alliance or congress of European sovereigns." It is said to contain the graves of forty-eight Scottish, two Irish, one French, and two Norwegian kings, and other powerful chieftains and ecclesiastics, but discrepancies occur as to the number.

According to tradition, the tombs were arranged in nine rows or "ridges," but these can scarcely be distinguished, owing to the levelling influences of time. The kings, it is recorded, were buried in three tombs in the form of small chapels, and were in the third row. The tombs have long since been swept away.

Among monarchs buried at Iona was Macbeth, who

Loch Brittle
Rudh' an Dunain
Soay Sound
Loch Scavaig
Soay
Strathaird Ho.
Kilmarie Lo.
Elgol
Loch Slapin
Loch Eishort
Dunscaith Cas.
Ord
Isleornsay
Isle Ornsay
Tokavaig
Teanga
Knock Cas.
Kilmore
Tarskavaig
Strathaird Pt.
Cuillin Sound
Ostaig Ho.
Armadale Cas.
Ardvasar
Calligarry
Tormore
Caradal
Aird of Sleat
Point of Sleat
Port Eachaggh
Sound of Sleat
Sandaig
Sandaig B.
Glen Beg
Brochs
Ben Screel
3196
Loch Hourn
Arnisdale
Inverguseran
2573
2227
Airor
Glen Guseran
Ladhar Bheinn
3342
Knoidart
R.L. Chapel
Glaschoille Ho.
2612
Inverie Ho.
Dulochan
3107
3083
Glen Meadoil
1709
2454
2803
Loch Nevis
Mallaig
Stoul
Tarbet
Kylesmorar
North Morar
Bracora
R. Morar
Morar
Loch Morar
Traumor Ho.
Port Ban
Eige
Scamadale
South Morar
L. na Ceilltean
Arisaig
Arisaig Ho.
Borodale
Arisaig Pt.
337
L. Beoraid
Arisaig
Lochailort
L. nan Uamh
Sound of Arisaig
Peanmeanach
Loch Ailort
Inverailort
L. Eilt
Glenfinnan
2852
2895
Glenuig B.
Samalaman
Roshven
Fros bheinn
2876
Moidart
943
2179
Loch Moidart
Shona
Kinloch Moidart Ho.
R. Moidart
Loch Shiel
2475
Ardtoe
Dorlin Ho.
Dalelea
Polloch
Canna
Tarbert
Compass Hill 450
Canna Har.
Sanday I.
Sound of Canna
Kilmory
Camas Pliasgaig
635
Orevál
1869
Kinloch Cas.
L. Scresort
Rum
Glen Harris
Allival 2365
Ashval 2552
Askival 2659
Sgor nan Gillean 2503
Glendibidil
Sound of Rum
Laig B.
Cleadale
Ben Tighe 1034
Eigg
Kildonan
Scuir of Eigg 1289
Galmisdale
E. Chasgie
E. nan Each
Gallanach
Muck
Carndearg
Ru Druimnich
Faskadale
Kilmory
Ru Sana
Glen Drian
Ockle
Gortenfern
Gorteneorn
Kentra
Shiel Br.
Acharacle
Ardshealoch
Ardnamurchan Pt.
Light House
Yash Ben
Ardnamurchan
L. Mudle
Ben Shalloch
Ardnamurchan
Kilchoan
Inn
Ben Hiant
1729
Glenmore
L. Laga
Glenborrodale
Mingary Cas.
Ardslignish
Salen
Inn
Ben Resipol
2774
Resipole
Scotstown
Sunart
Strontian
Ardnastang
Loch Sunart
Oronsay
Carna
Glencripesdale
Laudle
Liddesdale
Auliston Pt.
Rahoy
Ben Yadain
1873
Fuar Bheinn
2511
Black W.
Glen Dubh
L. Uisge
Kingairloch
Morven
Barr
Drimnin
Kinlochteacuis
Bunavullin
Morven
L. Durinemast
Shian
1808
Acharn
L. Aricuas
2423
Beinn Mheadhoin
Glen Geal
Ardtornish
Kinlochaline Cas.
Fiunary Ho.
Hotel
Loch Aline
L. Aline
Glashven
1516
Ardtornish
Eileraig Har.
Eilean Mor
Torrastan
Sodisdale
Arinabost
Clabhach
Coll
Arinagour
Ornsay
Fiskarg
Frisland
Ardmore Pt.
Dunara
L. Mingary
Quinish
L. Cuan
Glengorm Cas.
Ru na Gal L. Ho.
Tobermory
Calve
Caliach Pt.
Croag
Dervaig
Kilmore
L. Mishnish
Aros Ho.
Calgary Cas.
Calgary B.
Cairn Mor
1126
L. Frisa
Spyon Mor
1455
Spyon Beg
1155
Treshnish Pt.
Port Haunn
Kilninian
Torloisk Ho.
Aros W.
Aros Cas.
Sound of Mull
Salen
Inn
Fladda I.
Treshnish Is.
Lunga I.
Loch Tuath
Balligown
Killichronan
Gometra
Ulva
Laggan Ulva
Torosay K.
Pennygown
Ben Uan
1320
Knock
L. Ba
Barony Pt.
Scallasdale Ho.
Java Ho.
Back-mor
Dutchmans Cap
Little Colonsay
Ulva Ho.
Staffa
Fingals Cave
L. na Keal
Mc Kinnons Cave
MULL
Craignure
Duart Cas.
L. Ho.
Torosay Cas.
Sgeur Dearg
2505
Ben Talla
2496
Lochdonhead
Inch Kenneth
Maol Mhor
1420
1852
Ben More
3185
Lussa W.
Auchnacraig
L. Don
Erisgeir
Glen More
L. Ba
Kilfinichen Ho.
1621
Burgh
Tavool Ho.
Houran
Kinloch
Loch Buy Ho.
Creachbeinn
2344
Ben Buy
Loch Spelve
Crogan
Gylen Cas.
Kerrera I.
Loch Scridain
Pennyghael Ho.
Benbuy Lo.
Killinaig
Church
L. Uisk
Laggan
Old Ch.
& Mausoleum
Port Odhar
Lord Lovats Cave
Loch Feochan
Lerags
Barnacarry
Port Duriny
Kintra
L. Lathaich
"Cathedral"
Iona
Hotels
Village
Ardfinaig
Beach
Kilpatrick
Pennycross Ho.
Bunessan
Hotel
L. Assapoll
Kilvicuen
Ross of Mull
Quarries
Cuneas
Nuns Pass & Cave
Carsaig B.
L. Buy
Ardencaple
Sheep I.
Fidden
Iona Sound
Soay I.
Erraid I.
Chalman I.
Ardalanish
Port Uisken
Easdale I.
Cuan
Seil I.
Kilbrandon K.
Ardmaddy Ho.
Melfort Ho.
Cullipool
Slate Is.
L. Ho.
Luing I.
L. Melfort
Kilmelford
Garvelloch I.
Isles of the Sea
Coulie
Black Is.
Lunga I.
Shuna
Dunollie Cas.
Dunstaffnage Cas.
Lismore
Cas. Rachel
Cas. Tirafour
Auchindown Cas.
FIRTH OF LORN

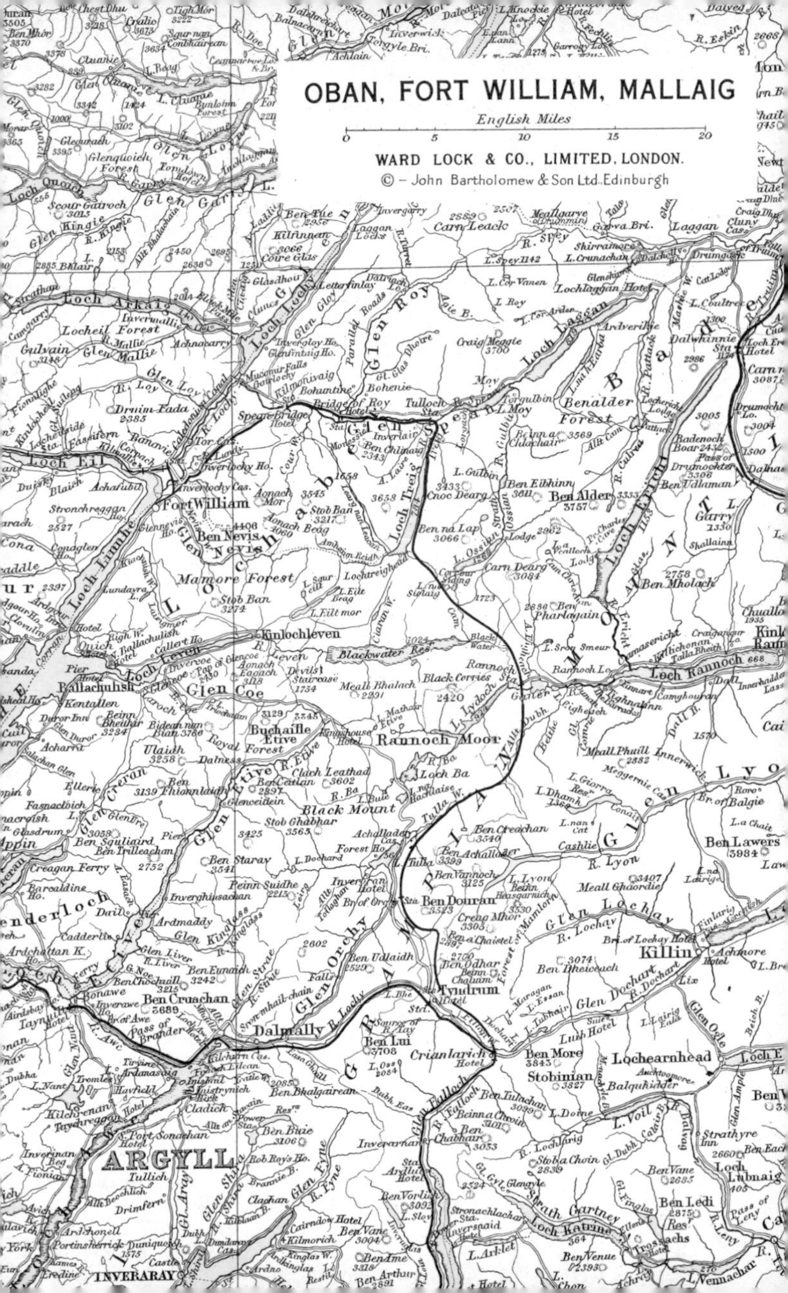

OBAN, FORT WILLIAM, MALLAIG
English Miles
0 5 10 15 20
WARD LOCK & CO., LIMITED, LONDON.
© – John Bartholomew & Son Ltd. Edinburgh
Loch Arkaig
Locheil Forest
Loch Quoich
Glen Garry
Loch Lochy
Glen Roy
Loch Laggan
Benalder Forest
Loch Ericht
Spean Bridge
Fort William
Ben Nevis
Glen Nevis
Mamore Forest
Loch Eil
Loch Linnhe
Loch Treig
Kinlochleven
Loch Leven
Blackwater Res.
Glen Coe
Ballachulish
Rannoch Moor
Loch Rannoch
Loch Ba
Black Mount
Glen Etive
Glen Lyon
Ben Lawers
Glen Lochay
Killin
Glen Dochart
Tyndrum
Dalmally
Ben Cruachan
Pass of Brander
Ben Lui
Crianlarich
Ben More
Lochearnhead
Balquhidder
Loch Voil
Loch Lubnaig
Ben Ledi
Loch Katrine
Trossachs
Ben Venue
Ben Vorlich
Glen Falloch
Glen Orchy
Glen Kinglass
Benderloch
Ardchattan K.
Taynuilt
ARGYLL
INVERARAY
Glen Shira
Glen Fyne
Loch Awe
Ben Alder
Ben Dorain
Bridge of Orchy
Kingshouse Hotel
Loch Moy
Dalwhinnie

was preceded here by Duncan I of Scotland, who began to reign A.D. 1034, and six years later was killed by Macbeth.

In the cemetery is **St. Oran's Chapel**, 40 feet long by 22 wide. It is the most ancient structure in the island, having probably been built late in the eleventh century by St. Margaret, queen of Malcolm Canmore. It is said to occupy the original site of St. Columba's Church. Its name is due to the tradition that Columba's disciple Oran was buried alive under the foundation as a sacrifice to the earth god.

On approaching the Cathedral we see, opposite the west door, the celebrated **St. Martin's Cross**. It is 14 feet high and 18 inches broad, and is ornamented by sculptured figures, including the Holy Family, David with the harp, Daniel in the lions' den, the Sacrifice of Isaac, etc. It was erected in memory of St. Martin of Tours, who lived in the fourth century, but the cross probably dates from the ninth or tenth century.

Near the west entrance of the Cathedral are the foundations of a small cell or chamber, called **St. Columba's Shrine**, restored by the Iona Community.

Iona Cathedral

was dedicated to St. Mary and was once the chief church in the Diocese of the Isles. In 1899 George, eighth Duke of Argyll, conveyed the ruins to a public trust that has carried out the restoration of the church and fitted it for worship. Further restoration is being carried out by the *Iona Community*, a fellowship of ministers and laymen who live and work together here in summer.

The building is 160 feet long by 70 wide. Its erection was begun in the twelfth century, and it is mainly of Norman and Early Pointed architecture, but from the mixture of styles it is evident that it grew, piecemeal, down to the days when, in the sixteenth century, it fell a victim to the iconoclastic zeal of the Reformers or to neglect. A square tower, at the intersection of the nave and transept, rises 70 feet, and is supported by four Norman arches and plain cylindrical columns, about 10 feet high and 3 in diameter. The proportions of the other pillars in the church are similar. Their capitals are short, and some are decorated with grotesque figures, still sharp and well preserved. Among the sculptures are representations of the Crucifixion and the Temptation.

Cloisters were enclosed on three sides by the nave, one of the transepts, and the refectory. The Monastery was situated north of the Cathedral, and north of the Monastery are the remains of the Bishop's House.

In 1965 the old Infirmary was restored. It now contains many ancient stones including the remains of St. John's Cross and St. Columba's Pillow.

Behind the Cathedral rises **Dun-I** ("the island fortress"), a grey hill, 332 feet high, from the summit of which more than thirty islands may be seen.

Iona contains much that cannot be seen in the time during which the steamer waits. Besides the objects which have been described, and which cannot be more than hastily glanced at unless at least a night is spent on the island, there are the **Spouting Cave, Port-na-Curaich** ("the port of the Coracle"—the traditional landing-place of St. Columba), **Port Ban,** the **Cell of the Culdees,** and the now disused **Marble Quarries.**

The island has a population of about 100, most of whom dwell in the village of **Baile-Mor,** signifying "the great city."

There are unlicensed hotels (*St. Columba* and *Argyll*) (*see* p. 215) and a golf course.

Leaving Iona, we steam along the **Ross of Mull** (*see* p. 215), the most southerly part of the island. The coast abounds with columns of basalt, indented with deep ravines and caves. From the quarries in the Ross of Mull was obtained the red granite used in the construction of the Albert Memorial, Blackfriars Bridge, and the Holborn Viaduct, London.

At first we thread our way through the **Torrins,** or **Torran Rocks,** a dangerous reef which stretches from the neighbourhood of **Erraid Island,** celebrated by "R.L.S.," half-way to St. John's Rock, 16 miles away, the site of **Dubh-heartach Lighthouse.**

After clearing the reef, and rounding Ardalanish Point, there comes into view, on the south shore of the Ross, a bold headland called **Gorrie's Head.** Beyond are the **Carsaig Arches,** formed in basaltic rocks by the action of the sea, and very similar to those at Staffa. The larger is 150 feet long, 60 feet high, and 55 feet in breadth.

The smaller arch is 70 feet in height, but only a few feet in length. Just eastward of the arches is the **Nun's Cave,** remarkable for carvings believed to be the original designs of the Iona Crosses. From its vicinity the freestone for Iona Cathedral was obtained and was sculptured in the cave.

Beyond **Carsaig Bay** we pass **Loch Buie,** at the head of which are the old and new castles of the Maclaines. Dr. Johnson and Boswell spent a night at Loch Buie on their way from Iona to the mainland, during their tour in the Hebrides.

A small and almost imperceptible hole in the cliffs, just east of the entrance to the loch, is pointed out as **Lord Lovat's Cave,** and is said to have been one of the hiding-places of that notorious schemer after the battle of Culloden. At Loch Buie Head the steamer turns from the Mull coast and shapes its course for the Sound of Kerrera, entering Oban Bay from the side opposite to that of its departure in the morning.

THE ISLAND OF MULL.

Daily, except Sundays, throughout the year there is a car ferry service between Oban and Craignure in Mull, with a coach connection to and from Tobermory *viâ* Salen. Craignure is 22 miles by road from Tobermory.

Mull is one of the largest islands of the Hebrides. In shape it is extremely irregular, and its coast-line is so much indented that it measures quite 250 miles in circumference, while the longest walk in a bee-line across the island would be but 30 miles, and the shortest only 3.

The southern and eastern part is mountainous, the peaks varying from 1,500 to over 3,000 feet in height. The northern portion of the island is hilly, but no eminence attains an elevation of 1,500 feet.

The greatest indentation of the island is **Loch na Keal,** on the western side. It is a favourite resort of seals and at its head is a beautiful sandy beach. Coal is found at Ardtun, on the shore of the loch, and the leaf-beds here are rich in fossils.

The columnar shores and promontories of Loch na Keal and the Sound of Ulva are clothed with ivy and with oak and ash copses. The shores of Loch na Keal, the long promontory called the Ross of Mull, and some other portions of the island, are particularly interesting to geologists.

There is a ferry for Iona from Fionphort on the Ross, 49 miles by road from Tobermory and 39 from Salen *viâ* Loch na Keal; 36 miles from Craignure by Glen More.

There are daily motor tours to Iona and other places of interest. Though much of the Island of Mull can be seen in the course of a day's excursion from Oban, the island deserves more time, if only for its legendary lore.

A description of the northern shore will be found on page 212, of the western on page 213, and of the south-eastern on page 211.

The island abounds in lochs, most of which contain brown trout. The rivers also provide sport for anglers. The residents at some of the hotels have the right of fishing in certain waters, and the proprietors of preserved waters will occasionally give permission for a day's fishing when application is courteously made.

Those who desire to climb Ben More should start from Salen, which commends itself to visitors by its central situation. (Postal address, Aros, to avoid confusion with Salen on Loch Sunart.) The village is connected (4 miles) by a good road, through Glen Aros, with **Loch Frisa**, providing good fishing. An easy road runs from Salen south-eastward to **Glen Forsa**, some 3 miles distant. In the woods of the glen and in the corries of the adjacent hills are many red deer.

Ben More (3,169 feet) is the highest summit in the island. The ascent can be made with comparative ease. The distance from Salen to the foot of the Ben is 7 miles, and, reckoning from that spot, the ascent and descent may be made in from 3½ to 4½ hours.

From Salen follow the road westward of the hotel for a trifling distance, and then turn to the left. Soon the road bends to the right, and leads across the low col separating the Sound of Mull from Loch na Keal. In about a mile it crosses the Ba, issuing from Loch Ba, and then at Knock turns sharply to the right. For the rest of the distance, some 3½ miles, the route lies along the south shore of **Loch na Keal.**

Before reaching a bend of the road in full sight of the island of Eorsa, leave the road near Dishig and make for An Gearna, the north-east shoulder of the mountain, from which the actual summit of Ben More is seen. The ascent thence to the summit is simple and requires no description.

By the same road one may reach **Mackinnon's Cave** at Ardmeanach, on the west shore. Its size is so vast that it has given rise to the legend that the cavern extends right across the island. It is supposed to be more than 100 yards long and from 50 to 80 feet high, and can be entered from the shore, near Gribun, only at low water. At the inner extremity is a huge stone called "Fingal's Table," which is believed to have been used as an altar by early anchorites. The southern part of Ardmeanach headland, known as *The Burg*, contains **MacCulloch's Tree**, one of the most famous fossil trees in the country, an old conifer embedded upright in rock. The Burg is National Trust for Scotland property.

Loch Scridain, a large inlet of the sea a few miles south of the cave, is famous for its fishing.

From Salen to Tobermory by land is 10 miles. The road, a pleasant one, lies along the Sound of Mull and passes the ruin of **Aros Castle** (2½ miles from Salen), an ancient stronghold of the Lords of the Isles.

Tobermory.

Access.—To and from Oban (daily, except Sunday) *viâ* Craignure (by coach) and car ferry. To and from Mingary (in Ardnamurchan) daily, except Sunday.
Early Closing.—Wednesday.
Hotels.—*Mishnish* (15 rooms), *MacDonald Arms* (14 rooms), *Western Isles* (50 rooms); *Springbank* (guest), *Strongarbh* (guest). *Youth Hostel.*
Population.—632.
Recreation.—Salt-water fishing, boating, bathing, tennis and golf (9-hole course).

Tobermory, "the Well of Mary," is the chief town in the island of Mull. Founded in 1788 by the Society for the Encouragement of the British Fisheries, it has not realized the hopes of its founders by becoming an important fishing station. It stands on the shore of a bay which affords safe and spacious anchorage and is protected by the small island of Calve, much as Oban is by Kerrera. On weekdays it is connected with Mingarry (*see* pp. 213, 238) in Ardnamurchan.

One of the ships of the Spanish Armada was sunk in the bay in 1588 by Donald Glas MacLean, who, retained as a hostage, set fire to the magazine. Brass and iron guns, shot, silver-plate and other relics have been recovered from time to time. The identity of the wreck and the presence of treasure aboard remain to be proved. Thomas Campbell's poem on *The Parrot in Exile* owes its origin to this historic wreck.

Dr. Johnson and Boswell paid a visit to Tobermory in October, 1773. A storm, a tiring ride to Ulva, and the loss of his oak stick put Johnson out of humour with Mull.

A small stream, which empties itself into the bay, tumbles over a pretty double cascade at the back of the town. Towards the north-west is **St. Mary's Well**, which gave its name to the place and was once believed to have healing virtues. The lighthouse on Rudhanan Gall (" Strangers' Point "), on the cliffs at the northern extremity of the bay, commands an extensive panorama.

OBAN TO BALLACHULISH AND FORT WILLIAM.

By rail to Connel thence road. For motorists the alternative to crossing Connel Bridge is the road by Glencoe (*see* pp. 226–9).

For the road from Oban to Connel *see* p. 199. Walking route up Glencruitten (*see* p. 203) by the old road which carries the telegraph wires all the way.

From the north end of Connel Bridge the road crosses the **Moss of Achnacree**, or Ledaig, supposed to be Ossian's " Plains of Lora." It is notable as the site of an ancient lake-dwelling and for the remains of two large cairns, one of which is said to mark the burial-place of the Gaelic Homer (*see* p. 326), but a spot near Killin and another in Galloway claim the same distinction.

Two miles from Loch Etive is the village of **Ledaig** or **Benderloch**, a charming place for a quiet holiday, with fishing, bathing, walking, etc. (Postal Address *Ledaig*; *Beachview* and *Loch Nell Hotel*, near Connel Bridge.) The rocky eminence above the village is ***Beregonium***, said to be the site of the capital of the Fingalian kings and the Dalriadic Scots. The view from the summit is superb. Westward lie the Tralee Sands and Ardmucknish Bay (the salt-water Loch Nell). There are remains of two fortifications on Beregonium, and traces of the vitrified wall of the one nearer the sea are yet visible. Where the boats lie on the pebbly beach at the base of Beregonium is **Port Selma**, and the locality around has been identified as the Selma of the Ossianic poems, which have been assigned to the time of the first coming of the Scots from Ireland, in the third or fourth century. The historicity of the Ossianic Poems is, however, more than doubtful (*see* p. 326).

Beyond Benderloch the main road turns north-eastwards, to make its way round Loch Creran.

Prominently placed about 2 miles north of Beregonium, between the Shian road and the main road, and at a short distance from the shore of Loch Creran, is **Barcaldine Castle,** the ancient seat of the Campbells of Barcaldine, cadets of the noble house of Breadalbane. The castle dates in part from 1579.

About 4 miles from Benderloch a road strikes up through woods on the right and through **Glen Salach,** between lofty hills. On the left is **Beinn Bhreac,** " the spotted mountain " (2,324 feet).

The ascent through the glen continues for fully 3 miles. From the highest point, 516 feet, there is a steep descent of over a mile, giving a fine view of Loch Etive, and of the more distant Ben Cruachan. When the road approaches the loch, turn to the right for the remains of **Ardchattan Priory,** a religious house of the Valliscaulian Order, founded in 1231 by Duncan MacDougall, Lord of Lorne. In 1308 King Robert the Bruce assembled within its walls the last national council conducted in the Gaelic tongue. It was burned by Cromwellian troops. The principal portion that remained standing was the Prior's Lodge, now forming part of Ardchattan House.

In the ruins of the ancient **Priory Church** are the tombs of two priors, and curious sculptured figures, one of which represents Death with a toad under his knees.

On the hillside is **Baile Mhaodian,** an ancient burial-place containing the ruins of a small chapel built by St. Modan, colleague of St. Ronan, in the eighth century.

Onwards from Barcaldine the main road skirts lovely **Loch Creran,** a long, winding arm of the sea, on whose low islets white sea-swallows make their nests and seals often bask. The road makes a detour round the heart of the loch, by Glasdrum—walkers and cyclists can use the ferry at Shian, near the entrance to the loch. Nearby is Invernahyle, now a farmhouse, but once the seat of Donald of the Hammer, who led the Stewarts of Appin at the battle of Pinkie in 1547. Under his territorial name, " Invernahyle," he figures as one of the characters in the Waverley Novels, and many particulars of him are given in Sir Walter Scott's *Tales of a Grandfather*. Sir Walter Scott stayed at the house in 1814.

Northward of Loch Creran, on an islet near Appin and *Portnacroish Hotel*, stands the square restored tower of **Castle Stalker**, built by Duncan Stewart of Appin as a hunting lodge in which to entertain his royal relative, James IV (1488–1513). In those days the Stewarts of Appin held the whole region of **Appin**—extending from Loch Creran to Ballachulish. At the ancient seat of the chief of the clan, visible a mile to the north of Appin, Sir Walter Scott, when a young man, acquired the knowledge of the region which he used in his *Lord of the Isles.*

For the part the Stewarts of Appin took in the rebellion of 1745 their estates were forfeited, and the management of these was entrusted by Government to Colin Campbell of Glenure (in the same district), whose assassination forms the notorious event known as the **Appin Murder**, familiar to readers of R. L. Stevenson's *Kidnapped.*

Alan Breck, one of the characters in Stevenson's novel, was suspected, but he managed to escape to France; and James Stewart of the Glens, the illegitimate half-brother of Stewart of Appin, who had been heard to utter words that were construed as a threat against the factor, was arrested, tried, found guilty, by a Campbell jury, as an accessory, and hanged on a little mound close to Ballachulish Ferry station. A monument on the mound commemorates the event.

From Castle Stalker the main road follows the shore of Loch Linnhe, and after going inland at Duror (*Duror Hotel*) comes out on the shore again at Kentallen and winds round the skirts of Ben Vair or Sgorr Dhonuill (3,284 feet) and of Creag Ghorm (2,470 feet) and the wood of Lettermore to **Ballachulish Ferry** at the entrance to Loch Leven.

Ballachulish Ferry (hotels on both sides of Ferry) is a little more than a mile to the west of Ballachulish village and Pier.

Ferry.—The ferry across the mouth of Loch Leven, between North and South Ballachulish, is in operation daily from 8 a.m. (Sundays 9 a.m.) to 9.30 p.m. Cars charged according to size. Transit 4–5 minutes. Cars towing caravans or trailers should go round Loch Leven by Kinlochleven (*c.* 20 miles).

Ballachulish (*Ballachulish, Laroch*), the distance by road from Orban is 39 miles, is a slate-built village situated on the south side of Loch Leven. It was noted for its exports of millions of roofing slates, the largest slate quarries, now disused, in Scotland being in its neighbourhood. It stands in the midst of magnificent scenery, and offers facilities for boating and sea-fishing besides being busy with the Glencoe traffic. For the Ferry, *see* above.

The most direct route between Oban and Fort William crosses Loch Leven by Ballachulish Ferry ; the alternative to the ferry is the 20-mile detour by Ballachulish village and Kinlochleven at the head of the loch—a good road and a pleasant ride.

The **Loch Leven** of this excursion is, of course, not the Loch Leven that held the prison of Mary, Queen of Scots, but a long narrow inlet on the eastern shore of Loch Linnhe. From its mouth to its farthest extremity it presents an unbroken succession of grand and romantic landscapes.

Opposite the slate quarries pier is the **Isle of St. Munda**, the burial-place of the Macdonalds of Glencoe. At the entrance to Glencoe (*see* p. 226) the road turns off to the left, keeping close to the loch-side and passing **Glencoe House**, built by the first Lord Strathcona and now a hospital. Half-way to the head of the loch are the narrows of Caolasnacoan and Corrynakeigh, where Alan Breck hid immediately after the murder of Campbell of Glenure (p. 224).

Kinlochleven (Kin = " head ") in 1900 was merely a pair of houses ; now at the head of this romantic loch are the factories of the British Aluminium Company and a town (*Mamore Hotel*). It cannot be said that man has acted up to Nature's example in the matter of beauty, for Kinlochleven is an ugly little industrial town. The factories produce aluminium and carbon electrodes. The raw material is an ore called *Bauxite*, because first discovered at Les Baux in France. The power for the works is supplied by the water, stored, in a reservoir 8 miles long, by means of a huge dam, three-quarters of a mile long, over 60 feet wide at the base, and with an average height of 80 feet. (*See* Blackwater Reservoir, p. 229.) In the neighbourhood is an impressive waterfall.

The walk (¾ mile) along the Old Military Road (which leads over by the " Devil's Staircase " into Glencoe, p. 228), to the right of the pipe track, is worth taking for the grand view of the surrounding country.

Onich, a mile west of North Ballachulish, is a pleasant little village with hotels (*Creagdhu*, *Allt-nan-Ros*) and other accommodation and endless amusement in boating, fishing and walking or driving through the grand scenery in the neighbourhood. The views across Loch Leven to Glencoe are exquisite. A Celtic cross commemorates the Rev. Alex. Stewart, LL.D., the enthusiastic and literary Celt, known by his *nom-de-plume*, "Nether Lochaber," who lived at Onich Manse.

North-westward from Onich are the Corran Narrows: *ferry* (*cars carried*) across Loch Linnhe to **Ardgour** (Corran) **Pier** (*hotel*). Continuous ferry service 8–8 in summer, till dusk in winter.

Farther north, on the far side of Loch Linnhe, is **Inverscaddle Bay,** on the shore of which is Conaglen House. On the right are glimpses of Ben Nevis, and straight in front is the Great Glen, through which runs the Caledonian Canal (*see* p. 239). For **Fort William** *see* p. 230.

GLENCOE.

Motors from all parts. Road routes from Oban and Fort William, *see* foregoing pages. Ski-ing facilities include chair lift and chair tow.

Glencoe, among the grandest and most magnificent glens in Scotland, is finely drawn in Macaulay's *History*:

"In the Gaelic tongue Glencoe signifies the Glen of Weeping; and in truth, that pass is the most dreary and melancholy of all the Scottish passes—the very Valley of the Shadow of Death. Mists and storms brood over it through the greater part of the finest summer; and even on those rare days when the sun is bright, and when there is no cloud in the sky, the impression made by the landscape is sad and awful. The path lies along a stream which issues from the most sullen and gloomy of mountain pools. Huge precipices of naked stone frown on both sides. Even in July the streaks of snow may often be discerned in the rifts near the summits. All down the sides of the crags heaps of ruin mark the headlong paths of the torrents."

Those who see the glen when the sun is shining brightly will be of opinion that Macaulay's description is exaggerated. The fact is that the glen is most impressive when viewed amid mists and storms.

On all but the gloomiest days it is a very fine sight, and if it be objected that the new road (a magnificent piece of engineering) is less romantic than the old, one must agree that the smooth travelling it provides does at least allow opportunities for admiring the fine array of rocks on either hand. And lest it be thought that the old road is no more, we can recommend it to walkers who hold that a slight extra distance is a small price to pay for walking undisturbed by motors.

At the time of the massacre, this desolate part of the country belonged to a branch of the clan Macdonald. William III had been seated on the throne from which James II had fled, but the change of sovereigns was not pleasing to all British subjects, and among the discontented were the Highlanders.

In 1691 the clans were required to take, before the end of the year, the oath of allegiance to William III. All submitted except the clansmen of Glencoe. Their chief, MacIan, an old man, held out to the last day. Then, realizing the folly of resistance, he hastened to Fort William to take the oath, but there was no magistrate in the garrison to receive it. The nearest was at Inveraray, and thither MacIan hurried, but the mountain passes were deep with snow, and it was not until January 6 that he reached his goal.

The magistrate administered the oath, and duly notified the fact to the authorities at Edinburgh. But by their raids the Macdonalds had made many enemies, who now seized the opportunity to have vengeance. The magistrate's explanation of MacIan's delay was withheld from the King's advisers, who were persuaded to cancel the certificate of submission and obtain the royal warrant for the extirpation of the clan.

The punitive force consisted of a hundred and twenty Campbells. At their head was the uncle of the wife of a son of MacIan. In 1907 the original order under which he acted was sold by auction for £1,400. The soldiers entered the glen under a plausible pretext, and the old chief, suspecting no evil, treated them with Highland hospitality. For twelve days they were entertained by the Macdonalds, and on the very night of the fell deed the commander was playing with the chieftain's sons.

At five o'clock on the morning of February 13, the massacre began. Old and young men, women, and children were indiscriminately slain, and nearly all who escaped the bullet or the sword were frozen to death among the precipices to which they fled. The old chief was one of those that were shot.

When the butchery was over the deserted huts were fired, and the executioners departed, driving before them the flocks and herds and Highland ponies that had belonged to the clan.

At the foot of the glen (where is the modern *Glencoe Hotel*) is a **Monument** in memory of the massacre, while for a mile or two up the glen on the same side clusters of green mounds and grey stones mark the sites of the ruined huts of the clan. At the head of the wider part of the glen rises the **Signal Rock**, which owes its name to the tradition that it was the spot from which was given the signal for the massacre. Close above this spot stands the *Clachaig Inn*, 6 miles from Ballachulish Ferry. Beyond Clachaig the two roads join. Travellers are recommended to take the old road *viâ*

Clachaig as it is the loveliest part of the whole glen. In front rises the precipice of the **Black Rock** of Glencoe, with lonely **Loch Triochatan** at its foot. High in the face of the Black Rock is a narrow but deep recess known as **Ossian's Cave,** and **Ossian's Shower Bath** may be seen in a corrie close by. Ossian is said to have been born beside Loch Triochatan. At the head of the pass, high above the river gorge through which the road now goes, is a parapet known as the **Study** (a Scots word for the Anvil). From it the best view of the glen—the upper part is National Trust property—can be obtained.

Looking down the glen from this point, one sees on the left three remarkable mountain masses commonly called the " **Three Sisters of Glencoe** " (or Faith, Hope and Charity). For geological note, *see* p. 40.

Beyond the summit of the pass, a track on the left, known as the **Devil's Staircase,** climbs over to the head of Loch Leven. The path was the route taken by the two young sons of the chief of the Macdonalds in escaping from the massacre of their clan.

The mountains here on the right are Buachaille Etive Bheag and Buachaille Etive Mor, the **Little** and **Great Shepherds of Etive.** Also on the right a rough, wild road strikes off over the moor and down to **Glen Etive,** ending by the pier at the head of Loch Etive. All around are grand, rugged mountains.

The road from Glencoe, after crossing the watershed (1,024 feet), crosses the River Etive and passes a quarter of a mile to the west of *Kingshouse Hotel,* which is on the old road on the other side of the river. The road now runs south-east on to desolate **Rannoch Moor,** 20 miles square, which R. L. Stevenson immortalized in *Kidnapped* as the scene of the escape of David Balfour and Alan Breck from the pursuing dragoons. For the route from Kinloch Rannoch, *see* p. 313. In the far recesses of the moor is the tarn **Lochan a'Claidheimh** (pronounced *Loch na Clive,* and meaning Sword Loch). Into its waters the Earl of Atholl, late in the fifteenth century, cast his sword, renouncing all claim to the adjacent lands in favour of the Camerons, until his brand should be recovered. Its waters flow into the great **Blackwater Reservoir,** 8 miles in length, impounding the streams that flow into the head of the salt-water Loch Leven, and supplying motive-power for the aluminium works at Kinlochleven (p. 225). The dam is 85 feet high and 62 feet thick at the base.

Rounding the north-east shoulder of Beinn Chaorach at a height of 1,143 feet, the new road descends to the west end of Loch Ba. After passing between that loch and Lochan na h-Achlaise the road strikes southward and after a short rise drops rapidly down to the east end of Loch Tulla, and thence along the south side of that loch to **Bridge of Orchy** (*hotel*). (*Inveroran Hotel* is 2½ miles distant on the old road at the west end of the loch.) From Bridge of Orchy the new road keeps to the west side of the glen containing the railway and, after crossing the county boundary at a height of 1,033 feet, reaches the Oban road at Clifton, half a mile west from Tyndrum.

From Bridge of Orchy another road runs south-westward down Glen Orchy to Dalmally (p. 197). For **Tyndrum** and the road thence to Oban *see* p. 196.

A mile or so south of Bridge of Orchy the railway makes a wide sweep to skirt a side valley; a track up this valley leads between **Ben Dorain** (3,524 feet) and Beinn a Chaisteil and Beinn Fhuaran, and climbs north-eastward for about 3 miles, and then swings to the east and crosses to the head of **Glen Lyon** (*see* p. 300): a very fine route—for strong walkers, as there is no accommodation between Bridge of Orchy and Fortingall, 35–40 miles, though vehicles can come up Glen Lyon to Loch Lyon, and shelter may possibly be found at Bridge of Balgie, 15 miles below the loch.

FORT WILLIAM.

Access.—Road from Oban, *see* pp. 222–6; from Newtonmore, *see* p. 321; from Inverness, *see* pp. 239–43. Rail *viâ* Tyndrum, Bridge of Orchy and Tulloch.
Distances.—Ballachulish (N.) ferry, 12 m.; Ballachulish (S.) *viâ* Kinlochleven, 24 m.; Oban, 48 m.; Inverness, 66 m.; Kingussie, 49 m.; Mallaig, 47 m.
Early Closing.—Wednesday.
Hotels.—*Station, Highland, Grand, Alexandra, Imperial, Croit Anna Motel, Nevis Bank*, etc.
Information Centre: Lochaber Tourist Association, Cameron Square, Fort William.
Museum of West Highland arts and crafts in Cameron Square, admission *fee.*
Sports.—Bathing, boating, bowls, fishing (permits from local angling association), tennis, golf.

THE town originated in a fort built by General Monk, during the Commonwealth, to overawe the Highlanders, and reconstructed in the time of William III, from whom the place derives its name.

The fort was unsuccessfully besieged during the rebellion of 1745, was garrisoned until 1860, dismantled in 1866, and levelled for the railway (1894).

Fort William, standing on important rail and road routes, and well equipped for such shipping as still comes its way, is not only a growing tourist centre, but also a busy market town with a successful branch in industry in the shape of the Lochaber works of the British Aluminium Company, a distillery, and a large pulp mill at Corpach.

The views from the higher portions of the town include Loch Linnhe in the foreground, with the Ardgour hills in the distance. To the north-west is Loch Eil; to the north-east are the Lochy and the River Nevis. Ben Nevis is too close to the town to be seen to advantage from it.

At Fort William the River Lochy terminates its brief life of 8 miles by flowing into the head of **Loch Linnhe.** The loch itself has a westward continuation in **Loch Eil,** and in the angle formed by the two lochs are **Corpach** (*Corpach Hotel*) and **Banavie,** of some importance as the southern terminal point of the Caledonian Canal and ranking as satellites of Fort William in the eyes of tourists, since they are excellent centres for steamer and motor trips as well as for walks.

BEN NEVIS.

The principal excursion in the neighbourhood is, of course, the ascent of **Ben Nevis** (4,406 feet), the highest mountain in Britain. It is most easily ascended from Achintee Farm (2½ miles from Fort William), which can be reached by road by *crossing* the Bridge of Nevis at the north end of the town and then turning sharp to the right by a fair road which follows the north bank of the River Nevis. There is a rough path to the summit (7½ miles from Fort William), but in spite of this there is some stiff climbing to be done after the first mile or so, and strong boots, preferably nailed, are needed on account of the rough rocks. Climbers should carry warm clothing to wear at the top, and sandwiches to eat. The stone building at the summit was, until 1904, a meteorological observatory. Hardy walkers often ascend in the evening and spend the night on the mountain for the sake of the glorious view at sunrise; but mists are apt to cause disappointment. For geological note, *see* p. 40.

From Achintee Farm the path climbs steeply up the hillside, crosses several shaky bridges and at a height of 1,750 feet crosses the south end of the little valley containing Lochan Meall an t-Suidhe. From here it turns sharp to the right, passes the remains of the Half Way House, crosses the Red Burn and then rises up in steep zig-zags to the summit.

The actual summit of the mountain is flat and is covered with loose stones of all shapes and sizes. To the south it slopes away gradually and then very steeply into Glen Nevis. But on the north-east it is cut off by a magnificent range of rock precipices a mile and a half in length and nearly 2,000 feet in height. To the east the summit descends rapidly to a very narrow *arête*, which circles round the head of the glen at the base of the precipice and rises to the summit of Carn Mor Dearg.

The great north-east precipice is furrowed with many chasms, some of which hold snow all the year round. This, if local tradition may be relied upon, is a fortunate circumstance for Cameron of Glen Nevis, who is said to hold his land by a charter which gives it him while there is snow on the mountain. The story is told of a winter in which but little snow fell being followed by a summer so hot that the Cameron of that day had to put a tent over a snow-wreath to keep it from melting, lest his tenure of the land should be lost.

On a clear day the **View** from the summit embraces a panorama almost 150 miles in diameter. Nearly all the highest peaks in Scotland are visible and it is claimed that Ireland can be seen 120 miles away. During summer the services of a guide are available for parties to the summit at an inclusive charge (including bus).

"In no other place," Sir Archibald Geikie observes, "is the general and varied character of the Highlands better illustrated, and from none can the geologist, whose eye is open to the changes wrought by subaerial waste on the surface of the country, gain a more vivid insight into their reality and magnitude.

"It is easy to recognize the more marked heights. To the south, away down Loch Linnhe, he can see the hills of Mull and the Paps of Jura closing in the horizon—Loch Eil seems to be at his feet, winding up into the lonely mountains.

"Far over the hills, beyond the head of the loch, he looks across Arisaig and can see the cliffs on the Isle of Eigg, and the dark peaks of Rum, with the Atlantic gleaming below them. Farther to the north-west, the blue range of the Coolins rises along the skyline, and then sweeping over all the intermediate ground, through Arisaig, and Knoydart, and Clanranald's country (where the Pretender landed, whence also he departed), mountain rises beyond mountain, ridge beyond ridge, cut through by dark glens, and varied here and there with the sheen of lake and tarn.

"Northward runs the mysterious straight line of the Great Glen, with its chain of lochs. Thence to the east and south the same billowy sea of mountain-tops stretches out as far as the eye can follow it—the hills and glens of Lochaber, the wide green strath of Spean, the grey corries of Glen Treig and Glen Nevis, the distant sweep of the mountains of Brae Lyon and the Perthshire Highlands, the spires of Glencoe, and thence round again to the blue waters of Loch Linnhe."

The name of Ben Nevis has been variously interpreted as meaning the "cloud-capped mountain," the "heaven-kissing hill," and the "hill of heaven," all alluding to the fact that its top is generally so obscured by clouds and mist as apparently to reach the sky.

A splendid alternative way of reaching the summit—much longer and harder, but perfectly feasible and safe for really strong walkers—is by the Allt a' Mhuilinn (pron. *Voolin*) and up the *arête* between Carn Mor Dearg and Ben Nevis. The rock scenery in the Allt a' Mhuilinn is of unparalleled grandeur and on a scale absolutely stupendous. Follow the ordinary path as far as the southern end of Lochan Meall an t-Suidhe, beyond which leave the track and proceed along the hillside, keeping the same level, in a northerly direction, having Lochan Meall an t-Suidhe on your left-hand side. In a short time you will come to a deer fence. Crossing this, you find yourself overlooking a wild glen, flanked by the red granite slopes of Carn Mor Dearg on the east side and by the north-east precipices of Ben Nevis on the west side. You now proceed to pick your way downwards in a slanting direction towards the head-waters of the stream which threads its way through the bottom of the glen, the Allt a' Mhuilinn. Having got down to the bed of the stream or near it, proceed upwards along its banks (past a Scottish Mountaineering Club hut—locked), crossing the burn at some suitable spot so as to get a wider view of the magnificent cliffs of Ben Nevis. Our route lies straight ahead south-east to the lowest part of the ridge or *arête* connecting Carn Mor Dearg with Ben Nevis. The slope at the top of the corrie seems at a distance somewhat formidable, but when one comes up and near to it, it will be found to consist mainly of rough screes and boulders, and a little care and judicious selection of the route will always find a way. On gaining the crest, turn to the right along its narrow edge towards Ben Nevis, and after a long pull up you will at length find yourself standing at the summit cairn of the Ben itself.

On the north-east precipice there are some of the finest and longest rock climbs in Britain; but they are difficult and for expert climbers only. Full and exact descriptions of them will be found in the Scottish Mountaineering Club's *Guide to Ben Nevis* (1936).

Glen Nevis, on the southern side of the mountain, is worth exploring; a road deteriorating to a track goes up it for several miles.

About 1½ miles from Fort William is a picturesque waterfall called *Roaring Mill.* About 2½ miles from Fort William is a rocking stone. Nearby is a Youth Hostel behind which, on the summit of a detached hill, are the remains of a vitrified fort. About a mile farther up the glen are the **Lower Nevis Falls**, spanned by an iron bridge. Beyond *Evans's Burn* is **Samuel's Cave**, in which fugitives from Culloden Moor are said to have found shelter. At a point about 7 miles from Fort William the driving road ends. Beyond this the glen narrows to a fine gorge through which a path leads to **Steall** (*Mountaineering Club Hut*), near which on the south side there are some fine waterfalls. The path may be followed eastwards to the head of Glen Nevis and on to the south end of **Loch Treig**, in the midst of a wild inhospitable area between Rannoch Moor and Glen Spean. From Lochtreighead a rough track leads in 3 miles to Corrour Station, from which the train could be taken back to Fort William, or the route may be reversed. From Lochtreighead a track leads through the wild Lairig Leacach to Spean Bridge (10 miles).

FORT WILLIAM TO KINGUSSIE BY GLEN SPEAN AND LOCH LAGGAN (50 miles).

The first few miles, along a Wade road (now rebuilt and modernized) to Spean Bridge, afford magnificent views of the northern flanks of Ben Nevis. The mountain is pierced by a tunnel 15 miles long and 15 feet in diameter, bringing water from Loch Treig (p. 322) for the production of electricity. Incidental to this scheme—one of the greatest engineering feats of its kind—are the raising of the level of Loch Treig and the elevation of part of the adjacent railway line by about 30 feet; also the diversion into Loch Treig (*viâ* the River Spean and a canal and tunnel 3 miles long) of the waters of Loch Laggan and of the River Pattack, the latter augmented in turn by a partial diversion of the headwaters of the Spey. The western end of the tunnel is plainly seen high up the face of the mountain. It is hardly picturesque, but demands respect as a monument to modern engineering skill and resource. On the banks of the *Lochy* stands old **Inverlochy Castle** and, beyond it, Nevis Distillery, and the modern Inverlochy Castle.

Spean Bridge has a railway station and has a good hotel. The bridge takes us across the river, where we turn to the right for *Roy Bridge (hotels)*. This is the starting-point for the excursion up **Glen Roy**.

The **Parallel Roads** are shelves or terraces formed by the waters of a lake that once filled the intervening glen. They begin about 5 miles north of Roy Bridge, and extend to Brae Roy Shooting Lodge (10 miles), to which there is a road. An excellent view of them is obtained from a point about midway. The highest " road " is, of course, the oldest, and those below it were formed in succession as the waters of the lake decreased in depth. The lake not only filled Glen Roy, but also some of the valleys adjoining it on the west. The water was held by a glacier in the glen and in the valley of the Caledonian Canal. The Great Glen was apparently filled to the brim with ice, which blocked the mouths of Glens Roy and Spean.

"When the lake," says Sir Archibald Geikie, "that must have thus filled Glen Roy and the neighbouring valleys was at its deepest, its surplus waters would escape from the head of Glen Roy down into Strathspey, and at that time the uppermost beach or parallel road (1,155 feet above the present sea-level) was formed.

"The Glen Treig glacier then shrank back a little, and the lake was thus lowered about 78 feet, so as to form the middle terrace, which is 1,077 feet above the sea. After the lake had remained for a time at that height, the Glen Treig glacier continued on the decline, and at last crept back out of Glen Spean. By this means the level of the lake was reduced to 862 feet above the sea, and the waters of Glen Roy joined those of Loch Laggan, forming one long winding lake, having its outflow by what is now the head of Glen Spean, into Strathspey. While this level was maintained, the lowest of the parallel roads of Glen Roy was formed.

"As the climate of the glacial period grew milder, however, the mass of ice which choked up the mouth of Glen Spean and pounded back the waters gradually melted away; the drainage of Glen Roy, Glen Spean, and their tributary valleys was no longer arrested, and as the lake crept step by step down the glen towards the sea, the streams one by one took their places in the channels which they have been busy widening and deepening ever since."

From *Turret Bridge*, 10 miles up Glen Roy, strong walkers have three routes: (1) Cross the ridge westward to the head of **Glen Gloy**, the foot of which is at Glenfintaig, on the Spean Bridge–Fort Augustus road; (2) follow the track to the *col* at the head of Glen Roy (14 miles from Roy Bridge) and 4 miles farther join the *Corrieyairack route* (p. 242) at Melgarve, thence either eastward to Laggan Bridge or north-westward to Fort Augustus.

For the route from Tulloch, 5 miles farther up Glen Spean from Roy Bridge, to Kingussie and Strathspey, *see* pp. 321–2.

FORT WILLIAM TO ARISAIG AND MALLAIG.

This run of just under 50 miles is through some of the most wildly beautiful West Highland scenery, but motorists must not expect to find roads comparable in surface and engineering to, say, the new road up Glencoe. The district is of historical interest, as Prince Charlie landed on its shores in 1745, and fourteen months later re-embarked from it, a " sair, sair altered man " after his failure to drive George II from the throne.

From Fort William the route crosses the Lochy and the Caledonian Canal to Banavie and Corpach, a little beyond which is **Kilmallie Church**, with an obelisk to the memory of Colonel John Cameron of Fassifern, who fell at Quatre Bras, 1815. The epitaph was written by Sir Walter Scott, who, in his " Waterloo," refers in touching terms to Cameron's death. Road and rail now run close to the shore of **Loch Eil.**

Near the centre of the north side of the loch is **Fassifern House**, where Prince Charlie spent a night. At the head of the loch is **Locheilside**, a district known also as Kinlocheil. Here it was that the Prince heard the Government had offered a reward of £30,000 for his capture, a proclamation to which he replied by another offering the sum of £30, afterwards increased to £30,000, for the capture of the "usurper," George II.

After traversing the strath stretching westwards from the head of Loch Eil to Loch Shiel, we pass through **Glen Callop to Loch Shiel**, a fresh-water lake about 17½ miles in length, less than a mile wide, and with a maximum depth of 420 feet. There are no roads along Loch Shiel.

A small steamer sails down the Loch from Glenfinnan to **Acharacle** whence motors run to Salen, on Loch Sunart, and Kilchoan, Ardnamurchan. Six miles down the Loch, Glenaladale (where Prince Charlie spent a night in the old family residence of the Macdonalds) is seen to the north. A delightful circular tour can be made by coach and steamer from Fort William.

Fishing in Loch Shiel can be enjoyed by visitors at the hotel known by the old name of the *Stage House*, at the head of the loch, and at *Loch Shiel Hotel*, at *Acharacle* at the foot of the loch.

By the head of Loch Shiel is the **Glenfinnan Monument**, marking the spot where Prince Charlie's standard was unfurled 19th of August, 1745. The inscription on the monument is in English, Gaelic and Latin.

From Glenfinnan road and rail pass through a winding, narrow valley towards **Loch Eilt**, a fresh-water loch studded with islets. We then reach the head of **Loch Ailort**, an inlet of the western sea, where there is a small hotel. From here there is an exceedingly beautiful walk, for strong walkers only, by a good track along the coast and through Glen Uig to Loch Moidart and on to Shiel Bridge, Acharacle (*hotel*) at the foot of Loch Shiel, and **Salen** (*hotel*) on Loch Sunart. After leaving Loch Ailort the road soon crosses the Arnipol Burn and then Gleann Mama. At this point there is a magnificent view of **Loch nan Uamh** (Loch of the Caves), with its rock-bound shores. Far out in the ocean is the island of **Eigg**, with the mountains of Rhum on its right, and Muck on its left. It was in Loch nan Uamh that the French frigate *Doutelle* anchored on July 19, 1745, with Prince Charlie and seven followers on board.

The oddly named group of islands comprising Eigg, Muck, Rhum and Canna—the Parish of the Small Isles—is of considerable geological interest.

The remarkable island of **Eigg** is, to a considerable extent, under cultivation. The *Scuir of Eigg* is, by reason of its extraordinary shape, the most conspicuous object for many miles round. It consists of a mass of basaltic shafts, rising from a steep rocky base. At the north side of the island is a long line of cliff presenting a similar phenomenon, but not attaining so great a height.

Muck (*Muic*, the sea-pig; "Porpoise island") is occupied by half a dozen families.

Rhum is the most mountainous of all these islands except Skye, and certainly the most barren. It consists almost entirely of rugged masses of rock and scree, rising to the most boldly defined outline in the Hebrides. The highest point is *Askival* (2,659 feet). Except near Kinloch there is no habitation. The island measures about 8 miles by 7, and the population is under 40. About 97 per cent. of the area is forest and moorland, the game comprising deer, grouse, woodcock, snipe, and wild-fowl. Rhum is now a Nature Conservancy and there are restrictions in force.

Canna, with a little harbour, pier, and verdant slope, is attractive. The island measures about 6 miles by 1½, and its western extremity is a fine cliff 425 feet high. The population is about 60. The high ground at the north-east of Canna is *Compass Hill*, a name due to the manner in which magnetic compasses are affected by the quantity of iron in the basaltic rock of which it consists.

The district known as **Borrodale** is inseparably associated with the final wanderings of Prince Charlie. After Culloden he fled to Glen Beasdale, where he waited till a boat could be obtained to convey him to the Outer Isles, hoping to find a ship there that would carry him to France. But from South Uist he returned to the mainland, piloted part of the way by Flora Macdonald. He landed near Mallaig, was conducted through the military cordon by his friends, and after many wanderings farther east came back to Borrodale, where he stepped on board the ship which carried him to France.

Proceeding over a low-lying moss and crossing the *Brunery Burn*, we reach **Arisaig** (*Arisaig Hotel*), a hamlet at a charming spot. The coast is studded with rocks, on which seals may be seen in large numbers on a calm summer day, and the view includes **Loch nan Cilltean**, with its countless rocks and islets, at the entrance to which, and 3 miles from the village, is Arisaig pier. There is good boating, bathing and fishing. **Morar** (*hotel: Youth Hostel*), 6 miles farther, is on the coast near the western end of Loch Morar, the deepest lake in Great Britain (987 feet). At the falls on the *Morar River* a small hydro-electric scheme, supplying power to surrounding districts, has its station commendably hidden in the hillside. The bay in which the river joins the sea has wonderful white sands. Road and railway end at **Mallaig** (*hotels: Marine* (20 *rooms*), *West Highland* (32 *rooms*). Mallaig is an important fishing port. During the fishing season dozens of steam drifters are to be seen in its harbour, where their freights are landed for dispatch to southern markets. The **Sound of Sleat** separates Mallaig from the **Isle of Skye** (*see* p. 244), 4½ miles distant.

Mallaig offers exceptional facilities for visiting other ports. Car ferry services daily (except Sunday) to Kyle of Lochalsh, Portree (Skye) and Raasay; to Kyle of Lochalsh and Stornoway (Lewis); twice weekly to Eigg, Rhum, Canna, Lochboisdale (South Uist), Loch Maddy (North Uist), Tarbert and other ports in Harris. Car ferry daily except Sundays to Armadale. Motor-boat service to Loch Brittle. Also motor-boat connection with Inverie and the head of Loch Nevis.

FORT WILLIAM TO ARDNAMURCHAN AND MORVERN.

About 10 miles from Banavie a very poor road doubles round the western end of **Loch Eil** and returns along the southern shore of the loch until opposite Corpach, whence it skirts the western shore of Loch Linnhe past Inverscaddle and Ardgour (*hotel*) to **Inversanda**, at the foot of Glen Tarbert. From Inversanda a road, very narrow, runs southwards along the west side of Loch Linnhe to **Kingairloch**, a beautiful spot, and thence inland to Loch Aline on the Sound of Mull (*small hotel*), where there is a pier. (Steamer and car ferry to Oban and Mull.)

At the western end of Glen Tarbert is **Loch Sunart** separating Morvern from Ardnamurchan. **Strontian** (*hotel*), near the eastern end, gave its name to the element strontium, first discovered in the lead-mines here. Farther west is **Salen** (not to be confused with Salen in Mull), with an hotel, and from here a road goes north to *Shiel Bridge* (4½ miles)—note there is another Shiel Bridge, in Glen Shiel, on the Invermoriston–Strome Ferry route, (p. 243)—at the foot of Loch Shiel (p. 236), and on to **Dorlin**, on Loch Moidart, a rugged arm of the sea. Westward from Salen the road wends its way along the southern shore of Ardnamurchan—a route which should fully satisfy the needs of any wishing to get off the beaten track. So remote is it, that the statement that James IV held a court **at Mingary Castle**, the ruins of which are a little way short of **Kilchoan** (*inn*), seems a fantastic invention; but the court was held, and here the island chiefs submitted in 1495. Southward, across the Sound of Mull, is Mull (p. 219), with Ben More towering to 3,169 feet; south-westward are Coll and Tiree; northward are Muck, Eigg, Rhum, and Canna (*see* p. 236), and beyond them the mountains of Skye.

THE GREAT GLEN.

Motoring.—A road (A 82) runs through the Glen all the way from Fort William to Inverness (66½ miles), and in recent years it has been modernized and rebuilt in connection with the great road scheme alluded to in connection with Motoring (p. 12). Between Fort William and Fort Augustus the road follows the east side of the glen with the exception of 4 miles along the west side of Loch Oich. Beyond Fort Augustus the road follows the west side of Loch Ness and the River Ness to Inverness.

There is a regular daily bus service between Fort William and Inverness, *viâ* Spean Bridge (where connection is made with trains from and to the South) and Fort Augustus all the year round.

Steamer.—Through Steamer services on the Caledonian Canal have not been resumed since the war and the railway line between Spean Bridge and Fort Augustus is completely abandoned. There are, however, occasional cruises from Inverness in to Loch Ness and various launches operate from different points. *See* local announcements or inquire Canal Office, Inverness.

The voyage through the Caledonian Canal is a favourite one for canoe-ers, but there is, however, a charge for taking a canoe from Fort William to Inverness.

THE **Great Glen** is a deep natural depression extending north-eastwards across Scotland from Fort William to Inverness, from Loch Linnhe, or the Firth of Lorn, to the Moray Firth (*see* pp. 39–40). The Glen provides the route of the **Caledonian Canal.**

The construction of the Canal was begun in 1804 under Telford. Much trouble was caused by the numerous rapid burns flowing from the west into the Lochy. Sluices had to be constructed through the solid rock to convey these waters under the Canal to the river, and the bed of the Lochy had to be raised 12 feet to cause that stream to fall into the Spean at Mucomir. But the greatest difficulty arose in connecting Loch Lochy with the sea at Corpach. The distance between the two points is only 8 miles, but the surface of the lake is 93 feet above sea-level. Telford overcame the difficulty by constructing a series of eight locks: "*Neptune's Staircase.*" Each has a drop of 8 feet, so that vessels passing through change their level 64 feet before again sailing in the open water. Altogether there are twenty-nine locks on the Canal.

The total length of the passage from Corpach to Muirtown (Inverness), the eastern terminus, is 60½ miles, of which only 22 miles are Canal, the remainder consisting of the lochs which the Canal connects. The Canal is 16 feet deep, 50 feet broad at the bottom, and can take vessels with draught not exceeding 13 feet 6 inches. The portions of the natural waterway are Loch Lochy (10 miles), Loch Oich (4 miles) and Loch Ness (24 miles). The whole length of the Canal, when extended on the map, measures only 4 miles longer than a straight line drawn from one extremity to the other. The summit is 105 feet above sea-level.

The first-class road (A 82) from Fort William to Inverness has already been described (*see* p. 234) as far as **Spean Bridge** (9 miles) as the start of the route (A 86) to Strathspey by Loch Laggan. With an all-the-year-round bus service to and from Fort Augustus and Inverness and trains running north and south, Spean Bridge is admirably situated.

Beyond the three-spanned bridge the Fort Augustus road swings sharply to the left and for a mile or so climbs to a moorland commanding magnificent views of Ben Nevis. Where a road branches off for Gairlochy (near the foot of Loch Lochy: canal locks: Mucomir Falls) stands an impressive *Memorial to the Commandos* trained at Achnacarry in the Second World War, the sculptor being Scott Sutherland.

From the monument the main road goes down to the shore of **Loch Lochy** (*Letterfinlay Lodge Hotel; Youth Hostel*). Across the Loch are Glengarry deer forest and **Ben Tee** (2,957 feet), and near the south-western end is the opening of **Loch Arkaig**, a long narrow sheet of water. Here was once a fine avenue of gigantic beech-trees called the **Dark Mile**, planted by Lochiel before he set out from Achnacarry House for the Forty-Five. It has now almost been cut away. High above one end is a cave in which " bonnie Prince Charlie " hid in his flight from Culloden. On Loch Arkaig was hidden the famous " treasure," the root of so much Jacobite intrigue and romance. A fair road runs along the northern shore of Loch Arkaig to the west end of the loch.

At the northern end of Loch Lochy a short length of Canal connects it with **Loch Oich**. Here are the Laggan Locks, and here the road crosses from east bank to west.

Loch Oich is a most beautiful lake forming the summit level of the Canal. Steep mountains fringe it on the south, and pretty islets dot its bosom. Near the south end of the loch is a strange monument, overlooking a spring called Tobar nan Ceann—the **Well of the Heads.** It was erected as a memorial of the vengeance inflicted on the murderers of some members of the family of Macdonell of Keppoch. The heads of the seven murderers were presented to the chief of the clan after having been washed in this spring.

Invergarry (*Invergarry* (14 *rooms*), *Glengarry Castle*) stands in the middle of the west side of the loch, amid charming scenery. On a rocky headland are the ruins of a Castle long the home of the MacDonells of Glengarry. Of interest in Invergarry is the salmon hatchery run by the North of Scotland Hydro-Electric Board (*visitors welcome*).

Invergarry to the West Coast.—This road is through scenery of great grandeur and beauty. The first portion is through woods and along the north side of **Loch Garry** (at far end of loch is *Tomdoun Hotel*). In 2 miles, however, a road strikes north over by the foot of Loch Loyne to meet the Glen Moriston road below the east end of Loch Cluanie (*see also* p. 243). Thence the road is westward through **Glen Shiel** to **Shiel Bridge** at **Loch Duich** (*Kintail Lodge Hotel*) and on to Dornie and Kyle of Lochalsh (*see* p. 243).

The road that continues along Loch Garry to *Tomdoun Hotel*, at its end, goes on to Loch Quoich and the head of **Loch Hourn** (27 m. from Invergarry), but the descent to Kinlochhourn is dangerously steep for motors, and there is no accommodation there. It may be better to explore the beautiful scenery of Loch Hourn by sea from Mallaig or from **Glenelg**, on the eastern side of the Sound of Sleat.

This wild corner is the western terminus of grand walks over the mountains. **Glen Lichd** (*see* p. 410), the foot of which is crossed by the road at Croe Bridge, near the head of Loch Duich, leads along the south-western flank of **Ben Attow** (3,383 feet), and by following the Croe stream to the head of the valley and thence skirting the eastern shoulder of the mountain, one can drop into the head of Glen Affric, and by Lochs Affric and Beneveian reach Invercannich (p. 411).

Another route from Croe Bridge ascends the glen on the northern side of Ben Attow and then drops to the southern end of Loch Beallach, whence Glen Grivie leads eastward to the head of Glen Affric and the above-mentioned route.

From the northern end of Loch Beallach the stream may be followed past the **Falls of Glomach** (highest waterfall in Britain —370 feet in one plunge), by a path high up on the west side of the chasm, to the road in Glen Elchaig, which is reached by a bridge across the foot of Loch na Leitreach. Westward from this point the road leads down Glen Elchaig to Killilan and the head of Loch Long and then along the western shore of that Loch to Ardelve; north-eastward, 1½ miles beyond Loch na Leitreach, a path climbs from the Iron Lodge beside a stream to little Loch an Droma; descending eastward (no path) to Loch Lungard and the shores of Loch Mullardoch, a road runs down Glen Cannich to Invercannich. (*See also* pp. 411–12.) Here a hydro-electric scheme was recently completed.

Fort Augustus.

Access.—Daily bus services to and from Inverness, Spean Bridge and Fort William.
Hotels.—*Lovat Arms, Caledonian, Inchnacardoch.*

The fort which gave name to the village was built in 1715. In 1867 it was sold to the Lord Lovat of that day, and in 1876 his son presented the site to the Benedictine Order for the erection of a monastery, which in 1882 was raised to the dignity of an **Abbey.** Visitors are admitted to the church and museum. The Abbey School is a well-known boarding school.

The pleasant township attracts visitors, with boating, fishing and golf, and it is a fairly good centre.

Fort Augustus is at the northern end of a rough track, a derelict Wade road, over the **Corrieyairack Pass** (2,507 feet) to the Spey at Laggan (p. 321), 25 miles of rough going, with no inns or shelter, but with glorious views.

About 2 miles from Fort Augustus, on the right, is **Glen Doe,** through which a very steep road leads to **White Bridge** (*hotel*) in Strath Errick and thence to Foyers and along the east side of Loch Ness to Inverness.

Fort Augustus is at the head of **Loch Ness,** second largest fresh-water lake in Scotland: 24¼ miles long, 1–1½ miles wide and with a maximum depth of 754 feet; and famed, among other things, for the " monster " which disturbs its peace from time to time.

Six miles from Fort Augustus is **Invermoriston** (*hotel*), on the west shore.

A few miles beyond Invermoriston, **Mealfuarvonie** (" the round hill of the cold upland "), a dome-shaped mountain, 2,284 feet in height, rises steeply above the western shore of the loch; it is well seen from **Foyers** (*hotel*) on the opposite side of the loch, where aluminium works have impaired the once-famed **Falls of Foyers.**

At the mouth of the rich Highland vale of **Glen Urquhart,** on the western shore of Loch Ness, are the picturesque ruins of **Urquhart Castle,** originally built in the twelfth century. The first castle was besieged by Edward I, in 1303, and in its place he erected this formidable-looking fortress. (*Admission to Castle, weekdays,* 10 a.m. *to* 7 p.m.; *Sundays,* 2–7; *charge.*)

The road here makes a loop round the mouth of the Enrick, passing through **Lewiston** (*hotel*) and **Drumnadrochit** (*hotel*), amid charming scenery.

A good road runs up Glen Urquhart to Invercannich, in Strath Glass (about 14 miles); and a pretty though hilly road goes northward from Milton and through to Beauly (*see also* p. 406). Some 2 miles south-west from Drumnadrochit are the Falls of Divach, higher than Foyers.

Four miles north of Temple Pier is **Abriachan.** At the north-eastern extremity at Loch Ness, beyond **Dores** Pier is **Aldourie Castle.** About half a mile beyond the outlet of the river *Ness* is **Dochgarroch.** Here is the termination of the northernmost stretch of the Canal, which 3 miles farther flows into Inverness Firth at Muirtown, on the western outskirts of **Inverness** (p. 403).

Invermoriston to Glenelg and Kyle of Lochalsh (60 miles). The road lies alongside the river Moriston and Loch Cluanie (enlarged by the Glenmoriston Hydro-electric Scheme) to *Cluanie Inn Hotel* (24 m.). Hence the way is down **Glen Shiel** to **Shiel Bridge,** at the head of Loch Duich. Here the main road swings to the right: that continuing straight ahead takes pedestrians and cyclists by a shorter and less hilly route to the ferry at Totaig, opposite Dornie, but at a short distance a fork left proceeds to climb the **Mam Ratagain Pass,** which by a series of sharp elbows with a general gradient of 1 in 7 carries one in 3 miles to 1,116 feet above sea-level. The road is safe, but an awkward place for cars towing large or heavy caravans. The views are glorious. Half a mile short of **Glenelg** village, bear right for the ferry across **Kyle Rhea** to Skye (*see* p. 244). The road beyond Glenelg is narrow and hilly (but suitable for cars), leading in about 10 miles to Arnisdale, on Loch Hourn.

From Shiel Bridge the main road rounds the head of Loch Duich and then, after a steep climb at Keppoch, descends to **Dornie,** with good views of **Eilean Donan Castle** (*open weekdays, charge*) now restored. At Dornie (*hotel*) a bridge (free of toll) has been built to carry traffic over Loch Long to Ardelve, superseding the ferry. Three miles west of Ardelve (*Loch Duich Hotel*) the road from Strome Ferry (p. 412) comes in on the right, and then we reach **Kyle of Lochalsh** (*Lochalsh, Kyle*), a small town, with hotels, banks and shops and glorious views across to Skye. It is of importance as the departure point of the ferry across to Kyleakin, but is also a centre for fishing and for sea trips, being connected by steamer with Mallaig, Armadale, Portree and Stornoway. Here too is the termination of the railway line from Inverness.

SKYE.

Access.—*By rail.*—From the south *viâ* Edinburgh, Glasgow and Fort William to Mallaig, thence steamer *viâ* Kyle of Lochalsh to Portree, or ferry from Kyle of Lochalsh to Kyleakin.

From the south and Glasgow *viâ* Stirling, Perth and Inverness to Kyle of Lochalsh, thence steamer to Portree, or ferry from Kyle of Lochalsh to Kyleakin.

By Boat.—From Mallaig and Kyle of Lochaish in connection with trains, and by ferry from Kyle of Lochaish to Kyleakin.

By Road.—From Fort William or Inverness by the Great Glen to Invergarry or Invermoriston and thence *viâ* Cluanie to Loch Duich. Thence to Dornie and Kyle of Lochalsh. From Inverness also *viâ* Garve to Strome Ferry and Kyle of Lochalsh.

Ferries.—Three ferries link Skye with the mainland, each carrying cars:

(1) Kyle of Lochalsh–Kyleakin, (2) Mallaig–Armadale and (3) Glenelg–Kylerhea.

KYLE OF LOCHALSH–KYLEAKIN.—Continuous services daily including Sundays. No advance booking.

[Note: To reach Kyle of Lochalsh by road it is necessary to cross either Dornie Bridge or Strome Ferry.]

MALLAIG–ARMADALE.—Car ferry service by MacBrayne steamers. Daily except Sundays. Rates from £1.35 according to car length. Advance booking advisable, but no telephone bookings accepted. Apply David MacBrayne Ltd., 302 Buchanan Street, Glasgow, C.2. Tel.: 041–332 9644.

GLENELG–KYLERHEA.—Continuous car ferry service May to September, daily except Sundays, from 8.30 a.m. to dusk.

STROME.—Continuous service from 8 a.m. till dusk (fare and a half if after 10 p.m.). No Sunday service.

NOTE: (1) There is limited communication with and in Skye on Sundays. (2) Pier dues may be charged in some places. (3) There is no air service except in special emergencies.

SO much has been written regarding the misty mountains of Skye that it is desirable to stress the fact that the attractions of the island are by no means solely for climbers. Skye has boating of all kinds, bathing, fishing, golf, tennis, and the Games are an important fixture. " Skye Week " (usually held at the end of May) is an annual event of " festivities and typical Hebridean celebrations "—Highland games, ceilidh, piping competitions, etc.

Nor is the weather so persistently wet as might be imagined. There are wet days, as in all mountainous districts (and visitors should not go unprepared for them), but there are also many fine days, particularly in June.

The island is of extremely irregular shape, some 50 miles from end to end with a width varying from 4 to 25 miles. The principal places are Portree, Broadford, Kyleakin and Dunvegan.

Visitors who cross from the mainland by the Kyle of Lochalsh ferry land at **Kyleakin** (*King's Arms*, *White Heather*, *Marine*, etc.), a pleasant little village bordering the broad strip of green turf through which the road runs and with grand views.

Overlooking the pier is the ruined **Castle Moil**, reputed to have been built by a Danish princess nicknamed "Saucy Mary," who stretched a chain across the Kyle and allowed no ship to pass without paying toll.

From Kyleakin to Broadford is a matter of eight miles. At Lusa the mountain road from **Kylerhea** comes in on the left. It is a steep narrow road, but those who have climbed the Mam Ratagain Pass (p. 243) in order to reach the Kylerhea Ferry will not be worried by this climb through Glen Arroch.

A few miles west of Lusa is—

BROADFORD.

Buses.—To Kyleakin, Portree, etc.
Distances.—Kyleakin, 8; Armadale, 16½; Elgol, 15; Portree, 26.
Hotels.—*Broadford*, *Dunollie*, etc.
Youth Hostel.—On north shore of Broadford Bay.

Broadford is the second largest community on Skye, though here as elsewhere on the island the term "parish" would be more aptly descriptive than "village," the houses and hotels being spread over a considerable area. The main portion overlooks Broadford Bay, where boating and fishing can be enjoyed.

Broadford to Loch Scavaig (15 miles).—Almost at once the Red Coolins—**Beinn Dearg** (2,323 feet) and **Beinn na Caillich** (2,403 feet)—spring into view, looking very shapely and forming a horseshoe suggesting a nice walk. The road winds past the ruined church of Kilchrist and the neighbouring loch and through hilly pastoral country and then comes a full-length view of **Blaven** (3,042 feet), its eastern face riven with corries. The beauty of the view is intensified by **Loch Slapin**, in the foreground, which on a calm morning mirrors the mountain delightfully.

From **Torrin** (or **Torran**) the road runs round the head of Loch Slapin (from which a path leads northwards through Strath

Mor to Luib) and then follows the western side of Loch Slapin past the entrance to Strathaird House and finally drops down to Elgol on the shore of Loch Scavaig.

Walkers making for Coruisk should leave the Elgol road by a path which starts by the entrance gates of Strathaird House and goes nearly due westward, keeping well up on the hill-side to avoid the boggy ground below, and in four or five miles arrives at **Camasunary**, a farmhouse at the head of a sandy little bay. Camasunary is an important meeting-point of routes: northward through Glen Sligachan to Sligachan Hotel; southward down the coast to Elgol (but this walk should be taken in the reverse direction, for the sake of the views) and westward to Loch Coruisk. This last walk is one of the excursions for which Skye is famed. From Camasunary take the narrow path on the far side of the stream, working round the steep and rocky headland at a considerable height above the sea. The distance is not more than four miles, but the walk is extremely rough and is not recommended to those who dislike narrow and exposed paths. The worst portion of all is at the notorious **Bad Step**, where the rocks over which one passes shelve steeply to the sea. However, by climbing above the rock face one can reach a heather track running about 70 feet above the crack forming the Bad Step.

The road from Broadford ends at **Elgol**, a small and very scattered upland village (boarding house and cottage accommodation) from which there is a steep descent to the beach (car park). The beach commands what is probably the finest sea and mountain view in Britain—that up Loch Scavaig to the heart of the Coolins. In the rocky amphitheatre beyond Loch Scavaig lies Loch Coruisk.

LOCH CORUISK.

Boats take parties from Elgol (and Mallaig) at prices varying according to the number of passengers on board. Time is usually allowed for an exploration of Loch Coruisk and its immediate surroundings, but special arrangements should be made for a longer stay. A landing is made during the weekly steamer excursion from Mallaig.

The real grandeur of this incomparable scene—the quint-essence of Skye—is only to be appreciated in the course of the approach to it across the waters of Loch Scavaig. Loch Coruisk itself is not visible, but the great rocky amphitheatre in which it lies is mirrored in the waves and the whole picture is so satisfying that even the most daring artist would not require to take liberties with any detail of the grouping or colour.

From the landing place a few minutes' walk bring us above the end of **Loch Coruisk** ("Coroosk") and the view from this point is such that most people decide to have their picnic here and to explore the loch-side afterward. There is a mountain hut on the shore.

For those who are not returning by boat we may mention that the path to Sligachan is by the east side of Loch Coruisk as far as the big burn (say about half a mile). Here turn to the right and (keeping burn and Loch Choire Riabhaich on the left) an easy climb leads to the summit of **Drumhain** (1,038 feet—a grand viewpoint). Here is a large cairn. The view of the Coolin ridge from Drumhain is most impressive; unfortunately it is often blotted out by mist and rain. By walking along the summit of Drumhain in a north-west direction for about a mile a very fine view into **Harta Corrie** may be obtained. This is one of the wildest corries in the Coolins, hemmed in by steep black rock peaks extending from Sgurr nan Gillean on the right to Bruach na Frithe and Bidean Druim nan Ramh on the left.

The direct descent from Drumhain to Harta Corrie is not easy and one should therefore retrace one's steps to the cairn at the pass. From the cairn a track leads northwards across an eastern shoulder of the hill and then descends into Glen Sligachan and joins the Camasunary path at a point about 1 mile north of Loch an Athain. From here the long and tedious walk down Glen Sligachan begins, and it will take one and a half to two hours' steady walking to reach Sligachan.

Broadford to Armadale.—Armadale is situated in the southernmost point of Skye, in the district known as Sleat. The run is interesting on account of the many beautiful views of the mainland after the first 6 or 7 miles have been covered, the mountains around **Loch Hourn** showing up particularly well. Between 8 and 9 miles from Broadford is **Isle Ornsay** (hotel), the name applying to the village as well as to the island off the coast. Beyond Knock and Kilmore we pass Armadale Castle and so come to **Ardvasar**, a small village with an hotel, and near to Armadale pier and the car ferry for Mallaig.

Broadford to Portree. This is one of the most interesting roads in the island, the views changing continually and being almost throughout of a high order. About 16 miles from Broadford is the **Sligachan Hotel**, famous as a headquarters for climbs in—

THE COOLINS.

The Coolins (or Cuillins) undoubtedly provide the most splendid mountain scene and the finest climbing in Britain. It is not a question of height or extent (for the highest point is but 3,251 feet above the sea and the main group measures only about 8 miles by 6 in extent) but of proportions, as a result of which the peaks seem to soar to a much greater height than they do in fact and possess a sublimity which is not encountered elsewhere in Britain.

It cannot be too strongly emphasized that walking and climbing about the Coolins is dangerous for those unaccustomed to such conditions. The steepness of the routes is such that in several cases there is no feasible alternative route, so that if one misses the right path one is almost bound to get into difficulties which might trouble even experienced climbers. The compass, owing to the magnetic rock (especially on the ridges), is unreliable. *See also* p. 20.

The best known and most popular of the Coolins is undoubtedly **Sgurr nan Gillean** (3,167 feet)—" the peak of the young men "—all in all, probably the most difficult " tourist " mountain in Scotland. The easiest way up it has some steps, especially nearing the top, that are distinctly trying to the uninitiated, and several people have lost their lives on it because they did not treat the mountain with the care and respect it deserves. *It should not be attempted without a guide.*

The ascent from Sligachan will take three to four hours, and the descent two to three hours. From the hotel follow the Dunvegan road for a third of a mile ; then turn off on the left by the track leading to Cuillin Lodge. Cross the Red Burn by the stepping stones (if this is not practicable a footbridge nearer the hotel may be used) and keep southward over the moor. Loch a' Choire Riabhaich is passed on the left, and the Coire nan allt Geala is gained by a rough, steep, stone shoot. Progress up this corrie is over a wilderness of boulders and screes to the ridge which extends south-eastwards from the summit. This ridge is struck at a point about 300 feet below the top. From this the route lies along and up the ridge, dipping over to the left-hand side in places where the direct ascent up the ridge is too steep. Hands as well as feet will here have to be constantly used, and a sharp lookout for the small cairns which indicate the right route : the nail marks on the rocks, too, are a useful guide. A little short of the summit a gap has to be crossed, which at first sight seems a bit sensational ; but the rock is firm and good, and the handholds and footholds are excellent. The top is a very narrow one, with precipitous cliffs all around. The descent is exactly by the way you came up.

Bruach na Frithe (3,143 feet)—" the ridge of the forest " —is not so well known as Sgurr nan Gillean, but the view from it is, if anything, finer than from Sgurr nan Gillean, and it is much more easily scaled ; in fact, there is nothing to prevent any tourist, with mountain experience, from ascending Bruach na Frithe. Time, about four hours up and three hours down. Turn off the Dunvegan road as for Sgurr nan Gillean (*see above*) but instead of crossing the Red Burn at the Lodge keep to the

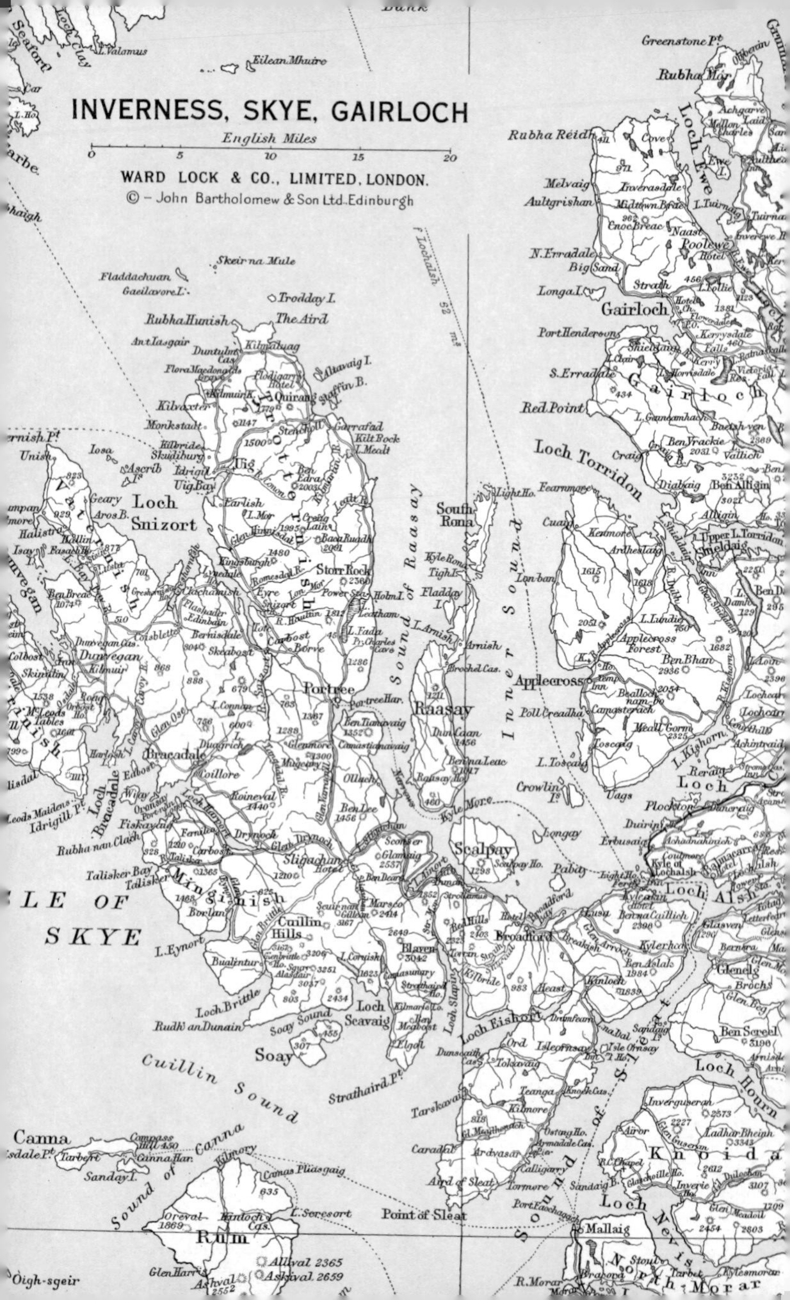
INVERNESS, SKYE, GAIRLOCH
English Miles
0 5 10 15 20
WARD LOCK & CO., LIMITED, LONDON.
© – John Bartholomew & Son Ltd. Edinburgh
ISLE OF SKYE
Loch Snizort
Vaternish
Dunvegan
Trotternish
Uig
Portree
Raasay
Sound of Raasay
Inner Sound
South Rona
Scalpay
Pabay
Broadford
Cuillin Hills
Sligachan Hotel
Minginish
Bracadale
Loch Bracadale
Soay
Soay Sound
Cuillin Sound
Canna
Sound of Canna
Rum
Point of Sleat
Sound of Sleat
Loch Eishort
Mallaig
Loch Nevis
North Morar
Knoidart
Loch Hourn
Glenelg
Loch Alsh
Kyle of Lochalsh
Applecross
Loch Torridon
Gairloch
Poolewe
Loch Ewe
Rubha Reidh
Greenstone Pt.
Staffin B.
Storr Rock
Skeir na Mule
Trodday I.
Rubha Hunish
Duntulm Cas.
Blaven 3042
Ben Screel 3196
Allival 2365
Askival 2659

ROSS AND CROMARTY
INVERNESS
Loch Broom
Ullapool
Rhidorroch Forest
Glen Achallt
Corriemulzie Lo.
Strath Cullenach
Strath Carron
Bonar Bridge
L. Migdale
Spinningdale
Freevater Forest
Seana Braigh
Glen Beg
Glen More
Diebidale Lo.
Ben Tharsuinn
Dundonnell
An Teallach
Ben Derg
Braemore
Measach Falls
Dirrie More
Glascarnoch Reservoir
Strath Vaich
Strath Rannoch
Kildermorie Lo.
L. Morie
Loch Glass
Wyvis Lo.
Boath
Dealty
Knock Fyrish
Alness
Novar Ho.
Evanton
Cromarty
Ben Wyvis
Inchbae
Altguish Inn
Fannich Forest
Loch Fannich
Fannich Lo.
Strathcrombie
Ben Fionn
Heights of Kinlochewe
Kinlochewe
Achanalt Sta.
Loch Luichart
Garve
Gorstan
Achterneed Sta.
Strathpeffer
DINGWALL
Conon Br.
Ferintosh
Black Isle
Achnasheen
Sgurr Vuillin
Strath Bran
Glenmeanie
Dalbreac Lo.
Strath Conon
Fairburn Cas.
Urray
Muir of Ord
Redcastle
Kessock
Beauly Firth
Beauly
Kilmorack
Kirkhill
Moruisg
Glen Evaig
Glen Orrin
Corrybauch
Achnashellach
Sgurr Chaoruinn
East Monar Forest
Loch Monar
Lurg Mhor
Glen Farrar
Strathfarrar
Struy
Eskadale
L. Bruiach
Beaufort Cas.
Kiltarlity
Belladrum
Lochend
Dochfour Ho.
Sgurr na Lapaich
Riabhachan
L. Mullardoch
Glen Cannich
Strath Glass
Corrimony
Glen Urquhart
Milton
Drumnadrochit
Lewiston
Balmacaan
Urquhart Cas.
Dores
Tomich
Guisachan Ho.
Cougie
L. Affric
Glen Affric
Mam Soul
Cain Eige
Balmacaan Forest
Mealfourvonie
Inverfarigaig
Foyers
Loch Ness
Aberchalder
Invermoriston
Glen Moriston
Ben Attow
Glen Shiel
Cluanie
Loch Cluanie
Loch Loyne
Fort Augustus
Ceann a' Mhaim
Whitebridge
Glen Doe
Corriyarrick Hill
Glengarry Forest
Glen Quoich
Loch Quoich
Tomdown Hotel
Glen Garry
L. Garry
Invergarry
Loch Oich
Ben Tee
Kilfinnan
Laggan Locks
Loch Lochy
Letterfinlay
Loch Arkaig
Glen Roy
Glen Gloy
Meallgarve
Garva Bri.
Laggan
Shirramore
L. Crunachan
L. Spey
Lochlaggan Hotel
Ardverikie
Carn Mairg
Carn Leack

track which follows its left bank to the Beallach a' Mhaim (pron. *Vaim*), 1,132 feet. From here turn south up over the long grassy slope for about 1,000 feet, and then over easy screes and rock to the summit. On nearing the summit keep below the ridge a little to the right, and so avoid all difficulties. The descent can be made by the east ridge towards Sgurr nan Gillean, and then down into Fionn Choire, where the walking is smooth and pleasant. It is worth while when on Bruach na Frithe to go round the head of Fionn Choire to the Bhasteir and Tooth.

Sgurr Alasdair (3,251 feet)—" Alexander's Peak "—is the highest peak in the Coolins, and in every way worthy of its reputation. It is climbed from Glen Brittle (*see below*). The best route of ascent is *viâ* the Sgumain Boulder Shoot from Coire Lagan (lower) and thence over Sgumain and along the intervening ridge between the two peaks. A " bad step " is present on this ridge, but may easily be avoided lower down in the Coire Ghrundda side. The descent may be made by a scramble down the Stone Shoot. The Stone Shoot is not easy to find and a guide is essential for all but thoroughly experienced climbers. Time from Glen Brittle, five to seven hours.

Full details of the ascents and climbing routes in the Coolins will be found in the Scottish Mountaineering Club's *Guide to Skye.*

To **Glen Brittle** (14 miles).—Either by the passable and hilly road from Drynoch, on the Dunvegan road, or *viâ* the Bealach a' Mhaim, a delightful and easy walk of three hours or so from Sligachan (*see* under Bruach na Frithe, above). The track becomes somewhat indistinct on the other side of the Bealach, until it joins the road near the head of Glen Brittle, but the view of the Coolins from the top of the pass before descending into Glen Brittle is unsurpassed. **Glen Brittle** is a mountaineering centre with accommodation (*Glenbrittle Boarding House*) (*Rhudunan P.O.*), Youth Hostel and S.M.C. hut. There are grand sands and safe bathing and motor-boat trips to Isle of Soay, Loch Coruisk, Canna, Eigg and Rhum. It should be added that the road from Carbost to Glen Brittle is narrow with occasional passing bays. Daily bus service from Glen Brittle to Carbost, Sligachan and Portree.

The route up the burn which comes down just beside Glen Brittle House, near the foot of the glen, leads in about two hours of pleasant walking into **Coire Lagan**, a scene of great grandeur. Cross the burn a little above the house, and then, after keeping the burn beside you on your left for a short distance —say 200 or 300 feet—bear away to the right until you reach a fair-sized loch—Loch an Fhir-bhallaich = " the loch of the spotted folk " (i.e. trout). Skirt along the side of the loch, and continuing on in the same direction Coire Lagan will come into view. Bear round to the left a little, and continue straight up, making for part of the corrie. After a little scramble up some extraordinary glaciated rocks you find yourself at the side of a small loch amid a scene of the wildest grandeur (**Loch Coire Lagan**, 1,845 feet). The descent should be made by precisely the same way as you came up.

Coire na Creiche (6 miles) is one of the wildest corries in the Coolins. From Sligachan follow the Bruaich na Frithe route (*see* p. 248) to the summit of the Bealach a' Mhaim. The corrie lies over this pass to the left, and to obtain the best view you must descend some distance down towards Glen Brittle, on the farther side of the pass.

For **Harta Corrie** *see* p. 247.

PORTREE.

Access.—By road from Kyleakin, etc. (*See above.*) Steamer connections with Kyle of Lochalsh and Mallaig. Road connection for Armadale-Mallaig car ferry.
Distances.—Sligachan, 9 miles; Broadford, 26; Kyleakin, 35; Staffin, 17; Uig (*viâ* Staffin), 32, direct, 14½.
Golf Links (9 holes) on west side of town.
Hotels.—*Royal, Caledonian, Coolin Hills,* etc.
Tennis.—Courts near Post Office.

Although its population numbers only about 1,700, Portree is the most considerable community on Skye. It is a compact little place on a hillside partly enclosing its Harbour—a bay on the picturesque Portree Loch. The immediate neighbourhood is well wooded, a few minutes away are heather-covered hills and beyond them on the one hand are the glorious Coolins and to the north the extraordinary Storr Rock. Portree is an excellent centre. There are motor, steamer and motor-boat trips, and walks of endless interest.

Prince Charlie's Cave (5 miles by boat; motor-boat trips run from the Harbour) is unremarkable in itself, and it is doubtful whether it ever sheltered the Prince. The boat trip along the coast to it, however, is very interesting. The Cave lies to the north of the harbour.

The **Storr Rock.** From Portree follow the Staffin road for 5 miles past Loch Fada and to the northern end of Loch Leathan, the Storr being in full view with its square-cut top and its Needle Rock, the veritable **Old Man of Storr**, on the right. The upper cliff of which the Storr itself forms the crown is best climbed by leaving the road at the far end of Loch Leathan and making away to the left over a succession of grassy humps for a stony little ravine, whence the ridge of the cliff begins to rise steeply for the mountain-top. A scanty rill flows down this ravine and into Loch Leathan. The final climb is short and steep, but its roughness makes it quite feasible. Once on top you have only to mount the long grass slope which bends round the tremendous black precipices forming the seaward front of the hills.

Portree to Uig *viâ* **Staffin.** For the first few miles the view is dominated by the Storr Rock, with the Old Man of Storr standing away to the right of the main mass. Where the road approaches the cliffs beyond **Loch Leathan**, it is worth walking across the grass for the sight of the grand falls by which the waters of the Loch precipitate themselves to the sea at Bearreraig Bay.

Loch Mealt, near Staffin, also spills its waters into the sea by a fine cataract, but the noteworthy sight hereabouts is the rock-formation composing the cliffs, its alternate horizontal and vertical bands having given it the name of the *Kilt Rock*. There are good views from the cliff edge a little south of the loch.

Staffin (*Staffin House*) is a scattered parish of smallholdings, which seem particularly colourful, set out on the slopes at the foot of—

QUIRAING,

one of the strangest and most fascinating mountains in Scotland. To describe its form briefly and accurately would be almost impossible, so confused is this mass of cliffs and pinnacles.

From the Staffin—Uig road it is a clear walk along the top to Meal nan Suiramach (1,779 feet), but this route misses the most surprising feature of Quiraing—*the Table*—an area of smooth green turf sunk, as it were, into the solid rock until it is surrounded on almost every side by huge cliffs. The path to the Table from the Uig road keeps along the south-eastern slope of the mountain just below the scree and passes between the main mountain and the projecting rock known as the Needle.

Beyond Staffin Bay the coast road comes to **Flodigarry**, where is an hotel occupying the residence built by a descendant of Flora Macdonald who herself lived in the adjacent cottage (the cottage is courteously shown to interested visitors). The views from this corner are exquisite.

From Flodigarry we continue to **Duntulm** (*hotel*), where the scanty remains of the castle rise gauntly above the cliff edge. Rather more than 2 miles southward a lane on the left of the road leads to the burying ground of **Kilmuir**, where is the large cross forming the Flora Macdonald Memorial.

Flora Macdonald (1727–90) was the daughter of a small farmer at Milton, in South Uist. Even as a child she showed unusual talents and was taken with the family of Sir Alexander Macdonald of the Isles to Edinburgh, so that she might there finish her education.

While she was visiting the Clanranalds in Benbecula, Prince Charles Edward landed there in the course of his flight after Culloden (1746), and after some persuasion Flora agreed to help in his escape. On the pretence of going to visit her mother (who had been abducted and married when Flora was only 6 years old, by Hugh Macdonald of Armadale), she obtained a passport for herself and a party which included "Betty Burke, an Irish spinning maid." Betty, of course, was the Prince in disguise. After a very rough passage the party proposed to land at Vaternish, in Skye, but on seeing militia there they landed instead at Monkstadt, the home of that Sir Alexander Macdonald who had befriended Flora. Militia were at Monkstadt also, but arrangements were made for the Prince to spend the night at Kingsburgh, and next day he left by boat from Portree to Raasay.

Unfortunately Flora's part in the escape became generally known and she was arrested and sent to the Tower of London, whence she was released under the Act of Indemnity. Returning to Skye, she married Alexander Macdonald of Kingsburgh and the pair settled down at Flodigarry. Here they lived for over 20 years, subsequently moving to Kingsburgh, where she was visited by Dr. Johnson. In 1774 the family emigrated to America, but returned in 1779–80, and they lived at Kingsburgh until Flora died there in 1790.

In front as we continue **Loch Snizort** appears, with Vaternish beyond—actually a part of Skye but seemingly so distant as to form part of a separate piece of country. The next few miles, however, will show increasingly how indented is the coastline of Skye, particularly the point just beyond the rise from Totscore where the whole of Uig Bay and many of the ramifications of Loch Snizort come into view. **Uig** (*Uig Hotel ; apartments ; Youth Hostel*) is a good place for a quiet holiday, with fishing, boating and walking and other excursions. There is car ferry connections between Uig and Lochmaddy (North Uist) and Tarbert (Harris).

Beyond Uig is **Kingsburgh**, with its memories of Flora Macdonald (*see above*), and then the road runs steadily down through Romesdal to Snizort and Borve and so to Portree.

Portree to Dunvegan (22 miles).

Dunvegan (*Dunvegan, Misty Isle*, etc.) is on the shore of Loch Dunvegan, with boating and fishing, but is mainly visited on account of its Castle, for centuries the seat of the Macleod chiefs. It stands to the north of the village on a rock having the sea on three sides, and formerly could be reached only by a boat and a subterranean passage, but access is now obtained by bridge. The Castle and its grounds are open to the public April to mid-October on weekday afternoons, 2–5.

It is said to have been founded in the ninth century, its high tower being added four hundred years later, and a third portion being built in the reign of James VI. In recent years it has been put into thorough repair. It is among the houses that claim to be "the oldest inhabited castle in Scotland." Johnson, Boswell and Sir Walter Scott are among those who have been entertained within its walls. One of the treasures of the castle is a "Fairy Flag," which on being waved will bring relief to the chief or any of his clan. The charm was to act three times and has twice been employed.

Prominent across the loch are two **isolated hills**, called on account of their curious flat summits **Macleod's Tables.** Each is about 1,600 feet in height.

The first part of the run from Dunvegan to Sligachan is of great interest on account of the views of **Loch Bracadale**—its coast extremely irregular and its surface sprinkled with islands large and small. Some of the cliffs are magnificent. At the southern extremity of Duirinish are **Macleod's Maidens**, three basaltic columns. The tallest is 200 feet high, whilst the others are only about half as lofty. They rise sheer out of the sea, and are backed by cliffs from six to seven hundred feet high. Beyond Bracadale village we round the long and narrow **Loch Beag** (walkers and cyclists can use the ferry) and then have before us the first of the magnificent series of views of the Coolins which provide such a splendid culmination to the run.

THE OUTER HEBRIDES.

The Hebrides, or Western Isles, are commonly divided into two portions, the Outer and the Inner Hebrides. The former comprise Lewis—with Harris—often called the Long Island, North Uist, Benbecula, South Uist, Eriskay, and Barra, with Vatersay, Mingulay, and Berneray, extending from the Butt of Lewis in the north to Barra Head, in the south, a distance of about 130 miles. Fifty miles west of the Outer Hebrides is the small island of St. Kilda.

The Inner Hebrides are more widely scattered along the coast (for descriptions *see* Index). The largest are Skye, Mull, Jura, Islay, Rhum, Eigg, Coll, Tiree, Colonsay and Oronsay.

Access.—Stornoway in Lewis reached by mail steamer (cars carried) from Mallaig or Kyle of Lochalsh. Tarbert in Harris and Lochmaddy in North Uist have car ferry connection with Uig in Skye. Lochboisdale (South Uist) and Castlebay (Barra) are reached from Oban on the Inner Isles mail service via Coll and Tiree. In addition to MacBrayne's steamers the islands are served by coasting steamers from Glasgow, etc.

Car ferry from Uig to Tarbert and Lochmaddy.

Daily bus service between Stornoway and Harris.

Air Routes from Glasgow and Inverness (*see* p. 16).

The Outer Hebrides consist chiefly of bleak stretches of bog or moorland, and the scenery is only saved from being monotonous by the numerous lochs and inlets of the sea, and by picturesque ranges in Harris, South Uist and Barra. Sporting visitors to the Outer Hebrides are mainly attracted by the salmon and trout in the streams and lochs. Some of the beaches on the western coasts, however, are among the best in Britain.

Stornoway, with a population of 5,300, is the only important town in **Lewis**, the northern part of the principal island of the Outer Hebrides. It is a busy fishing port, and the centre of an extensive Harris Tweed industry. Stornoway Castle, just over a hundred years old, is now a technical college ; the former Castle, by the steamer pier, was destroyed by Cromwell. (*Hotels : Caledonian, Crown, Royal, County, Newton House, Lewis, Caberfeidh, Hebridean*). A golf course (18 holes) is laid out in the castle grounds.

The **Standing Stones of Callernish,** at the head of Loch Roag, on the west coast, 15 miles from Stornoway, form one of the largest and most perfect Stone Circles in Scotland. Eight miles west of Callernish is the famous **Broch of Carloway.**

Holm Head, near Stornoway, was the scene of a terrible disaster on January 1, 1919, when the naval yacht *Iolaire* ran ashore during a storm, there being only about 50 survivors out of a party of some 280 Service men returning home for New Year's leave.

Harris, the southern part of the island, is in Inverness-shire, is mountainous in surface, and is chiefly occupied as deer-forests. From it come the true Harris tweeds. The chief town is **Tarbert** (*Harris Hotel*). *Clisham* (2,622 feet), the highest mountain in the Outer Hebrides, can be conveniently ascended from Tarbert. There is some good salmon and sea-trout fishing held by the hotels at Tarbert and Obbe or Leverburgh, also sea-fishing, etc. Near Leverburgh at **Rodel,** on the southern extremity of the island, are the considerable remains of an ancient church.

Some 52 miles west of Harris, its nearest neighbour, is the lonely island of **St. Kilda,** now in the possession of the National Trust for Scotland and used as a nature conserve.

Lochmaddy (*hotel*) is in **North Uist,** the third largest of the Outer Hebrides. It is in effect the county town for the portion of the Outer Hebrides from North Harris southwards which form a part of Inverness-shire. The island abounds in wild life, including red deer, wild cats, wildfowl, otters and seals. The principal occupations are crofting, seaweed processing and wool spinning. From Lochmaddy a road leads across the island to **Carinish** (*hotel*) at the south end of the island and continues by a new causeway (1960) across the *North Ford,* which connects North Uist with **Benbecula.**

Benbecula is traversed by a road 5 miles long from north to south, with an hotel at Creagorry at the South Ford. The South Ford is about ¾ mile wide and is now spanned by a long single-track bridge.

South Uist, 21 miles long, is the second largest of the Outer Hebrides. A fair road runs along the west side of the island from **Carnan** (*hotel*) at the South Ford to **Pollachar** (*inn*) at the south end of the island. Near the road are the ruins of the Birthplace of Flora Macdonald. **Lochboisdale** (*hotel*) is a favourite resort for anglers. The principal hills on the island are **Ben Mhor** (2,034 feet) and **Hecla** (1,988 feet). The ascent of the former is worth doing.

Eriskay, south of South Uist, is interesting as being the first place in Scotland on which Prince Charlie set foot and is celebrated as having been the principal source from which the late Mrs. Kennedy Fraser obtained "The Songs of the Hebrides."

Barra, the island south of Eriskay, has an important fishing station at **Castlebay** (*hotel*) which is served by steamer from Oban, and car ferry from Mallaig. On a small rocky islet in the bay is Kisimul Castle (*open Sats,* 2–5), the largest of such in the Outer Hebrides. **Heaval** (1,260 feet) is the highest hill on the island and may be easily ascended from Castlebay in an hour or so. It commands a good view of the southern islands. These latter are small and many of them are uninhabited. Their best features are the magnificent cliffs on the Atlantic sides of **Mingulay** and **Berneray.** Biulacraig on the former is almost vertical and has a height of 753 feet. The lighthouse at Barra Head on Berneray is perched almost on the edge of a high cliff and shows its light at a height of 683 feet above sea level. If a suitable boat can be obtained at Castlebay and the weather is favourable it is worth while to make a visit to these southern islands.

EDINBURGH TO STIRLING AND PERTH.

LEAVE Edinburgh by Dean Bridge and the Queensferry Road (*see* Map, pp. 120–1), passing Daniel Stewart's College on left and on far right Fettes College, conducted on the lines of an English public school. **Lauriston Castle,** to the right of Davidson's Mains (which formerly rejoiced in the name of Muttonhole), was the birthplace of John Law, the financier, founder of the Bank of France (1716) and originator of the bubble Mississippi Scheme (1719). The Castle is now national property (*admission,* 11–1, 2–5*;* Nov.–March, weekends only, 2–4*; closed Fridays. Castle and grounds,* 5p.; *grounds only,* 11–dusk, 2p.). Hence, passing two golf courses, to the newly widened **Cramond Bridge** over the *Almond.* The scene of the historic adventure of James V was, however, at old Cramond Brig, an ancient structure, visible a little lower down the river.

James V, fond of mingling incognito with his people, had, according to the popular tale, been making love to a peasant girl, when he was attacked by her suitor and several relatives. He was on the point of being overpowered when a peasant named Jock Howieson, crying, "What, sax agens ane! I'm for the ane," rushed forward, brandishing the flail with which he had been at work. He soon dispersed the assailants, and the monarch in gratitude bestowed upon him the lands of Braehead, on the condition of presenting a ewer, basin and towel for the king to wash his hands whenever he passed Cramond Brig. The service is still binding on the owners of Braehead.

There was a Roman station at **Cramond,** now a quaint little village at the mouth of the river. In Cramond House grounds is the Dunfermline College of Physical Education.

Across the *Almond* is the Dalmeny estate (Earl of Rosebery); then, on left at fork, a road leads to **Dalmeny** village, with a most interesting little Norman church—the finest example of the style in Scotland. It has recently been carefully restored. Here are buried Sir A. Primrose, founder of the Rosebery family, and his successors, including the Earl of Rosebery, the eminent statesman (d. 1929).

Dundas Castle, an ancient double tower, with a modern mansion beside it, stands upon an eminence above **South Queensferry** (*Hawes Inn, Sealscraig*), a small but interesting old-world burgh. The famous ferry across the

Forth at this point which ceased to operate on the opening of the Forth Bridge in 1964 received its name from the fact that Margaret, Queen of Malcolm Canmore, often crossed here on her frequent journeys between Edinburgh and Dunfermline.

The Forth Bridges.

The intrusion of the Firths of Forth and Tay into the East Coast formerly prevented a direct seaboard railway route and necessitated a considerable deflection to the west. The Tay, after one failure, was successfully bridged ; and in 1890 the scheme was augmented by the opening of the magnificent railway bridge over the Forth.

The projection of the North Queensferry peninsula brings the opposite banks of the Firth of Forth to within a mile of each other, and midway is the rocky island of Inchgarvie. The channels (each 570 yards wide) north and south of the islet are upwards of 200 feet deep, prohibiting a supported bridge.

The Forth Railway Bridge consists of north and south approach viaducts and three huge steel double cantilevers, the arms of each of which extend 680 feet north and south from central piers with two lattice girder suspended spans of 350 feet between the ends of the cantilevers of the two main spans. The central towers of the cantilevers are higher than St. Paul's Cathedral and are each supported on four huge main piers. The length of the bridge is 5,349½ feet, or with the approaches, 8,295 feet, or nearly 1½ miles. The spans are of colossal dimensions, two being 1,710 feet (the Sydney Harbour arch is 1,650 feet in span) and two 680 feet. The permanent way is carried by rail troughs and cross girders at a height of over 150 feet above high water. The bridge cost nearly three and a quarter millions sterling and was designed for a wind pressure of fifty-six pounds to the square foot, a wind force unknown in these islands.

Half a mile west the new **Forth Road Bridge** crosses the Forth from beside Port Edgar to North Queensferry, near the Mackintosh rock. It was begun in November, 1958, and opened for traffic during 1964. It is the longest suspension bridge in Europe, having a length with approach viaducts of 1½ miles. The central span is 3,300 feet, the two side spans 1,340 feet each, while the steel towers rise to a height of 500 feet above the water. It was completed at an estimated cost of £18,000,000.

On the north shore of the Firth, west of the Forth Bridges, is **Rosyth Naval Base.**

Two and a half miles west of Queensferry is **Hopetoun House,** the beautiful home of the Marquis of Linlithgow. The house was begun in 1699 by Sir William Bruce, and completed by William Adam and his two sons. (*May to September, daily except Thursday and Friday,* 1.30–5.30. *Admission charges. Teas.*)

From Queensferry it is 8 miles to—

Linlithgow,

(Hotels : *Star and Garter, St. Michael's, Bonsyde, West Port*)

whose palace-walls, somewhat square and heavy-looking, are seen on the right. The town has many historical associations. In its palace Queen Mary was born, James IV, James V and Mary of Guise held court and Parliament and Councils sat ; in its church James IV was forewarned by the apparition of the disasters of Flodden ; in its streets the Regent Moray was shot.

A feature of the town is its wells—the *Cross Well* (a copy (1807) of an earlier structure) and *St. Michael's Fountain* are the most noteworthy.

St. Michaei's Church, just outside the palace, has striking features. It is Gothic of the fifteenth century and is still in use as a parish church.

The *Palace Grounds* are entered by a gateway surmounted by the insignia of the Orders of the Thistle, the Garter, the Golden Fleece, and St. Michael, forming the four Orders borne by James V.

The oldest parts of the **Palace** (*open* 9.30–7, *Sundays* 2–7, *closes winter at* 4, *fee*), the east and west sides, were mostly built in the fifteenth century ; the newest, the north side, in 1620. The original entrance was by a drawbridge on the east, where is still an archway surmounted by the Royal Arms, and the remains of a protecting forework.

On entering by the present doorway on the south side we have the *Guard Room* on the right. In the centre of the quadrangle is a *fountain,* erected by James V, of which that in front of Holyrood is a copy. To the original eastern entrance we cross and inspect the *Kitchens,* with a huge fireplace. On this side, too, is the *Lyon* or *Great Hall,* 100 feet long, with a noteworthy triple chimneypiece, the finest of its kind in Scotland, and well restored. It had a minstrels' gallery, and a long passage by the side of it leads to the *Chapel.* From it we pass through the royal apartments to the chamber in which (December 7, 1542) Queen Mary was born—a great contrast in point of size to that which witnessed her son's birth in Edinburgh Castle. A spiral staircase at the north-west corner leads up to *Queen Margaret's Bower*, the most perfect little room in the palace, square within, hexagonal without. There is a fine look-out from it, and here the Queen is fabled to have watched for the return of her husband, James IV, from Flodden.

Falkirk (*Royal, Temperance*), 7 miles west of Linlithgow, occupies a strategic position at the south end of the "pass" between the hills and the Forth. It stands near the eastern end of the **Antonine Wall** (*see* p. 147). Two battles were fought here: in 1298 Edward I defeated Wallace, and in 1716 Prince Charlie, retreating northward, won a welcome victory. Once famed for its cattle markets ("Falkirk Trysts") the town is now noted for its iron-works. The town Steeple is prominent.

North of the road connecting Linlithgow and Falkirk is **Grangemouth** (*Queen's, Lea Park*), a busy port with oil refineries, at the mouth of the old Forth and Clyde Canal (p. 147). The road to Grangemouth (continuing to Stirling) also serves the bridge over the Forth to **Kincardine** (p. 271).

Beyond Falkirk routes to the Highlands swing northward—the roads by Larbert or by Denny reuniting near the village of **Bannockburn**. The battlefield (*see* p. 262) whereon Robert the Bruce gained his crowning victory over the forces of Edward II in 1314 lies to the west of the road. Ahead the Ochil Hills have for some miles been increasingly prominent, and as we approach Stirling the strength of its position as a key to the routes to and from the Highlands is very apparent. To the right of the town the lofty Wallace Monument crowns the Abbey Craig.

STIRLING.

Early Closing.—Wednesdays.
Hotels.—*Station, Royal, Allan Park, Garfield* (unl.), *Golden Lion* (85 rooms), *St. Hilda's House. Youth Hostel.*
Railways.—London Midland Region from London (Euston), and from Edinburgh and Glasgow. Connection with Perth, Inverness, Aberdeen, etc.
Sports.—Bowls, fishing, golf, tennis, putting. Festival in May

The principal features of the town can be visited in the course of a short circular walk from the junction of Port

Street, by which Stirling is entered from the south, with King Street on the left. Looking up King Street are the old *Burgh Buildings*, with a statue of Wallace. Proceeding to the right up Baker Street and turning right into Broad Street, with **Darnley's House** at the foot, the Mercat Cross and Old Town House in the middle, the way leads to a curiously sculptured ruin called "*Mar's Work*," erected by the Earl of Mar in the sixteenth century, on the left of which is the Church of the Holy Rude (p. 262). Farther on the right is Argyll's Lodging (1630) (now in use as a Youth Hostel), built by Sir William Alexander, Earl of Stirling, poet and statesman, who founded the colony of Nova Scotia. Hence steps lead up to the *Esplanade*, from which there is a magnificent view. Here, too, is a good statue of Robert the Bruce. Crossing the drawbridge, one enters the precincts of the Castle itself.

Stirling Castle

Open April, May, Sept., 10–6.45 (Sundays from 11); June, July, Aug., 10–8; Oct.–Mar., 10–5 (Sundays from 1). Admission *fee*.

dominates the scene and is the chief feature of the town. A fortress from time immemorial, it was formerly a Royal residence of the Kings of Scotland. Within its walls were born James III, and perhaps James IV, and it was the scene of the coronations of James V and of Mary. The Castle contains the *Parliament Hall*, built by James III, once used as barracks; the *Palace*, built by James V, and the *Chapel Royal*, rebuilt by James VI for the baptism of his son, Prince Henry. In the *Douglas Room* (restored in 1856 after a fire) the eighth Earl of Douglas was murdered by James II. On the battlements are *Queen Mary's Look-out*, with the initials "M.R., 1561"—Mary lived in the Castle, or in the neighbourhood, from two until five years of age—and the *Victoria Look-out*, from which Queen Victoria and Prince Albert admired the scenery in 1842. From the Castle seven battlefields may be seen—including the scenes of the victories of Wallace and Bruce, Stirling Bridge (1297) and Bannockburn, near at hand.

The eye ranges over the Carse of Stirling, through which the Forth, above and below its junction with the Teith, meanders in a succession of bewildering curves from the far-off hills. Of these, Ben Lomond rises in the west, with The Cobbler beyond it; much nearer and just over a line of cottages below, Ben Ledi appears; between the two is Ben Venue; and to the right of Ben Ledi, just in sight, the peaks of Ben More and the broken summit of Ben Vorlich, and the rival one of Stuc-a-Chroin. Over Bridge of Allan is Ben Chonzie, beyond Crieff. The Wallace Monument, on its frowning crag, rises in front of the green Ochils in the north-east, in which direction the foreground is much richer than westwards. Then, due east, we have the tower of Cambuskenneth Abbey, about which the windings of the Forth are more perplexing than ever.

A fuller view southwards is obtained from the Ladies' Look-out,

entered by the south-west corner of the upper quadrangle, and from the Ladies' Rock in the Cemetery (*indicator*). In this direction, the Gillies Hill, west of Bannockburn (so called from the sudden appearance of the camp-followers on its ridge at a critical moment of the battle), may be seen from both viewpoints. From other parts of the ramparts we look across the plain of the Forth to Arthur's Seat at Edinburgh, just over the Alloa railway bridge, with the Pentlands to the right of it.

Notable in the Cemetery is the glass-protected *Virgin Martyrs' Memorial.* It represents two sisters, Margaret and Agnes Maclachlan, the Wigtown Martyrs (*see* p. 105). Hard by is a large pyramid known as the Covenanters' Monument. The *Church of the Holy Rude*, the ancient Parish Church, is situated south of the Cemetery. It is a beautiful and interesting Gothic building. The nave dates from 1414, and the choir from 1507. James VI (when 13 months old) was crowned in it (John Knox officiating on this occasion). For many years the interior was partitioned off into two separate churches but under a recent restoration scheme this has been discontinued. The tower commands a fine view.

The Guildhall (Cowane's Hospital), close at hand, contains some interesting relics, including John Cowane's chest, standard weights and measures of Scotland, etc.

From this point Port Street is regained by the **Back Walk**, a promenade along the west side of the hill. The Walk passes the Municipal Buildings, from which by Dumbarton Road we reach the **Smith Art Gallery and Museum** (*Weekdays* 10–5, *fee*), containing the *Stirling Heads* and a collection of Scottish folk material.

Excursions around Stirling.

Shore Road (just north of the station), the continuing Abbey Road and footbridge across the river lead to ruins of **Cambuskenneth Abbey**, founded by David I (1147) for Augustinian canons. Within its walls the Scottish Parliament once sat, and James III and his queen, Margaret of Denmark, were buried here: the present tombstone was placed over the grave by Queen Victoria. Little remains of the Abbey beyond the west doorway, fragments of the walls, and a striking tower, which is a good viewpoint. (*Open daily, no charge.*)

The Bore Stone and the **Field of Bannockburn**, 2 miles.—The road itself is of no particular interest, but the view from the Bore Stone is very good, and the gorge of the Bannock is surprisingly deep.

From Stirling the main road to the south leads in 2 miles to St. Ninian's, where take the Glasgow fork and a little farther again go to the right along a by-road leading to the **Bore Stone**. It is a square stone with a grating: a rotunda encircles the spot now in National Trust keeping. An equestrian statue of Bruce by Pilkington Jackson stands nearby. Hence Bruce is said to have superintended the battle, which took place on June 24, 1314, and resulted in the utter discomfiture of the English. According to one modern version the battle was fought much farther north, the English having crossed the Bannock lower down on the night of June 23/24, and being penned in by the Scots, who were the aggressors. But it is hard to see how, or why, the English could have got into so disadvantageous a position, and as the Bore Stone is on the edge of the ancient "New Park" of Stirling, in which Bruce passed the night, the traditional view has much to commend it, though the traditional figures 100,000 to 40,000 must be abandoned. Certainly the Bore Stone commands a wide view, the prospect including the plain of the Forth, the hills of Fife, and the Ochils, and, over the cliff and trees westward, the peaks of Ben Ledi, Ben Vorlich and many others. The first-named is most conspicuous. Stirling Castle and the Wallace Monument are also seen. The *Gillies Hill*, so called from the panic caused to the English by the sudden appearance of the gillies upon it, is a little north of west. Half a mile south, and left of the road, is the ruin of the cottage where James III was stabbed after the Battle of Sauchieburn (1488).

The **Wallace Monument at Causewayhead** is reached by passing along the main street of Stirling to the **Bridge** (the Battle of Stirling Bridge (1297) was, however, fought around a more ancient structure some distance higher up). The Monument (220 feet high) crowns Abbey Craig and commands a view only equalled by that from Stirling Castle (*admission, fee*). The little Museum contains a number of statues, etc., but the most interesting exhibit is a sword said to have belonged to Wallace: it was stolen in 1936 but found again in the Clyde in 1939.

STIRLING TO PERTH.

Dunblane (*Stirling Arms, Dunblane Hydro, Ardleighton, Neuk*), pleasantly situated on the Allan Water, is principally remarkable for its *Cathedral*, a noteworthy Early English building with a tower that is partly Norman. There was a church here in the sixth century and David I made Dunblane the seat of a bishopric; but for a long period after the Reformation only the choir of the Cathedral was used. The nave has since been re-roofed (1893).

Dunblane has golf, tennis, bowling and good angling facilities among its attractions.

East of Dunblane is the field of **Sheriffmuir**, where the Earl of Mar fought an indecisive battle on behalf of the Old Pretender against the Duke of Argyll (1715).

For the road to **Callander and the Trossachs**, *see* p. 285.

From Dunblane the Perth road runs high above the Allan Water through a country of trim farmsteads and with good distant mountain views. Just over 11 miles from Stirling, at *Greenloaning*, a road goes off on the left for Crieff (p. 281), passing in about 2 m. over the very fine Roman remains at **Ardoch**. The especial point of interest at Ardoch is the series of five ramparts and ditches on the north and east sides of the rectangular camp. A little north, the road passes right through another enclosure known as the *Great Camp*, connected with which is a smaller camp.

The Perth road continues eastward through Blackford to **Gleneagles** (the sumptuous hotel belongs to British Rail), famous as a golfing centre. There are three courses: the King's Course (18 holes); the Queen's Course (18 holes); and the "Wee" Course (9 holes). Each is open to visitors and there is Sunday play.

Gleneagles has been for over 700 years the ancient home of the Haldanes, of whom there are memorials in St. Mungo's Chapel, at the mouth of the glen which runs southward over the **Ochil Hills**, connecting with Glen Devon and so to the Rumbling Bridge (p. 268).

At the foot of Gleneagles a road goes off on the left to **Crieff** (9 miles) by way of *Tullibardine*, which gives the courtesy title of Marquis to the eldest sons of the Dukes of Atholl. Beyond Muthill is **Drummond Castle** (Earl of Ancaster)—the old Castle, built in the fifteenth century, stands apart from the modern mansion, which is celebrated for its pictures and its very fine gardens. On from Gleneagles the Perth road goes to **Auchterarder**, spread out on either side of the highway, and with fine views on the left of the hills beyond Crieff. Then through Aberuthven and on to the bridge over the Earn. Among trees on the hillside ahead is the house of *Gask*, with many memories of Bonnie Prince Charlie.

PERTH.

Angling.—The Tay is famous for its salmon. Apply Secretary of the Perth Anglers' Club, 1 Scoonieburn, Perth, or Town Council.

Distances.—Aberdeen, 82 m.; Braemar, 50 m.; Dundee, 21 m.; Edinburgh, 42 m. *viâ* Forth Bridge, 70 m. *viâ* Stirling; Glasgow, 61 m.; Inverness, 116 m.; Oban, 95 m.; Stirling, 34 m.

Early Closing.—Wednesday.

Golf.—Three courses. *King James VI Course*, on the Moncreiffe Island (50p per day; £1.50 per week); (week-end £1). *Craigie Hill Course* (50p per day; £1 Saturday). *Public Course*, on the North Inch: 25p per round. (Public *Putting Courses* have been laid out on both Inches.) For *Gleneagles*, 15½ miles south from Perth, *see* p. 264.

Hotels.—*Station* (56 rooms), *Salutation* (85 rooms), *Victoria*, *Queen's* (54 rooms), *Atholl* (unl.), *County*, *Royal George* (52 rooms), *Waverley*, *West End*, etc. *Youth Hostel*.

Population.—41,650.

Post Office.—Near centre of High Street. Open 9 a.m. to 5 p.m. Saturday, 9-4.30 p.m.

Railways.—From Glasgow *viâ* Larbert, Stirling and Gleneagles on the West Coast Route from England. From Edinburgh (Waverley Station) *viâ* the Forth Bridge, in continuation of the East Coast and Midland Routes from England, Carlisle and the South direct by Stirling.

Sports.—Golf and angling (*see above*); bowls, tennis, cricket, ice rink, etc.

Perth is an attractive city, nobly situated on the right bank of the Tay. Its dye-works are famous, and it has also several textile factories and important cattle markets.

Though formerly the capital of Scotland, and of great antiquity, it is almost destitute of ancient relics. This is in great part due to the destruction of the religious houses by the populace in 1559, after listening to the fiery harangues of John Knox, and to the removal of other visible evidences of the city's historic glories by the civic authorities in the early years of the nineteenth century. The buildings destroyed by the religious fanatics comprised the Blackfriars Monastery where James I was killed; the Carthusian Monastery which he founded, and where he and Joan Beaufort, his Queen, and Margaret, the Queen of James IV, were buried; the Greyfriars Monastery, which stood on the present churchyard of that name. The house of the Carmelites or Whitefriars House, situated a little west of the city, may have been sacked at the same time. The nineteenth-century demolition included the removal of Earl Gowrie's Palace (*see below*) to make room for the County Buildings; the destruction of the Mercat Cross (erected in 1668 in place of one taken down by Cromwell; a copy has been erected in memory of King Edward VII); and the clearing away, in 1818, of the Parliament House, where the ancient Diets of Scotland were held. Until the seventeenth century Perth was also known as *St. Johnstoun* in honour of the patron saint of the city.

Most of the show-places of Perth are within a few yards of the river. Towards the southern end is the **South Inch**, a large recreation ground, with the **Railway**

Station close to one side and at the other **Tay Street**, which runs alongside the river to the **North Inch** at the opposite end of the city. In midstream is Moncreiffe Island, on which is one of the golf courses. Following Tay Street northward one reaches the **County Buildings**. They occupy the site of old Gowrie House, in which, according to the generally accepted story, James VI was seized in 1600 by the Earl of Gowrie and his brother, the Master of Ruthven, who had enticed him thither, and was on the point of being murdered or kidnapped when rescued by his attendants. Opposite the County Buildings and spanning the Tay is the **Queen's Bridge**, opened in October, 1960, when the city celebrated the granting of its first Royal Charter in October, 1210.

St. John Street, a turning on the right out of South Street, near the County Buildings, leads to the principal church, and the oldest building in Perth, **St. John's Church**; here John Knox preached his famous sermon against "idolatry" (1559). Its records go back to the twelfth century; it has a nave and transept dating from the thirteenth century and a choir of fifteenth-century design. For many years the Church sheltered three separate congregations, but as part of the latest restoration (a War Memorial scheme) the partitions have been removed and one sees the fine cruciform building as a whole. From the other end of St. John Street a return can be made to Tay Street, which leads north to the **Perth Bridge** of nine arches, built by Smeaton in 1771. Near it, in George Street, is the **Art Gallery and Museum**, and here the North Inch begins. (At Bridgend, on the opposite bank, in a house now bearing a commemorative tablet, John Ruskin spent part of his childhood.)

From the Bridge, Charlotte Street may be followed to North Port (on the left), which quickly brings one to Pullar's Dye Works and Curfew Row, where, marked by a tablet, stands **Simon Glover's House**, the supposed home (now Corporation property) of the "Fair Maid of Perth." Readers of her story, as told by Sir Walter Scott, will regard the **North Inch** with special interest as the scene of the memorable combat (1396) between the clan Chattan and the clan Quhele (Kay). The spacious greensward is now a public golf course and recreation ground. From its south-western corner Atholl Street leads to **St. Ninian's Cathedral**, which is an Episcopal Cathedral.

Methven Street leads the visitor westward to the Railway Station, near which are large cattle-markets.

The best view of Perth is obtained from **Kinnoull Hill** (729 feet), a great part of which was presented to the town by Lord Dewar in 1924. It is about three-quarters of an hour's walk eastward from the station across the river (buses in summer). From the summit of the hill a

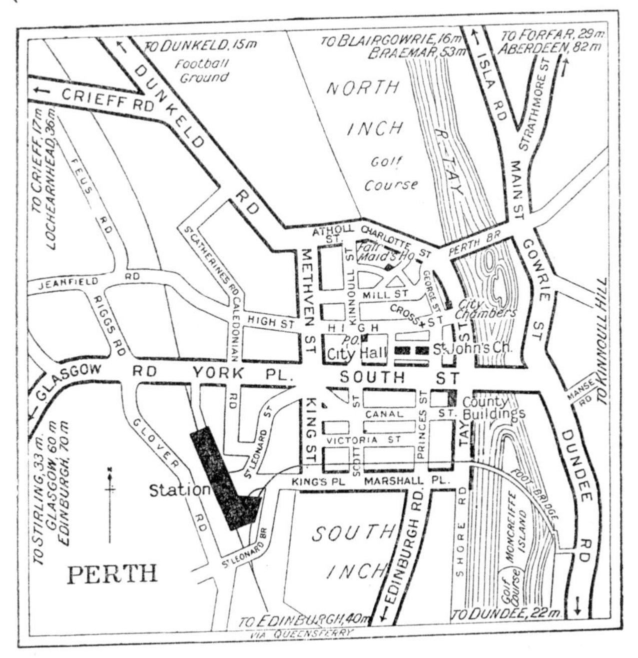

spacious view is obtained of Strathearn, the Ochils and the Grampians, and the Firth of Tay, widening between the fertile shores of the Carse of Gowrie and of Fife.

STIRLING TO ST. ANDREWS DIRECT.

Railways.—The Fife and Kinross promontory is served *viâ* the Forth Bridge, the main line running north to Dundee across the Tay Bridge. There is a loop line between Inverkeithing and Markinch.

Instead of turning to the right immediately on arriving at **Causewayhead,** 2 miles from Stirling (*see* p. 263), go straight on for another quarter of a mile with the Wallace Monument high on the right, and on meeting the main road turn to the right. For some miles the road skirts the southern edge of the **Ochil Hills,** with the rugged **Dumyat** (1,375 feet) away to the left, above Menstrie. **Alva** (*Johnstone Arms*) is notable for a pretty glen with a good waterfall. From **Tillicoultry** (*Crown*) the ascent of **Ben Cleuch** (2,363 feet) is easy. Go up the beautiful Tillicoultry Glen by an excellent path and then follow the Daiglen Burn to the foot of the upper slope of the hill and so to the summit. The summit (view indicator) commands a grand panorama, especially of the Grampians from Ben Lomond to the Cairngorms. By keeping northward beside the Broich Burn, one comes to Glen Bee and so to Blackford, an excellent walk over the Ochils. The name Tillicoultry, by the way, is singularly expressive, meaning literally " the knoll of the back-lying place." Then comes **Dollar** (*Castle Campbell Hotel*), with a well-known Academy. The principal attraction in the neighbourhood is **Castle Campbell,** a mile to the north and reached by a pretty walk alongside a romantic stream. The Castle (*admission, fee ; children, half*), an ancient stronghold of the Argylls, restored in recent years, is a square tower, which contains the old hall, with a fine stone roof. The track to Ben Cleuch goes off to the left at the Castle, which lies between the Burn of Sorrow and the Burn of Care : a path beside the latter goes over the hills to Glen Devon.

Between Dollar and the village known as Pool of Muckart a road goes off on the right for **Rumbling Bridge,** a place of some beauty, bearing a resemblance to the scene of the Devil's Bridge in North Wales. The view from the parapet of the modern bridge is very fine ; below is an ancient bridge without parapets, which, however, once carried the main road. Above and below the bridges are charming walks, tickets for which are obtainable at the hotel. The *Devil's Mill* is the name given to a very picturesque cataract rushing through a narrow chasm.

From this point a road goes off over the Ochils up **Glen Devon** to Gleneagles (*see* p. 264). The River Devon rises to the north-west of Ben Cleuch, tumbles eastward down Glen Devon, and a mile or so east of Rumbling

Bridge makes a remarkable change of direction at a point which has accordingly been named **Crook of Devon.**

We now approach **Kinross** (*Hotels : Green* (41 *rooms*), *Bridgend, Kirklands, Muir's*), a small, quiet county town on the western shores of **Loch Leven.** Scotland has so many romantic lochs that it seems almost a pity that for such an episode as the imprisonment and escape of Queen Mary history should have chosen this quite ordinary sheet of water.

The *Castle* wherein she was imprisoned stood on the island nearest to Kinross : in those days boats could draw right up to the Castle walls. The Queen was brought here after her surrender at Carberry (p. 55), in June, 1567. Several fruitless attempts at rescue were made ; but in May, 1568, young William Douglas, son of the doughty Lady Douglas, who was Mary's gaoler, got hold of the castle keys, helped the prisoner to escape, locked the castle doors behind him and threw the keys into the loch. Friends awaited the Queen as she landed on the shores of the loch and carried her away to Niddry Castle, but a week or so later her cause was definitely defeated at Langside (*see* p. 33). The escape is thrillingly described by Scott in *The Abbot.* (Ferry service crosses to the island in June. The loch is well known for its trout, which average 1 lb., while fish up to 9½ lb. have been taken with fly. Season extends from April to September. Apply to the Manager, Loch Leven, Kinross. The loch is now a Nature Reserve.

The largest island is towards the eastern end of the loch and is named after St. Serf, a follower of St. Columba, to whom it is said to have been granted by the Pictish kings.

From Kinross the main road runs northward to Perth by way of the romantic **Glenfarg,** which cuts right through the Ochils. Near the northern end of the Pass is **Abernethy,** with a round tower, 74 feet high (*admission* 1p.). It has an entrance door 6 feet from the ground and is built of hewn square stones—unlike the generality of Irish towers. It is not so fine a specimen as the Brechin tower (p. 350). Abernethy itself, once an important place, has declined to a village. Three miles north-west is *Moncreiffe Hill* (725 feet). **Elcho Castle** (*weekdays,* 10–4 *or* 7 *; Sundays,* 2–4 *or* 7 *; admission, fee*) stands, a somewhat mournful ruin, beside the Tay to the north-east on Moncreiffe Hill. Eastward of Abernethy, near the shore of the Firth of Tay, is **Newburgh** (*George*), an attractive little place with a harbour and a "lion" in the guise of the ruined *Lindores Abbey.*

Bridge of Earn (*Moncreiffe Arms*), where the main routes to Perth cross that river, is a pleasant resort with charming views and access to much varied scenery. A mile westward of the Bridge are the Pitkeathly Mineral Wells.

From Kinross to St. Andrews the route is by Strathmiglo, Auchtermuchty and Cupar (*see* p. 280).

From Strathmiglo a road goes south-eastward for 3 miles to **Falkland**, where is the remnant of a Palace that was long a favourite residence of Scottish sovereigns (*open weekdays*, 10–6, *Sundays*, 2–6 ; *charge*). It occupies a fine position at the foot of the Lomond Hills, but only the south wing is now intact, the remainder having succumbed to fire in 1654, when Cromwell's troops were billeted here. The Palace is a fine example of French Renaissance work. The Chapel, with unique oak screen and painted ceiling, and the tapestry gallery are worth seeing, and the external appearance is very attractive.

The Palace was built on the site of an old castle of the Earls of Fife, and was occupied by Robert Duke of Albany and Earl of Fife, the Regent Albany, who imprisoned here his nephew David, Duke of Rothesay, and according to tradition starved him to death. (See *The Fair Maid of Perth.*) When the house of Albany fell, the crown obtained possession and Falkland became a favourite " Hunting-box " of the Stewarts. The present Palace may have been begun by James III or James IV but its keenest memory, perhaps, concerns James V, who here came to his deathbed, after the crushing defeat at Solway Moss, and a few days later received news of the birth of Mary Queen of Scots. " It came wi' a lass and it'll gang wi' a lass " was his oft-quoted comment. Mary resided at the Palace on various occasions.

STIRLING TO ST. ANDREWS BY DUNFERMLINE.

The counties of Kinross and Fife occupy the promontory between the Firth of Tay on the north and the Forth on the south. The " gateways " are Stirling and Perth on the west ; and on the south the Forth Bridges and Kincardine Bridge and on the north, Dundee and the Tay Bridges. Defoe's recommendation that the coast tour exhibits the best scenery and the most interesting places still holds good, so we will follow the shore round from Stirling to Perth.

The road leaves routes already described at Causewayhead (p. 263), where is the lofty Wallace Monument. **Alloa** (*Crown*) is the first place of any consequence : a manufacturing town (beer, yarn, etc.) with a little harbour and a thirteenth-century Tower in Alloa House grounds (Earl of Mar and Kellie). Then comes **Clackmannan,** former "capital" of Scotland's smallest county and with memories of the Bruce. **Kincardine** assumed greater importance with the opening, in 1936, of the bridge (over ½ mile) which saved the long detour by Stirling and greatly reduced the road distances from Edinburgh to Fife and the North prior to the completion of the Forth Road Bridge.

Beyond Kincardine our road approaches the shore at Blair Castle. *Dunimarle Castle*, a little farther east, is noted for its collection of paintings, which can be seen on Monday, Wednesday and Saturday afternoons in summer. **Culross** (*Dundonald Arms*) is a quaint old place with the remains of a Cistercian abbey (*weekdays, admission fee*), of which the choir now forms the Parish Church. The National Trust have acquired many old houses in the burgh and the Palace (*admission, fee*) is of special interest on account of the mural paintings, which have been treated by the Department of the Environment.

Beyond Torry the road goes inland, heading straight for—

DUNFERMLINE.

Distances.—Alloa, 14 m.; Edinburgh (by Forth Bridge), 14 m. Perth, 30 m. St. Andrews, 41 m.; Stirling, 21 m.
Early Closing.—Wednesday.
Hotels.—*City* (25 rooms), *Brucefield, Belleville, Pitbauchlie House, Elgin, Charlestown.*

This ancient and historical town occupies an effective site on the brow of a hill about 3 miles north from the seaboard of the Firth of Forth at an elevation of about 300 feet rising farther towards the north, and is one of the pleasantest towns in Scotland. The prospect it commands is extensive and beautiful. The town is especially associated with the manufacture of linen and, more recently, terylene. The house in which Andrew Carnegie was born has been preserved and alongside it is a Museum containing many interesting articles. The town is headquarters of some of the Trusts concerned with the administration of the Carnegie funds. Its interest to visitors centres mainly in Pittencrieff Glen (gifted to the town by Andrew Carnegie), the Abbey and the ruins of the adjoining Palace.

Dunfermline Abbey is a combination of different periods of architecture, the east portion consisting of a pretentious Gothic tower dating from about 1821, the general character of which may be surmised from the fact that the stone network round the top of the tower shows in huge letters "King Robert the Bruce." The nave, however, with its aisles, is amongst the finest examples of Norman in Scotland. The west end, with its doorway surmounted by a Decorated window, and again, over that, by Norman details, is notable. The pillars and nearly all the windows, aisles, triforium and clerestory are severe Norman. Two of the pillars are strangely fluted in zigzag fashion, with the peculiar effect that they appear to the eye to decrease in thickness from top or bottom according to the position from which you see them, the decrease being in the direction of the point of the zigzag.

Under the pulpit in the New Church (the east end) lie the remains of the Bruce ; over them is an elaborate brass, set in Italian porphyry. The front of the royal pew of James VI (1610), which is now fixed to the wall of the north transept of the modern church, exhibits a full list of the royal personages buried here.

Note the beautiful sculptures of the wife of Dean Stanley and other members of the Elgin family, in the south transept. Beneath the ruined *Fratry* or *Refectory*, south of the Church already mentioned, are a number of cells. *The Abbey is open, free,* 10–7, *Sunday* 2–7, *closing at* 4 *in winter.*

In the **Palace** (*free*), of which one wall only remains, Robert Bruce resided, Charles I was born, and Charles II signed the Dunfermline Declaration regretting his father's opposition to the Solemn League and Covenant and his mother's idolatry.

South and west of the Abbey lies the beautiful **Pittencrieff Glen,** extending to about 60 acres, managed and maintained by the Carnegie Dunfermline Trustees. It contains many attractions and in particular beautiful gardens. There is a tea-room. There are also an Aviary and Paddling Pools for children. Pittencrieff House, a good specimen of a seventeenth-century Scottish mansion, now serves partly as a Costume Museum and partly as an Old Men's Club.

South of Dunfermline, but included in the burgh, is **Rosyth Naval Dockyard.**

For the purpose of forming the yard, the Government purchased from the Marquis of Linlithgow the shore lands surrounding **Rosyth Castle,** built by a branch of the Stewart family in 1560 on a rock which was an island at high water, but at low tide was connected by a causeway with the mainland. The castle is mentioned by Sir Walter Scott in *The Abbot.* The position of the Base is about 30 miles from the mouth of the Firth. The Base became one of the largest in the world, capable of docking and repairing all classes of warships.

For its main purposes as a Naval Base, Rosyth was, however, abandoned in 1925, Port Edgar being offered for sale, and the place became more notable on account of the "Garden City," one of the most attractive housing developments in Scotland.

With the coming of the Second World War, however, Rosyth once again assumed a rôle of considerable importance.

For the **Forth Bridges** *see* p. 257.

On the small island of **Inchcolm**, which has been dubbed "the Iona of East Scotland," are the remains of an Augustinian Abbey, founded by Alexander I in the twelfth century. The church is almost completely ruinous, but a portion of a remarkable mural painting of early date was discovered during preservation work. There is an octagonal chapter-house and the cloistral buildings are more complete than those of any other Scottish monastery. In some ways this is the most interesting monastic ruin in Scotland. The oldest building on the island is the small hermit's cell in the north-west corner of the grounds. *Boat from Aberdour: steamer from Granton in summer. The landing fee includes admission. Open* 10–4 *or* 7, *Sundays from* 2 *p.m.*

Aberdour (*Woodside, Star, Seabank*) is a popular resort, with golf, boating, bathing, fishing, bowls and tennis, and Edinburgh is within easy reach. It has a restored Norman Church and the ruins of an ancient Castle. A mile or so eastward is **Burntisland** (*Greenmount, George*). Burntisland is one of the principal centres of the manufacture of aluminium. Shipbuilding is important here, but the harbour is no longer a ferry port. *Rossend Castle* (purchased by the Town Council and included in a housing scheme) incorporates parts of the fifteenth-century castle in which Queen Mary was staying at the time Chastelard was visiting her. The old parish church is interesting as a copy of the North Church of Amsterdam.

On the way to **Kinghorn** (*Kinghorn, Anchorage* (*temp.*)), a popular little place with golf links, on the eastern side of the Point of Pettycur, is seen a monument marking the spot where Alexander III fell from his horse and was killed, 1286 (*see* p. 29).

Kirkcaldy (*Anthony's, Station, Ollerton, Abbotshall, Dunnikier Arms, Victoria, etc.*) is a busy manufacturing town and good seaport. It has associations with three celebrated men: Adam Smith, who here wrote *The Wealth of Nations*; Thomas Carlyle, and Edward Irving, who taught in the school. At *Dysart* are the ruins of a church dedicated to St. Serf, a fifth-century hermit; West and East Wemyss (pronounced *Weems*) take their name from the numerous caves ("weems") in the neighbourhood; it was in **Wemyss Castle** that Mary and Darnley first met. Thence by the busy seaport of **Methil** to **Leven**, where the river of that name enters the Firth. **Leven** (*Hotels: Caledonian, Beach, Star*) is a favourite resort of Edinburgh folk. In addition to golf there is bathing in the open sea and in a pool, tennis, bowls, fishing and a series of interesting short excursions. It stands on the western end of the bay of **Largo.** Alexander Selkirk ("Robinson Crusoe") was born at Lower Largo (*Crusoe Hotel*) and a monument commemorates the fact. There is a grand view from *Largo Law* (953 feet), a mile or so north of the town. Its golf course and beach bring many visitors to **Lundin Links** (*Lundin Links, Beach*), which adjoins Upper Largo. At the eastern end of the bay are **Earlsferry and Elie** (*Marine, Golf, Victoria*), bordering a small bay and with golf links and other attractions which make them popular little resorts.

St. Monance, farther east, is principally notable for the remains of a fourteenth-century church; thence by Pittenweem, Anstruther (with its subjoined Anstruther Easter) to **Crail** (*Croma, East Neuk, Marine, Balcomie Links*) a quaint little place that even modern transport seems unable to deprive of an ancient air. There are fine sands for bathing, and golf and tennis. The road past the church continues to *Fife Ness*, off which are the lighthouse-guarded Carr Rocks.

The *Coves of Crail* (Caiplie Coves), now high above the sea, are caves driven into the cliff, and rest on a platform (raised beach) cut by the waves when the land stood at a lower level.

Southward from Crail, out in the mouth of the Firth, is the **Isle of May,** also with a lighthouse (white flash every twenty seconds, visible 21 miles). On the island (a mile long) are the ruins of a thirteenth-century chapel and a bird-watching station. So by Kingsbarns and Boarhills to St. Andrews.

ST. ANDREWS.

Access.—The most direct routes from the South are by the Forth Bridge (rail to Leuchars, 4 miles, or road).
Buses.—Bus station off City Road. Services to all neighbouring places.
Caravan Sites.—At Kinkill Braes and Cairnsmill.
Distances.—Edinburgh (by Forth Bridge), 47 m.; London, 427 m.; Cupar 9 m.; Dundee (by bridge), 14 m.; Perth, 30 m.; Stirling, 50 m.
Early Closing.—Thursday.
Golf.—Four first-class links (*see below*).
Hotels.—*Rusack's* (67 rooms) *Reden* (17 rooms), *Rufflets* (20 rooms), *Golf* (21 rooms), *Star* (18 rooms), *Cross Keys* (25 rooms), *Station* (40 rooms), *Scores* (40 rooms), *Crown* (5 rooms), *Kinburn* (20 rooms), *Ardgowan*, *Dunvegan*, *Imperial*, *Old Course* (68 rooms), and numerous private hotels, boarding houses, and apartments.
Car Parks.—North Street, Queen's Gardens, Murray Place, West Sands, etc.
Population.—10,083.
Sport.—Golf (*see* p. 276), bathing, boating, bowls, fishing, tennis (the Scottish Hard Court Championships are played at St. Andrews, during August).

The fame of St. Andrews has been so nicely apportioned between Golf and the University that the stranger may be pardoned for asking whether the city has other attractions. It has. But first let us review its history.

The earliest name of St. Andrews, Rigmund or Kilrymont, suggests a royal seat. It early received a Columban Church, and after Iona had been repeatedly sacked it became, soon after 900, the Ecclesiastical capital of Pictland. In the twelfth century, when St. Peter of York advanced dangerous claims, St. Andrew was chosen as the patron saint of Scotland. By this time St. Andrews had a priory of Regular Canons, founded 1144, existing side by side with the Culdee foundations whose ruined Church may still be seen on the Kirkhill. In 1472 it was made an archbishopric. One of the oldest buildings still extant in the city is the St. Regulus Tower, erected by Bishop Robert in the middle of the twelfth century. This tower stands in the Cathedral enclosure. The Cathedral itself was commenced a few years later by Bishop Arnold, but not finished till 1318. The signal for its stripping is said to have been a series of characteristic discourses by John Knox in 1559, and from that time till the last century the work of destruction was carried on by the appropriation of its stones for all manner of secular purposes.

The Castle was originally founded in 1200, but was entirely rebuilt nearly two centuries later, having been destroyed from fear of its being taken by the English. In it the celebrated

Cardinal Beaton was murdered in 1546 by a number of the followers of George Wishart, who had been burnt for heresy. The murderers, joined later by Knox, defended themselves within its walls for more than a year, until a successful attack was made upon it by French and Scottish troops, and the garrison were sent as prisoners to Nantes. After the Gowrie conspiracy, James VI took refuge in it, but soon afterwards it was deserted and gradually fell to ruin.

The University was founded in 1411 by Bishop Wardlaw, and is the oldest in Scotland. It long consisted of three colleges—*St. Mary's* (founded 1537), entirely devoted to theological studies, and *St. Salvator's* (1450) and *St. Leonard's* (1512), which were amalgamated in 1747 under the name of the *United College*, but now generally known as *St. Salvator's*. To these was added, in 1954, *Queen's College* (incorporating Dundee University College). St. Leonard's School (1877) is a well-known residential school for girls.

Golf at St. Andrews.

The Bishops of St. Andrews were powers in the land; nor was their power always exclusively ecclesiastical. When, for instance, in the fifteenth century the law went forth that "Fute ball and golfe be utterly cryit downe and nocht usit," the Bishop of St. Andrews is said to have championed the playing of golf on the local links. The Royal and Ancient Club was founded in 1754, and to-day St. Andrews holds a proud position as the capital of the world of golf.

All four courses, the Old and New and the Jubilee and Eden, are open to the public. They are maintained by a Joint Committee of the Royal and Ancient Golf Club and the Town Council.

St. Andrews is venerated as the Mecca of Golf, and in Britain the Royal and Ancient Club is the recognized ruling authority for the game, which from Scotland has spread all the world over. Each year the new Captain "plays himself in" ceremoniously at the Autumn Meeting (late September).

The famous links with the "**Royal and Ancient" Club House** are at the western end of the town, adjoining the shore. A little eastward of the club-house is the obelisk in memory of four victims to religious bigotry, who perished at the stake between 1528 and 1558—among them George Wishart, the leader of the Scottish Reformation. He was burned by order of Cardinal Beaton, and the Protestants revenged themselves by murdering the Primate as he lay in St. Andrews Castle and exposing his body on the battlements. The incident probably had far-reaching effects, for some ten months later the defenders of the Castle were joined by John Knox, and when, after several months, the castle was recaptured by a French force, the captives were dispatched to France to sharpen their bitterness in the galleys.

The Castle—or what is left of it—is reached by following **The Scores**, as the Promenade is called, past a pro-

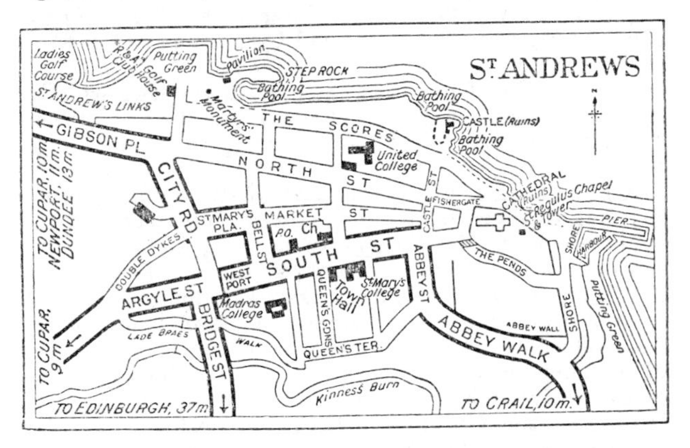

jecting rock, known as the *Step*, a favourite bathing-place. Situation rather than architecture is the feature of the **Castle.** (*See above. Weekdays, summer* 10–7, *winter* 10–4 ; *Sundays*, 2–7 *or* 4 ; *admission, fee, children, half.*) There is some tracery in the walls, but the only object of special interest is the *Bottle Dungeon*, so called from its shape. There is also an Underground Passage, formed probably by the mine and counter-mine of the siege of 1546–7.

From the Castle the shore-road continues to the **Old Pier,** which protects the harbour and the fishing boats. From this point we turn back townwards, passing along the south side of the Cathedral cemetery, under a round archway, and through a Pointed arcade, 25 yards long, with a finely groined roof, to the point at which the principal streets of the town converge. This arcade is called the **Pends**, and is one of the most beautiful architectural features of the city.

The Cathedral.

Weekdays, summer 10–7, winter 10–4. *Sundays*, 2–7 or 4. *The Museum closes at* 4 *p.m.*

The history of the building has already been alluded to. All that remains is a portion of the east and west ends, and parts of the south nave and transept walls. The large area which the building once occupied is apparent. The full length inside was 356 feet. The west end has one octagonal turret standing, supported by a flying buttress.

The east end is almost complete, and consists of two turrets 100 feet high, with three small rounded windows surmounted by one large pointed one between them. The style is earlier and less elaborate than that of the west end.

A few yards south of this part of the building stands **St. Regulus** or **St. Rule's Tower** (*admission, fee*), of which we have already spoken as being perhaps half a century earlier than any part of the Cathedral itself. Attached to it are the walls of a small Romanesque chapel.

Now descending South Street, increasingly attractive, we soon come to **St. Mary's College**, a regular range of buildings on the left. This is the Theological College of the University of St. Andrews. The buildings to the left house the **University Library**, dating from 1612, and now comprising over 500,000 books besides many rare manuscripts. A hawthorn, now propped up in the courtyard, is said to have been planted by Mary, Queen of Scots. Adjoining the College are the *Botanical Gardens*, the *Bute Building*, the *Bell-Pettigrew Museum* and departments of botany, geology, zoology, and anatomy, biochemistry and physiology.

Nearly opposite the College and exactly opposite the Town Hall is the **Parish Church**. The fine pre-Reformation tower is original; the rest of the building has been restored (from old fragments and old drawings) to what it was in pre-Reformation times and enriched with many windows and memorials.

Continuing along South Street we come to **Madras College**, standing back from the street just beyond the

Royal Hotel. It is a fine Jacobean building and was founded as a school, in 1832, by the Rev. Dr. Bell, Prebendary of Westminster and ex-Chaplain of the Orphan Hospital, Madras. The School is now concerned with Secondary Education under the Fife Education Authority. The Black Friars Chapel—one of the chief adornments of St. Andrews—is all that is left of a Monastery founded here in 1274. The destruction of the chapel by the "rascal multitude" in 1559 was due to an inflammatory sermon preached in the old church by John Knox. At the west end of South Street is the **West Port,** one of the old city gateways.

St. Salvator's College, in North Street, originated in the foundation here in 1450 of the College of St. Salvator, to which was united, in 1747, the College of St. Leonard. Adjoining is **St. Salvator's Chapel,** founded by Bishop Kennedy in 1450, and the most interesting and beautiful of his buildings that have survived to our time. It contains Bishop Kennedy's Tomb, one of the most elaborate specimens of ancient Gothic architecture in Scotland. The interior of the Chapel underwent extensive restoration in 1930. It is used by the students for morning prayers and Sunday services.

In close proximity is the palatial **Younger Graduation Hall,** the gift of Dr. James Younger and Mrs. Younger, and opened in 1929 by the Queen Mother, then Duchess of York. To the rear of the Hall and facing the Scores is the fine St. Salvator's Hall of Residence for men students. This handsome edifice was given to the University by Dr. Harkness of New York.

East of the town is the *Gatty Marine Laboratory,* a centre of research in marine biology.

On the shore near St. Andrews is that unique igneous formation, the *Rock and Spindle,* the relic of an ancient volcano, from which apparently no lava ever flowed, but from which dykes of basalt were intruded into the debris. The Spindle is a spheroidal mass of basalt which flowed into a cavern, and on cooling developed basaltic columns radiating from the centre outwards.

St. Andrews Bay faces north-east, and beyond the estuary of the Eden and Leuchars the long Tents Moor extends to **Tayport,** where the Firth of Tay narrows to less than 2 miles.

At the western end of the strait the famous **Tay Bridge** carries the railway across.

The distance from shore to shore is 3,593 yards, and the bridge is a double-line iron lattice structure with eleven main spans of 245 feet and two of 227 feet and 74 other spans of smaller size. Over the navigable channel there is a clear headway of 77 feet at high water.

There are in all 85 piers, 73 of which are founded on twin wrought-iron cylinders sunk into the river bed.

Some distance to the east is the fine new *Tay Road Bridge*, opened to traffic in 1966 at a cost of four and a half million sterling. Stretching from Craighead of Newport across the Tay to King William Dock, Dundee, it has a total length of 1½ miles.

Leuchars Church (7 miles from St. Andrews) is one of the most interesting in Scotland. The chancel, terminated by a dome-crowned apse, is of the early part of the twelfth century, and in its two rows of arches, one beyond the other, displays what is possibly the purest specimen of Norman architecture in Scotland.

Some 3 miles west of Wormit (at the Fife end of the Tay Bridge) are the ruins of Balmerino Abbey, now National Trust property. The ruins are of a Cistercian Abbey founded in 1229. It has a lovely position overlooking the Tay.

Inland from St. Andrews is the ancient town of **Cupar** (*Royal, Station*), with, however, little of ancient interest. The town is frequently referred to as Cupar Fife, to distinguish it from Coupar Angus (p. 346). At one time all Fifeshire legal cases were tried at the courts at Cupar, a fact which gave rise to the saying, " He that will to Cupar maun to Cupar " (i.e. " an obstinate man must have his way ").

PERTH TO CRIEFF AND LOCHEARNHEAD.

This is part of the direct east–west route from Perth to Oban. Distance to Crieff, 18 m.; to Lochearnhead, 26 m.

The first object to attract interest is **Huntingtower** (*admission, fee ; weekdays,* 10–4, 6 *or* 7 ; *Sundays from* 2), lying to the right of the road about 2 miles from Perth. Formerly known as Ruthven Castle, it was the scene of

PERTH
Forest of Atholl
Monadhliath Mts
Aviemore
Kingussie
Newtonmore
Kincraig
Feshiebridge
Rothiemurchus
Cairn Gorm
4084
Cairn Gorm Mts
Braeriach
Ben Macdhui
4296
Cairn Toul
4241
Ben Avon
3843
Glen Avon
Glenavon Forest
Beinn-a-Bhuird
Inchrory
Balmoral
Braemar
1100
Balmoral Forest
Beinn Chiochan
(Lochnagar)
3768
Broad Cairn
Tolmount
Glas Maol
Cairnwell
Mayar
Driesh
Glen Feshie
Glen Feshie Forest
Glen Dee
Linn of Dee
Inverey
Sgarsach
3300
Carn Bhac
3014
Gleney Forest
Falls of Tarf
Ben Dearg
3304
Glen Tilt
Ben-y-Gloe
3671
Spittal of Glenshee
Glen Shee
Glen Isla
Dalwhinnie
Loch Ericht Hotel
Dalnaspidal
Dalnacardoch
Glen Garry
Blair Atholl
Ben Vrackie
Killiecrankie Pass
Pitlochry
L. Tummel
Kinloch Rannoch
Schiehallion
3547
Forest of Alyth
Kirkmichael
Blairgowrie
Alyth
Rattray
Meigle
Coupar Angus
Ballinluig
Aberfeldy
Kenmore
Fortingall
R. Lyon
Ben Lawers
3984
Loch Tay
Dunkeld
Birnam
R. Tay
Strath Braan
Amulree Hotel
Glen Almond
Ardeonaig Inn
Cargill
Stanley
Bankfoot
Methven
Scone Palace
New Scone
PERTH
Glen Lednock
St Fillans
Loch Earn
Comrie
Crieff
Ben Vorlich
3224
Forest of Glenartney
Glen Artney
Muthill
Auchterarder
Dunning
Forteviot
R. Earn
Abernethy
Auchtermuchty
Strathmiglo
Gleneagles
Callander
Loch Lubnaig
Carse of Gowrie
Errol
Kinnaird
Sidlaw

PERTH TO ABERDEEN
English Miles
0
5
10
15
WARD LOCK & CO., LIMITED, LONDON.
© – John Bartholomew & Son Ltd. Edinburgh
ABERDEEN
Old Aberdeen
Girdle Ness
Nigg
Cove Bay
Findon
Portlethen
Downies
Newtonhill Sta.
Skateraw
Muchalls
STONEHAVEN
Dunnottar Cas.
Crawton
Catterline
Kinneff
Inverbervie
Gourdon
Johnshaven
St Cyrus
Montrose
The Ness
Ferryden
Lunan B.
Red Hd
Auchmithie
Arbroath
Elliot Jun.
East Haven
Carnoustie
Buddon Ness
Monifieth
Broughty Ferry
DUNDEE
Tayport on Tay
Abertay (Light Ship)
Newport-on-Tay
Tents Moor
Leuchars
Leuchars Jun.
St Andrews Bay
St Andrews
Kinkell Cas.
Babbet Ness
Kingsbarns
Carr Bks
Fife Ness
Crail
(Inchcape)
Bell Rock
Light House
Leith to Aberdeen 85 m. to Kirkwall 215 m. to Lerwick 265 miles
KINCARDINE
NGUS
Brechin
Forfar
Kirriemuir
Glamis
Friockheim
Laurencekirk
Marykirk
Edzell
Fettercairn
Drumlithie
Banchory
Aboyne
R. Dee
R. Don
Stonehaven
Alford
Tarland
Lumphanan
Torphins
Peterculter
Mt Battock
2555
Mt Keen
3077
Kerloch
1747
Cairn O'Mount
Hill of Fare
1545
Glen Dye
R. North Esk
R. South Esk
Montrose Basin
Hillside
Dubton Jun.
Bridge of Dun
Guthrie Jun.
Inverkeilor
Lunan
St Vigeans
Kingennie
Dyce Jun.
Woodside
Cults
Milltimber
Durris
Drumtochty Cas.
Auchinblae
Arbuthnot
Roadside
Benholm
Lauriston
Garvock
Craigo
Stracathro
Careston
Tannadice
Aberlemno
Letham
Inverarity
Carmyllie
Arbirlot
Monikie
Tealing
Strathkinness
Dunino
Cameron
Ceres
Pitscottie
Radernie
Carnbee

"the Ruthven Raid" (1582), when the sixteen-year-old James VI was invited here on the pretext of hunting and found himself detained a prisoner by the Earl of Gowrie and his friends. The terms for ransom virtually made Gowrie and his companions rulers of Scotland for the time being. It will be recalled that a later Earl of Gowrie was also concerned with a plot against the freedom of James VI (*see* p. 266).

A less authentic bit of history attached to the castle concerns the space between the two massive towers. This is said to have gained its name of The Maiden's Leap from the tradition that a daughter of the first Earl jumped across it in order to escape discovery in a love affair.

From the vicinity of **Methven** (*Star*, *Methven Arms*), 4 miles on, roads run off on the right to Glen Almond, joining the Crieff–Dunkeld road (p. 282) at the foot of the **Sma' Glen.** About 10 miles from Perth is *Trinity College*, a public school in connection with the Scottish Episcopal Church. *Logiealmond*, across the river, is the "Drumtochty" of Ian Maclaren's novels, Methven being "Kildrummie."

Beyond Balgowan House a road on the left leads to the ruins of **Inchaffray Abbey** (literally, "the Isle of Masses"). It was the Abbot of Inchaffray who blessed the Scottish army before Bannockburn, raising aloft the most treasured possession of the Abbey—the arms of St. Fillan.

Also on the left are the lovely grounds of **Abercairny.** At Gilmerton an important road goes off on the right for Amulree, *viâ* the Sma' Glen (p. 282), but our road keeps to the left of the hill known as the Knock of Crieff (911 feet), passing Crieff Golf Course.

Crieff.

Access.—By road from Stirling *viâ* Greenloaning (p. 263) and from Perth *viâ* Methven.

Early Closing.—Wednesday.

Golf.—A splendid 18-hole course, open to visitors. *Gleneagles* (p. 264) is within 9 miles.

Hotels.—*Arduthie*, *George*, *Birches*, *Star*, *Murraypark*, *Leven House*, *Ancaster*, *Tower*, *Victoria*, *Hydro*, *Drummond Arms*, *Waverley*.

Population.—5,773.

Recreation.—Golf, bowls, tennis, mountaineering, etc.; fishing (salmon and trout) in the Earn and other waters. There is also a library, and the Strathearn Institute has billiard and reading rooms; cinema.

Crieff claims to be the most picturesquely situated hill-town of Scotland and is a very popular health resort.

Built close to the river *Earn*, on the southern face of a wooded hill called the Knock, one of the first slopes of the Grampians, it is sheltered from cold winds, has a gravelly subsoil, and is the centre of a district full of historical and general interest and of great scenic beauty.

At the door of the Town Hall, in High Street, are the ancient stocks, and near them is the Cross of the Burgh of the Regality of Drummond, an antiquarian relic associated with exploits of Rob Roy. The **Cross of Crieff** is believed to be a ninth-century Celtic preaching cross.

The **Knock of Crieff** (911 feet: view indicator), to the north of the town, commands a view of nearly the whole of Upper and Lower Strathearn.

Two miles south-east of Crieff between the Earn and the Auchterarder road is the quaint *Innerpeffray Library*, to which is attached an old chapel and school. Founded from a will in 1680 of the third Lord Madertie it was one of the first public libraries in Scotland.

From Crieff, walkers may follow **Glen Turret** past Loch Turret to **Ben Chonzie** (3,048 feet), whence one may descend southward to Comrie by way of Glen Lednock: a way can be found through Gleann a' Chilleine to Ardtalnaig, on Loch Tay.

Crieff to Gleneagles.—On the Muthill road are glass and wrought-iron works which may be visited. The road continues past **Drummond Castle**, the seat of the Earl of Ancaster. The old castle, built in the fifteenth century and restored in the nineteenth, stands apart from the modern house. The gardens are very attractive. (*Occasionally open.*) From **Muthill**, a pretty village containing an ancient tower and the ruins of a fifteenth-century church, a road runs south-west to **Braco** (near the Ardoch Roman camp, p. 264). For **Gleneagles**, *see* p. 264.

Crieff to Dunkeld and Aberfeldy viâ Amulree.

Rounding the Knock hill, the road strikes northward from Gilmerton up the **Sma' Glen**, a rugged, deep and narrow valley, small only in name, where Ossian (p. 326) is said to sleep. The colouring of the glen is very beautiful, and beyond Newton Bridge, where the Almond is crossed, the route is over wild moor to **Amulree** (*hotel*), which looks inviting in its solitude. From this little hamlet there is a rough hill-road, passing *Loch Freuchie*, to **Kenmore** (p. 300): the final stages open grand views of the mountains beyond Loch Tay. Two miles below Amulree a road climbs out of Strath Braan by the long

Glen Cochill and descends to Aberfeldy (*see* p. 306). For the road between Amulree and Dunkeld, *see* p. 305.

From Crieff to Comrie two roads follow on opposite banks, a green strath watered by the winding *Earn*. On the hill of **Tomachastle** is a prominent monument to General Sir David Baird, who overthrew Tippoo Sahib at Seringapatam in 1799, and died at Ferntower, Crieff, in 1829. South of Tomachastle is *Forlum Hill* (1,291 feet). On either side wooded hills contribute to the general beauty of the valley, which at Comrie widens to receive Glen Artney from the south-west and Glen Lednock on the north.

Comrie.

Hotels.—*Ancaster Arms* (10 rooms), *Comrie* (10 rooms), *Royal* (11 rooms), *St. Kessac's* (6 rooms), *Craggish House* (7 rooms).
Sports.—9-hole golf course, bowling green, and pleasant angling in Earn and other waters.

Comrie, charmingly placed among the hills, has a reputation for cleanliness and neatness; also for harmless earthquakes, which geologists recognize as an aftermath of the Highland Boundary Fault. While the climate is genial in winter and spring, it is bracing during the warmer months through breezes from the uplands. The best views are obtained from **Dunmore** and the so-called *Druidical Stones*. The former is a hill (839 feet) to the north, crowned by a monument of the first Lord Melville.

South of the town is a "*Roman Camp*," which has by some been identified as the scene of a memorable fight narrated by Tacitus; but the remains are especially inconsiderable in view of their proximity to the fine camps at **Braco** and **Ardoch** (*see* p. 264), reached by a road southward from Glen Artney in about 15 miles.

From Comrie a fairly good road runs south-westward up **Glen Artney** for about 10 miles, and from this point there is a walking route over to Callander (p. 286), passing near the Bracklinn Falls on the way down to that place. Sir Walter Scott laid the opening scenes of *The Lady of the Lake* in Glen Artney.

Northward from Comrie **Glen Lednock** winds up into the hills and is continued by a path leading past Loch Lednock to Loch Tay (p. 298). At the foot of Dunmore Hill is the *Deil's Cauldron*, where the water tumbles over the rocks very attractively. Five miles from Comrie, at

Invergeldie, a mile short of the fall known as *Spout Rollo*, a path goes off to the summit of **Ben Chonzie** (3,048 feet), the presiding mountain of the district. The River Turret rises on the south-eastern slopes of the mountain, and from the little Loch Uaine may be followed past Loch Turret and down **Glen Turret** to Crieff. In a north-westerly direction there is a track which crosses the upper waters of the Almond and leads down to Ardtalnaig (*see* p. 299).

From Comrie to St. Fillans (6 miles; bus to Balquhidder) the hills close in upon the road. To the left is Aberuchill Castle, and on the right *Dunira*, an estate which originally belonged to Henry Dundas, first Viscount Melville and Baron Dunira, who practically ruled Scotland for many years in the days of George III.

We are now in the pass made famous by the Ettrick Shepherd's poem, *Bonny Kilmeny*. About 2 miles nearer St. Fillans, but on the south side of the river, is the green hill of **Dunfillan** (600 feet), on which St. Fillan, the patron saint of Robert Bruce, is said to have prayed so assiduously as to leave the marks of his knees in the rocks. At the foot of Dunfillan, a few feet from the Dundurn Burn, is **St. Fillan's Well**, formerly believed to possess miraculous healing powers.

St. Fillans.

Distances by road.—Oban, 65 m.; Perth, 29½ m.; Stirling, 37 m.
Hotels.—*Drummond Arms, Achray, Four Seasons.*
Sports.—Angling (in the Earn and Loch Earn); boating on Loch Earn; golf (9 holes); water ski-ing.

This delightful village of cottages and villas lies along the eastern end of Loch Earn and the outlet of the river. The houses extend in a long line on the narrow strip between the mountains and the water. The scenery of the vicinity is remarkably fine.

Saint Fillan, to whom the village owes its name, lived in the eighth century, and was the son of an Irish princess. After being abbot of a monastery on the Holy Loch he wandered about the West Highlands and built churches at Killin and Dundurn. He died at Dundurn, on the other side of the Earn from St. Fillans, and his original chapel remained there until about 1500, when the building now in ruins took its place.

For **Loch Earn and Lochearnhead,** *see* p. 295.
Lochearnhead to Killin, p. 296; to Crianlarich, p. 297; thence to Oban, pp. 196–9.

STIRLING TO CALLANDER AND THE TROSSACHS.

THE busier route is by the Callander road, which from Stirling drives straight across the flat lands between the Forth and the Teith, turning right at Kincardine (6 miles) for Doune. More interesting is the road crossing Stirling Bridge and turning to left at Causewayhead, close to the lofty Wallace Monument.

Bridge of Allan.

At 3 miles Bridge of Allan is a deservedly popular resort on the southern slopes of a hill overlooking the Allan just above its junction with the Forth.

Distances.—Crieff, 18 m.; Perth, 30 m.; Stirling, 3 m.
Early Closing.—Wednesday.
Hotels.—*Allan Water* (60 rooms), *Queen's* (18 rooms), *Old Manor* (7 rooms), *Royal* (37 rooms), *Walmer*, etc.
Sports.—Golf, fishing (Allan Water for trout, grilse and salmon), bowls, tennis, boating, curling. *Games Meeting:* 1st Saturday in August.

The mountain views westward are lovely. The village came into prominence on account of its mineral springs, but its modern fame is at least as much due to its position as a centre for excursions long and short. Eastward are numerous fine rambles over the Ochil Hills.

At **Dunblane** (*see* p. 263) the Callander road turns westward for **Doune.** On the left, as the village is approached, is *Doune Castle,* less famous (and consequently less besieged by visitors) than many in Scotland, but nevertheless very interesting. *Open daily, March to November, except Thursdays in Spring and Autumn,* 10–6, *charge.*

The Castle dates from the beginning of the fifteenth century and consists of two towers and a large court on a strong position between the *Teith* and the *Ardoch,* which unite their waters just below its walls. During the 1745 rising, the Castle was held by the adherents of Bonnie

Prince Charlie, and among the prisoners confined here was John Home (author of *Douglas*), who made his escape by means of a rope of bedclothes. At other times the Castle served as a royal palace and state prison, and a number of historic personages have found more or less welcome security within its walls; but the modern interest of the Castle results largely from the thorough restoration of some of the apartments carried out during the last sixty years by the Earl of Moray, the Baron's Hall, the Banqueting Hall, the Kitchen and Queen Mary's Room affording very interesting glimpses into the habits of bygone days.

From Doune to Callender the road at first runs close to the River Teith, on the far side of which is *Lanrick Castle*. At the house of *Cambusmore*, passed just before the road crosses the Keltie Water, Sir Walter Scott spent some time collecting material for *The Lady of the Lake*.

Callander.

Distances.—Glasgow, 35 m.; Edinburgh, 51 m.; Stirling, 16 m.; Trossachs Pier, 10 m.; Lochearnhead, 13 m.
Hotels.—*Dreadnought* (75 rooms), *Caledonian* (24 rooms), *Ancaster Arms Crown, Bridgend House, Coppice, Glengarry,* and numerous others.
Sports.—Golf (18 holes), tennis, bowls, angling (salmon and trout).

Proportionately to its population (less than 1,800) Callander has a greater number of hotels and boarding-houses than any other place in Scotland. It is, of course, the "jumping off" place for the celebrated Trossachs Tour, but it deserves attention also as a very good centre for road and rail excursions in all directions, being equally in touch with Edinburgh and Glasgow and the finest loch and mountain scenery. The town itself needs no description. As to the surrounding country, no Guide Book can compete with the glowing pictures in Scott's *Lady of the Lake*.

Apart from the Trossachs Tour the two principal excursions from Callander are the walk to the **Bracklinn Falls** and the ascent of Ben Ledi. The falls occur in the *Keltie*, rather more than a mile east of the town in a direct line. The route begins by a road which leaves the Stirling road at the east end of the town, and thence one follows well-marked paths over a hillside covered with gorse and bracken and commanding good views. (The best views are from Beacon Craig, or Willoughby's Craig (1,100 feet), to which signposts point the way.)

Where the river is spanned by a footbridge the water tumbles over a succession of huge sandstone blocks which form a rough natural staircase. The colouring is rich and all about is a profusion of mountain ash, oak and other trees.

Ben Ledi (2,875 feet) lies west of Callander, between the Trossachs road and the Lochearnhead highway. The ascent is not arduous, and the view from the top has that peculiar charm which characterizes the frontier heights of mountain districts. The easiest route is from Coilantogle Farm, 2½ miles from Callander (*see below*), whence the way over the heather and bracken slopes to the smooth green summit is obvious.

A more striking route leaves the Lochearnhead road nearly 3 miles from Callander, passing over the river by an iron bridge.

Ascend the track up the knoll on the left, bending to the right round the knoll, the top of which is crowned by a small cairn. Hence is a beautiful little view in both directions. Northwards the lower reach of Loch Lubnaig is seen, and southwards through the wooded dingle of the Leny Pass appear the Teith and Callander Bridge. The bridge continues to be a more or less prominent feature in the scene during the whole ascent.

The rocky escarpment of Ben Ledi itself now appears in front. Beneath it are a few yards of a winding track about a quarter of a mile ahead. Make for this track, and when you have climbed it, turn to the left so as to get on to the main ridge at the south end of the scarp and nearly a mile from the summit.

When once the ridge is gained, turn to the right and an easy grass-slope takes you to the top of the mountain.

The **view** is fine and varied. Callander Bridge is, perhaps, its most telling feature. Beyond it the windings of the Forth may be seen, with the Ochil range on their left. Nearer at hand are Doune Castle and Dunblane Cathedral. To the south-east is Arthur's Seat behind Edinburgh. In the north and west rises an endless billowy range of Highland hills. Ben Lomond displays by no means his most pleasing outline, being conspicuous by three small lumps. To the left of him Goat Fell, in Arran, may be discerned, and to the right of him the "Cobbler" somewhat resembles in profile a cat's head, the ears being prominent. Then farther north rise the two peaks of Ben Cruachan, some way apart as seen from here. Ben Nevis shows a curved outline terminated southwards by a peak, in the extreme distance and beyond the triangular-shaped summits of Ben More and Stobinian. The two last named, almost close at hand, are easily recognized by the V-shaped depression between them. Ben Lawers is the most prominent peak northwards, and to the right of it the outline of the Cairngorms cut the horizon.

The lochs visible are Lubnaig, Menteith, Vennachar, Achray, and the upper end of Katrine. Beyond Vennachar and Katrine respectively the tarns of Drunkie and Arklet are seen.

CALLANDER TO THE TROSSACHS.

One mile beyond Callander, at the old *Kilmahog Toll*, the Trossachs road leaves the main road and turns sharp to the left over the bridge, to run south-westward towards Loch Vennachar.

A shorter route from Callander is by the road turning down to the bridge in the village, and crossing the Teith again to join the main road about a mile west of Kilmahog Bridge.

The first part of the route to the Trossachs from Callander owes more of its interest to Sir Walter Scott than to its own merits. Almost every house on the way is associated with the hunt described in *The Lady of the Lake.* Immediately after crossing the railway we have the farm-house of *Bochastle* on the left. Here the pace began to tell decisively; the "tailing" had already commenced at Cambusmore on the other side of Callander:

"'Twere long to tell what steeds gave o'er
As swept the hunt through Cambusmore;
What reins were tighten'd in despair,
When rose Ben Ledi's ridge in air;
Who flagg'd upon Bochastle's heath,
Who shunn'd to stem the flooded Teith."

At the foot of **Loch Vennachar** is, or rather was, *Coilantogle Ford*, where Roderick Dhu flung down his gage to FitzJames:

"See here all vantageless I stand,
Arm'd, like thyself, with single brand
For this is Coilantogle Ford,
And thou must keep thee with thy sword."

Had the "Black" Roderick lived now, he would probably have chosen another spot for the dramatic episode herein described; otherwise his historian would have had to substitute for "Coilantogle Ford" "the great sluice of the Glasgow Waterworks," and to give this a poetic ring would have puzzled even such an eminent word-painter as Sir Walter Scott. The sluice, however, terrible dissipater of romance as it is, has its advantage: it keeps back the water in and above Loch Vennachar against a drought.

The peculiar colour-charm which is more conspicuous in Perthshire than in any other Scottish county is nowhere more so than around Callander. Not only are the hill-sides all aglow with the light purple of the ling, but also the rocks, and consequently the roads, are deeply tinged with the same hue.

Loch Vennachar (the "Lake of the Fair Valley") is pleasing without having any striking features. It is 4 miles long, and from a half to three-quarters of a mile wide. Beyond it is a charming view over Loch Achray to the Trossachs and Ben Venue. Then comes a short descent to Brig of Turk.

From the hamlet among the trees a short way east of Brig of Turk a rough road strikes to the right up *Glen Finglas*, by which the pedestrian may in 10 miles reach **Balquhidder,** at the east end of Loch Voil, climbing to a height of 1,400 feet, and descending by *Glen Buckie*. After wet weather a formidable stream has to be waded about 2½ miles short of Balquhidder. There is little or no track between the farm-house of *Achnahard*, about 1½ miles up the glen, and that of *Bailemore*, 2 miles short of Balquhidder. The intervening 6 miles will take from two to three hours.

At Brig of Turk is *Lendrick Youth Hostel.*

The Trossachs.

Loch Achray, whose side the road now skirts, is one of the most charming little lochs in Scotland, when seen from its eastern end. At its head commences that un-rivalled mingling of purple crag, silver-grey birch, oak-copse, and green herbage which we call the **Trossachs** (the "bristly country"). Ben Venue rising directly behind it, broken, rugged and precipitous, adds a grandeur to the scene far greater than its actual height (2,393 feet) would lead one to anticipate. It is, perhaps, the glossiest mountain in Scotland, rivalling in this respect, and even surpassing in richness of colour, the fells of the Coniston and Langdale portion of English Lakeland. Ben Venue is as different from the ordinary run of Scottish mountains as velvet is from calico.

At a bend of the road along the loch-side there is a fine point of view, from which Turner took one of his pictures, and a little farther we reach the *Trossachs Hotel* (80 rooms).

The vast area of hills to the south of Loch Achray and Loch Katrine are now vested as the **Queen Elizabeth National Forest Park.** Where before the hills were bracken-covered the Forestry Commission have planted forest by the square mile. There is public access on the forestry roads for walking and picnicking.

WALKS THROUGH THE TROSSACHS.

(1) To the foot of **Loch Katrine,** and back by the **Pass of Achray** (3½ miles; about three hours). Proceed along the main road for nearly a mile, and 70 paces beyond the ninth milestone from Callander take a road to the left. In 1¼ miles this reaches the sluices, after crossing which (*a*) you return by a path to Achray Hotel, on the Aberfoyle road, or (*b*), taking a path to the right, you at once cross a foot-bridge and, turning up the hollow, join the path from Achray Hotel (p. 147) to the **Pass of Bealach nam bo,** which is seen strewn with boulders, and here and there a stunted tree, high up to the right. After a pleasant up-and-down walk of a mile or so, the stiff ascent begins. From the top, by climbing the little knolls on the right, you get a lovely view of Loch Katrine, with Ellen's Isle just below, the Trossachs, Ben A'an opposite, Lochs Achray and Vennachar, and a host of mountains.

Bealach nam bo (" Pass of the Cattle ") is so called from the fact that the old " caterans," or cattle-rievers, used it as a pass through which to drive their stolen flocks and herds.

(2) By the **Old Trossachs** track to **Loch Katrine,** and back by the present road, 3¼ miles. Old track very sloppy after rain. Quit the main road a quarter of a mile beyond the hotel, opposite the divergence of the Aberfoyle road. After a good mile of up-and-down through woods you enter the road along the north side of Loch Katrine, by the side of a burn, a quarter of a mile beyond the steamer-pier.

(3) **Round Loch Achray,** re-entering main road just beyond the Brig of Turk, 4 miles (*see map*).

The following climbing excursions are also fully worth the time and exertion required by them :—

(1) **Sron Armailte** (1,187 feet), a commanding viewpoint just behind the *Trossachs Hotel,* one hour up-and-down. Go up the grounds on the east side of the hotel and pass to the right of an outhouse ; then straight up.

(2) **Ben A'an** (about 1,500 feet, an hour's brisk walk to the top ; splendid view). Cross the beck behind the hotel ; follow up the stream for two minutes or so, and then bear to the left by a narrow path which soon begins to wind up steeply amongst the crags above the woods. The cone of the mountain soon appears ahead. When past the crags, bear right to the ridge, and follow its ups-and-downs until you get almost under the

summit, which is gained by making a detour to the right round a gully. The view includes Loch Katrine, the Trossachs, and the surrounding mountains.

A descent may be made in the direction of the length of the loch, through at first deep heather, crossing two small burns, and dropping steeply into the north-shore road of Loch Katrine a little beyond the point at which it is opposite Ellen's Isle. Hence back to the hotel either by the present road, or the old Trossachs track (*see above*), entered a quarter of a mile short of the steamer-pier, 2½ miles. *N.B.*—In descending be careful to avoid the crags on the left.

(3) Ben Venue (2,393 feet; four to five hours up-and-down, a circular walk). Either (*a*) take the *Path of the Sluices* to the top of *Bealach nam bo* (*see* p. 290), and thence follow a faint track that bears up the left towards the ridge; or (*b*), taking the reverse way, ascend by the ridge from Achray Hotel. The walking is up-and-down and rough, but the view of the three lochs and the fertile plain of the Forth beyond is very fine.

Trossachs to Aberfoyle, 7 miles (*see* pp. 145–7).

From the *Trossachs Hotel* to the Steamer Pier the road passes through the heart of the Trossachs. The distance is about a mile, and the country traversed is a rich copse wood dingle, which admits of little distant view except the peak of *Ben A'an*, whose rocky crest rises to a height of 1,500 feet on the north. The Trossachs glen is best appreciated either out of season or early or late in the day, when one's admiration of the scenery is not interrupted by the fumes of the busy traffic. The pier and its surroundings are the very essence of rustic beauty. Here, indeed, "every prospect pleases"—and here, alas, man (or some men) earn the epithet "vile" for the manner in which they dispose of orange peel, tins and cartons. So abruptly do the purple crags rise out of the water, and so closely do the trees—birch, hazel, dwarf-oak, and others, that love to burrow their roots through the rocky chinks—grow to their edges, that even under a noontide sun deep shadows are cast on the still waters of the land-locked bay.

At the Pier-head are refreshment-rooms and a space for car parking.

The road itself (pedestrians only) is continued along the northern shore of the loch, passing *Ellen's Isle* and the *Silver Strand*, the latter a mile beyond the pier. So far the tourist should certainly stroll. The entire route (about 8 miles in length) takes one to the farmstead of *Portnellan*, about a mile beyond that part of the loch which is opposite Stronachlachar. Here the public road ends. The Glasgow Water Department have, however, constructed a private road (available to cyclists and walkers) round to Stronachlachar, meeting up with the Inversnaid–Aberfoyle road. There is also a good walk up Glen Gyle and over the hills to Ardlui, at the head of Loch Lomond. The walk along the loch side admits of a fine view of Ben Venue, but otherwise nothing can be seen to greater advantage than from the steamer.

From Trossachs Pier steamers leave for Stronachlachar, towards the far end of Loch Katrine, about twice daily (not Sundays) (*cycles carried, but not cars or motor-cycles*).

The steamer usually passes to the right of **Ellen's Isle**, on the beach of which the "blighted tree," against which the Harper reclined, is still pointed out. For beauty of outline and delicacy of foliage—mainly birch—this island is certainly unsurpassed. Opposite is the **Silver Strand**, a promontory which has been made an island by the raising of the water. The *Goblin's Cave* (*Coire na Uruisgean*) and, above it, Bealach nam bo, "Pass of the Cattle" (p. 290), are seen well up the slope of Ben Venue. The mountain ahead, as we look up the loch, is *Stob a Choin*.

Loch Katrine is called by Scott "Loch Cateran," or the loch of the "robbers"; and the name, though less pleasing to the southern ear, is supported by others of similar import in the neighbourhood, *Bealach nam bo* (p. 290) to wit. If the tourist can throw himself back to the time when there was no road from Stronachlachar to Inversnaid, and "no mode of issuing from the Trossachs except by a sort of ladder composed of the branches of roots and trees," while of houses of entertainment the nearest and best was the clachan of Aberfoyle, he will realize the probable appropriateness of the name. The loch is 8 miles long and, on an average, three-quarters of a mile wide. The whole beauty is concentrated at the Trossachs end, the rest of it being singularly destitute of distinctive features, though it is surrounded by wild hills of considerable height. During the sail up it, Ben Lomond comes into view on the left, and, soon after, the Glasgow Waterworks, marked by a villa amid fir-trees, are passed on the same side.

The length of the aqueduct from the Loch to Glasgow is about 30 miles. The Thirlmere aqueduct to Manchester is 95¾ miles long; the Lake Vyrnwy to Liverpool, 67 miles; the Rhayader to Birmingham, 73½ miles. In addition to Loch Katrine, the waters of the enlarged Loch Arklet (*see below*) are also requisitioned.

The steamer stops at **Stronachlachar** ("the Stone-mason's Point"), 2 miles short of the head of the loch. (*Note:* There is no longer a hotel at Stronachlachar.) From this point buses convey the passengers through **Glen Arklet to Inversnaid,** a distance of 5 miles. Loch Katrine being 378 feet above the sea, and the highest part of Loch Arklet scarcely 500, the climb is very slight, but at the far end of Glen Arklet there is a sharp descent to Loch Lomond, which is only 23 feet above the sea: this part of the route is by far the most interesting, as the Arklet cascades down a pretty glen to finish finally at the site of the loch in the Inversnaid Falls. The road is steep with hairpin bends, but from it is obtained an excellent view across Loch Lomond to Inveruglas with Beinn Ime at its head and flanked by Ben Vane, Ben Vorlich and Beinn Narnain. At the foot of the glen can be seen Loch Sloy hydro-electric power station. The view in front is also the chief feature of the journey alongside Loch Arklet, on the southern shores of which Rob Roy's wife, Helen MacGregor, is said to have been born. At the western end of the glen is a small clachan: the farmstead known as *The Garrison* commemorates the fortress erected to overawe the MacGregors in 1713: no less a celebrity than General Wolfe once was its commander. (*See also* p. 194.)

A little-used route, giving good views over Glen Gyle and the wild country at the head of Loch Katrine, strikes up from Glen Arklet beside the Corrarklet Burn, passes round Beinn a' Choin and Stob nan Eighrach and suddenly discloses a grand "bird's-eye view" of Loch Lomond before descending to its shores at Ardleish, opposite Ardlui.

Half a mile from Stronachlachar the pretty road from Aberfoyle strikes in on the left (*see* p. 145). For **Loch Lomond,** *see* p. 191.

CALLANDER TO KILLIN, CRIANLARICH AND ABERFELDY.

FROM Callander the route is westward to Kilmahog, where the Trossachs road (p. 288) goes off on the left, and beyond which we enter the lovely **Pass of Leny.** It is well seen from the road, though it is fully appreciated only by leisurely pedestrians. On the left hand Ben Ledi flings down his most precipitous side almost to the foot of it, and on the right more gentle heights, clad in a parti-coloured vesture of silver-birch, hazel, oak and heather, rise in a succession of irregular and picturesque knolls. Nowhere in " bonnie Scotland " is the scene more enhanced by her characteristic flower than in the neighbourhood of Callander.

The valley widens out to Loch Lubnaig near a small walled-in churchyard, remnant of the *Chapel of St. Bride,* in whose precincts young Angus handed over the fiery cross to Norman, dispatching him on a solitary honeymoon. In 1932 the foundations were verified and restored and an entrance gate erected in connection with the Scott centenary celebrations.

Loch Lubnaig (the " crooked lake ") till lately provided Callander's water-supply. The road skirts the shore for its entire length of 4½ miles. The road has good vantage points of view, being opposite to the most effective side of the lake, and bringing into greater prominence the central rock, which is the keynote to its beauty. This rock, projecting high and steep, and boldly rounded at the top, divides the lake into two reaches, and saves it from that monotonous appearance which it would otherwise wear.

About half-way along the loch, beside *Ardchullarie Mor,* a path climbs the western flank of Beinn Each and descends by Glen Ample to Loch Earn at **Edinample,** passing **Edinample Falls** near the lower end of the glen, which is about 2 miles from Lochearnhead.

A mile beyond the head of the loch, and a long eight from Callander, is the pleasant hamlet of **Strathyre** (*Ben Sheann, Munro,* and boarding houses). Here the Forestry Commission have a nursery where trees are grown from seed.

Strathyre to Balquhidder.—Cross the river, and follow an up-and-down course parallel to the main route to Balquhidder (4 miles). Walkers should take this route, returning by the direct road to the King's House. The entire round measures 6 miles.

From the bridge over the Balvag a fine full-length view of **Loch Voil** is obtained. It is a long narrow lake, with lap after lap of dark green mountains descending abruptly to its shoreline, and well clothed with wood in their lower parts. Those on the north are the famous "Braes of Balquhidder." There is a road along that side of the lake. Looking eastward from the Balvag Bridge the eye catches the cone of Ben Vorlich rising above the level ridge behind the *King's House Inn.*

Balquhidder (*Baile-cul-tir*) means "the village of the back-lying country." The *Old Chapel* is a mere shell, in front of the new one. It is ivy-clad, and has a picturesque little open bell-turret. Inside is a little grove of Irish yews growing on a carpet of grass, and outside, a few yards from the east end, are the reputed tombs of **Rob Roy**, his wife, and sons. They consist of flat slabs inscribed with quaint devices—swords, mystic knots, and animals—the whole bearing the stamp of an antiquity greater than that of Rob Roy, who died in 1734 at a house near the far end of the loch—one of that class of men, who according to Andrew Fairservice, are "ower bad for blessing and ower good for banning." The scene, by the way, in which Rob made his thrilling escape by slipping off at his horse's tail is on the Forth, not by the side of Loch Voil, as some writers would have it.

The nearest hostelry to Balquhidder is the *King's House Inn*, 2 miles east, on the main Callander–Killin highway, 2 miles north of Strathyre.

From this point the main road continues north-eastward to **Lochearnhead,** a pretty and attractive hamlet with hotels (*Lochearnhead, Auchraw*) at the western end of **Loch Earn.** The loch is 7 miles long and about half a mile broad, and is singularly attractive, although it is difficult to say exactly wherein lies its charm. The west end of the loch is famed for national and international water-ski-ing championship events which attract many spectators, while at the St. Fillans end dinghy-sailing is popular. The main road to Crieff passes along the northern shore, but a narrow though more attractive route is available on the south side.

About 5 miles from Lochearnhead, **Glen Tarken** strikes up from the northern side of the loch; a couple of miles up the glen is a curiosity in the form of a huge mushroom-shaped boulder. That part which rests on the ground is 70 feet in circumference, while 10 feet higher the circumference is 120 feet. For **St. Fillans**, *see* p. 284.

On the south side of the loch, a mile from Lochearnhead, are the **Edinample Falls**, at the lower end of **Glen Ample.**

Ben Vorlich (3,224 feet) may be ascended without difficulty from Lochearnhead. Follow the road along the south shore of Loch Earn as far as Ardvorlich House (4 miles); thence ascend on the near side of the burn until the ridge on the right can be conveniently climbed. This ridge leads to the summit. An interesting but very up-and-down descent may be made to the *King's House Inn*; a longer route is down the valley southward to Loch Lubnaig; or one can turn northward and follow the Edinample valley to Loch Earn (*see* p. 294).

For the first 5 of the 7 miles between Lochearnhead and Killin, the road (the A85) is occupied with the passage of steep and forbidding **Glen Ogle** (probably *Gleann Ogluidh*, the "gloomy valley"), which attains an elevation of 948 feet (631 above Loch Earn). Though thoroughly Highland in character, it is somewhat wanting in decisive features. At its summit, on the left hand, is a small tarn—a favourite curling rendezvous in winter—from which the water flows northward into Glen Dochart.

For **Crianlarich** keep ahead (*westward*) up Glen Dochart (*see below*) on emerging from Glen Ogle and passing under the bridge; for Killin turn sharp to right. During the descent to Killin there are views of that village, the head of Loch Tay, and Ben Lawers—the last-named forming a noble background, with an array of fine peaks to the left of it.

Killin (pronounced Kill-*in*), with good hotels (*Killin* (36 rooms), *Bridge of Lochay, Falls of Dochart, Tighnabruaich, Clachaig*) and other accommodation, is a very attractive little place, situated at the head of Loch Tay and between the rivers Lochay and Dochart, which here flow into the loch. It derives its name from the two words *Cil Fhinn*, signifying the "burial-place of Fingal," whose supposed grave is marked by a stone in a field a quarter of a mile from the present church, at the foot of Sron a' Chlachain.

Sron a' Chlachain (1,708 feet; 1,440 above Killin) rises due west of Killin, about a mile distant as the crow flies. Its name, signifying "stony point or projection," well describes its position as the most easterly point of the range which separates Glen

Lochay from Glen Dochart. From the top the lower reaches of both Glen Lochay and Glen Dochart are seen, and the entrance to Glen Ogle, to the south. Ben More in the south-west, and Ben Lawers in the north-east, display their bold forms to great advantage.

A good road up beautiful **Glen Lochay** strikes off on the near side of Lochay Bridge, and a few yards before the hotel. About 3 miles up it are the **Falls of Lochay**, more picturesque than grand.

Finlarig Castle, an ivy-grown ruin, embosomed in trees, beside the road to the pier, was the burial-place of the Breadalbane family.

KILLIN TO CRIANLARICH, BY GLEN DOCHART.

Glen Dochart is softer in style than neighbouring Glen Ogle, but the generally dark green of its strath gives it a strangely gloomy appearance.

On the south side of the glen rise **Ben More** and **Stobinian** (*see below*), and towards Crianlarich is **Loch Dochart**, consisting of two sheets of water connected by a half-mile stream, the whole company measuring about 3 miles in length. The lower loch is also known as Loch Iubhair, " the Loch of the Yew tree." A ruined castle on an island in the more western loch is said to have served Bruce as a retreat. For **Crianlarich** and on to **Tyndrum, Dalmally** and **Oban**, *see* pp. 196–9.

Ben More (3,843 feet), in conjunction with its fellow height, **Stobinian** (3,821 feet), is the most conspicuous mountain in Perthshire. The two summits are separated by a V-shaped depression, and form, when seen from either the east or the west, a pair of almost similar triangles, the only difference being that while the apex of **Stobinian**, the more southerly of the two, is cut off by a short and perfectly straight line, that of Ben More itself is slightly rounded.

From four to five hours should be allowed for the walk up and down from the point at which the high-road through Glen Dochart is left. The ascent is best commenced near the place where the burn threading the hollow on the east side of the mountain is crossed—i.e., about 1½ miles from old Luib Station, 2½ from *Luib Hotel*, and 5½ from Crianlarich. Hence the shortest way up is by the ridge all the way, a climb of unrelieved steepness. An easier plan is to follow more or less the course of the burn until the eastern ridge of the mountain is gained, whence turning sharply to the right, a steep pitch leads directly to the top. Another ascent may be made from the Ben More Farm, 2 miles east of Crianlarich ; but the slope is terribly steep all the way to the top : the route from Luib is easier.

The view from the summit comprises an endless array of mountain-tops, prominent amongst which are Ben Lui and Ben Cruachan to the west; Ben Ime, The Cobbler, Ben Vorlich (Dumbartonshire), and Ben Lomond to the south; Ben Ledi, Ben Vorlich (Loch Earn), and Ben Lawers south-east, east, and north-east respectively; Ben Dorain and the mountains of Glen Lyon to the north. The softer features of the scene are Loch Tay and Loch Voil.

The descent may be varied by climbing over the top of Stobinian and then descending into the valley at the west end of Loch Voil, and thence walk or drive to Balquhidder.

Loch Tay.

Salmon fishing begins on January 15, and may be enjoyed by visitors to the following hotels: Kenmore (Breadalbane Hotel), Killin, and Ardeonaig.

Trout fishing on the loch is free.

Loch Tay is one of the largest and most beautiful of the Scottish lochs, while for salmon fishing it is second to none. The trouting is also sometimes excellent. The loch is about 15 miles long by 1 mile broad. Roads (bus services throughout the year) skirt both north and south shores; that on the north having the better surface, that on the south a superiority of outlook.

After crossing the Bridge of Lochay the north shore road climbs steeply and in about 3 miles a rough hill road goes off on the north to Bridge of Balgie, in **Glen Lyon.** Hence the way down Glen Lyon is very fine; for really good walkers a rough track continues northward, from Innerwick, a mile east from Bridge of Balgie, to the southern shore of **Loch Rannoch,** but it is a route to be avoided in mist unless one knows the way.

About 4 miles farther east, on the northern shore, is **Lawers** (*hotel*), the most convenient point from which to ascend **Ben Lawers** (3,984 feet), which is, considering its great height, as easy a mountain to ascend as any in Scotland. Only the last few hundred feet of the ascent are at all steep. Ben Lawers is mainly National Trust property, and has good ski-ing slopes, much frequented in the winter sports season. The *Ben Lawers Hotel* is itself 600 feet above the sea. Those who do not care to make the whole ascent may with advantage climb the subsidiary height of Meall Odhar (*see below*), about a third of the way up, and just above the hotel.

Follow the Kenmore road for a few hundred yards, and just beyond the first burn take to the open fell, and climb with the burn close by on the left hand. In about forty minutes after leaving the hotel cross a wall by a stile. Hence proceed straight forward, leaving the fir-planted **Meall Odhar** (1,794 feet) some way on the left, and still keeping the burn on the same side. The top of Ben Lawers is seen, also to the left of the general direction of the route up. To reach it scale the eastern ridge a considerable distance from the summit, so as to avoid the steep slope which intervenes in the direct course. On attaining this ridge follow it all the way up. Below, on the right hand, you will look across the deep valley containing Lochan nan Cat, out of which the Lawers Burn flows, to a lofty range of steep hills beyond. View indicator on summit of the Ben.

View.—Very fine and extensive, including the full length of Loch Tay with Killin and Kenmore at either end. Southwards the Loch Earn Ben Vorlich is the conspicuous height, and to the right of it the twin peaks of Ben More and Stobinian. On the north-east rises Schiehallion with its cone modified into a long ridge on the eastern side, and, far away beyond it, the flat-topped summits of the Eastern Grampians—Braeriach, Cairn Toul, and Ben Macdhui rising slightly above the general elevation. North-west, over the Black Moor of Rannoch, the equally flat top of Ben Nevis may be discerned, and the same distance south of west Cruachan is recognizable by its sharp peaks, with, and much nearer, Ben Dorain (flat-top peak) to the right and Ben Lui to the left. Ben Ime is seen exactly between the peaks of Ben More and Stobinian, and Ben Lomond considerably to the left. Ben Ledi is almost due south. The upper part of Glencoe is visible, with Buachaille Etive on its left; also north-east, over the right shoulder of Schiehallion, the farther part of Glen Tilt. In clear weather the eye may range south-east over and to the left of the Ochils to the Peaks of Fife, North Berwick Law, the Bass Rock, and Largo Law, in the order named.

The rough and crumbling schist formation of which the higher part of Ben Lawers consists is very favourable to the growth of rare plants—including gentian and many kinds of saxifrage—and the traveller who is a botanist as well as a climber will prolong his stay on the mountain-slopes with great satisfaction. It is said that there are, or were, more Alpine plants than on any other Scottish mountain, but collectors have sadly depleted them. Specimens should *not* be taken away.

In *descending*, the route may be varied by taking a rough and rather steep shoulder considerably to the west of the route by which we have described the ascent, and overlooking the depression which separates Ben Lawers from the next mountain, Beinn Ghlas. From the bottom of this shoulder cross the comparatively level and, perhaps, swampy ground to **Meall Odhar**, whence you may descend almost in a bee-line to the hotel.

An easy and delightful descent is direct for **Killin** over Beinn Ghlas, entering the road near *Edramucky*.

Beinn Bhreac (2,341 feet), Ben Lawers' less lofty *vis-à-vis*, can be climbed easily from **Ardtalnaig** on the south side of Loch Tay. On its eastern side the Acharn Burn runs down to Acharn, making a pretty cascade just above the village of Acharn, on the loch-side, about 2 miles from Kenmore.

From **Fearnan,** a picturesque village with hotel on the northern shore about midway between Lawers and Kenmore, a road goes over to **Fortingall,** at the foot of Glen Lyon. Beside the road about half a mile above Fearnan is the baptismal font of the long-vanished church of St. Ciarnan.

Fortingall is a pleasant village with hotel and a famous yew-tree that is supposed to be the oldest specimen of vegetation in Europe. The tree stands in an enclosure at the west end of the church and is believed to have been flourishing when Solomon was building his temple and the Greeks were besieging Troy. The church has been rebuilt: within is preserved a Celtic bell. In the fields opposite are the remains of a supposed Roman camp. Garth Memorial Youth Hostel is a mile east of Fortingall.

Glen Lyon is 30 miles long and for the greater part of its length is narrow and rugged. The lower part is particularly fine: indeed, many who find the Trossachs rather overrun during the height of the season rate Glen Lyon as definitely equal, if not superior. A road goes up the glen to Bridge of Balgie and on to lonely **Loch Lyon,** more than a thousand feet up among the hills, and a path continues south of Ben Dorain to the road connecting Tyndrum and Bridge of Orchy (*see* p. 229). From Glen Lyon one may reach Loch Tay and Killin by the steep and narrow road from Bridge of Balgie. Northward an inviting track goes from Innerwick to the shores of Loch Rannoch.

Kenmore is a placid and attractive village at the eastern end of Loch Tay. It is gathered around a neat green (on which were executed the chief of the MacGregors and other " limmers "), at one end of which is the church and at the other an entrance to Taymouth Castle, a former seat of the Marquis of Breadalbane, but no longer used as such; on the north side of the green is the picturesque *Breadalbane Hotel* (38 *rooms*). A pretty island in Loch Tay opposite Kenmore contains the ruins of a Priory founded in 1122 by Alexander I, whose first queen, Sybilla, daughter of Henry I of England, was buried in it. There is a golf course in the grounds of *Taymouth Castle.*

At Kenmore the main road crosses the Tay, hence following the south side of the river, past a Stone Circle known as *Craig Monach* (from the vicinity of which there is a grand view of Schiehallion, to the north-north-west), and on through park-like scenery to **Aberfeldy** (p. 306).

Kenmore to Loch Tummel.—From the road-angle just north of the Tay Bridge at Kenmore a reasonable road runs north-east for 3 miles to the vicinity of the ruined keep of *Comrie Castle*, where the Lyon is crossed. Turn left, and at *Coshieville Hotel* go to the right. This road climbs, with the Keltney Burn on the left, and shortly there are increasingly good views to the left, over Garth Castle, a stronghold of the "Wolf of Badenoch." Two miles from Coshieville a narrow road goes off on the left for **Schiehallion**, the ascent of which is made by its long eastern ridge.

Those unable or unwilling to climb Schiehallion (*see below*) may enjoy at least a great part of the view northward by continuing for another 2 or 3 miles along the road towards Tummel, which attains a height of over 1,200 feet and unfolds a panorama which for grandeur and extent would be hard to surpass among views which can be enjoyed from the seat of a car. The road itself, too, has been reconstructed, and the long run down to Tummel Bridge is very enjoyable. For the route hence either to Pitlochry or to Kinloch Rannoch, *see* page 310.

Whether to look at or to look from, Schiehallion (3,547 feet) is one of the finest of Scottish mountains. As seen from other eminences its cone is always a graceful and distinctive object in view, while its commanding position over the strath which extends from Loch Tummel to Loch Rannoch gives to the view from it a diversity that contrasts strongly with that obtained from many Scottish mountains of greater altitude. In addition to the approach mentioned above, it may be ascended also from Kinloch Rannoch or from Tummel Bridge (*see* p. 310).

The View. The feature is Loch Tummel and the glen beyond it, through which the River Tummel makes its way into the Garry, near Pitlochry, and beyond which Ben Vrackie rises to a graceful peak. In the opposite direction a part of Loch Rannoch is seen, and the "Shepherds of Etive" at the head of Glencoe. Northwards, over Strath Tummel, the dull line of the Eastern Grampians is only relieved by Ben-y-Gloe, rearing itself on the far side of Glen Tilt, which is visible above Forest Lodge. The loftier mass of Ben Lawers shuts out a good deal of the prospect southwards.

PERTH TO INVERNESS.

(The Great North Road.)

FOR the first 30 miles of the route the hurrying waters of the Tay and Tummel are close at hand and provide views of unceasing interest; then, beyond the Pass of Killiecrankie, the scenery begins to open out. Struan is near the beginning of the long and splendid climb through Glen Garry and the Pass of Drumochter (1,504 feet) by which the Grampians are crossed. For the next 25 miles we run down to and along broad Strathspey, with grand views of the Cairngorms on the right and a succession of attractive villages besides the river; for the final 30 miles the road is concerned with crossing the Monadhliath mountains—wild scenery which forms a splendid preface for the picture of Inverness, backed by the soft beauty of Beauly Firth, which is the feature of the final stage of the journey.

Road and railway use the same route, and each, in its turn, provides features of interest for the other, as by good engineering it overcomes gradients or surmounts sharper natural difficulties.

Perth (p. 265) is left by the Dunkeld road, beside the North Inch. A mile or so out a glimpse may be caught, across the river, of Scone Palace (p. 357). Then, between the river and our road, comes the field of *Luncarty*, whereon Kenneth II defeated Danish invaders.

Legend has it that the Danes, contrary to practice, determined upon a night attack, but that the alarm was given by the involuntary cry of one of them who trod with bare foot upon a thistle. Hence the elevation of the humble weed to the proud position of national emblem. In actual fact, however, the thistle does not appear as a national emblem until very much later, and the battle itself is something of a myth.

The river now makes a wide bend to eastward, but the road cuts across the promontory by Bankfoot to regain the valley near **Murthly Castle** (demolished) and at the entrance to the **Pass of Birnam**, to which the railway arch forms a gateway. High on the left rises Birnam Hill, with the ruins of Duncan's Castle (*see Macbeth*), and then a bridge crosses the river to Dunkeld (15 miles from Perth).

Dunkeld and Birnam.

Hotels.—Dunkeld: *Atholl Arms, Dunkeld House, Royal, Taybank, Cardney House.* Birnam: *Birnam, Merlewood.* Birnam Youth Hostel.

Sports.—Tennis, bowls, golf (9-hole course. No introduction necessary), angling (visitors at the Birnam Hotel can fish 1½ miles of the Tay for salmon and its tributary, the Braan, for trout. There are also waters open to visitors at the Atholl Arms Hotel, Dunkeld, whilst the Dunkeld House Hotel has a private stretch of the Tay for salmon.)

Dunkeld and Birnam are charmingly situated on opposite banks of the Tay and are the centre of many delightful walks and drives. Dunkeld (i.e. Fort of the Culdees; according to others, Hill of the Caledonians) was an early seat of Scottish sovereignty and of Celtic Christianity. The first turning to the left beyond the Bridge leads to the **Cathedral**, the earliest portion of which dates from the thirteenth century. It is a venerable ruin in lovely grounds, overlooking the river. It was wrecked by the Reformers in 1560, and lay in ruins until 1600, when Stewart of Ladywell repaired and re-roofed the choir. In 1691 the Cathedral was repaired by the Atholl family, and fitted as the Parish Church. In 1908 the choir was restored after the original design through the munificence of Sir Donald Currie. The building was, in 1927, handed over to the nation by the Duke of Atholl (*open daily, fee; 10–4 or 7; Sundays, 2–4 or 7. Guide.* The roofless nave is now a burial-ground: in the Church is the tomb, with effigy in armour, of "The Wolf of Badenoch." A curiosity of the west front is the west window, which is considerably out of line. One of the bishops of Dunkeld was the Scottish poet, Gawain Douglas (*c.* 1474–1522), son of Archibald Bell-the-Cat. To many, however, Dunkeld Cathedral is chiefly memorable for its lovely situation amid shaded lawns beside the Tay. The National Trust for Scotland owns many of the "little houses" in Cathedral Street and High Street.

Adjoining are the grounds of **Dunkeld House** (now an hotel, once seat of the Duke of Atholl). Among many fine trees within the grounds is a remarkably fine larch, one of two that grew side by side and were known as "the mother larches," as they were said to be pioneers of the kind grown in Britain. They were brought from Tyrol in 1738. (The tree is near the churchyard.)

EXCURSIONS FROM DUNKELD AND BIRNAM.

1. **Birnam Hill** (1,324 feet).—Easily ascended by a path starting from a lane at the north end of the railway station.

From the summit the view extends to Ben Lawers and Schiehallion 25 miles away in a direction rather north of west—the latter recognizable by its conical peak, and the former presenting a broken ridge to the left of it. Still more to the left the top of Ben More may be descried in the distance. Northward Ben Vrackie is not more than a dozen miles distant. Behind it rise Ben-y-Gloe and the other heights of Glen Tilt, and farther to the east are Mount Blair and the mountains which separate the Dee from the Tay basin (Glas Maol, etc.). A group of lakelets on the Blairgowrie road is a pleasing feature in the prospect to the north-east; and just over Dunkeld, whose cathedral, bridge, and couple of streets appear as in a bird's-eye view, Craigie-Barns, the guardian rock of Dunkeld, shows its abrupt yet graceful outlines, softened by their head-to-foot covering of trees. Turning more to the east and south-east, the eye ranges over the rich plain of Strathmore (the "great flat") to the Sidlaw Hills, on the right of which lies Perth. Due south are the Ochils.

2. **Craigie-Barns,** a rocky height clothed with woods through which are beautiful walks. The entrance is at Cally Lodge on the Blairgowrie road.

3. **The Hermitage Bridge.** Follow the Aberfeldy road to Inver Bridge and take the road to the left just before reaching the bridge. After crossing the railway go through a gate on the right and take a rough track across the fields. Where this dips down to some low ground keep straight on by a faint path which soon improves and affords fine views of the Hermitage Bridge. This is a delightful spot and on the far bank of the river is a large summer house known as *Ossian's Hall.* Beyond it the path on the left bank of the stream is joined.

4. The **Rumbling Bridge** and the **Falls of Braan** (2½ miles) and **Inver** (1 mile).

(*a*) By path from Inver. Take the Aberfeldy road to Inver (*see below*) and about ¼ mile beyond the last house take a path which strikes off to the left. This path follows the left bank of the stream, passes close to the Hermitage Bridge, latterly becomes a grassy track across some fields, and finally joins a road at a point about ¼ mile from the Rumbling Bridge.

(*b*) By road. Follow the main Amulree road for 2½ miles and then take a branch road to the right which leads down to the Bridge. The return to Dunkeld may be made by either of the routes mentioned above. **Inver** was the birthplace of

Neil Gow, the celebrated Scottish violinist (1727–1807), whose cottage is pointed out. (His grave is at Little Dunkeld, at the south end of the bridge.) In the same house was born Charles Mackintosh (1839–1922), the " Perthshire Naturalist."

From the northern end of Dunkeld a road goes off eastward to **Blairgowrie**, 12 miles (p. 358), a romantic and interesting route following for the greater part of the way the river Lunan and passing several lochs. An island on **Loch Clunie** contains the ruined Castle of Clunie, an early home of " The Admirable Crichton."

DUNKELD TO PITLOCHRY VIÂ ABERFELDY.

The direct route for Ballinluig and Pitlochry follows the left (eastern) bank of the Tay; but those who wish to visit Aberfeldy *en route* for the North may do so with hardly any loss of scenery and at the cost of not more than 20 extra miles, by taking the road along the western bank of the river. The main route is rejoined at Ballinluig. This route passes Inver, Dalguise, Balnaguard and *Grandtully* (*hotel*), the last-named village adjoining, some say, the original of Tullyveolan, the Castle of Bradwardine in Scott's *Waverley*.

Another route to Aberfeldy is *viâ* Strath Braan and **Glen Cochill**, which strikes up to the north about 8 miles from Dunkeld. A little farther up Strath Braan is **Amulree**, whence are routes to Kenmore and to the **Sma' Glen** and Crieff (p. 281).

DUNKELD TO PITLOCHRY BY BALLINLUIG.

Swinging left at the far end of Dunkeld's main street we pass beneath the wooded slopes of Craigie-Barns and make northward for Ballinluig. Below the road, on the left, is the Tay, and beyond that the hills arrange and rearrange themselves in ever-interesting formation.

Ballinluig is important as the meeting-point of the Tay and the Tummel and of the interesting roads which accompany those rivers over this part of their courses. It stands at the junction of the Great North Road with the very fine road to the west coast at Oban by Kenmore and alongside Loch Tay to Killin, and on by Crianlarich to Dalmally, Loch Awe and the Pass of Brander as described on other pages.

From Ballinluig rail and road follow the east bank of the *Tummel*, which except after continued rain occupies but a small part of its wide and stony bed. On the lower spur of a hill on the left is a monumental Celtic cross to the sixth Duke of Atholl. *Moulinearn* is 1¾ miles from Ballinluig, an important inn in days gone by, but now a farm. Here, in the rebellion of 1745, Prince Charles breakfasted when northward bound, and almost a century later (1844) Queen Victoria partook of "Atholl brose" (a mixture of oatmeal, honey and whisky) while on her way to Blair Castle.

BALLINLUIG TO ABERFELDY AND KENMORE.

From Ballinluig an interesting road runs west along the north side of the Tay to Aberfeldy. **Logierait**, a mile west of Ballinluig on the Aberfeldy road, was the seat of a Court of Regality in which the Lords of Atholl administered feudal justice. The ancient prison once held that famous outlaw Rob Roy. A statue of the sixth Duke of Atholl (died 1864) marks the site of a Royal Castle (the Rath) which was used by Robert III as a hunting lodge. In the *Hotel* garden a hollow oak-tree, estimated at a thousand years old, is used as a tea-room. Opposite the village there is a ford across the Tay, which is also crossed by a chain-boat.

Aberfeldy.

Angling.—The local Angling Club issues permits for its waters for day or season, for trout fishing. Salmon and trout fishing on the Tay is offered by the Weem Hotel.
Distances.—Perth, 32 m.; Crieff, 23 m.; Dunkeld, 17 m.; Gleneagles, 31 m.; Killin, 22 m.; Tummel Bridge, 13 m.
Early Closing.—Wednesday.
Golf.—A 9-hole course along the banks of the river. The course in the grounds of Taymouth Castle is also open to the public (*see* p. 300). Sunday golf from 1 p.m.
Hotels.—*Palace* (18 rooms), *Breadalbane Arms* (20 rooms), *Station* (12 rooms), *Crown* (20 rooms), *Moness House* (30 rooms), *Weem* (19 rooms). Several guest houses, etc. Municipal caravan site on banks of Tay.
Sports.—Angling, putting and golf (*see above*); bowls, tennis, etc.

Aberfeldy, pleasantly situated amid good scenery, is a very convenient centre. Robert Burns was here in 1787, having come over the hills from Crieff by Amulree and Glen Quaich. Of the lovely scenery in the neighbourhood he sang in his *Birks of Aberfeldy*. The song is to the air of an older lyric, "The Birks of Abergeldie." The birches at the latter place, on Deeside, are famous, but curiously there are very few at the Falls of Moness.

The Bridge (1733) is one of the best examples of the work of General Wade: note the inscription relating to its erection. Near the bridge a Monument to the Black

Watch marks the place where that gallant regiment was originally enrolled.

The three **Falls of Moness**, which inspired Burns's song, are a short distance south of the town. The entrance to the path leading to them is opposite the *Breadalbane Arms*. About two hours are required in making the circuit of the falls. The lowest fall is a mile from the entrance, and is inferior to the others. The next is a quarter of a mile farther, and the third half a mile beyond that. A rustic bridge, a little above the last fall, leads back by a gentle descent. Admission is free.

From Aberfeldy a road runs south by **Loch na Craige** and Glen Cochill to Kinloch Lodge, and then down Strath Braan to Dunkeld (p. 305) or *viâ* Amulree (p. 282) to Crieff.

From Aberfeldy to Kenmore ($6\frac{1}{2}$ miles) the road is a fine avenue passing through park-like scenery, of which the grand climax is reached opposite the grounds to Taymouth Castle. A little short of this, looking up the glen of the *Keltney Burn* on the right, we obtain a fine glimpse of Schiehallion. Then, after passing a stone circle on the left, we obtain from the *Fort*, a mile or so before Kenmore is reached, a justly celebrated view of the Castle and surrounding scenery, including a portion of Loch Tay and Ben Lawers. For **Kenmore** and Loch Tay, *see* pp. 298–300. Thence to Killin, Crianlarich or Callander, etc., *see* pp. 296–9.

ABERFELDY TO TUMMEL BRIDGE (14 miles).

From the far end of Aberfeldy Bridge an avenue of poplars leads to the village of **Weem** (*Weem Hotel*), behind which rises the **Rock of Weem** (800 feet), a fine view-point. Nearly half-way up is **St. David's Well**, the original stonework of which, a memorial of the Menzies family, is now in the mausoleum of Sir Robert Menzies.

From the Weem Rock the walk may be extended to the top of **Farragon** (4 miles ; two and a half hours from Weem ; 2,559 feet) by an obvious route. Fine all-round view—Schiehallion very prominent, with the " Sugar-loaves " of Glencoe over its north slope ; Ben Nevis (far away to the right of it) and Ben Alder, and to the left Ben Lawers (south-west), Ben More (far away), Ben

Chonzie (south), Ochils, Sidlaws (south-east), Braemar Mountains, Ben Vrackie, the Cairngorms, Ben-y-Gloe, etc. A fine extension of the walk takes one over **Ben Eagach** (2,259 feet) to the east end of Loch Tummel.

A little beyond Weem village the road passes **Castle Menzies,** a fine old baronial mansion bearing date 1571. Hence the road follows the green Strath of Appin past Dull and the ruins of Comrie Castle (on the far side of the river Lyon just above its junction with the Tay), and so to *Coshieville Inn,* where the road to Fortingall and Glen Lyon goes off westward (*see* p. 300) and that to Tummel Bridge strikes up to the right beside the Keltney Burn (*see* p. 301).

Pitlochry.

Distances by road.—Inverness, 88½ m.; Kingussie, 44½ m.; Perth, 27¼ m.; Blair Atholl, 7 m.; Dunkeld, 13 m.; Aberfeldy, 15 m.
Early Closing.—Thursday.
Festival Theatre.—April to September.
Hotels.—*Atholl Palace* (114 rooms), *Hydro* (63 rooms), *Moulin* (20 rooms), *Scotland's* (54 rooms), *Fisher's* (70 rooms), *Dundarach* (23 rooms), *McKay's* (16 rooms), *Green Park* (28 rooms), *Pine Trees* (30 rooms), and many others.
Population.—2,501.
Sport.—Good fishing for trout and salmon in Loch Faskally and the Tummel. Tennis (a feature of the *Atholl Palace Hotel* season is the Highland Lawn Tennis Championship Meeting). Bowls. Golf (18-hole course on high ground, with good turf; 60p. per day; £2 per week. There is a private 9-hole course in Atholl Palace Hotel grounds). Highland Amateur Golf Championship 3rd week in August. Recreation Ground with putting green; boating on Faskally Loch.

Pitlochry is situated on the sunny slopes of the Grampians, on the north bank of the river Tummel, and is one of the most attractive and convenient resorts in the Highlands. It has a bracing air. The vicinity is exceedingly lovely, the valleys of the Tummel and the Garry affording some of the finest examples of glen scenery in Great Britain, and within a short distance are a number of excellent mountain excursions. For indoor entertainments there is a Cinema, and an enterprising Festival Theatre (with Restaurant) enlivens the holiday season.

The main street forms part of the road made by General Wade to the Northern Highlands across the Grampians. The railway station is on the main Perth–Inverness line.

One of the most interesting features is the Pitlochry dam, with the Fish Pass. The buildings of the Power Station are open to the public. **Loch Faskally** was formed as the result of the damming of the River Tummel. There is an observation chamber for the unique fish pass, which enables salmon to get to the upper reaches of the river.

Nestling at the foot of the hills about a mile north of Pitlochry is the charming little village of **Moulin**, with a delightfully situated hotel. Moulin Church, reconstructed in 1874, stands on what has been a sacred site from time immemorial. In the churchyard are several curious tombstones, and an ash-tree to which culprits were chained while waiting sentence by the Council of Lairds, the old-time administrators of justice. Kinnaird Cottage, 1 mile east of Moulin, was the residence of Robert Louis Stevenson in 1881, when he wrote *The Merry Men* and *Thrawn Janet*.

Above Moulin is **Craigower** (1,300 feet), one of the loveliest viewpoints in Scotland. To reach it turn left behind the hotel at Moulin and follow the sign-posts. It is an easy climb.

The knoll commands a glorious prospect. Eastward it is limited, but westward it extends over the entire length of Strath Tummel, including the loch, beyond which the graceful peak of Schiehallion forms the southern flank of the valley, and Beinn a' Chuallaich the northern. Nearer to hand, and a little to the left of Schiehallion, is Farragon Hill. If the weather be clear, the vista is continued over Loch Rannoch to the far-off hills of Glencoe, the "Shepherds of Etive." Southwards the valley is seen almost as far as Dunkeld, the Tummel and the Tay uniting their waters about half-way down it. Close at hand, to the north, are the steep wooded slopes flanking the deep-cut Pass of Killiecrankie.

From Pitlochry a visit may be paid to the *Black Spout*, a picturesque waterfall in a densely wooded ravine about a mile south-east of the town.

Ben Vrackie (2,757 feet).

From Pitlochry, three and a half to four and a half hours, up and down.

This excursion may be turned into a tour by descending to Killiecrankie and returning to Pitlochry through the Pass of Killiecrankie, an easy walk of five or six hours.

Take the left-hand turn behind the hotel at Moulin, and continue along the road, which soon degenerates into a rough cart-track, till trees and cultivation are left behind (three-quarters of an hour; 1,000 feet). The cart-track continues, but corners are cut off by climbing alongside a broken-down wall to a depression a mile farther, in which there is a gate. Here take a track to the left, which enables you, without descending, to gain the top by a steep green hollow just south of it.

The strong points of the view, which is exceedingly delightful, are the Garry valley up and down, and the vista up the Pass of Tummel —the latter, however, not so perfect as from Craigower (*see above*)—to Loch Tummel, Loch Rannoch, and, in clear weather, the Buachaille Etives. Schiehallion rising on the left, above Strath Tummel, is a fine object; and some way to the left of it is Ben Lawers with the twin peaks of Ben More peeping over its left shoulder, and the Loch Earn Ben Vorlich still more to the left. The two masses of Ben-y-Gloe block a deal of the northward prospect, but between them one of the Cairngorm group may be detected. To the right of them Lochnagar and Glas Maol are the chief heights, and southward, in clear weather, Arthur's Seat may be seen just left of the Ochils.

The descent to Killiecrankie is due west, and rather steep at first. The distance is nearly 3 miles, and another 4 from Killiecrankie to Pitlochry (or 3 to Blair Atholl).

By Aldour Bridge, about a mile south of Pitlochry (pedestrians can cross over by the Dam, a suspension bridge below it, or the long aluminium bridge at the head of Loch Faskally) one joins the pleasant road which from Logierait (*see* p. 306) runs up the west side of Tummel and Loch Faskally to Clunie Power Station and the Falls of Tummel and then along Loch Tummel to meet the Tummel Bridge–Coshieville road (p. 301). The **Falls of Tummel** were formerly among the finest cascades in Scotland, but the flow is now affected by the Tummel–Garry hydro-electric scheme. A footbridge above the Falls allows walkers to cross the river and return to Pitlochry by the Bridge of Garry (*see* p. 311).

PITLOCHRY TO KINLOCH RANNOCH.

In no other part of Scotland is there a high-road, of equal length (21 miles) to that between Pitlochry and Kinloch Rannoch, passing through scenery more beautiful or more varied.

The first 3 miles lead north to the entrance to the Pass of Killiecrankie (*see* p. 314). Here the Rannoch road turns to the left across the new Garry Bridge over the railway and the river, with grand views along the Pass and down the valley. (Entrance to walks through Pass a short way above the footbridge which now replaces the old Garry Bridge.) Beyond the new bridge, the road climbs above the north bank of the *Tummel*, passing the mansion of Bonskeid (used as a Y.M.C.A. holiday home). Branching off the road to the north-west is the mouth of the little **Glen of Fincastle.** At the far end of this charming Glen of Tummel is a parking place for the cars of those visiting the **Queen's View,** a lofty projecting rock that affords a magnificent prospect over Loch Tummel (*view indicator*). Strathtummel Youth Hostel is half a mile east of Queen's View.

Loch Tummel is about 7 miles long by half a mile broad. It contains pike and large trout.

From the Queen's View the road runs parallel with the loch, with fine views across its colourful shores and waters to Schiehallion, rising ever gracefully ahead. Ten miles from Pitlochry is *Loch Tummel Hotel,* a favourite resort of anglers. Three and a half miles beyond the hotel is **Tummel Bridge,** where a road strikes south past a power-station to Fortingall, Aberfeldy and Kenmore. On a clear day the view northward from the highest point of this road is extraordinarily fine.

The high-road to Kinloch Rannoch does not cross the Bridge, but continues along the northern bank of the river. A short mile from the Bridge the road from Trinafour and Struan comes in (p. 318), and 3½ miles farther is the western fork of the same route. *Dunalastair House* stands on a lovely stretch of the Tummel, opposite to the base of **Schiehallion,** and near by it is the Hydro-electric Board's *Dunalastair Reservoir.*

Kinloch Rannoch is a flourishing little village situated —despite its name—at the lower end of **Loch Rannoch.** (*Hotels : Bunrannoch, Dunalastair, Loch Rannoch.*) Buses daily to and from Pitlochry ; and also to and from Rannoch Station (18 miles) on the Crianlarich–Fort William line.

Loch Rannoch is a fine sheet of water, 1 mile wide and 9½ miles long. It is bordered by gently sloping hills in regular and unbroken outline, on the north ; on its southern side the hills are higher and steeper. The main road runs along the north side of the loch, but a secondary road skirts the southern shore, passing the **Black Wood**

of Rannoch, famed for its grand Scots pines. On the shores are some beautiful shooting lodges.

The water is famous for brown trout of large size ; it also contains small trout in abundance. Upon it are boats belonging to the landlords of the three hotels at Kinloch Rannoch. The guests have the privilege of fishing the loch and also part of the Tummel which flows from it. Near its western extremity (the better end for trout) is the mouth of the *Ericht,* which comes from the loch of the same name. Into the head of Loch Rannoch flows the *Gaur,* which has its origin in Loch Laidon (*see* p. 313), in the Moor of Rannoch ; it is one of the best trouting lochs in the country.

Loch Rannoch has become a participant in ambitious hydro-electric schemes. The power-house near the western end of the loch is operated by water drawn (through a great tunnel) from a dam on the River Ericht a little below its outlet from Loch Ericht. The schemes involved, amongst other things, the creation of dams and reservoirs on the Tummel, between Loch Rannoch and Loch Tummel, the lengthening of Loch Tummel, and the erection of power-houses at Tummel Bridge and at Gaur.

ROUTES FROM KINLOCH RANNOCH.

1. To **Struan** (*see* p. 318), 13 miles by road.

2. The ascent of the sharply pyramidal peak of **Schiehallion** (3,547 feet) : from two to three hours. Variety may be had by ascending from Tummel Bridge (on the bus route) and descending to Kinloch Rannoch, or *vice versâ.* The ascent from the Bridge takes about an hour longer. From Kinloch Rannoch follow the road on the south side of the river for 2 miles to the farmhouse of *Tempar.* Hence ascend by the *Tempar Burn* until you are below the cone, and then climb to the summit. The last part is fairly but not awkwardly steep. From Tummel Bridge.—(*a*) Follow the Aberfeldy road for 4 miles until the road from Kinloch Rannoch converges beyond *Loch Kinardochy.* The White Bridge is a quarter of a mile farther ; hence proceed due westward, skirting the north side of Dun Coillich, close at hand, and climb by the ridge all the way to the top.

3. The **circuit of Loch Rannoch** (22 miles).—The road is almost level and is shaded by trees for a great part of the way.

4. To **Rannoch Station** on Crianlarich–Fort William line

(18 miles: bus service). The road along the north side of the loch affords fine views of Schiehallion. A mile short of the western end of the loch, beyond the power-house, it crosses the Ericht at **Camasericht**, so called from its situation at a "bend of the Ericht." At the head of the loch *Rannoch Lodge* is passed, and a mile westward, on the Gaur River, *Dunan Lodge*. Loch Eigheach has been doubled in length for hydro-electric purposes. Beyond is bare moorland to Rannoch Station, where the road ends and at which there is a small inn (*Moor of Rannoch*).

A very rough and indistinct track runs from Rannoch Station by the north shore of Loch Laidon to **Glencoe** (*King's House Inn*), 15 miles, right across the Moor of Rannoch from east to west. The path is, however, very indistinct in places and is frequently very wet. The route is emphatically one for hardy walkers only, and then only in clear weather. The route crosses the Nature Reserve, the **Moor of Rannoch**, a vast area of peat, bog and old forest, covered with lochans of "black moss water," intersected by a chain of larger lochs, and surrounded on all sides by grim, boldly shaped mountains. The uninitiated and superficial person may call it "dreary," but it has a power and a charm all its own, and every season of the year brings to it its own peculiar beauty. (*See also* p. 229.)

In winter the Moor is simply 20 miles square of a study in sepia; but in summer the brilliance of the colouring is marvellous. The purple heather, the green mosses, the yellow grasses, and the rich brown of the peat-hags, with here and there the delicate azure of the harebell—by itself, all but unseen—combine to form a luminous mass of lovely tints. The whole Moor appears to be covered with one colossal Turkey carpet, so rich and oriental is the colouring.

Great difficulty was found in constructing the railway across the Moor. No firm bottom could be got until the ingenious device was adopted of laying on the soft peat a thick layer of brushwood, upon which the permanent way was built, making one of the most satisfactory stretches on the line.

On reaching **Loch Laidon**, a quarter of a mile west of the Rannoch station, gradually leave the shores of the loch, but do not get too high up on the right unless you find the lower ground very swampy. After an hour's walk you may hit a regular track about half a mile above the loch. This track soon passes a shepherd's hut, 7 miles from King's House.

Hence there is a fair narrow track all the way, keeping a western arm of the loch and the stream by which several other moss-water lochs are connected with it, from half a mile to a mile on the left, and in 4 miles passing a shooting lodge, from which the *King's House Inn* is reached by an indifferent road in about an hour. The scenery for the last 10 miles is the acme of desolation, only enlivened by the towering masses of *Buachaille Etive* and other wardens of Glencoe in front.

On the far side of the mountains to the north of the track is the great Blackwater Reservoir (p. 229), supplying the aluminium works at Kinlochleven.

5. To **Glen Lyon** (Innerwick, 12 miles), by **Dall**, on the south side of the loch, and thence afoot by a glorious hill path through the Lairig Chalbhath (1,650 feet). There is no inn at Innerwick, but a bus runs from there to Fortingall and Aberfeldy (*see* p. 300).

PITLOCHRY TO BLAIRGOWRIE (24 miles) AND THE SPITTAL OF GLENSHEE (32 miles).

This route forms a very convenient link between Pitlochry and the Eastern Highlands and Deeside.

Walkers may reduce the distance to Spittal of Glenshee by striking north-eastward across the hills to the Spital from the road at Ennochdhu, 3 miles short of Kirkmichael. The path climbs to over 2,000 feet, thence dropping sharply down to Glenshee just opposite the hotel. The path is not so good as it looks on the map, and strangers should not attempt the walk in misty weather or if there is the slightest prospect of being overtaken by night.

The beauty of this excursion is mostly retrospective. Leaving Pitlochry by the Moulin road (p. 309), we enter an avenue at that village and soon bend to the right. In another mile a farm-road to the left and then right cuts off a corner. Hence the road continues to climb for a mile or so till it gains an elevation of 1,250 feet. It then descends Glen Brerachan to Straloch, about 1½ miles beyond which the foot-route to the Spittal strikes off to the left at Enochdhu, a few yards short of a burn. **Kirkmichael** (*Hotels : Kirkmichael, Aldchlappie*) is 3 miles farther. Hence the descent of Strath Ardle to Bridge of Cally calls for no description. For Bridge of Cally and the rest of the road, *see* p. 358.

PITLOCHRY TO BLAIR ATHOLL.

(*Main Route Resumed.*)

Three miles north of Pitlochry the road begins to run high above the famed **Pass of Killiecrankie**, and from openings among the trees on the left one can look down to where the river rushes along its rocky bed. The railway viaduct is prominent at the end of the vista, and beyond rises the pointed peak of Ben-y-Gloe.

The walks along the hill-side are best begun from the gate by the National Trust for Scotland's Information Centre and car park by the main road (*Hotel : Killiecrankie* (10 *rooms*)). So excellent is the road that many motorists doubtless hurry by without realizing the presence of the Pass, but, to quote Macaulay : " In the days of William III Killiecrankie was mentioned with awe by the peaceful and industrial inhabitants of the Perthshire lowlands. It was deemed the most perilous of those dark ravines through which the marauders of the hills were wont to sally forth. The sound, so musical to modern ears, of the river brawling round the mossy rocks and among the smooth pebbles, the dark masses of crag and verdure, the fantastic peaks, suggested to our ancestors thoughts of murderous ambuscades and of bodies stripped, gashed and abandoned to the birds of prey. The only path was narrow and rugged ; a horse could with difficulty be led up ; two men could hardly walk abreast."

Through this dark defile, General Mackay led the royalist force which encountered the rebellious Highlanders under Claverhouse (Viscount Dundee) on the plain about half a mile north of Killiecrankie Station, July 27, 1689. It will be remembered that while King William's soldiers were routed, Dundee fell mortally wounded, and his death was the ruin for the time of the Jacobite cause.

Opposite Killiecrankie Cottage, at the top of the Pass, is the **Soldier's Leap.** A fugitive royalist, pursued by one of Dundee's Highlanders, is said to have cleared the river here at a bound—a feat emulated by an English visitor in 1912.

From opposite the railway station a path goes off on the right for the ascent of **Ben Vrackie** (2,757 feet ; p. 309).

Blair Atholl.

Angling.—Trout fishing in the River Garry, a tributary of the Tummel. Permit necessary from local angling club.
Golf, etc.—9-hole course at Invertilt. Bowling green.
Hotels.—*Atholl Arms* (30 rooms), *Tilt* (24 rooms). *Dalgnreine, The Firs, Invergarry, Laggan* (guest houses), all at Bridge of Tilt.

This pleasant village affords excellent headquarters to tourist and sportsman. It stands 450 feet above the sea, and has a climate even more bracing than that of Pitlochry.

Blair Castle (*open daily May–September, Sundays and Mondays in April. Admission charge. Tea room*), the home of the Dukes of Atholl, dates from 1269. In 1644 it was garrisoned by Montrose; stormed by a Cromwellian soldier, Colonel Daniel, in 1653; occupied by Claverhouse in 1689; besieged by the Jacobites in 1746. It was afterwards dismantled and deprived of its battlements and upper storeys. In 1869 it was restored. Queen Victoria was more than once a guest within its walls, and her *Journal* contains an account of her first visit in 1844.

About a mile south-west of Blair Atholl is the **Hill of Tulloch, or Tulach,** "The Knoll" (1,541 feet).

Blair Atholl to Braemar by Glen Tilt.

(During the stalking season there may be restrictions on the Linn of Dee road. Inquiries to Estate Office, near Corriemulzie. Permission to use the Glen Tilt road must be obtained from the Estate Office, Blair Atholl.)

This is the easiest route across the Eastern Grampians, being 2 miles shorter, 1,200 feet lower, and not nearly so rough as the alternative route from Aviemore to Braemar. There is a rough road as far as *Forest Lodge* (8 miles), and a rough bridle-path thence to the upper waters of the Dee at *Bynack Lodge* (18 miles from Blair), from a mile beyond which a very poor road (hardly suitable for motors) leads to the Linn of Dee and the beginning of the good road to Braemar (30 miles).

Turn out of the main road opposite the *Tilt Hotel*, and follow the course of the stream for half a mile to the *Old Bridge of Tilt*. Those walking from Blair Atholl station should turn right at main road (past Blair Castle) and cross river bridge, immediately turning left along path following river bank. This leads into the road in about ½ mile. Shortly take left fork, cross bridge over stream and under small bridge. Continue for about ½ mile until just short of a single grey-stone house on right and take road on right running back at an angle (marked "Private—Speed limit 10 m.p.h."). Follow this road, with river below on right for several miles all the way through to Marble Lodge. Hence is a straight course with green mountains of a pastoral "Lowland" character on both sides, and the river below for many miles. The bridle-path begins at *Forest Lodge*, the principal shooting-box of the district, and pursues an almost straight course as far as the bridge over the Tarf. The stream in descending from the desolate mountain wilderness on the left leaps over a ledge of rock. In conjunction with another burn which comes down from Glas Tulaichean on the right, a little farther on, it forms the main waters of the Tilt, which, considerably reduced in volume, is itself crossed about 2 miles farther on in its descent from Loch Tilt. The highest part of the route is now reached, and the track passes into Aberdeenshire. In 2 miles *Bynack Lodge* is reached, and farther on, after crossing the Geldie Burn, the rough road to Braemar commences. In front Ben Macdhui and its dependent summits, almost equal in height, appear. Prominent amongst them, and dropping precipitously into Glen Dee, is the Devil's Point. A mile beyond the Geldie Burn the River Dee is crossed by the White Bridge and 3 miles farther the Dee is again crossed at the **Linn of Dee**, a narrow rock-ravine through which the river tumultuously plunges. Here the track from Aviemore converges, and the road, now excellent, continues along the south side of the river to Braemar, passing *Inverey* and the picturesque, richly wooded *Linn of Corriemulzie* (p. 370). Youth Hostel at Braemar and Inverey.

Ben-y-Gloe (*Beinn a' Ghlo*) (3,671 feet).—From Blair Atholl, 7–8 hours up and down. The Ben-y-Gloe (the "mountain of the mist") group attains a greater height than any other in the Eastern Grampians, except that of which Ben Macdhui is the culminating point, and the double peak of Lochnagar. Consequently it commands an uninterrupted view to the south and east, and in other directions a prospect only obstructed by the hills above-named, and by Ben Alder and Ben Lawers in the west and south-west respectively. The ascent from Blair Atholl, which is itself 400 feet above sea-level, is long and somewhat complicated, but not difficult. In outline, as seen from a distance, Ben-y-Gloe is the boldest of all the Eastern Grampians.

Follow *Glen Tilt* as far as the *Fender Bridge* (*see above*). Instead of crossing this, proceed by the road which ascends the right-hand side of the burn, and after passing through a wood about a mile long, turn up a track on the left opposite Loch Moraig to *Monzie* (pronounced *Monee*) *Farm*, 3 miles from the *Tilt Hotel*. The route now lies up past the old shooting-lodge to the *beallach* between Carn Liath (3,193 feet) and the unnamed peak marked 3,505 feet. You now contour along the east side of this latter peak to the second *beallach* between it and the true summit of Ben-y-Gloe, from which the said summit is easily reached.

Another and probably better route is to continue for nearly 2 miles up the road beyond the divergence for Monzie Farm, and thence climb to the summit of Carn Liath and then along the ridge to the *beallach*. The distance from Monzie Farm to the top of Ben-y-Gloe is about 6 miles.

The ridge of Ben-y-Gloe continues northwards till it drops into Glen Tilt, a mile short of the point at which the Tarf is crossed. Those who wish to vary the descent in any way should satisfy themselves as to the manner in which this can be done before starting. It is a "far cry" to the nearest place of entertainment on the other side of the mountain.

In descending you may make almost due south for Loch Valican as far as the bed of the stream, down which, after the first tributary, a track can be found, gradually enlarging into a peat-road (capital bathing-pools down this valley).

BLAIR ATHOLL TO NEWTONMORE.

(Main Route Resumed.)

Three miles beyond Blair Atholl a wide parking place in a bend of the Great North Road marks the proximity of the **Falls of the Bruar,** the path to which leaves the road just beyond the bridge and passes under the railway. A little way up the stream are the lower bridge and one of the falls, and from this spot there is a good path on each side of the burn to the upper bridge, which is about a mile from the main road, and just beyond the highest and best of the three falls, which consists of three cascades, having a combined height of 200 feet.

The banks of the Bruar are clothed with fir plantations, thanks to the " Humble Petition of Bruar Water to the noble Duke of Athole," penned by Burns.

A mile westward of the Bruar Water the road crosses the railway to **Calvine,** a small hamlet at the foot of Glen Garry (*below*). To the left is **Struan** (*hotel*), whence a steep road goes off by *Glen Errochty* to Kinloch Rannoch (p. 311), climbing to over 1,000 feet beyond Trinafour and providing grand views over the Tummel Valley.

For the next 20 miles the main route is concerned in crossing the Grampians. It is a grand road, through scenery that so increases in its impressiveness as the summit is approached that even the electric cables on their striding pylons are dwarfed into insignificance. Between Struan and Dalwhinnie—some 20 miles—is neither hotel nor garage, hardly, indeed, any permanent habitation. The first 12 miles are through **Glen Garry,** railway, road and river travelling side by side.

From *Dalnacardoch Lodge* (6 miles beyond Struan) a rough road runs 6 miles over the hills to the south to Trinafour and so to Kinloch Rannoch (*see above*) ; while, on the north, a private road follows the Edendon Water, and is continued, as a footpath, along a chain of lochs, to the secluded **Gaick Forest,** noted for its deer, at the head of the *Tromie,* whence there is access to the valley of the Spey at Kingussie (20 miles from Dalnacardoch).

The old right of way route by the **Minigaig Pass** from Blair Atholl to Kingussie makes an almost straight line across the hills. From Old Blair the route lies up Glen Banvie and over into **Glen Bruar,** which is followed to its head. From here the route lies slightly west of north over the hills (summit level **2,750 feet**) and then descends along the Allt Bhran to join the

Glen Tromie road 2 miles north of Loch an t-Seilich. This route is, however, not so interesting as the Gaick Pass described above.

Loch Garry is now impounded for the Hydro-Electric Power Station on Loch Rannoch. A delightful footpath runs from Dalnaspidal, *viâ* Loch Garry, over to Loch Rannoch, about a dozen miles to the south. Just beyond **Dalnaspidal** (bus from Dalwhinnie or Blair Atholl), the summit level of the railway is reached. This is 1,484 feet above the sea, the highest level attained by any ordinary type of railway in the British Isles. The point coincides with the boundary between the counties of Perth and Inverness, and is marked by a notice-board giving the height of the pass. Dalnaspidal means "the field of the spital or hospice," and the name is thought to indicate that the spot was once the side of a hospice—a feature which many weary travellers have wished to revive, for now the place is uninhabited, bleak—the reverse of hospitable. Snow lingers late on the neighbouring mountains, and the stoutly built fences which protect the railway and road from snow-drifts in winter add further to the wildness of the scene.

Beyond Dalnaspidal, road and rail run in close company through the **Pass of Drumochter** (" the upper ridge "), a narrow gap in a long range of hills. On the west are two mountains, the Atholl Sow and the Badenoch Boar (2,422 feet). Running down to Dalwhinnie the views open out and there is a grand panorama of the Monadhliath mountains. Just before reaching **Dalwhinnie** (58 miles from Perth, and 1,169 feet above sea-level) the War Memorial is conspicuous on the right, and a little short of it is a concrete dam (with salmon ladder) in connection with the hydro-electric schemes. Dalwhinnie itself is a small village with two hotels (*Grampian, Loch Ericht*), filling stations, and a distillery.

There is a track across the hills from Dalwhinnie into **Strath Mashie** (7 miles), entering the Fort William road 4 miles beyond Drumgask and 3 east of *Loch Laggan* (*see* p. 321).

Dalwhinnie lies near the head of **Loch Ericht,** 15 miles long, and situated partly in Perth and partly in Inverness. It is one of the wildest and most solitary lakes of Scotland. In many places it is extremely deep. Its water, though very cold even in the hottest days of summer, seldom freezes. Loch Ericht is now being used in connection with the local hydro-electric scheme (*see* p. 312). **Cluny's Cage,** where Prince Charlie sheltered in 1746, is on the west side, towards the foot of the loch, where it is overshadowed by **Ben Alder** (3,757 feet). Loch Ericht is the home *par excellence* of the bull trout (*salmo-ferox*), and therefore a great attraction to anglers. Small trout also abound. It may be fished by visitors at the *Loch Ericht Hotel,* Dalwhinnie, where boats are also available for hiring.

From Dalwhinnie to Newtonmore by **Glen Truim** the road is downhill practically all the way, and the mountain views are extremely fine. Shortly after leaving Dalwhinnie and crossing the railway a hilly branch road leads due north and joins the Fort William road at Drumgask near Laggan Bridge—a useful short cut. The Monadhliath range is in front; to the right the Cairngorms come more and more clearly into view; and as the road enters Strathspey, 8–9 miles below Dalwhinnie, a glimpse may be caught of Ben Nevis, far away in the west. The country nearer at hand, too, takes on a different character; after miles of stern, boulder-strewn mountain-sides, we look with renewed pleasure on plantations of trees and green fields, among which cattle browse.

Newtonmore (*Balavil Arms* (38 *rooms*), *Badenoch, Glen, Main's, Craig Mhor*) borders the highway for some distance and makes a very attractive touring centre. It has many apartments and hotels, and a Clan Macpherson museum. There is a good golf course of 18 holes, bowls and tennis, pony-trekking, which originated here, and winter sports. Angling is another attraction, there being good trout fishing in the Spey and smaller streams. Situated not far below the junction of the *Truim* with the Spey—the scene of a famous clan battle between Camerons and Mackintoshes in 1386—it has nearer access than Kingussie to the scenery of the Upper Spey.

Among the best short excursions are the walk over **Craig Dhu** (*Creag Dhubh*) (*see* p. 321) and that to **Falls of Truim** (5 miles south-west). Follow the Dalwhinnie road till, 3 miles from Newtonmore, you turn on to the road to *Mains of Glen Truim,* beyond which a rough road followed by a path leads to the falls, close to which you recross the river, returning by road to Newtonmore.

From the Mains of Glentruim a road leads in 5 miles to Drumgask and Laggan Bridge.

Calder River to Loch Dubh, Cairn Mairg (3,087 feet) **and back to the river by the Bhealaich path** (*Glen Balloch*), **16 miles in all.**

This is a fine wild walk. From Newtonmore there is first a road, and then a distinct track (5 miles). The loch is not seen till you are quite on it, as, just before reaching it, you have to ascend out of a hollow in which you think the loch should be. Once at it, you find yourself in a scene of striking impressiveness and solitude. Hence it is easy to ascend on to the ridge north-west of the loch, and so on to **Cairn Mairg** (*Carn Ban*) (3,093 feet), whence is a very fine view, especially in the Loch Laggan (south-south-west) direction. The return may be made east by the side of the ridge, hugging the slope of the hills to the cottages, and so into the road again.

NEWTONMORE TO SPEAN BRIDGE (37 miles) AND FORT WILLIAM (46 miles).

This road forms a most important connecting link between the Central and Western Highlands. The scenery around Loch Laggan is very fine, and the views of the distant mountains are most impressive. A characteristic Highland run.

From Tulloch the railway accompanies the road.

The route is along the north side of the river. On the right are **Craig Dhu** (*Creag Dhubh*) (2,350 feet), the "black crag," whose name was the gathering cry of the Macphersons, and **Cluny Castle** (9 miles), formerly the seat of Cluny Macpherson. Chiefs of the Macphersons have contested with The Mackintosh the headship of the Clan Chattan, whose chanter (now in Clan Macpherson House) is said to be that used in the battle on the North Inch at Perth.

Two miles beyond the Castle is the hamlet of **Laggan Bridge,** whence a hilly but motorable road runs to Dalwhinnie (8 miles; p. 319).

A mile west of the Bridge a hilly track crosses the Mashie and ascends beside the Spey past Loch Crunachdan. This is the beginning of the wildly magnificent route to Fort Augustus (24 miles) which goes over the **Corrieyairack Pass** (2,507 feet). The route is dignified by the name of "General Wade's Road," but most of it is a rough track. Prince Charlie marched from Invergarry to Dalwhinnie by this route, August 27–29, 1745. There is no inn on the way, and the route is for strong walkers only.

Westward of Laggan Bridge the main valley of the Spey is left for that of the *Mashie*, one of its tributaries. In the angle between the rivers are the remains of the British fort of **Dundalair,** having thick walls of slate and said to be one of the most perfect British strongholds in Scotland. Strath Mashie, in its turn, is soon left, and then the road attains its greatest height near a point where the river Pattack, flowing northwards from the wild inhospitable regions of Ben Alder and Loch Ericht, describes an acute angle and turns south-westwards to Loch Laggan, thus forming the head-waters of the Spean.

Loch Laggan is a beautiful sheet of water 820 feet above the sea, and some 7 miles long, by ½ a mile wide, but lengthened by 4½ miles artificially at the west end as part of the Lochaber Water Power Scheme (*see* p. 234). It contains an abundance of small trout and a great many *salmo-ferox*, fishing for which is free. Boats may be obtained from the *Loch Laggan Inn* at its eastern end. Around the lake are lofty, well-wooded mountains, and on its surface are two small islets, named respectively *King's Isle* and *Dog's Isle*, from the tradition that Fergus, "the first of the Scottish kings," lived on one and kept his dogs on the other.

From the hotel a track runs in a north-easterly direction to the Corrieyairack track to Fort Augustus (21 miles; *see above*), which it strikes at the end of 3 miles; and running in a south-easterly direction there is a wild track to Dalwhinnie.

A grand mountain ramble begins about half-way along Loch Laggan, at *Aberarder*. Follow the path up the right hand of the stream to **Coire Arder**, where at its head, at the Lochan a' Choire Arder, a scene of wild and massive grandeur presents itself. The rocks descend into the loch almost perpendicularly for 1,000 feet, several vertical black gullies dividing up the cliff face, locally known as the "posts" of Coire Arder. From the loch go due west up to the prominent V-shaped gap in the main ridge. This is *The Window*, an old pass and right of way. Prince Charlie twice passed through this "Window" in his wanderings after Culloden on his way from Lochaber to Badenoch. From the Window the way is easy by the ridge to the summit of Creag Meaghaidh (3,700 feet), from whence a descent can be made south, rejoining the road at Moy.

Four and a half miles beyond Moy Lodge is the great **Laggan Dam** across the Spean, by which the waters of the Spean and Loch Laggan are impounded and led by a 2¾ mile tunnel into Loch Treig as part of the Lochaber Power Scheme. The dam is constructed of concrete and is 700 feet long with a height of 130 feet. At the road-side is a relief model of the surrounding district.

At **Tulloch** the Spean is joined by the Treig, running down from **Loch Treig**, one of the most remote lochs in Scotland—a deep trough 5½ miles long and three-quarters of a mile wide, through steep bare mountains, with a house or two at its head. For the "harnessing" of the Treig, see p. 234. From Tulloch a track crosses the Treig just below the foot of the loch and makes a wide sweep eastward around Cnoc Dearg (3,433 feet) to Loch Ghuilbinn, and thence by Strath Ossian to **Loch Ossian,** 1,269 feet above sea-level, one of the highest lochs in Scotland (*Youth Hostel*).

Tulloch to Fort William, *see* pp. 235–6.

Kingussie.

Distances by road.—Inverness, 44 m.; Pitlochry, 44½ m.; Perth, 71¾ m.
Golf.—An 18-hole course, open to visitors. Sunday play. Licensed. The course at Newtonmore is also convenient.
Hotels.—*Duke of Gordon* (60 rooms), *Royal* (30 rooms), *Star* (27 rooms), *Silverfjord* (12 rooms), and Board Residence, Youth Hostel, Caravan Site.
Population.—About 1,100.

The name (pronounced *king-yew-sie*) is derived from the Gaelic equivalent of " the end of the pine-wood."

Kingussie is the centre of a wide district of great beauty. It is situated at a height of 764 feet above sea-level, and is a capital point from which to explore some of the most magnificent Highland scenery. A notable **Highland Folk Museum** is housed in a Georgian dwelling near the station and is now in the care of the Scottish Universities (*weekdays in summer*, 10–1, 2–5 ; *admission charge*).

Near the far end of the bridge crossing the river are the ruins of **Ruthven Barracks**, which supplanted the residence of the Comyns, lords of Badenoch. They were erected in 1718 to overawe the Highlanders. In February, 1746, they were captured by a band of Highlanders under Gordon of Glenbucket.

Creag Bheag (1,593 feet; 1½ miles).—There are two ascents—one from Loch Gynack, which may be reached by crossing the golf course, and is a stiff scramble, the other from West Terrace, along easy paths. The view extends to Braeriach, just visible over the nearer and almost equally lofty range beyond Glen Feshie; farther north are Cairn Gorm and a wide tract of the Spey valley. In descending the wood may be avoided by bearing south into the Newtonmore road.

There is a splendid mountain-view from a hill called **Croidh-la** (2,099 feet). The most direct route to it is across the hill to *Glentromie Lodge*, 3 miles south-east from Kingussie, whence, after crossing the stream by an iron bridge, you reach the summit, due south, in 1¼ miles, after a rise of 1,130 feet. Another way is by Tromie Bridge, as in the route to Glen Feshie (*below*).

Glen Feshie.—A pleasant circular drive or walk of 14

to 16 miles may be made into this romantic glen, and a good walker may cross the *col* (nearly 1,800 feet), between it and Glen Geldie, entering the Blair Atholl and Braemar route (p. 316), 3 miles short of Linn of Dee and 9 of Braemar.

Cross the line at the station and then the river, and bear left. Two miles farther the road crosses the *Tromie* at a remarkably pretty spot, the stream rushing through a romantic rocky channel below. From the bridge go a few yards to the right, and cut off a corner by a path through the wood. Re-entering a road, you come to some cottages, and going straight on emerge on to open moor, over which there is a good road as far as the farm of *Baileguish* (1,000 feet above sea-level), where cross the burn by a footbridge. Proceed over a slight ridge into **Glen Feshie** (7 miles) opposite Achlean.

For the route through Glen Feshie to Braemar, *see* p. 372.

To vary the return to Kingussie, take the road down Glen Feshie, and in 1½ miles, just after crossing a tributary stream—the one previously crossed at Baileguish—enter a path that goes straight ahead across a pleasant open country, with a wood on the left, and so to the little village of Insh.

Insh Church, which lies at the east end of Loch Insh, is said to be one of the oldest in Scotland, a place of worship since the sixth century. An old bell preserved inside passes as one of the finest relics of Culdee worship. Dedicated to St. Adam Columnare, biographer of St. Columba, Abbot of Iona, 679.

Glen Tromie, 3 m. ; **Gaick Lodge,** 12 m. ; **Edendon Lodge,** 17½ m. ; **Dalnacardoch Lodge,** 22¼ m. ; **Dalnaspidal Station,** 28 m. Ten to eleven hours.

From Tromie Bridge (*see above*) it is 11 miles up **Glen Tromie** to *Gaick Lodge,* half a mile beyond *Loch an t-Seilich,* a loch 1,400 feet above the sea, and enclosed by precipitous cliffs.

The upper part of Glen Tromie is very lonely, the way being completely shut in by surrounding hills. Two miles short of the Loch, the Allt Bhran is crossed by an iron bridge.

After leaving Gaick Lodge *keep to the path,* which bears round to the left, and so on to *Loch Bhrodainn.* The walking now becomes rough, and the scenery is very wild.

The path is well defined, and skirts the east side of Loch **Bhrodainn**, winding on till it reaches *Loch an Duin* (1,592 feet), which it skirts on the west side. The view across this loch is, perhaps, the best bit of wild scenery along the whole route.

After leaving the loch, keep on the east side of the stream to **Edendon Lodge** (17½ miles). From the lodge a cart-track leads southward beside the Edendon Water to the main road at Dalnacardoch Lodge (22¼ miles; no accommodation), whence it is 5 miles to Dalnaspidal, and 6 miles to Struan. Kingussie may then be regained by motor (but before setting out from Kingussie inquire about bus services to guard against disappointment).

A very pleasant excursion from Kingussie is to take motor or train to Aviemore and walk back by **Loch an Eilean** (16 miles all told). On reaching the shore of Loch an Eilean (*see* p. 327) keep the water on the left, and at the far end of it turn to the right. Very soon you come to a gate and, practically, the end of the road. Bear to the left and pass, on the same side, a ruined cottage. Half a mile or so beyond the gate you come into the road that leads from Aviemore to Kingussie. A very picturesque spot on this road is **Feshie Bridge**, 3 miles from the point at which you enter it.

To **Struan** or **Blair Atholl** across the mountains.

From the iron bridge in Glen Tromie (2 miles short of Loch an t-Seilich; p. 324), take the hill-path for Glen Feshie, but instead of going to Feshie, take the south track (the Minigaig Pass) and walk past Bruar Lodge to Struan. This is a hard walk of about 30 miles. The **Minigaig Pass** is about 2,750 feet up, and half-way. The route passes Bruar Lodge (1,500 feet), whence one may follow the Bruar to Struan, or cross the hills by the right of way path to Glen Banvie and Blair Atholl (*see* p. 318).

Tromie Bridge, 3 m.; **Glen Feshie,** 7 m.; **Carn Ban** (3,443 feet), 11 m.; **Sgoran Dubh** (3,658 feet), 12½ m. A bracing walk with a grand mountain view. Fine weather essential. *For route as far as Glen Feshie, see* page 323.

Cross the Feshie by a footbridge just opposite a cottage with the name *Stronetoper*. Hence a pony-track leads due east right up to the top of the **Carn Ban** ridge. Half-way up you strike another path—*take the higher one* (both are rough walking)—and after a stiff one and a quarter or one and a half hours' climb you get to the top, and it is plain sailing by map and compass to **Sgoran Dubh** (3,658 feet), whence is a very fine view of the Cairngorms. The look down into Loch Einich, 2,000 feet below, is also very fine. West and south-west, too, there is a fine mountain prospect, Ben Nevis being visible a little south of west; Ben Alder, Ben Lawers and Schiehallion more south; while south of Cairn Toul you look through a gap to Lochnagar and others of the Braemar Highlands. The top of the ridge about Carn Ban is a vast grassy plateau.

From Carn Ban it is a long but quite practicable walk of 6 to 7 miles round the cliffs that overlook Loch Einich to Braeriach (4,248 feet; *see* p. 336).

KINGUSSIE TO AVIEMORE.

(*Main Route continued from* p. 323.)

Looking across the strath from Kingussie, we see the Glen Feshie mountains, which hide the loftier Cairngorm group until they come into view 3 miles beyond Kincraig—a most magnificent panorama—Braeriach to the right, Cairn Gorm to the left, with the plateau of Ben Macdhui between them. These heights are all more than 4,000 feet above the sea-level, and together constitute the loftiest group of mountains in the kingdom. As, however, the part of the Spey valley which we are now traversing is itself 700 feet up, and there is a considerable breadth of strath for a foreground, they do not present so imposing an appearance as many others of less elevation—notably those which rise with unbroken steepness from the sea on the west coast.

Two miles from Kingussie, in a small larch plantation on the left, is a *Monument to James Macpherson* (1736–96), the translator or compiler of the ancient Gaelic poems attributed to Ossian.

In 1760 Macpherson published *Fragments of Ancient Poetry* and followed this book with "translations" of *Fingal* and *Temora*, poems which he attributed to an ancient bard, Ossian. Dr. Johnson challenged the authenticity of the poems in characteristic manner, and controversy became hot. The final blow was struck when a subscription was raised to print the originals, and no originals were forthcoming. Many will consider that the point was of relatively minor importance, and in any case Macpherson was buried in Poets' Corner, Westminster Abbey.

Close by is *Balavil House*, occupying the site of the old Castle of Raits, originally a stronghold of the Comyns, and for a time in the possession of "Ossian Macpherson," and afterwards of his son-in-law, Sir David Brewster.

About a couple of miles farther on, we pass on the right **Loch Insh**, a beautiful sheet of water—an enlargement of the Spey—roughly a mile long by three-quarters of a mile wide. Its pike are noted. (*Fishing by permit.*) Just beyond the lake is **Kincraig** (*Suie Hotel*), convenient centre for Feshie Bridge and Glen Feshie. (Nine-hole golf course.)

Three miles beyond Kincraig, the road skirts pretty **Loch Alvie**, and opposite is **Tor Alvie**, or the **Hill of Kinrara**. Upon it are two monuments—a lofty pillar in memory of the last of the old Dukes of Gordon, and a cairn in memory of Highland soldiers who fell at Waterloo. The summit of the hill commands a magnificent view of Strathspey. *Kinrara House*, at the fcot of the Tor, was the favourite residence of the mother of the fifth and (before the re-creation of the title in favour of the Duke of Richmond) the last Duke of Gordon. She was the beautiful Jean Maxwell, the friend and hostess of Robert Burns.

So past the clachan of **Lynwilg**, in which is a comfortable hotel that may serve as headquarters for walkers wishing to explore the Grampians. On the left is the **Rock of Craigellachie** (pronounced *craig-ell-achy*), the trysting-place of the Grant clan, whose slogan or war-cry was "Stand fast, Craigellachie."

Aviemore.

Distances.—Carrbridge, 7 m.; Grantown, 15 m.; Inverness, 30 m.; Kingussie, 12 m.; Perth, 83 m.; Pitlochry, 54 m.
Hotels.—*Cairngorm* (30 rooms), *High Range* (24 rooms), *Coylum Bridge, Alt Na Craig; Dell*, at Rothiemurchus.
Recreation.—Tennis, fishing, ski-ing, pony-trekking.
Railway.—On main Perth–Inverness line.
Ski facilities. Youth Hostel.

Aviemore is an excellent centre for tourists. It is a good starting-place for the summits of the Cairngorms, and also has attractions of its own, including a Stone Circle and other archæological remains. Previous to the opening of the direct route to Inverness, *viâ* Carrbridge (p. 338), it consisted mainly of a general shop, a post office, and an old inn, in which Burns had stayed. Now it is expanding rapidly and attracting skiers, climbers, etc.

Loch an Eilean ("Loch of the Island," 3 miles south

of Aviemore station) is the gem of this neighbourhood, and decidedly the loveliest of all the little lochs of Strathspey. To reach it, cross the river by the bridge a quarter of a mile south of the station, and three-quarters of a mile farther, where the road forks at *Inverdruie*, just beyond a modern new church, take the right-hand branch. Gradually bending to the right, you will reach the loch in a short 2 miles. It lies secluded in a forest of pine and birch-clad hills, with a picturesque castle. The castle has no association with the notorious " Wolf of Badenoch " (Alexander, Earl of Buchan) during the later fourteenth century, as is popularly believed. It was probably used as a place of refuge. The ruin is the home of a fine echo.

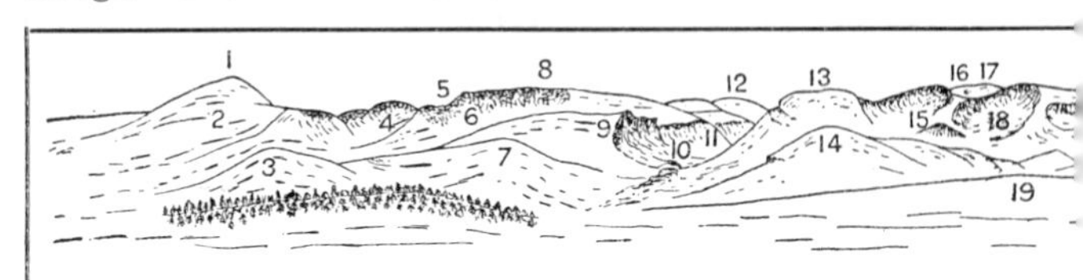

THE CAIRNGO

1. CAIRN GORM, 4,084 feet ; 8½ miles.
2. COIRE CAS.
3. AIRGIOD MEALL.
4. COIRE AN T-SNEACHDA.
5. FIACAILL COIRE AN T-SNEACHDA.
6. COIRE AN LOCHAIN.
7. CAISTEAL SGROBACH. [CASTLE HILL.]
8. CAIRN LOCHAN.
9. CREAG AN LETH-CHOIN. [LURCHER'S CRAG.]
10. LARIG GHRU.
11. MARCH BURN.
12. BEN MACDHUI, 4,300 feet ; 10 miles
13. SRON NA LAIRIG.
14. CARN ELRICK.
15. COIRE BEANAIDH. [CORRIE BENNIE.]

Loch Gamhna, a small loch at the upper end of Loch an Eilean, is adorned with water-lilies, which visitors must leave untouched. **Polchar** was for many years the summer and autumn residence of Dr. Martineau, in memory of whom a road-side column was erected in 1913. The **Doune** is the ancestral home of the Grants of Rothiemurchus. Between Rothiemurchus and Braemar is a vast National Nature Reserve.

An interesting 15-mile road excursion is round by **Boat of Garten** (p. 340) and Coylum Bridge. The return is made by the eastern side of the river, passing **Kincardine Church**, an old building with a " squint " or leper window, and a rude stone font. (From Kincardine one can return on foot to Aviemore by the **Sluggan Pass**, which runs southward up the Milton Burn and through the delightful Queen's Forest to Loch Morlich.) Two miles short of Aviemore, after leaving Loch Pityoulish behind, the road passes over **Coylum Bridge,** the centre of very picturesque scenery.

To Loch Einich.—The route is *viâ* Inverdruie, and, if on foot, the return journey may be made *viâ* Loch an Eilean. Loch Einich is a long, narrow sheet of water about 9 miles from Aviemore. It is 1,650 feet above sea-level. Above it tower the rocky ridge of **Sgoran Dubh** (3,658 feet) and the lower slopes of **Braeriach** (4,248 feet). The loch contains char and brown trout.

Glen Einich is a good starting-point for the ascent of Braeriach, Cairn Toul (4,241 feet), and Sgoran Dubh.

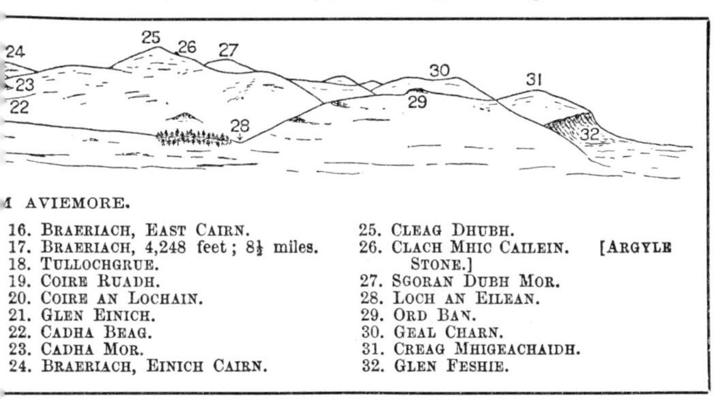

CAIRN GORM AND BEN MACDHUI.

The motor road to Glenmore Lodge now climbs boldly up to **Coire Cas** on Cairn Gorm. From the Car Park at its end a **Chair Lift** mounts (all year round: weather permitting) to **White Lady Shieling** (2,520 ft.: restaurant) and on up to 3,600 ft., within easy reach of the top of Cairn Gorm. The panorama is magnificent.

From Glenmore Lodge, now a Youth Hostel, it is 5 miles to the summit of Cairn Gorm (4,084 ft.). Here, too, in the midst of a grand National Forest Park, are the outdoor training centre of the Scottish Council of Physical Recreation and facilities for camping, climbing and ski-ing.

The easiest excursion is up and down Cairn Gorm by Glenmore Lodge. For the best circular route we recommend the ascent of Ben Macdhui; then the plateau walk to Cairn Gorm—one of the finest high-level walks in

Britain—whence descend to Glenmore Lodge, 6½ miles by road from Aviemore. The whole round is one of about 30 miles, and will take a full day. It is best taken in this direction, because you thus have the easiest part last. A careful study of the map and good local advice should be added to the following instructions.

From Aviemore cross the river and by Inverdruie proceed to *Coylum Bridge.* The Nethy Bridge road goes off on the left and the Larig Ghru track on the right; our route is straight ahead. **Loch Morlich** is skirted about 3 miles beyond the bridge and at the far end of the loch is Glenmore Lodge. From near the Lodge go off to the right and ascend beside the Allt Mor by road and a well-defined path all the way to the summit of Cairn Gorm.

Aviemore to Ben Macdhui (13 miles, 6½ hours); **Cairn Gorm** (17 miles, 8½ hours); **Glenmore Lodge** (22 miles, 10 hours); **Aviemore** (29 miles, at least 12 hours). Good walking.

The first 5 or 6 miles through the *Forest of Rothiemurchus* are described in connection with the Larig Ghru (p. 332). Climbers of Ben Macdhui should leave that track about 1½ miles after entering the "rough foot-track," and where the ground begins to rise in earnest on the left hand, just beyond the first summit, Castle Hill. The finer but more difficult route is by ascending along the edge of the crag of the Lurcher's Rock, and following its ridge to its southern end. This route gives admirable views into and along the Larig Ghru, and across it to the east face of Braeriach. An easier, but longer, route is obtained by turning eastward from the Larig Ghru path to the south of Castle Hill and of the notch that separates it from the Lurcher's Rock; this notch or "Eag" is a remarkable bit of wild rock scenery, by the way. We thus reach the east slope of the Lurcher's Rock, and get easy foot-tracks ascending the valley of the Allt Creag an Leth-choin. At the head of this valley these two routes converge, and the summit-cairn is in view, 2½ miles away to the south. The way is tiresome, and it is 6 long miles from the beginning of the steep part of the climb, at the edge of the forest, to the top of **Ben Macdhui** (4,300 feet). The summit of the mountain is a vast wilderness of red granite. The highest point is marked by a large cairn near which is a Cairngorm Club view-indicator.

The view cannot be gained all at once, the wide extent

of almost level ground on nearly every side of the actual summit hiding the depression which would otherwise form the foreground. A short walk to the west, however, enables us to look down into the depths of the Larig Pass, on the other side of which the towering forms of Braeriach, Cairn Toul and the Devil's Point together constitute the most imposing mountain spectacle in the Eastern Grampians. The wild Garbh Choire between Braeriach and Cairn Toul is specially fine and is reputed to contain a patch of perpetual snow in one of its inner recesses. Westward, over the expanse of Strathspey, the Monadhliath range—high moorland—between that valley and the Caledonian Canal is seen. Northwards over Cairn Gorm, the prospect *may* extend to Morven (a cone), in Caithness, and the Sutherland hills, while in the south-west lies Ben Nevis. Due south Ben-y-Gloe is the commanding height, and south-eastwards Lochnagar rises pre-eminent among the Braemar Highlands. A portion of the Dee and its tributary valleys are included in the panorama.

The easiest walk between Ben Macdhui and **Cairn Gorm** involves a dip of only a few hundred feet. The two peaks lie almost due north and south, but the ridge trends somewhat to the west, skirting the head of several depressions which converge at the south-west end of **Loch Avon,** or *A'an,* where, near the stream, is the *Clach-Dhian,* or "**Shelter Stone,**" the only possible protection against wind and rain for miles round. It is formed of three blocks of granite, the largest of which has tumbled on the top of two smaller ones. It is worth while to diverge a little to the east so as to look down upon Loch Avon and the Shelter Stone, especially fine from a "chimney" overlooking the most westerly point of the loch just north of the Feith Bhuie burn. This stream descends in a succession of cataracts to Loch Avon and alongside it lies the best route to the Shelter Stone from the plateau. As a resting-place for tourists travelling the route we are now describing, the stone suffers from the disadvantage of involving an extra up-and-down journey of 1,500 feet each way, or a circuit of several miles by the foot of Loch Avon, and into the track from Glen Derry to Nethy Bridge (p. 334). The "Stone" is best reached from Cairn Gorm by going in a south-west direction from the summit down into the corrie, which lands you at the shores of Loch Avon about half a mile from its western end.

The **view from Cairn Gorm** is obstructed southward by Ben Macdhui, but Cairn Toul and Braeriach are visible south-west, to the right of "Dhui," though the Larig Pass is hidden by the great plateau. As compensation Cairn Gorm offers a much fuller prospect northwards and over Strathspey. Ben

Rinnes is a conspicuous figure north-east, as is the far-off cone of Morven, in Caithness, due north. Loch Avon, south-east, is not seen from the summit-cairn.

Descents from Ben Macdhui.—(1) *For Braemar by Glen Derry.* From the summit strike off a little south of due east, past the ruin of the Sappers' Bothy, for half a mile to near a rocky top, at the edge of the precipice overlooking the Coire Sputan Dearg, where a well-marked path will be joined which leads in a north-easterly direction to the foot of Loch Etchachan and thence down Coire Etchachan to Glen Derry and on to Derry Lodge, 8 miles from the summit. Or alternatively from the top mentioned above strike south (no path) by the Sron Riach down into the Luibeg glen, where a path will be found leading to Derry Lodge, 6½ miles from the summit.

(2) For *Aviemore* keep along the ridge parallel to and above the *Larig Pass* till well beyond the summit of the Lurcher's Rock and then drop down easy slopes to join the Larig Ghru path. For the rest of the way, *see below.*

Aviemore to Braemar by the Larig Ghru.

This is about the longest day's march (30 miles) in the Highlands, and the only one which displays the full grandeur of the Eastern Grampians. Height of Pass, 2,733 feet. There is no hotel, inn or teahouse on the way, but at Luibeg Cottage, near Derry Lodge, 10 miles short of Braemar, refreshment may be available. Between Coylum Bridge, 2 miles from Aviemore, and Derry Lodge there is no regularly occupied habitation whatever (*see* p. 334). The path is good, bad, and indifferent by turns. From Derry Lodge there is a road to Braemar (10 miles).

It is better to make the journey in this than in the reverse direction, because in the latter case, should the traveller by any chance get belated, he will have some difficulty in extricating himself from the mazes of Rothiemurchus forest during the last part of the walk, whereas the last 10 miles of the road to Braemar are quite unmistakable. The middle portion of the route is excessively rough, but there can be no real difficulty about finding the way, except in the forest, through which the cart-tracks and paths twist about in a manner which makes it impossible to form any judgment as to the destination of any one of them.

From Aviemore to Coylum Bridge (2 miles) as already indicated. Turn to the right at a finger-post just short of the bridge, and proceed for one-third of a mile by road to a cairn, beyond which on the left in front of you a wooden house can be seen. Leave the road and take the path past this house, and then by a narrow and, in places, almost overgrown footpath, follow the stream for another 2 miles, at the end of which, at another guide-post, cross an iron footbridge.

Two deep depressions in the huge mountain-barrier now appear before us. The left-hand one is our route, he right-hand one being Glen Einich. Beyond the foot-bridge the path crosses a greensward in front of a tenantless building (*Alltdruie*); a little farther on it breaks off into two cart-tracks, which must be avoided. Close to the diverging point there is a guide-post, from which a rough foot-track bears away to the right through the heather, parallel to and some distance above the stream. This is our path, and here the rough walking begins, but the difficulty of finding the way ceases. We are about half-way to the top of the Pass, and the mountain-walls on both sides prevent our straying any distance from the path until we are far down the other side of it.

From the summit of the **Larig Ghru** one looks upon a scene of such rude grandeur and wildness as is hardly to be surpassed in Scotland. The *col* forms the division-line between the counties of Inverness and Aberdeen. The prospect extends far away in both directions—northwards to the lone moorland between the Spey and Loch Ness, and south ward to the lofty heights which separate the basin of the Dee from that of the Tay. The vista in the latter direction is decidedly the finer of the two, and, as we descend, it becomes still more striking. Ben Macdhui occupies the whole of the eastern side of the valley, but opposite to it Braeriach and Cairn Toul, with its two flanking peaks, the Devil's Point and Sgor an Lochan Uaine ("Angel's Peak"), have all separate claims on our admiration, the outline of the two last-named being very bold; in fact, it is only by thus plunging into the very heart of the Eastern Grampians that we can fairly appreciate their vast proportions. In the interstices of the boulders about here the beech fern and other polypodies find a congenial home.

A short distance beyond the summit are the **Pools of Dee**, a succession of icy-cold pools between which the water, as in limestone countries, finds its way beneath the surface of the ground. Near the lowest pool is a good halting-place, but the pedestrian should not forget that he has still some six hours' walking before him. Beyond the Pools, the path, which is henceforth fairly marked, crosses this headwater of the Dee.

On the right-hand side, a little farther on, the *Garrachorry Burn*, which is really the main source of the Dee, comes down a desolate valley between Cairn Toul and Braeriach.

For 4 miles or so after leaving the Pools of Dee the path keeps along the valley. Below **Devil's Point**, on the right, is the *Corrour Bothy*, a small, untenanted hut which has more than once been a welcome harbour for the night. Beyond it **Glen Geusachan**, short but deep, opens on the same side. From opposite this glen are two tracks : one continuing down Glen Dee, and the other bending to the left round the southern shoulder of Carn a' Mhaim, and dropping into *Glen Lui Beg*, as it is called to distinguish it from the more important division of the valley lower down. The *Glen Dee* route is at the best a sheep-track, the commencement of which, at all events, is quite undiscoverable. Care, too, is required in quitting the valley for the Glen Lui route, which, however, though far from obvious at first, very soon develops into an excellent track of white granite, and continues so till it reaches the bottom of the valley, a couple of miles farther. If the traveller fails to see the track he is probably too low down for it. It keeps a stream and a lakelet or two at a considerable distance on the right, and crosses the *Lui Beg Burn* by a wooden bridge. From this point the actual summit of Ben Macdhui is nearly but not quite visible at the head of the glen, on the left. Our path now keeps the stream on the right as far as **Derry Lodge**, a shooting-box, just short of which the path crosses the *Glen Derry Burn* and, passing to the right between the grounds of Derry Lodge and the stream, enters the road close to the south lodge-gate. From here a private road leads down Glen Lui to a gate (locked) at the public road along the north bank of the Dee, half a mile east of the Linn of Dee. Note :—The keys of the above gate may be had, on payment of a small charge, at the Lodge at the Victoria Bridge and this arrangement enables one to order a car from Braemar to meet walkers at Derry Lodge.

Aviemore to Nethy Bridge by the Revoan Pass (17 miles).

As far as Glenmore Lodge the route has already been described. Beyond the lodge the track ascends the pretty

Revoan Pass at the head of which is the charming little *Green Loch* (the colour is due to fine mica in suspension). There is a grand view of Speyside from the height to the west of the Pass, known as **Meall a' Buachaille** (The Shepherd's Hill; 1,400 feet above the Pass, 2,654 above sea-level). From the Pass an undulating course brings us to Rynettin, a keeper's lodge, and so to Forest Lodge. Here turn left, and in half a mile to right, and so through Abernethy Forest to **Nethy Bridge** (*Nethy Bridge* (74 rooms), *Grey House* (11 rooms)).

At the **Revoan Pass** a cart-road leads eastwards to a bridge (bothy nearby) across the Nethy. From this point **Loch Avon** may be reached in 5 rough miles by tramping straight up the glen and over the watershed known as the **Saddle** (2,707 feet). The first part is tiresome and very marshy. After that there is a broken track.

A well-marked path begins at the little bridge that spans the stream, and ascends steeply to the ridge of Bynack (2,536 feet), crossing it diagonally. The ascent of **Ben Bynack** (3,574 feet), which has two peaks—the greater and less, separated by a shallow depression—is obvious. About the summit are groups of castle-like rocks. The finest group, the *Barns of Bynack*, are about half a mile south-east from the summit, from which they are not visible. They are quite remarkable and worth visiting. From it you may proceed to Loch Avon, or by a steepish descent rejoin the Braemar route without going back to the point at which you left it. The only risk about here arises from the utter absence of accommodation for many miles.

By the **Larig an Laoigh** (the Pass of the Calves) to Braemar. The route from the bridge over the Nethy is the same as for Ben Bynack till near the foot of the peak, but it then strikes off towards the south-east, descends a little and skirts the east slopes of Ben Bynack, with the Barns well seen high up on the right, and runs through a narrow pass between Ben Bynack and Creag Mhor to the River Avon, which is reached at a place known as Avonford. Loch Avon lies 1 mile to the west. Even here the Avon, so near its source, is a considerable stream from 10 to 15 yards wide, and at times unfordable. This is the best place for a halt for refreshments. The height above sea at which we cross is about 2,250 feet, and beyond it, continuing due south, we ascend a rough valley, passing to the left of two lakelets and between the towering heights of Beinn Mheadhoin and Ben a' Chaorruinn. From the watershed (about 2,450 feet), 2 miles beyond the Avon, the path, not always very clear, descends, with Corrie Etchachan, up which runs the path to Ben Macdhui, on the right, and we are now on the route up that mountain described on p. 375.

Braeriach and Cairn Toul.

From Aviemore Braeriach (4,248 feet) is 12 miles, and Cairn Toul (4,241 feet) 16 miles. A hard and full day's work.

The access to these heights is by road, marked " private," and during the shooting and stalking season the tenants not unreasonably object to casual wandering.

Follow the Glen Einich road, which turns south just short of Coylum Bridge, to ruined bothy (7½ miles), where the Allt na Beinne Beg comes down on the left to join the Beinne Mor. The road crosses the Beinne Beg by a bridge, about 75 yards up from its junction with the main stream. Right opposite the site of the bothy turn to the east, keeping on the north side of the stream and gradually bearing away from it on the higher ground, which will be drier and less boggy than close to the stream. The north face of **Braeriach** has three great corries, separated from each other by two buttresses. Our way is up the western of these buttresses, and when we have reached a point due north of this western buttress, we cross the stream and follow the ridge of the buttress. This is decidedly rough, but quite safe. In a mile from the stream we look down on our right on to the loch in the western corrie, and shortly after arrive on the general plateau of the mountain. Rising ground to our left, at the head of the middle corrie, hides the summit, but by working to the south round this we see the summit to the east-south-east, and less than half a mile away.

The cairn marking the summit of Braeriach stands close to the edge of the Garrachorry, and this edge or the ridge may be followed round to **Cairn Toul,** the real source of the Dee being passed on the way.

Alternative (*a*).—Start from ruined bothy as directed above, but follow the Beinne Beg to its source, high up on the left, crossing to the south side of the stream opposite to the eastern buttress. The Coire Beinne is a delightful open stretch of greensward, frequented by red deer. From its eastern corner a steep and rough but easy track leads up to the ridge of Sron na Lairig, which can be followed southwards and then westwards on to the main mass of Braeriach. The views into and across the Lairig and the Garbh Choire during the latter part of the walk are very fine. The reversal of this route makes an easy and pleasant descent from Braeriach.

Alternative (*b*).—Follow the Glen Einich driving-road to the ruined bothy. Looking along the western side of the near corner of Braeriach, a long somewhat flat shoulder is seen dropping from the west side of the western corrie towards the mouth of the Beinne Beg. By following the course of the Beinne Beg for nearly half a mile the lower end of this shoulder may be reached, and the shoulder itself followed southwards for about a mile. This will bring us to an altitude of about 2,500 feet, and we may get on to the zigzag path, which we see in front of us. This leads to the plateau, above and a little west of the western corrie containing the loch. The summit may then be reached by crossing the plateau due east for about a mile.

Cairn Toul, direct, 15 miles.—A long and hard day's work. The view is similar to that from Ben Macdhui (p. 330), except that the two mountains are mutual "obstructives," south-west and north-east respectively. While the north-east and east is blocked by Ben Macdhui from Cairn Toul and Braeriach, the south comes out much more strongly.

(*a*) Follow the Glen Einich road to the *upper* bothy (9½ miles), which is within a quarter of a mile of Loch Einich. The road ends a little farther on, but at the bothy a path leaves it and ascends on the left, crossing several streams, and gradually bearing off into the eastern corrie, *Coire Dhondail.* This path is rough and steep, but perfectly plain, and at the top of the corrie rises by a very steep but easy scramble to the plateau. Then a walk of just under a mile due east will bring us to the edge of the southern scallop of the Garrachorry. The view of the corrie is very striking, coming as it does so suddenly and unexpectedly. In mist the approach must be made with care, as we *rise* to the edge of the corrie. This edge may now be followed to the right as far as the summit of Cairn Toul. This involves the ascent and descent of the **Angel's Peak,** which gives 250 feet additional up and down, but is very well worth doing, as the view from it of Braeriach, Cairn Toul, Lochan Uaine and the Garrachorry is fine. But both it and the upper part of Cairn Toul are piles of granite blocks, and the going is *very* rough and heavy. **Cairn Toul** has two cairns, about a furlong apart, the northern one, which we first reach, being the higher.

Alternative.—At the head of Coire Dhondail two streams unite, falling together over the rock that is ascended by the steep but easy scramble just mentioned. The northern of these two streams may be followed to its source. Half a mile more of very easy walking in the same direction, north-east, will take us over the low ridge and down to the real "**Wells of Dee,**" the true sources of that river at a height of 4,000 feet above sea-level. These are small well-eyes rising from the granite detritus with which the great plateau is covered. About a quarter of a mile to the east is the edge of the *Garrachorry*, and this may be followed either way to **Cairn Toul** or **Braeriach**, the summits of which are in full view. In going to the latter the head of the great fall of the Dee is passed.

AVIEMORE TO INVERNESS VIÂ CARRBRIDGE.

The Great North Road takes this direct route from Aviemore to Inverness (33 miles), running now on one side of the railway, now on the other, and making straight for Inverness across Drummossie Moor from Daviot without any detour such as the railway is obliged to make.

Carrbridge (*Carrbridge, Rowan-Lea, Struan House*) is a pleasant village, 850 feet above sea-level, 25 miles from Inverness by road. It is surrounded by pine-clad hills and is built on a subsoil of gravel, and the climate is particularly salubrious. Some fifty yards above the road bridge over the Dulnain are the carefully preserved remains of an old arch built by the Earl of Seafield of two hundred years ago to facilitate access to Duthil churchyard across the often-swollen Dulnain. Carrbridge is a popular ski-ing centre and has a golf course.

Duthil, 2 miles eastward, was known in ancient times as Glencarnie, or Glencharnoch ("Glen of Heroes"), from the number of illustrious dead who were laid to rest under cairns, many of which remain. The churchyard has been the burial-place of families of Grant for three hundred years. The history of the church goes back to the thirteenth century. From Duthil a road with grand views runs northward into the pretty country around **Lochindorb** (*see* p. 342); a haunt of anglers.

For a charming walk the right bank of the river should be followed above Carrbridge. Within 2 miles is **Sluggan Bridge**, in a pretty spot. A little farther along the Dulnain there come into view, on the shoulder of the hill at the upper end of the dell, the ruins of **Inverlaidnan House**, which in its days of grandeur gave a night's shelter to the Young Pretender.

From Carrbridge (7 miles) we begin to ascend the southern slope of the Monadhliath mountains. At the deep **Pass of Slochd Mor** (railway summit, 1,315 feet) there is a remarkable echo. Emerging from the Pass, we reach an open, trackless expanse of furze and heather. In excavating the enormous railway cutting on this portion of the route, there were discovered at a depth of 25 feet below the surface three successive crops of pine-trees, showing that in prehistoric times the region was tree-clad, although now there is not a twig to be seen. From about the summit there is a grand retrospect of the Cairngorms, including Ben Macdhui, while in front the elephantine form of Ben Wyvis soon comes into view. A viaduct, a quarter of a mile in length, carries the line across the *Findhorn*, a river that has always been famed for its salmon and trout fishing. On 2 miles of the stream, visitors at the *Freeburn Hotel* at **Tomatin**, the very heart of the Mackintosh country, have the privilege of fishing both for salmon and trout. Three miles farther is **Moy Hall**, the residence of The Mackintosh of Mackintosh. Two swords used in the Clan fight on the North Inch at Perth (1396) are preserved here. Among many other relics are a blue bonnet and a canopy bed used by Prince Charlie. Dry rot necessitated the abandonment of the previous larger Moy Hall at the northern end of **Loch Moy**.

In February, 1746, Prince Charles arrived at Moy Hall in advance of his army and was entertained by The Mackintosh's Lady, who had raised the Clan for the Chevalier and was consequently known as "Colonel Anne." Only a few servants and retainers were within call, and one of these, Donald Fraser, a blacksmith, realizing the Prince's peril, posted himself with a few companions on the road along which danger was to be feared. On the approach of Lord Loudoun's force, the hidden men fired their muskets as quickly as possible and raised the slogan of various clans. Darkness concealed their number, and the royalists, thinking they had come upon a strong body of the Prince's supporters, retreated to Inverness. In this curious engagement, which is known as the *Rout of Moy*, only one man was killed. The unfortunate individual was McCrimmon, the hereditary piper of McLeod of Skye, some of whose clansmen were with Lord Loudoun. Before he left home he had a presentiment of his fate and composed the famous pipe tune known as *McCrimmon's Lament*.

Living Man's Glen is so called from the tradition that a living man was buried in it, the supposed grave being marked by a small cairn. According to the story, there was a dispute between The Mackintosh and MacGillivray of Dunmaglass respecting the boundary of their lands. Dunmaglass undertook to produce a man who would declare on oath the exact boundary under the penalty of being buried alive if he swore falsely. The man, on being brought to the spot, swore by the head under his bonnet and the earth under his feet that he stood on Dunmaglass's land. Inspection of his shoes and headgear showed that he had partly filled the former with soil from the acknowledged property of Dunmaglass and that he had a cock's head in his bonnet. The Mackintoshes adjudged him guilty of perjury and inflicted the penalty agreed upon.

On approaching **Daviot,** a glorious panorama of mountain scenery comes into view. Beyond Daviot (*Meallmore Hotel*), the Great Glen opens on the left, and far away in the north-west rises the huge mass of Ben Wyvis (3,429 feet). From Daviot the road climbs over Drummossie Muir, and then comes the grand view of Inverness, backed by the waters of the Beauly Firth. Soon there may be seen towards the north, across the River Nairn, a lofty ridge, a site of great historic interest, for it is the battlefield of Culloden. From Daviot the railway swings northward in a wide detour, giving glorious views, and crosses the Nairn river by a very fine stone viaduct of 29 arches and a third of a mile in length.

AVIEMORE TO GRANTOWN.

The Grantown road leaves the main road 4 miles north of Aviemore and in about a mile a small right turn leads to **Boat of Garten** (*Boat, Craigard*), a very popular little resort, with fishing and an excellent golf course. The name commemorates the ferry which preceded the bridge which now crosses the Spey. Beside beautiful **Loch Garten,** on the east side of the river, is a bird sanctuary where ospreys have their eyrie. Close to the road and river about 2 miles beyond Boat of Garten is the farm of **Tullochgorum,** a name familiar to Scots as that of a celebrated "reel," and of the Rev. John Skinner's verses, which Burns declared to be "the best Scotch song that Scotland ever heard." At Dulnain Bridge the road from Carrbridge (*see* p. 338) is joined. So to—

Grantown.

Angling.—The Strathspey Angling Improvement Association has 13 miles of fishings on the Spey and the Dulnain. Salmon and trouting tickets are issued by the Secretary (77 High Street, Grantown). Trout fishing in Loch Garton. There is free trout fishing in certain tributaries of the Spey, and there are many streams and lochs in the vicinity.

Bowls.—A green adjoins the golf course.

Bus service to Elgin and to Carrbridge and Aviemore.

Camping and Caravanning.—Modern site with good facilities.
Distances.—Aberlour, 21¾ m.; Aviemore, 15 m.; Ballindalloch, 13 m.; Boat of Garten, 8 m.; Carrbridge, 10 m.; Forres, 22 m.; Inverness, 33 m.; Nairn, 23 m.; Nethy Bridge, 6 m.; Tomintoul, 14 m.
Early Closing.—Thursdays.
Golf.—A sporting 18-hole course.
Hotels.—*Grant Arms* (66 rooms), *Palace* (57 rooms), *Spey Valley* (19 rooms), *Strathspey*, *Holmhill* (9 rooms), *Craiglynne* (60 rooms), *MacKay's* (10 rooms), *Ben Mhor*, *Coppice*, *Garth*, *Seafield*, *Dunvegan*, *Waterford*, *Rosehall*, and numerous guest-houses.
Ski-ing facilities.
Tennis.—Tournaments are held in August.

Grantown, or Grantown-on-Spey, to distinguish it from Granton, near Edinburgh, stands in Morayshire, upon a plateau having an elevation of 712 feet above sea-level. It is an exceptionally neat and attractive town, with a population of about 1,500.

To the south, the grandest feature of the landscape is the Cairngorm range, the nearest height about 12 or 14 miles distant in a direct line, while to the right and left the valley of the Spey is seen for many miles, with all its varied sylvan and romantic scenery.

The town takes its name from its founders, members of the Grant family, and is comparatively modern, the first houses having been erected in 1766.

Grantown is an excellent centre for sport, walks and motoring excursions. It has a bracing climate, the salubrity of which is increased by the presence of extensive pine-woods. It stands on gravelly soil, and has an abundant supply of good water. With its many advantages as a place of residence, there is no room for wonder that as a Highland health and pleasure resort it rivals Ballater and Braemar. In winter it is a popular centre for ski-ing.

Queen Victoria called **Castle Grant**, in her *Journal*, "a very plain-looking house, like a factory," and that description exactly fits it. The oldest portion is a picturesque tower bearing the name of Babie's Tower (after some old-time Barbara), and dating from the fifteenth century.

The Castle is the ancient seat of the chiefs of the Clan Grant, the Earls of Seafield, but the seventh Earl and his son, who succeeded him, broke the entail, and the eighth Earl, who died in 1884, left the estates to his mother. Since then there have been landless chiefs of Grant and Earls of Seafield, but the Dowager Countess justified her long possession by planting extensive woods and in other ways improving the territory. She died in 1911, and left the estates in trust, ultimately to revert to the holders of the Seafield Earldom. The eleventh Earl, James Ogilvie Grant, was killed in action in 1915 and was succeeded in the Seafield title by his daughter Nina. In 1969 the present Earl succeeded. Part of the castle has been damaged by fire.

Lord Huntly's Cave (3½ miles).—Follow the Forres road past the Castle Grant gateway until just beyond the third milestone. A footpath on the right leads to the glen, at the bottom of which, on the left-hand side, is a cave. It derives its name from a tradition that it was the hiding-place of the second Marquis of Huntly, who espoused the cause of Charles I, but fled at the approach of his brother-in-law, the Earl of Argyll, commander-in-chief of the Scottish forces.

The return to Grantown may be made by following the path down the glen for about a mile and then taking a by-road on the right that joins the main road some 2 miles north of the town.

Grantown to Bridge of Broun (10 miles) and **Tomintoul** (14 miles).

Cross the river by the fine new bridge and turn to the left along the Cromdale road. The Tomintoul route goes off on the right after the Nethy Bridge turn. The scenery is very interesting and a Pass of nearly 1,500 feet is scaled. **The Bridge of Broun** is in a most romantic spot, where the water flows through a rocky channel some 2 feet wide at the surface of the stream, and 8 or 10 feet wide at the upper surface of the rocks some 40 feet above the water. This part of the stream is known as the **Linn of Broun.** The road then climbs up over the hills to the east and crosses the Avon by the Bridge of Avon and there joins the road, *viâ* Strath Avon, from Ballindalloch to Tomintoul. For **Tomintoul,** *see* p. 344.

Lochindorb, to the north-west of Grantown, may be reached by tramping across the moor, or by a road (some 10 miles) doubling back from Dava. The loch is a fine sheet of water. On an island is a castle that in 1303 was captured by Edward I of England. Forty years later it became the prison of William Bullock, a favourite of David Bruce, who, being suspected of tampering with the English, was starved to death in its dungeon. Still later it was a stronghold of the Wolf of Badenoch. A causeway connecting it with the shore is now submerged. On the eastern side is **Craig Tiribeg** (*Cheerepeck*), 1,586 feet, one of the heights on which bonfires are lighted to celebrate great events in the Grant family.

Cromdale Hills (over 2,000 feet).—Cross Spey Bridge, turn to the left, and follow the road running parallel with old railway. In about 2 miles, take road on right by the edge of a wood, leading to Burnside farm, from which it is 2 miles south-east to the summit, *Creagan a' Chaise* (2,367 feet), on which there is a large cairn. Magnificent view. On these hills, after the battle of Killiecrankie, the Jacobites were surprised and routed (1690).

Grantown to Nethy Bridge (6 miles).—By the road running up the right bank of Spey, **Nethy Bridge** is reached. This tiny village, beautifully situated on the verge of Abernethy Forest, has charming woodland walks, a golf course, angling and ski-ing to attract visitors (*hotel:* 74 rooms). Loch Garten (p. 340) is within easy reach. Long mountain tracks lead to Aviemore and to Braemar (*see* p. 335).

Grantown to Forres (22 miles) and **Nairn** (23 miles).—From Grantown the route is past the entrance to Castle Grant and the glen containing Lord Huntly's Cave. The road soon rises to the summit level of 1,097 feet, and the views become extraordinarily good. A little short of the road-fork at Dava (left for Nairn (as on p. 387); straight on for Forres; a road on left leads to **Lochindorb** (*see* p. 342).

Beyond Dava the road runs alongside the lovely **Findhorn Glen**, as described on p. 386.

Grantown to Ballindalloch (13 miles).—The road now passes through the choicest portion of **Strathspey**, the "thundering Spey" rolling wide and deep through a circumscribed valley, abundantly wooded and backed by softly swelling hills and high mountains. This pleasant road follows the course of the river with its multitudinous twinings, at many places running on its very brink, and innumerable stretches of the stream are disclosed to view. The **Spey** is one of the most rapid rivers in Scotland, and the third of Scottish rivers in point of length (110 miles), and, next to the Tay, it is the grandest river in the country. It ranks high as a salmon stream, and on that account most of it is preserved. Trouting is not permitted in those parts that are let for salmon fishing. It also contains finnocks. (*See under* Grantown, p. 340.)

The main road leaves Grantown by the new bridge and winds above the southern bank; less used is the road turning out of the Forres road near the Golf Links and running along the northern side of the valley, the Spey being crossed at Cromdale or Advie.

As far as Advie, the "Haughs of Cromdale" (p. 343) are on the right bank. Beyond Advie the scenery closes in upon the road and is particularly fine.

Near **Ballindalloch** the Spey is joined by the *Avon* (or A'an), a river so pellucid as to give rise to the couplet:

> "The water o' A'an it rins sae clear,
> 'Twould beguile a man o' a hunder year.'

On the right bank of the Avon is **Ballindalloch Castle:** The picturesque entrance gate fills the space between a steep rock and the end of the parapet wall of a bridge over the river. Over the keystone of the arch above it are the family arms and the motto, "Touch not the cat bot a glove," i.e., without a glove.

The castle, which has been added to and modernized, is considered one of the finest specimens of Baronial architecture in the north of Scotland.

Ballindalloch guards the Avon, alongside which a road goes past *Delnashaugh Hotel,* Drumin Castle ruins, the mouth of the *Livet* and the entrance to **Glenlivet,** and the Bridge of Avon (p. 342) and so to **Tomintoul.**

The road ascends the pleasant wooded valley of the *Avon,* to the entrance to Glenlivet, where is a choice of routes. One crosses the Livet and follows the Avon closely to Tomintoul while the other follows the Livet for several miles, passes the *Pole Inn* and crosses the moor in a south-westerly direction to Tomintoul. **Glenlivet,** best known for its distillery, is of historical interest as the scene of a fierce battle in 1594 between two Scottish forces, one being commanded by the Earl of Huntly, the other by the Earl of Argyll. The Earl of Huntly having caused the murder of the "Bonnie Earl of Moray" and entered on an attempt to overthrow the Protestant cause, the King commissioned Moray's brother-in-law, the young Earl of Argyll, to bring him to account, but the avenging army was defeated with a loss of 500 men, while the loss on the other side was trifling.

From Glenlivet a road runs down to Dufftown (p. 345) by way of **Glen Rinnes,** skirting the southern base of **Ben Rinnes.**

Tomintoul is the chief centre of population in the extensive parish of Kirkmichael, in Banffshire. The highest village in the Highlands (1,124 feet), it has bracing air; the district abounds with trout streams, and the place is making a name for itself as one of the holiday resorts of the North. (*Hotels: Richmond Arms* (23 rooms), *Gordon Arms* (30 rooms), *Glenavon* (12 rooms), *White Heather* (9 rooms). Youth Hostel.

Bus service (not Tues., Weds.) Tomintoul and Dufftown (32 m.) *viâ* Glen Livet and Glen Rinnes. For routes between Tomintoul and Dee-side by the rebuilt Lecht Road, *see* pp. 367, 371 and 401; between Tomintoul and Grantown, *see* p. 342; between Tomintoul and Strathdon, *see* p. 401.

At Delnashaugh the main road turns very sharp to the left, and for several miles road-travellers see little of the river. **Blacksboat** derives its name from a ferry, now replaced by a bridge across the Spey. **Aberlour** (*Aberlour, Lour*) has a fine waterfall (Linn of Ruthrie). There is a 9-hole golf course and good fishing.

At **Craigellachie** (accent on second syllable) (*hotel*) the Fiddich joins the Spey, which farther north makes a grand sweep round the base of **Ben Aigan** (1,544 feet).

The road crosses the Spey by a fine cast-iron bridge (Telford) and then the way is cut along the face of the lofty precipitous rock called **Craigellachie**, which forms the boundary in this direction of Strathspey, as the more famous Craigellachie Rock, near Aviemore, marks the southern end of this section of the Spey valley. In both directions the valley is extremely lovely.

For the routes northward from Craigellachie to Elgin, Forres, Nairn and Inverness, *see* pp. 379–92.

From Craigellachie, **Glen Fiddich** winds very charmingly to **Dufftown** (*Commercial*), famous for its distilleries. There is good fishing, golf, bowls and tennis. It has benefited by the generosity of Lord Mount Stephen (born here in 1829), and is in high favour with visitors on account of its bracing climate—its altitude is over 600 feet—and the charming walks and drives in the vicinity. Mortlach Church (restored) dates back to very early times. Auchindoun Castle, a gaunt towering ruin, was a Gordon stronghold. A little to the north of the town is the old **Castle of Balvenie** (*open weekdays*, 10–4 *or* 7; *Sundays*, 2–4 *or* 7; *small charge*).

Ben Rinnes (2,755 feet).—The summit is 7 miles from Dufftown. The ascent presents no difficulty. The descent may be made to Aberlour, 7 miles from the top, or to Ballindalloch, 8 miles. The two **Convals** offer nearer and easier ascents.

PERTH TO ABERDEEN BY FORFAR, BRECHIN AND STONEHAVEN.

Distance.—90 miles.

For the coast route *viâ* Dundee and Montrose, *see* p. 354 ; for that *viâ* Blairgowrie and Braemar, *see* p. 357.

CROSS the river at Perth and turn to the left, bearing to right at fork a few hundred yards north of the Old Bridge. Two miles out is **New Scone** (for historic Old Scone, *see* p. 357). The Sidlaw Hills are on the right, and beyond Balbeggie we are opposite **Dunsinane Hill**, the traditional site of Macbeth's Castle. **Coupar Angus** (*Royal* (14 *rooms*), *Moorfield* (14 *rooms*), *Red House* (5 *rooms*)) has vestiges of the wealthy Cistercian Abbey founded here by Malcolm IV in 1164. " Angus " is the old name, now officially re-adopted, for the county of Forfar, and is here used to distinguish the town from Cupar in Fife. Coupar Angus, formerly partly in Forfar, or Angus, and partly in Perthshire, is now considered wholly in Perthshire.

A good road goes northward to **Blairgowrie** (p. 358); southward there is a road to **Dundee** (p. 354).

Five miles east of Coupar Angus is **Meigle**, with a museum containing sculptured stones of much interest to archæologists and Arthurians, for they are said to mark the grave of Queen Guinevere, who was imprisoned on Barry Hill, a mile or so from Alyth.

Alyth (pronounced *ail-lith*) is a featureless but thriving town on the south slopes of the Grampians. There is golf and fishing, and the place is a centre for some good local excursions. (*Hotels : Lands of Loyal, Alyth.*)

1. **Airlie Castle** (5½ miles north-east), an ancient home of the Ogilvys, Earls of Airlie, is prettily situated at the junction of the picturesque Melgam and Isla. The old castle, " *The Bonnie Hoose o' Airlie*," was burned in 1640 by the Earl of Argyll.

2. **The Slug of Auchrannie**, 2 miles from Airlie Castle by path beside the Isla, a series of falls in a fine sandstone gorge.

3. **Reekie Linn** (5 miles north).—Walkers may follow the old road over the **Hill of Alyth** (966 feet) ; motors turn to left out of road to Airlie Castle. The routes unite about 3 miles from the town ; take the right-hand branch at fork, and a mile

farther turn up a lane through a farm-gate. At the end of the lane pass through a wicket, from which the linn is but a short distance. The river, in three plunges, falls sixty feet.

4. **Kirkton of Glenisla** (10 miles).—This excursion may be a continuation of that to Reekie Linn. Opposite the lane referred to in No. 3 is a road on the left. Follow that to its junction with a high-road from Alyth, and then follow the latter for 4 miles. It leads up a hill called the **Druim Dearg** (" Red Ridge "). Near the summit (1,487 feet) a track on the right leads down to **Kirkton of Glenisla** (*hotel : Youth Hostel :* skiing). The best road, however, leaves the main road half a mile beyond the Reekie Linn and strikes due north to Dykend, where it joins the road from Kirriemuir to Glenisla. Glenisla is the habitat of many flowers and ferns—among the latter the rare holly fern—and is a good trout-fishing centre. A motor-coach leaves Alyth for Glenisla and Folda in the morning and returns in the afternoon (time about 1¼ hours each way).

5. **Mount Blair** (2,441 feet).—From Alyth to the summit is 14 miles. Proceed, as in No. 4, as far as the track near the summit of Druim Dearg. There is then a choice of two routes. For the Kirkton Hotel follow the track ; otherwise keep to the main road, as by so doing a mile is saved. Beyond a stone bridge enter a lane leading to the buildings of a farm called Alrich, thence make for the middle of the eastern shoulder of Mount Blair, from which there is an easy climb to the summit. The descent may be made to the Spittal of Glenshee, in a north-westerly direction, or to Blairgowrie, in a south-westerly direction. About a couple of hours' walking will take one to Spittal of Glenshee Hotel (an anglers' and skiers' " howff "), while Blairgowrie is about 15 miles from the summit of Mount Blair, and some 12 miles from the point at which the high-road is reached. A motor runs in the afternoon from Glenshee to Cally Bridge and Blairgowrie (time, 2 hours).

6. **Braemar** (35 miles).—Proceed up Glenisla to Folda (14 miles), near the ruins of **Forter Castle** (supposed by some to be the scene of the ballad of " The Bonnie Hoose o' Airlie ") and the shooting lodge of **Tulchan,** 5 miles farther. Follow the Isla a mile beyond the lodge, and then take a path by the Glas Burn on the left that leads to the ridge of **Monega Hill** (2,917 feet). The path then bears north-west to near the top of **Glas Maol** (3,502 feet), where three counties meet. This, perhaps the highest hill-path in Scotland (3,250 feet), was at one time much used by smugglers. The descent is made into **Glen Clunie,** joining the Cairnwell road at the Sheann Spittal Bridge, 7½ miles south of Braemar.

Motorists should proceed *viâ* Blairgowrie, Spittal of Glenshee, and the Devil's Elbow. For Braemar, *see* p. 369.

Eastward from Coupar Angus the road passes through Meigle, to the south of which, above **Newtyle,** a ruined watch-tower on **Kinpurney Hill** (1,134 feet) is prominent. Six miles farther is Glamis (*Glaams*), with **Glamis Castle** (Earl of Strathmore), a magnificent baronial pile, which for seven centuries has looked across the richly wooded valley of Strathmore to the Grampians. *The historical parts of the castle and the grounds are open during summer on Wednesday and Thursday afternoons (Sundays, July–Sept.).*

The Castle is not well seen from the main Forfar road, but by diverging for about a mile, at the road junction on reaching Glamis, along the Kirriemuir road, a good view of the Castle may be had from the road.

The Castle was the headquarters of the Covenanters' army and later of the forces of the Young Pretender. The latter deemed it one of the fairest castles he had seen, and he knew some of the stately palaces of France and Italy. Part of it was rebuilt after a fire in 1800. A beautiful avenue and a wonderful crypt are notable features, and the popular belief is that there is a secret chamber known only to the Earl, his heir-apparent when he comes of age, and his factor. The association of Glamis with Shakespeare's *Macbeth* is well known. The place also awakens memories of a Lady Glamis, falsely accused by a discarded suitor of practising the art of witchcraft against the life of James V, and dragged to death at the stake on the Castle Hill of Edinburgh, in the year 1537. Lady Glamis's real offence was probably that she was by birth a Douglas. A happier page in the family history was written in 1923, when Lady Elizabeth Bowes-Lyon, daughter of the fourteenth Earl of Strathmore, married the then Duke of York. Here, in 1930, was born their second child, the Princess Margaret Rose, the first royal baby born in Scotland for three hundred years.

In the village of Glamis is a Folk Collection with a range of exhibits representing the lives of Angus people over the past 200 years ; it is housed in four seventeenth century cottages in Kirk Wynd (National Trust). (*Daily*, 1–6 *p.m.*)

Some 5 miles north of Glamis is **Kirriemuir** (" Thrums " —the birthplace in 1860 of Sir J. M. Barrie, O.M., who was laid to rest in the cemetery " up the hill " in June, 1937). It is a small town of about 3,500 inhabitants, 6 miles by road from Forfar, pleasantly situated on the southern slopes of the Braes of Angus. (*Hotels : Airlie Arms* (8 *rooms*), *Ogilvy Arms, Thrums, Newton, etc.*) It is within easy reach of salmon and trout streams, and has an 18-hole golf course. The house in which Barrie was born has been thoroughly repaired by the National Trust for Scotland, and part forms a *Museum*. The Wash-house that was Barrie's " first theatre," the " Window," the " Den," Caddam Wood and other scenes in the Barrie novels are in the town or the immediate vicinity.

Northward from Kirriemuir Glen Clova winds far into the Grampians, **Glen Prosen** coming in from the north-west at Cortachy (5 miles). Buses daily as far as **Clova** (15 miles ; *hotel*), a hamlet that is the centre of the mountain district known as the *Braes of Angus*. Ski-ing facilities at Glendoll Youth Hostel.

Clova to Braemar (18 m.).—Follow road to beyond Braedownie (3 miles), cross the river and take a path which passes to the left of the Youth Hostel and strikes up Glen Doll to Jock's Road at the head of that Glen. The path then goes north-west, passing high above Loch Esk (on the right) and with **Tolmount** (3,143 feet), on the left, and then drops down into the glen leading to Loch Callater, from the north-west end of which a rough road leads down to join the Cairnwell road, 2 miles short of Braemar.

Clova to Ballater (16 miles).—Proceed as above to Braedownie Bridge. Do not cross it, but follow the cart-track for three-quarters of a mile and there strike up Capel Mount, on the right. The path is more distinct in its upper than its lower part, and is indicated by poles and occasional cairns. On either side is a swamp. Descend to the Spittal of Glen Muick, half a mile beyond the end of Loch Muick, from which a road leads down the glen to Ballater. Four miles beyond the Spittal the road passes the Linn of Muick, a fine waterfall, and 5 miles farther reaches Ballater.

Forfar

(**Hotels :** *Queen's, Commercial, County, Jarman's, Royal*)

Forfar is the county town of Angus and is situated in the heart of Strathmore, 7 miles east of Glamis and 14 miles north of Dundee. It was created a Royal Burgh by David I and was the site of royal residences until its castle was razed by Bruce's men in 1308. The town charters were destroyed by Cromwell's troops in 1651 and restored by Charles II in recognition of the town's loyalty to the Stewarts. There is a fine Town Hall (1788) with old masters (Romney, Raeburn, Thorwaldsen). The Meffan Institute houses a local reference library and museum. Forfar rock (a sweet) and Forfar Bridies (meat pasties) are well known.

The town stands at the east end of the Loch of Forfar (sailing, fishing), the traditional scene of the drowning of the murderers of Banquo or Macbeth II.

About a mile east of Forfar are the remains of **Restenneth**

Priory (thirteenth century; *admission fee*), an offshoot of Jedburgh Abbey. Two miles farther is **Rescobie Loch** and still farther eastward is **Guthrie Castle, built in** 1468, and much enlarged in modern times.

About 10 miles north-east of Forfar is—

Brechin.

Angling.—In the Cruick, the South Esk, North Esk and West Water by permission.
Early Closing.—Wednesday.
Population.—6,750.
Golf.—An 18-hole course.
Hotels.—*Dalhousie* (7 rooms), *Northern* (18 rooms), *Star* (8 rooms), *Jolly's*.

Brechin, pleasantly situated on the *South Esk*, is a busy manufacturing centre. The **Cathedral**, founded in the twelfth century, was restored in 1901, and is used as a parish church. It contains some perfect specimens of Early English architecture, and is of great interest. At the south-western corner is a **Round Tower** (one of two in the mainland of Scotland, the other being at Abernethy, in Strathearn), a hundred and six feet high, similar to the round towers of Ireland. It dates from the tenth or eleventh century. In the centre of the town is a fragment of a thirteenth-century Maisondieu chapel.

Brechin Castle held out for three weeks against Edward I. It was then in possession of Sir Thomas Maule, and is still the residence of the representative of the Maule family, the Earl of Dalhousie.

On the **Caterthun Hills** (5 miles north-west of Brechin) are the remains of Pictish forts under the care of the Department of the Environment. The largest, known as the *White Caterthum*, is on the left-hand side of a road which crosses the hills and consists of concentric rings of loose stones; to the right is the *Brown Caterthun*, concentric rings of earthworks. Similar earthworks are on the next height, Lundie Hill.

Brechin is mainly of importance to tourists and other holiday-makers in Angus on account of the access through Edzell into Glen Esk and Glen Lethnot.

Edzell (*Glenesk, Panmure, Central, etc.*), a small village 6 miles north of Brechin, in the valley of the *North Esk*, is famed for its beauty. There is a fine golf course (with a resident professional); and a mile away is the *West Water*, a good trout stream. James Inglis, author of *Oor*

Ain Folk, etc., was born in the manse at Edzell. A mile or so west are the ruins of **Edzell Castle.** The ornamentation of the garden walls is unique in Scotland, the garden attractively laid out in keeping with its early seventeenth-century period, and is now in the care of the Department of the Environment. (*Weekdays,* 10–7 *or* 4. *Sundays,* 2–7 (*October–March* 2–4). *Admission charge to garden.*)

There is a nice walk from **Gannochy Bridge** (1¼ miles north), with a charming view of the river gorge. Cross the bridge and apply at the lodge on the left for permission to enter. Follow path by river-side for nearly a couple of miles, to the road 3 miles from Edzell.

Edzell to Ballater (30 miles), *viâ* Tarfside (12 miles), Loch Lee (16 miles), and Mount Keen (3,077 feet).

The road leads up Glen Esk from beyond Gannochy Bridge and in about 17 miles reaches the ruined Invermark Castle, at the junction of Glen Mark and Glen Lee. The bridle path goes up Glen Mark and in a mile or two reaches the Queen's Well, whence the route (the **Mounth Road**) lies through beautiful and varied scenery. The path, well marked, strikes steeply up the west side of the Ladder Burn and in 2½ miles reaches the watershed (2,504 feet) just to the west of the peak of **Mount Keen,** well worth ascending for the little extra effort required. The path now dips into Glen Tanar and crosses the stream to the remains of a ruined house. From this point a good private road leads down the Glen to Aboyne. The Ballater path strikes northward up the hill-side and when above Etnach turns north-west and passes through the fence on the sky-line by a gate. Thence west, very indistinct, across the head of the Pollagach Burn to cross the next ridge by a dip about half a mile north of Cairn Leuchan. From here a rough road leads down to the south Deeside road, which it joins near the bridge over the Muick, ¾ mile from Ballater.

To **Banchory** (24 miles), by road. *Viâ* Gannochy Bridge to the pretty village of **Fettercairn** (4½ miles) (*hotel*). Then by the west side of **Finella Hill** (1,358 feet) to **Clattering Bridge** (8 miles); **Cairn o' Mounth,** 1,488 feet high and commanding a fine view; **Bridge of Dye** (14 miles); **Bogendreep Bridge** (18 miles); the village of **Strachan** 20½ miles); and past the **Bridge of Feugh** into **Banchory**.

Montrose.

Distances.—Aberdeen, 37 m.; Brechin, 8 m.; Dundee, 29 m.; Stonehaven, 24 m.
Early Closing.—Wednesday.
Hotels.—*Star, Madeira, Park, Central, Corner House.* Caravan Sites.
Sports.—Bathing, bowls, tennis, cricket, boating, fishing, golf (*see below*).

Montrose, a town of great antiquity, is entered from the south by a bridge over the lagoon-like Montrose Basin, nearly 2 miles square. It is prettily laid out and possesses many attractions for visitors. Its golf links include one "Championship" Course, an 18-hole auxiliary course, and a 9-hole pitch-and-putt course. A magnificent indoor swimming pool was completed in 1962. A very fine sandy bathing beach extends for 4 miles. William the Lion, Balliol and James VI are among the many historical personages associated with its Castle (now vanished), and Joseph Hume was among its "sons."

The principal road from Montrose to Stonehaven is by the coast (the other goes inland through Marykirk and joins the Brechin–Aberdeen road just short of **Laurencekirk** (*Royal*), a town once famous for the manufacture of snuff-boxes). The coast road needs no description, though motorists who are not in a hurry will find it worth while to turn down some of the side roads for the sake of the unsophisticated villages overlooking the sea and, particularly in later stages of the journey, for the fine coast views. The most remunerative halt is at **Dunnottar Castle** (*open all year, admission fee*), a mile or so short of Stonehaven, and approached from a new gateway with car park, etc. Before beginning the walk down to the Castle inquire at lodge regarding the admission, as unless the Caretaker is there one has a long and rather tiring walk to small purpose.

The best view of the Castle is from the edge of the cliff a few hundred yards from the road, and even those unable to explore the interior of this fine old stronghold—one of the most impressive ruins in Britain—should come thus far.

Long the stronghold of the powerful Keiths, Earls Marischal of Scotland, the Castle stands on the summit of a cliff washed on three sides by the sea ; on the fourth it is almost separated from the mainland by a deep chasm, from which the ascent is steep and rugged. The ruins cover about three acres and consist of the great square tower, which is almost entire, broken towers and turrets, remains of the palace and the chapel, long ranges of roofless buildings and broken arches, and many dismal halls, vaults and chambers.

The Castle was taken from the English by Wallace in 1297. To the church which then stood on the crags some of the English soldiers fled for sanctuary, but only to find death in awful forms, for the building was set on fire.

Forty years later Edward Balliol garrisoned the Castle with English soldiers, but it was again re-taken. In 1645 it was besieged by Montrose. Among those in it were sixteen Covenanting ministers, who urged the Earl Marischal to be firm in its defence, and to come to no terms with Belial, as they styled their foes, assuring him that the smoke of his farmsteads and villages burning on the mainland would be "a sweet smelling incense in the nostrils of the Lord." Six years later the Castle was besieged by a Parliamentary force, and as starvation threatened to compel surrender, the ancient Scottish Regalia, which had been sent to it for safety, were in danger of being lost. They were smuggled out, through the blockading forces, and until the Restoration the Regalia lay buried under the floor of Kinneff Church.

The last of the cruel memories attached to Dunnottar is of the treatment of imprisoned Covenanters in 1685, when confined in one dungeon in the height of summer were 167 men, women and children. Those who died were interred in Dunnottar churchyard, where the **Covenanters' Stone** recording their names may still be seen. It was while clearing the inscription on this stone that Robert Paterson, the original of "Old Mortality," was seen by Sir Walter Scott, who was passing the night in the manse (*see* p. 100).

A mile or so beyond Dunnottar the road swings round a headland to reveal **Stonehaven** spread out below. Originally a fishing port, this place has of recent years taken its place among Scottish seaside resorts, and the quaint old town is now pinned against the Harbour and the protecting cliff by streets of more modern houses. Tennis, boating and golf, bathing and fishing, are the principal amusements, and there is a swimming pool. (Hotels: *Royal* (21 *rooms*), *Alexandra, Crown, Marine, Belvedere, County, Station, Queen's, Heugh, Commodore, St. Leonard's*, and numerous boarding-houses and apartments.)

The "**Slug**" **Road** to Banchory (16 miles; p. 364) climbs to 757 feet, giving good views of the Cairngorms, and is a handy "short cut" into Deeside. *Raedykes*, a Roman camp about 5 miles out from Stonehaven, has been identified as the site of the Battle of Mons Graupius (A.D. 86), in which Agricola decisively defeated the Caledonians under Galgacus.

About 5 miles north of Stonehaven turnings on the right lead to **Muchalls** (*hotel*), a former fishing village perched on the cliff near some of the finest rock scenery in the north-east of Scotland. **Findon** or Finnan, farther north, was once famed for smoked haddocks, which perpetuate its name—"Finnan haddies."

Now the spires and towers of Aberdeen break the skyline in front and shortly the road crosses the sixteenth-century Bridge of Dee. Turn to the right along Holburn Street for Union Street and the city centre.

(*Note.*—The by-pass road to Inverness and the North (Anderson Drive) continues straight on and avoids the city.)

For **Aberdeen**, *see* page 359.

PERTH TO ABERDEEN VIÂ DUNDEE.

Distance: 88 miles.

CROSS the river at Perth and turn to the right, the road skirting *Kinnoull Hill*, now public property and a good viewpoint. Then past Kinfauns Castle (Co-operative Holiday Association) on the left and with the river at hand on the right the road runs out upon the flat Carse of Gowrie.

About 10 miles from Perth a road on the left leads to the house of *Fingask*, in the grounds of which are some remarkable statues hewn out of granite, the best group representing Burns, Allan Masterton and William Nicol—" Willie brew'd a peck o' maut." There is also a collection of well-cut yews. (*The lovely grounds are open to the public occasionally on behalf of local charities.*)

DUNDEE.

Access.—*Rail:* Dundee is on the main line from Edinburgh (Waverley) to Aberdeen *viâ* the Forth and Tay Bridges. It is also connected with Perth (through the Carse of Gowrie).

Bus.—Services daily to Broughty Ferry, Carnoustie, Arbroath, Montrose, Aberdeen, Forfar and Brechin, Glamis, Kirriemuir, etc., etc.

Early Closing.—Wednesday.

Hotels.—*Queen's Royal* (76 rooms), *Tay Centre* (100 rooms), *Invercarse, Tornaveen, Tayview, Angus* (57 rooms).

Population.—183,000.

Post Office.—Meadowside (centre of town), 9.00 a.m. to 5.30 p.m.; Saturdays till 4.30 p.m.

Stations.—*Tay Bridge* for Edinburgh, Arbroath, Montrose and Aberdeen; and also for Perth and Glasgow.

Youth Hostel.—77 Constitution Road.

Dundee, the fourth Scottish town in population, has a finer site than Aberdeen, but has not the same hold on visitors as " the Granite City." Its main industries are jute, flax and linen, engineering, textile machinery, shipbuilding—whalers were long a speciality—canning, marmalade, confectionery, etc. On the left of the Perth Road as the city centre is approached is the **Queen's College**, founded in 1883, and now forming part of Dundee University.

Perth Road becomes Nethergate, where, at the head of Union Street, is the **Old Steeple**, a handsome and massive tower, decorated in style, and more than 150 feet high, surmounting the City Churches (three under the same roof). It dates from the fourteenth century, and was restored by Sir Gilbert Scott.

In the south-west corner of the churches' grounds is a copy of the **Old Town Cross** (1586).

In the City Square is the magnificent **Caird Hall** (1914–23), due to the generosity of Sir James Caird; it has a fine façade of ten Doric columns and includes the City Hall (seating 3,300) and the municipal chambers.

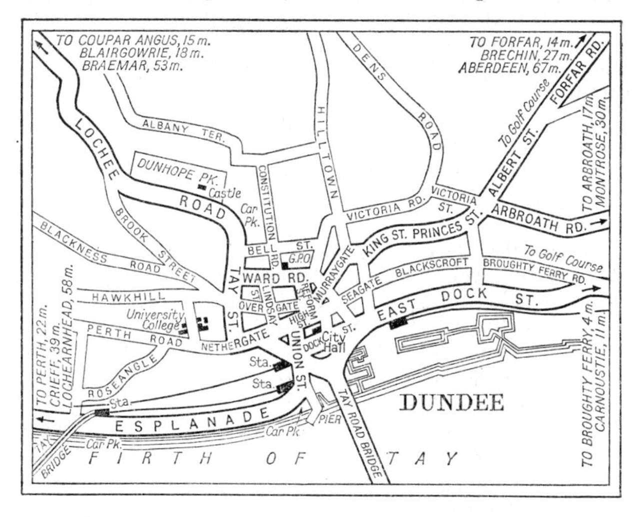

At the northern end of Reform Street, and fronted by a good statue of Burns, is the **Albert Institute**, one of Sir Gilbert Scott's modern Gothic buildings. It contains a Library, Art Gallery, and Museum (*open daily, free*). Around the Institute are congregated the **Howff**, a quaint old burying-ground given to the city by Mary Queen of Scots, the Post Office, the **Royal Exchange** and the **High School**, with a Greek portico. Panmure Street leads to the **Cowgate** and the **East Port**—the only one remaining—over which is recorded the preaching of George Wishart during the plague of 1544. In 1546 the preacher was burned at St. Andrews.

Riverside Drive, extending from Tay Bridge Station to Ninewells and passing under the Tay Bridge (*see* p. 280), affords pleasant views across the Firth.

Dundee Law (572 feet) is a mile north of the Post Office by way of Constitution Street and Law Road, which latter goes right to the summit of the hill. On the way one passes near the **Royal Infirmary** and **Dudhope Park,** in which is **Dudhope Castle,** dating from the sixteenth century, and formerly the residence of the Constable of Dundee. From the top of the Law—on which is situated the city's rather striking War Memorial—there is a most extensive view of the city and surrounding country, including some of the distant Grampians. There is a useful view indicator.

In Caird Park are the ruins of **Mains Castle** and golf courses of 18 and 9 holes.

In Camperdown Park is the famous *Spalding Golf Museum.* The Mills Observatory in Balgay Hill is open daily.

The modern **Tay Road Bridge** was completed in 1966 at a cost of over five and a half million pounds sterling. It is about 1½ miles long and extends from King William Dock, Dundee, across the Tay to Craighead of Newport. The former well-known ferry has now been suspended.

From Dundee a good road crosses the Sidlaw Hills to Coupar Angus and so to Blairgowrie; whence either to Braemar or Dunkeld the routes are described on pages 358 and 305 respectively.

East of Dundee is **Broughty Ferry** (*Castle*), a popular resort taking its name from the ferry formerly plying across the Tay to Tayport. Once a Burgh, it was incorporated with Dundee in 1913. The Waterloo Monument between Newport and Tayport is prominent across the river. Broughty Castle (reconditioned) dates from the fifteenth century.

Between Monifieth and Carnoustie is a triangular promontory terminating in Buddon Ness and used for artillery camps and ranges. **Carnoustie** (*Bruce, Station, Glencoe, Kinloch Arms*) has come to the fore as one of Scotland's premier golfing resorts, but it has fine sands and other attractions which render it a very popular holiday resort. A dozen miles out at sea may be discerned the lighthouse which has superseded the Bell on the *Inchcape Rock*, with which readers of Southey are familiar.

Arbroath (*Windmill*), 6 miles north-east of Carnoustie, is a busy town, with a small harbour and many attractions for summer visitors, including a swimming pool. The Abbey was founded in the twelfth century. (*Admission fee; weekdays: summer* 10–7, *winter* 10–*dusk; Sundays,* 2–4 *or* 7.) The ruin has grand features, but, as a whole, is vast rather than beautiful. It is of red sandstone. The deeply recessed western doorway, by which we enter after passing through a Gothic arcade, is Norman, but the rest is Early English. The three pointed windows at the east end help to emphasize the great length of the building. Besides these the south wall of the nave, the south transept and the Chapter House, hard by and still roofed, are nearly all that remain, if we except the pointed arches and the lower segment of a large rose window over the western doorway. A plain stone in the chancel is said to cover the bones of the founder, William the Lion. The last Abbot was Cardinal Beaton. The Abbot's House has been adapted as a Museum of objects of local interest.

Between Arbroath and Montrose the main road runs some way inland, but those interested in caves and rock formations might well turn aside and visit the vicinity of *Red Head.* At either end of Lunan Bay are collections of fantastic rocks.

For **Montrose**, and thence to Aberdeen, *see* pages 351–3.

PERTH TO ABERDEEN VIÂ BLAIRGOWRIE AND BRAEMAR.

Perth to Aberdeen, 108 miles. This route is not served by railway.

Of the three routes between Perth and Aberdeen, this is much to be preferred, since it introduces some of the finest examples of Highland scenery.

Cross the river at Perth and turn to the left, keeping to the left at the fork a quarter of a mile beyond the old bridge.

Scone Palace, 2½ miles from Perth, is a modern residence adjoining the site of the ancient Abbey of Scone wherein the Scottish Kings, from Kenneth II to James VI, were crowned. Charles II was also crowned here two years after his father's execution. The famous Coronation Stone, said to have been brought from Dunstaffnage (p. 205), was removed to Westminster by Edward I, there to be placed beneath the chair made for that monarch and used for the coronation of every English monarch since. (*Scone Palace is open daily except Fridays, fee.*)

Meikleour, some miles farther on, is famous for its lofty beech avenues, and then the road crosses the green lands of Strathmore to **Blairgowrie,** a favourite summer resort with good fishing, golf (18 and 9), and a variety of interesting excursions. (Hotels: *Queen's* (28 *rooms*), *Royal, Angus* (54 *rooms*), *Glen Ericht, Station* (7 *rooms*), *Kinloch House, George.*)

(For the routes between Blairgowrie and **Dunkeld,** *see* p. 305; **Alyth,** p. 346; **Coupar Angus,** p. 346.)

Since the reconditioning of the fine road over the mountains to Braemar, Blairgowrie has attracted increasing attention from motorists. The first few miles of this road are on the western side of the Ericht to **Bridge of Cally,** where a road goes off on the left for Pitlochry. At Cally Bridge we cross the Ardle, which with the Blackwater composes the Ericht, and begin the ascent of **Glenshee.** The green pastoral scenery of Strathmore gives way to wild and rugged mountain-sides; trees become rarer, and it is not difficult to realize that in bygone days the "Spittal" of Glenshee was a very welcome feature of the route. ("Spittal" is a corruption of "Hospital," a shelter for travellers.) There is little else but the hotels, a church and a cottage or two, but, in season, the top of Glenshee is a popular centre for ski-ing. The old hotel has been rebuilt with observation lounges on the Swedish pattern. At the Spittal the road takes us into **Glen Beg,** still climbing relentlessly towards the pass between the Cairnwell and Glas Maol, at which point it is all but 2,200 feet above sea-level. The final rise to the summit is by way of **The Devil's Elbow,** far less fearsome than formerly, thanks to the Ministry of Transport. At the **Cairnwell Pass** the road reaches a higher point than any other road of its class in Britain. The views are magnificent; countless mountain peaks rising on every hand. The road passes from Perthshire to Aberdeenshire, and runs gently down all the way to **Braemar** (p. 369). The Deeside road hence to Aberdeen is described on pages 364–70.

ABERDEEN.

Access by *Rail;* The most direct route to Aberdeen from Edinburgh and the South (East Coast) is *viâ* the Forth and Tay Bridges, joining the route from London (Euston), Crewe and Perth at Dundee.

Road; viâ Perth and Stonehaven (*see* pp. 346–57); from Blairgowrie *viâ* Ballater and Deeside (*see* p. 357). Buses run to Aberdeen from Glasgow *viâ* Stirling and Perth, from Edinburgh and from Inverness.

Airport at Dyce, 5½ m. north of the city. Air terminal at 335 Union Street.

Amusements.—Cinemas are numerous; *His Majesty's Theatre* is in Rosemount Viaduct. There are also modern dance halls, headed by the fine modern ballroom on the Beach Esplanade. Ice Rink in Spring Garden. Ten-pin bowling in George Street.

Angling.—Inexpensive and good angling in the lower part of the *Dee. Don, Ythan* and *Ugie* are within easy reach. Information can be had from the various tackle makers in the city. Excellent sea-fishing.

Bathing—Good open sea bathing. Corporation Bathing Station on the sea front. *Bon Accord Baths* in Justice Mill Lane, modern swimming pool, Turkish baths.

Buses connect the most important parts of the city; and there are also numerous buses connecting with places around.

Car Parking.—Thistle Street, Castle Street, Lower Denburn, Crown Terrace, Golden Square, Stell Road, Spa Street, Sea Beach Esplanade, Bridge Place, Guild Street, etc.

Distances.—Banchory, 18 m.; Banff, 46 m.; Birmingham, 434 m.; Braemar, 58 m.; Edinburgh, 131 m.; by rail, Forth and Tay Bridges: 125 m. by road *viâ* Perth and Forth Bridge; Elgin, 66 m.; Glasgow, 152 m.; Inverness, 108 m.; Liverpool, 356 m.; London, 540 m.; Perth, 82 m.

Early Closing.—Wednesday and Saturday.

Market Day.—Friday.

Golf.—The principal courses are: *Balgownie Links*, 18 holes, 2 miles from the centre of the city, the magnificent private course of the *Royal Aberdeen Club.* Visitors may be introduced. Adjoining it on the north is the course of the *Murcar Club.* Also open to visitors. There is also a ladies' course of 9 holes. There are *Municipal Courses*—the old course (18 holes) on the King's Links alongside the Beach Esplanade, and the 9- and 18-hole inland courses at Hazlehead, 3 miles west from Castle Street, and at Balnagask. At Bieldside is the course of the *Deeside Club.*

Guide Book.—See the Ward Lock *Guide to Northern Scotland.*

Hotels.—*Imperial* (100 rooms), *Caledonian* (70 rooms), *Douglas* (110 rooms), *Station* (60 rooms), *George* (45 rooms), *Northern* (37 rooms), *Royal, Guild* (23 rooms), *Gloucester* (87 rooms), *Bell's* (private), *Atholl, Central,* and many others. *Youth Hostel,* 8 Queen's Road.

Population.—180,625.

Post Office.—The head office is in Crown Street, on south side of Union Street, half a mile west of City Centre. There are numerous branch offices.

Library (Public) in Rosemount Viaduct. Reading-room open from 9 a.m. to 9 p.m. Reference Department, 9.30 a.m.–9 p.m. (Saturdays, 5 p.m.). Various branch libraries and reading-rooms throughout the city.

Tennis, Bowls, etc., in public parks. Sunday play.

ABERDEEN is at once an ancient Cathedral and University city, a very popular seaside resort and a busy seaport with a thriving fishing industry. It lies between the *Don* and the *Dee,* the mouth of the latter river forming also the entrance to the Harbour.

The principal thoroughfare is **Union Street,** running south-west to north-east, and ending in Castle Street, on

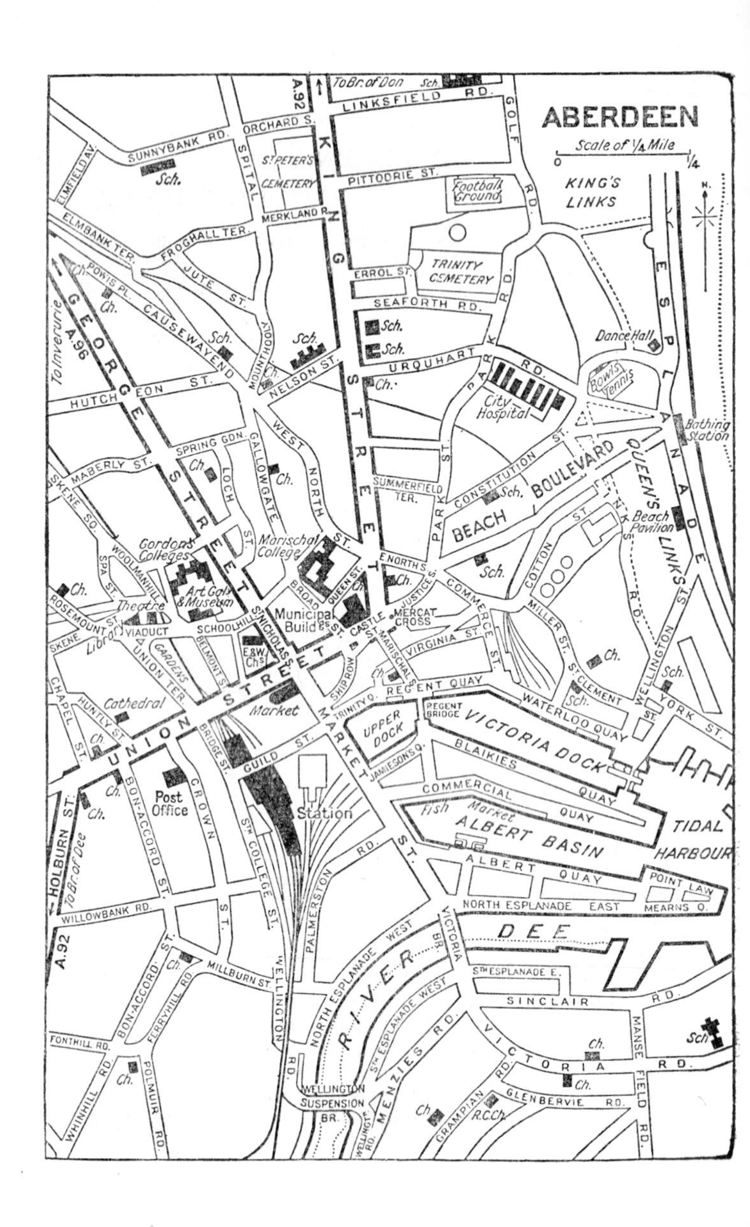

ABERDEEN
Scale of 1/4 Mile
0
1/4
N.
KING'S LINKS
To Br. of Don
A.92
LINKSFIELD RD.
GOLF RD.
ORCHARD S.
SUNNYBANK RD.
ELMFIELD AV.
SPITAL
ST. PETER'S CEMETERY
PITTODRIE ST.
Football Ground
MERKLAND R.
KING STREET
ELMBANK TER.
FROGHALL TER.
JUTE ST.
ERROL ST.
TRINITY CEMETERY
SEAFORTH RD.
POWIS PL.
CAUSEWAYEND
MOUNTHOOLY
NELSON ST.
URQUHART RD.
PARK RD.
PARK ST.
City Hospital
Dance Hall
Bowls Tennis
Bathing Station
ESPLANADE
To Inverurie
A.96
GEORGE STREET
HUTCHEON ST.
SPRING GDN.
GALLOWGATE
WEST NORTH ST.
LOCH ST.
MABERLY ST.
SKENE SQ.
SUMMERFIELD TER.
CONSTITUTION ST.
BOULEVARD
BEACH
QUEEN'S LINKS
Beach Pavilion
COTTON ST.
LINKS RD.
Gordon's Colleges
Marischal College
WOOLMANHILL
SPA ST.
BROAD ST.
QUEEN ST.
E. NORTH S.
JUSTICE S.
COMMERCE ST.
MILLER ST.
WELLINGTON ST.
Art Gally & Museum
Theatre
ROSEMOUNT
Library
VIADUCT
SCHOOLHILL
ST. NICHOLAS ST.
Municipal Build gs
CASTLE ST.
MERCAT CROSS
VIRGINIA ST.
SKENE
UNION TER.
GARDENS
BELMONT ST.
E&W. Chs.
SHIPROW
MARISCHAL ST.
REGENT QUAY
WATERLOO QUAY
ST. CLEMENT
YORK ST.
CHAPEL ST.
HUNTLY ST.
Cathedral
UNION STREET
Market
TRINITY Q.
UPPER DOCK
REGENT BRIDGE
VICTORIA DOCK
BRIDGE ST.
MARKET ST.
GUILD ST.
JAMIESON'S Q.
BLAIKIES QUAY
COMMERCIAL QUAY
Post Office
CROWN ST.
BON-ACCORD ST.
HOLBURN ST.
To Br. of Dee
Station
STH COLLEGE ST.
Fish Market
ALBERT BASIN
TIDAL HARBOUR
ALBERT QUAY
POINT LAW
MEARNS Q.
NORTH ESPLANADE EAST
WILLOWBANK RD.
PALMERSTON RD.
A.92
DEE
RIVER
VICTORIA BR.
NORTH ESPLANADE WEST
MILLBURN ST.
WELLINGTON RD.
STH ESPLANADE E.
STH ESPLANADE WEST
SINCLAIR RD.
FERRYHILL RD.
FONTHILL RD.
MENZIES RD.
VICTORIA RD.
MANSE FIELD RD.
WELLINGTON SUSPENSION BR.
WHINHILL RD.
POLMUIR RD.
GRAMPIAN RD.
GLENBERVIE RD.
R.C.Ch.
Sch.
Ch.

the north side of which are the Town House and Sheriff Court House. Passing along the Beach Boulevard one comes to the Beach Esplanade, 2½ miles in length and extending beside the sands from the mouth of the Dee to the mouth of the Don. Here are the public golf links, tennis courts, a bathing station, pavilions and other accessories of Aberdeen's pleasure beach; and turning southward by the Esplanade and then along one of the byways on the right one comes to the busy quays surrounding the Harbour. Such a tour includes most of the Aberdonian "lions"; notable exceptions being St. Machar's Cathedral, King's College and the Old Brig o' Balgownie, which lie to the north and are reached by way of King Street, branching off from Castle Street at the beautiful **Mercat Cross.** The Cross was erected in 1686 and was designed as a reproduction of an old Edin burgh cross.

The **Municipal Buildings,** with a lofty tower (200 ft.), are a few yards westward of the statue (*daily*, 10–4; *tower is a fine viewpoint*). There are some good pictures by Jamesone, "The Vandyke of Scotland" (1587–1644), Wm. Dyce, R.A., John Phillip, R.A., and Sir George Reid, P.R.S.A., all Aberdonians. The Burgh Records are the most complete collection of civic documents in Scotland. At the east end of the Municipal Buildings is the old **Tolbooth,** the former Townhouse.

Behind the Municipal Buildings, and fronting on Broad Street, is—

Marischal College.

Visiting Hours.—Mitchell Tower, Mitchell Hall and Portrait Gallery (*admission, free*), throughout the year, but viewing time restricted according to examination requirements. The Anthropology Museum is open daily (*free*).

This fine pile, 420 feet in breadth and 548 in depth, and with an array of soaring pinnacles, is probably the largest and most imposing granite building in the world.

The site once held a monastery and gardens belonging to the Order of Grey Friars, who were dispossessed; their property being assigned by James VI to George Keith, fifth Earl Marischal, who, in 1593, converted the monastery into a college. The present buildings were begun in 1840, but were greatly extended between 1890 and 1906.

Entrance from Broad Street is by a finely carved gateway giving on to a courtyard, from the far end of which rises the *Mitchell Tower* (235 feet), which gives entry to the Mitchell Hall, Picture Gallery and Museums.

The **Mitchell Hall** is very fine, granite and carved oak being well blended, and giving rich effect to the coloured glass in the windows.

The University of Aberdeen was founded in 1494–5 by Bishop Elphinstone, who also founded within it King's College, owing its name to the favour of James IV. Marischal College was founded as a separate university in 1593. After an abortive union in 1640, the two were united in 1860.

King's College, which lies a mile to the north of Marischal College, is prominent for its delightful open lantern in the form of the Imperial crown surmounting its Chapel tower. The Chapel is a good example of Scottish Flamboyant Gothic, begun in 1500, and remarkable for its original timber ceiling and carved stalls and screens. The **Library** is rich in treasures and now possesses over half a million books.

The University of Aberdeen has some 60 professors, a large number of lecturers, and some 6,000 students. King's College is mainly devoted to Arts and Divinity, Marischal College being chiefly concerned with Science, Medicine, Engineering and Agriculture.

The curious Oriental gateway of the former *Powis House*, opposite King's College, serves as entrance to modern halls of residence and to the Music Department.

Up till 1891, when an Amalgamation Act was passed, Aberdeen consisted of two separate burghs, Aberdeen proper and what was known as **Old Aberdeen,** in which are situated St. Machar's Cathedral and King's College. Originally merely the precincts of the Cathedral, Old Aberdeen was in 1498 erected into a Burgh of Barony, and for nearly four centuries it remained a separate burgh with its own municipality.

A little north of King's College is—

St. Machar's Cathedral,

(Open weekdays, 10–8 or dusk. Sunday services at 11 a.m. and 6 p.m.

now consisting of nave and aisles only, built of granite, and used as the parish church of Old Aberdeen and Old Machar.

The building occupies the site of a rude church, said

to have been erected about 581 by St. Machar, one of Columba's contemporaries, who, according to tradition, was sent towards the northern part of the land of the Picts, with instructions to proceed until he came to a spot where the river took the form of a bishop's crook, and there he was to found a church.

The existing structure was begun about 1378 and completed in 1552. The most striking external features are the twin battlemented towers with short sandstone spires, at the west end, and the round-headed portal and the seven-lighted window of the west end.

The third " lion " in this northern outskirt of the city is **The Auld Brig o' Balgownie,** or old Bridge of Don, a picturesque structure noteworthy as being the oldest first-class bridge in Scotland still in full use. It spans the river with a high, single-pointed Gothic arch, 57 feet wide, and was erected early in the fourteenth century. In 1605 Sir Alexander Hay devised for its maintenance a small property producing a trifling annuity, but so great became the increase in the value of the legacy that the proceeds sufficed for the erection of the New Bridge, and left a handsome sum in hand.

Westward of the Municipal Buildings, in Union Street, is the building known as **the East and West Churches,** and which at the Reformation was the largest parish church in Scotland. It was then divided into separate churches, but each half has been rebuilt since. North of the churches are *Robert Gordon's Colleges,* now a secondary day school and technical college ; the **Art Gallery and Regional Museum** (daily, 10–5 ; Sundays, 2–5), which specializes in modern painting and sculpture. There is a series of artists' self-portraits probably unique in this country ; print room and art library ; the **Theatre** and the **Public Library.**

The **Fish Market,** when in " full cry," is by no means the least interesting spot in Aberdeen. The best time to come is at 8 a.m., when often as much as 1,000 tons of fish are auctioned.

Rubislaw Quarries, near Hazlehead Park on the western outskirts, provided the bulk of the bright grey granite which has earned Aberdeen the title of the Granite City. The quarries are no longer worked.

For a full description of Aberdeen and its many interests see the *Ward Lock Guide to Aberdeen.*

DEESIDE.

Aberdeen to Ballater and Braemar.

Five important routes go westward and northward from Aberdeen :—
The Deeside road (*see below*).
The direct road north-westward to Fochabers and Elgin—the principal route for Inverness, Strathspey and the far North (*see* p. 376).
The Strathdon road (*see* p. 401) which joins the foregoing route at Huntly.
The coast route *viâ* Cruden Bay to Peterhead (*see* p. 392).
The road driving north *via* Turriff to the coast at Banff (*see* p. 396).

AS a touring centre Aberdeen is chiefly renowned for its proximity to the grand road through **Deeside,** past Balmoral to Braemar, and although the improvement of the Glenshee route from Blairgowrie has led to a greater use of this route as a means of *reaching* Aberdeen, Deeside scenery at its best is revealed only to those travelling westward, towards the high mountains instead of away from them. There are road services connecting Aberdeen with Banchory, Aboyne and Ballater (43 miles). As far as Banchory motorists have a choice of routes, roads following either side of the Dee.

Beyond **Cults,** 5 miles from Aberdeen, there is an extensive panorama of pleasant scenery, and on the left, almost hidden from view, is Blairs Roman Catholic College. Ten miles from Aberdeen, on the right, is **Drum Castle,** the seat of the ancient family of Irvine. It is a large Tudor edifice, built in 1619, with a keep said to have been erected by William the Lion at the end of the twelfth or beginning of the thirteenth century. Another 5 miles and there appears on the right **Crathes Castle,** National Trust property and one of the finest of the ancient castellated buildings in the country (*daily in summer : the gardens, open daily, dating from* 1702, *are famous*).

Banchory, 17 miles from Aberdeen, nestles in one of the prettiest spots on Deeside (Hotels: *Banchory Lodge, Tor-na-Coille, Raemoir, Burnett Arms, etc.*). There are bowls, tennis and golf. Trout-fishing may be had on the *Feugh*, which enters the Dee at Banchory, and the Shiach, which enters the Dee at Crathes.

The south Deeside road from Aberdeen crosses, a mile short of Banchory, the narrow **Bridge of Feugh**, one of the sights of the neighbourhood.

The **Hill of Fare** (1,545 feet), 5 miles to the north, is a fine viewpoint.

An interesting road runs southward through **Strachan, Glen Dye** and over **Cairn o' Mounth** to Fettercairn (19 miles), Edzell (24 miles), and Brechin (30 miles). (*See* p. 351.)

Westward from Banchory the road follows more or less the windings of the Dee. North of **Kincardine O'Neil** a few miles is **Lumphanan**, where there are the remains of a peel castle associated with Macbeth and a cairn that is said to mark his grave. According to Wyntoun, the chronicler, he fled hither after his defeat at Dunsinane, and was killed here, and not at Dunsinane as Shakespeare has taught us to believe.

So past the **Loch of Aboyne** to **Aboyne**, 31 miles from Aberdeen, an attractive village built around a large green between the road and the river, here crossed by a bridge. The neighbourhood is thickly wooded. Aboyne is about 400 feet above sea-level. The climate is bracing, and there is a good 18-hole golf course. (*Hotels : Birse Lodge, Charlestown, Huntly Arms, Abercorn, Balnacoil.*) There is good fishing to be had from both banks of the Dee. The *Aboyne Highland Games*, held in the first week of September, are the great event of the holiday season. **Aboyne Castle**, long the family seat of the Marquises of Huntly, stands close to the village. Within the policies are the remains of a Druidical circle, a sculptured stone, and what is known to archæologists as the Aboyne Ogham Stone.

There are many delightful walks in the neighbourhood, particularly one through the glen known as the **Fungle**, skirting the *Ault-dinnie Burn*. From the resting-place at the head a magnificent view is obtained. Another pleasant walk is on the **Hill of Mortlich**, formerly crowned by a monument to the tenth Marquis of Huntly. Other pedestrian excursions recommended are : to **Glen Tanar**, a highly picturesque glen running towards the south-west from the vicinity of Aboyne Bridge ; to **Mount Keen** (3,077 feet), at the head of the deer forest of Glen Tanar ; to the **Forest of Birse**, and to **Lochs Kinord** and

Davan. Further particulars will be found in the Ward Lock *Guide to Aberdeen and Deeside.*

From Aboyne the road runs through woods and across Dinnet Moor to **Dinnet** (*hotel*), a picturesque hamlet, near which is a pretty lake. A short way up the stream running into the west side of Loch Kinord, beside Dinnet, is a singular granite chasm which has given to the stream the name of "The Burn of the Vat." Westward of Dinnet is **Cambus o' May** (*hotel*), where the pink granite was once quarried. On the other side of the Dee, 3 miles west from Dinnet Bridge, is **Ballaterach,** where Byron spent some of his youthful days, and on this south side of the river, but 2 miles farther west, is **Pannanich Wells** (*hotel*), where are some old chalybeate springs.

Ballater.

Angling.—Salmon and trout in the *Dee*; fishings rented during the season, so that local inquiry is desirable.
Distances.—Aberdeen, 42 m.; Aboyne, 11½ m. Banchory, 24 m.; Braemar, 16½ m.
Early Closing.—Thursday.
Golf.—The course has a setting of some of the wildest and grandest scenery in the Highlands. 18 holes; Sunday play.
Hotels.—*Invercauld Arms* (25 rooms), *Loirston* (44 rooms), *Alexandra* (*unl.*), *Craigendarroch* (20 rooms), *Craigard, Tullich Lodge* (9 rooms), etc.
Population.—1,056.
Youth Hostel.—Deebank Road.

Ballater is a modern, well-built village, 660 feet above sea-level. It stands like a sentinel at the entrance to the upper and, for many, most characteristic portion of Deeside—the lovely valley between wooded hills which winds past Crathie and Balmoral to Braemar. In addition to golf, fishing, tennis, etc., indoor entertainments are organized during the season, and the village is an admirable centre for walkers. The Highland Games take place on the third Thursday in August.

Rising between the present main road and the Pass of Ballater is the hill of **Craigendarroch,** 1,250 feet above sea-level, but only 600 feet above Ballater, a good viewpoint.

About midway between Ballater and Cambus o' May, on the south side of the Dee, is **Pannanich Wells** (*see above*).

Southward from Ballater **Glen Muick** winds up to the flanks of Lochnagar. Six miles up the glen is the **Linn of Muick**; at 10 miles is Loch Muick. The path along the south-east side of the loch climbs to cross into the valley of the stream leading into Glen Clova, which can be followed to Clova (19 miles) and **Kirriemuir** (*see* p. 348). The more direct path, the Capel Mounth, leaves the road to the Loch about half a mile beyond the Spittal of Glen Muick (*see* p. 349).

About 2 miles from Ballater Bridge a track climbs eastward, passing just north of **Cairn Leuchan** (2,293 feet) and into **Glen Tanar**, at the foot of which is Aboyne (p. 365). In the other direction the path leads out of the head of Glen Tanar and by the **Mounth Road** crosses the west shoulder of Mount Keen at a height of 2,504 feet to the Queen's Well in Glen Mark, and so to Tarfside (16 miles) and **Edzell** (30 miles).

The Ascent of Lochnagar.

Lochnagar (3,786 feet) (so called from the lochan beneath its northern precipice—*Loch-na-gar*, the "goat's loch") is a finely shaped mountain, and its ascent is pleasant.

For the ascent from Ballater allowance of from 4–5 hours should be made.

The summit is about 13 miles from Ballater by the route here described. From Ballater a public road on the east side of the Muick leads to the Spittal of Glen Muick (9 miles), whence a footpath crosses the glen to Alltnagiubhsaich, where the Lochnagar path commences. The lower part of **Glen Muick** is very beautiful but the upper part, beyond the Linn, is rather bare. The path up Lochnagar is very well defined and perfectly easy although rather steep at one place known as "The Ladder." From the top of The Ladder the path passes close to the edge of the magnificent northern precipice, passes to the right of the first summit (3,768 feet), and ¼ mile farther on reaches the highest summit, on which there is an excellent View Indicator. The ascent from Alltnagiubhsaich should take from 2½ to 3½ hours.

The foreground shows but little variety, the only break in the general barrenness being supplied by the Dee valley, a strip of which is visible near Balmoral. The distant prospect, however, is enhanced by the contrast between the rich lowlands of Aberdeenshire, reaching away to the North Sea, and the wild assemblage of billowy mountain-heights, which stretch as far as the eye can travel in every other direction. To the north-west, the giant family of Ben Macdhui closes the view. Northwards there is no material object, except atmosphere, to obstruct the view over Ben Rinnes and the Moray Firth to the headlands of Caithness. In the north-east the prominent hill is Morven, a featureless height beyond and a little to the left of Ballater. Mount Keen is conspicuous in the east. Beyond it the hills dwindle down to the plain of Forfar and the Ochils, between which and Ben Macdhui, Ben Lawers, Schiehallion, with its graceful peak, and Ben-y-Gloe rise above their fellows.

Northward from Ballater a wild road climbs Glen Gairn and **Glen Fenzie** to Strathdon near **Cock Bridge** (p. 402). The accomplishment of long-discussed improvements of this road and the continuing *Lecht Road* to **Tomintoul** has opened a very fine route from Deeside to Speyside for motorists.

Ballater to Braemar.

As far as Balmoral, some 8 miles from Ballater, there is a road on each bank of the river ; that along the north side is shorter and better, and is that generally used by motors. The view along the south side is frequently restricted by hills and woods, but at the same time the route is highly picturesque, and the round from Ballater, up the north side and down the south side, is very popular.

Six miles from Ballater, on the south side of the river, is **Abergeldie Castle** (cf. p. 306). A mile farther on the north side is **Crathie Church**, the foundation-stone of which was laid in 1893 by Queen Victoria. This is the church attended by the Royal Family when staying at Balmoral. It is a plain building of grey granite, with red roof and spiret, and contains a handsome altar and reredos in memory of Edward VII, the busts of George V, George VI and Queen Victoria and the mural memorial to her son the Duke of Edinburgh.

Across the river from Crathie hamlet is—

Balmoral Castle.

(*From May* 1 *to July* 31, *the grounds are open to the public, in the absence of the Court, daily, except on Fridays and Sundays, from* 10 *a.m. to* 5 *p.m. Small fee, devoted to charities. The interior of the castle is not shown.*)

The site is nearly a thousand feet above the level of the sea, but a belt of trees (thinned somewhat by wind) screens it from the road, and for the best view (especially on such days as the grounds are not open) turn up the Strathdon road on the right some 500 yards beyond Crathie post office ; in three-quarters of a mile turn back to left, and then the Castle is suddenly revealed among the trees below, "dark Lochnagar" grandly terminating the view. This part of the road is not suitable for cars, but the round trip from the car park at Crathie starting as described, continuing down to main road and so back to Crathie is only 3 miles and a pleasant walk.

The Castle was erected by the Prince Consort in 1854, the Prince himself designing the principal features. It is of light-coloured granite, in the Scottish Baronial style of architecture, and comprises two blocks with connecting wings, bartisan turrets, and a projecting tower, a hundred feet high, in which is a clock.

Among other objects of interest are a massive granite fountain erected to the memory of King Edward VII by his tenants and servants, and statues of Queen Victoria and the Prince Consort.

Westward of Balmoral Castle the Braemar road passes **Carn na Cuimhne** (the Cairn of Remembrance), on the south side of the road. Its Gaelic name is the slogan of the Farquharsons, and the spot is said to have been the rendezvous of the clan when summoned to battle.

Hereabouts there have been great clearances of timber in recent years. Those who look eastward during this part of the journey will catch a glimpse of Balmoral Castle along the river.

A mile farther on (52 miles from Aberdeen) is **Inver,** with a hotel and granite quarries.

On the left, south of the river, is the magnificent pine **Forest of Ballochbuie.** It is said that Farquharson of Invercauld became possessed of it in exchange for a tartan plaid. In allusion to this tradition, Queen Victoria, when she became the owner, erected a stone inscribed: " Queen Victoria entered into possession of Ballochbuie on the 15th day of May, 1878. The bonniest plaid in Scotland."

Nearly a mile farther, the Dee is crossed by **Invercauld Bridge,** a short distance west from the picturesque old bridge, and another mile brings us abreast of **Invercauld House,** away to the right—the ancestral home of the Farquharsons of Invercauld.

On the right, between road and river where they turn south to Braemar, is **Braemar Castle.** This historic castle was built in 1628 by John Erskine, Earl of Mar, but has been in the Farquharson family since 1731. (*Open daily, May to October,* 10–6. *Charge.*)

Braemar.

Angling.—The hotels have several miles of fishing (salmon) on the *Dee,* while the fishings can be rented by local arrangement.
Golf.—An 18-hole course. **Tennis.**—Courts available.
Hotels.—*Invercauld Arms, Fife Arms, Callater Lodge, Braemar Lodge, Mar Lodge,* and *Mayfield Guest House* (unlicensed).
Population.—500.
Youth Hostel.—In Corrie Feragie Lodge.
Winter Sports.—Good conditions for skiing in season.

Braemar, or, to give its full title, *Castleton of Braemar,* is 1,100 feet above sea-level, and is surrounded by well-wooded, lofty hills, which effectually shield it from winter winds. It is a particularly attractive place with first-class hotels; the climate is dry, the air remarkably pure and bracing. As the village is situated in the midst of fine scenery, and is the best centre from which to make excursions in the Eastern Grampians, it is a very popular resort. Its "Gathering" or Highland Games held in September attracts large crowds.

In recent years Braemar has also attracted attention as a Winter Sports centre, and certainly here the snowfall is less fickle than elsewhere in Britain. At *The Cottage* R. L. Stevenson spent the summer of 1881, and wrote *Treasure Island*, his first great work.

EXCURSIONS FROM BRAEMAR.

Strangers must bear in mind that, where excursions into the surrounding countryside are concerned, their movements are liable to considerable restriction, especially during the stalking season (from August onwards).

1. **Morrone Hill**, 2,819 feet above the sea, but only about 1,700 above Braemar. It lies to the south-west of the village. The simplest route of ascent is by the Chapel Brae to Tomintoul, a few crofts on the shoulder of the hill, and thence by a well-marked path to the summit. Time up and down about three hours. The Tomintoul crofts may be also reached by paths from near the golf course. The prospect includes a most charming view of the valleys of the Dee and the Quoich and a magnificent panorama of the Cairngorms.

2. **Linn of Quoich.**—The *Quoich* is a stream entering the Dee a short distance west of Braemar. The only access for cars is by a fair road on the north side of the Dee, from the Linn of Dee, which passes the back of Mar Lodge. Pedestrians may go eastward to Invercauld Bridge and thence by a right-of-way track that runs across the low ground between Invercauld House and the river. The Linn is about a mile above the confluence. The falling water has formed cavities or "pot holes" in the rock; "Quoich" is the Gaelic for "cup." The falls are under 3 miles from the village in a *direct* line.

3. **Linn of Corriemulzie and Linn of Dee.**—Follow the high-road westward. Three miles from Braemar the Corriemulzie Burn passes under the road and into a narrow glen, in which is the picturesque **Linn of Corriemulzie.** Half a mile farther the Dee is crossed by the Victoria Bridge which leads to Mar Lodge, built for the Duke of Fife in 1898 and now a hotel. The **Linn of Dee** is 6 miles from Braemar. The river runs through a very narrow channel in the rocks.

4. The **Falls of Garrawalt** (*Garbh allt* = rough stream). A walk of 8 miles there and back, but the falls can be visited only on certain days. Follow the Ballater road to a point a few yards

below **Invercauld Bridge**, and there pass through a gateway on the right, across the old Bridge of Dee, beyond which the route lies through Her Majesty's private grounds.

5. **Ascent of Lochnagar** (3,786 feet; time, 4–5 hours). The great features of "dark Lochnagar" are the precipices and corries on the north side, where snow generally lies all the year round.

Follow the Cairnwell road (A93) for 2 miles to where it crosses the *Callater Burn*; then turn off to the left and follow the burn to the foot of **Loch Callater**, from which the summit of Lochnagar is distant about 7 miles. At the Loch Lodge the road comes to an end, and the track slants up the slope to the north-east of the loch and in 1½ miles reaches a pass west of Cairn Taggart (Carn an t-Sagairt Mor on the maps). The path is somewhat indistinct here, but by climbing directly east up the side of Cairn Taggart the path will be found running round the south slope of that hill. In due course there comes into view on the right a desolate glen containing the stream which flows into the **Dubh Loch**, i.e. the Black Loch. After crossing this stream the track, which is well marked, runs in a fairly direct line north-eastwards to the summit of Lochnagar. The only spot at which there is any probability of the track being missed is where the turn to the right must be made to round Cairn Taggart.

To **Blairgowrie** (35 miles), one of the finest drives in Scotland.—Bus service to Perth on Saturdays and Sundays only. The highest point on the route is reached 10 miles from Braemar —**Cairnwell** (3,059 feet) on the right and **Glas Maol** (3,502 feet) on the left—at an altitude of 2,199 feet. (Chairlift to summit of Cairnwell, summer and winter.)

From the top of the pass there is a steep descent through **Glen Beg** to the *Spittal of Glenshee Hotel*, the shoulder of the Cairnwell being crossed by the once notorious **Devil's Elbow** now much less formidable thanks to the Ministry of Transport. Thence the road is along **Glenshee**. In about 9 miles it passes on the left **Mount Blair** (2,441 feet), and 5½ miles below is the **Bridge of Cally**, which affords a fine view of the *Ardle*, that here unites with the Shee, the stream so formed being called the *Ericht*. Four miles from the bridge the Ericht flows through a rocky ravine, along one side of which is the road, while on the other stands **Craighall**, which Lockhart tells us was the original of Tullyveolan of *Waverley*, "the habitation of the Barons of Bradwardine." Two miles farther is **Blairgowrie** (p. 358).

To **Loch Builg** (13 miles) and **Tomintoul** (24 miles), and **Ballindalloch**, on the Charlestown of Aberlour–Grantown main road (40 miles), or **Grantown** (38 miles). There is a cart track all the way, with the exception of 4 miles between Loch Builg and Inchrory Lodge. (For the through road route, *viâ* Cock Bridge, *see* p. 367.) Follow the Ballater Road to a point a little beyond Invercauld Bridge and there take a road on the left. Keep to the right at the fork a few hundred yards on, and at the fork 2 miles farther on go to the left. (The right-hand branch leads to the Inver Hotel.)

The road crosses the Feardar Burn, climbs steeply up to the north, and when a height of about 2,200 feet has been reached strikes away in a north-westerly direction across the east slopes of *Cullardoch* (2,953 feet) and drops down to the River Gairn which is crossed about half a mile short of **Loch Builg.** The Loch, about a mile in length, is on the borders of Aberdeen and Banff. Apart from the ruins of a shooting bothy on its uninteresting shores, the nearest habitation is Corndavon Lodge, 8 miles down Glen Gairn by a fair road.

At Loch Builg the road ceases and a track runs along the eastern side of the loch and continues in a northerly direction until it strikes the *Builg Burn* (about half a mile from the loch), which it then follows to the road in the vicinity of Inchrory Lodge. Thence a fair road (private for the greater part of the way) follows the course of the *Avon* to **Tomintoul** (p. 345). The scenery is particularly fine at the gorge of the *Ailnack*, 1½ miles short of Tomintoul.

For route between Tomintoul and Ballindalloch (15 miles), *see* p. 344 ; Dufftown, *see* p. 345 ; **Grantown,** *see* p. 342.

Braemar to **Blair Atholl** *viâ* **Glen Tilt** (30 miles ; *see* p. 316). The road passes the Linn of Dee but is private beyond this point. By arrangement a car can be hired to await at Forest Lodge, 8 miles from Blair Atholl, thus reducing the walking distance to 16 miles. There is no house of refreshment between Blair Atholl and Braemar. Near Inverey, 5 miles west of Braemar, is *Mar Lodge Hotel,* while some houses in the village may offer accommodation. (*Youth Hostel at Inverey.*)

The bridge at the Linn of Dee is crossed, and the road to the left is followed. Three miles from the Linn the Dee is again crossed at the White Bridge, and the route thence lies along the western side of the Geldie Burn for 1½ miles, crosses it and then strikes due south, passing Bynack Lodge on the right, and crossing the watershed at a height of about 1,500 feet and 2 miles south from the Lodge. The descent is through **Glen Tilt,** the track following closely the course of the river on its right bank, with **Ben y Gloe** (*Beinn a Ghloe*) (3,671 feet) towering on the other side.

Rough as is this route in its central portion, it is easier and much less rough than the Larig Ghru route (*see* p. 373), between Braemar and Aviemore.

To **Kingussie** (30 miles).—Follow the Blair Atholl route to the crossing, 1½ miles beyond the White Bridge. From this point a rough road, washed out in places, leads along the north side of the Geldie Burn for three miles to opposite a ruined lodge. The road should be left near where it dips down to the stream and a poorly marked path followed westward across the moor, keeping well up, for three miles to the River Eidart. There is a footbridge across the Eidart, beyond which a good path runs along the north side of the Feshie to the bridge near Glenfeshie Lodge.

To **Clova** (19 miles), thence to **Kirriemuir** (34 miles) or to **Brechin** (42 miles).—The route at first is along Glen Clunie and then by the side of the Callater Burn past Loch Callater. It has been described as far as the loch on p. 371. The track keeps along the north bank of the lake, a dark-looking sheet of water nearly a mile long, and thence is fairly plain on the north side of the burn to the ridge of the **Tolmount** (3,143 feet), 9 miles from Braemar. The descent is made by "Jock's Road" to the left of the *White Water*, down Glen Doll. Although there is a right of way, there is not, in all parts, a well-defined track, but by keeping the White Water in view on the right, the head of Glen Doll will be reached and the road in Glen Clova will be struck 3 miles short of **Milton of Clova** (*hotel*). For Clova and the route to Kirriemuir, *see* pp. 348–9.

Brechin may be reached from Clova by a rough walk of 10 miles in an east-north-east direction to Loch Lee, where connection is made with the route from Ballater (*see* p. 367); or by crossing the South Esk at Cortachy, some 3 miles short of Kirriemuir, and following the road which runs thence to Brechin.

To **Kirkton of Glenisla** (25 miles) and **Alyth** (31 miles).—Follow the Cairnwell road for about 8 miles. A few yards short of a bridge over the main stream take a track that goes up the bank of the Clunie, swings left up the long ridge of Sron na Gaoithe, then passes close to the summit of the Glas Maol. This point is about 2 miles from the spot where the Cairnwell road was left. From it the track proceeds to **Monega Hill** (2,917 feet) and from the ridge of that follows a small stream (the Glas Burn) to the *Isla*. The course is then along the latter, and in a mile is the shooting lodge of *Tulchan*, while a couple of miles farther down the glen are some picturesque falls near the confluence of the Glencally Burn with the Isla. Three miles lower are the ruins of **Forter Castle**, a stronghold of the Earl of Airlie (perhaps the "Bonnie Hoose o' Airlie" destroyed by Argyll in 1640). Thence the route is along the left-hand side of the stream, and at the end of 4 miles it reaches **Kirkton of Glenisla** (*hotel; mail motor between Glenisla and Alyth*).

By the **Larig Ghru to Aviemore**.—The central portion of the walk (30 miles) is extremely rough. At various points finger-posts have been erected by the Rights of Way Society, but the roads in the Rothiemurchus Forest, at the latter end of the route, are very bewildering. (*See also* p. 332.)

From Braemar the route is to the Linn of Dee and across the bridge there, then go a quarter of a mile down by the Dee and up by the side of the Lui Water. There is a locked gate across the road leading up Glen Lui. The **Bridge of Lui** is crossed and the road is followed up the stream to **Derry Lodge** (10 miles).

The route thence is across the *Derry Burn* and along the north side of the *Lui Beg Burn*. Just beyond the bridge that spans the Derry Burn a track (the **Larig Pass** or *Larig an Laoigh*) runs off on the right to Nethy Bridge, while on the south side of the Lui Beg Burn is the keeper's cottage. Apart from the Corrour bothy below the Devil's Point and the Sinclair hut near the northern end of the pass, the traveller will not see another house for 16 miles.

The Larig Ghru (" Gloomy Pass ") route lies along the north side of the burn for a couple of miles and then crosses it. (The track that continues with the burn goes over Ben Macdhui.) It keeps its westward direction for a mile or so and then inclines towards the north and leads into **Glen Dee** opposite the **Devil's Point** (3,303 feet). (There is a footbridge across the Dee leading to the Corrour Bothy.) It crosses the Dee about half a mile above the inflow of the *Garrachorry Burn*, an important feeder that comes from the west between Cairn Toul and Braeriach. After crossing the Dee, the traveller must keep close to its western side and will then soon come to the **Pools of Dee** —four tiny ice-cold tarns. Just beyond them is the summit of the pass (2,733 feet), from which the way for about a mile is over rough boulders on the left side of the stream. The latter is then crossed to the right bank and the path, now good, followed for 2½ miles to its junction with a rough road at which there is a sign-post. Turn sharp to the left along the road and follow it past a ruined cottage, half a mile beyond which the stream, the Allt-na-Beinne-Mhor, is crossed by an iron bridge, which was erected by the Cairngorm Club in 1912. The traveller has now the choice of two routes. He may continue by the side of the burn for a couple of miles to **Coylum Bridge**, and thence by the high-road to Aviemore, 2 miles distant, or he may take the road westward to **Loch an Eilean** (2 miles), and then take either the first or the second road on the right past that, turning to the left when it joins the road which leads to Aviemore. The route *viâ* Coylum Bridge is about half a mile shorter than that *viâ* Loch an Eilean, but is not so beautiful.

Ben Macdhui (4,296 feet) and Cairn Gorm (4,084 feet).

The high level walk between these two heights is very well worth doing, but in any case the excursion is long and for strong walkers only. Snow may be encountered on the plateaux and corries up to the month of June.

To Derry Lodge, as above.

From the *Lodge* you may proceed by either of the valleys which converge there. The shortest and finest way is by that to the left, by the *Lui Beg Burn*. By this route the summit is little more than 6 miles distant, and the sloppiness of parts of the Glen Derry track is avoided. From Derry Lodge follow the Larig Ghru path to about a furlong short of the footbridge across the Lui Beg Burn. Here a path, marked by a small cairn, strikes up to the right and follows the east side of the Lui Beg Burn for about 1¼ miles, to a fork in the stream. Cross the first branch and then strike up the ridge in front, the Sron Riach, skirting the precipices above *Lochan Uaine*, where the ground is for a bit very rough, and then making straight for the summit.

The *pony-track* from Derry Lodge crosses the Derry Burn just beyond the Lodge and follows Glen Derry for 4 miles, after which it bears to the left up Coire Etchachan to *Loch Etchachan*. For the first 1½ miles from Derry Lodge the path leads through magnificent pine trees, a remnant of the Caledonian Forest, after which the Glen is rather desolate. The last half mile or so up Coire Etchachan is steep, but the path is quite good and is well marked by cairns all the way. On the opposite side of Loch Etchachan the ground rises very steeply, but the track bends away still more to the left and climbs to the plateau of the mountain by the side of the streamlet which feeds the loch. The Lui Beg valley opens on the left, and to the north, 4 miles away, rises Cairn Gorm over a depression, at the bottom of which, unseen, lies Loch Avon. Behind us, eastwards, the lofty table-land of Beinn a' Bhuird rises to a height almost equal to that on which we are standing. The remaining half-mile or more of the ascent is over comparatively level ground, past the ruins of the Sappers' Hut to the Ordnance Survey pillar on the summit. Near the cairn there is a useful View Indicator which was erected by the Cairngorm Club in 1925.

For the view from the summit and the walk over to Cairn Gorm, *see* p. 330.

By the Larig an Laoigh to Nethy Bridge. This walk (31 miles) is described, in the opposite direction, on page 335. *See* also page 374.

ABERDEEN TO INVERNESS VIÂ HUNTLY.

For the route *viâ* Cruden Bay, *see* p. 392 ; *viâ* Old Meldrum, *see* p. 396.

THIS is the principal road route between Aberdeen and the north-west of Scotland. The route is followed by the railway throughout.

Leave Aberdeen by George Street, which in a mile or so turns westward beside the *Don*. Beyond Bucksburn is the Rowett Research Institute, where research into animal nutrition is carried out. In a little over five miles a lane on the right leads to the *Standing Stones*, twelve in number and the largest Druidical circle in Aberdeenshire. Just over a dozen miles from Aberdeen is **Kintore** (*hotels*), an ancient place with a quaint town hall. A mile to the west are the ruins of *Hallforest Castle*, said to have been a hunting tower of the Bruce, who gave it to Sir Robert Keith, from whom were descended the Earls of Kintore. Vast numbers of seagulls nest in the vicinity. A mile or so beyond Kintore the Don valley (p. 402) goes off on the left, but our road crosses the river and turns into **Inverurie** (*Gordon Arms, Kintore Arms*), a pleasant little royal burgh in a fine agricultural district. Golf and fishing are among its attractions. On the eastern side of the river is modernized Keith Hall, the seat of the Earl of Kintore.

The neighbourhood of Inverurie has been the site of two important battles. One was fought on *Barra Hill*, between Inverurie and Old Meldrum (p. 396) in 1308, the Bruce overthrowing his great rivals the Comyns. The second battle was fought at **Harlaw**, in 1411, when Aberdeen was threatened with pillage by a Highland host gathered by Donald, Lord of the Isles. The opposing force, under the Earl of Mar, was reinforced by citizens and the invaders were repelled. A monument marks the battlefield, about 2 miles north-west of Inverurie.

Now there comes into view on the left the *Mither Tap*,

Rogart
Sta.
L. Lundie
Dunrobin Castle
Golspie
Little Ferry
Coul
Embo
Pronoy
Astail
Evelix
Clashmore
DORNOCH
Dornoch Firth
Skibo Cas.
Tarbat Ness
Light Ho.
Tarbat H.
Portmahomack
Rockfield
Inver
TAIN
Tarlogie Ho.
Baladie
Hill of Fearn
Geanies Ho.
Cadboll
Hilltown
Balintore
Shandwick
Ankerville
Barachie
Balnagown Cas.
Kildary
Delny
Kilmuir
Barbaraville
Nigg
Nigg Bay
Dunskeath Ho.
Invergordon
CROMARTY
Firth
Udale B.
Navity
Jemimaville
Ethie
Glenurquhart
MORAY FIRTH
Fort George
Rosemarkie
Fortrose
Chanonry Pt.
Avoch
Gollanfield
Dalcross
Petty K.
Croy
Cantray
NAIRN
Delnies
Ardersier
Auldearn
The Bar
Culbin Sandhills
Kintessack
Findhorn Bay
Findhorn
Dyke
Brodie
Inshoch Cas.
Darnaway Cas.
Forres
Kinloss
Alves
Mosstowie
Burghead
Burghead Bay
Coltfield
Cummingston
Hopeman
Covesea Scars
Halliman Scar
Branderburgh
Lossiemouth
Gordonstoun
Duffus Ho.
Drainie
Spynie Cas.
New Spynie
ELGIN
Kingston Port
Garmouth
Urquhart
Lhanbryde
Speymouth
Spey Bay
Portgordon
Longmorn
Orbliston
Birnie
Pluscarden Abbey
Blervie Cas.
Rafford
Altyre
Dallas
Kellas
R. Lossie
Findlay Seat
Orton
MORAY
Rothes on Spey
Rothes Glen
Dandaleith
Arndilly Ho.
Craigellachie
Aberlour
Dufftown
Mortlach
Archiestown
Knockando
Blacksboat
Ballindalloch
Inveraven
Ben Rinnes
BANFF
Achnastank
Advie
Tulchan Lo.
Derraid
Dalvey
Cromdale
Cromdale Hills
Grantown-on-Spey
Inverallan Cas.
Lethendry
Lyne
Glenlivet Distillery
Corryhabbie
Cooks Cairn
Tomnavoulin
Kirkmichael
Knockandhu
Threestone Hill
Tomintoul
Carn Mór
Delnabo
Caulrig
Conglas W.
Strathdon
Invernan
Carn Ealasaid
Allargue Inn
Cock Bridge
Tornahaish
R. Don
Carn a Bhacain
Inchrory
Glen Avon
Glenavon Forest
Ben Avon
Ben Bynac
Cairn Gorm
Cairn Gorm Mts
Beinn-a-Bhuird
Cairn Eas
Culardoch
Glen Gairn
Crathie
Balmoral
Abergeldie
Ben Macdhui
Braeriach
Cairn Toul
Carn Ban
Dunphail
Edinkillie K.
Relugas Ho.
Coulmony Ho.
Ardclach
Logie Br.
Ferness
NAIRN
Cawdor Cas.
Urchany
Barevan
Clava
Culloden Moor
INVERNESS
Strath Nairn
Daviot
Craggie Inn
Ben Bhuidhe Mhor
Drynachan Lo.
R. Findhorn
Moy Hall
L. Moy
Moy
Tomatin Ho.
Corrybrough
Carn Glas
Freeburn Inn
Findhorn Bri.
Slochd Mhuic
Clune
Duthil
R. Dulnain
Dulnain Bri.
Broomhill
Carrbridge
Abernethy K.
Nethybridge
Boat of Garten
Abernethy Forest
Dorback Lo.
Kincardine
Geal Charn
Aviemore
Inverdruie
Glenmore Lo.
Rothiemurchus
L. Morlich
Dalmigavie
Inverlaidnan
Dalnahaitnach
Coignafearn
Coignashie
Monadhliath Mts
Carn Dulnan
L. Alvie
Alvie
Kincraig
Insh
Feshiebridge
Kingussie
Newtonmore
Ruthven
Spey Bri.
Lochindorb
Dava
Summit
Knock of Braemoray
Larig Hill
Aitnoch
Baillieward
Castle Grant

ABERDEEN TO INVERNESS

English Miles

0 5 10 15 20

WARD LOCK & CO., LIMITED, LONDON.

the most striking in appearance of the six peaks of **Bennachie** (*benna-hee*) (1,698 feet).

A remarkable old hill fort on the summit is approached by the "Maiden Causeway," an ancient paved road. Each of the six summits of the ridge, which extends for 4½ miles, commands an extensive view. *Oxen Craig*, the loftiest, has a height of 1,733 feet. Though the mountain presents a steep face to the north, the ascent is easy. From Pitcaple or Oyne Stations by road to Pittodrie and thence good path to the summit. Motorists from the south should leave the main road at Drimmies, 2½ miles beyond Inverurie, and proceed by a steep road to Chapel of Garioch and Pittodrie. One mile beyond Chapel of Garioch an interesting sculptured stone 10 feet high stands by the roadside. It is called the **Maiden Stone.**

The **Garioch** (pronounced *Gairy*, the *g* hard), one of the ancient territorial divisions of Aberdeenshire, is celebrated for its exceeding fertility—it is the "girnel," or granary, of Aberdeenshire.

Three and a half miles beyond Inverurie we pass Inverramsay. Three miles farther on the road forks. The right-hand branch is the more direct and the better road to Huntly, but it is not so interesting as that *viâ* Oyne and Insch. At **Newton House**, near Insch, there are two stones, one bearing inscriptions in Ogham and minuscule characters and the other prehistoric designs. One mile beyond the little town the **Hill of Dunnideer** rises like a pyramid from the plain. It bears the ruins of an ancient hill fort. *Christ's Kirk*, the hill on the left of the road, is supposed to be the place referred to in the old poem, "Christ's Kirk on the Green." A mile from Kennethmont is the seventeenth-century mansion, *Leith Hall* (National Trust) with a lovely rock garden (*open in summer*, 11–6, *Sundays from* 2.30 ; *garden from* 9.30).

Now the route gets more among the hills as we pass from the Garioch into **Strathbogie.** Nearing Gartly there is a good view of the **Tap o' Noth** (1,851 feet) on the left. The summit is marked by a very fine vitrified fort, the walls of which rise in some places 8 feet from the ground.

Forty miles from Aberdeen is **Huntly** (*Gordon Arms, Castle, Huntly*), a neat town at the meeting-points of roads running in every direction and with golf and good fishing in the vicinity. (Apply Town Clerk.) The chief sight of the town is the ruin of **Huntly Castle,** the cradle and seat of the Gordons, Earls (afterwards Marquises) of Huntly and Dukes of Gordon. (*Admission : weekdays*, 10–7 ; *Sundays*, 2–7 ; *fee*.) The principal feature is a large keep with a great round tower at the south-west corner and a smaller round tower at the opposite corner.

The earliest castle here was a Norman peel built in the latter part of the twelfth century by Duncan, Earl of Fife, who, following a grant of land from William the Lion, became the first lord of Strathbogie. In the peel Robert Bruce found shelter in 1307, but shortly before Bannockburn the then lord of Strathbogie turned against Bruce and his lands were taken from him and given to Sir Adam Gordon of Huntly, in Berwickshire, whose descendants became Lords of Huntly, Marquises and Dukes of Gordon, and were for many generations all-powerful throughout a wide district, the head of the family being for centuries known as "The Cock of the North." A successor to the Norman building was the scene of the marriage of Perkin Warbeck. It was despoiled by Mary's troops in 1562 and "cast down" by James VI in 1594 : only the underground basement and dungeon of this work are left, the remainder of the ruin dating from about 1550–1600. Ordinary processes of disintegration were assisted by the builders of Huntly Lodge in 1742, who found the Castle a convenient quarry. The ruin is, however, now under the care and administration of the Department of the Environment.

To many Huntly is interesting as the birthplace of George Macdonald (1824–1905 ; a tablet marks the house in Duke Street), who sketched it and its castle in *Alec Forbes of Howglen*.

Westward from Huntly a road runs over to **Dufftown** (14 miles). From it, nearly half-way, a branch follows the Deveron valley southward from the *Haugh of Glass* to the wild, mountain-girt **Cabrach,** whence one can regain Huntly by the Dufftown road to Rhynie (*Richmond Arms*), thence northward by Gartly—a most enjoyable round.

Ten miles north-west of Huntly is **Keith** (*Queen's, Commercial*), a busy town in Banffshire on the *Isla*, a good trout stream. The pediment of the Roman Catholic Church is distinguished by two colossal figures of St. Peter and St. Paul.

In 1650 the churchyard of Old Keith was the scene of the unmanly ranting of the parish minister at the fallen Marquis of Montrose, who was compelled to attend the service in the ragged and unkempt condition in which he was captured. Fifty years later it was the scene of the capture, by Duff of Braco, of the freebooter James Macpherson, whose manner of facing his subsequent execution inspired Burns to the lines :

> " Sae rantingly, sae wantonly,
> Sae dauntingly gaed he ;
> He played a spring an' danced it round,
> Below the gallows tree."

Keith proper is connected with Fife Keith, across the Isla, by a bridge dating from 1609. Near the churchyard of Fife Keith is the *Gaun Pot*, or Pool, in which witches were drowned. **Newmill**, a mile northward, was the birthplace in 1794 of James Gordon Bennett, founder of the *New York Herald.*

From Keith an increasingly fine road runs south-west to **Dufftown** (*see* p. 345) and so to Strathspey ; north and east roads run to **Cullen** (p. 399) and **Banff** (p. 397) ; westward a road runs to Spey at *Boat o' Brig*, once the site of a ferry. From Mulben, 6 miles from Keith, a pretty road goes south-west to Craigellachie (p. 345).

The main Inverness highway, however, goes north-westward from Keith, throwing off a branch to **Portgordon** (p. 401) in about 2 miles, and thence running beautifully through woods to **Fochabers** (*Gordon Arms, Spey Bank*), a prettily situated village (population: 1,200) at the entrance to the grounds of *Gordon Castle.*

For many years the seat of the Duke of Richmond and Gordon, this was one of the finest places in Scotland. In 1937, however, the estate—together with many other of the neighbouring Ducal properties, including the townships of Fochabers and Portgordon and the villages of Kingston, Garmouth, Spey Bay and Tomintoul—was sold to the Crown and demolition of the massive pile followed. The desolate remains stand in a well-wooded park.

At Fochabers the Spey is crossed by a bridge from which there are good views upstream, Ben Rinnes being seen to advantage. One and a half miles south of Fochabers there is a remarkable gorge on the east bank of the Spey, the *Allt Dearg*, where there are some fine examples of rain-eroded pillars of old red conglomerate and boulder clay. From Fochabers to Elgin the way is pleasant but unremarkable.

A road on the right leads to **Garmouth** and **Kingston**, at the mouth of the *Spey*, the former a quaint little village with some historical interest as the landing-place of Charles II in 1650. There is no way across the river for cars below the bridge at Fochabers. For **Spey Bay**, *see* page 400. For **Lossiemouth**, to which another right-hand turning leads, *see* page 383.

ELGIN.

Distances.—Aberdeen, 66 m. Inverness, 38 m.; Forres, 12 m.; Keith, 18 m.; Lossiemouth, 5½ m.
Early Closing.—Wednesday.
Hotels.—*Gordon Arms, City, Thunderton House, Braelossie, Sunninghill, Laichmoray, Royal, St. Leonard's,* etc.
Population.—16,500.
Railway Access.—From the south *viâ* Aberdeen, or *viâ* Aviemore and Inverness.
Sports.—Fishing in the Lossie and Millbuies Lochs, bowls, boating, golf, tennis. Indoor swimming pool.
Youth Hostel.—West High Street.

Elgin is an attractive little city (it claims the title as a Cathedral town of old) on the south bank of the Lossie, about 5 miles from the coast and some 38 east of Inverness and 66 from Aberdeen. It is the centre of a fertile district known as the Garden of Moray. It has a mild climate and many attractions, including good educational facilities.

The ruins of the **Cathedral**, the principal object of interest, are reached by turning out of the High Street at the Little Cross by North College Street. The ruins are accessible weekdays from 10 a.m. to 4 or 7; Sundays, 2–4 or 7 (*tickets from Office in north-west Tower*), but at other times a very good idea of their beauty can be gained from the road skirting the enclosure. The most notable feature is the fine western doorway.

The Cathedral, the "Lanthorn of the North," was founded in 1224 by Andrew, Bishop of Moray, but of the structure then erected the remains of the transepts and the towers are the chief portions, the rest of the church as it exists to-day having been built after a fire in 1270.

The building again suffered from fire in 1390, through the act of Alexander, Earl of Buchan, commonly known, on account of his rapacity, as the Wolf of Badenoch, who, having been excommunicated for deserting his wife, sought to be revenged. Under compulsion by his half-brother, Robert III, who feared terrible ill might follow the outrageous sacrilege, the earl helped to repair the damage.

In 1506 the great steeple—rebuilt by Bishop Innes (1407–14), fragments of whose monument remain—fell. With the Reformation came the beginning of the final destruction of the beautiful building, for in 1568 the Regent Moray and his Privy Council, being hard pressed for money wherewith to pay their soldiers, ordered the lead to be stripped from the roof and sold for their benefit. It was bought for about a hundred pounds by a mercantile company in Amsterdam, but was sunk with the ship off the rocky headland of Girdleness, just outside the harbour of Aberdeen. After this act of vandalism the building was allowed to fall into decay as "a piece of Romish vanity too expensive to keep in repair."

For nearly a hundred years the ruins lay utterly neglected, except by those who found the fallen walls a convenient quarry and, near the end of the period, by an enthusiastic antiquary, one John Shanks, who set himself the task of removing what had become mere rubbish and laying bare the ground plan of the building.

The style of architecture is the First Pointed Order, and the building is perhaps the best specimen of ecclesiastical architecture in Scotland. When entire, to quote an authority, Elgin Cathedral was "a building of Gothic architecture inferior to few in Europe." The edifice was 289 feet long; greatest breadth, 87 feet; western towers, 84 feet in height.

The best preserved portion is the early fifteenth-century **Chapter House**, at the north-east corner. In the centre is a massive pillar, some 9 feet in circumference, having the form of a cluster of sixteen slender shafts.

Between the Chapter House and the vestry is the Sacristy, containing a lavatory, the water basin of which was the cradle of General Anderson, the founder of the local institution bearing his name (*see below*).

In the Chancel is the tomb of the founder of the Cathedral, and to the right, in St. Mary's Aisle, is the burial-place of the Gordon chiefs. The first Earl of Huntly lies here and also the last Duke of the male line.

A portion of the Deanery has been incorporated with the house known as North College; South College is the Archdeacon's Manse, modernized. The wall at the rear of South College garden leads to *Panns Port,* the only one remaining of the four entrances to the Cathedral precincts. Close at hand is **Anderson's,** now a home for old people and which is also the memorial of the romantic career of Lieut.-General Anderson. At his father's death his mother was so destitute that she was forced to find a dwelling among the Cathedral ruins (*see above*). Later the boy enlisted as a drummer in the Honourable East India Company, rose to the rank of Lieut.-General and died in 1824, leaving about £70,000 for the foundation of the institution which bears his name.

In **Cooper Park**, across the road from the Cathedral, is *Grant Lodge*, the dower house of the Earls of Seafield; the mansion contains a public and rural library. The policies of the house now form Cooper Park (named in honour of the donor). Towards the eastern end of the main street of Elgin is the **Little Cross**, supposed to have marked the limits of the Cathedral sanctuary; opposite is the *Museum* of the Elgin Literary and Scientific Institution (*weekdays*, 10–12.30; 2–5 (*Tues*. 10–1: *fee*). Also in the street is the **Muckle Cross**, beside the Parish Church, a large Classic building. To the north side of the street is **Lady Hill**, crowned by a monument commemorating the last of the old Dukes of Gordon, "a benefactor of agriculture in the North." A Charter of 1106 mentions a Castle which stood upon the hill and which was the residence of early Scottish kings. The remaining fragment is named *Duncan's Castle* (King Duncan, of *Macbeth*, is believed to have died a few miles away, at Pitgaveny).

The ruins of an old *Greyfriars' Abbey* (founded by Alexander II) have been restored and incorporated with a chapel. For permission to view apply at Convent in Abbey Street.

The *Ladies' Walks* are an attractive series of paths beside the Lossie.

Southward from Elgin a road traverses the **Glen of Rothes** to Rothes and Craigellachie, in Strathspey. **Birnie**, to the west of this road, about 3 miles from Elgin, has "the oldest bishop's church in the diocese of Moray." It belongs to the twelfth century, and is still strong and perfect. It has no east window, contains a copper bell, called the "Ronnel Bell" (the only one in Britain), and has a distinct chancel and nave with separate roofs—a feature unique in the north of Scotland.

Rothes, a distilling centre, is commanded by a ruined Castle of the Leslies, in which Edward I quartered himself in 1296 during his southward march from Elgin. For **Craigellachie**, *see* page 345.

Pluscarden Priory, 6 miles south-west of Elgin, was founded by Alexander II, in the thirteenth century, and the walls of the church having remained in a good state of preservation, the edifice was restored and part of it fitted up for Divine service in 1898 by the Marquess of Bute, who acquired the building by purchase. The fittings are rich in carving and the altar is one of the finest in the north of Scotland.

The Priory is beautifully placed in the narrowing glen of the Lochty, and the road may be followed onward to Forres (p. 385), passing **Blervie Tower**, an ancient structure five storeys high, commanding a grand view.

The road north from Elgin to Lossiemouth passes near the remains of **Spynie Palace**, for many centuries the residence of the Bishops of Moray. It was inhabited by Roman Catholic Bishops up to 1573, and then for upwards of a hundred years by Protestant Bishops. Its extensive ruins comprise a very fine keep. *Spynie Loch*, on the east side of the highway, was originally an arm of the sea, but has been gradually drained or silted up and for the most part is rich meadow land. *Pitgaveny*, near the south end, has already been mentioned as the traditional scene of Macbeth's murder of Duncan.

Lossiemouth.

Bus connection with Elgin, etc.
Early Closing.—Thursday.
Golf.—The Moray Golf Club has a very fine course of 18 holes, and a 9-hole relie course.
Hotels.—*Stotfield* (50 rooms), *Laverock Bank* (18 rooms), *Rock House* (7 rooms) Numerous apartments.
Population.—6,400.

Lossiemouth is composed of the ancient fishing settlements of Seatown and Old Lossie, the newer settlement of **Branderburgh**, which dates from about the middle of last century, when a new harbour was constructed, and, lastly, the ancient hamlet of **Stotfield**, now a district of modern villas. It is built on and around a headland rising from the Laich o' Moray.

Modern Lossiemouth is almost entirely a creation of the present century. James Ramsay MacDonald (1866–1937), the first Labour Prime Minister of Great Britain (1924), was a native of Lossiemouth. His residence was " The Hillocks." A Memorial plaque marks the cottage (1 Gregory Place) where he was born.

Lossiemouth has bracing air ; a low rainfall (an average

of only 20¾ inches); a long, broad sandy beach; and around are extensive prospects which charm the eye. It also offers golf, bowling, putting, tennis, trout and sea-fishing.

West of Lossiemouth, about 3 miles, is **Covesea** (pronounced *Cowsie*), with a tall white lighthouse and interesting rocks and caves with old-time smuggling associations. Half a mile away is Gordonstoun with its famous school at which the Duke of Edinburgh and the Prince of Wales attended. In this direction also are *Drainie* and **Duffus.** The few ruins of Duffus Castle are noteworthy. The ruins of Spynie Palace mark the original extent of Spynie Loch, which once lapped the palace walls.

Westward again from Covesea are the fishing village of **Hopeman** and the busy little port of **Burghead,** where is the British Broadcasting Corporation's transmitting station for the North of Scotland. Burghead is also interesting to the antiquary.

Across the neck of the elevated promontory are the remains of a triple breastwork and of inner ramparts, within which is a chamber cut in the solid rock, with a cistern and spring in the centre—the so-called *Roman Well.* All these were formerly reputed to be of Roman workmanship, but are now regarded as Celtic. On the crest of the promontory—supposed to be the "Ptoroton" of Ptolemy—the *Clavie,* a relic of ancient fire-worship, is kindled by the fishermen on New Year's Eve (Old Style, i.e. January 12), to ensure a successful year's fishing.

Burghead and Hopeman have fine bathing sands. There is a golf course at Hopeman.

The 12-mile run from Elgin to Forres is across the fertile *Laich o' Moray*; to the left are good hill views; all around are prosperous farms—many of considerable extent. The hill known as the **Knock of Alves** is crowned by a monument to the Duke of York, son of George III. Nine miles or so from Elgin roads on the right lead off to **Kinloss,** where are the ruins of an Abbey founded by David I in the mid-twelfth century. Edward I and Edward III lodged here, and the Abbey was able to provision the entire army of the former monarch for three weeks. After the Reformation the Abbey, like so many others, became just a builders' quarry. From Kinloss a straight road goes north-west for 3 miles to **Findhorn**

(*Culbin Sands, Crown*), lying on a lagoon-like bay. There is bathing, boating, fishing and golf, and with good accommodation, Findhorn is finding favour as a popular little resort.

Findhorn Bay is actually the result of the difficulty the *Findhorn* river has had in finding a way through the sand-hills to the sea. The river is bridged by the main road about a mile west of Forres, above which point it provides some of the finest scenery in the north of Scotland. (*See* p. 386.)

Forres.

"How far is't call'd to Forres ?"—*Macbeth.*

Angling.—For salmon, grilse, sea-trout and finnock fishing in the lowest 5 miles of the Findhorn, between Red Craig and the sea, apply *Forres Angling Association.*
Distances.—Aberdeen, 78½ m.; Elgin, 12 m.; Grantown, 22 m. Inverness, 26½ m.; Nairn, 10½ m.; Perth, 121 m.
Early Closing.—Wednesday.
Golf.—18-hole course. Putting in Grant Park.
Hotels.—*Carlton, Royal Station, Victoria, Queen's* (18 rooms), *Cluny Hill* (68 rooms), *Red Lion, Park, Newbold, Ramnee,* etc.
Population.—4,860.

Forres, dating from very ancient times, stands on gently rising ground on the eastern bank of the Findhorn, and is largely resorted to by sportsmen and tourists—the former for the salmon and trout fishing, the latter by reason of the exquisite scenery and the sweet and balmy climate of the district. The **Market Cross**, erected in 1844, was modelled upon the Scott Monument at Edinburgh. The **Falconer Museum** in Tolbooth Street is open weekdays, 10–5, *fee* (Saturday, *free*). Two sons of Forres who have been benefactors of the place are Lord Strathcona (1820–1914) and Sir Alexander Grant; the former was born in a thatched house which once stood at the west end of the town, between the *Burn of Mosset* and the mound that is the site of " King Duncan's Castle," the foundations of which have been excavated. A monument to Nelson crowns the summit of Cluny Hill and affords grand views. At the foot of the hill is charming Grant Park.

At the eastern end of the town, a few hundred yards along the Kinloss road, is one of the most remarkable stone obelisks of old-world date in Britain. Known as **Sueno's Stone,** it stands 23 feet above ground and bears carvings of warriors, animals and Celtic knots. In popular belief it records the final defeat of the Danes in 1014.

Between Forres and Nairn (10 miles) the direct road (*see below* for preferable route) passes **Brodie Castle**

(4½ miles), the seat of Brodie of Brodie. The splendid park, in which is a noteworthy "Pictish Stone," with Oghams, is always open to the public. The Castle (admission by appointment: Tel. Brodie 202) is of great antiquity.

Away to the right are the **Culbin Sandhills,** with *Buckie Loch,* famous for its aquatic plants. These sandhills were formed in 1694, when during a violent storm the sand began to drift inland and overwhelmed the barony of Culbin, a fertile tract of land formerly known as the granary of Moray. Of this estate (including the mansion house of Culbin and sixteen prosperous farms), only a single farm escaped. Since then the dunes have been steadily moving eastwards, but by planting brushwood and Corsican pine, etc., the Forestry Commission have succeeded in halting the movement. Culbin Forest is a monument to man's fight against Nature. The once insidious desert waste has been transformed into quite productive woodlands.

West of the Culbins, between road and railway, comes **Hardmuir,** the "blasted heath," now cultivated land, where Macbeth is supposed to have met the witches, the traditional spot being a knoll on the left known as **Macbeth's Hill.** The ruins of Inshoch Castle, also popularly associated with Macbeth, are a mile westward.

Auldearn was the scene of a battle in which Montrose brilliantly defeated the Covenanting General Hurry in 1645, and it has an interesting old churchyard.

For **Nairn,** *see* p. 388.

Motorists not pressed for time, however, are recommended to travel from Forres to Nairn by way of the **Findhorn Valley,** one of the most charming roads in Scotland, with good and varied scenery all the way.

The road turns off from the main highway by the War Memorial at the west end of Forres and soon reaches an area of rich heath and woodland—**The Forest of Altyre.** The *Findhorn* runs below on the right, and beyond the valley a glimpse may be caught of *Darnaway Castle,* one of the seats of the Earl of Moray. It is a modern building incorporating fragments of a castle built by Randolph, Earl of Moray, Regent of Scotland. At the fork about 6 miles from Forres turn down to the right. Here is **Relugas,** one of the points at which admission is gained to the lovely **Findhorn Glen.**

The most charming part is between Sluie and Relugas, though to visit Altyre or Relugas grounds special permission would have to be obtained. On account of the winding of the stream, the length of the Glen between the places named is 3 miles. So long as no trees are damaged or litter left, admission is granted daily to Randolph's Leap, except on Monday. (On that day those coming from a distance may be admitted.) Visitors who proceed to the Glen in hired vehicles are either set down at Sluie and picked up at Relugas, or *vice versa*. Considerable forestry planting in the area, and periodic flooding having washed away the former path along the river, restrict movement in the Glen. A bridge over the Divie at Relugas (1½ miles north of Dunphail) gives on to a wall with steps over. Then follow a path which leads back to the bridge, past **Randolph's Leap**, a narrow rocky gorge in the grounds of Relugas House, a short distance above the confluence of the Divie with the Findhorn. It takes its name from a supposed feat of Randolph, the first Earl of Moray and the builder of Randolph's Hall at Darnaway Castle. From the bridge follow the path above the east side of the Findhorn to Sluie, where the high-road may be reached, or the river bank may be followed to a point only 3 miles from Forres.

Even those who do not leave the highway can enjoy the fine scenery of the Glen, beyond which the road climbs to heathery uplands about *Ferness.* From the Ferness cross-roads it is 11 miles to Forres; 10 to Nairn; 13 to Grantown by Dava; and 15 to Carrbridge by the Duthil road, which continues west of **Lochindorb** (*see* p. 342) across the moors.

For Nairn, however, turn sharp back to right at the fork at Ferness and after crossing the river by Logie Bridge climb the far side of the valley for the lovely run onward. Just beyond Logie Bridge a road on the right runs down the west side of the valley to the main road about 3 miles west of Forres, passing through Darnaway Forest and near the Castle. All delightful scenery.

The road to the left at Logie Bridge leads in about 4 miles to **Dulsie Bridge,** a very beautiful part of the Findhorn. It may also be reached from the Forres–Duthil road. The Tomlachlan Burn is now crossed by a concrete bridge.

Those bound for Inverness and with no special reason for visiting Nairn should turn off on the left about 2 miles south of that town by a road following the southern side of the Nairn valley and passing **Cawdor Castle** (p. 388). The river may then be crossed at various points: the third turning on the right, about 9 miles west of Cawdor, leads up from near the

Clava Stone Circles (p. 391) to the main road close to the Cumberland stone on **Culloden Moor** (p. 391).

Nairn.

Access.—Rail connection *viâ* Inverness or Aberdeen. Inverness airport at Dalcross.
Angling.—Trout and salmon fishing in the *Nairn*. (Apply *Nairn Angling Association.*)
Distances.—Forres, 10½ m.; Elgin, 22 m.; Fort George, 8 m.; Inverness, 16 m.
Early Closing.—Wednesday.
Golf.—There are three courses, the *Nairn Club* has an 18-hole course, 3½ miles in length, close to the seashore, with the *Newton* 9-hole course nearby. There is also the *Nairn Dunbar Golf Club* with an 18-hole course eastward of the town.
Hotels.—*Highland* (65 rooms), *Royal Marine* (52 rooms), *Golf View, Royal, Washington, Victoria, Ardgour, Braeval*, etc. Numerous private lodgings and furnished houses.
Museum.—Viewfield House.
Population.—About 4,800.
Sports.—Golf, bowls, cricket, tennis, pleasure cruises on Moray Firth, coach trips, rowing and bathing. Highland games, golf and tennis tournaments are held during August. Swimming baths.

Nairn is a prosperous-looking town situated on the *Nairn* river, where it flows into the Moray Firth. The western end has been very attractively laid out, with a large green, known as the Links, overlooking the shore and used as a cricket ground in summer. There is splendid bathing, the beach extending for miles. There are three golf courses and facilities for tennis, bowls and other sports, and the residential portion of the town is very pleasant. The main street is dominated by the Town and County Buildings, beyond which it runs to the harbour.

The surrounding district has many historical associations. To the east is *Hardmuir*, Macbeth's "blasted heath"; to the west is the *Height of Balblair*, the site of Cumberland's last camp before proceeding to the battlefield of Culloden; Cawdor Castle is within easy reach, and on the hills south of the town are the vitrified remains of Castle Finlay and the ruins of Rait Castle (fourteenth century).

Cawdor Castle is 5 miles south-west on the Nairn–Cawdor road.

Cawdor Castle.

(Not on view. The gardens are occasionally opened to the public.)

The seat of Earl Cawdor, the Castle is built on the rocky bank of a mountain stream which flows into the River Nairn. The original castle was built about 1390 and consisted of a very plain square keep surrounded by a curtain wall, parts of which still exist, and outside which was a dry moat. The outer courtyard is approached over a drawbridge, the most perfect specimen, perhaps, of such entrances now in existence. In 1454 the sixth Thane of Cawdor was granted a Royal Charter by James II to complete the fortification of the building, including the battlements and a copehouse on top of the tower. Additions were made between 1660 and 1700 by Sir Hugh Campbell of Calder and his wife, Lady Henrietta Stuart, daughter of the third Earl of Moray.

There was a small castle at " Old Calder " which probably occupied the site of the present Brackla Distillery. There is a legend that the then Thane of Calder wanted to build a larger tower. He is said to have had a dream in which a magician appeared, telling him to place his treasures on a donkey. The donkey would come to the bank of a burn, where three hawthorn trees grew. It would rub itself against the first, eat grass at the foot of the second and lie down under the third. He should build his castle round the third hawthorn tree, and the fortunes of his family would flourish. The dried-up stem of the tree is still in the vaulted ground floor room of the existing tower. The abduction in 1499, by a party of Campbells, of little Muriel Calder, " the red-haired lassie," gave rise to the saying, " It's a far cry to Lochow," according to one story. This child was the sole heiress, and her marriage with Sir John Campbell, 3rd son of the 2nd Earl of Argyll, founded the house of Campbell of Cawdor. (*See also* pp. 208–9.)

Across the river a mile west of Cawdor is *Kilravock Castle* (*not shown*), dating from 1460, and with additions said to have been designed by Inigo Jones. The Castle has been in the possession of the Rose family since 1290.

Some 3 miles from Nairn is the *Loch of the Clans*, to which Prince Charlie's army marched on the day before Culloden, intending to give battle to Cumberland's forces. The loch contains curious examples of crannogs or lacustrine dwellings.

From a fork on the main road 2 miles west of Nairn a road runs out to quaint little **Ardersier** (aforetimes known as *Campbelltown*) and **Fort George**, depot of the Royal Highland Fusiliers, but built soon after the rising of 1745 to overawe disaffected clans. The Chapel contains a three-decker pulpit.

The main road to Inverness from Nairn is characterized by some long straight stretches, but on account of the views over the Firth, the slightly longer road across Culloden Field and Drummossie Muir is preferable, apart from its historic interest.

The Battle of Culloden.

Many of the Culloden Memorials are in the care of the National Trust for Scotland. There is a small museum at Leanach with warden in attendance.

In 1745 Prince Charles Edward, grandson of James II, determined to regain the crown which James II had lost for his father, the "Old Pretender." After narrowly escaping a British cruiser, which disabled a French warship that was accompanying his vessel, the Prince, with seven or eight followers, landed on the west coast of Eriska island, in the Outer Hebrides, on July 23. Two days later he reached the Scottish mainland at Borrodale, in Arisaig, and set up his standard at Glenfinnan on August 19. Cameron of Lochiel, against his better judgment, joined the Prince. Other Highlanders followed the example, but on August 20, when Charles began to march through the country, his force numbered only 1,600. The Government was unprepared for the outbreak, and Charles reached Edinburgh, where he took possession of the Palace of Holyroodhouse, and caused his father to be proclaimed King as James VIII. A royalist force, under Sir John Cope, was defeated at Prestonpans. Early in November the Prince's force began to march southwards. In England he took the town and castle of Carlisle, evaded the royal forces, and advanced as far south as Derby. There he unwillingly turned back, Lord George Murray and other chiefs deciding that further advance spelt disaster. Few adherents had joined him south of the Border. At Clifton Moor, near Penrith, he checked the pursuit of the Duke of Cumberland. The Prince entered Glasgow on December 26, and having made the city, which was unfriendly, pay him £10,000, he went on to Stirling. Despite a victory at Falkirk on January 17, 1746, the Jacobite army, discouraged by failure to capture Stirling Castle, retreated to Inverness, which was reached on February 18. Two days later, the garrison surrendered and the Castle was razed to the ground. As the spring advanced numbers of the Highlanders scattered to their homes.

The Duke of Cumberland had been advancing, and on April 14 reached Nairn. The following day, his birthday, was spent in rejoicing. The Jacobite force, which had been drawn out from Inverness to Culloden, attempted a night attack, but Nairn was 10 miles or more away and they had not reached it when day began to break. Tired, dispirited and half-starved, they were forced to turn back. At Culloden there was nothing for them to eat, and while many were away foraging the Hanoverian army arrived. With the Prince were about 5,000 men. The Duke of Cumberland had 9,000 men and he was reputed one of the ablest tacticians of the day. The two forces were drawn up 400 or 500 yards apart. The battle began at 1 o'clock and lasted but forty minutes. The Highlanders broke the first of the three enemy lines, but were repulsed by the second and utterly routed. No mercy was shown to the fugitives. There are many sad stories of the brutality with which they were treated, and Cumberland, from the measures he took after the battle, gained the name of "the Butcher." The estimate of the Jacobites' loss on the field and in flight varies from 1,000 to 2,000. The royalists had only 310 killed and wounded.

Accompanied by a few friends, the Prince fled from the field and for five months wandered about the Highlands, while a reward of £30,000 was offered for his capture. On September 20 a French vessel bore him away from the vicinity of the spot on which he had landed thirteen months before. It will be remembered that he sank into sottishness, and died in 1788.

Besides the road from Nairn, about half a mile west of Culloden Moor, is the **Cumberland Stone,** a hugh boulder which owes its name to the tradition that from the top of it the Duke of Cumberland directed the movements of his army.

The principal cairn is about 400 yards westward, and in a rough semicircle on the other side of the road are the graves of the Jacobites, buried according to their clans. The English were laid to rest in the only arable land then upon the Moor.

The road that runs past the Jacobites' graves has been made since the battle. That which existed at the time was about a quarter of a mile farther north. It ran along the edge of the depression known as the **Stable Hollow,** from the tradition that some of the Duke of Cumberland's cavalry were rested and fed in it. The ragweed, which is a common plant here, is said to have sprung from seed introduced by the hay brought for the horses.

In the valley north of the Moor, 2 miles from the battlefield, and surrounded by plantations, stands **Culloden House.** The old Castle was partly burned not long after the Rising, and the present mansion has to a large extent replaced the house in which Prince Charlie lodged the night before the battle; but the old portion contains a small apartment in which seventeen officers of the Jacobite army were confined for three days before being shot by order of the Duke of Cumberland.

The road south-east from the Cumberland Stone leads in a mile to the **Clava Stone Circles,** "the most splendid series of circles and cairns on the eastern side of the island." Each of the principal cairns is surrounded by great pillars or standing stones, and contains a central chamber some 12 feet high and

12 feet in diameter. Near one of the cairns is what has been held to be the foundation of an early Christian church or oratory.

Near the western end of Culloden Moor the road joins the main highway from Carrbridge and Aviemore (pp. 338–40). All the way down are splendid views of Inverness and the Black Isle, with Moray Firth between.

For Inverness, *see* p. 404.

ABERDEEN TO INVERNESS BY THE COAST.

Though longer (143 miles) than the direct route (104 miles) *viâ* Huntly, already described, this puts one in touch with good coast scenery, and along the north coast there are several quaint little fishing villages well worth a detour.

The way out of Aberdeen is by King Street, opposite the Cross. The Don is crossed by the New Brig, about a quarter of a mile farther downstream than the picturesque old Brig o' Balgownie (p. 363).

North of Aberdeen, between *Don* and *Ythan*, is the district known as **Formartine.** North of that again, between *Ythan* and *Deveron*, is the old territorial division of **Buchan,** the most easterly knuckle of Scotland. The Buchan district is for the most part flat and treeless, but is richly cultivated, and to the tourist appeals chiefly through its coast scenery and its historical associations. The richness of its Doric is at once the delight and the despair of strangers.

Places in these regions are connected by motor-bus services, the former railway having been discontinued.

Newburgh (*Udny Arms* (18 *rooms*), *Ythan* (3 *rooms*)), a dozen miles north of Aberdeen, stands beside the mouth of the *Ythan*, and was formerly of greater importance as a port. The Ythan is a good angling stream, and the various villages in its valley are favourite headquarters. Besides salmon, sea and lake trout, brook trout, whiting, grilse and pike, the river contains pearl mussels : one of the largest gems in the ancient crown of Scotland was obtained from this stream. **Ellon** (*New Inn*, *Station*, *Buchan*), a few miles inland from Newburgh, has a municipal golf course and other sports facilities in addition to fishing. A mile or so farther upstream is *Haddo*

House (the Earl of Haddo); and to the south is **Udny** (an angling centre), overlooked by a castle rebuilt some sixty years ago.

The wide estuary of the Ythan is crossed a little above Newburgh, and then the road runs past the sands of Forvie, among which are the remains of a building said to have been the parish church. **Collieston** is a quaint but thriving fishing village famous for its speldins (small fish split, salted and dried in the sun). The village is sprinkled over the cliffs surrounding a small beach, and in the vicinity are interesting caves (lights necessary for exploration). On a headland a mile or so north of Collieston are the remains of the old *Castle of Slains*, destroyed after the Counter-Reformation under the personal direction of James VI.

Between Udny and Tarves are **Pitmedden** (remarkable seventeenth-century garden: Nat. Trust) and **Tolquhon Castle** (*admission fee; summer*, 10–7, *winter*, 10–4; *Sundays*, 2–7 *or* 2–4), built on the courtyard plan and an excellent example of Scottish architecture in the late sixteenth century.

CRUDEN BAY.

Distances.—Aberdeen by road, 23 m.; Peterhead, 9 m.
Golf.—A course of 18 holes. Sunday play.
Hotels.—*Kilmarnock Arms, Red House.*
Sports.—Bathing, golf, angling in the *Cruden Burn*, boating and sea-fishing, tennis, bowls.

Cruden Bay is situated in the very centre of the most picturesque part of the Buchan Coast, noted for its bold and precipitous cliffs, its fantastically shaped rocks, and its numerous caves.

The bay itself is fringed with a clean hard sandy beach, over 2 miles in length, admirably adapted for bathing, and backed by an extensive stretch of sand dunes on which is the **Golf Course** of eighteen holes. The full-sized course is nearly 3½ miles long. Its greens are a special feature.

It was at Cruden Bay where was fought the legendary final battle (1012) between the Scots and the Danes. The relics found include a neck-chain and a battle-axe that have been deposited in the museum at Peterhead.

Moat Hill, on Ardiffery Farm, is said to have been the seat of justice in feudal times.

To the south of the beach is a long low promontory, off which is a reef of sunken rocks called the **Scaurs**, or Skerries, running far into the sea. Over them the waves break at high water in misty foam, and upon them many a gallant ship has been wrecked. About the middle of the bay is a lofty headland, called the **Hawklaw**, from which there is a magnificent prospect. Inland from the Scaurs is **Whinnyfold**, a picturesque village in some favour as a quiet resort and a favourite haunt of picnic parties.

Aulton Road connects with the village of **Port Erroll**, which lies along the Cruden Burn and has a harbour that can accommodate a number of fishing boats.

On a granite headland above Port Erroll is the site of the now demolished **Slains Castle** (1836), formerly the residence of the Earls of Erroll. The old Castle of Slains is 5 miles south (*see* p. 393).

The neighbouring coast scenery is very fine. A little to the north of the site of the more modern Slains Castle is a rock pierced with two openings which is known as the *Twa Een* (i.e., two eyes), and a little farther north is the *Dun Buy* (Yellow Rock). Near this is a cave with two openings, one of them a little way inland, which has earned the name *Hell's Lum* (lum = chimney) from the way in which, during an easterly gale, the spume is forced out of the inner opening. The most striking feature of the coast, however, is at **The Bullers of Buchan**, a huge circular cavern, or basin, open to the sky and entered from the sea through a narrow arched opening. It is in a promontory on the north side of a narrow creek, at the head of which are a few cottages. The sides of the cavern are perpendicular walls of rock that in places are less than a couple of yards wide. In calm weather it is possible for those who have strong nerves to walk round the cauldron, but during storms the sea dashes high up the lofty sides, and any human being in its way would be swept to destruction. One can well believe, on such an occasion, that " Bullers " is a corruption of " Boilers." In calm weather boats may be taken inside—a trip graphically described in Dr. Johnson's *Journey to the Western Isles.*

Cruden Bay is a popular resort. The nearest villages are *Longhaven*, 2 miles north, and **Boddam,** at Buchan Ness, the most easterly point in Scotland. Boddam is given up to fishing. The headquarters of fishing in these parts, however, is **Peterhead** (*Palace, Imperial, Royal, North-Eastern*), 35 miles from Aberdeen and the most easterly town in Scotland. Two hundred years ago Peterhead was celebrated as "the Tunbridge Wells of Scotland," and at various periods since it has enjoyed some fame as a health and pleasure resort. To-day it is one of the principal Scottish ports engaged in the white fish industry. In the bay south of the town is a huge National Harbour of Refuge. 18- and 9-hole golf courses.

From Peterhead a road runs westward to Macduff and Banff by way of *Longside* (John Skinner, 1721–1807, author of *Tullochgorum* and other favourite Scottish poems, was minister of the Episcopal church for over sixty years) and **Mintlaw**, near which are the remains of the *Abbey of Deer* (*weekdays*, 10–7, *Sundays*, 2–7. *Closed in winter.*) A Cistercian Abbey was founded here in the thirteenth century, but fell to decay after the Reformation; in 1927 a re-dedication of the property took place. Long before the Cistercians came here, however, there was a Celtic Christian monastery at Old Deer; the most treasured relic is the celebrated ninth-century Book of Deir, now in Cambridge University Library.

Between Peterhead and Fraserburgh the road runs at some distance from the coast. Just outside Peterhead are the ruins of Inverugie Castle and those of Ravenscraig Castle. The landscape is flat, relieved by the lone height of *Mormond Hill* (769 feet), on one slope of which is a white horse made in 1700 and on the other the figure of a stag made in 1870. Eastward of the road is the uninteresting *Loch of Strathbeg.*

Fraserburgh (*Royal, Saltoun Arms* (17 *rooms*), *Alexandra, Station*) was founded in 1546 by Sir Alexander Fraser, ancestor of the Saltoun family, and is almost entirely given up to the fishing industry. During the season its normal population of about 10,600 is increased by the innumerable workers who follow the shoals down the coast. The sight of the industry in full blast is memorable. There is an 18-hole golf course and good angling.

The northernmost part of the town is on *Kinnaird Head*, where are the remains of Sir Alexander Fraser's Castle, surmounted by a lighthouse. Near it is the Wine

Tower, the origin and use of which are unknown. The only entrance is on an upper storey, the wooden stairway to which is modern.

From Fraserburgh to Macduff the road winds among numerous hamlets, now almost on the cliffs, now some way inland. Along by **Rosehearty, New Aberdour** and Pennan (11 miles) the cliff scenery is wonderful and compensates for the shortcomings of the road. Near Rosehearty are the ruins of ***Pitsligo Castle,*** the residence of Alexander Forbes, Lord Pitsligo, outlawed after Culloden. Two miles west is a cave where he stayed in hiding. New Aberdour has the ruined Dundarg Castle and St. Drostan's Chapel and Well to interest antiquaries.

For the rest of the way to **Banff,** *see* pp. 398–9.

ABERDEEN TO BANFF VIÂ OLD MELDRUM AND TURRIFF.

This is the shortest route to the Moray Firth coast and serves several of the most popular resorts along that shore.

Aberdeen is left by George Street and so to Bucksburn (p. 376), where we take the right-hand road at the fork. Approaching **Old Meldrum** we have Udny (*see* p. 392), away to the right, and to the left the hill of **Barra** (*see* p. 376). In Old Meldrum turn off to the right and so to **Fyvie,** beyond which the road skirts the lovely grounds of Fyvie Castle, a very fine example of "the rich architecture which the Scottish Barons of the days of King James VI obtained from France." On one of the turrets is the stone effigy of Andrew Lammie, celebrated in a "waeful" ballad taking its name from the Mill o' Tifty, half a mile north-east of the Castle. Eastward from Fyvie is *Gight Castle,* once in the possession of Byron's mother's family.

Some 4½ miles along the main road north of Fyvie the square keep of *Towie Barclay Castle* (1300) may be seen through the trees on the left just before reaching Auchterless. Yet another 2 miles, and the red sandstone castle of Hatton is on the right.

Turriff (*Commercial*) is a busy little place, the centre of a prosperous agricultural district. The Old Church belonged to the Knights Templar, but only the choir and belfry remain. The "Trot of Turriff" on May 14, 1639, was a Royalist surprise and a Covenanting flight, but this skirmish saw the first blood shed in the Civil War in Scotland. There is a good 9-hole golf course (Sunday play), and good facilities for tennis, bowls and angling.

From Turriff the road runs down the east side of the beautiful valley of the *Deveron* to Banff.

About 4 miles from Turriff is the ruin of **Eden Castle**, the ancient seat of the once powerful Earls of Buchan.

The name of **King Edward** (5 miles from Banff), a corruption of *Ceann-eadar*, is pronounced *Kin-edart*.

Banff and **Macduff** are twin towns respectively on the west and east sides of the mouth of the Deveron, across which is a seven-arched bridge designed by Smeaton. Each town has its harbour, each has its golf and its residential portions.

Banff.

Angling.—There is good sea-fishing. The Banff and Macduff Angling Association controls both banks of the Deveron from its mouth for three-quarters of a mile. The Fife Arms Hotel also has beats on the river.

Golf.—18-hole course in the grounds of Duff House. Sunday play. The Tarlair Course (*see* p. 398) is within easy reach.

Hotels.—*Fife Arms* (29 rooms), *Crown*, *Royal Oak*, *Links*, *Seafield*, and several unlicensed hotels, including *Dunvegan*, etc.

Population.— 3,570.

Tennis, Bowls, Boating, Cinema.

Banff is the capital of the county of the same name and was the site of a royal castle which on three occasions was the headquarters of the English king Edward I. James Sharp—"Sharp of that ilk"—the famous Archbishop of St. Andrews was born in it in 1618. The present **Banff Castle** (community centre) was erected in 1750. The old churchyard contains remains of the ancient Parish Church and interesting gravestones. The shaft of the **Market Cross** is reputed to date from pre-Reformation days. Westward of the town is a beautiful sandy beach, excellent for bathing (shelters are provided), and a modern caravan site.

Duff House, formerly a seat of the Earls of Fife, dates from the middle of the eighteenth century. In 1906 it was presented to the two towns of Banff and Macduff by the Duke of Fife, who gave with it that portion of the park immediately surrounding the house, covering an area of about 140 acres and including the gardens. In the grounds is the very fine Duff House Royal Golf course (18 holes).

Through the park is a path by the side of the *Deveron* to the **Bridge of Alvah,** 2 miles, where the river has scooped out a deep channel, the surface of the water being 40 feet below the bridge. **Montcoffer House,** a residence formerly of Princess Arthur of Connaught, on the east bank of the Deveron, overlooks the bridge.

Macduff (*Fife Arms, The Knowes, The Shore, Bay View, Rosedale House*) as a town dates only from 1783, when through the influence of the second Earl of Fife with King George III the existing hamlet of Doune was made a burgh under the name of Macduff, Viscount Macduff being one of his lordship's titles.

At Tarlair (where the Royal Tarlair Golf Club has its course: Sunday play), about a mile to the east, is the *Howe of Tarlair*—a picturesque bay enclosed on three sides by high cliffs. Within the Howe was Tarlair Spa (chalybeate); a Swimming Pool has been constructed under the shadow of the famous "**Needle's E'e**" **Rock.**

Eastward of Tarlair the coast is rocky and precipitous.

Specially conspicuous features in the contour of the coast are three promontories—Gamrie Head (or Mhor Head), Troup Head and Pennan Head.

On **Gamrie Head** are the ruins of **Gamrie Church,** said to have been built in 1004, in fulfilment of a vow made during a Danish raid.

In a narrow bay on the eastern side of Gamrie Head is the fishing village of **Gardenstown,** named after its founder, Alexander Garden, of Troup. It presents a very picturesque appearance, as it slopes up from the shore and clings to the steep side of an overhanging hill.

A little farther around the cliff is the smaller fishing village of **Crovie.**

Troup Head, a mile from Gardenstown, is the most northerly projection on this part of the coast. Hereabouts is "a rugged mass of broken hills, forming a cluster of remarkably wild glens, rich to exuberance in plants and flowers—a very garden of delights to the botanist." In the vicinity of the Battery Green a narrow opening on the slope of the hill bears the somewhat common name of *Hell's Lum.* From it a subterranean passage, nearly

100 yards in length, extends to the sea, and along this, on the occasion of a storm, the spray is forced till it finds its escape by the lum, or chimney, appearing like dense smoke. Not far from Hell's Lum is another subterranean passage, called the *Needle's Eye.* It is some 15 to 20 yards long, exceedingly narrow, and terminates in a large cavern called the Devil's Dining-Room, supported by huge columns of rock, and facing the sea, which runs into it.

Pennan Head protects a small harbour and the quaint little fishing village of **Pennan.** Hence to Fraserburgh, *see* pp. 395–6.

Westward from Banff the Elgin road runs past a succession of villages and small towns that for most of the year are immersed in the fishing industry and during summer are popular little holiday resorts. From Banff the main road runs inland behind rising ground and the sea is out of sight for some miles. In about 2 miles a road on the right leads over the ridge to **Whitehills,** a quaint fishing village with two harbours—one used by the fishing boats, the other a miniature affair into which only the smallest craft could wriggle and not now used. The coast is wild and rocky. There is an hotel and lodgings can be had.

Hence to Portsoy the only feature of outstanding interest in view is *Durn Hill* (651 feet). **Portsoy** (*Commercial, Station*) is a clean little fishing town with the double harbour characteristic of this part of the coast and excellent rock scenery in the neighbourhood. A beautiful serpentine, formerly quarried in the neighbourhood, is known as Portsoy Marble, some of which has a place in the Palace of Versailles. Portsoy is a favourite holiday resort.

Two miles west of Portsoy is the tiny hamlet of **Sandend,** on a fine bay, and between that and Cullen are the ruins of *Findlater Castle,* perched on the cliffs and reached by a somewhat intricate path. The Castle ceased to be inhabited about 1600. South of the main road, at Fordyce, is *Fordyce Castle* (1592), still inhabited, and those with time to spare might detour by Fordyce to Kirktown of Deskford and reach Cullen by the charming little glen extending to the coast a little west of the town. Deskford has a remarkably fine sixteenth-century sacrament house.

Cullen is finely situated at the eastern end of its extensive bay. A feature of the main street is the manner in which the viaduct which carried the railway was designed to imitate an ancient gateway—an excellent effort which might well have been followed elsewhere. The town stands on high ground, and the road to the sands winds down above the harbour and the fishing quarter. Adjoining the sands is the golf course, and light refreshments may be obtained at the pavilion by all. The rocks on the shore are dignified by the name of the *Three Kings of Cullen*. The house and grounds of **Cullen House** (part of which is 700 years old), with several miles of lovely walks, are open to the public on certain days. Hotels include *Seafield Arms, Grant Arms, Royal Oak, Cullen Bay, Waverley*. There is a popular municipal caravan site. The **Bin of Cullen** (1,050 feet), 3 miles south-west, commands a wide view, including the distant Cairngorms.

From Cullen to Fochabers the main road runs inland, through woods and with charming views, but an even more interesting road follows the coast closely and introduces one to a number of delightfully quaint, unsophisticated little fishing villages which make excellent quarters for a quiet holiday. **Portknockie, Findochty** and **Portessie** have accommodation for visitors.

Buckie (*Commercial, St. Andrews, Rathburn House, Strathlene, Marine, Highlander's*) is a fishing port with an interesting harbour. The largest town in Banffshire, it has a swimming pool, two golf courses and cinema among its attractions.

So by **Buckpool** and **Portgordon** to Spey **Bay**, a little east of the point where the *Spey* completes its long and adventurous journey from the Monadhliath Mountains beyond Kingussie and flows quietly into the Firth. The principal attraction at Spey Bay are the fine golf links (18 holes ; Sunday play). Close to the rivermouth is the *Tugnet*, the headquarters of the Crown salmon fisheries, which extend for 10 miles along the coast. Spey Bay is four miles from **Fochabers** (p. 379), where the river is crossed by a bridge giving fine views up and down river.

Hence to **Inverness,** *see* pages 380–91.

THE ALFORD VALLEY.

This provides an alternative to the direct route between Aberdeen and Keith by Inverurie, and also provides the eastern portion of the fine cross-country route by way of

Cock Bridge and Tomintoul to Strathspey. The road north of Cock Bridge, called the **Lecht Road**, rises very steeply to a height of 2,114 feet.

From Aberdeen *viâ* **Kintore** (p. 376) or *viâ* Skene to **Tillyfourie**, where the two routes unite. Some 5 miles south-west of Kintore and between the two routes is **Castle Fraser**, a grand specimen of Flemish architecture in perfect repair, although mainly built about 1617, while the square tower is ascribed to the fifteenth century. **Cluny Castle**, a mile or so westward, is fifteenth century, rebuilt in 1836. To the north is **Monymusk**, with Monymusk House, one of the finest mansions in Aberdeenshire. The mansion as well as the parish church is said to have been built from the materials of an Augustinian priory that stood near; a carved stone by the roadside is also ascribed to the priory. From Tillyfourie the road runs through a gap in the hills and enters the fertile *Howe of Alford*. A road on the right some 2 miles from Tillyfourie leads to **Keig**, where is Castle Forbes, and in the vicinity of which the river scenery is particularly delightful. Beside the main road half a mile short of Alford is the ruined Balfluig Castle (1556).

Alford (*Forbes Arms* (20 *rooms*), *Allargue Arms*, *Haughton Arms*) is a pleasant village which offers good fishing and forms a very fair centre for a number of attractive short excursions. About 5 miles to the north is **Terpersie Castle** (1561); 5 miles south is **Craigievar Castle** (National Trust) in a fine position overlooking the Leochel Burn. It is a capital example of the Scottish castellated style. Over the staircase is a coat of arms with the date 1668 and the injunction " Do not vaiken sleiping dogs." Still farther south is **Aboyne** (p. 365), on the Dee, and westward from Alford the main route continues to the old toll of **Mossat** (7½ miles from Alford), where the main road goes off northward through Strathbogie to meet the road from Aberdeen *viâ* Inverurie a few miles short of Huntly (p. 378). The Tomintoul road bears to the left at Mossat, and in a couple of miles reaches **Kildrummy**, where are the extensive ruins of a castle that is connected with the old Kings of Scotland and the history of the Bruce. Edward I captured the castle in 1306 and cruelly put to death Bruce's youngest brother. Thence through the narrow sylvan **Den of Kildrummy**, and the Deeside height of **Morven** is seen ahead. About

12 miles from Alford is the *Glenkindie Arms Inn,* not far from **Towie Castle,** the scene of the pathetic Scottish ballad *Edom o' Gordon.*

The *Kindie Water* is crossed, and not far beyond is Glenkindie House. In a small plantation in the second field on the right beyond that is a **Picts' House** containing two chambers—the most interesting of the many Picts' houses in the district. Farther westward the road crosses the mouth of the *Buchat,* which flows for 7 miles down a wild glen, in which are **Badenyon,** famous in song, and **Glenbuchat Castle.**

In the next 3 miles there are first the farm of **Buchaam,** with an earth house in the garden, and then the grounds of Castle Newe (now taken down). About 2 miles beyond the latter Upper Strathdon is entered at Bellabeg (*hotel*). The church and manse of Strathdon are on the right bank. The ruined **Colquhonnie Castle** (begun in the sixteenth century) is said never to have been completed, because during its construction three of the lairds fell from the top and were killed. Hard by is the **Doune of Invernochty,** a once fortified mound. (A footpath, from the Glen of the *Nochty,* crosses Cairnmore and descends by the Ladder of Glenlivet into the valley of the Spey.) The road rises rapidly, and passes **Corgarff Castle.** Corgarff Youth Hostel is on the south side of the Don, 1½ miles below **Cock Bridge** (*Inn*), 28 miles from Alford.

Cock Bridge to Braemar (22 miles) and **Ballater** (15 miles).—A first-class, though hilly, road—an old military route—runs south from the upper Don to the upper Dee valley. It crosses the Don some 3 miles down the river from Cock Bridge. At Rinloan a branch goes off down the right bank of the *Gairn* to Ballater (*see* p. 368), the main road continuing by Bridgend of Bush to join the Deeside road above **Crathie.**

Cock Bridge to Braemar (23 miles) *viâ* **Inchrory,** which is situated in the valley of the Avon, 6 miles to the west of Cock Bridge, and is reached by following the road that runs close to the south side of the Don. The track from Inchrory Lodge to Braemar is described in the reverse direction on p. 371.

At Cock Bridge the highway leaves the Don and goes northward by a very precipitous moorland route across the **Lecht** into Banffshire, attaining a height of 2,114 feet.

INVERNESS.

Airport.—Municipal Airport at Dalcross. Services to Glasgow, London, to Stornoway, and to Orkney and Shetland.

Angling.—That portion of the River Ness known as the *Four Cobles Water* is open for fishing from January 15 to October 15. Sea trout and salmon. (Brown trout from March 1.) The *Cobles Water* (or Bught) is owned by the Corporation and leased to the Inverness Angling Club, who issue tickets to visitors. Salmon, sea trout, brown trout, finnock, on stretch of 3 miles. Other fishings available through tackle-dealers.

Baths.—Corporation Swimming Baths, Albert Place. Open daily, 9–7.15 (Saturday, 4.15). Sundays, 8–9.15 and 2–4.15. Sea-bathing in the Firth,

Bowls.—Public Greens at Waterloo Place, Planefield Road and MacEwen Drive,

Buses.—To and from South Kessock Ferry. (From North Kessock buses run several times daily to Fortrose and Cromarty.) There is a good service to Beauly and Dingwall; Ullapool, Dornoch, Wick and Thurso are all attainable by bus from Inverness. There are daily bus services to Fort Augustus, Spean Bridge and Fort William (in connection with West Highland trains); to Nairn, Forres, Elgin and Aberdeen; and to the villages on either side of Loch Ness (Drumnadrochit, Foyers, Whitebridge, etc.).

Distances.—Aberdeen, 104 m.; Edinburgh, 160 m.; Fort William, 66 m.; Glasgow, 165 m.; London, *viâ* Forth Bridge, 541 m.; *viâ* Carlisle, 594 m.; Perth, 116 m.

Early Closing.—Wednesday.

Golf.—18-hole course at *Culcabock*, three-quarters of a mile from the station. 18-hole municipal course at Torvean.

Guide Book.—See Ward Lock's *Guide to Inverness and Northern Scotland* for fuller details than can be given here.

Hotels.—*Station* (76 rooms), *Caledonian* (69 rooms), *Albert*, *Queen's Gate* (48 rooms), *Columba* (70 rooms), *Palace* (46 rooms), *Royal* (37 rooms), *Glencairn*, *Rannoch Lodge*, *Windsor*, *Haughdale*, and others.

Population.—About 33,000.

Tennis.—Public Courts at Bellfield and at Fraser Parks. Club courts at Bishop's Road.

Youth Hostel.—In Old Edinburgh Road.

INVERNESS, the northernmost town of any considerable size in Scotland, occupies a beautiful site at the head of the Inverness Firth and at the north-eastern end of the Great Glen, which contains the Caledonian Canal. Through it flows the river *Ness*.

Prominent in every view of the town are the County Buildings, of red sandstone. They are generally spoken of as the **Castle**, although the Castle that figures in *Macbeth* (as well as the earlier residence of King Brude, according to some) is believed to have stood on the summit of the ridge to the east of the station.

Beside the Town Hall at the foot of Castle Hill, is the **Town Cross**. The upper part is modern; the lower part

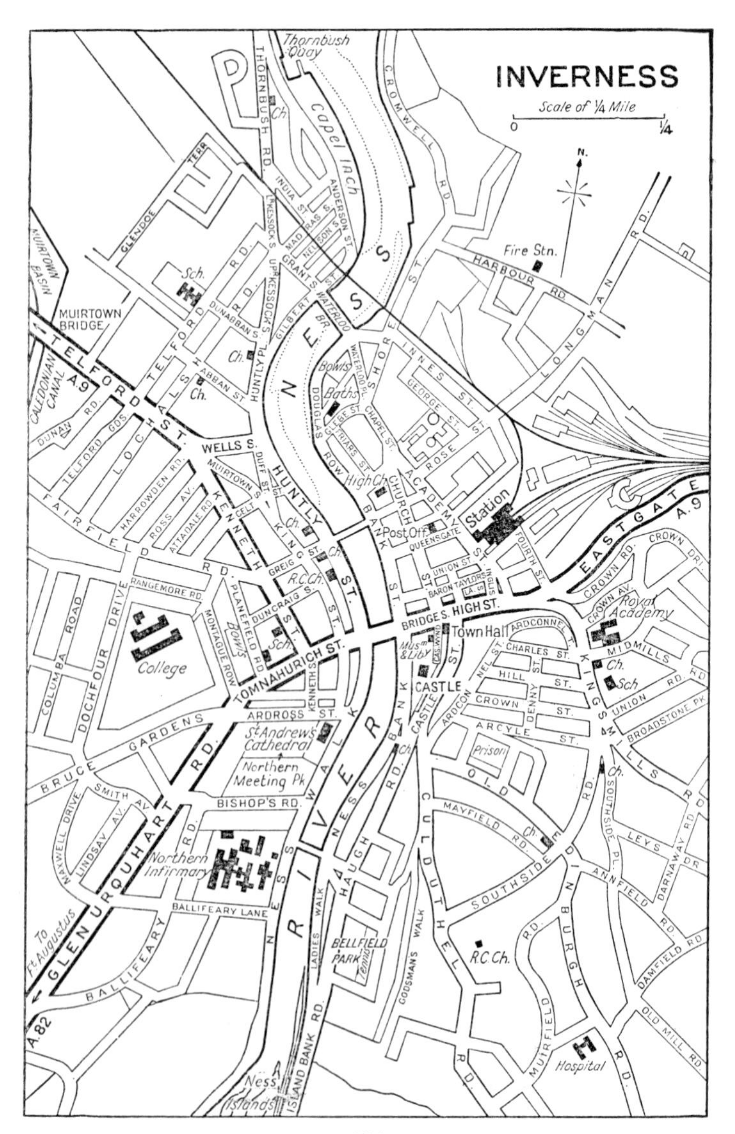
INVERNESS
Scale of 1/4 Mile
0
1/4
N.
Thornbush Quay
Capel Inch
RIVER NESS
Fire Stn.
HARBOUR RD.
LONGMAN RD.
CROMWELL RD.
THORNBUSH RD.
MUIRTOWN BASIN
MUIRTOWN BRIDGE
CALEDONIAN CANAL
TELFORD ST.
A.9
GLENDOE TERR.
Sch.
Ch.
TELFORD RD.
DUNABBAN S.
ABBAN ST.
HUNTLY PL.
HUNTLY ST.
WATERLOO BR.
Bowls
Baths
SHORE ST.
INNES ST.
GEORGE ST.
CHAPEL ST.
ROSE ST.
ACADEMY ST.
Station
EASTGATE A.9
WELLS S.
MUIRTOWN S.
DUFF ST.
KENNETH ST.
LOCHALSH RD.
FAIRFIELD RD.
HARROWDEN RD.
ROSS AV.
ATTADALE RD.
DUNAN RD.
High Ch.
CHURCH ST.
BANK ST.
Post Off.
QUEENSGATE
UNION ST.
BARON TAYLORS LA.
INGLIS ST.
FOURTH ST.
CROWN RD.
CROWN DRI.
CROWN AV.
Royal Academy
MIDMILLS RD.
KINGSMILLS RD.
Ch.
Sch.
UNION RD.
BROADSTONE PK.
RANGEMORE RD.
MONTAGUE ROW
PLANEFIELD RD.
Bowls
GREIG ST.
R.C.Ch.
DUNCRAIG S.
Sch.
KING ST.
College
COLUMBA ROAD
DOCHFOUR DRIVE
BRIDGE S.
HIGH ST.
Town Hall
Musm & Liby
ARDCONNEL ST.
CHARLES ST.
HILL ST.
CASTLE ST.
CASTLE WYND
ARDCONNEL ST.
NELSON ST.
DENNY ST.
CROWN ST.
ARGYLE ST.
Prison
TOMNAHURICH ST.
KENNETH S.
ARDROSS ST.
St Andrew's Cathedral
Northern Meeting Pk
GARDENS
BRUCE
SMITH AV.
MAXWELL DRIVE
LINDSAY AV.
BISHOP'S RD.
Northern Infirmary
GLENURQUHART RD.
NESS WALK
RIVER NESS
NESS BANK
CASTLE RD.
OLD EDINBURGH RD.
MAYFIELD RD.
SOUTHSIDE RD.
SOUTHSIDE PL.
LEYS DR.
DARNAWAY RD.
ANNFIELD RD.
CULDUTHEL RD.
HAUGH RD.
BALLIFEARY LANE
BALLIFEARY RD.
To Ft. Augustus
A.82
LADIES WALK
BELLFIELD PARK
Tennis
GODSMANS WALK
R.C.Ch.
DAMFIELD RD.
OLD MILL RD.
MUIRFIELD RD.
Hospital
Ness Islands
ISLAND BANK RD.

incorporates a curious blue lozenge-shaped stone, called the *Clach-na-Cudainn*, " the stone of the tubs," and for centuries regarded as the palladium of the burgh. It derives its name from having been the resting-place for the water-pitchers by bygone generations of women as they passed from the river. It is said to have been used by the earlier Lords of the Isles at their coronation, but how it came into the possession of the inhabitants of Inverness is unknown.

On the western bank of the river, nearly opposite Castle Hill, is **St. Andrew's Cathedral** (Episcopalian), the most imposing ecclesiastical structure in the place. Its style is Decorated Gothic, from designs by Alexander Ross, LL.D., himself an Invernessian.

About three-quarters of a mile up the river are the wooded **Islands**, connected with each other and with the roadway on either bank by suspension bridges, and forming a favourite resort in the summer evenings.

Not less worth a visit is the Cemetery on fairy-haunted **Tomnahurich Hill**, a thickly wooded height rising 223 feet above the level of the sea, and commanding good views. Another good viewpoint is **Craig Phadrig** (550 feet), a wooded height on the farther side of the Canal and about a mile from the Cemetery. On the top is a vitrified fort, identified with the home of the Pictish King Brude, who is said to have been visited here in the sixth century by St. Columba and converted to Christianity.

Five miles east of Inverness is **Culloden Moor** (p. 389), now National Trust property. The trip to the Battlefield may be combined with a visit to the **Clava Stone Circles**, a mile south of the Cumberland Stone (p. 391), or, in the opposite direction, a road runs down to the shores of the Firth by Allanfearn, providing lovely views.

The most direct route from Inverness to the Black Isle (p. 417) is *viâ* the ferry (cars carried) between **North Kessock** and **South Kessock**, reached by following the road on the western bank of the river down to the river-mouth.

FROM INVERNESS TO THE WEST.

INVERNESS TO STRUY AND GLEN AFFRIC.

THIS introduces some very fine scenery, but is a through route to the west coast *only for good walkers*, who can cross the mountains from Glen Affric (*see* p. 408) or Glen Cannich (p. 410) to Croe Bridge, on Loch Duich or to Ardelve, on Loch Long, on the road to Kyle of Lochalsh (*see* p. 243). Motorists can make a good circular run of about 55 miles by turning eastward from Invercannich, climbing over to Glen Urquhart and running down it to Drumnadrochit, thence regaining Inverness by the shores of Loch Ness.

From Bridge Street, Inverness, cross the river, keep straight forward for 250 yards and then turn to the right. At Muirtown the **Caledonian Canal** (*see* p. 239) is crossed close to the steamer quay.

At Clachnaharry (" the watch stone " : the site of a memorable clan battle in 1454) the road approaches the shore of the **Beauly Firth** and for the next few miles the running is very pleasant indeed, especially at evening, when the sun sinks behind the mountains far beyond the head of the Firth. Leaving the shore, the road runs past a charming district of small wooded hills, dotted with farmsteads and cottages. At *Kirkhill*, north of the road, is shown the grave of Simon Fraser, Lord Lovat.

About a mile short of Lovat Bridge a road goes off on the left for *Glen Convinth* and so to *Milton*, in Glen Urquhart, through varied and picturesque scenery ; the road to the right at the fork about 1½ miles from the Inverness–Beauly highway leads *viâ* Eskadale to Struy and is an interesting variation to the direct road to Kilmorack from Lovat Bridge.

Just beyond Lovat Bridge the main road for the far North swings to the right, but our road keeps straight ahead, rising through the woods to **Kilmorack** in the Aird district. Extensive hydro-electric installations here have caused the disappearance of the former Kilmorack falls. Across the river is *Beaufort Castle*, set in some very fine grounds. The castle is the seat of Lord Lovat, the head of the Clan Fraser.

Beyond Kilmorack Church the road runs very finely along the sides of the rocky valley through which the Beauly river finds its way, and the views are good compensation for those who have not left the car to see the river at Kilmorack. The narrowest portion of the pass is known as the *Druim* (dreem). Then the road rounds a corner, widens, and passes the gateway of Aigas House. *Eilean Aigas*, an island in the river, was long the hiding-place of Simon, Lord Lovat, when letters of fire and sword were issued against him and the principal families of his clan by King William in 1697.

As the road winds westward the scenery becomes increasingly beautiful, the river now passing through rich pasture land between hills that are softer in outline, and backed by the sterner hills beyond the hamlet of Struy. It is at **Struy** (*hotel*) that the rivers Glass and Farrar unite, and are henceforth known as the Beauly river.

STRUY TO STRATHCARRON BY GLEN FARRAR (35 miles).

A road goes as far as Loch Monar (15 miles); beyond that the route is for walkers (strong walkers only).

The only accommodation to be had on this route is at the keepers' houses in the glen, and naturally this is barred during the shooting season. The birch woods in the lower part of Glen Farrar are extremely graceful. Above Deannie Lodge the glen becomes barer, but **Loch a' Mhuillinn** is a gem of beauty. Sgurr na Lapaich (3,773 feet), a most prominent and beautiful peak, is well seen above Ardchuilk. A wild and rough gorge (*Garbh-uisge*) leads to Monar Dam, where the road ends. Since the conversion of Loch Monar to reservoir purposes the level of water fluctuates widely, and there is virtually no path as far as the head of Strathmore. From there, a faint path leads westward through the Bealach an Sgoltaidh (1,847 feet), to Loch an

Laoigh, and south to Bendronaig Lodge and then over the hills to the west by the Bealach Alltan Ruairidh to *Strathcarron Station* (*hotel*). The expedition leads through some magnificent scenery, but is only suitable for good and hardy walkers. From Pait Lodge (pronounced *Patt*), west end of Loch Monar, there is a bridle-path to the head of Glen Elchaig, where it joins the road to Lochalsh *viâ* Killilan and Ardelve.

CANNICH TO LOCH DUICH BY GLEN AFFRIC (30 miles).

About 7 miles south-west of Struy is **Cannich** (*Glen Affric Hotel ; Cannich Youth Hostel*)—a splendid centre for hill-walkers, being situated at the meeting-point of Glen Affric, Glen Cannich, Strathglass and Glen Urquhart. The area has, however, undergone great change due to the Mullardoch–Fasnakyle–Affric hydro-electric scheme, the road up Strathglass being greatly improved.

The public road on the south side of the River Glass ends at **Tomich** (*hotel*), at the entrance gates of Guisachan Estate. From Tomich there are very beautiful routes to the head of Loch Affric, although not so well marked.

(1) Cross the river at the Guisachan gate and follow a rough road (2½ miles) to opposite the very fine **Plodda Fall.** The track then strikes westwards past Loch an Eang, becoming very faint in places, and passes through very fine forests high above Loch Beneveian, and latterly along the south side of Loch Affric to Athnamulloch at its western end. This route is believed to be the old right of way track.

(2) From Tomich follow the road through the Guisachan policies to the lonely house called Cougie, passing through a magnificent forest of Scots pine containing some trees which must be 400 years old. From Cougie the path leads westwards through the hills and joins the previous route at the Allt Garbh, to the south of Glen Affric Lodge.

Two miles from Cannich the main road enters the *Chisholm's Pass*, as the first part of **Glen Affric** is called. Here at **Fasnakyle,** with its impressive power station and sad memories of Prince Charlie, the road leaves Strath Glass, and climbs to the right, displaying more and more the grandeur of the glen. As we begin to look over the trees instead of through them, we catch glimpses of a rapid stream far below, rushing over a rocky bed and fringed to the water's edge by trees of every description. The woods at first rise to the summits of the hills on both sides, but are afterwards overtopped by the long mountain-ridges which ascend through them from the level of Strath Glass to the culminating peaks of Mam Soul and Scour Ouran and a host of other magnificent mountains.

The best viewpoint for Glen Affric is 4 miles from Invercannich, where the road comes close to the water near the **Dog Fall.** The glimpses of the river in this vicinity are exquisite in richness of colour and variety of rock contour. In places the stream seems scarcely to stir as it passes over some deep black pool overarched by threatening crag and drooping foliage. Then it emerges into a bright, sunlit scene, edged by narrow belts of emerald verdure and luxuriant tufts of fern. Those unable to explore the glen farther should at any rate ascend it to this point.

Approaching Loch Beinn a' Mheadhoin (the " middle lake "), now more familiar as **Loch Beneveian,** road and river arrive at the same level. The old road is now submerged, but a new road constructed at a higher level enables motorists to proceed as far as the western end of the loch. The old Scots pines around Loch Affric are particularly fine. The view westwards from the east end of the loch is as fine as anything in the kingdom. The road ends at the lodge, but there is a bridle-path along the north shore of the loch—at some distance from it—as far as the cottages of Aultbeath (" burn of the birches "), 8 miles farther. Here is a small *youth hostel,* and half a mile farther the path crosses a burn along which, on the far side, the route up **Glen Grivie** strikes to the right. We are here 900 feet above the sea. The path, turning west, then ascends Glen Grivie between bare mountains, that on the left being Ben Attow, for three miles to **Loch a' Bhealaich.**

The more distinct route along the south side of Ben Attow by the river Croe continues for another furlong alongside the main stream ; then crosses another burn (at which a most indistinct track strikes south across a *col* 1,400 feet high to **Strath Cluanie,** 5 miles). It rises gradually for nearly 2 miles to a ruined cottage called Camban, 1,100 feet above the sea. Still ascending, we reach in another short mile the watershed (1,200 feet) between the eastern and western seas, and after a sharp descent and a bit of level, drop several hundred feet very steeply into **Glen Lichd.** Hereabouts the scenery attains its wildest grandeur. Great care should be taken in descending to keep well to the right or north side ; any other way is dangerous. A fine *waterfall* enhances the scene. At the foot of the steep part the path crosses to the south side of the stream by a footbridge at a keeper's house, and thence continues to Croe Bridge (p. 242), where it joins the Glen Grivie route. If anything, this route by Glen Lichd is the finer of the two, but both ways have their distinctive features.

The **Falls of Glomach.**—From Loch Beallach a level, desolate valley strikes to the right, and along it a rough track diverges a little short of the loch. Follow this track, and when it ceases, pick your way along the riverside. About one to one and a half hours' walk will bring you to the top of the celebrated *Falls of Glomach*, second highest and wildest in Britain. Except after heavy rain they are apt to disappoint, however, the depth of the fall being hardly sufficient compensation for the lack of picturesque surroundings. The Falls are the property of the Scottish National Trust. For routes from Glomach, *see* p. 241.

After leaving **Loch a' Bhealaich,** our track ascends about 400 feet in one mile to the top of the **Pass** of the same name (*Beallach* signifies a " pass "), whence it makes a very rapid descent of about 1,400 feet in 2 miles to the small alluvial strath at the head of Loch Duich, joining the highroad to Balmacara at Morvich, a short distance from *Croe Bridge*, and 4 miles from the top of the pass.

BY GLEN CANNICH TO ARDELVE (37 miles).

This is another of the beautiful cross-routes of Inverness-shire. From Cannich (or Invercannich) the road goes around the huge reservoir formed by the raising of the waters of Loch Mullardoch and Loch Lungard by a mighty dam, half a mile in length. Apart from *Mullardoch Hotel* there are no hostelries between Invercannich and Ardelve.

Glen Cannich vies with Glen Affric and Glen Farrar in characteristic combination of mountain, stream and native wood. The word " Cannich " has reference to the cotton-grass which grows on the rough green pastures of the glen. The waters at Invercannich itself run through a narrow defile, neither long nor deep, but so placed that the rising ground on either side of them shuts out the glen from Strath Glass. A short climb, however, brings us in full sight of its lowest part, a wilderness of rock, birch, heath and pasture, threaded by a turbulent stream, and hemmed in by mountains which grow higher and higher as far as the eye can trace their peaks in front. A few miles' walk up the glen will enable the traveller to appreciate its style, but he should proceed, if at all possible, till he gets a good view of **Loch Mullardoch.** The path along the northern shore of Loch Mullardoch extends as far as *Ben Ula Lodge.* The track now follows the north side of the stream at some distance above it, and in 3 miles crosses the *col* (1,100 feet), whence it rapidly descends into *Glen Elchaig*, keeping the stream close at hand on the left all the way to *Carnach*, where a fair road begins, thence coasting along the north side of *Loch Long* to **Ardelve** (*see* p. 243). There is a short cut from Glen Elchaig, by a good path from Camus-luinie by the River Glennan, to Dornie. To use it one must cross the Elchaig by a footbridge 2 miles east of Camus-luinie. At Dornie a road bridge has superseded the ferry across Loch Long, thus making easier access to Kyle of Lochalsh.

INVERNESS TO STROME FERRY AND KYLE OF LOCHALSH.

At Lovat Bridge (p. 406) the road from Inverness to the North swings to the right for **Beauly** (*Lovat Arms*), a pleasant little town with mineral springs (sulphated alkaline waters) at Brigend and some claims as a touring centre. The town is built around a large square, at the far end of which are the remains of a priory founded in 1230 for Valliscaulian monks and now cared for by the Department of the Environment. (*Open daily*, 10–4 *or* 7, *Sundays*, 2–4 *or* 7. *Free.*)

Two miles north of Beauly the road comes to **Muir of Ord,** a modern village with a golf course laid out on the site of an ancient "cattle tryst." *Tarradale House,* on the shores of Beauly Firth, was the birthplace of Sir R. Murchison and the residence of orientalist Sir Henry Yule ; it is now a hostel for students.

(For the Black Isle, *see* p. 417.)

At Muir of Ord the railway is crossed, and the road to the west leaves the Dingwall road. The Orrin is crossed near Urray, and some 2 miles farther a road on the right leads to **Moy Bridge,** over the Conon. [From Marybank, just south of Moy Bridge, a very pleasant road leads westward for 17 miles up **Strath Conon** to Loch Beannacharain. It commands fine views of **Tor Achilty** and the beautiful glen at the foot of **Loch Luichart.** A vast hydro-electric scheme has added dams and reservoirs, fish passes and power stations to the scene in the Conon and Orrin valleys.] At Moy Bridge our road turns sharp to the left and in 2½ miles reaches *Achilty Inn*, from which a pleasant excursion may be made to Loch Achilty and the **Falls of Conon.** From the latter there is a walking route by Loch Luichart to Lochluichart Station.

(For Strathpeffer and excursions therefrom, *see* p. 421.)

From *Achilty Inn* the main road runs up the valley of the Blackwater, passing the **Falls of Rogie,** to **Loch Garve,** through which the river flows and alongside which run road and railway. *Garve Hotel*, at the far end of the loch, is 30 miles from Inverness.

Four miles beyond Garve we run along the northern end of **Loch Luichart,** the source of the river *Conon*. The loch is about 5 miles in length by a mile in breadth. Beyond the Loch we cross the *Grudie* and enter **Strath Bran,** bare and bleak, through which we travel to **Achnasheen** (46 miles from Inverness, 27½ from Dingwall). Even in summer Achnasheen is a lonely hamlet, consisting of little more than a station, a hotel, and a petrol station.

Achnasheen to Loch Maree and Gairloch, see page 413.

At the western end of Achnasheen bear to the left over the *Bran* and follow the valley of its tributary, the Ledgowan. Beyond **Loch Gowan,** among wild moorland, comes pretty **Loch Scavan,** or Sgamhain, and a fine run down the valley of the *Carron* to **Doule,** or Dughaill, with Achnashellach station and Youth Hostel nearby. The grand Torridon Mountains are here well in sight. We approach the salt-water **Loch Carron** about a mile before which a left turn leads to **Strathcarron** station and hotel. Now rail and a new road follow the eastern shore of the loch to touch the southern terminal of Strome Ferry from which our road turns south to connect with the Ardelve road for Kyle of Lochalsh (p. 243).

Beyond the Strathcarron turn the main road continues along the northern shore of Loch Carron a few miles down which is **Lochcarron** village, or *Jeantown* (*hotel*), whence runs a road to **Shieldaig,** on Loch Torridon, or (with a daunting climb to 2,000 feet in 5 miles) to **Applecross.** From Loch Carron the shore road continues to **Strome Castle** (*hostel*) where the **Car Ferry** (*weekdays only*) must be crossed for this approach to Kyle of Lochalsh.

INVERNESS TO LOCH MAREE AND GAIRLOCH.

By rail or road to **Achnasheen**, as described above, thence by car or motor-coach.

For the first half of the journey from Achnasheen the road is on the rise, then it runs alongside **Loch Rosque,** a rather tame, river-like lake, some 3 or 4 miles in length. From the farther end may be seen, on the left, a hill shaped like a recumbent face, and called **Cairn-a-Crubie.** The watershed is reached about 6 miles from Achnasheen. It has an altitude of 815 feet, and from it there bursts upon the view the beautiful Loch Maree. From this point the route is full of interest. Descending **Glen Docherty,** a wild and narrow ravine, bounded by steep mountains and extending for about 4 miles, during which the road falls 700 feet, we enter the hamlet of **Kinlochewe** (*hotel*).

From Kinlochewe a road goes west to **Torridon** (10 miles), at the head of a beautiful sea-loch, whose shores and guardian mountains—the highest, *Liatach* (3,456 ft.) —are a delight for the hiker and the nature-lover (Youth Hostel at remote Craig, on the north side, facing Skye). Shieldaig, on the south side, is reached by road from Lochcarron (p. 412) or by a new road from Torridon.

A couple of miles beyond Kinlochewe begins—

Loch Maree,

one of the finest lochs in Scotland. It is about 12½ miles long and from 1 to 3 miles broad. The river *Ewe* flows from it and enters the sea at Poolewe and the road runs for 10 miles along the south shore. Across the loch presides majestic **Slioch** (3,217 feet). On the southern side **Ben Eighe** (3,309 ft., Nature reserve), one of the Torridon Hills, attracts attention by its peak of white quartz rock and beautiful form.

On **Eilean Suthainn** (1 mile long and three-quarters of a mile broad) are three lochs. **Garbh Eilean** (" rough island ") and **Eilean Ruairidh** (pronounced *rory*), towards the west, are generally regarded as the most beautiful. The most celebrated of the group is **Isle Maree.** It lies near the northern shore, directly opposite the Loch Maree Hotel, and contains a primitive burying-ground and the scanty ruins of an ancient chapel, said to have been erected in the seventh century by St. Maelrubha, a monk of Bangor in Ireland, after whom the lake and island are named. Loch Maree is as famous for the sport it yields to the angler as for its beauty. Salmon freely enter, and there are plenty of sea trout and brown trout.

Two miles beyond Loch Maree Hotel the road leaves the loch side and strikes westwards across the hills to the River Kerry, alongside which it runs through very charming scenery to **Flowerdale**, just beyond which is **Gairloch.** This village, at the head of the sea loch of the same name, is the centre of a beautiful district, and has established itself in popular favour. Bathing, boating, and fishing may be enjoyed in the bay. Excellent trout fishing may be had on several lochs within an easy walk, and there is a 9-hole golf course. There is a good hotel and a Youth Hostel (*Carn Dearg*).

The places and objects of interest in the district include the picturesque village of **Strath**; the **Vitrified Fort,** *viâ* Leabaidh-na-Ba-ban (" Bed of the White Cow "); **Inverewe**; the drive to **Opinan** along the southern shore of Gairloch; **Sand,** with its sand mountains; **Cliff House,** built and occupied by Hugh Miller; caves in the vicinity of **Stirkhill** and **Cove**; **Loch Maree.**

From Gairloch the main road continues eastward to **Poolewe** (*hotels*), on the strip of land separating Loch Maree from Loch Ewe. **Inverewe House** (7 miles from Gairloch) has a wonderful garden famed for its rare and sub-tropical plants (National Trust: *daily to dusk, including Sundays; charge; restaurant*). Thence by **Aultbea** (*hotels and Youth Hostel*), a small village on a bay in Loch Ewe. Then descending to **Gruinard Bay,** by a very steep hill (average gradient 1 in 7·8) with a sharp turn at the foot. The hamlet of Laide is on the left. It may save disappointment to note that camping is prohibited on the shores of this delightful Bay, and there is practically no accommodation for staying visitors.

Leaving Gruinard Bay the road crosses another promontory and proceeds to skirt the southern shore of **Little Loch Broom.** Here and there the hillsides spout fine waterfalls, but one is too close to its flanks to appreciate the rugged red mountain, **An Teallach** (" The Forge "). The Loch is left at **Dundonnell** (*hotel; Youth Hostel*) at its head and thence the road climbs over to the Garve–Ullapool road at Braemore (*see below*), 45 miles from Gairloch. **Ullapool** is about 12 miles westward.

Garve to Ullapool (32 miles). Bus service daily.

The road, which branches to the right about a mile beyond Garve (p. 412), runs through one of the wildest districts in Scotland. It first traverses the pretty **Strathgarve,** with the long slopes of Ben Wyvis reaching up on the right, and at the end of 10 miles reaches Altguish (*Inn*). Thence it rises to the new dam and *Loch Glascarnoch* skirting the reservoir thus created by the flooding of Strath Dirrie. The summit level is reached at **Loch Droma,** 15 miles from Garve. On the right is **Beinn Dearg** (3,547 feet). About 21 miles from Garve a road goes off to the left for Dundonnell, Poolewe and Gairloch (*see above*).

At this point, too, the Droma forms the **Falls of Measach.** The uppermost fall is difficult to see well owing to the narrowness of the ravine in which it roars, but thanks to the National Trust, a suspension bridge spans the ravine and enables the Falls to be viewed to great advantage. The mile-long Corrieshalloch Gorge is 200 feet deep, and the falls have a drop of 150 feet.

From Braemore to Ullapool the road commands a succession of beautiful views, and the eye gratefully rests upon cultivated fields, patches of woodland, and the grass-clad hills of **Loch Broom,** a fine sea loch. The name signifies " the lake of showers."

Ullapool

(*Caledonian* (30 *rooms*), *Morefield*, *Riverside House*, *Royal* ; *Youth Hostel*), on a peninsula running into the loch, is a village established by the British Fisheries Association in 1788. The vicinity is very beautiful, and visitors may enjoy good and safe bathing, sea-fishing and trouting. There are motor-boat trips to the Summer Isles.

On the northern shore of the inlet rises **Ben More Coigach,** and at the mouth of the loch are the **Summer Isles,** favourite resorts of picnic parties, and **Achiltibuie** (*hotel and Aucheninver Youth Hostel*).

Ullapool to Lochinver. The usual route is by the wild and adventurous road, with magnificent scenery, running northward by Ledmore (where the route from Lairg is joined) to **Inchnadamph** (*hotel*), and then westward beside **Loch Assynt.** Those who enjoy an even more adventurous route may prefer to take the Inverkirkaig road, striking off to the left from the Inchnadamph road at Drumrunie, some 10 miles from Ullapool. The mountain scenery at this point of the route is extremely fine : on the left **Ben More Coigach** (2,438 feet) presents a continuously changing form—especially striking is the jagged promontory on its northern face ; on the right are **Cul Beag** (2,523 feet) and **An Stac** (2,009 feet). The latter, usually known as Stac Polly, has a long ridge from west to east. The ascent of the western bastion and this ridge are for rock climbers only. Ordinary pedestrians may reach the eastern top quite easily.

By Loch Lurgainn and Loch Bad a'Ghaill, and at the western end of the latter we leave the road to Achiltibuie (8 miles, *hotel*, fine seascapes) and swing sharp to the right and enter upon a series of twists and turns, ups and downs and sudden transitions from rocky gorges to open moorland as is seldom encountered in so short a journey. **Cul Mor** (2,786 feet) is seen beyond Loch Sionascaig but the mountain which holds the eye is **Suilven** (2,399 feet), which from this point is seen to have a ridge-like shape. When seen from the west, however, it appears to be a sheer cylinder of rock, apparently unscalable. East of it is **Canisp** (2,786 feet).

From the side of Loch Assynt (*see* above) a road strikes off northwards, rising to a height of some 850 feet between Quinag and Glasven ; it leads *viâ* the **Kylesku Ferry** (daily service, free : approach roads on both sides require care) to **Scourie** (p. 425), whence a road goes to Laxford Bridge (p. 425) and Durness, from which Cape Wrath may be visited, and thence eastward to Tongue, Bettyhill and Melvich to Thurso ; a magnificent run. At the head of Loch Glencone to the east of Kylesku is Eas-Coul-Aulin, the highest waterfall in Britain (658 feet).

Lochinver (*Culag*, at pier), at the head of the sea loch of that name, is popular with all classes of tourists, but the chief attraction is the angling on numerous lochs in the neighbourhood. There are no fewer than 280 named lochs in the parish. The sea-fishing is very good, and there is abundant trout fishing in the neighbourhood, but salmon fishing in the Kirkaig is controlled by the Culag Hotel. By the **Falls of Kirkaig** (5 miles south) one reaches Suilven, the " Sugarloaf," beloved of climbers, photographers and geologists (p. 38). Northward, a switchback road winds round the rocky coast by Stoer and Drumbeg (*hotel*) to join the main road south of Kylesku. *Youth Hostel, and caravan site at Achmelvich.*

THE BLACK ISLE.

Approaches.—(*a*) By *road* the usual approach from the south, for those who have not crossed Kessock ferry, is through Beauly and by a road cutting east about half a mile short of Muir of Ord. From the north the approach is by Conon—straight on for Fortrose, turn left (2 miles up hill) for Cromarty.

(*b*) By *ferry* from South Kessock (*see* p. 405) (continuous service daily; cars carried.

THE Black Isle is neither black nor an island. It is really a peninsula, and so far from being black it is green—a pleasant country of woods, meadows and corn-fields. It contains some of the best agricultural land in the Highlands and is famous for its crops (especially potatoes) and cattle.

The Black Isle—also called Ardmeanach, or the "middle ridge"—lies between the Cromarty, Moray, Inverness and Beauly Firths.

Kilcoy Castle, a few miles from **Muir of Ord** (p. 411), is a good example of the residences that were erected by owners of great estates in the fifteenth and sixteenth centuries.

Redcastle, on the shore of the Firth, is said to have been built by William the Lion in 1179. Queen Mary is said to have visited the castle, and the vicissitudes it has experienced include a burning in Cromwell's time.

Munlochy, a pretty village, is snugly situated in a valley at the head of a picturesque little bay, empty, however, at low tide. South of the village is **Drumderfit,** "the Ridge of Tears," the site of a fierce clan conflict in 1372, commemorative cairns of which remain. On the south side of the entrance to Munlochy Bay is the headland of **Craigiehowe,** with a cave, the reputed den of a giant; and on the other, the wooded **Lady** or **Ormond Hill,** on which stood the castle of the Thanes of Ross.

To the east a few miles from Munlochy is seen, on the left, **Arkendeith Tower,** an ancient fortalice.

Eleven miles from Muir of Ord is **Avoch** (*awch*—" ch " as in " loch "), a fishing village at the head of a small bay.

FORTROSE.

Early Closing.—Thursday.
Hotels.—*Royal Station, Oakfield, Rosevale.* Caravan sites.
Population.—About 900.
Sports.—Bathing, boating, tennis, bowls, golf, sea-fishing and a little trout fishing. The Chanonry Sailing Club welcomes visitors.

Fortrose, with its close neighbour, Rosemarkie, enjoys high favour as a seaside resort. The curvature of the coast-line, with its fine sandy beach, forms a sheltered bay, adjoining the harbour, the Chanonry promontory acting as a natural breakwater and thus affording smooth and calm waters in nearly all conditions of weather. The royal burgh claims to have the highest average for sunshine and the lowest average for rainfall in Scotland, over a long spell of years.

Fortrose (locally pronounced with the accent on the first syllable) was formerly the cathedral town of Ross, and had a bishop's palace and a castle, of which all traces have disappeared. It was also in bygone days a famous seat of learning.

Fortrose Cathedral, completed at the end of the fifteenth century, is for the most part a ruin, a condition due chiefly to the Reformation, although Cromwell is said to have carried off much of the stonework to Inverness to be used in the construction of his fort there.

The Cathedral formerly consisted of choir and nave with aisles to each, lady chapel, western tower, and a detached Chapter House. This last and the south aisle of chancel and nave are all that is left.

Acting as a buttress at the junction of the south aisle of nave and chancel is the rood turret, " a very elegant though singular composition." The top is modern. On the large bell in the spire is the name of Thomas Tulloch, Bishop of Ross in 1460. In this aisle or transept are the graves of the famous Rory Macleod (" Rory More ") and of many chiefs of the Mackenzies.

The Chapter House, renovated some years ago, has a beautiful groined roof. The upper storey is used as a Masonic Hall.

Rosemarkie (*Marine* (52 *rooms*) ; *Marita* (14 *rooms*)) is of greater antiquity than Fortrose. A monastery was founded here in the sixth century by the Culdees, and in 716 an endowment for it was obtained from the King of the Picts in northern Scotland by St. Boniface, or

Curitanus, who is said to have come from Italy, and to have visited Scotland for the purpose of inducing the ecclesiastics to conform to the practice of the Church of Rome. In 1125, David I founded the Bishopric of Ross in Rosemarkie, but in 1250 the See was transferred to Fortrose. In the middle of the fifteenth century the two towns were united by royal charter.

Rosemarkie has good sands for bathing, shares a golf course on Chanonry Point with Fortrose and is a regional transmitting station of the B.B.C. There are tennis courts and fine caravan sites.

A sculptured stone, with Pictish carving and symbols, in the churchyard is supposed to have marked the grave of St. Maluag or Moluog—" My Luke "—a follower of St. Columba, and the reputed founder of the monastery in Rosemarkie.

The **Burn of Eathie,** the scene of Hugh Miller's early discoveries, from which it has been well said he " dug his geological reputation," is 5 miles eastward from Rosemarkie, along the shore of the Moray Firth, and may be reached by boat or on foot. In Miller's *Old Red Sandstone* it is dealt with at length.

The **Fairy Glen,** half a mile from Rosemarkie, is in the valley through which flows the **Rosemarkie Burn.**

Cromarty.

Access.—*Ferries* to and from South Kessock (p. 405) in connection with trains. *Bus* from Kessock Ferry, Fortrose and Dingwall.
Early Closing.—Wednesday.
Hotel.—*Royal.*
Population.—About 720.
Recreation.—Safe bathing, sea-fishing, bowls, tennis, pony-trekking, etc.

Cromarty is a quaint, quiet little town that has lost its importance through the diversion to other ports of its trade and the decline of its fishery. It stands on a magnificent bay forming a safe harbour and entered between the **Sutors,** two bluff headlands exactly one mile distant from each other.

The thatched cottage which was the **Birthplace of Hugh Miller** (who gives a delightful description of his native town in *My Schools and Schoolmasters*) stands in Church Street (National Trust: *open*). Within are relics of the great geologist—fossils, manuscripts, and letters from eminent contemporaries, including Carlyle,

Darwin, Agassiz, Sir Thomas Dick Lauder and Chalmers. Adjoining is the house occupied by Miller on his marriage.

At the head of what is known as "the Pêys" (or the Paye) is a small cottage on which Miller made his start as a journeyman mason, while his last work with the chisel was a small headstone for the grave of his first child, Elizabeth. This, with its simple inscription, can still be seen in the old burying-ground of St. Regulus.

On high ground behind the town is the **Miller Monument.**

The Parish Church is one of the oldest in Scotland.

The **South Sutor** (463 ft.) is approached from the east end of the town, and footpaths lead to the summit. The views during the ascent and from the **Look-out**—a level moss-covered point overhanging the sea—are delightful. "A fine range of forest scenery stretches along the background, while in front the eye may wander over the hills of seven different counties, and so vast an extent of sea, that, on the soberest calculation, we cannot estimate it under a thousand square miles."—(*Hugh Miller.*)

The **Eathie Burn** (*see also* p. 419), 3 miles distant, may be entered from the seaside by following the highroad westward for about a mile, there taking a branch road, crossing over to Navity, and thence by the next turning reaching the beach, which must be followed westward until "where a mossy streamlet comes brattling from the hills," one sees "on turning a sudden angle, the bank cleft to its base, as if to yield the waters a passage." The nearer, and perhaps easier, way is by following the main road to a cottage in the corner of a field adjacent to the burn, and then proceeding along the track at the edge of the stream until a pathway is reached leading into the burn.

INVERNESS TO JOHN O' GROATS.

THIS route has been described as far as Muir of Ord on pp. 406–7 and 411. Eighteen miles from Inverness is **Dingwall**, the county town of Ross-shire, a royal burgh (dating from 1226), and, through its Academy, an educational centre for the north and west. (*Hotels: National, Royal, Caledonian.*) It has an old town hall and cross, tennis and bowls, and is a good centre, but to tourists it is chiefly important as the junction of road and rail routes to the West Coast and for its proximity (5 miles: bus) to—

Strathpeffer.

Angling.—The *Conon* and the *Blackwater* are good salmon streams, but permits are required. Some of the hotels have fishings.
Distances.—Inverness, 23 m.; Oban, 122 m.; Aberdeen, 131 m.; Edinburgh, 200 m.; London, 573 m.
Early Closing.—Thursdays in winter. June–September shops remain open till 10.30 p.m.
Golf.—There is a course of 18 holes on high ground, about 15 minutes' walk from the town square.
Hotels.—*Ben Wyvis, Highland, Holly Lodge, MacKay's, Richmond, Strathpeffer, Balmoral Lodge.* Caravan park.
Youth Hostel.—On the Garve Road. 97 beds.

Strathpeffer is a prettily situated village of modern creation on the sloping sides of a fertile valley near the foot of Ben Wyvis, and in the centre of some of the finest scenery in the Highlands. For long well known for its waters, the Strath is now chiefly known as a centre for tours in Northern Scotland.

After a lapse of many years, the Spa facilities have been revived. The famous Pump Room, newly re-opened in 1960, houses four wells from which sulphur and chalybeate waters are available.

Beside the square is the entrance to the **Gardens**, in which are putting and bowling greens, and the **Pavilion**, with concert room, dance hall and restaurant.

Among the best short excursions are—

1. **Knockfarrel** (720 feet) and the **Cat's Back** (822 feet). The shortest ascent of Knockfarrel is by a path from the Ben Wyvis Hotel garage. On the summit is one of the best-preserved vitrified forts in the country. The Cat's Back is the western end of the same ridge. To the summits and back is about 4 miles. In the valley behind them are the wood-fringed shores of **Loch Ussie**.

2. **Raven's Rock** (874 feet), a good viewpoint about 2 miles north-west, and best reached by walking along by the railway from Achterneed.

3. **View Rock** (500 feet) is picturesquely situated 2 miles from Strathpeffer *viâ* **Loch Kinellan.** (From it Loch Achilty and the Falls of Rogie can be conveniently visited.)

4. **Falls of Rogie,** 3 or 4 miles west, on the Ross-shire Blackwater. Famed for their leaping salmon, they are seen to most advantage from a chain bridge which spans the river below them.

5. **Loch Garve.**—About 4 miles beyond the Rogie Falls. The road lies through mountainous and romantic scenery. The return can be made by train from Garve station.

6. **Loch Achilty** (5 miles) is a beautiful sheet of water surrounded by birch and fir-clad hills, including the wooded pyramid of **Tor Achilty.** Farther on the same road are the **Lily Loch,** the **Falls of Conon** and **Loch Luichart** (10 miles).

7. **Circular Route by Brahan and Dingwall** (16 miles).—This excursion lies through varied and beautiful scenery. The road is by Contin (or Kinnahaird) to within a short distance of Moy Bridge. Instead of crossing the bridge it keeps straight on and passes up a shaded hill-road to the left of **Brahan Castle,** the former stronghold of the Earls of Seaforth, Chiefs of Clan Mackenzie. (Grounds open twice weekly in summer—usually Tuesday and Thursday ; admission *fee*, for the benefit of charity.)

8. **Ascent of Ben Wyvis** (3,429 feet).—The summit can be reached by pony, or on foot from near Achterneed station. Distance about 10 miles.

From Dingwall the route skirts Cromarty Firth. From Evanton village the *Black Rock* can be visited, and there is a track up beside the Glass river to Loch Glass. Crowning Knock Fyrish is a representation of the Gates of Negapatam—erected (to give employment in bad times) by Sir Hector Munro of Foulis (1726–1805), who won distinction as a General (and a fortune) in India.

A little way beyond Novar a good, though somewhat hilly, road branches off to the left and strikes almost due north across the hills *viâ Aultnamain Inn* to the Dornoch

Firth at Wester Fearn. This road reaches a height of 782 feet above sea-level and commands magnificent views.

Those desirous of seeing all that is to be seen, however, should disregard this road and continue by **Alness** to **Invergordon** (*Royal*, *Bisset's* (*unl.*), *etc.*), a town (naval depots) on either side of a wide main street. There is a modern swimming-pool, facilities for tennis, bowls, golf and boating.

On by **Saltburn**—a waterside village in marked contrast to its great Yorkshire namesake—and by the shore of Nigg Bay. **Nigg** has some fine sands. In the churchyard is a Celtic sculptured stone. There is another at **Shandwick**, two miles to the north.

At Barbaraville the road turns inland and crosses the promontory to **Tain**, an ancient and thriving town on the southern shore of the Dornoch Firth (*Royal*, *Balnagowan*, *Mansefield House*, *St. Duthus*). A quarter of a mile from the station is a particularly good golf course. Visitors welcome.

A massive tower forms the entrance to the Court House and County Buildings, but the architectural treasure of Tain is the restored ruin of **St. Duthus' Chapel.** The saint, often known as St. Duthac, is said to have been born on the site of the building. He became known as "the godly Bishop of Ross," and was reburied within the precincts of the chapel in 1253. The church, as now restored, was built in 1487. The Papal Bull authorizing its erection is in the archives of the burgh. The pulpit was presented by Regent Moray in recognition of the zeal of the inhabitants for the Reformation.

The story that James IV was born in the Abbey of St. Duthus in 1473 lacks confirmation, but for twenty years at least he made regular visits to the venerated shrine of St. Duthus, to do penance, it is supposed, for the part he took in his father's death. In 1527 James V made a pilgrimage barefooted to the shrine.

Four miles south-east, not far from Fearn station, are the remains of the **Abbey of Fearn**, a portion of which is still used as the parish church. Ten miles east of Tain, not far from Tarbat Ness Lighthouse, is **Portmahomack**, a fishing station and bathing resort.

Meikle Ferry no longer works across Dornoch Firth and cars must go westward, to Bonar Bridge (some 12 miles), in order to cross the Firth. The route is along the southern shore of the Firth by Edderton and Wester Fearn (where the direct route from the south by Aultnamain comes in on the left) to **Ardgay** (*Fearn Lodge*,

Commercial), where it branches off to the right for **Bonar Bridge** (*Dunroamin, Caledonian*). (*Main Route Resumed on p.* 425.)

BONAR BRIDGE TO LOCHINVER (49 miles).

The first few miles westward are along the northern shore of the Kyle of Sutherland. At **Inveran** (4½ miles) cross the river Shin and strike up Strath Oykell to **Oykell Bridge** (18 miles), where are some fine falls. Hence the road continues to climb, past Loch Craggie, reaching its highest point about 2 miles farther. It now descends through increasingly grand scenery to **Loch Borrolan** (*Altnacealgach Hotel*), beyond which the road from Ullapool comes in on the left. (*See* p. 415.)

Five miles north of Inveran and 11 miles from Bonar Bridge is **Lairg** (*Sutherland Arms*), at the southern end of **Loch Shin**, a fine sheet of water, 17¼ miles long, containing trout and *Salmo-ferox*. It can be fished by visitors at the hotels at Lairg and **Overscaig**. A huge dam near Lairg has greatly raised the level of Loch Shin.

From Lairg buses run to **Tongue** (2¾ hours), to **Scourie** (3¼ hours), and to **Lochinver** (3½ hours).

MOTOR ROUTES FROM LAIRG.

1. **Lairg to Tongue** (37 miles).—The route is up Strath Tirry, over the *Crask* (870 ft.) to the foot of **Ben Klibreck** (3,154 feet), and winds round the western side of that hill to Altnaharra, at the upper end of **Loch Naver**, a sheet of water 7 miles long. The loch contains salmon, large trout, and brown trout. It can be fished by guests at the *Altnaharra Hotel*. Half a mile north of the hotel a road leads along the north side of Loch Naver and then down Strath Naver to Bettyhill. The Tongue road strikes north and after rising to about 750 feet makes for the southern end of **Loch Loyal**. The lake is about 5 miles long, and is surrounded by high hills. One of these, Ben Loyal (2,504 feet), has a curiously splintered summit. The loch contains splendid trout and large *Salmo-ferox* and may be fished (on permit) by residents at the Tongue Hotel, as can also the neighbouring Loch Craggie and other lochs. The road skirts the western shore of Loch Loyal and then runs due north to Tongue (*hotel*), on the east side of the **Kyle of Tongue**, and in the neighbourhood of much mountain scenery of a grandly picturesque character. Near the village are the ruins of **Castle Varrich**, an old feudal keep. The *Borgie Lodge Hotel*, between

Cape Wrath
Light Ho.
370
Clash Carnoch
Cnoc-a-ghuish
982
Keisgag B.
Eilean Bulgac
The Shepherd
Sandwood
Sheigra
397
Oldshoremore
Roan I.
Loch Inchard
Kinlochbervie
Badcall
Kincaile
Achriesgill
Rhiconich
Loch Larford
Achlyness
Handa
406
Scourie B.
Scourie
325
Eddrachillis B.
Badcall
Badcall B.
Ben Stack
2367
Eddrachillis Bay
L. Cairnbawn
Oldany I.
Pt. of Stoer
Rhu Stoer
L. Culfruichie
Culkein
Oldany
Nedd
Clashmore
Balleladdich
Clashnessie
Quinag
Stoer
Clachtoll
Glasven
813
Achmelvich
Loch Inver
Lochinver
Soya I.
I. Kirkaig
Inverkirkaig
Canisp
2786
Suilven
2399
Coigeach
Enard Bay
Achnahaird B.
Rhubha Mor
Reiff
Polbain
Achiltibuie
Badenscallie
Coigach
Tanera More
Horse I.
Dubh I.
Bottle I.
Ben More
2438
Strathkanaird
Martin I.
Cailleach Hd.
Scoraig
Annat B.
Loch Broom
Little Loch Broom
Ullapool
Rhidorroch Forest
Glen Achallt
Leckmeln
Ardcharnich
Dundonnell
Sail Mhor
Badrallach
Gruinard
Dinan Mor
Kearvaig
Stac Chlo
Cleit Dhu
Garve I.
Castle Rock
Kyle of Durness
Farrid or Far out Hd.
Balnakeil
Durness
Smoo Cave
Eilean Hoan
Loch Eriboll
Kennageall or Whiten Hd.
Scrishven
The Parph
1504
Ben Derg-veg
1390
Fashven
Keoldale Hotel
Rispond
Ben Derg More
1427
Strath Shinary
Glasven Cottage
Mealmeanach
Portaneon
Heilim
Ben Spionn
2537
Carn Stackie
2630
Strath Dionard
Eriboll
Creag na Baolinn
Foinaven
2980
L. Dionard
Cashel Dhu
Ben Arkle
2582
L. Stack
Meall Horn
2548
Saval More
2283
Reay Deer Forest
Meall-garve
Achfary
Glashah
L. More
Ben Strome
L. Glendhu
Kyle Strome
Unapool
L. Glencoul
Ben Leod
Eas Coul Aulin
Ben Uie
Skiag Bri.
Ardvreck Cas.
L. Assynt
Inchnadamph
Hotel
Conivaill
Ben More
3273
L. Fad
Cam L.
L. Awe
Elphin
Knockan
L. Urigill
Cromalt Hills
Ledmore
Altnacealgach
L. Sionascaig
Coulmore
Coulbeg
2523
Stac Polly
L. Lurgain
Drumrunie
L. Craggie
Meall an Uran
1895
Oykel Bridge
Inn
Strath Oykel
Rappach W.
Gl. Einig
Ben Ulamhie
1816
Corriemulzie Lo.
Strath Mulzie
Freevater Forest
Badach Mor
2689
Alladale Lo.
Glen Alladale
Amat Lo.
Croick
Strath Carron
R. Carron
Balnagown Arms
Kincardine
Ben Hutick
1540
Talmin
Rabbit Is.
Kyle of Tongue
Tongue
Hotel
Moin Ho.
The Moin
Melness
Loch Hope
Hope Lodge
Ben Hope
3040
L. Derry
Cas. Varrich
Ribigill
Kinloch Ho.
Ben Laoghal
2504
(Ben Loyal)
Alltnacaillich
Dun Dornadilla
Strath More
L. Meadie
Gobernuisgach
Ben Dirach
Ben Hee
2864
L. Merkland
Forest
Altnaharra
Inn
Mudale
Coulside
L. Ellanach
Grubbeg
Loch Naver
Clibreck
Ben Clibreck
3164
SUTHERLAND
L. Griam
Glen Fiag
The Crask
Inn
Str. Crask
Strath Tirry
Loch Shin
Rhian
Shinness
Overscaig Inn
Maol-vealy
Ben Screavie
Ben Skerrach
Glen Cassley
Ben Eoin
1785
Rossal
Sallachy
L. Doula
Lairg
Torroboll
Achness
Invercassley
Rosehall
R. Oykel
Tutumtarvach
Achinduich
Invershin
Sta.
Achnahanat
Carbisdale Cas.
Culrain
Braelangwell
Strath Cuilenach
Bonar

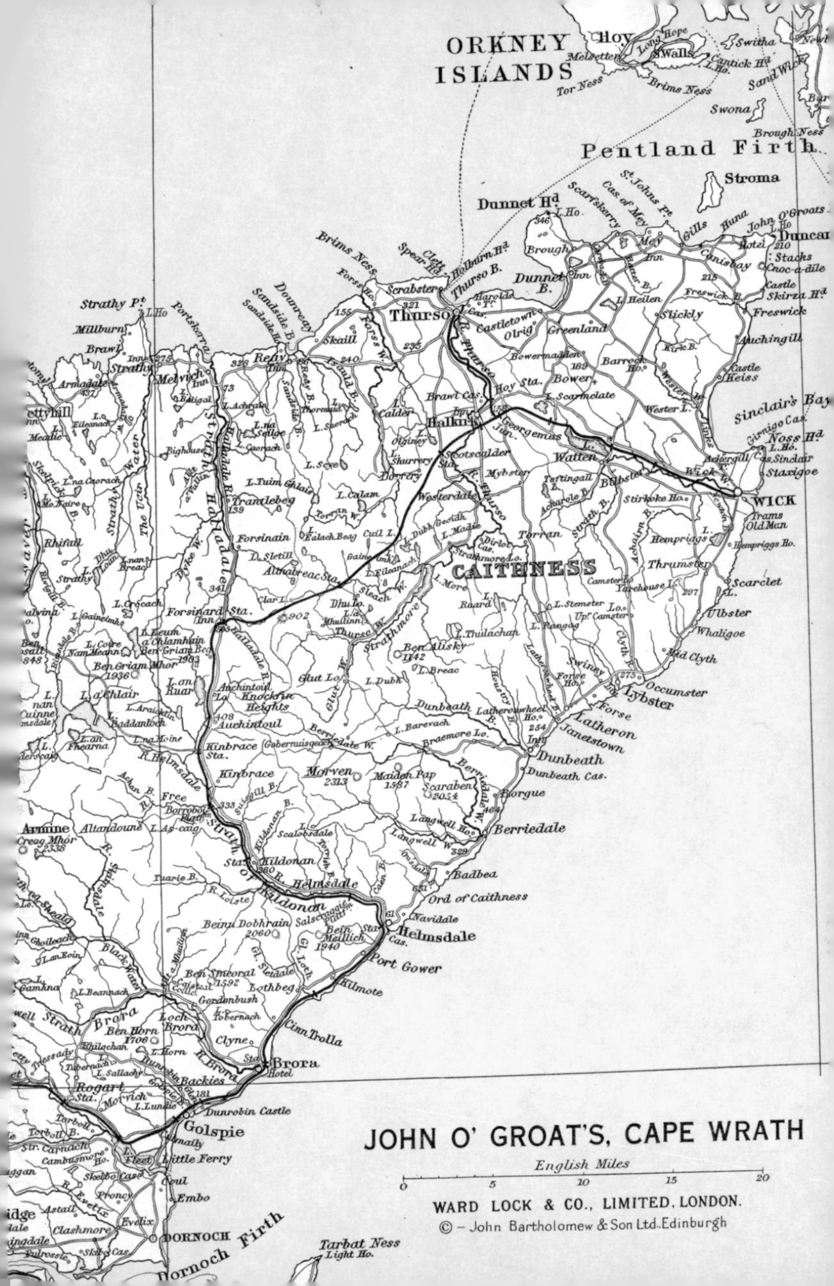
ORKNEY
ISLANDS
Hoy
Long Hope
S.Walls
Melsetter
Cantick Hd
Tor Ness
Brims Ness
Switha
Sand Wick
Swona
Brough Ness
Pentland Firth
Stroma
St Johns Pt
Scarfskerry
Cas. of Mey
Dunnet Hd
L.Ho.
Brough
Mey
Inn
Gills
Huna
John O'Groats
Duncan
Canisbay
Stacks
Cnoc-a-dile
Castle
Skirza Hd
Freswick
Freswick B.
Brims Ness
Spear Hd
Clett
Holburn Hd
Thurso B.
Dunnet B.
Scrabster
Forss Ho.
Thurso
Harolds Tr.
Cas.
Castletown
Olrig
Greenland
L. Heilen
Slickly
Auchingill
Strathy Pt
L.Ho
Portskerra
Sandside B.
Sandside Ho.
Dounreay
Skaill
Forss W.
Millburn
Brawl
Strathy
Melvich
Inn
Reay
Inn
Bowermadden
Barrock Ho.
Kirk B.
Castle Heiss
Bower
Hoy Sta.
Brawl Cas.
L. Calder
L. Scarmclate
Wester L.
Sinclair's Bay
Halkirk
Georgemas Jun.
Girnigo Cas.
Noss Hd
L. Ho.
Cas.Sinclair
Staxigoe
Armadale
Bettyhill
L. Meadie
L. Baligal
L. Achrain
L.na Seilge
L. Caorach
Bighouse
L. Sleve
Olginey
L. Shurrery
Dorrery
Scotscalder Sta.
Mybster
Watten
Achergill
Wick
Bilbster
Toftingall L.
WICK
Trams
Old Man
Strath Halladale
Halladale R.
Trantlebeg
L.Tuim Ghlais
L. Calam
Torran W.
Westerdale
Strath B.
Stirkoke Ho.
Acharole B.
Achairn B.
Hempriggs
Hempriggs Ho.
Dirlot Cas.
Torran
Strathmore Lo.
CAITHNESS
Thrumster
Forsinain
L. Sletill
Altnabreac Sta.
L.Eileanach
L. More
Camster
Yarehouse L.
Scarclet
Forsinard Sta.
Inn
Clar L.
902
Dhu Lo.
Thurso W.
Raard
L. Stemster
Lo.
Upr Camster
Ulbster
Whaligoe
L. Rangag
L.Thulachan
Strathmore
Ben Alisky
1142
L. Breac
Mid Clyth
Clyth B.
Swiney
Forse Ho.
Lybster
Occumster
Ben Griam Beg
Ben Griam Mhor
1936
1903
L.an Ruar
L. a'Chlair
L. Baddanloch
L.na Moine
Auchintoul
Knockfin Heights
Auchintoul
Glut Lo.
L. Dubh
Dunbeath
Latheronwheel Ho.
Latheron
Forse
Janetstown
Kinbrace Sta.
R. Helmsdale
L. Barevach
Berriedale W.
Braemore Lo.
Dunbeath
Dunbeath Cas.
Kinbrace
Morven
2313
Maiden Pap
1587
Scaraben
2054
Borgue
Free
Armine
Creag Mhór
2338
Altandoune
L. As-caig
Strath of Kildonan
Langwell Ho.
Berriedale
Langwell W.
Kildonan
Sta.
Scalobsdale
R. Helmsdale
Badbea
Ord of Caithness
Navidale
Helmsdale
Cas.
Beinn Dobhrain
2060
Salscraggie
Bein Meillich
1940
Port Gower
Black Water
Ben Smeoral
1592
Gordonbush
Lothbeg
Kilmote
L. Tobernach
Loch Brora
Strath Brora
Ben Horn
1706
Clyne
Cinn Trolla
Brora
Hotel
Rogart Sta.
Morvich
L. Lundie
Dunrobin Castle
Backies
Golspie
Little Ferry
Coul
Embo
Skelbo Cas.
Proncy
Evelix
Clashmore
DORNOCH
Dornoch Firth
Tarbat Ness
Light Ho.
JOHN O' GROAT'S, CAPE WRATH
English Miles
0
5
10
15
20
WARD LOCK & CO., LIMITED, LONDON.
© – John Bartholomew & Son Ltd. Edinburgh

Tongue and Bettyhill, offers exclusive fishing (on five lochs) and shooting.

From Tongue there is a good road eastward (44 miles) to Thurso (p. 430), by **Bettyhill** and **Melvich**, each with hotel accommodation.

A road runs westward from Tongue to **Durness** (*hotel*) (about 20 miles).

2. **Lairg to Scourie** (44 miles).—The first portion of the road is along the northern side of **Loch Shin**. Then the road skirts **Lochs Griam** and **Merkland**, both of which can be fished by guests at the Overscaig Hotel, 16 miles from Lairg. Beyond Loch Merkland is **Reay Deer Forest**, of which **Ben Hee** (2,864 feet) is the highest point. Then comes **Loch More**, the nearest hotel to which is at **Overscaig**, 11 miles distant. At 31 miles from Lairg is **Achfarry**. Soon afterwards the road reaches **Loch Stack**, under the cone of **Ben Stack** (2,364 feet), and the river *Laxford* that flows from it. The loch is one of the most famous in Scotland for its fish, but it is not open to the public. The Laxford, a fine salmon river, also is strictly preserved. At 37 miles from Lairg is **Laxford Bridge**. From it a road runs northward to **Durness** and one south-west to **Scourie** (*hotel: Youth Hostel*), a village on the coast.

Northward from Laxford Bridge a very interesting road runs to Durness (19 miles) by way of *Rhiconich* (*hotel*) at the head of Loch Inchard, alongside which a road runs to Kinlochbervie, on the edge of the wild and lonely coast terminating in Cape Wrath.

Durness, with sands and cliffs that rival those of Cornwall, is the most north-westerly parish on the British mainland, the principal village being **Durine** (*hotel*). One mile east is the remarkable limestone *Smoo Cave*. Close to **Balnakiel** (1½ miles) are some ancient stones and the ruins of a church. At Balnakiel a former R.A.F. camp has been converted to use as a Crafts village.

3. **Lairg to Lochinver** (47 miles).—From Lairg to **Rosehall** (11 miles), thence by the side of the *Oykell* to **Oykell Bridge** and hotel (16 miles), and thence over the watershed of Sutherland, with mountain peaks pricking the skyline in all directions, and numerous lochs within easy reach, all containing trout, to *Altnacealgach Hotel* (26 miles), a good resting-place, close to **Loch Borrolan**. Hotel guests can fish Loch Borrolan and the *Ledbeg*, which flows out of it, and also numerous near-by lochs and trouting streams. **Lochinver** is described on p. 416.

BONAR BRIDGE TO THURSO.

Main Route Resumed.

Having crossed the Dornoch Firth at Bonar Bridge, the road now runs seaward again along its northern side to

Dornoch, a few miles from which is Skibo Castle, to which Andrew Carnegie retired. Dornoch, created a Royal Burgh by Charles I in 1628, is the capital of Sutherland and almost the smallest county town in Scotland (population less than 1,000). It has a Cathedral, erected in the first half of the thirteenth century; its ancient castle, once used as the bishop's palace, is now an hotel; some good hotels (*Dornoch* (80 *rooms*), *Burghfield House, Dornoch Castle, Royal Golf*) and good boarding-houses offering accommodation; miles of links with an 18-hole and a 9-hole golf course; and extensive sands sloping gently to the water, ensuring perfectly safe and pleasant sea-bathing. Close to the beach is a good caravan and camping site. On three sides are heath-clad mountains and pine-covered hills. The climate is bracing and invigorating. Salmon and trout fishing can be had in the neighbourhood. But it is as a "Golfers' Paradise" that Dornoch most strongly appeals, and has become so popular that during the season the accommodation is unequal to the demand. Golf at Dornoch dates back to 1616, and the Dornoch Golf Links are the third earliest mentioned in history.

Like the railway, the main road to Wick and Thurso bypasses Dornoch. While the former runs north from Bonar Bridge to Lairg, then east down Strath Fleet to the coast, the road turns east till short of Dornoch, then north to meet the line again at the Mound (17 miles from Bonar Bridge).

North of Dornoch lies **Loch Fleet,** almost landlocked, and the Trunk road crosses its head by an embankment known locally as the *Mound.* Hence to the left a road goes up beside the Fleet river to **Lairg** (p. 424); the main route swings eastward once more.

A colossal statue of the Duke of Sutherland, erected by the Sutherland tenantry, comes into sight on the left.

Golspie (84¼ miles from Inverness, 70 miles by using A836) is a pleasant village with an 18-hole golf course and an excellent beach for sea-bathing. Visitors at the *Sutherland Arms Hotel* may fish Loch Brora, which contains trout averaging one pound. Also available is the fishing in Lochs Lundie and Horn. At a short distance are two of the best-preserved *brochs* or Pictish towers in the Highlands. Golspie is a mile and a half from **Dunrobin Castle,** where the Countess of Sutherland has established a new public school. Admission to the grounds is readily granted, but the house can be seen only by special order.

Beyond Golspie comes **Brora** (*Links, Royal Marine, Sutherland Arms, Grand, Bayview*) situated on a beautiful bay, stretching for miles, and perfect for bathing or boating. The river *Brora*, containing brown and sea trout, is available on permit, half a mile from its mouth, and visitors at the hotels may fish **Loch Brora,** 4 miles distant, one of the choicest sheets of water in Sutherlandshire. The golf course extends along the seashore for more than 3 miles, with turf of the finest order.

Just 100 miles from Inverness (by rail) is **Helmsdale,** which has long been an important fishing centre. On the right are the ruins of a castle, formerly a hunting seat of the Sutherland family. (*Hotels: Belgrave Arms* (14 rooms), *Bridge* (28 rooms), *Navidale House.*) *Youth Hostel.*

The railway and a good road turn northward from Helmsdale through Strath Ullie, a bare valley, having little to interest the traveller after the first few miles. At Kildonan attempts have been made (sometimes with a measure of success) at gold-mining. Near **Forsinard** is an hotel, visitors at which may fish several neighbouring lochs. The road reaches the north coast at **Melvich** (*hotel*), a popular trout-fishing resort on the main road between Thurso and Tongue. The proprietor of the Melvich Hotel has fishing rights on a score of lochs.

From Helmsdale the main road, now rather taxed by heavy traffic, follows the coast and immediately after leaving Helmsdale climbs steeply up to a maximum height of 747 feet in order to surmount the **Ord of Caithness.** The road then descends steeply to the picturesque village of **Berriedale,** just before reaching which there is a very fine view to the left up the **Langwell Glen** to the conical mountain of **Morven** (2,313 feet), with the three humps of **Scaraben** (2,054 feet) to the right. (For permission to climb these two hills apply at the Factor's Office at Berriedale.) At the entrance to the Glen is Langwell House, the shooting-seat of the Duke of Portland.

Beyond Berriedale the road climbs up very steeply with hairpin bends and then follows the coast through not very interesting country past Dunbeath (*hotel*), **Latheronwheel** (*hotel*), also called Janetstown, and Lybster (*hotel*) to Wick, 37 miles from Helmsdale.

Wick.

Airport.—The most northerly on the mainland. Services to and from Inverness in 45 minutes, Orkney 25 minutes, Shetland 1 hour 10 minutes.
Angling.—May be arranged for in the river *Wick* and neighbouring burns and lochs.
Early Closing.—Wednesday.
Golf.—18-hole course at Reiss Links, 3 miles distant.
Hotels.—*Mackay's* (27 rooms), *Nethercliffe* (10 rooms), *Queen's* (5 rooms), *Station* (57 rooms), and various guest houses.
Population.—About 7,800.

Wick is the county town of Caithness. It was once a busy herring fishing station, but this has given way to a thriving business with white fish which are iced at a factory, boxed and sent to the south.

In the neighbourhood are several interesting ruins, including Castle Sinclair and Castle Girnigoe on the coast at Noss Head, 3 miles north of Wick, and an ancient tower called the **Old Man of Wick** on the edge of the cliffs, 1 mile to the south of Wick Bay. Near the Old Man of Wick is some magnificent rock scenery, especially at the spot called the Brig o' Tram, where a narrow natural bridge connects the main cliff to what would otherwise be a detached skerry.

From Wick to John o' Groats, the road, about 16½ miles, for the most part runs along the coast. Objects of interest *en route* are the modern **Keiss Castle** and the ruined ancient castle.

Near Keiss are some of the finest brochs in Scotland, several of which have been opened up. One of them which may be readily visited is near the shore at Brough Head, 2 miles north of Keiss. It is conspicuous from the road by reason of a peculiar cairn which has been erected in its centre.

Two miles beyond Brough Head is **Bucholly Castle**, a most picturesque ruin, on the edge of the cliffs. It stands on an almost completely severed mass of rock which is only connected to the mainland by a narrow neck of rock. It is a sort of miniature Dunnottar Castle and was once a stronghold of Swayne the Pirate. **Freswick Castle,** on the shore, is the next object of interest and beyond it the road climbs up to a height of 325 feet on Warth Hill and commands a magnificent view, better seen from the top of the hill (412 feet) a short way off. The road then descends to Duncansby and John o' Groats.

John o' Groats (*John o' Groats House, Seaview*) is not, as is popularly supposed, the most northerly point of the mainland ; for that it is necessary to go to **Dunnet Head,** nearer Thurso. John o' Groats is, however, 876 miles from Land's End in the very far south-west, and even the facility of modern motoring cannot banish altogether some feeling of achievement on the part of those who have come thus far. There are grand views across to **Stroma** island and to Ronaldsay and Hoy in the Orkneys. The beach is thickly strewn with shells, particularly with a kind of cowry, known as Groatie buckies.

According to tradition, John de Groat was one of several Dutch brothers who settled in Caithness in James IV's reign, and prospered until fratricidal strife threatened over the question of precedence at the annual family banquet. The wily John averted the danger by designing a house with eight walls, eight windows and eight doors, and a table with eight sides, so that each of the eight claimants could enter by his own door and assert that his was the seat of honour—like the Highland chieftain who haughtily declared, "Wherever the Pherson sits, that's the head of the table!" A room in John o' Groats Hotel commemorates this legend.

At Canisbay Church, at Kirkstyle on the coast, there is built into the south wall of the south transept a slab (dated 1568) commemorating various members of the Groat family.

Two miles east of John o' Groats is **Duncansby Head** (210 feet), the most beautiful headland in the north of Scotland. About a mile south of the Head are two immense pillars of rock, called the **Stacks of Duncansby.**

ALONG THE NORTH COAST.

Good roads serving the north coast make it easy and comfortable for motorists and cyclists to reach a number of places with great potentialities as holiday resorts. None of them is large—few are more than hamlets—but for cliffs and sands with fine mountain backgrounds this coast is worth exploration.

From John o' Groats the way is by **Canisbay Church**—outside which is a large inscribed slab *said to be* the gravestone of the veritable John o' Groats—through relatively uninteresting country, passing on the right, Mey, where is the sixteenth-century **Barrogill Castle** (Castle of Mey) which belongs to Queen Elizabeth the Queen Mother. On next to Dunnet, at the southern end of **Dunnet Head,** 341 feet, which is the most northerly point of the mainland. **Dunnet Bay** (*hotel*) has a splendid stretch of firm sands divided from the road by dunes of almost mountainous proportions.

Thurso (*Royal, Pentland, Holborn, St. Clair*) is the most northerly town on the mainland. Objects of interest are the house of Robert Dick, baker, botanist and geologist, whose life was written by Smiles, and the Museum bequeathed to the town by Dick. Though the town will not long detain the visitor, Thurso has excellent natural advantages as a seaside resort. The bathing is good and the long stretch of firm sands one of the finest in the North. Steamers run daily between Scrabster Harbour, 2 miles from Thurso, and Stromness, Orkney.

At Dounreay, 8 miles from Thurso, is the United Kingdom Atomic Energy Authority's experimental Atomic Station with a striking steel sphere housing the atomic pile (*museum*).

Two miles farther west is **Reay,** a hamlet near the head of the aptly named **Sandside Bay,** and then comes **Melvich** (*hotel*). There are good sands in the bay; there is plenty of fishing—sea and freshwater—and all along the coast are rocky coves well worth visiting. **Strathy, Armadale, Farr** are representative of other places along this coast—humble hamlets yet in splendid holiday surroundings.

At **Bettyhill** (*hotel*) are fine sands and fishing of all kinds.

From **Borgie Bridge** (*Borgie Lodge Hotel* half a mile to the north) to **Tongue** there are magnificent views of **Ben Loyal** and this most shapely mountain dominates the southward prospect as the road rounds the Kyle of Tongue, and makes for the bridge at the northern end of **Loch Hope.**

Loch Eriboll is a fiord-like inlet of sea, surrounded by great grim mountains.

At the entrance to Loch Eriboll is **Rispond** (*hotel*) and from there the rocky coast runs up to **Far-Out Head,** at the foot of which are **Sango Bay** and **Durness** (*see* p. 425).

Cape Wrath, the most north-westerly point on the mainland, is 523 feet above sea-level (lighthouse).

THE ORKNEY AND SHETLAND ISLES.

ALTHOUGH these two groups are at least 50 miles apart they have certain features in common. In the first place, so far as holiday-makers are concerned, the climate of both Orkney and Shetland is much milder than one might suppose from a consideration of their latitude (Shetland is in approximately the same latitude as Bergen, and farther north than Oslo). The mean temperature of Orkney is about 46 degrees ; the average annual rainfall from 30–37 inches. A happy effect of the northern latitude is the length of the day in summer. In June, the sun rises about 3 a.m. at Kirkwall and does not set until nearly 10.30 p.m., and even then daylight is not succeeded by the darkness of night, and it is often possible to read by ordinary light at midnight.

As to attractions for visitors, the saying is " Shetland for scenery, Orkney for antiquities "—and one might add " either for angling." There is also golf, tennis and bowls and the two " capitals " have their cinemas and local newspapers.

The place-names recall that for centuries the Islands were part of Norway, and the vigour with which the Norwegians sailed the neighbouring seas is illustrated by the Norse tinge in many place-names on the mainland. The isles belonged to Norway after the Hebrides had been ceded to Scotland in 1266 (p. 153), but in 1468 they were pledged by Christian I for the payment of the dowry of his daughter Margaret, who married James III. The dowry was not paid and the isles were annexed by Scotland in 1472.

In extent, the **Orkney Isles** are 48 miles from north to south and 35 miles east to west. Only about a score of the islands are inhabited. The total area is 376 square miles, and the population about 18,400. The **Shetland Isles** measure nearly 70 miles from north to south and 30 miles from east to west. Of the hundred islands only eighteen are inhabited. The mainland is 55 miles long, but so irregular is its outline that a walk round the coast would cover 480 miles, although no part of the island is more than 3 miles from the sea. The area of the group is 550 square miles, and the population some 18,000. From the north of Orkney to the south of the mainland of Shetland is 50 miles, and half-way lies lonely Fair Isle. From the mainland of Scotland to the south of Orkney is a matter of 7 miles.

THE ORKNEY ISLES.

Access.—Steamer between Scrabster (near Thurso) and Stromness every weekday, and on Sundays in July and August, the crossing taking just under 3 hours. From Leith and Aberdeen by steamer about twice weekly in summer; less frequently in winter. For current details apply *North of Scotland and Orkney and Shetland Shipping Company,* Matthews' Quay, Aberdeen. *Air Services* from Aberdeen and Inverness *vid* Wick.

The Orkney Isles number sixty-seven, of which twenty-nine are inhabited, and they extend northward for upwards of 48 miles. The western coasts present to the Atlantic an almost unbroken front of lofty cliffs, the abode of innumerable sea-birds. Everywhere the coast teems with fish; and seals, otters, whales, and porpoises are by no means uncommon.

In calm weather the stretches of sea that, like Scapa Flow, are land-locked by the islands, resemble a vast lake, clear and bright as a mirror, and are without a ripple, save for the gentle impulse of the tide. But during a storm the grandeur of the Orkney land- and sea-scapes is fully revealed. Thick driving mists sweep over the hilly districts, and upon the weather shore, especially if this be on the west side, beat waves of a magnitude and force of which few strangers can have formed any conception. On the west side of Hoy, and at the Black Craig, north of Stromness, they climb cliffs 300 feet and more in height, tear away the soil and hurl large boulders through the air.

Kirkwall and Stromness, the largest towns in the Orkneys, are on **Mainland**, sometimes erroneously called Pomona. Both towns have 18-hole golf courses open to visitors.

KIRKWALL.

Kirkwall (*Royal, Queen's, Kirkwall, Albert, West End,*

Ayre, Lynnfield) stands at the head of a fine bay which indents the centre of the north side of the island. Its narrow streets and lanes, and its houses, with thick strong walls and small windows, which turn their crow-stepped gables towards the street, seem to speak of its Norwegian origin. The grand old **Cathedral** was begun in 1137 and dedicated to St. Magnus. (*Admission, free, in summer every weekday,* 10 *a.m. to* 6 *p.m. and in early mornings, on arrival of Aberdeen steamer; winter* 10 *a.m. to* 4 *p.m.*) Its architecture resembles that of Trondhjem, in Norway. The oldest parts are the transepts and three bays of the choir; the first five bays of the nave are only slightly later. The nave is interesting on account of its massive Norman pillars. It is less than 50 feet wide, but this very narrowness gives an impression of height. Note the various "mort brods," each with name of the deceased and various symbolic designs. The whole of the Cathedral has been thoroughly restored.

In 1263 Haakon, King of Norway, was buried here, but his remains were afterwards removed to Trondhjem. Twenty-seven years later the Maid of Norway (*see* p. 29) died on board ship off South Ronaldsay, but there is no foundation for the legend that she was buried in Kirkwall Cathedral. Among the tombs in the nave-aisles are those of two nineteenth-century explorers: W. B. Baikie (1824–65: Africa) and John Rae (1813–93) "the intrepid discoverer of Franklin." In the vestry are some old brazen alms plates, one engraved with a picture of Paradise and inscribed, "Had Adam gedaen Gods woort wys soo vaer hy gebleven int Paradys Anno 1636" ("Had Adam obeyed God's word we should have been in Paradise"). Two skeletons, discovered in 1926 in pinewood chests within two pillars, are held to be those of St. Magnus (ass. in 1114) and his nephew St. Rognvald.

The view from the top of the tower is interesting, and useful to those who find difficulty in getting their bearings in this island of extremely irregular coastlines.

Close to the Cathedral are the remains of the Bishop's and Earl's palaces; the latter a fine specimen of sixteenth-century domestic architecture. **Wideford Hill (741 feet)**, in the neighbourhood of the town, commands an uninterrupted view of all the Orkney Isles. On the north-west slope of the hill is a prehistoric chambered cairn which is cared for by the Department of the Environment. A similar structure may be seen on Cuween or Kewing Hill, Finstown. Across a narrow isthmus, where the main island is nearly cut in two, and nearly 2 miles from Kirkwall, is **Scapa Pier**, on the wide expanse of **Scapa Flow**, well known as a Naval base. Here the Germans scuttled their Fleet in May, 1919.

Buses run between Kirkwall and Stromness, at the south-west corner of the island. The winding road is about 15 miles long. There is an inn at **Finstown**, about half-way. A little beyond the ninth milestone is the far-famed **Mound of Maeshowe**, a large, chambered construction, which can be explored by visitors. (Key at the neighbouring farm of Tormiston, *fee.*) Close to Maeshowe, where two large lochs, Harray and Stenness, open into each other, are the greater and the lesser circles of the **Standing Stones of Stenness**, objects of supreme archæological interest, although " The Stone of Odin," mentioned in Sir Walter Scott's novel, *The Pirate*, no longer exists. The principal circle, the *Ring of Brogar*, has a diameter of over 120 yards and is surrounded by a deep trench. Twenty-seven of the stones still stand, the average height being about 10 feet. Nearer the road and the hotel three stones, two of them 15 and 18 feet high, and a tablestone, are remains of another circle.

Stromness (*Stromness*), the " Venice of the North," contains much that is of interest ; as does **Birsay** (*hotel*), at the north-west corner of the island, where are the ruins of the Earl's Palace. On the Brough of Birsay, which is accessible at low tide, are the remains of a Viking settlement and of a mediæval monastery. On the west coast of the island and at the southern edge of the Bay of Skaill is the exceedingly interesting prehistoric village of **Skara Brae.** Active excavations since 1928 have revealed a group of stone huts connected by covered passages, besides furniture, implements, ornaments, and one or two skeletons of the former inhabitants. The settlement probably belongs to a Stone Age later than that of the Scottish mainland. Other notable early monuments which have been developed by the Ministry in charge of ancient monuments are the Knowe of Gurness on Aiker Ness, 11 miles north-west from Kirkwall, and the broch and neolithic burial construction at Mid Howe on the island of Rousay.

Two miles south-west of Birsay is **Marwick Head,**

off which sank, on June 5, 1916, H.M.S. *Hampshire*, while conveying Lord Kitchener and his staff to Russia. On the headland is a monument to their memory.

The island of **Hoy** comes next in size to Mainland. Its steep, dark-tinted hills are the highest in the group, and its cliff scenery is the most imposing in the British Isles. It is, however, difficult of access, and lacking in accommodation for travellers, at least at the northern end, where most of the wonders of its cliffs, mountains and antiquities are situated. It contains the **Dwarfie Stone** and the **Carbuncle** (a mass of sandstone) on Ward Hill, the legends attached to which play an important part in the plot of *The Pirate*. But the most noteworthy feature of the island is the **Old Man of Hoy**, an isolated pillar of rock, 450 feet high, facing the Atlantic about 2 miles south of St. John's Head. The latter is 1,141 feet high and is probably the loftiest vertical sea cliff in the British Isles.

The Isle of **Egilsay**, one of the most interesting of the group, contains the ruins of *St. Magnus Church*, in which the patron saint of Orkney and Shetland, St. Magnus, was murdered by his colleague in the government of the two archipelagos, in the early part of the twelfth century. It possesses a round tower. On **Eynhallow**, the Holy Isle, in the strait between Rousay and Mainland, are the remains of an ancient monastery.

South Ronaldsay, the most southern of the group, has an area of about 18 square miles. It is linked with **Burray** and Burray with Mainland by a causeway built during the 1939–45 War. It contains the village of **St. Margaret's Hope**, near which is the Broch called the **Howe of Hoxa**. Other islands deserving mention are Shapinsay, Stronsay, Sanday, Eday, **Westray** (on which is the ruined Castle of Noltland) and North Ronaldsay. **Stroma**, in the Pentland Firth, belongs to Caithness.

THE SHETLAND ISLES.

Access.—Communication between the mainland and Shetland is maintained by the *North of Scotland and Orkney and Shetland Shipping Company*, whose steamers run between Lerwick, Aberdeen and Leith (Edinburgh) three or four times weekly. Current particulars respecting fares and times of sailing may be obtained from the Manager, Aberdeen.

Air Services to Sumburgh from Glasgow, Edinburgh, Aberdeen and Inverness.

The Shetland (or Zetland) group lies 48 miles to the north-east of the Orkneys. Midway between lies the

Fair Isle, a lonely island battered constantly beneath the assaults of the Atlantic and the North Sea. These two oceans join forces south of Sumburgh Head, where they form the turbulent tideway of the " Roost," which may be avoided by travellers taking the direct route from Aberdeen to Lerwick. Fair Isle gives its name to the patterned knitted wear for which Shetland is famous; in 1588 it was the scene of the wreck of *El Gran Grifon* of Armada fame, one of a host of vessels which have found an untimely grave on the rocky shores. Fair Isle has a noted Bird Observatory, with hostel.

The Shetland group (pop. 18,000) consists of about a hundred islands; some eighteen are inhabited. The surface of the larger islands is hilly, the trend of the ridges north and south, broken here and there by narrow transverse valleys. The hills are covered to their summits with moorland, their dark surface contrasting strongly with the deep green of the valleys and cultivated coast lands, their monotony intensified rather than relieved by numerous small lochs—in winter sombre treeless wastes, in summer and autumn a medley of contrasting colours. The highest point in the islands is **Ronas Hill**, a mass of red granite, 1,486 feet high. From its summit a magnificent panorama of the whole islands may be obtained, and at midsummer the sun may be observed to sink slowly below the horizon, reappearing in an hour or two a little to the east. In June and July it is never really dark; indeed it is this aspect of the islands, the " simmer dim," the long twilight with its everchanging shadows, that lingers longest in the memory.

The coastline is broken and rugged. Long winding sheltered voes or inlets of the sea, bordered by cultivated fields, run far inland. Bold headlands jut out into the ocean, rising at times into lofty cliffs that for grandeur and sublimity have few rivals. The Noup of Noss (592 feet), Fitful Head (928 feet), the Kame of Foula (1,220 feet), all sheer cliffs, form conspicuous landmarks. Lofty stacks, natural arches and deep caverns abound along the coast; some caves run inland for some distance and may reach the surface as pit-like openings, known locally as " kirns," at the bottom of which the sea foams and swirls. The Holes of Scraada in Eshaness is a well-known example, the Round Reeva in the Fair Isle is another. The small island of Papa Stour, owing to the columnar jointing of its rocks, is honeycombed with caves.

There is good angling to be had in Shetland. Some fishings are under the control of the Shetland Anglers' Association, while others are held privately, but in all cases permits are readily issued on payment of the low fees applicable.

MAINLAND,

the largest of the islands, is 54 miles long, but of very irregular outline. On it is **Lerwick,** the capital, a busy, cosmopolitan town in the herring fishing season, when its capacious harbour is crowded with vessels of many nations. There is a golf course (9 holes) on the island of Bressay, a mile by motor-boat. (*Hotels : Queen's, Grand.*)

On the west coast about 30 miles from Lerwick, **Hillswick** (*St. Magnus Hotel*) is placed near some magnificent rock scenery. To the north of it is **Ronas Hill** (1,486 feet), the highest hill in Shetland.

Scalloway (*Royal, Scalloway*), formerly the capital, is chiefly visited for the sake of the ruins of its castle, built in 1600 by Earl Patrick Stewart of evil fame.

To the east of Lerwick is **Bressay,** with the adjacent islets of **Noss,** a Nature Reserve, and the smaller **Holm of Noss,** formerly reached by a rope bridge, the Cradle of Noss. A pleasant excursion, when the weather is suitable, is the circuit of these islands by motor-boat or steamer from Lerwick ; the cliff scenery is magnificent.

South of Lerwick is—

The Island of Mousa,

which contains the most perfect specimen of a Pictish broch in existence. This, known as Mousa Castle, is about 40 feet high and 158 feet in circumference at the base. It gradually decreases in width till within about 10 feet of its top and then again expands—an arrangement which effectually prevented an attacking force scaling its walls, while the small size of the doorway, which could be built up in case of attack, rendered access in that way impossible. Upwards of eighty of these brochs, all in ruins, occur in Shetland, occupying strategic positions on headlands or in lochs. That of Clickimin, near Lerwick, ranks next to Mousa.

The most northerly spot in the British Isles is a conical rock, the **Muckle Flugga**, rising nearly 200 feet out of the sea off the coast of Unst. On it stands a lighthouse, which in spite of its height—250 feet above the water—is sometimes swept by the waves. At the other extremity of the group is **Sumburgh Head**, bearing a lighthouse, and its loftier neighbour Fitful Head. This district figures largely in *The Pirate*. At Jarlshof, near Sumburgh, are the remains of an interesting succession of settlements which recent excavations have proved to be of Bronze Age, Iron Age and Viking periods. The site is under the care of the Department of the Environment, and is open to visitors at the usual hours (*charge*). Sumburgh (*hotel*) is the airport for Shetland (bus to Lerwick).

The inhabitants of these islands are engaged chiefly in fishing, farming, knitting and the rearing of sheep and ponies, for which the islands are renowned. Whaling was prosecuted from several stations on the west coast, but has been discontinued.

For rough shooting and all-round fishing, Shetland offers an attractive field. Rabbits are fairly abundant in many of the islands. There are also snipe, wild duck and golden plovers. The sea-fishing is splendid, and fine sport may be had with saithe off the rocks. Sea trout run large, and the lochs are full of brown trout. At most of the outlying islands seals are to be seen in great numbers. To the bird-lover and the geologist the islands are also of especial interest.

INDEX

Fraserburgh
Peterhead
ABERDEEN
Dee
Aboyne
Buckie
Wick
Helmsdale
Thurso
Dornoch
Moray Firth
Forres
Spey
Cairngorm
Balmoral
Inverness
Aviemore
Dingwall
Ness
Cape Wrath
Scourie
Lochinver
Fort Augustus
Strome
Kyle of Lochalsh
Stornoway
LEWIS
HARRIS
SKYE
Dunvegan

James Patterson is one of the best-known and biggest-selling writers of all time. Among his creations are some of the world's most popular series, including Alex Cross, the Women's Murder Club, Michael Bennett and the Private novels. He has written many other number one bestsellers including collaborations with President Bill Clinton, Dolly Parton and Michael Crichton, stand-alone thrillers and non-fiction. James has donated millions in grants to independent bookshops and has been the most borrowed adult author in UK libraries for the past fourteen years in a row. He lives in Florida with his family.

Maxine Paetro is a novelist who has collaborated with James Patterson on the bestselling Women's Murder Club, Private and Confessions series, *Woman of God*, and other stand-alone novels. She lives with her husband, John, in New York.

Meet The Women's Murder Club

EXCLUSIVE PROFILES **by Our Crime Desk**

LINDSAY BOXER

A homicide detective in the San Francisco Police Department, juggling the worst murder cases with the challenges of being a first-time mother. Her loving husband Joe, daughter Julie and loyal border-collie Martha give her a reason to protect the city. She didn't have the easiest start to life, with an absent father and an ill mother, but she didn't shy away from a difficult and demanding career. With the help of her friends, Lindsay makes it her mission to solve the toughest cases.

CLAIRE WASHBURN

Chief Medical Examiner for San Francisco and one of Lindsay's oldest friends. Wise, confident and viciously funny, she can be relied on to help whatever the problem. She virtually runs the Office of the Coroner for her overbearing, credit-stealing boss, but rarely complains. Happily married with children, her personal life is relatively calm in comparison to her professional life.

CINDY THOMAS

An up-and-coming journalist who's always looking for the next big story. She'll go the extra mile, risking life and limb to get her scoop. Sometimes she prefers to grill her friends over cocktails for a juicy secret, but, luckily for them, she's totally trustworthy (most of the time...). She somehow found the time to publish a book between solving cases, writing articles for the *San Francisco Chronicle* and keeping together her relationship with Lindsay's partner, Rich Conklin.

> "When your job is murder, you need **friends you can count on**"

YUKI CASTELLANO

One of the best lawyers in the city, she's desperate to make her mark. Ambitious, intelligent and passionate, she'll fight for what's right, always defending the underdog even if it means standing in the way of those she loves. Often this includes her husband – who is also Lindsay's boss – Lt. Jackson Brady.

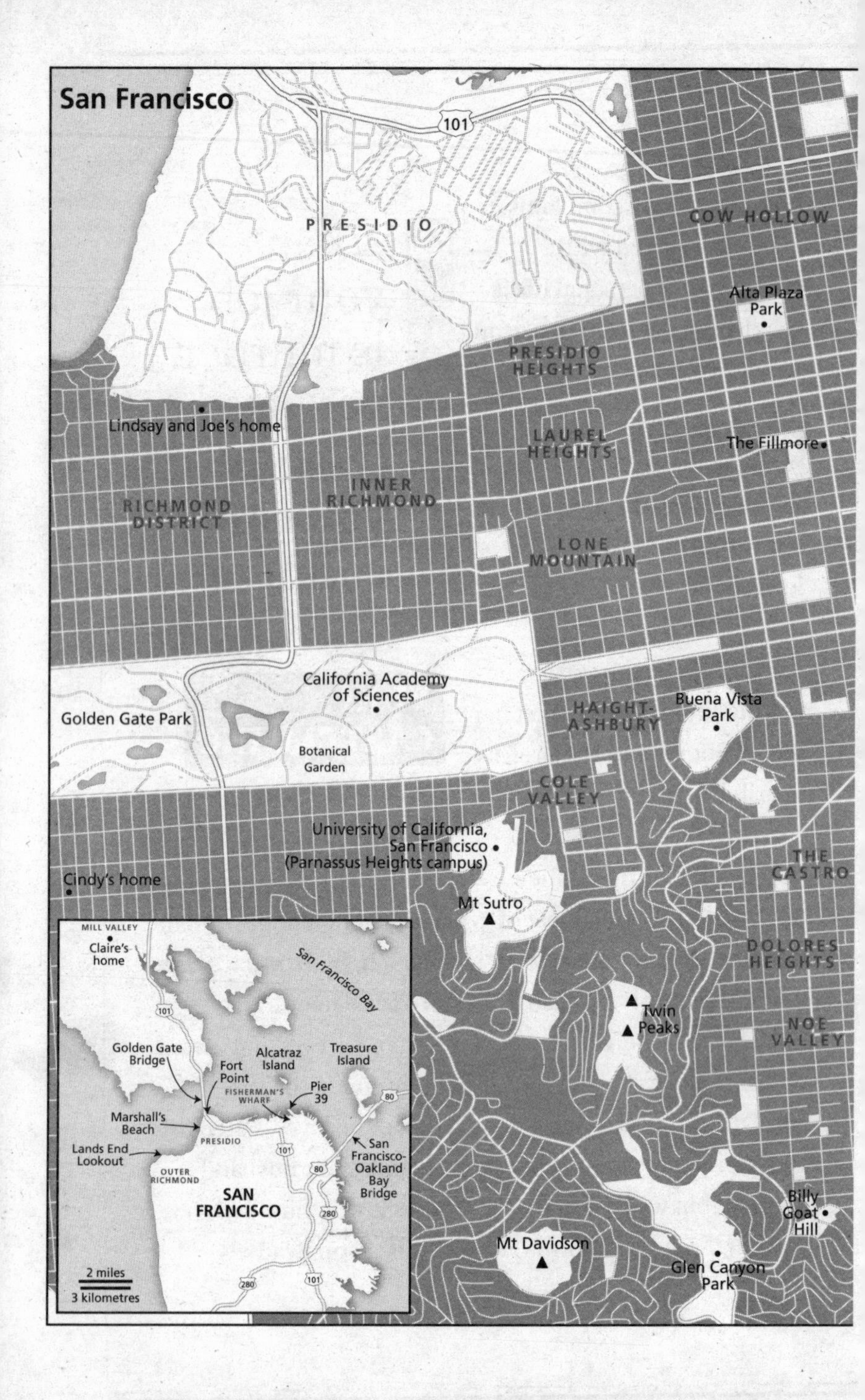
San Francisco
101
PRESIDIO
COW HOLLOW
Alta Plaza Park
PRESIDIO HEIGHTS
Lindsay and Joe's home
LAUREL HEIGHTS
The Fillmore
INNER RICHMOND
RICHMOND DISTRICT
LONE MOUNTAIN
California Academy of Sciences
Golden Gate Park
HAIGHT-ASHBURY
Buena Vista Park
Botanical Garden
COLE VALLEY
University of California, San Francisco (Parnassus Heights campus)
THE CASTRO
Cindy's home
Mt Sutro
DOLORES HEIGHTS
Twin Peaks
NOE VALLEY
Billy Goat Hill
Mt Davidson
Glen Canyon Park
MILL VALLEY
Claire's home
San Francisco Bay
101
Golden Gate Bridge
Alcatraz Island
Treasure Island
Fort Point
FISHERMAN'S WHARF
Pier 39
80
Marshall's Beach
PRESIDIO
San Francisco-Oakland Bay Bridge
Lands End Lookout
101
80
OUTER RICHMOND
SAN FRANCISCO
280
2 miles
3 kilometres
280
101

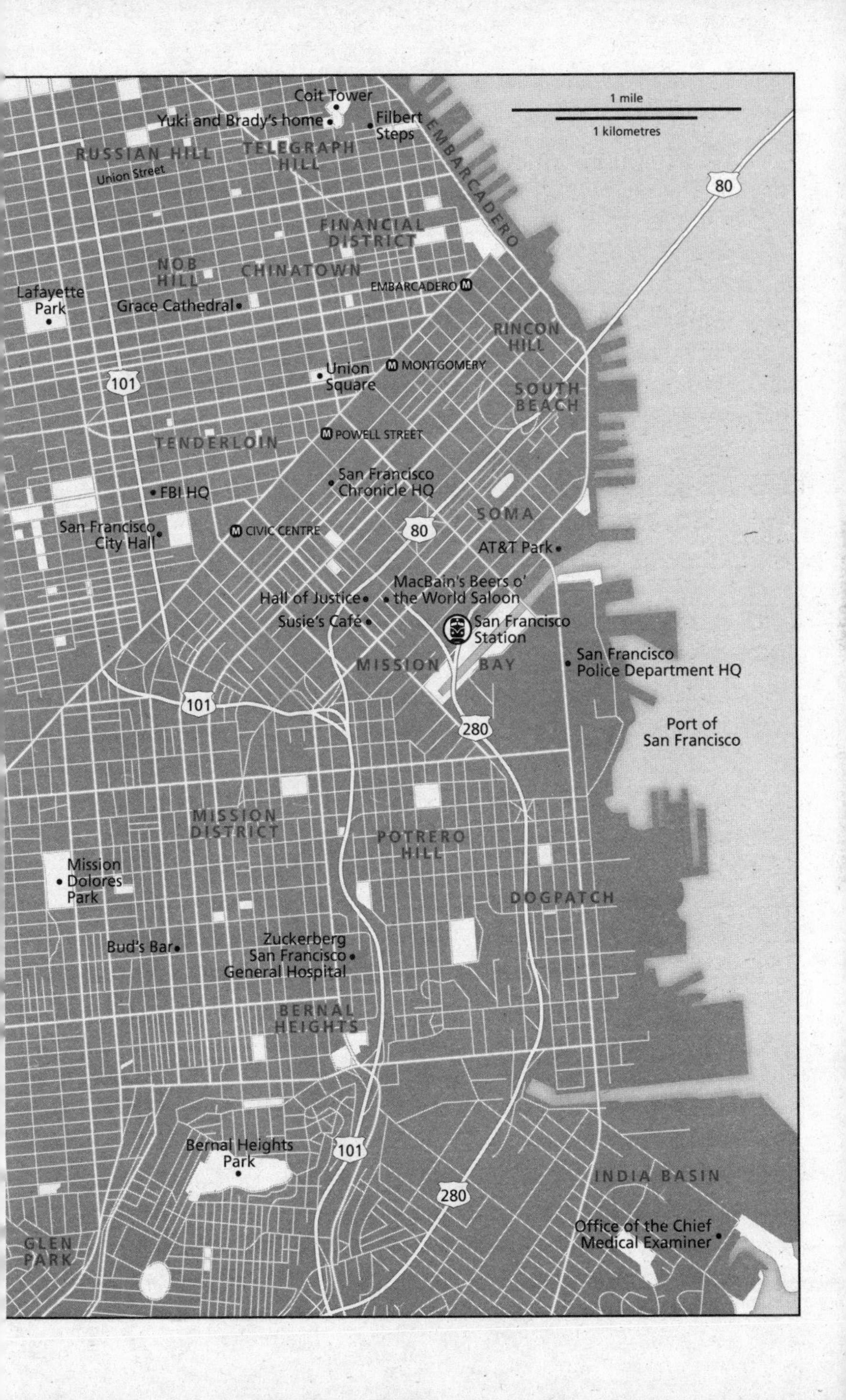
1 mile
1 kilometres
Coit Tower
Yuki and Brady's home
Filbert Steps
EMBARCADERO
RUSSIAN HILL
TELEGRAPH HILL
Union Street
80
FINANCIAL DISTRICT
NOB HILL
CHINATOWN
EMBARCADERO
Lafayette Park
Grace Cathedral
RINCON HILL
Union Square
MONTGOMERY
101
SOUTH BEACH
TENDERLOIN
POWELL STREET
San Francisco Chronicle HQ
FBI HQ
SOMA
San Francisco City Hall
CIVIC CENTRE
80
AT&T Park
MacBain's Beers o' the World Saloon
Hall of Justice
Susie's Café
San Francisco Station
MISSION BAY
San Francisco Police Department HQ
101
280
Port of San Francisco
MISSION DISTRICT
POTRERO HILL
Mission Dolores Park
DOGPATCH
Bud's Bar
Zuckerberg San Francisco General Hospital
BERNAL HEIGHTS
Bernal Heights Park
101
INDIA BASIN
280
Office of the Chief Medical Examiner
GLEN PARK

A list of titles by James Patterson appears
at the back of this book

JAMES
PATTERSON
& MAXINE PAETRO

THE 24TH HOUR

PENGUIN BOOKS

PENGUIN BOOKS

UK | USA | Canada | Ireland | Australia
India | New Zealand | South Africa

Penguin Books is part of the Penguin Random House group of companies
whose addresses can be found at global.penguinrandomhouse.com

First published in the UK by Century in 2024
Published in Penguin Books 2024
001

Typeset in 11.37/15.47pt Janson MT Std by Jouve (UK), Milton Keynes
Printed and bound in Great Britain by Clays Ltd, Elcograf S.p.A.

The authorised representative in the EEA is Penguin Random House Ireland,
Morrison Chambers, 32 Nassau Street, Dublin D02 YH68

A CIP catalogue record for this book is available from the British Library

ISBN: 978–1–529–16013–0

www.greenpenguin.co.uk

In memory of Laurie Catherine Birney

THE 24TH HOUR

PROLOGUE

SIX MONTHS EARLIER

ONE

I WAS LATE getting back from the men's jail in San Bruno. I braked the squad car in front of the Hall of Justice, where my good friend Assistant District Attorney Yuki Castellano was waiting at the curb.

She got into the car and asked, "How'd it go?"

Yuki is a prosecutor. Interrogation is her thing.

I said, "An inmate called Brandt got word to me that he knew who shot Holly Fricke and wanted to make a deal. It should have been one-stop shopping, but I had to sign six forms, wait for a free room, wait some more for Brandt to be brought down . . ."

"And then?" Yuki asked.

"He's a pathetic liar. I heard him out, laughed, and left. Anyway, sorry, Yuki. You called ahead?"

"Yep, yep, yep. Claire said don't worry. She and Cindy are having fun. Said something about caviar."

Yuki grinned into my sour expression.

"Did she tell you?" she asked.

I smiled for real. "Cindy? No. But I have confidential informants."

Yuki laughed her high-pitched musical chortle.

"It's going to be great," she said.

"What part?"

"Allllll of it."

I agreed. Cindy and my longtime friend and partner, Rich Conklin, had finally both committed at the same time to getting married. It was a bell ringer. The two of them had been living together, playing house, for several years, both in love, but still stuck on an obstacle. Cindy was building her dangerous, satisfying career and didn't want to have children—yet. Richie was from a big family, and to him children had to happen. The obstacle had somehow been sidelined. But Cindy was keeping the details to herself. Besides, today's celebration was for Claire.

Cindy, Yuki, and I had saved up for Claire's birthday, and today was the day.

Yuki was perfectly dressed in a pencil skirt and a blazer over a silk blouse just right for Xe Sogni, the hottest and most expensive place to eat in the entire Bay Area.

I hadn't had time to change out of my everyday Homicide detective gear: blue pants, button-down shirt, blue blazer, badge on a chain around my neck. I freed my lapel from the shoulder belt and tipped the rearview mirror toward me.

"You look fine," Yuki said.

I said, "Well, hair and makeup didn't show up this morning."

"It's just lunch. Okay?" she said.

"This time with a cake and candles."

We both laughed and I turned my mind to Claire. I wanted her to have a birthday she would remember for years. If we *got* there this year.

As I sweated the noontime rush, traffic slowed even more. Horns blew. I was tempted to hit my lights and sirens, but instead, I pounded the wheel with my palms. "Come onnn."

Yuki looked at me like, *Chill, Lindsay.* And just then the traffic moved.

"And we're off," she said.

I floored it and five minutes later we saw the restaurant just up ahead, a plain brick building disguising a culinary gem. I pulled up to the curb and valets opened doors and whisked the squad car away.

The restaurant's main room was dimly lit, banked on our right with an open kitchen, lined to our left with mahogany dining tables and large contemporary artwork. The air smelled indescribably delicious.

Yuki said, "The Women's Murder Club is in the house."

I followed her finger and saw Cindy and Claire sitting at a table for four near a spiral staircase. They were both grinning. Claire, dressed in navy-blue silk, had never looked happier. Yuki and I pulled out chairs and joined them. Waiters fussed. As Yuki predicted, we were in time for the caviar course presented with a curl of salmon in a scallop-shell dish.

God, this was good.

We were joking and roasting the birthday girl as the next course was served—then a woman screamed, loud enough to lift the roof.

"Noooooo!"

Our waiter dropped a water glass. I grabbed his sleeve and showed him my badge.

"What's up there?"

"Staff ch-ch-changing room."

I got to my feet, knocking over my chair, and started up the corkscrew staircase. I took two steps at a time, and when I was halfway up, I heard a man shout, "You crazy bitch!"

I pulled my gun and, with my left hand on the railing, I raced to the top of the stairs.

TWO

AS OUR WAITER had said, the second floor was a changing room. It was carpeted, about thirty feet square, densely packed with rows of lockers and benches between the rows. The lockers formed barricades and I couldn't see between them from where I stood in the doorway. Even though I was armed, it was dangerous as hell to be here without my partner.

I listened as I scanned the maze of a room. I heard nothing, saw no movement, and then a shadow shifted in a far corner to my left. The shadow was a woman, lying on her side with her back pressed against the wall twenty feet away. I saw that, except for her pink bra that had been pushed up above her breasts, the woman was naked. The dim overhead lighting flickered. The rheostat was to my left and so I dialed up the lights. I reached the woman in seconds and identified myself. She didn't seem to notice.

But I was taking mental notes of her. She was in her twenties; her eyes were puffy and partially closed and she was wheezing out little cries. I spoke to her again, asked her name, but she didn't respond. That's when I saw the fresh bruises encircling her neck and wrists.

She'd been choked and beaten, but she was alive.

I whipped my head around, scanned the area. Where was the damned attacker? Invisible.

I pulled my radio from my blazer pocket, connected to dispatch, and barked out a request for backup and an ambulance. If the attacker was still in the room, he'd heard me and would know that the cops were on the way.

Where was he?

I scoped out the room again from this new angle. There had to be an exit that led down to the kitchen, but I couldn't leave the victim alone to look for it.

Taking a chance, I stood up and shouted, "SFPD! Step out with your hands in the air."

That didn't happen. Restaurant sounds had resumed on the floor below. China clanked, diners laughed. Where was the man who'd cursed loud enough to be heard downstairs over the music and chatter?

And then I saw movement at the far end of a row of lockers. A man was half hidden behind an open locker door. Was this the attacker, or a waiter changing into his work clothes—or one and the same?

With just a sliver view, I made him as a white male, mid-twenties, average height and weight, dirty-blond hair, and he was half naked. The tails of his white dress shirt hung down to mid-thigh, front and back. His underwear and trousers were coiled around his feet.

It was him.

We made eye contact and he panicked, hopping, stumbling, bouncing off lockers as he tried to pull up his pants.

I shouted, "Stay where you are. Show me your hands."

He stopped and, leaning against a locker, held out his palms. He didn't have a gun. I let out a breath and said, "Turn around, close that locker, and put your hands on the door."

"I'm going to get dressed, okay?"

"What'd I just say?"

The subject shut the locker door with a bang, then hesitated. He tried to pull up his pants and I could see him thinking of making a run. I guess I'm psychic. He pushed off from the bank of lockers and, heading away from me, took one step and immediately tripped and fell hard to the floor with a yowl of pain. He was where I wanted him. I holstered my gun and, kneeling alongside him, pulled his arms around to his back and cuffed him.

"Hey," he said with his cheek pressed to the floor. "Listen to me. She set me up. I want to tell you what happened . . ."

"You have the right to remain silent. You have the right to an attorney . . ."

"Am I under arrest?"

"Yes, you are. What's your name?"

"Tyler. I work here."

"Tyler what?"

"I'm done talking."

"Fine. Tyler Doe, you're under arrest for aggravated assault, other charges pending."

He spat, "Jesus Christ, what is this? She set me up, god-damnit. I'm telling the truth, okay?"

I finished reading him his rights and he acknowledged none of them. I needed help to get him out of here and the victim needed medical attention.

Where was my backup?

THREE

THE VICTIM LOOKED to be in her late twenties. Her body was marked with fresh contusions and lacerations and the bruises around her neck were livid.

I stooped down and again tried to get a response from her. "I'm Sergeant Boxer. SFPD. Can you tell me your name?"

She groaned and wheezed. If she'd heard me, she was unable to answer or even look up. I pulled my phone from my pocket and speed-dialed Claire, who was still at our lunch table on the main floor.

When Claire picked up, I said, "There's an injured woman up here. Yeah, I called it in. Can you come up and take a look? And tell the manager that the locker room is off-limits to everyone but cops and EMTs. Yes, Yuki can come up."

The victim's backpack was half buried in a pile of her clothes. I unzipped the bag, saw makeup and pens and an assortment of small office supplies. I rooted around for a moment looking for her wallet and phone, then dumped the whole lot of stuff onto the floor. I opened her wallet and, after finding her driver's license, compared her DMV photo to her face. The woman on the floor was named Mary Elena Hayes, age twenty-eight.

"Mary Elena," I said. "Can you tell me what happened?"

Her voice was raspy, but I could make out what she said.

"He raped us."

What?

"There's another victim? Where is she?"

Mary Elena struggled to sit up.

"Lie still," I said. "Help is coming."

She croaked, "I'm Loretta. My name is Loretta." She rolled onto her stomach and sobbed onto the carpet.

Tyler was looking at me from the floor. He said, "Let me talk."

I said, "Hey! We'll take your statement at the station."

Claire and Yuki stepped through the locker room doorway and went directly to the victim. Claire spoke first.

"I'm Dr. Washburn. Can you show me where you hurt?"

Yuki grabbed a towel from a stack on a nearby bench and covered the young woman's body as I asked Ms. Hayes, "How do you know this man?"

Finally, she looked at me. "I just wanted to use the b-b-bathroom."

"Tyler" had said he was done talking, but he was still trying to get his story out. "Listen. Sergeant. I work here. She saw me, and she followed me. She *wanted* this. Understand? This was her idea."

"I hear sirens," Yuki said. "And Cindy's heading up."

I sighed. Cindy is an investigative crime reporter, and although I love her to pieces, she's dogged, and once she saw this scene she'd call it news and would be working. It was the wrong time to talk to the press.

Tyler Doe spoke. "She said her name was Olivia and that I was hot."

"No. Did not," the woman mumbled.

"She did," said our only suspect. "She said she wanted it hard and fast, and right now. I'm just human, Sergeant. She begged me. And another thing—"

Footsteps pounded up the stairs and two uniforms appeared; Nardone and Einhorn, both good cops I'd known for years.

"*Another thing,*" Tyler shouted as the two cops pulled him to his feet. "She's *nuts*. First, she tells me her name is Olivia. Then, it's Loretta. Or is it Mary Elena? She lies."

Nardone got a grip on the suspect's shoulders while Einhorn hoisted and zipped up the man's trousers, leaving the belt dangling.

I began opening unlocked locker doors. A jacket hanging from a hook in one of them looked like it could be Tyler's.

I showed it to him. "Is this yours?"

He looked away from me and Nardone slapped the back of his head.

"Answer the sergeant."

"Yes. It's mine," he said.

Tyler's wallet was inside his jacket pocket. His ID told me that his full name was Tyler Richard Cates, showed him at five ten, 160, with green eyes and a Gough Street address. I said to Nardone, "Voucher this and take him to booking. I've charged him with aggravated assault."

"So leave him in lockup."

"You got it."

As the two officers left with Cates through the rear exit, Cindy, panting from the climb, arrived in the changing room and called out to me.

"Lindsay. What happened?"

"Hey, Cindy. You know I can't tell you."

"Off the record?"

"Hah."

"Okay. I know. Anyway, I'm here to tell you that our waiter needs to clear our table. There's a cake. With candles. Oh, and here you are, Claire. We didn't even sing 'Happy Birthday to You.'"

Claire said, "It's okay, Cin. Medical emergency."

The ambulance driver appeared in the locker room with a pair of EMTs who went to Mary Elena Hayes and lifted her onto a stretcher. While Claire filled in the EMTs on her observations, I thought about what Mary Elena Hayes had told me.

"He raped us." What had she meant by that?

Cindy sighed as the room cleared out, leaving her without a story. She put her arm around my waist.

"Trouble always finds you, Linds."

I hugged her and said, "Look who's talking."

Cindy smiled at her feet, then said, "We can still kinda make this work. Let's bag the gifts. Box up the cake. Pay up. And then you tell me everything."

"Girl Reporter," I said, giving her a squeeze. "You're incorrigible."

PRESENT DAY

MONDAY

CHAPTER 1

THE *DAYDREAMER* WAS ninety feet of streamlined fiberglass, teak, and chrome. I'd never been on a yacht like this, but today was the day. Bob Barnett, Cindy's agent and lawyer, had treated her to a three-hour excursion on the bay because her just-published book, coauthored with a twisted serial killer, had topped the *New York Times* Best Seller list.

We grouped around Cindy on the main deck as she read Barnett's card out loud.

"Writing Burke's book was an act of admirable courage and determination, Cindy. You're a winner and your book is a new true crime classic. Promise me that you'll relax and have fun today. Try, okay? Love, Bob."

Cindy called out, "Thank you, Bob. Wherever you are."

I seconded that emotion.

A ship's officer showed us through the lounge and passageways to the aft deck, where a cushioned bench rounded the stern and lounge chairs were set up under the shade of the overhanging deck.

As the yacht cast off, Cindy took a lounge chair at the center. Claire and Yuki settled into the chairs flanking hers and I stretched out on one of the long side benches across from them. We were all beaming. It was a picture-worthy moment.

I took a selfie with my friends waving their hands behind me. Phones were passed around for portraits of a memorable day and the breeze blew away the worries of the last week. Yuki lifted her glass, saying, "To a life of happy days."

"Hear, hear."

Claire reached her hand over to Cindy's chair, saying, "So we're soon to become the Women's Married Club."

"Who told you?" Cindy joked.

Claire laughed. "Let's see that blinding green bling on your finger again."

Cindy stuck out her hand theatrically and Claire said, "Wow oh wow."

Yuki said, "Let me see," and Cindy showed her, too.

"It's too gorgeous, Cindy. It's stunning."

"He bought it for me. I don't even want to know what it cost him," Cindy said, first time I'd ever seen her looking shy.

"Really suits you, Cin," I said. I'd first seen the ring years ago. When Rich asked me what I thought of the square cut emerald I'd said, "It's perfect!" The next day, he'd proposed to Cindy at Grace Cathedral. She'd said yes but then later changed her mind.

It had killed Richie, but he'd hung in for love.

Now, Cindy was wearing the ring again. She was getting married.

And she was marrying the perfect man.

CHAPTER 2

CLAIRE PROPPED HERSELF up on the chaise and asked Cindy, "So, tell us again, but this time fill in some details. The juicier the better. What did Richie say?"

"Aw, I don't think I can tell you that."

Yuki said, "You can tell us, Cindy. It's off the record."

We all laughed, Cindy included. So many times we'd discussed a case in front of her and she'd started taking notes. One or all of us would shout, "Off the record."

I said, "Not fair, Cindy. Come on. We've been talking about you and Richie for years."

Cindy said, "Okay, okay."

She let it all out and we didn't interrupt. She said that the other night she'd opened the bedroom closet door and a pile of gun catalogs had slid down from the top shelf, hitting her in the face. Rich was asleep but when she grabbed up the catalogs and dropped them into the trash, the noise woke him up.

"We had a shouting match about whose closet it

was—his—and how sick I was of living in that dark hole with him, and I threatened to move out."

Claire said, "But this was bull, right? You were fighting about something else, am I right?"

Cindy nodded her head. "I was fuming, packing up, and wondering what the hell I was doing when Rich sat me on the bed, grabbed my hands, and said, 'I want to marry you, Cindy.'" She stopped to cough, then went on.

"He said, 'I love you more than anything, more than closet space, more than a clean fridge, more than a dozen kids.' Something like that," Cindy said, looking at each of us. "And he said, 'Marry me? Will you please?'"

We swarmed over her, congratulating her, practically pulling her finger off her hand to see the ring. One of us was crying. I think it was me.

About then, the waiter came out and said that lunch was served. We four grabbed onto one another and staggered against the surprising roll of the deck.

Claire said to Cindy, "By the way, Cin. This is what marriage is like."

We were all still giggling when we reached the dining salon. A large round table was set for eight in the center of the room and four of the places were taken.

It took a few seconds for my eyes to adjust to the darkened interior, and by then, the men at the table had gotten to their feet. They were grinning because they'd totally blindsided us.

"How'd you get here without us seeing you?" I asked Joe, my dearly loved husband.

"I'm a G-man, remember?" he said.

We reached out to our husbands. Cindy hugged Rich, her

husband-to-be. Claire gave Edmund a big smack. Joe hugged me and got in a butt grab while he was at it. Yuki's husband, my commanding officer, Homicide Lieutenant Jackson Brady, swept Yuki off her feet—literally—then toasted the newly engaged couple.

TUESDAY

CHAPTER 3

AT SEVEN THE next morning, Yuki sat in the small conference room in the DA's suite of offices at the Hall of Justice. Tyler Cates's trial would begin tomorrow, and she was polishing her already buffed opening statement.

There was a mug of black coffee at her right hand and her laptop was open to the voluminous Cates folder, filled with depositions and videos and her own notes.

The note on the first page of the folder was the key point of her case against Cates: "Show that Tyler Cates knew that Mary Elena Hayes has a severe mental disorder known as dissociative identity disorder (DID), and therefore cannot, could not, give informed consent to sex."

Yuki had put a star next to this point because it was critical to her case. She would maintain that Cates knew Hayes had a mental condition, and she also knew that Cates's attorney would challenge this claim to the bitter end.

Yuki had listed the proofs of rape in bullet points: That although Mary Elena had no firsthand memory of the event, there was abundant medical proof that Tyler Cates had raped her: The bruises, the vaginal tearing, Cates's semen inside her body. The screams of protest witnesses heard down on the ground floor, rising above the ambient sounds in the restaurant. Cates's admission to Lindsay that he'd had sex with Hayes at the scene of the crime. And that the woman he'd had sex with had said her name was Olivia, while the woman who told Lindsay she'd been raped said her name was Loretta. *Anything else?* Cates had ignored his victim's multiple names and identities, and instead had congratulated himself that he was having a lucky day.

Yuki's second chair, Nick Gaines, pulled open the conference room door, and took a seat beside Yuki.

"I read it. I like it," he said of the draft of her opening statement.

"You only like it? Not love it? You're not blown away?"

Gaines had been Yuki's second chair on dozens of trials. Based on his GPA from Harvard Law, he could have been fast-tracked up the ladder at any prestigious firm, but that's not who Gaines was. He was sharp, insightful, had attack-dog instincts and a genuine soft spot for victims of violent crime.

He said, "I'm this close to being blown away, Yuki. I don't doubt you. It's Mary Elena and company. I don't know if there is a defense against Olivia. From the tapes, she's charming and likable. If Olivia comes forward when Mary Elena is on the stand, the jury will love her, and she'll say she was crazy about Cates."

"Schneider will underscore that on cross and we'll have to cancel out our own witness on redirect." Yuki sighed, continuing Gaines's line of thought.

But could she redirect if the house was on fire?

Gaines handed over the thumb drive of interviews psychiatrists had done with Mary Elena, and said he was ready to meet her.

"If you don't mind, Yuki, I want to push her buttons a little."

Yuki thought about it, said, "Risky. But maybe it's worth trying before we go to court."

Gaines said, "Send me the Cates transcripts and video again, okay?"

Yuki tapped some keys on her laptop as Gaines got out of his seat. "Done," she said.

She was gathering up her laptop, handbag, and coffee mug, planning to go back to her office, when her boss, Len Parisi, walked through the conference room door. Yuki sat back down.

San Francisco district attorney Leonard Parisi was known as Red Dog for his grizzled red hair and unflagging "winners win" mentality. As he took a chair across from Yuki, saying, "How's it going?" a cell phone rang. "Wait a second. I have to take this."

Parisi put his phone to his ear, giving Yuki another few moments to order her thoughts. The boss got snappish if she didn't give him a clean-to-the-bone summary of the matter at hand.

Red Dog growled into the phone, "Right. Call me when you have something real," and hung up.

"Sorry, Yuki. This day is shaping up to be a multicar pileup on Route 101."

CHAPTER 4

YUKI CHECKED HER watch. Eight fifteen already.

She said, "It's complicated, Len. Mary Elena has dissociative identity disorder, formerly and still commonly called multiple personality disorder. Much of the time, she's like the rest of us. Has a job, memories—"

Parisi said, "I know, you've told me this before. Several times."

"This time I'm telling you as if you're a juror. See how it plays."

"As I've been saying for months, Yuki. This is a weak, circumstantial case. Your best witness is Tyler Cates and he's not going to convict himself. So, you're at the mercy of Mary Elena's invisible friends."

Parisi had made his point, but she still wanted his support. A loophole. Or a story of a no-win case that he'd turned into a touchdown. But he wasn't going there. He was itemizing all the reasons the Hayes case was doomed. Yuki listened while looking Red Dog in the eye.

When Parisi ran out of gas, Yuki said, "Hear me out, Len. I was with Mary Elena immediately after she was raped. She'd been choked and punched, and fingerprint-shaped bruises were coming up on her inner thighs. The DNA inside her body matched Cates's DNA. We need to convict him—"

Parisi cut her off, saying, "Olivia was behind the wheel when Cates got busy."

"True."

"And she may have seduced him."

"That's what *he* says. But there's more to it than that. How much time do you have?"

"You'll have to discredit Olivia without discrediting Mary Elena. How are you going to do that?"

Yuki pictured it. Cates had told Lindsay that he'd had sex with Olivia and only heard the name Loretta after the fact. Still, it was indisputable that sex had been forced. Though Cates would say Olivia directed him to be rough.

Parisi cut into her thoughts. He said, "Can you bring out the personality who took the attack? Loretta?"

"If only," said Yuki. "It doesn't exactly work that way with Mary Elena. If I stress her out—or Cates's counsel goes after her, accuses her of being a liar, say—in that case, one of Mary Elena's alters might step in to protect her, but we don't know which one. More than one could front her on the stand."

"What's 'front her' mean?"

"Become the dominant personality."

"Okay. So, you're saying that Loretta or Olivia could come out, and Mary Elena wouldn't be there. Consciously. Or another of her alternate personalities could take control, a personality that you don't know?"

"Possibly."

"I don't like this, Yuki."

Yuki thought that was at least the fourteenth time he'd told her that.

Parisi slapped the conference table and stood up.

"You want to ride this case into a box canyon, it's your horse. Go right ahead. I have a meeting."

Yuki nodded and Len Parisi left the room. He was a great prosecutor. He'd never told her she was crazy to take on a case before, no matter how bad the odds of winning. But this one was brand-new territory. She didn't know a single prosecutor who'd ever been dealt a stack of wild cards like this one.

Then again, she'd never had an easy case in her life.

CHAPTER 5

MARY ELENA SAT in a visitor chair across from Yuki's desk, relating a dream she'd had.

"We're in court," Mary Elena said. "TV movie–type courtroom. I'm sitting next to you and someone says, 'Has the jury reached a verdict?' And the jury foreman says, 'We have, Your Honor.' The foreman looked like Sean Penn and I woke myself up like three times."

"How did you feel in the dream?" Yuki asked.

"Scared, I guess," she said. "Who wouldn't be?"

Yuki nodded. Mary Elena said she was "grounded," but Yuki saw fear in her eyes.

"It'll be all right, Ms. Hayes. I read that Sean Penn is shooting a movie out of the country."

Mary Elena grinned and said, "My grandmother called me Mary Elena."

Yuki said, "My grandmother called me *chiisana neko.* Which means 'little cat,' but you can call me Yuki."

They both laughed and then Yuki said, "I'd like you to

meet Nick Gaines. He's working with me as second chair in our case against Mr. Cates."

"He knows all about . . . ?"

"Absolutely. And he's got a few questions for you."

Yuki grabbed the desk phone and called Gaines. He picked up, and, by the time Yuki had clicked off, was at her open door. He pulled the second visitor chair around so that he triangulated both Yuki and Mary Elena.

He smiled, said, "We have a good case, Mary Elena, but the defense is prepared and they're going to try to win. Here's what we figure is going to be the defense's position. Shall we talk about it?"

"I'm ready. I think."

"Nothing to worry about. This is just you and your legal team doing a practice run. Not a problem, right?"

"Okay."

Gaines said, "Good," and kept going. Yuki thought Mary Elena was not exactly okay, but she let it go. Gaines was smart and even if Mary Elena didn't know him, this was a safe place.

"Here we go," Gaines said.

Yuki saw Mary Elena's face flatten and she heard Parisi's warning in her mind.

This is a weak, circumstantial case . . . You want to ride this case into a box canyon, it's your horse.

Yuki watched Gaines lean closer to Mary Elena, who, under the force of his stare, pushed her chair back flush against the wall. If Gaines felt her withdrawing from him, he showed no sign.

"Now, Mary Elena. Ed Schneider, Tyler Cates's attorney, is a pit bull."

Mary Elena said, tersely, “I heard.”

Gaines nodded and went on.

“The jury is going to want to hear your side. Schneider may call you to the stand and pummel you with questions. So, it’s far better if we call you. The defense will still question you, but they won’t have as much control.

“Now, according to Cates, you followed him to the second floor. You asked him for rough sex, then when he hurt you, you said that he raped you. Schneider is going to push hard on that. Quoting his client, he’ll say that Cates met a woman named Olivia who told him, ‘I want you to take me hard and fast and now.’ In other words, the defense position will be that the sex was your idea but that you changed your mind after the fact. And that you were in full control of Olivia.”

“I didn’t know she was out,” Mary Elena said. “She doesn’t talk that way. I only remember that when I went into the room and was looking for the ladies’ room, that guy asked me who I was. I said, ‘Elena.’ I don’t remember anything else until the police came.”

“This is important, Mary Elena. Did any of your alters tell Cates that you have DID?”

Mary Elena said, “I can only tell you what I know and what I’ve said. I went into Xe Sogni to use the ladies’ room. A waiter said it was upstairs, so I climbed that spiral staircase. Then I woke up on the floor, naked and hurting everywhere.”

Gaines said, “You told Sergeant Boxer that your name was Loretta. You told her, ‘He raped us.’ You’ve just said that you were on your way to the bathroom, then woke up on the floor without memory of this rape. That’s a contradiction, isn’t it?”

“Noooo. I remember going up to the ladies’ room. I

remember being on the floor. I remember hurting. But I don't remember talking with Sergeant Boxer."

"So, it was a different personality—Loretta—who was attacked by Cates? Where was the personality called Olivia? Did either one of them tell Cates that you have dissociative identity disorder?"

"*I don't know.* Do you understand, if an alter comes out, she is protecting me? I don't know what happened when Olivia or Loretta were fronting. But I knew from the *pain* that I had been raped and beaten. And that had happened. *Do you understand that?*"

CHAPTER 6

THE ATMOSPHERE IN the room was still quivering in the wake of Mary Elena's anguished protest. Yuki tried to signal Nick Gaines to take the intensity down, but he didn't see her. His eyes were fixed on Mary Elena and he kept talking at her.

"Schneider is going to try to trip you up, Mary Elena. You said, 'He raped us.' Forgive me for saying so, but while your body bore the physical evidence of rape, you don't remember a thing about that attack, who said what to whom, if another person was present, if that person was a facet of you, or even if Cates got Olivia's okay. You don't remember what happened in that room, isn't that right?"

Yuki was as transfixed as Mary Elena, who stared at Gaines with her mouth hanging open. She pushed up against the back of her chair, pulled her legs up to her chest, gripped them hard with her forearms—and then blasted Gaines.

"Who are you?"

Shockingly, her voice had changed. To Yuki, she sounded like a very young girl.

Yuki said, "Mary Elena?"

Without looking at Yuki, Mary Elena shouted at Gaines. "*You're badddd. Mama and I don't like you.*"

Gaines put out his hand to stop Yuki from interfering.

"Who are *you?*" he asked Mary Elena.

"I'm Lily. You know I'm Lily. Don't talk to my mama like that."

Yuki said, "Nick, I'll stay with Lily."

Gaines gave Yuki a look like *I've got this,* but Yuki said his name again, louder. He stood up and left the room, closing the door behind him.

Yuki turned back to the formerly composed woman of twenty-eight, now crouched in a desk chair, panting like a frightened child.

"Lily, I want to help. What can I do for you?"

"Go away. Leave me alone."

"Okay. I'll be right outside the door."

Lily didn't answer. Yuki didn't want to leave Lily alone, but witnessing Mary Elena assume a new persona while sitting across from her was unnerving. She needed a plan.

Hesitating, Yuki left Lily in her office and closed the door. She startled when she saw Gaines standing only feet away.

He said, "That wasn't pretty, but we know a lot more about Mary Elena now, don't we?"

"Yep. If she freaks on the stand . . ."

"Our case flames out of control."

CHAPTER 7

YUKI'S MOTHER HAD once said, "Yuki-eh, you have three trains of thought at same time."

It was true enough. At the moment, those three trains were on parallel tracks, converging on a one-track tunnel. Yuki told Gaines she'd get back to him in a while, then slid into an empty cubicle. Phone in hand, she took her best shot. She called Mary Elena's psychiatrist, Dr. Stuart Aronson.

By the fourth unanswered ring, Yuki prepared herself for a useless, leave-a-message recording, but before that happened, a masculine voice growled in her ear, "Stu Aronson."

Yuki said, "Doctor, this is ADA Yuki Castellano—"

"I've got a patient in the waiting room," Dr. Aronson said. "I'll call you back—"

"I've got an emergency here and need direction," Yuki cut him off.

"Make it fast," said the doctor.

Yuki explained Mary Elena's immediate condition quickly and finished with "What should I do?"

"Put her on the phone. Has to be quick," Dr. Aronson said. "I can only give her five, six minutes."

Mary Elena was still curled up in the side chair, but she looked more relaxed. Her eyes were closed and one foot touched the floor.

Yuki said, "Mary Elena?"

She opened her eyes. "Did I fall asleep?"

"Yes and that's okay. But I was worried about you so I called Dr. Aronson—"

"You called my shrink?"

"Yep. He's here on my phone right now."

Mary Elena unfolded her limbs and sat up in the chair. "But why? He's very busy."

"He's free now for a few minutes."

Mary Elena said, "I've never spoken with him on the phone before. Why did you call him? I'm okay."

Yuki said, "If I say you were speaking as Lily, do you know who I mean?"

"Oh. Lily. She thinks of me as her mother. Did something happen?"

"I think so. I want to be sure you can go through this trial without harm. I'm on your side entirely, and so is Nick. Do you remember Nick?"

"I don't think so."

"Please take the phone. Speak with your doctor."

"And say what?"

Yuki said into the phone, "Dr. Aronson, Mary Elena is here. Please ask her to hand you off to me before you go. I would appreciate it."

She passed her phone to Mary Elena, and leaving her

office, Yuki went back to the empty cubicle. Gaines peered over the top of the partition, and said, "Hey."

Yuki looked up and said, "She's talking to Dr. Aronson. She doesn't remember you, so probably best if you . . ."

"Got it."

Gaines was back in his office when Mary Elena appeared and said to Yuki, "Dr. Aronson didn't have time to talk with you, but he says he sent you something by email. A video. I told him it was okay."

After Yuki had walked Mary Elena to the elevator, she stopped off at Gaines's office, saying, "I need you, Nicky. We've got work to do."

Yuki woke her computer and clicked on the email from Dr. Aronson.

"It's a therapy session," Yuki said as Gaines pulled up a chair. "Dated a month ago."

"Aronson sent this to you?"

"With Mary Elena's permission."

Yuki opened the attachment and a video began playing. Dr. Stuart Aronson sat in an easy chair. Mary Elena was in a chair across from him, talking.

Yuki and Gaines watched as the session streamed.

CHAPTER 8

CONKLIN'S FOOT WAS heavy on the gas as we sped to the scene of a fatality on Pacific Avenue. The victim had been identified as James Fricke III: well-known billionaire, middleweight philanthropist, sole owner of a Belgian soccer team, and a narcissistic SOB. The man in his early sixties was now a deceased SOB, shot in the street a block away from where his wife, former Olympic gymnast Holly Bergen Fricke, had been killed six months before.

We still had no leads in Holly Fricke's murder investigation, and I was willing to bet that soon we'd be looking at another no-clue homicide—the kind of crime that would go unsolved for years, then become a cold case that haunted good cops and turned them into humorless drunks.

Conklin's mood mirrored mine, but he was expressing his frustration out loud, ranting that Jamie Fricke, the most likely suspect in his wife's death, had gotten himself killed "on purpose." Richie's uncharacteristic outburst shifted into overdrive when traffic suddenly stopped, boxing us in at the intersection of Franklin Street and Geary Boulevard.

My partner swore, got out of the car, and took off at a run toward the bottleneck. I stayed in place with the radio and thought about Holly Fricke. I'd been a fan. I'd cheered her on when I was in high school and she was in the Summer Olympics, picking up the gold medal in gymnastics for Team USA.

I'd followed her when she founded *Spike,* a women's sports magazine, and became a familiar face on late-night talk shows. Then Holly married Jamie Fricke. He was a large man, square-faced, dark-eyed. He exuded power the way Holly radiated goodness. They'd looked happy together. And although they hadn't had any children, babies were named after Holly and deserving high schoolers went to college on her dime.

But now we still didn't know *why* Holly Fricke had been killed or by *whom,* though Medical Examiner Claire Washburn had told us *how.* Holly's cause of death was an onslaught of .40-caliber rounds from an unregistered handgun, every shot fatally precise. Neither her new Bentley nor the jewelry she'd been wearing, estimated to be worth a low seven figures, had been recovered.

Unofficially, we'd chalked up Holly Fricke's murder to armed robbery, but privately none of us really bought that. It was excessive. Holly had been shot in broad daylight. No witnesses. Nothing from her husband or friends. Now that Jamie had been killed the same way, I knew we'd missed all of it: means, motive, opportunity—and suspect.

On day one, Holly's case had been assigned to senior Homicide team sergeants Cappy McNeil and Paul Chi.

Cappy is a wise old hand, a walking chronicle of murders in San Francisco over the last twenty years. His partner, Paul Chi, is as thorough and obsessively detailed an investigator as is humanly possible. It's said he can find a hair in a haystack. Yet a thousand cop-hours spent working her homicide had yielded zip, not even a theory. If Cappy still had hair, by now he'd have torn it all out. Chi had gone dark and quiet, as though in some fathomless funk.

Conklin and I had been brought in to back up this first-class team, but all we'd been able to surmise was that Holly's killer knew her movements, had a strategic mind, titanium nerves, and perhaps, a cloak of invisibility.

When questioned, Jamie Fricke had told us as little as possible. He didn't like cops, which he made clear with his clipped answers and negative attitude. He'd previously been accused of sports crimes, but had skirted the law with handshake deals and payoffs. He brought in his squadron of high-priced lawyers and threatened to hire private investigators.

Somehow, Cappy and Chi had kept the PI threat at bay. But Fricke had offered a quarter of a million dollars as a reward for evidence leading to the arrest and conviction of Holly's killer, which opened our hotline to an unending plague of useless tips.

My thoughts were derailed as horns blew behind the squad car. Conklin came back to the car and got behind the wheel, released the brake, and I called dispatch to say we would be at the crime scene in ten minutes.

I hit the switch that loosed the lights and siren.

CHAPTER 9

CONKLIN PULLED OUR car over on Steiner Street, at the intersection of Steiner Street and Pacific Avenue. The smart, well-kept homes and small businesses in this upscale neighborhood were now penned in by cruisers with flashing lights, the ME's stolid van, and the CSU mobile with its panel doors wide-open.

"Ready?" Conklin asked me.

Ready or not, I opened my door.

Walking toward the barrier tape, I saw CSU investigators in hazmat suits pitching an evidence tent and placing halogen lights around the perimeter for the night shift. Techs put out markers, snapped shots of shell casings, close-ups of the deceased, and of faces in the gathering crowd.

It was only nine thirty in the morning, but from the amount of manpower working in and around the scene, it was clear to me that CSU would be here throughout the night.

Jackson Brady glanced up when Conklin and I ducked

under the tape and became part of the too-real crime scene. Conklin and I stepped gingerly around the inner perimeter until we were a few feet from the bloody corpse of James Fricke III.

Claire stood up from where she'd been crouched beside the victim.

She said, "In my professional opinion, he's dead."

I said, "Duly noted."

She went on, "The shooting was called in by a bystander about an hour ago, so that's our approximate time of death. I count five bullet wounds, one each to head, heart, liver, back, groin. The head shot was probably the kill shot. I'll let you know after I've done the post. Brady has Fricke's wallet, but his watch and wedding ring are missing. His car wasn't here when we arrived. The shooter may have driven it off."

Same as Holly's car, confirming my earlier thoughts that Holly and Jamie Fricke's murders were virtually identical. Both had been shot on Pacific Avenue, both robbed, both murders were overkill. Since Holly and Jamie were married, and both shot to hell, it made me wonder if these had been crimes of passion. But we hadn't heard even a whisper about anyone wanting to kill either of them, let alone both.

Brady's shadow fell across me. He said, "Here ya go," and handed me a man's slim wallet inside a plastic evidence bag.

"Boxer. You're the lead. You and Conklin assemble a task force that includes McNeil and Chi. I know I don't have to say this . . ."

So, *I* said it. "Don't blow it."

"*Please,* don't blow it," he said.

Crime Scene Unit director Gene Hallows made his way over

to me. He is astute, salty, and after decades of science-based crime-busting in our forensics lab, was recently elevated to the top job when former CSU director Charles Clapper was promoted to chief of police.

"Tell me something good," I said to Hallows.

My guess, CSU had found shell casings at this crime scene of the same caliber bullets as those that had killed Holly.

Reading indignation on my face, Hallows said, "I know you'd like me to say I found Fricke's signed confession in his breast pocket along with a suicide note."

"Good one, Gene."

"Have faith, Boxer. We've been here for under an hour."

Car doors slammed to my right along Pacific Avenue. Reporters exited their vehicles and headed toward the crime scene. More vehicles arrived, more press joining the swarm that soon filled Pacific Avenue from side to side. Uniforms formed a cordon outside the yellow ribbon of tape and held back the crowd shouting questions at Brady.

"Is that Jamie Fricke?" "How did this happen?" "Do you have a suspect?" "Lieutenant. Say a few words to our viewers . . ."

Brady turned and scanned the crowd. I saw what he saw: cameras held high, mics and phones pushed forward, a sound truck that had parked halfway on the sidewalk. Brady shouted back, his voice colored with a southern twang he'd picked up during his earlier years with Miami PD.

"Listen up, y'all. You, Mr. Clancy, Ms. Blume. You know I'm not gonna feed you reporters guesswork while the case is ongoing. Soon as we can clear the area we can open a lane to traffic. You get any verifiable leads, call Homicide, SFPD. You know our number."

A man's voice came at us from the back of the crowd. "I saw it happen. I live right over there."

I snapped my head around until I located the tall, bearded white man pointing to a three-story, white stucco house with bay windows down the street.

He was saying, "I'm Dan Fields. I'm the one who called the police. I was looking at the view when I saw a guy on foot jump out in front of Jamie Fricke's car. Fricke gets out of his Jaguar. Late model. Black. I recognized him from TV. I heard shots and he dropped. The shooter was on foot with his back to me. The whole thing happened so damn fast. Shooter got into Fricke's car and took it east on Pacific."

Brady said, "Thanks for coming forward, Mr. Fields. We'll be needing you to come to the station to make a statement."

I stepped toward the witness, introduced myself and Conklin, and, after escorting Mr. Fields home to lock his doors, we drove him back to the Hall for a long interview—which went nowhere.

CHAPTER 10

I ARRIVED HOME at just after 7:00 p.m. I parked in my usual spot on Eleventh and Lake, took the elevator up, then paused at our front door before letting myself inside.

My mind was still swimming with fresh images of Jamie Fricke's bloody corpse face down on the street, followed by his unveiling on the table in Claire's autopsy suite. I didn't want to carry those images into my home. I've taught myself a little trick that often works: Before I turn the key in the lock, I roll my shoulders forward a couple of times, then back. And last, I shake myself like a wet dog. Then, I go inside.

Tonight it worked.

I walked into a place that was warm and alive with Dean Martin singing "Volare," his voice filling the loft-sized room, accompanied by my husband's glorious baritone. Martha, my elderly border collie and pal since before I met and married Joe Molinari, woofed at the sound of the door opening and welcomed me inside.

I shouted, "Mommy's home!" as I stowed and locked my

gun in the case in the foyer. Then I stooped to gather my five-year-old daughter, Julie, and Martha together into a noisy hug before walking to the kitchen area where Joe was making something with pesto sauce. We hugged and kissed, and after I took a peek inside the pot on the stove, he put a glass of Cabernet in my hand and we all headed to the sofa at the far side of the room.

The next few hours went by way too fast.

We talked, laughed, ate. If dinner had been only half as good, it would have gotten five stars. Julie had made cookies with Mrs. Rose, our neighbor and part-time nanny. Once the cookies had turned into a plate of chocolate crumbs, I took our little girl into her bedroom.

I read to her and then she told me a story that she made up as she went along. Allie the Alligator had a toothache, and he had to go to the dentist.

I asked, "So what happens?"

Julie said, "Allie might eat the dentist, maybe."

Joe was listening at the doorway. He said to Julie, "If Allie does eat the dentist, does he have an escape plan?"

"Oooh," said Julie. "Escape plan? I know. He grows wings!"

Joe said, "Really good, Julie Bug." He walked into the room and we both kissed Julie good night and Joe said he'd take Martha for a walk.

Good. Great. I wanted a shower and I was going to have one.

When Joe came back with Martha, he woke me up. I'd fallen asleep on the bed, still wearing my clothes.

"I just lay down for a second," I mumbled to Joe.

"Stand up," Joe said, using his law enforcement voice. I struggled to my feet.

"Arms up," he said.

I held up my arms like a child and let Joe peel off my clothes. He had some trouble with the hooks of my bra, and I laughed at him.

"I'm out of practice," he said.

"Try again. I'm begging you. I can't get my hands around that far."

"Tough day, hmmm?"

"I can be talked into telling you all about it."

"Later. Take your shower or don't. Up to you."

I left the room, promising that I would be quick, but it felt so good to stand under the hot water, I struggled with turning off the taps. When I was finally steeped and steam-cleaned, I stepped out of the shower stall and shuffled into the bedroom semi-draped in a hand towel.

Joe was in bed, lights out, but I could see him by street light. I dropped the towel and slid under the covers and my G-man pulled me close. I put my arms around him and he kissed me between my neck and shoulder.

"You feel so good," he said.

I reached up to kiss him, but he put his hands on my shoulders and held me back. I looked into his eyes.

"I love you, Lindsay," he said. "All the way."

"Prove it," I said.

I can't be sure why our lovemaking only gets better. I wasn't thinking anymore that night. I was lost in Joe, somewhere near heaven.

CHAPTER 11

THE NIGHT BEFORE the trial, Yuki's sleep was split between waking anxiety and frightening dreams. At some time during that fractured night, she had a nightmare that stayed with her. Mary Elena as Olivia was prancing in front of the jury box wearing a pink bra and ripped leggings, flirting with the jurors.

Yuki woke when a siren screamed past the bedroom window, shattering the night irreparably.

Brady stirred, asking, "You okay?"

"Uh-huh. Fine. Go back to sleep, sweetie."

It was 3:17 a.m. In six hours, she would be in court with a clear-cut mission: convict Tyler Cates and get justice for Mary Elena. Disturbingly, sensational reporting on the case had made her the butt of late-night TV jokes and social media wisecracks. Yuki would need to utilize every bit of her law school training and on-the-job experience with the San Francisco DA to send Tyler Cates to jail.

She knew what she had to do, but still one piece eluded

her—and it was critical. Did Cates know that Mary Elena had a dissociative disorder, or that she had more than one functional personality? Or did he really believe that he'd had sex with a woman called Olivia?

Yuki stared up at the ceiling and pictured the jurors as she rehearsed her opening statement, reviewing what she knew about them, imagining their faces. She thought about Mary Elena sitting at the counsel table, listening to Yuki tell strangers about the deeply personal traumatic assault that she didn't remember happening.

She thought about Parisi shaking his head, saying, *Yuki, I warned you.*

Yuki closed her eyes and moments later, it seemed, opened them. It was just after 5:00 a.m., and from the hints of pale light filtering through the windows, it would soon be dawn. She rolled onto her side and moved closer to Brady, tucking her knees behind his, exhaling as she laid her cheek against his bare back.

When he felt Yuki's body against his, Brady turned over, reached his massive arms around her, and drew her close. This was what she loved: the scent of him and how she was able to fit so comfortably against him, and how he could slip back into sleep while surrounding her with the best safety zone she'd ever known.

The next time Yuki's eyelids flew open, it was almost six thirty. It took a few seconds to orient herself and remember that she was meeting Mary Elena at eight. She tried to slip out of Brady's grip but he tightened it, cupping the back of her head with one hand, throwing a leg over her hip.

Yuki said, "Lover, I gotta go."

"Court," he acknowledged. Brady opened his eyes and relaxed his hold on Yuki. "Call me at lunch recess," he said. "You're going to do great."

"There are many unknowns," she said.

"You're not one of them."

He tipped her chin up and kissed her. Yuki wanted more but couldn't take the chance. She kissed him lightly and squirmed out of his arms.

WEDNESDAY

CHAPTER 12

ONCE YUKI'S FEET touched the floor, she moved quietly through the apartment. She'd once lived here with her mother. The carpeting was soft and thick, and so were Yuki's memories of Keiko Castellano, bride of an Italian soldier who had died before Yuki was old enough to know him. Keiko had also since passed away, but not before she'd imparted volumes to her daughter over the years on how to be a good wife.

Keiko had been a spiritual woman. Yuki sometimes still heard her mother's voice, even if it was only in her imagination. And sometimes, she answered her.

Now, Yuki stared down at the two suits she'd laid out on the green slipper chairs in the spare room before going to bed last night.

Her mother's voice was in her head. *The striped one, Yuki-eh. Save red for closing.*

"Done," Yuki said out loud.

She dressed in the gray striped suit, projecting herself toward lunch recess, hoping that when she called Brady, she could tell him, "It's all good."

CHAPTER 13

IT WAS JUST after seven forty-five in the morning when Yuki pulled her car into the All Day lot on Bryant Street. She reached out her hand to the shy young man in the booth, who gave her a ticket and without making eye contact said, "Go get 'em."

Yuki said, "Count on it, Lanny, and wish me luck."

"You know I do," he said. "Hurry though. It's fixin' to rain."

"Hmm. Well, I have to wait for someone," she said.

Yuki parked at the rear of the lot in the only spot facing the street. The Hall of Justice, a large, gray, granite block of a building, was directly across Bryant. Yuki undid her seat belt and got out of the car.

Mary Elena would be meeting her in the lot at eight, giving them enough time to go upstairs and meet with Nick Gaines again before heading to the courtroom doors at a few minutes to nine. Yuki hoped that despite Mary Elena's earlier interaction with Gaines, she would recognize that he was a good guy and valuable to them both.

There was still time, but Yuki paced, looking up and down the street for Mary Elena's car. A new potential obstacle appeared to her: it was possible that one of Mary Elena's alternate personalities would tell her to stay in bed, and she'd go for that; ditch the trial due to stress and outright fear.

She pictured Olivia on Dr. Aronson's tape: a vulnerable-looking, very feminized version of Mary Elena. Olivia twisted her hair, crossed and uncrossed her legs, and spoke in a soft voice while looking at the doctor.

Yuki hated the thought, but *had* Mary Elena as Olivia come on to Tyler Cates, as he maintained? Even so, flirting wasn't consent, not for rape, not for aggravated assault, not for sex at all. Legally, if the attacker knew that the would-be sex object had a mental disorder and could not give informed consent, it was a serious crime with a jail sentence penalty.

The sky darkened with rain clouds. Checking the time, Yuki saw that it was ten after eight. *Where are you, Mary Elena?*

She watched the morning rush on Bryant, frozen at the traffic light. A mob of press gathered across the street, reporters from local news stations as well as unfamiliar faces. This much attention to the People versus Tyler Cates was unexpected and a little daunting.

Yuki heard someone call her name over the street uproar. It was Cindy, looking for an opening in the stream of traffic, and about to step off the sidewalk and cross the street toward her.

Yuki waved her off, *no, no, no,* but called Cindy's phone.

"I can't talk now, Cin. Later, okay?"

"Promise?"

"Cross my heart."

As Yuki walked back to her car, a silver Camaro took a turn into the lot and pulled up to the ticket booth.

It was Mary Elena. Shouts came from the gaggle of reporters across Bryant waiting for the light to change.

The young woman looked alarmed as Yuki got into the passenger seat. "Quick," Yuki said, buckling her seat belt. "Make a U-turn and take a right. I'll tell you where to go."

"What's wrong?"

"Hungry press," Yuki said. "I don't want them to interview you. They can't follow us through the back door."

Mary Elena followed Yuki's directions and parked under the overpass on Harriet. Yuki then hurried them down the breezeway to the Hall's back entrance. But her diversionary tactic didn't stop a dozen reporters from racing ahead, blocking their way. Mary Elena spun on her heels yelling, "Go away!"

Her voice was that of a little girl. Her face was flushed and her eyes stretched wide-open. The reporters stopped, a few backing up. Before they could make another move, Yuki had opened the lobby's rear door. Security guards let her and Mary Elena into the building but the press was shut out.

Yuki said, "Lily?"

"Mary Elena," she said. "I'm Mary Elena."

"Oh, good."

Twenty minutes later, Yuki, Mary Elena, and Nick Gaines settled into their seats at the prosecution table in Courtroom 8G. Soon enough, the courtroom would be called to order.

CHAPTER 14

JOE WAS PATCHING a leak under the kitchen sink when his phone rang. He was alone in the apartment—Lindsay was at work and Julie was at school.

He backed out of the cabinet, banging his head on the lip of the counter. Banged it hard. Calling himself an effing dummy, he reached his phone on the third ring and said, "Molinari."

The voice on the line belonged to Craig Steinmetz, section chief of the FBI's San Francisco office.

"Can you come in? I want you to meet someone."

"I can be there in an hour."

"Half hour would be better."

"Okay," Joe said. "If I don't shave."

"Come as you are," Steinmetz said, and hung up.

A half hour and a couple of aspirins later, Joe was signing in at the fifteenth-floor desk when Steinmetz called out to him. The chief stood behind him at the doorway between the offices and reception area. Joe crossed the blue, insignia-embossed carpet to shake hands.

Steinmetz was sixtyish but looked seventy. He'd put on some weight and lost some hair since they'd last worked together, and the older man looked worried.

"I've got an assignment for you, Molinari. I think you'll like it. Even if you don't, you're needed. We've got a situation . . ."

The chief's voice trailed off as he and Joe entered the corner office. While Steinmetz had changed, his office looked as it always had: a worn blue carpet, plain government-issue oaken desk, two flags—California and USA—and a picture window behind them. Bookshelves were to his left and right, and a half a dozen photos of Steinmetz shaking hands with high-ranking government officials hung on the wall near his desk.

Yet one thing was new.

A well-turned-out thirtysomething Chinese woman sat in one of the chairs facing the chief's desk, hands clasped in her lap. She turned her head to look at Joe as he came toward the desk. He noted her charcoal-gray pantsuit, white men's tailored shirt, minimal makeup, and short wash-n-go hair. He, having dressed for speed, was wearing a khaki shirt, chinos, and work boots. Plus an untrimmed twenty-four-hour-old beard and plumber's putty under his fingernails.

Steinmetz said, "Joe. Have a seat. Meet Bao Wong, director of cyberterrorism, DC office. Bao, this is Joe Molinari."

Joe dusted off his hands on his back pockets, shook hands with Director Wong, and took the chair beside her. Steinmetz gave Bao the thirty-second version of Joe's decades in government service; first, a few years with the FBI, then even longer with the CIA, followed by getting drafted by DHS as deputy director.

"Later, he went back to DC for another tour," Steinmetz said.

Joe said, "I'm a risk assessment consultant specializing in port security, and I have background in cyber threats."

"Actually, I've followed your career, Joe," Bao said. "Great to meet you in person."

Coffee was served in FBI-branded mugs as Steinmetz told the agents about the case that had brought them together.

"Two weeks ago, Oakland Pediatrics' computer network was breached, for Christ's sake. The hospital had a cybersecurity system in place, but some dope in a back office—a doctor, actually—clicked on a phishing site and let the dogs in. The hackers called themselves 123 Boom. Whoever they are, they put Oakland Pediatrics in a twenty-four-hour choke hold. Then, *boom*."

Steinmetz swiveled his chair so that he faced the street and talked to the glass.

"They input incorrect medical formulas and protocols, resulting in four neonatal deaths. The hospital was underinsured. The ransom was seventeen million in Bitcoin to get their data back. The hospital paid. The encryption keys were returned. The hackers evaporated. The babies stayed dead. Lawsuits pending."

Bao Wong said, "The hackers can take what they got from Oakland, tweak it, and use it on them again. Or they can use it elsewhere."

"'Elsewhere' called an hour ago," said Steinmetz, swiveling back to face the two people who might be a hospital's last resort. "Joe, now they're threatening St. Vartan's. Boom is demanding eighteen million dollars in"—Steinmetz looked at his watch—"forty-seven hours. By 9:00 a.m. Friday, we've either shut these killers down, or St. Vartan's lights go out. They lose all of their patient records, past and present, and whatever archived information they've stored on dead patients. As a sweet farewell, 123 Boom will also have embedded digital land mines in the network."

Steinmetz stood up, seizing his coffee mug. "Please tell Joe the rest, Bao," he said. "I'm meeting with the governor to fill him in. Contact me the moment you have something, and good luck."

CHAPTER 15

JOE AND BAO got into Joe's old Mercedes and headed out to St. Vartan's by way of Van Ness Avenue.

Bao said, "Gotta make a quick call."

She took out her phone and, seconds later, said, "It's me." She listened, then said, "That's so good, Cam. You did it!"

When she clicked off, she said, "My son Cameron's nine. Got the lead in a class play. Lines *and* singing."

She beamed at Joe.

Joe said, "Hey. That's great."

"You'd think so. The lead role is a talking frog. Cam's been practice-belching for weeks now. Driving his mother crazy."

Joe laughed along with Bao. "I've got a little girl. I think Julie would also love to be a frog."

Bao said, "I just don't see the attraction to amphibians."

Joe laughed again, and relayed Julie's alligator-going-to-the-dentist story. Then, with the ticking clock in mind, he asked, "So what do we know about 123 Boom?"

Bao said, "Well, they set off alarms in DC months ago. My

team has been working up their methods, embedding moles, tracking this gang's footsteps ever since. Their IP addresses are always in motion, hopping from one country to another. New threats, new names, but we recognize their patterns."

Joe thought how the public perception of ransomware was a hairy guy in Russia making a digitally distorted phone call: *Give me all your money or people will die.*

He said, "Remember when cyber theft was buying and selling credit card numbers on message boards? Some years ago, an airline called me. Their network was frozen. Flights canceled. Even the elevators were dead. And there was a demand for twenty million in crypto, which they paid."

Bao said, "That was huge. I remember it."

"Now," said Joe, "these digital terrorists don't care about stealing data. They're screwing up chemotherapy orders. Killing without leaving fingerprints. And still walking away with the dough."

The two were silent as Joe took a right on Bush Street and headed east.

Bao said, "One of these businesses we're tracking makes kids' toys, goes by the name Skylark. You look at them, it's a functioning, medium-sized company of seven hundred based in Amsterdam. They have a manufacturing floor. Marketing. Sales. And a floating crew of Americans and other foreign nationals, all tech geniuses, one of whom appears to be in or near Northern California with dark web access to the Dutch mother ship. This holdup at St. Vartan's could be part of Skylark's ransomware wing. The pattern fits."

"What's his job? Does he have a name?"

"All we know is that he's the negotiator, likely American,

may have lived in this area for years unnoticed. He has an IP address like a chameleon. We want that guy with his phone and computer. If he would just stand still."

The traffic light turned red and Joe turned to Bao.

"More on that," he said.

"After we meet with St. Vartan's response team, their corporate officers, lawyers, and IT head, we'll see how bad the situation is, what can be retrieved. We'll plug in to home base and try to take these killers down before they turn St. Vartan's network into local phone calls only."

Joe was thinking of the hundreds of patients lying helpless and unaware in hospital beds. "Tell me the truth, Bao. What are our chances of stopping them?"

"I just don't know. I really don't, Joe. But we're not alone in this. Our mother ship is bigger and smarter than theirs."

CHAPTER 16

JOE SAID "HELLO" to the unsmiling woman who was waiting for him and Bao when the elevator doors slid open on St. Vartan's top floor.

"I'm Christine, Mr. LaBreche's PA. Please come with me."

Christine's expression was pained, and she walked as if she had broken glass in her shoes. She didn't speak again, just took the lead, put her head down and struck out for the northern end of the corridor.

Joe and Bao followed Christine along the length of the executive floor. When they reached a glass-walled conference room at the far corner, Christine knocked on the door. A blue-suited man wearing a loosened tie around his collar got up from his chair at the head of the table, opened the door, and stepped back as the two-person FBI team entered the room.

"I'm Rob LaBreche, CEO," he said. "The guy that gets hung for this disaster."

He pulled the ends of his tie up under his jaw and, after

fake-hanging himself, shook hands with Bao and Joe and offered them seats at the table. LaBreche introduced the seated semicircle of corporate officers by name and function. Joe made a mental note of the heads of the legal and IT departments. Next, LaBreche introduced Sveinn Thordarson, a stocky man in his sixties and the head of Cyber Security Incorporated, a well-known anti-cyberattack firm. He wore a dress shirt and blue tie, no jacket, good quality trousers, and had a short, trimmed beard. Thordarson in turn introduced his partner, Peter Wooten, as an anti-ransomware genius in a young but growing industry, expanding around the world. Wooten was about forty, a wiry six feet tall, red-haired, wearing square, rimless eyeglasses, chinos, and a Hawaiian shirt.

In the all-suited assemblage, Thordarson and Wooten stood out, as did Joe in his khaki shirt and work boots.

LaBreche said to Bao, "You know what I'm praying? That somehow through the arcane tricks of their trade, Sveinn and Pete will quickly restore our system and wall off our permeable network without loss of life. That's what I've been praying for over the last hour. And that you," he said, indicating Bao and Joe, "will find this filth and nail them to the walls of a maximum-security cell for the rest of their lives."

"Amen," said Thomas Walters, the head of IT. "This is madness. Obviously, it's evil to hold hospitals hostage, and more personally, we had an incident response plan in place. Within ten minutes of getting the threat, Thordarson and Wooten were on the phone."

Thordarson said, "Why don't I take it from here, Mr. Walters? First, nice to meet you both," he said to Bao and Joe.

"Director Wong, I believe we worked together on that Chem Con breach . . . ?"

"Five years ago. In Santa Rosa," she said. "Right you are. It was a squeaker."

LaBreche tapped his watch. "Sveinn?"

Sveinn Thordarson said, "Let me give you the streamlined summary. The ransom demand was sent to the hospital's top-tier mailboxes this morning. At 8:00 a.m., everyone at St. Vartan's with an executive function or a stethoscope, say two hundred people, received it. Some messages were sent to St. Vartan's email addresses. But at least half of our executives got the warning in their personal mailboxes. That was the panic button.

"Here's a printout of the email," he said, separating it from a pile of papers in front of him.

LaBreche had immediately forwarded the email to Steinmetz upon receipt. Joe and Bao had already seen the one-page printout that read, "Because you hired a low-rent response team, we've got the goods. We can take the entire hospital down below dead pool in five minutes: computers, medical equipment, refrigeration, everything but the flush toilets. Or you can find twenty million in crypto in the next forty-eight hours and deposit it into our wallet in outer space. See link below. Do that and most of your patients will survive. We'll also educate your lame IT director and tell you how to protect yourself in the future. You'll get a call from us at 1:00 p.m. today. Keep your lines open. All we want to hear from you is, 'We sent the crypto.'"

Thordarson exhaled and said, "It's signed 'Apocalypto.' This is an active start-up group and has some of the hallmarks of the older 123 Boom. Possibly it was seeded by Boom.

Pete and I have been in touch with Apocalypto, identified ourselves. We let them know that the hospital cannot raise twenty million in any form within the time allowed and if they don't play this straight, we will hand off our investigation to the FBI."

Joe asked, "How much time did you buy?"

"We deposited seven million in exchange for two days' extension," said the head of the premier incident response company west of the Rockies.

"The deposit went to a virtual account on the dark web that is effectively a ghost bank. They can see it but they can't access it until we have proof they're out of our system."

LaBreche wasn't listening. He cut into the conversation, saying, "We've called for any external backup drives that may exist outside the hospital. We're in the process now of transferring as many patients out as we can find beds for, but other hospitals are packed. We have surgery patients on vents—my PA Christine's mother is one of them—and on heart-lung machines. Pete says that Apocalypto has been inside our systems for months. Is that right?"

Bao said, "Very likely."

LaBreche spit curses, paced, and shoved chairs as he circled the conference table.

"So, for sure they've burrowed into everything we have and do. We're not safe until Apocalypto is out of business and the people who ruined this hospital are in prison. Or worse."

Joe said, "That's why your cybersecurity team called us. Sveinn, Pete, tell us where we can help. We're ready."

CHAPTER 17

JOE WATCHED PETER WOOTEN square the papers and pens in front of him. Then he squared them again. Joe thought, *Precise, maybe OCD.* Perfect mental tic for a man in Pete's field. Check it. Check it again. And again.

Pete said, "We've tracked Apocalypto to a server in Bruges . . ."

"No longer there?" Bao said.

"Correct."

"Lucky guess," she said.

Christine came into the room and whispered to LaBreche, who said to her, "Might as well." Christine wheeled in a coffee cart and several people rose from their places for coffee, but Bao and Joe, the professional hack prevention team, and four top hospital executives who were sweating and making notes on their phones remained seated. They were fighting an enemy they didn't know and couldn't see, while trying to save lives and a very good hospital on an extremely tight deadline.

Pete Wooten said, "So, this morning at 9:03, after extending the deadline and funneling crypto into their blind Bitcoin wallet, we began to drill down on the malware. As I said, Apocalypto was pinging a server in Belgium. Then the signal hopped to another location.

"The program began seeking its point man on the West Coast from somewhere within a hundred miles of the Anglo-Scottish border, then the signal bounced around here in San Francisco."

"Sounds like an airplane was involved," said Joe.

LaBreche, who'd been pacing since accepting an offered cup of coffee, asked, "This hopping is some kind of 'Catch me if you can' kind of thing?"

"Exactly," said Thordarson. "By disguising their location and the program itself, we don't know who and where they are. Makes it hard to erect a defense. But we will locate the source and the target, Mr. LaBreche. That's what we do."

LaBreche looked hopeful, then a blink later, entirely depressed. He stopped his pacing near Joe's chair and said, "I might as well tell you, I had to be talked into working with the FBI. We don't want this to, you know, get out, but Pete convinced me to call in the Feds. Can you actually keep this quiet?"

Joe said, "Honestly? The fact of the attack may leak, Mr. LaBreche, but we won't be advertising our involvement. We understand what's at stake and we'll do everything possible to contain the situation. Maybe we'll come up with something that hasn't been done before. Anything else?"

LaBreche shrugged and Joe took that to be a no.

He said, "We'll check in when we have something to tell you. Pete? Sveinn? Your place or ours?"

CHAPTER 18

RILEY BOONE WAS the bailiff, the law enforcement officer in charge of maintaining court procedure. He was short but stood tall, and Yuki was always surprised by the volume and resonance of his voice as his announcement "Allll rise" caromed off the oak-paneled walls of Courtroom 8G.

A hundred and twenty people noisily stood as one—the counselors and their clients and deputies, the jurors, and the audience in the gallery—as the Honorable Henry William St. John entered through the door from his chambers into the courtroom.

A handsome man in his forties, Yuki thought Hank St. John had classic good looks, like an adman from the sixties—tall, fit, with a pencil mustache, always carrying a book. He stepped up to his enviable desk chair behind the bench, adjusted his robes, and took his seat.

Judge St. John motioned for all but the jurors to be seated. After Boone had sworn in the jury, they filled the jury box and Boone called the court to order. Two court officers took their places with their backs to the double doors of the entrance.

Nick Gaines, Mary Elena Hayes, and Yuki adjusted their chairs, pulling them up to the prosecution table. To Yuki's mind, Mary Elena looked perfectly composed in her nice brown skirt suit, understated makeup, and unruffled expression. She wondered if Mary Elena was recalling the dream she'd told to Yuki days ago about the movie courtroom, unreal but real, although the actual foreperson looked nothing like Sean Penn.

Across the aisle to their left, criminal defense attorney Edward Schneider—six two, 250 pounds—spoke behind his hand to his second chair. The defendant, Tyler Cates, checked out the courtroom. He leaned forward and peered around the bulk of his lawyer, stared across the aisle at Mary Elena. He continued to stare until Schneider's number two whispered, "Stop doing that."

Judge St. John put his hand over his mic and exchanged a few words with his clerk and then his voice broke into Yuki's thoughts.

"Ms. Castellano. Are the People ready to begin?"

Yuki got to her feet. "Yes, Your Honor."

Two seats down from her at the counsel table, Mary Elena moaned softly. "Oh, no."

Yuki turned her head, following Mary Elena's gaze, and saw two women in the gallery dressed like lunatics. They both wore hats, one with springs coming out of the top, the other with a cross-eyed cat perched on top. They were laughing.

Yuki stood, said, "Your Honor, may I approach?"

St. John waved her in. She spoke with him quietly but urgently, then returned to her table. The bailiff, Riley Boone, went directly to the gallery. Although the women having fun with the idea of a plaintiff with a mental disorder promised to keep their hats under their seats, they were firmly shown out of the courtroom.

Judge St. John addressed the room, saying, "This is a trial. Serious work is done here and I will not brook funny business. Understood?"

Murmured affirmation buzzed through the room and St. John banged his gavel, returning silence to the courtroom.

"Ms. Castellano?" he said. "Shall we try again?"

Yuki walked to the jury box and put her hands on the rail. She smiled and made eye contact with all twelve jurors and the two alternates, many of whom she'd chosen during voir dire. They made a diverse mix of male, female, blue-collar, and white-collar, from multiple ethnic groups, with ages spanning thirty-six to sixty-eight. Nine were married with children.

Yuki cared about reaching every one of them.

The jurors lifted their eyes to hers and waited for her to speak. She let the silence grow until it was nearly intolerable.

CHAPTER 19

YUKI WAS VERY good at opening statements, laying out the facts of the crime chronologically without actually arguing the case. And now she was sure she was ready. If she rehearsed her opening once more, she'd risk scrambling the entire bowl of eggs.

Keiko's voice was in her head: *Keep it simple, Yuki-eh. You know this.*

Right. After formally introducing herself to the jurors, Yuki brought them back to six months earlier, when victim Mary Elena Hayes had been brutally attacked and raped in the changing room of a tony restaurant in the financial district.

"Here's what happened to Ms. Hayes on that day six months ago," she said. "Ms. Hayes had been to her dentist and was returning to her job at Raymond James, where she works in human resources. It was a long walk and Ms. Hayes needed to use a ladies' room pretty badly.

"She was coming up on a five-star restaurant called Xe

Sogni and took a chance. A valet opened the door for her and she quickly found the maître d', Jules Lenoir. She asked him if she could use the facilities. Mr. Lenoir said yes to this well-dressed young lady and pointed her to a spiral staircase."

Yuki continued, "Ms. Hayes took the stairs up to a carpeted room, furnished with lockers and benches—the staff changing room, where at opposite sides of the room are two bathrooms, one for men and one for women.

"Ms. Hayes never reached the ladies' room.

"Within minutes after she'd climbed the stairs, diners on the floor below heard a loud scream and '*Nooooo!*' Mr. Lenoir will testify that he took this scream to be a distressed cry for help."

Yuki let the echo of that virtual scream hang over the jury box, then said, "One of Xe Sogni's clientele that day was a police sergeant having lunch with friends. I was one of those friends, and I, too, heard that scream. The police officer, Sergeant Lindsay Boxer of SFPD Homicide Division, will testify that she ran upstairs. She will tell you in her own words that she saw a nearly naked woman lying on the floor wearing only a pink bra pulled up over her breasts and that this woman had an assortment of fresh bruises on her arms and inner thighs as well as finger marks around her neck. Her eyes were swollen nearly shut and she had a large fist-sized bruise coming up on her left cheek.

"Sergeant Boxer asked this semiconscious young woman what had happened to her and she said, 'He raped us.' Let me repeat that. Ms. Hayes, the victim, said, 'He raped us.' "

Yuki paused to let Mary Elena's words work on the jury and saw surprise on several faces. Images of Claire's birthday lunch and Mary Elena Hayes's bruised body lit up Yuki's own mind, and for a moment she was as good as there at Xe Sogni six months ago.

Back in the present, Yuki walked along the front of the jury box and stopped at the center of the rail, looking into the eyes of the forewoman, Gayle Grabo, and the other jurors. What she saw in their faces confirmed what she'd anticipated. Fully attentive, they waited to hear more.

CHAPTER 20

JUDGE ST. JOHN cleared his throat with meaning and Yuki got the message. *Get on with it.*

The expected time limit for an opening statement is fifteen minutes. Yuki glanced at her watch. She was six minutes shy of fifteen, so she picked up the story where she'd left off, this time with more energy.

She said, "The apparent victim told Sergeant Boxer that her name was Loretta, but when the sergeant located her wallet, the name listed was Mary Elena Hayes. Apart from Ms. Hayes, there was only one other person in the changing room: the defendant, Tyler Cates, who worked in the kitchen. Sergeant Boxer located him half hidden behind a locker door. He was also naked from the waist down.

"At that point, Mr. Cates told Sergeant Boxer that the name of the woman on the floor was Olivia, not Loretta, that she was a liar, and that she had asked him for rough sex. He admitted, and we have his sworn statement, that he'd had sex with Olivia but insisted that she was the one who'd initiated it and directed him as to when and how."

Yuki continued the narrative, stating that Sergeant Boxer had called for help from a doctor. San Francisco's chief medical examiner, Dr. Claire Washburn, then came upstairs. Dr. Washburn gave Ms. Hayes a cursory examination while she waited for an ambulance to arrive. At about that time, backup in the form of two uniformed officers took Mr. Cates into custody to SFPD's Southern Station, right here in this building two floors up.

Yuki said, "Mr. Cates was questioned and he gave a statement to detectives before hiring an attorney. This interview was videotaped and will be entered into evidence by Sergeants McNeil and Chi, who interviewed Mr. Cates, and who will testify and show the videotape.

"But here's the main point. Mr. Cates told the detectives that when Mary Elena came into the room, he called out, 'Hey. Who are you?' And Ms. Hayes told him that her name was Mary Elena.

"That is a seemingly innocuous verbal exchange but let me repeat it again. When asked her name, Ms. Hayes told Mr. Cates that her name was Mary Elena. The answer is pivotal to determining what happened in Xe Sogni that day.

"Let me shift gears for a moment. Ms. Hayes has a mental disorder known as dissociative identity disorder, or DID. It was formerly known as split personality, or multiple personality disorder. In the course of this trial, you will hear from two highly qualified psychiatric experts who will tell you about this disorder and what it means to have alternate personalities. It's possible that while Ms. Hayes is testifying, one or more of those personalities will emerge.

"But for now, the critical point to know and remember is that this syndrome is the psychological result of severe childhood trauma. Some of those afflicted with this disorder may have two or even dozens of alternate personalities who exist to protect 'the body'—in this case, Ms. Hayes—from danger."

Yuki explained to the jurors that it was a crime to have sex with a person whose mental disorder makes it impossible for them to give informed consent.

"Here's how we know that Mr. Cates understood that Ms. Hayes had a psychological disability: Mary Elena Hayes told Mr. Cates her given name, Mary Elena. But she almost immediately felt threatened by Mr. Cates, which caused Olivia, one of her alternate personalities, to emerge. Olivia is a peacemaker and a people pleaser, and she moved Mary Elena out of the picture and dealt with Mr. Cates as best she could.

"But Olivia was no match for Mr. Cates. When she couldn't distract him or otherwise hold him off, another of Ms. Hayes's personalities, a tougher personality called Loretta, stepped in to fight back. Instead, Loretta absorbed the violent abuse. It was Loretta who told Sergeant Boxer, 'He raped us.'

"*Us.* Mary Elena, Olivia, and Loretta."

Yuki turned her head and briefly took in the gallery, the counsel table, and the defense table, where Tyler Cates's expression was as flat as a wall. As Yuki walked back to the prosecution table, she felt all the people in the courtroom watching her.

CHAPTER 21

CINDY THOMAS AND a dozen other avid journalists had stampeded around the Hall of Justice to the back entrance and, once there, had been flatly turned away by security guards. No surprise, really, but Cindy felt personally attached to Mary Elena, who'd been attacked and raped while the Women's Murder Club had been lunching on caviar.

Trying again to get into the courtroom, this time through the front door, Cindy maintained her pole position in the lead while Alison Kiel from the *American Enquirer* questioned her, trying to make friends, hoping to follow her into the Hall. Cindy put on extra speed. By the time she and the rest of the pack reached the Hall's front entrance and cleared security, court was in session.

Cindy adjusted her computer bag, hoisting its weight onto her shoulder as she took the elevator up to the second floor. Clearly, she'd wasted time trying to snare a quote from Yuki or Mary Elena, but hell, she'd had to try. She hoped that Louie Mack, one of the two court officers who manned the doors to Courtroom 8G, would hold "her" seat in the last row and would admit her to the court while it was in session.

Cindy didn't see Louie outside the courtroom as she headed toward it, and then, as if he could see through six inches of oak—he opened the door.

"Anybody else would be left standing in the hall," he said.

"Thanks, Louie. I was chasing a scoop. How'd you know?"

He said, "ADA Castellano texted me. Get in here. Quick."

Cindy edged into her seat, closest to the door. She plugged her devices into the socket in the baseboard and checked the time, again. It was later than she'd thought. Yuki was winding up her opening statement. Damn it. Cindy loved to watch Yuki work and now she'd missed her setup for the trial.

"Shit."

The woman sitting in the seat to her left gave her a hard look. Cindy ignored her and concentrated on Yuki.

CHAPTER 22

YUKI SUBMITTED THREE copies of each of her exhibits to the clerk: the photos of Mary Elena's injuries, the transcript and a thumb drive of the police interview with Tyler Cates before he lawyered up, with a video of the interview. The clerk logged the exhibits and passed them to the judge for his approval. Defense counsel had already seen them so the clerk delivered the exhibits to the jury, who, to Yuki's eye, still looked a little shocked from her opening.

When the exhibits had been viewed and returned to the clerk, Yuki addressed the jurors again.

"As you saw from the photos, Ms. Hayes suffered a vicious attack. Mr. Cates punched her, strangled her, pulled her legs apart, and forcibly penetrated her. As you will see on the videotape, Mr. Cates claimed that Ms. Hayes 'asked for it.'

"It will be up to you to decide if her screams contradict this statement.

"During the course of this trial, we will introduce noted psychologist Dr. Laurie Birney, a specialist in the field of dissociative identity disorder. We will also introduce you to Dr. Stuart Aronson, Ms. Hayes's treatment psychiatrist, who will testify about her condition and how it affects her emotions and behavior."

Yuki explained, "Alternate personalities, Olivia and Loretta, took over for Ms. Hayes when she was experiencing terrible fear, pain, and stress. This happens when the dominant personality, Mary Elena, is 'bumped' into a dark place that people with this disorder often call 'lost time.' This lost time is a form of amnesia and a hallmark of DID. Accordingly, Ms. Hayes does not remember what happened to her in the changing room at Xe Sogni, but it cannot be disputed. The beating and the rape did occur, and we will prove this to you with medical reports and forensic evidence showing a 100 percent match to Mr. Cates's DNA."

There was a murmur in the gallery that was shut down of its own accord. What would the ADA say next?

Yuki was pacing now, looking down at the floor as she collected her thoughts. Keiko's calming voice was in her head: *Okay now, my daughter, you are doing very well.*

Yuki launched the next and last part of her opening. "The defendant did indeed assault and rape Ms. Hayes. And whether or not he knew what Ms. Hayes's mental disorder was called, he knew that her name and personality changes that took place in his presence were not normal. Still, he violently assaulted her, sexually penetrated her as she screamed for help. Mr. Cates chose to take advantage of the situation, possibly thinking that it was his lucky day."

Ed Schneider objected to Yuki's putting her thoughts into his client's mouth and Judge St. John sustained his objection, ordering Yuki's last comment stricken from the record. Yuki felt it was a price worth paying.

She thanked the court and said, "We've concluded our opening statement."

Yuki returned to the counsel table, nearest to the jury box. She took her seat on the aisle and leaned across Gaines and whispered to Mary Elena, "Okay?"

Mary Elena said softly, "We're fine."

Gaines gave Yuki a hearty thumbs-up and then Judge St. John addressed the defense.

"Mr. Schneider, please proceed with your opening statement."

CHAPTER 23

YUKI HAD NEVER met Ed Schneider, but he was well-known in California as a cutthroat criminal defense attorney with an impressive batting average. Now, Tyler Cates's attorney rose to his feet. He buttoned his jacket and staked out a position behind the podium in the center of the well. Facing the jury box, he began to dismantle Yuki's platform, one board at a time.

"Your Honor, good people of the jury. I don't intend to take an hour to give the defense opening statement. The witnesses will fill you in on the events that took place in Xe Sogni because they were there.

"For now, let me say this.

"The defendant did not know that the plaintiff had a theoretical mental illness that blocks out real words and actions happening in actual present time. Why is knowledge of this theoretical mental illness critical to the prosecution's case?

"It's critical because my client has sworn that he did not know that there was anything wrong with Ms. Hayes. If he had known, it would have meant that Ms. Hayes could not give consent to having sex with him. That is the prosecution's case because sex without consent with a disabled person is a crime.

"There was no witness to the commission of the sex act, let alone that the defendant believed Ms. Hayes was mentally disabled. Ms. Hayes told my client that she wanted to have sex.

"Furthermore, when I say that Ms. Hayes's disorder is 'theoretical,' I mean there is no scientific proof that DID even exists. It's simply theory. Guesswork and make-work for untold numbers of psychiatrists, psychologists, psychiatric researchers, and social workers. However well-meaning, the expertise of these people lies in detecting and analyzing symptoms, then labeling them as mental disorders. They are not scientists, and I repeat, scientific evidence of DID does not exist.

"For example, a theory of another psychological disorder: It's been posited by psychiatrists for decades that depression is caused by a shortage of serotonin, a feel-good neurochemical produced in the brain. Until lately, the theory has been that early trauma causes the human brain to create additional *receptors* for this neurochemical. The effect of many additional receptors, according to this theory, is that the serotonin is sucked up into those receptors so quickly that it does not sufficiently bathe the brain cells with feel-good serotonin, and so the individual becomes depressed.

"Ever hear of a book called *Listening to Prozac*? This book posits that if a patient responds to selective serotonin reuptake inhibitors, like Prozac, they are therefore suffering from a shortage of serotonin, ergo, their depression is a psychiatric disorder and can be treated by serotonin.

"Manufacturers of a huge class of these selective serotonin reuptake inhibitors sold them by the boatload. Not long ago, it was proven that this theory—sold as 'science'—is faulty. SSRIs cured nothing. But Big Pharma pushed the theory disguised as proof and made billions.

"Back to the case at hand. Actually, there is no medication for DID. Psychoanalysis is recommended. Meditation. Learning what trauma triggers the presence of so-called alters. Tranquilizers. In other words, there's no standard of proof that DID exists. I could go down the list of psychological disorders where the proof is in the interpretation of symptoms, not in physical structures or provable disorders.

"Tyler Cates has common sense and a tenth-grade education. He washes vegetables and dishes for a living. He did not know if Mary Elena Hayes had dissociative identity disorder or a vivid imagination or just wanted to get roughed up by an attractive stranger. He didn't know, I don't know, and whatever Ms. Hayes says, I honestly say to her, 'You have a big and active imagination. You put yourself in a situation you couldn't control. You shouldn't do that again.'

"Mr. Cates couldn't take advantage of this so-called mentally disabled person who could not or did not give consent, because only the two of them were present in that changing room. There is no way to establish if Ms. Hayes has such a mental condition or if it just makes for good fiction or a rationale after the fact. At any rate, Tyler Cates didn't know a thing about it. Mary Elena Hayes, by any name, came on to him. He complied with her wishes."

Ed Schneider strode heavily back to the defense table, roughly pulled out his chair, and when it snagged on the table leg, he wrangled it into submission and sat down.

Schneider didn't intimidate Yuki and she'd remained unfazed while he spoke. Now it was time for Yuki to call her first witness.

CHAPTER 24

JOE WRENCHED THE steering wheel, sending his old Mercedes into a hard right turn around the curve on California Street. Bao fell against her seat belt, then was thrown back in her seat as Joe, staying close to Cyber Security Incorporated's Tesla, climbed the forty-five-degree incline of Jones Street. Bao hung on to the armrest, and as Joe took the hilly roads, she told him what she knew about Thordarson and Wooten.

"Sveinn Thordarson graduated MIT with honors in math—Jeez, Joe."

"Sorry, Bao. Keep talking."

"Where do you keep the barf bags?"

"Seriously?"

"Nooooo. As I was saying, Thordarson was then recruited by the Secret Service. Wooten graduated Harvard in the top 1 percent; majored in science and technology. He was snapped up by Intel and was on a management track. By then

Thordarson had started his new business and offered Wooten a partnership in his cyber threat defense start-up."

Joe said, "That fits. I see Thordarson as a risk taker. Wooten's precise. I'd guess an intellectual."

"Here," said Bao, reading from her phone. "One of their clients says, 'Wooten can see threats in five dimensions, in or out of the sandbox.'"

"That fits."

"Good guess," Bao teased, bracing against the next curve with her hand on the dashboard.

Joe knew that in tech jargon, a sandbox was an isolated testing environment for trying out code changes and other experimental work. Like tracking cyber threats.

The Tesla pulled up to a ten-story office building on a mixed-use block in the Rincon Hill district. Joe parked behind the CS Inc. company car, and he and Bao joined Sveinn Thordarson and Pete Wooten at the building's entrance.

Inside, the lobby was fronted with a manned security desk, lined with white stone, and punctuated by a half dozen elevators. One of them was marked with a nameplate inscribed CYBER SECURITY INCORPORATED and had a biometric palm print reader below it. Thordarson cleared his guests through security, and Wooten put the flat of his hand on the palm reader. There was a *buzz,* a *thunk,* and the lift doors opened. The four got in and the car sped them directly to the top floor. The doors opened again, this time into a long white room taking up most of the tenth floor.

Joe was temporarily stunned by the pure white light evenly illuminating six long tables, running lengthwise, from back to front of the room, the SOC, or security operations center. Each of the tables held multiscreen computers from end to end. Behind them sat dozens of technology operators wearing headsets, their chairs pulled up to the tables, their eyes fixed on the screens. There was a soundtrack, the clacking of keyboards and chatter of speech to fellow operators nearby.

Joe and Bao followed Thordarson and Wooten to the office at the rear of the room. Wooten closed the door behind them and Thordarson offered chairs and cold drinks. After all were seated, Joe asked how their process worked.

Thordarson squared the empty space in front of him with his hands. Then he said, "St. Vartan's wants us to work with the Feds and that's what I always recommend. We can track the evildoers but have no authority to arrest them."

Thordarson gave Joe and Bao his full intense attention. He said, "So, our charge is to eject Apocalypto's payload, reset what's been damaged or altered in St. Vartan's network, and set up the next level of protection. In this case, shutter all of the faulty protocols that Apocalypto has put into place in the last weeks or months, malware that is set to drop the instant the two-day extension period expires if the ransom doesn't drop into their bank. Once we've restored their systems, put blocks in place, St. Vartan's is going to be impermeable, and Apocalypto knows it."

"Smart of the hospital to have you at the ready," Bao said.

"Thanks, Director. It's still impossible to stop attacks before they happen, but our warning system did its job and we've been actively working since LaBreche called me three hours ago. Right now we're collecting indicators of compromise. When we're done, God willing, we'll have an impermeable hospital and we'll turn over the attackers' names or pseudonyms, IP addresses, a report on the malware, and other types of indicators to you guys."

"Stupendous," Bao said with a smile. "Now, I think I'll take a diet-something with caffeine. Jet lag."

CHAPTER 25

PETE WOOTEN OPENED the fridge under the table, took out a Diet Coke, held it up.

"Ice?"

"A nice cold can is fine," said Bao.

Wooten handed off Diet Cokes to Bao and Joe, grabbed a Red Bull for himself and one for Thordarson, then clinked cans with all three.

"To Fidelity, Bravery, Integrity," Wooten said, quoting the FBI motto. Bao grinned and Wooten returned a grin, then sat back down in his chair.

Thordarson said to the FBI visitors, "We brought you here to see our process in action. Pete and I developed a real-time attack map for locating cyberattacks."

"Real time how?" Bao asked.

"As you know, the current best practice is to have one person, say FBI or NSA, watching the attackers' end and the internal security folks watching the target—in this case the hospital. Our dream tracker watches both sides at the same time."

"Oh, wow," Bao said. "You're going to give us a demo?"

"Exactly. This is its actual maiden launch. We'd be interested in your read on CS Inc.'s just-minted attack catcher.

"Created right here."

He pointed a remote-control device at the eighty-inch screen on the wall to his right. A diagram appeared on the screen. Joe peered at it. Couldn't quite make out what he was looking at.

Thordarson said, "Can everyone see okay? I'll sharpen the contrast."

Wooten cut the overhead lights, and after Thordarson brightened the picture, Joe walked over to the screen and Bao rolled her chair closer. Now, the 3D diagram was clearer.

"Beautiful," said Joe.

"This program is part sandbox, part dream catcher. It's a perfectly in-scale diagram of the globe. Right now, we're viewing the northern hemisphere. Those pinpoint clusters of light represent individual devices signaling at 1,000 Hz or higher. Here's a sparse concentration of pinpoints in the Arctic," Wooten said. "Those are biologists' devices likely studying and recording life-forms deep under the ice. And here, this is a military base in Croatia. These blips are coming from search engines powerful enough to hop over continents without being boosted by an outside network. And of course, they use the submarine fiber-optic cable backbone."

Wooten toggled a switch on the remote and the map rotated.

"We're seeking a signal of an IP address launched from a known location in Amsterdam or Bruges or Eastern Europe and coming toward a known location in Northern California, USA."

Sveinn said, "Pete, roll back the tracking record to two weeks ago."

Pete Wooten made some adjustments to the projector, winding back the time stream. The symbols on the diagram rapidly reassembled.

"Here we are," said Wooten. "Two weeks ago."

He jabbed a button on his remote, which brought the rotation and all other movement to a halt.

Wooten said, "Now, retroactively, we've identified devices that have been pinging the IP addresses of companies, individuals, targets of all kinds in Bruges, Amsterdam, Glasgow, and finally setting course for the City by the Bay. We developed an AI program that alerts us to a pair of hits that include Eastern Europe and Northern California. That's when our SOC team"—he pointed to the room outside the office—"runs the IP addresses through our programs to get IDs on the signal. That signal carries the payload and starts the destruction when directed. So far, we don't have those hits."

Wooten pressed a button and the program sped up to present time. Joe found it mesmerizing to watch computer signals break apart and reform. He was impressed by the display, but unless it produced a suspected attacker, it was all lipstick and no pig. As he watched the light array cross the East Coast of the US, the machine beeped.

"There—and none too soon, I should add," Wooten said, pointing to one glowing dot in a cluster. "That dot represents a device bearing a known twelve-digit IP address. It launched from Amsterdam and is searching now from a point in San Francisco."

"It's on the move," said Bao.

Joe added, "Unless my eyes are failing, it's crossing the bay."

Thordarson said, "We're monitoring that signal now. And this tag on the dot identifies the signal as a blacklisted entry. Not necessarily an attack, but an IP address that's pinged a hospital server before. Oakland Pediatrics, I'm guessing. And we watch to see if the next stop is St. Vartan's. Pete and I think that Apocalypto has at least one agent frequenting or living in this area."

Wooten pushed in on the blinking dot. All watched as a dot the size of a pinhead slowly crossed the San Francisco Bay, heading toward the mainland.

CHAPTER 26

I WAS PACING the corridor outside the dozen courtrooms on the second floor of the Hall, waiting to testify in the Tyler Cates trial. Like most detectives, I took all of my cases personally, and I wanted Cates off the street and in a cell for what he'd done to Mary Elena Hayes, and possibly others. I would tell the court what I knew to the best of my ability, while keeping any trace of disgust from my face.

The double doors leading to Courtroom 8G opened. Louie Mack, one of the court officers, said, "Sergeant Boxer? You're up."

He held the door as I walked through. I squeezed Cindy's shoulder and she touched my hand as I passed her sitting in her regular seat on the aisle of the last row. I kept walking, going through the gate in the bar and across the well to the witness box.

Bailiff Riley Boone extended the Bible. I put my left hand on the Good Book, raised my right, and swore to tell the whole truth and nothing but. Then I stepped up to the witness box and took my seat. Below and across from me, my dear friend Yuki Castellano walked toward me. I stole a quick look at Mary Elena, sitting at the prosecution table beside Nick Gaines. Did she remember me? The lights were on, but was she home? I didn't note any flicker of recognition in her eyes.

Yuki stepped over to the witness box in her smart suit and stiletto heels. Suppressing a smile, she said "Good morning, Sergeant Boxer."

I acknowledged her greeting and Yuki asked me if I had responded to a scream for help on the second floor of Xe Sogni on the date in question. I told her that I had, and Yuki questioned me for about fifteen minutes. She asked me about the scream, what I'd found when I arrived upstairs, what I'd seen in the dim light, and if I could identify Mary Elena Hayes. I said I could and did.

"Sergeant, do you remember asking Ms. Hayes to tell you what had happened to her?"

"Yes. She told me, 'He raped us,' and that her name was Loretta."

In response to Yuki's questions, I told the court about finding Tyler Cates half naked at the end of a row of lockers and arresting him for aggravated assault. And that I had asked the ME, Dr. Claire Washburn, to come upstairs, evaluate the victim, and call an ambulance while I kept Cates restrained while awaiting backup.

I said, "Mr. Cates told me that Mary Elena had informed him her name was Olivia, not Loretta, and that she had begged him for sex, 'hard and fast and right now.' I had cuffed him and called dispatch for a team of police officers to come to the restaurant. He was read his rights and arrested, then Mr. Cates was brought back to the station for booking."

"He was questioned at the station?"

"He was," I said. "By two inspector sergeants."

"And apparently, sometime after that, he was arraigned and pleaded not guilty."

"Correct."

"Do you see him in court today?"

"Yes. Mr. Cates is wearing a blue jacket and is sitting at the defense table."

Yuki had no further questions and defense counsel had none, reserving the right to call me at some other time. I was dismissed and left the courtroom.

I found Claire sitting on a bench in the corridor, her ankles crossed, wearing a blazer over her scrubs, reading her phone.

I said, "Hey, girlfriend."

"How'd it go, Linds?"

"Regular," I said. "Just the facts, ma'am."

The guard said to Claire, "Dr. Washburn? You've been called."

Claire has some arthritis in her right knee. She stuck out her arm, asking me, "Mind giving me a hand up?"

I braced and pulled Claire to her feet. Then we hugged, kissed cheeks, and I headed for the fire stairs.

The Fricke task force was waiting for me.

CHAPTER 27

IT ONLY TOOK two minutes for me to take the stairs to the Homicide squad room. I checked in with Bobby Nussbaum, our gatekeeper and squad assistant. He used hand signals to indicate that one of my shirt buttons was open while handing over a short stack of junk mail addressed to me.

I re-buttoned my shirt, then said, "Thanks, Bob," putting a little barb in it. He laughed. Bobby loves his job. I crossed in front of his desk, then walked four paces to the three-desk pod I share with Inspectors Rich Conklin and Sonia Alvarez.

Alvarez is the most recent addition to our Homicide squad. She was previously with Las Vegas Metro's Vice squad, where she'd starred in undercover work. Then she'd been hand-picked for the SFPD by our chief, Charles Clapper.

Not long after joining us, she'd proven her tough-cop chops when she and I faced off against a mass murderer in the basement of the Bellagio Resort and Casino. She was all that; good with a gun, as well as being upbeat, fearless, a sharp interviewer, and she can carry a tune. In short, Sonia Alvarez is a pleasure to work with.

I asked her if the task force meeting had started.

"Not yet, but Cappy, Chi, and Conklin are all in Swanson's old office. But that's not all." She pointed to Brady's glass-walled office at the far end of the bullpen. I looked down the center aisle and saw Brady was meeting with two other men, all three standing and filling most of the usable space in that glass bread box. I made out DA Len "Red Dog" Parisi by the color of his tweeds. Chief Clapper filled in the rest of the eight-by-seven room.

Parisi rarely comes upstairs to our bullpen, but no doubt he was here to meet with Clapper and Brady about James Fricke's murder.

I squeezed in behind Alvarez's chair to reach my own so I could check my mail. I couldn't help but notice that Alvarez had her hand inside a bag of potato chips, specialty type, baked in truffle oil. This was her weakness and she'd gotten me hooked, too.

"Please take these," she said shoving the large foil bag over to my desk.

"Hey," I said, "pushing truffle chips is a felony."

She laughed, saying, "I never make you *eat* them."

"Okay. Pushing truffle chips is a misdemeanor in the first degree," I said, pulling open the bag. While feeding my new habit, I peered over Alvarez's shoulder and saw the dazzling image on her computer.

"Fricke Cottage," I commented as the immense mansion in Pacific Heights filled the screen.

"Fricke's man Bevaqua called for you," said Alvarez, referring to Jamie Fricke's house manager, Arthur Bevaqua. "How about taking me along for the ride?"

"Have you heard the expression 'Never volunteer'? Well, too bad for you, Sonia. I'm putting you on the Fricke task force. Dust the chips off your shirt and come with me to the meeting."

Alvarez beamed. She cleaned up, put the chips in a file drawer, and downed her coffee. I pulled my phone from my pocket, texted Conklin that I was at my desk and would be down the hall in a minute. Then I called Arthur Bevaqua. Bevaqua picked up but his voice cracked so much I could hardly understand him.

After six months of working Holly Fricke's case, I'd logged in so many hours with Bevaqua, I almost felt we were related.

"I'm sorry this happened, Arthur. Stay in the house. I'll be there as soon as possible," I told him.

"Good," he said. "Very good."

Alvarez and I headed down the long corridor to the conference room that had once been Ted Swanson's corner office. Swanson was now deceased but his activities as a sociopathic renegade, responsible for the estimated deaths of more than a dozen cops and crooks and innumerable drug users, had left a stain on Southern Station's reputation. I didn't know if solving the Fricke murders would redeem us, but it would certainly be good for morale.

As we walked, I told Alvarez, "We've inspected every one of the thirty rooms in the Fricke house, spoken with everyone who worked there and is connected to Holly and Jamie. Cappy and Chi went farther afield."

"I'm fresh, Lindsay. Expect the unexpected."

She was right. We could use new eyes on the Fricke family tragedy and Alvarez was something of a lucky charm.

"Task force meeting first," I said. "Then, chez Fricke."

CHAPTER 28

TED SWANSON'S FORMER office was easily the gloomiest office in the Hall of Justice. That's how he'd liked it. Dark. Cold. Out of the way. He hadn't planned on dying in prison but it was what he deserved.

Post-Swanson's-mortem, the walls of his office were used to display crime-scene evidence, and Holly Fricke's morgue photos were still taped where I'd put them. The timeline was sketched in marker pen on the whiteboard. Soon we would fill in James Fricke's movements as we knew them and tape up his morgue shots and pictures of the place where he had died.

Chief Clapper stood by the whiteboard, still speaking with Brady and Red Dog. He nodded a hello toward me and I pulled up a chair at the table. Charlie Clapper's background was Homicide, then head of CSU, and now chief of police. Clapper is the ultimate pro, immaculate in his work and his person. He used to have a sense of humor but left it in the crime lab when he was promoted to the top cop job.

Now, he said to the task force, "I'll make this brief. If we don't find the Frickes' killer or killers, the FBI is taking over the case. Jamie was a white-collar criminal, fixing soccer games overseas. Now that frickin' James Fricke is dead, the CIA is starting an investigation overseas where his soccer team is based and where he surely had enemies. We'll take all the help that's offered," he said. "Northern Station is volunteering two of their three teams from the night shift. They'll report to Lieutenant Brady, who will be keeping me advised."

My old friend and current chief turned to me and said, "I'll be waiting for you to tell me, 'We got him.'"

Next, Parisi spoke to the half dozen of us. "What the chief said. I'll assign an ADA to this case, TBD, PDQ."

Then he spun his 350-pound girth around and left the room, creating a breeze in his wake.

Brady said, "Anyone have anything to add? Any questions? Beefs? Theories? Awright, then. Sergeant Boxer is primary. Cappy is chief firefighter. He and Chi go where needed. Conklin is point man, working from here. Lemke and Samuels as well as Michaels and Wang will pick up new cases that come in and will back us up on Fricke-related incidents. Northern Station cops will become available shortly."

After Brady had scheduled everyone assigned to the Fricke nightmare, he welcomed Alvarez to our task force. Then he dismissed us.

I was determined not to let the Frickes' killer—or killers—evade us, but that was my pride getting brassy. I couldn't afford to either doubt myself or be overconfident. I had to lead.

The sky was overcast, and by the time we signed out an unmarked car, rain was coming down hard. Alvarez took the wheel. The *thwack-thwack* repetition of the windshield wipers and low visibility concentrated my mind, and I turned my thoughts back to Holly Fricke. I pictured her on the parallel bars, on Jimmy Kimmel's late-night show. I had stored an image of her in the audience with schoolkids taking in the Cirque du Soleil. And I saw her lying dead on Pacific Avenue, wearing gray gym wear, her body drilled with bullets, five lethal shots, all of the wounds still oozing red.

Now her husband had suffered precisely the same kind of death. I turned every fold in my brain inside out looking for what I, we, might have overlooked in Holly's case to date. The woman had been admired and loved. She had no record. There had been no unanswered questions except why and whodunit.

I had a sick feeling that working Jamie's murder was going to be just as fruitless as working Holly's had been.

CHAPTER 29

ALVAREZ SPED UP the windshield wipers and was singing a song about rain. I didn't know the song and she only knew some of the words, but it was upbeat and so was she, filling in with "dah dah dah dee dah dah RAIN" when she lost the lyrics.

But I knew why she was so happy. She was getting out of the "house," and I had a feeling that, to her, working on this case was like being assigned to the Zodiac Killer task force.

I turned up the car radio, filling the front compartment with staticky calls from dispatch, and Alvarez didn't seem to notice. A half hour after leaving the Hall, she pulled the unmarked Chevy up to the front gates of a house that looked like a cross between a castle and a wedding cake.

I checked my gear, unbuckled the seat belt, swung my legs out of the car, and bounded up to the intercom at the gates. I pressed the button and said my name. There was an answering buzz and the gates swung open wide.

I got back into the unmarked and Alvarez drove through,

then around the circular drive, stopping at the broad steps that rose to the wide expanse of the portico. We walked together to the front door—which sprang open. Arthur Bevaqua stood in the doorway.

Bevaqua was forty and had been with Jamie Fricke for twenty years, working his way up from kitchen aide to right-hand man in charge of the staff at the Fricke house on Pacific Avenue. He was tall, fit, and well-groomed, but his face was swollen from crying, just as it had looked right after Holly was killed.

Our task force had interviewed him for days at a time after Holly's death and he wanted to be questioned more. Anything he could do, he would do. We'd double-teamed him every time we'd gone to the Frickes' home. He had a solid alibi for the time of Holly's death and swore that Jamie hadn't and couldn't have killed her. He hadn't had any clues, leads, hunches about who would have hated Holly or even who could have killed her just to hurt Jamie, who'd been embraced by the 1 percent but widely disliked by regular folk. Theft had been part of Holly's case; neither the very pricey jewelry that she'd been wearing nor her car had turned up. Jamie's watch, wedding ring, and new Jaguar had also been stolen and disappeared.

Had they both been killed for personal property?

People had been killed for much less. But I just didn't believe it.

I looked at the impeccably attired Arthur Bevaqua as water dripped from my hair and soaked my jacket. Alvarez introduced herself and Arthur welcomed us both.

He said, "Step in. Give me a second. I'll get towels."

Alvarez and I took off our shoes and jackets, accepted slippers and towels for our hair, and Arthur told us that he'd set up a light lunch in the solarium.

"Patty insisted," he said of the cook, Patty Delaney.

"Please join us, Arthur."

"I think I will," he said.

He walked us through the high-ceilinged rooms hung with what to my eye looked to be millions of dollars in museum-grade art, including a few old masters featuring rearing horses on gory battlefields. Victorian furniture looked quite at home and Oriental rugs softened and enlivened the stone floors. We followed him through an arched entrance at the western end of the ground floor and entered an enormous solarium with a rounded thirty-foot-high glass-paned ceiling.

Arthur showed us to a wrought-iron table set with linens and silver, surrounded by tall potted palms and hanging succulents. Beyond the glass walls was a stupendous view of the Golden Gate Bridge, Alcatraz, and San Francisco Bay. Arthur pulled out chairs for us, saying, "I'll be right back."

He left and I said to Alvarez, "Train your instincts on him."

CHAPTER 30

ARTHUR RETURNED WITH an ice bucket filled with bottles of sparkling water. He pulled up a chair and joined us as a subdued Patty brought out aromatic bowls of chili—vegetarian for Arthur, with ground, grass-fed beef for us girls—and a basket of warm sourdough rolls. I introduced Patty to Alvarez, offered our condolences, and said we'd catch up with her later.

I was grateful for the lunch, but I was distressed, picturing Jamie Fricke's crime scene washing away in the downpour. That, and knowing I was going to have to question Arthur Bevaqua and the staff again, reopening old wounds.

After the blond, thirtysomething cook had left the solarium, Arthur said, "Sergeant Boxer. Yesterday, I was with Mr. Jamie in his office straightening up, when he got a call on his cell. He told me that he had to leave but he'd be right back."

"Do you know who called him?"

"He didn't say. I got a feeling he'd been expecting the call. And of course, he took his phone with him."

The phone that's now in SFPD's property room, I thought, then asked, "What did you hear him say?"

"He said, 'Seriously? Yes. I'll meet you there in five.' He told me to have Rafe bring his car around. I watched Mr. Jamie get into the Jag and drive off. I never saw him alive again."

I said, "What's Rafe's last name?"

"Talbot."

"Where is he now?"

"He has an apartment over the garage."

Chi and Cappy had interviewed him twice before and found nothing suspicious about him. Their notes mentioned that he had a Kimber handgun and it was registered. Rafe's number was likely in Cappy's notebook, but I took it for mine. To my right, Alvarez asked Bevaqua, "How did Jamie seem to you? Scared? Excited? Pissed off?"

"Excited," Arthur said. "And there's this."

Arthur pulled a sheaf of papers, folded lengthwise, from his inside jacket pocket and handed the sheaf to me. It was a document printout, a work in progress, and it was out of order. A quick look showed me that some lines had been struck out and other lines written in the margins with a ballpoint pen. The new lines had been initialed and dated.

But it was the title on the first page that chilled me.

Alvarez saw the look on my face and tugged the papers out of my hand. I watched her expression and saw that she was as stunned as I. This might be the clue of clues, the piece I'd never seen before that could unravel the mystery of the Fricke murders.

Centered on the top line of the front page were the words "Last Will and Testament of James R. Fricke III."

CHAPTER 31

ALVAREZ, ARTHUR, AND I stood in the doorway of Jamie Fricke's office. I was desperate to read his will but I wanted to do it privately. I clutched the pages and said to Arthur, "How about giving Inspector Alvarez a tour of the place?"

"My pleasure. Downstairs first?"

As they headed for the parlor, I reentered Jamie's office and shut the door. Rich Conklin and I had been in this room with Jamie about a dozen times in the last months. Each time I'd steeled myself for what I knew was coming. Jamie would deflect our questions in the way he had of being rude without crossing the line. No name-calling. No actual bullying. He was just cold, contemptuous, and used as few words as possible.

I'd always let the chill roll off my shoulders into the corners of the room while I watched and listened for tells or accidental self-indicting utterances. Which never happened. Fricke saw himself as some kind of royalty and this room was his seat of power. It felt that way to me, too. More than an office, the room was also a two-story-tall library, a trophy parlor, and a private sanctuary. Fricke's large mahogany desk was at the center of the room resting on a jillion-dollar Oriental carpet. Neat stacks of papers and magazines were piled on a credenza behind the desk, and a multiscreen computer sat in the center of it with the power turned off.

I leaned over and pressed the On button. Light blazed. One screen filled with soccer scores and the other was taken up with a TV show, a pair of sports commentators giving excited play-by-plays to enthusiasts in French.

A fireplace was centered on the wall across from the desk, dominated by a large oil painting of Jamie and Holly, his sons from a previous marriage, and his soccer team, the Bleus, arrayed around them. The trophy case was opposite the door and a pin light beamed down from the ceiling onto the gold cups and photos of winning games behind the glass.

I looked out the window onto the front of the house and called Rich on my cell. I asked him to get Jamie's phone out of the property room and dump the calls, incoming and outgoing.

I said, "He took a call and left the house about five minutes before he was shot."

"Crime lab has the phone now. You okay?" asked my partner, a man I loved like the brother I'd never had.

"Uh-huh. Why do you ask?"

"Your voice."

I cleared my throat. "Is that better?"

"Loads," he lied.

My throat was tight. I hadn't yet gone through the will but I wanted to, badly.

I said, “Rich, ask Red Dog to put a hot rush on a search warrant. The one in my pocket expires at midnight.”

“He’s done it. Judge Hoffman signed off. I’ve got it in Brady’s desk.”

“Thanks. Anything I need to know, text me. I’ll check in with you after I’ve read Jamie’s will.”

He whistled through his teeth.

“Yeah. His will,” I said. “I don’t want to get overexcited. But ten minutes after we hang up, I’m going to know a lot more about Jamie Fricke than I do now.”

“Do read. Call if you need me. I’m at Brady’s desk making paper clip chains.”

I laughed. “I’ll call you soon.”

There was a leather chesterfield sofa and a pair of matching deep brown leather chairs across from Jamie’s desk. I switched on a table lamp, sat in one of the chairs, and tried to ready myself for the twenty-six pages of Jamie’s last will that were calling out to me from my lap.

CHAPTER 32

I SAT IN the fine leather chair in Jamie Fricke's office, going through his will, cycling old thoughts and new, sure that the motive for Jamie's murder and maybe, God willing, Holly's, too, was just one blink away.

Feelings of imminent solution like this seem real and true and flatter you with your own genius. But I knew not to bet on them. I got a grip on myself, put the pages in order, and flipped to the last one. *Thank you, James*—he'd signed it, and had had it witnessed by Arthur Bevaqua while Holly was still alive.

If only Bevaqua had told us about it sooner.

I kept reading, skipped over long paragraphs of dense legalese, and halfway through found paragraph VI, the bequests. There. "If my wife survives me . . ."

I skimmed quickly, then forced myself to back up and slow down. In summary: If Holly had lived, she would have inherited the Pacific Heights manse and seventy million dollars in US T-bills and certificates of deposit. There was a two-page list of equities in Jamie's brokerage account that would also have gone to her. A big black X had been drawn with a marker pen through everything Jamie had planned to leave to Holly. He'd dated the changes four months ago and initialed them "JFIII."

But there was so much more to the Fricke holdings, all printed single-spaced, full of "heretofores" and "whereins," and sprinkled with Latin. I kept reading. Well, I skimmed. Assuming Holly's share had been returned to the whole, an enormous sum was now to be divided between Jamie's two adult sons, Leo and Rodney Fricke, the children he'd had with his first wife, Talia.

Two houses in Lucerne, Switzerland, were to be sold, the proceeds bequeathed to Holly's younger sister, Rae Bergen. Why? "For her many kindnesses," he'd written. "God Bless." And there was a margin note, an addendum to Rae's bequest that was too hard for me to read but had been cosigned "J. Borinstein."

Jamie's share in the team would revert to the team's manager. And there was more. Jamie had left three million each to Arthur Bevaqua, Patty Delaney, and two other women: Judy Borinstein, the Frickes' financial manager, and Marilyn Stein, who'd worked as Holly's assistant.

The size of the bequests to the women and to Jamie's right-hand man raised red flags. Why so much to the women? Were they girlfriends? Did the women have something on Jamie that I ought to know? Or did he just love them millions of dollars' worth? No better time than now to look into this munificent transfer of wealth.

CHAPTER 33

THE FIRST NAME on Jamie Fricke's list was Patricia Delaney, the Fricke family cook. Rich Conklin and I had interrogated Patty after Holly's murder and found no reason to suspect her, let alone hold her. She didn't have a police record, she was in the kitchen when Holly had been shot, and the whole household vouched for her—but I absolutely needed to speak with her again.

Judy Borinstein had signed as executor and financial manager. It was likely she wouldn't tell me anything that would betray a confidence, but maybe she had a clue that would break the case. I'd never met her, but I would, as soon as possible.

I'd previously interviewed Marilyn Stein, Holly's former assistant, quite intensely after Holly's death. She'd hired a lawyer, cried throughout the interviews, and said repeatedly, "You don't understand what it's like to work in such close proximity to this family."

I had asked her to please explain, but she would only say, "It's complicated."

I'd wondered if she'd been romantically involved with one of the Frickes. I'd pressed her. I'd asked if she was more than a friend to Jamie and she refused to answer, just sobbed and kept her arm across her eyes. "Do you have feelings for Jamie?" I'd asked her. *No, no, no.*

Marilyn Stein had quit her job forthwith and moved to New York, where as far as I was aware, she still lived. I had no cause to arrest her, but I got less from Marilyn Stein than from the fortune cookie that comes with my wonton soup.

Her lawyer had said, "That's enough, isn't it, Sergeant? Ms. Stein loves this family. She has a solid alibi for the time of Mrs. Fricke's death. You've checked her alibi so unless she's under arrest, Ms. Stein has a plane to catch."

I was folding up the will when I noticed a margin note on the reverse of the back page. It read, "To Judy Borinstein, my executor: I've left personal notes to Arthur, Patty, and Marilyn in my desk, center drawer."

The postscript was signed, witnessed, and dated only a few weeks after Holly's murder. Judy Borinstein might know Marilyn's relationship with the Frickes. I had to know.

CHAPTER 34

I HOISTED MYSELF up from the deep brown chair and moved to Jamie Fricke's massive chair behind his massive desk. There was a photo beneath the lamp: a great snapshot of Jamie and Holly looking in love, framed in sterling silver. They had been a handsome couple. Jamie clearly had the charisma of Hollywood leading men like Clooney, Bale, Pitt, Craig. In this picture, he wore sports casual attire and had his arm around Holly, gripping her shoulder in a way that made me feel that he not only loved her, he'd never let her go.

Holly glowed in his embrace. She wore a tennis outfit, her streaked blond curls adding a girlish note to her picture-perfect features. She looked every bit the winner in everything she did.

I was struck again by the sense I'd had at the scene of Jamie's murder, that his death and Holly's were so similar, so closely tied, there had to be a killer—or a reason—in common. Arthur had never given me a hint that would put both Holly and Jamie in a killer's crosshairs. Now, for the first time, I wondered if Arthur could have been looking through those crosshairs himself.

It was a big ugly idea, but as Marilyn Stein had sobbed, "You don't understand what it's like to work in such close proximity to this family." Had Arthur loved Holly? Had they been involved and she'd dropped him? Had he had her killed? Or had Jamie hired a hit man to put her down for cheating on him with Arthur? If so, had Arthur paid Jamie back in kind?

It was another hunch only. But it checked a number of boxes and I couldn't quite shake it. Maybe Jamie had left the answer in a note inside his desk drawer.

CHAPTER 35

THE DRAWER WAS LOCKED.

I had latex gloves in my pocket, so I put them on before I patted the surface of the desk, unplugged the computer, and examined each piece as I put the parts on the floor. I looked under the drawer and opened the paper files in the desk's double pedestal. I did it carefully and thoroughly. I did not find a key even inside the file marked "K." I looked under the lamp, took it apart from base to harp and shade. I still didn't find the key.

I leaned back in the chair, swiveled it, and looked up. I took in the thousands upon thousands of books, pressed together in the stacks twenty feet high. Wheeled ladders on rails reached up to the top shelves. The proper key was probably on Jamie's key chain out at the crime lab. But if Jamie Fricke had hidden another key inside a book, I would need twenty people committed to opening each one, fanning the pages for weeks on end.

Or I could break the drawer from the underside and would

be disciplined for doing that, or even sued. But if I found evidence, it would be worth it.

In tossing Jamie's desk, I had cleaned off the surface, thrown the bits and pieces onto one of the leather chairs. I was looking at the fireplace mantel and the painting above it when a small idea bloomed. The framed photo of Jamie and Holly in love that had been on the desk under the lamp was now on the chair face down. I reached that chair in ten seconds, picked up the framed photo, and turned the lovebirds over.

The back of the frame had small catches all the way around, keeping the frame's back in place. After opening half of the catches, I got my fingers under the backing and ripped it off. Then I said "hello" to a small silver key taped behind the photo.

I peeled off the tape, sure that the key would open the drawer and at the same time sure that it wouldn't. Still, I fitted the key into the keyhole in the center drawer and with fifty-fifty odds in mind, I turned the key and the tumblers tumbled. I slid the drawer open.

The contents were disorganized, the drawer filled with business cards and bills and other office litter. I pawed around until I found five cream-colored envelopes each about five by four inches, all bound together with a blue rubber band.

A note to Patricia Delaney was on top of that little stack. I removed it, and using a short, plain letter opener, slipped the blade under the glued flap, pulled out the card, and flipped it over.

CHAPTER 36

THE NOTE CARD to Patricia Delaney read:

"To my darling Pattycakes,

"You know that I love you so very much. I've left you enough money to support you for many years. And I've left you a remembrance of all we've shared. Judy Borinstein has access to my safe deposit box. I hope when you read this, I am in my dotage and yours is the last face I see before closing my eyes forever. Your loving bear-man. J."

What was that?

Jamie and Patty were in love?

As that bombshell exploded in my boggled mind, I opened the next note, addressed to "Dearest Marly." Was Marly a pet name for Holly's assistant, Marilyn Stein?

"Marly, I hope you will always remember that you are the brightest of stars. Some of my best hours on earth were spent with you, our minds and bodies joined, and the earth indeed did move when we were together. My regret that we couldn't formalize our love is profound. That you are reading this note means we will have no more time together. I'm not sure I made it clear how much of my heart and soul belong to you. All my love. James."

I was trying it on. Was that dog, Jamie Fricke, really capable of heartfelt love for Holly, Patty, and Marilyn all at the same time? I wondered if he'd faked it all or if somehow, he was able to split his love many ways. No woman I knew or had ever known would have accepted that. And the next question was, who among them would have had him killed for his infidelities? Or was there a reason that had nothing to do with love?

The third note, inside an envelope the same size as the other two, was addressed to Arthur Bevaqua.

I'd just taken it into my gloved hand when my phone rang. It was Alvarez.

"You have to come out of there, Sergeant. Right now!" she shouted through my iPhone.

I heard scrabbling on the floor above my head, and then the tail end of a scream.

CHAPTER 37

YUKI STOOD BEHIND the prosecution table and watched her friend Claire Washburn raise her hand and swear on the Bible. Once she'd settled into the witness box, Yuki stepped forward and began questioning Claire about her job.

"Dr. Washburn, as San Francisco's chief medical examiner, how often do you examine living patients?"

Claire said, "Going to have to estimate the number."

"Of course. As best you can."

Claire told the court that she did postmortems on roughly a thousand bodies a year, but occasionally when she was called to the scene of an accident or a crime, there were survivors.

"For example?" Yuki asked.

"Say there's been a mass shooting or a fire, with both deceased and living victims at the scene. In that case, I call an ambulance and do first aid immediately; tourniquets, wound compression, chest compressions . . . The EMTs take it from there."

Yuki said, "Now, taking you back six months to the day in Xe Sogni. How did you come to examine Ms. Hayes?"

Claire explained the birthday lunch, the scream, and the call. "We were having lunch, four of us, including Sergeant Lindsay Boxer. There was a scream for help from the second floor. Sergeant Boxer ran up, and a short time later called my cell, saying, 'Can you come up and take a look?' I went."

Claire was interrupted by a loud yawn from the defense attorney. Yuki turned to glare at Ed Schneider, who didn't give a flip. He actually grinned back at her. Even Tyler Cates cracked a smile.

The judge leaned across his bench and said, "Restrain yourself, Mr. Schneider. Or else. You get me?"

"Yes, Your Honor. My apologies."

The judge told Claire to go on.

Yuki asked Claire, "Can you tell the jury what you saw on the second floor?"

"Well, it took a moment for my eyes to focus. The light was dim."

Claire described the locker room, and how Sergeant Boxer had cuffed the defendant, who was naked from the waist down.

Yuki asked, "Did you see Ms. Hayes?"

"She was lying on the floor in shadow," said Claire, "but I could see from her contorted position that she was in bad shape. An ambulance was already on the way, so I gave Ms. Hayes the best examination I could do without instruments."

"And what did you find?"

"Ms. Hayes showed signs of trauma from a beating. She was bruised all over her body and there were handprints around her neck. Clearly someone had manually strangled her and stopped just short of killing her."

Yuki prompted Claire to go on and Claire commented that "Ms. Hayes seemed disoriented."

Yuki asked for details and Claire explained that along with giving a different name than the one on her ID, Ms. Hayes was suffering from acute disorientation.

"I asked her to follow my finger with her eyes and she couldn't track it. That lack of eye motility can indicate a concussion or other brain injury. It can also indicate trauma or some form of mental disorder."

"Is the person you found in the locker room inside this courtroom?"

Claire swung her eyes to the prosecution table and said, "Ms. Hayes is sitting right there, wearing a brown suit."

Yuki thanked Claire, and Judge St. John asked the defense if they'd like to cross. Schneider replied in the negative.

The judge asked Claire to step down.

Claire looked up to the judge and said, "Your Honor, okay if the bailiff gives me a hand? I've got arthritis in my knee . . ."

"Of course, of course."

Bailiff Riley Boone came over to the witness box, offering Claire his arm and a nice smile. Claire leaned on the court officer and got to her feet, thanking him.

"Anytime, doctor."

When Claire had left the courtroom, Yuki called her next witness.

CHAPTER 38

YUKI HAD CHOSEN Dr. Laurie Birney carefully. She was a well-known and highly respected psychologist in her fifties, a top expert in the field of dissociative identity disorders as a practitioner and an educator, and often called as an expert witness in cases like this.

After Dr. Birney was sworn in, Yuki asked questions that elicited her credentials and accomplishments. Then Yuki turned her head to see how Mary Elena was doing. She couldn't read her client's expression—which she thought was a good thing. Yuki also saw Red Dog standing at the back of the gallery. She caught his eye before turning back to her witness.

"Dr. Birney, have you ever treated or even met Ms. Hayes?"

"No, I have not."

"Have you had patients with dissociative identity disorder?"

"Oh, yes. I wrote my first thesis on DID when it was still called 'split personality' or 'multiple personality disorder.' "

"And you're an expert on other dissociative disorders?"

"It seems immodest to say so."

"That would be a yes?"

Dr. Birney smiled and said, "Yes."

Yuki still felt the burn of Schneider's smug opening statement, in which he claimed that psychology was bull. Yuki was damned sure he would use that same argument in his closing statement, too. And it would only take one holdout on the jury to crash her ease against Tyler Cates into a wall.

But Schneider hadn't yet gone up against the authority of Laurie Birney. Her soft ways might fool him into taking a chance.

As Yuki turned back to her witness, she noticed peripherally that DA Parisi had moved from the courtroom entrance to the prosecution table and had taken her seat next to Nick Gaines. Parisi was watching. Not signaling. So Yuki walked closer to her witness.

"Dr. Birney, please tell the jury about DID, what was once called multiple personality disorder."

"You don't have to ask twice," said Dr. Birney. "It's my life's work. How long have we got?"

There was appreciative laughter in the courtroom followed by complete silence as Dr. Birney explained DID.

"DID is notable for the patient's missing chunks of memory that cannot be explained by forgetfulness. And the hallmark of DID, the inspiration for movies like *The Three Faces of Eve,* is the presence of at least two distinct and as many as dozens of personalities that are enduring parts of the individual's main personality.

"These fragmented personalities are generally utilitarian in nature in that they come into being to protect 'the body' by serving as a line of defense against further attack or fear of attack."

"This is recognizable, is it not?" said Yuki.

"It can be. Memory loss, disorientation, depression, suicidal thoughts are a number of symptoms that are common in dissociative disorders—and from the point of view of the afflicted person, awakening inside your main personality in a situation you don't recognize, or similarly coming into real time in an alternate personality, can be disabling, especially if the individual has been physically assaulted. With DID, you have no memory of this situation, this assault or circumstance. That's devastating."

There was a loud shriek from the prosecution table behind Yuki. She whipped around to see Mary Elena standing, facing and screaming at DA Parisi, who rose awkwardly to his feet, stepping backward.

Mary Elena yelled, "You go. Go away, Oompah!"

Parisi said, "I'm sorry. I didn't mean . . ."

"Go away!" Mary Elena yelled again.

Judge St. John banged the gavel and said to the court, "Court is in recess for a half hour. Does that give you and your client enough time, Ms. Castellano?"

Yuki said, "Your Honor, I can't be sure. If that's not enough time, we'll return without the plaintiff."

Bailiff Riley Boone escorted the jurors out the side door to the jury room and at court officer Louie Mack's direction, those in the gallery complied as the room was emptied.

Yuki said, "Mary Elena, come with me."

"My name is Ana. Don't you know me?"

Yuki understood that an alter named Ana was present. Ana

seemed larger than Mary Elena. She stood straighter, making her shoulders appear wider. She was angry, furious actually.

Nick Gaines said, "I'll walk Dr. Birney to her car."

Yuki put her hand loosely around Ana's upper arm in order to guide her and said, "Ana. My office is just at the end of the corridor. We'll talk, okay?"

Ana ripped away from Yuki and, glaring at the foot traffic in the corridor, walked alongside, stayed with her to the DA's office suite. Yuki thanked God that they had not run into Parisi.

CHAPTER 39

SONIA ALVAREZ SHOUTED at me, "Quick! Patty's room. Second floor, second room on the right."

I slammed the desk drawer shut, put the key in my front pants pocket, drew my gun, and followed Alvarez up the stairs. Bevaqua lunged past me, stiff-arming Alvarez out of his way and kicking open Patty Delaney's door. Alvarez held her weapon in a two-hand grip. Bevaqua was halfway across Patty's room when Alvarez yelled, "Arthur! Stop! Hands up. Stay where you are."

I didn't get it. "What's happening here?"

"I'd really like to know," said Alvarez.

We were in Patty's bedroom, a peach-colored chamber with a view of the bay through a pair of French doors. It had changed since I'd been here last. Patty had redecorated with a romantic bent.

I looked across the room to Patty, a cherubic blonde in her thirties, about five six, 140, now sitting naked on the edge of her four-poster bed. She pulled a floral quilt around her up to her chin, while heaving deep, wailing sobs. Alvarez had maneuvered Bevaqua so that he was facing the closed bedroom door.

I looked around. The gas fireplace opposite the bed was lit. An oil painting of an entwined nude couple on a chaise longue hung above it. The man's face was hidden in his partner's pale blond hair. There was a full-sized beveled mirror on the ceiling positioned over the bed.

I looked back to Patty, who was sobbing *no, no, no,* hugging pillows and crying into them.

Bevaqua shouted at Alvarez as she patted him down.

"I'm not armed. Don't be crazy, Inspector. I was trying to . . . Listen, Sergeant, I meant no harm. I'm in charge of the staff. Now more than ever. Okay if I put my hands down?"

"No," I said.

"I'm sorry I shoved you," he said to Alvarez. "Very sorry. I just didn't want for Patty to . . ."

"To what?"

I was processing slowly, like a first-generation computer, running theories, computing possibilities, weighing scenarios in the absence of facts. According to the note card I'd found in Jamie's desk, he and Patty were in love. The question that seemed to have an obvious answer: Was Bevaqua also involved with Delaney? Of course.

"I want to *console* her," Bevaqua shouted. "To *befriend* her, goddamnit."

"Arthur," I said. "Put your hands on your head."

Alvarez had holstered her gun and frisked Bevaqua up and down, front and back.

"He's unarmed," she said.

I had to be sure. I stooped beside Arthur and checked his ankles, didn't find a gun or any kind of weapon there, either. I said, "Arthur, go downstairs with Alvarez and wait for me at the kitchen table."

"You've got this all wrong."

"Do it or I'm taking you in."

"Okay, I'm going downstairs now. I'm doing what you say."

CHAPTER 40

ARTHUR BEVAQUA SHOT a look over his shoulder at Patty as he left the room with Alvarez. Her gun was in her hand again and she was walking right behind him.

I was confident Alvarez would be sitting across from Bevaqua at the granite kitchen table when I got down there. But at this minute, Patty was still under the covers clutching a blue garment to her face. It was a pajama top. Large man–sized. She was keening now—a terrible sound of bottomless grief that I didn't think could be faked.

I holstered my gun, switched on the overhead light, and looked around the room again. I was seeing things I hadn't noticed while crashing through the doorway with my gun drawn. Baby-blue thong panties on the floor near the Victorian bed; a horse whip over the back of the armchair. I toed a diaphanous curl of a nightgown with my shoe. I said, "Quite a party here, Patty. You and Arthur?"

Patty rolled toward me, propped her upper torso on her elbow, shook her head vigorously, and cried again. "Arthur?

Noooo. It was Jamie!" she bleated. "We made love until sunup. He was right here yesterday morning, his final hours alive. Now I want to die, too."

I'd just seen Patty an hour ago when she served lunch. I had noticed she was downcast but I hadn't imagined this. I had to reorder my thoughts—yet *this* Patty matched with "my darling Pattycakes."

"Do you know who killed him?" I asked this woman who looked vulnerable enough to bleed through her skin.

She shook her head no.

"Patty, you must have some idea. Was Jamie afraid of anyone? Had he been threatened? Did he have anything to do with Holly's murder?"

"*No, no, no.* But he didn't love her anymore. They had no secrets, though. Jamie and I—you're not going to believe me."

"I'm on your side, Patty. Talk to me."

"We were going to get married," she sputtered. "Holly knew, and they were going to get a divorce."

"Who else knew that?"

"It wasn't time to tell. Then Holly got shot . . ."

Patty searched my face looking to see if I believed her. I hadn't decided. I said, "Please get dressed. We need you to come to the station and give a formal statement."

"Again? You've got to be kidding."

"Arthur's coming, too."

"Why? Arthur didn't do anything."

"Let's go, Patty,"

"Do I need a lawyer?"

"You always have the right to a lawyer."

While Patty pulled on jeans and a cardigan, I opened

drawers in her nightstand, then her dresser. Looking for what, I didn't know. A diary. A weapon. Letters from Jamie. Drugs. I had a search warrant for the house and I figured that covered individual rooms. If not, bad on me.

I found nothing but fancy dildos and lubricants along with her workaday outfits and lacy underclothes.

I turned on the closet light, gave her laundry basket a good tossing, moved on to the overhead shelves, feeling up handbags for the weight and shape of a gun. Nothing, nada, zero.

The red-eyed blonde turned to give me a questioning look.

"Do you have a gun, Patty? Tell me now if you do."

"No. I don't have a gun. Arthur doesn't have a gun. He's my friend. He's the only one who knows, knew, about me and Jamie."

She ran from the room and down the stairs. I followed as she turned toward the kitchen. She went into Arthur's arms while Alvarez and I looked on.

CHAPTER 41

THE KITCHEN WAS one of those to-die-for rooms one sees in glossy home decor magazines—marble-tiled walls and floor, with a stone table in the middle of the room—but I focused on Arthur Bevaqua, who had his arms around Patty, cooing, "It's going to be all right."

"Never," she said. "It will never be all right, Arthur."

I pulled out a chair for Patty and one for myself. She sat next to Arthur and I sat beside Alvarez. Arthur looked grief-stricken, as if he'd accidentally backed his car over his dog. The house was big and empty and quiet, except for the sound of Patty's thick breathing and the distant sound of a lawn mower.

I asked the two sitting across the table from us, "Who's caring for the grounds?"

"Joe Casey and Mike Thomas. They're here once a week. They don't come into the house. I hired them. They never met Jamie or Holly."

I asked Alvarez to go outside and get their information and

IDs. "Call for a car and ask them to come to the station for questioning. We know they didn't do it. We just want to know what they've observed."

Alvarez got up from the table and headed out.

I asked Arthur and Patty if they knew or had a good guess about who'd killed the Frickes.

Arthur answered. "Don't you know that I would do anything to know? If only I had a hint or a suspicion as to who killed Mr. Jamie and Mrs. Holly, I would give it up. You wouldn't have to ask. I loved them both."

"Arthur. Think. Who hated them? Who'd been swindled? Who'd been ditched? Who was jealous?"

He said, "Sergeant, no offense. There's a whole world of people the Frickes knew that I never met, or only met to bring a drink to. I opened doors. I hung up coats. I supervised the staff and sometimes I served meals. I kept the press from the door. I was a utility. I knew from things Jamie told me or dictated to me that a lot of people didn't like him. Players and fans from any city with a soccer team that lost to the Bleus. Any man with a woman Jamie had slept with. There were many."

"No," said Patty, fresh tears starting. "You're wrong about that."

"Patty, it's true."

He put his arm around her again and she put her elbows on the table and cried into her sleeves. Then she got up and unloaded the dishwasher.

I said, "Anyone you think we should be looking at?"

"This is just talk," Arthur said, "because I don't know anyone who would have killed either of them. I'm a house manager. Understand? Talk to Marilyn Stein again. She knew everyone who knew Holly."

"Anyone else?"

"Talk to Mr. Jamie's driver. Rafe Talbot. He was totally checked out and cleared before he got this job."

Alvarez poked her head back in the room. She said to me, "Backup is here."

Perfect timing.

CHAPTER 42

I SPOKE WITH Alvarez while standing in the Frickes' semicircular driveway. "Turn Bevaqua over to Brady, Cappy, and Chi for interrogation, in whatever order." I pictured Cappy or Brady interviewing Arthur, surrounded by morgue shots of the deceased Frickes. He might open up. How many ways could he say, "I have no idea. I have no clue"?

Would Arthur confess? Would he finally spill a name?

I went on, saying to Alvarez, "Turn Delaney over to Conklin."

She and I both knew that Conklin was the best cop with women ever born.

"Brief Brady and sit in on as many interviews as possible," I said. "I'm going to call him and say to take his time getting their statements. Never mind tears and 'swear to God's. If anyone knows who killed the Frickes, it's these two."

I continued, "Keep the gardeners apart. Ask anyone on the team to talk to Casey and Thomas. Lemke and/or Samuels would both be good. If no one else is around, you do the interviews. I'm standing by," I said.

I called for another couple of units. Dispatch said, "On the way, Sergeant."

I walked to the garage, stepped through the open roll-up door. A muscular guy with thick white hair was inside sweeping the floor.

"Rafe Talbot?"

"Yes, ma'am."

I showed him my badge and we went together into his upstairs living quarters.

CHAPTER 43

RAFE TALBOT'S QUARTERS were as plain as a block of wood. Plain double bed covered with a gray sherpa blanket. Sink with a towel bar. A shelf of paperback books.

The kitchen table had a white linoleum top and looked like it had come from a used furniture store. A refrigerator hummed. The few posters on the wall were of rock groups from the 1980s. Beneath the posters sat what looked like a very pricey entertainment unit: a huge TV, abundant sound equipment.

There was no mess anywhere, no laundry, no dirty dishes. I saw no tattoos on Talbot's neck or arms but the shape of his nose suggested that he'd been a fighter or that at least someone had gotten in a punch. I judged him to be fifty-something.

"Sergeant, I have no idea who killed Jamie."

He looked like he wanted to talk, but couldn't find the words. He just couldn't do it. He shook his head.

Finally, he said, "What can I do? How can I freaking help when I don't know and can't even imagine it?"

Jamie Fricke had never warmed any part of me, so clearly there were things about him I just didn't get.

"It was my fault," Rafe Talbot said over and over again. "I should never have let him take the car without me."

And then he started talking in paragraphs.

"Yesterday morning, a little before eight thirty, Arthur told me to bring the car around. But Mr. Jamie said he was just driving over to Steiner Street. He'd be back in five minutes. He didn't say who he was meeting, and I didn't ask. Just drove the Jag to the front door, got out, handed him the keys."

Using my phone as a recorder, I spent an hour with Rafe going over the same well-trodden ground. Holly was loved. Jamie had many women and was apparently loved by some, feared by others. Rafe had only had this job for a couple of years. He knew the staff casually. No one confided secrets to him.

Rafe also had a girlfriend, Greta Schmidt, who worked as a caregiver, day shift. He spent his nights off at her place over in the Sunset district. She spent some nights, like last night, with Rafe. She'd left this morning while it was still dark.

He continued by saying he didn't know of anyone who would have killed the Frickes, but he listed several people who thought that Jamie was a son of a bitch, people Rafe had picked up or dropped off in the car, people who made a comment or two. He started writing names on the back of a grocery store receipt.

"Once I knew who we were picking up, where we were going, I'd close the barrier between the seats and put my earbuds in. I listened to my music when I was driving Mr. Jamie and guests.

"Everyone liked Holly," he continued. "I drove her, too."

I asked, "Did she ever step out on Jamie?"

"She had men friends. And she traveled. This coast, the other one. Overseas. I would drive her to the airport once a month. But if she had a boyfriend, I knew nothing about it."

"You have a record?" I asked him.

"When I was nineteen, I stole a car."

"How much time did you get?"

"Sixteen months at Wasco State, but six months off for good behavior. It was my first and only offense. Nothing since. Not even for speeding. I called Mr. Jamie when I was looking for a job two years ago, and he gave me this one. He knew my father years back."

"What happened to the guy who had the job before you?"

"He moved to Wisconsin to take care of his mother. Robert Corazzo. I have his number."

He wrote it down on the receipt.

"Rafe, our notes on you say that you have a gun?"

"Yes. A Kimber .40. It's registered. Only fired at a range and not in the last two months."

"I need it."

Rafe took the gun out of a high kitchen cabinet and gave it to me. I sniffed the muzzle. Smelled like nothing. Still, I confiscated it and the box it came in. I told him I was going to need an official statement from him at the station later today and to please not get lost.

"I won't go anywhere. Here's a present for you," he said.

He wrapped his hand around an empty ceramic coffee mug, put the mug in a paper bag, and handed it to me.

"My prints. I didn't wash it. My DNA should be all over the lip of it."

"Thanks, Rafe. It's all safe with me."

I let myself out of Rafe's garage apartment, checked out his nondescript gray Nissan just outside, typed the tag number into my phone, and returned to Jamie's office.

CHAPTER 44

JAMIE'S OFFICE LOOKED as I had left it. I gloved up and then opened the desk's center drawer, fished around, and found the other cream-colored envelopes. One was addressed to Marilyn Stein, Holly's former assistant; another to Judy Borinstein, financial manager; and another was addressed to Arthur Bevaqua.

I held the envelope for a moment. The letter opener again did the job. The note card inside had Jamie's handwriting on both sides.

I read every word fast. On the second read, after "Dear Arthur," I fell down the rabbit hole with the rabbit. As we tumbled like weightless astronauts, the rabbit said, "Wrong, wrong, wrong. You got it all wrong. You don't know anything."

CHAPTER 45

I WAS GOING through Arthur Bevaqua's bedroom, which was on the second floor, down the hall from Patty's. Like Patty, he had a bay view. Unlike Patty, his room was painted white. Photos on the wall were of pastel sunrises and blooming sunsets, and a very nice shot of Arthur sitting on a seawall between Jamie and Holly.

Arthur's closet was lined with pressed trousers and white shirts, dress coats and sports jackets. Ties hung from a rack inside the door, and a basket of laundry sat on the floor.

His dresser drawers were filled with neat stacks of underwear and rolled balls of socks organized by color. No evidence of frisky fooling around. His desk faced the windows and had two deep file drawers. I'd started to go through the one on the right when my phone rang. I recognized the name on my caller ID.

I took the call.

A woman said, "Sergeant Boxer? This is Judy Borinstein, James Fricke's financial manager. Your office told me that you're at the house. I'm only five blocks away. Okay if I come over to speak with you?"

I said, "Absolutely. I'll be in Mr. Fricke's office. I'll leave the door open."

When Ms. Borinstein arrived fifteen minutes later, I was sitting in Jamie's chair, going through his files. She was a fifty-something brunette, wearing a mauve-colored silk dress and a silver cross on a heavy chain. The diamond on her ring finger looked large enough to serve as a weapon in a fistfight. She looked formidable and at the same time stressed out, exhausted, and pretty sad.

I came around the desk, and after we'd shaken hands I offered her one of the chairs opposite Jamie's desk and took the other. She didn't look around the museum of Jamie's life, which told me that she'd been here before.

She got right to the point of her visit.

"Sergeant, can you authorize the release of Mr. Fricke's body? He was a congregant at St. Thomas Presbyterian and owns a family plot in their cemetery. As his emergency contact, I'm getting calls about his funeral."

I said, "I'll check with the ME. Hang on."

I speed-dialed Claire and we had five seconds of personal greeting, followed by one question and an answer. I signed off with my BFF and told Ms. Borinstein that the funeral home could pick up Jamie's body tomorrow morning, unexpected circumstances permitting.

"Thank you. My office phones are making us insane."

I said, "Do you have five minutes to talk, Ms. Borinstein?"

"Call me Judy. Of course, I've got time for you. And no, I

don't know who killed James Fricke. I don't know who would have had the nerve."

Nerve wasn't the point. Motive was. But now that I had Judy Borinstein's attention, I thought she might tell me a few things I hadn't known before she'd walked through the door.

CHAPTER 46

JUDY BORINSTEIN LOOKED at her sports watch, then turned her blue-gray eyes on me.

I said, "I've been speaking with women who were in love with Jamie. What can you tell me? No judgment, Judy. I'm trying to understand him and the people he knew."

"If you're looking at me, Sergeant," Judy Borinstein said, "I don't go that way. Meaning, married men. Or clients."

I said, "Patty Delaney told me that Jamie wanted to marry her. I suspect he might also have been involved with Marilyn Stein. Both women were torn up by his death. Arthur Bevaqua told me that there were others who were emotionally, sexually involved with Jamie and believed that Holly was old news. Then, someone shot her dead. Judy, do you think Mr. Fricke was planning to divorce Holly?"

Judy said, "In my opinion, absolutely not. And I don't have any idea what bastard might have killed her. It was a sin. Okay. But, between us girls . . ."

"Yes?"

"I had a one-week 'thing' with James years ago. One week. In Bermuda. I was single and he was persuasive. The week was memorable, but it wasn't life-changing. I didn't think he was going to ditch Holly then or ever. While we were there, he proposed, which was ridiculous, and we parted as friends. Five years ago, Jamie called me and asked me if I would be his financial manager, handling his estate. Why, yes, I would. Then, after Holly was murdered, I'd say three weeks after, he wanted to update his will. Reallocate his bequests.

"Holly wasn't my client, but always came with Jamie when we met to discuss his business. She was a terrific person. Why was she killed? Why? Why? Anyway, James and I were still cutting and pasting his will when he was shot down. He did sign the hand-edited will that was in progress. I witnessed it."

I said, "Arthur gave me that last draft. I read the lines and between them and didn't see anything about a future new Mrs. Fricke."

Judy Borinstein looked at her watch again and sighed. She said, "When it came to spinning a fairy tale, no one could spin like James Fricke. It was his ego, Sergeant. He loved to sweep women off their footsies, make their sexual fantasies come true."

"Great sex, you're saying."

"Wish fulfillment. Stories were if the girl dreamed of a knight charging through the gates to the village, he'd have a steed and full-dress armor. If she wanted to be treated like a whore or a virgin on successive nights, James was never too bored or too tired to experiment. In my experience, most men treat sex as a form of masturbation. But James liked having a knockout effect on women."

What I was hearing was that Jamie was not just a womanizer; he specialized in creating the feeling of real-life love, but it was entirely contrived.

I said, "He was a narcissist."

Judy laughed. "World champ."

"And how did Holly handle her husband taking his love to town?"

"You know about Holly's parents, Bill and Sassy Bergen?"

"Some."

I'd read Cappy's interview notes and some magazine articles. Bill and Sassy Bergen were party people who'd held major charity events, were world travelers. I'd seen a hundred wedding pictures of Holly and Jamie and read dozens of interviews. But I hadn't met Holly in person and didn't know the Bergens.

"What should I know?" I asked Judy Borinstein.

"Okay, here's what I know or have heard. It was rumored that Bill and Sassy Bergen were hedonists. So, Holly had enough exposure to their lifestyle to be drawn to Jamie and not be affronted by his dalliances. And Jamie told me that Holly didn't get crazy, and neither did he, if either spent a night out. Or a week. That may have been a pitch but I wasn't catching."

I thought about my marriage to Joe. A safe haven. Husband, lover, father of our little girl, all of us eating take-out dinners, watching TV. Joe and I brainstormed our cases, occasionally had a week away together. We were happy.

Judy was digging in her bag for her car keys.

"Just one more question," I said. "Tell me about Arthur Bevaqua."

CHAPTER 47

JUDY BORINSTEIN SAID, "Walk me out to my car?"

I got to my feet. "Sure."

As we left the office, Judy said, "Arthur is a sweetie. You probably know he's been working for Jamie ever since he graduated from Cal State. Jamie bought him a house not far away in Cow Hollow."

"Wait. I thought Arthur lived here. He has a room on the second floor."

"I don't know about that, but Arthur is married. His husband, Simon Bevaqua, is a writer. If I remember correctly, he's been working on a book about the relationship between animals and humans since the Garden of Eden."

My jaw didn't drop, because I'd read the card Jamie left for Arthur.

"I couldn't have left home without you. Wishing you and Simon continued love, health, and a very happy life."

Judy laughed. "I made up the biblical reference," she said. "But as I understand it, Simon's been writing the book for years and years. Arthur signs off on the household expenses, does administrative duties, writes employee checks for Jamie. That's all I know about Arthur except that he was considered invaluable to the Fricke family. Ran things while the Frickes were away, managed the staff and the household budget. I know what he was paid—a lot—and I'd guess he needed the money."

We stopped at her car, a BMW, in the driveway.

Borinstein said, "I just got it. You're thinking of Arthur as a suspect? That's your wheelhouse, Sergeant, but I don't see it. What I see is that pretty soon Arthur's going to have to find another job."

I stood by as Judy Borinstein got into her sharp little Beemer. We mutually agreed to check in with each other as the curtain fell on her visit to the house of Fricke.

I turned back to the house, climbed the steps to the portico, and called Conklin, who was running point for Team Fricke.

He said, "Time check, Lindsay. Nothing new to report."

CHAPTER 48

THERE WAS THE usual scuffle as the folks in the gallery jostled for seats, put away their phones, slid handbags and computer cases under the benches, coughed, whispered, and settled in. His Honor Henry William St. John entered the courtroom through his private door from his chambers to the bench. All rose, then sat back down. The judge exchanged greetings with the clerk and bailiff, who escorted the jury in. Twelve jurors plus two alternates stood while Riley Boone swore them in, announced the trial part and docket number and that court was now in session.

As the room quieted down, crime writer Cindy Thomas of the *San Francisco Chronicle* turned on her recorder. It was a repeat of earlier. Only one thing had changed: Mary Elena Hayes was not in her seat between second chair, Nick Gaines, and ADA Yuki Castellano.

Judge St. John made his customary warnings to the gallery about keeping quiet and penalties for disturbances. Ready to begin, he said, "Over to you, Ms. Castellano."

Yuki stood, saying, "Thank you, Your Honor. The People call Dr. Stuart Aronson."

Dr. Aronson was the reason Yuki had decided to exclude Mary Elena from the proceedings today. The witness was Mary Elena's treating psychiatrist, and although she had given permission for him to explain her condition to a room full of strangers, Yuki felt it safer for her client's mental health that she not be present for the sharing of these intimate details. The reaction from the defense would surely flip her out.

Bailiff Riley Boone stepped out into the corridor for Dr. Aronson, who entered the courtroom, came up the center aisle, and took the witness stand. Dr. Aronson was of slightly less than average height and weight and had less hair than most men in their forties, but his severe expression and firm step communicated that he was to be taken seriously.

After Dr. Aronson had been sworn in and seated, Yuki asked softball questions about his Ivy League education, his teaching hospital background, and how long he'd been treating Mary Elena Hayes. While they were so engaged, Nick Gaines set up a computer on a stand in front of the counsel table.

Yuki said, "Dr. Aronson, it's true, isn't it, that you have permission from the plaintiff to share details of her disorder?"

"That's correct."

"And how is this disorder classified?"

Aronson said, "Mary Elena suffers from dissociative identity disorder, abbreviated as DID. Under extreme stress or danger, her full personality is fragmented, dissociated from her core personality, and one or more alternate personalities come forward and take over, in a sense, to protect her. These alternate personalities are often referred to as alters."

Yuki asked, "Is Ms. Hayes aware of these alters?"

"Sometimes," said Dr. Aronson. "Not all people with DID have the same awareness of their alters. Mary Elena is not generally aware of their behaviors because when they become present, they 'bump her away,' and take over for her main personality. She does know a few and sometimes interacts with them. And some of these alters know one another."

"Was Mary Elena born this way?"

"Not at all. DID is a protective mechanism developed by some victims of abuse and severe trauma. As with many patients I've seen who present with DID, the cause was gross sexual assault, which Mary Elena experienced as a child. I videotaped one of our recent sessions and I've given it to the prosecution. I think seeing this video will explain to the jury how Mary Elena's psychological disorder came about."

Defense Counsel Ed Schneider was on his feet. "Objection, Your Honor. Irrelevant. Dr. Aronson was not under oath and neither was his patient while this demonstration was made. It has nothing to do with my client or the charges against him."

Yuki objected.

"Your Honor, Ms. Hayes's disorder has everything to do with the case against Mr. Cates. We maintain that several of the plaintiff's alters appeared during his assault on her and that he was aware that she was psychologically impaired. As such, she could not stand up to him and he took advantage of her mental disability."

The judge said, "Objection overruled. Carry on, Ms. Castellano."

CHAPTER 49

YUKI SAID, "DR. ARONSON, please continue."

Aronson said, "By way of background, Mary Elena Hayes was under ten years old when she first suffered repeated sexual abuse by her grandfather, whom she called Oompah. Oompah lived in a house behind the Hayes house and would take care of the child in the afternoons while her parents were at work."

Aronson continued, "I've brought a tape of a session I had with Mary Elena taken not long after she was beaten and raped in Xe Sogni."

Yuki nodded at Gaines, and one of the court officers dimmed the overhead lights. Her number two positioned the projector toward a whiteboard that was visible to the jury, the judge, and a portion of the gallery.

A light was projected. The fan whirred and then a moving picture appeared on the whiteboard. In the video, Dr. Aronson sat in a lounge chair in a room painted pale blue. Mary Elena looked as she had looked in the courtroom but was dressed more casually, wearing a large pullover, leggings, and moccasins. She sat in a chair across from Dr. Aronson.

On the tape, Aronson asked his patient, "What do you remember about Oompah?"

Mary Elena shook her head no.

"I'm recording this session, Mary Elena. Please talk to me so I can compare your early memories with your current ones and evaluate your progress."

Mary Elena looked down at her clasped hands in her lap and very softly said, "Okay."

Her psychiatrist said, "Try going back in time. Place your younger self in the kitchen of the house where you grew up. Tell me what you see and hear and feel."

"I've told you."

"I know. Please tell me again."

"'K. The school bus has just brought me home," said present-day Mary Elena in a childlike voice Yuki recognized as belonging to Lily. "The house is empty except for Oompah."

"How old are you?"

"I think, second grade."

"Seven or eight?"

Mary Elena nodded, and her doctor asked, "What does he say to you?"

"Oompah says, 'Hello, darling, how did school go today?' I say, 'It was good. A dad came in for show-and-tell and showed us how to make a whistle, with two fingers and a blade of grass.'"

Dr. Aronson said, "And then?"

"I start to go to my room, but Oompah gets between me

and the kitchen doorway. He says he's gotten me my favorite snack. Chocolate pudding and Oreos."

The camera in Dr. Aronson's office was steady. A phone rang in an outer room and was answered. Traffic sounds came into the room from the street, but the camera stayed on Dr. Aronson leaning forward in his chair to better hear Mary Elena, speaking in Lily's high-pitched and wispy little-girl voice.

She told her doctor that Oompah gave her the snack in the kitchen and said that he'd spent all morning sorting out inventory in his hardware store and he was awfully tired. He then asked Mary Elena if she was ready for her nap. From the expression of stark fear on Mary Elena's face visible on the recording, she knew what was coming from her previous experience with Oompah. And she was remembering that resisting him would fail.

In the courtroom now, Dr. Aronson spoke up. "See this. On the tape, Mary Elena is her current age of twenty-eight. But her fear has thrown a switch in her mind. She's mentally in the second grade. She backs into her chair and hugs her knees."

On the tape, Mary Elena was saying, "Let's go outside, Oompah. Let's go for a ride in the car. I want to go to the park."

Then her voice changed, though it still sounded young. She said, "He came toward me and I pushed back and the chair fell over and Oompah picked me up. 'What hurts?' he asked me. I told him, 'I just want to go outside. Please, Oompah.' We went to the park."

On the tape, Aronson asked, "Who are you now?"

"My name is Olivia."

In the courtroom, Dr. Aronson said, "Mr. Gaines, please freeze the frame."

Gaines pressed a button and the scene froze.

CHAPTER 50

YUKI STOOD TEN feet away from Dr. Aronson and continued her direct examination.

She asked, "Did you ever call the police about Mary Elena's grandfather, or tell her parents?"

The doctor said, "Oompah had died by the time I started seeing Mary Elena in therapy. Both her parents are now dead, but at that time, she didn't want to tell them, particularly her mother, who was Oompah's only child. But she told me how she tried to protect herself. One of the signal traits of DID is the use of alters."

Yuki asked, "Can you explain more about these alters?"

Aronson described four alternate personalities he'd either met or been told about by Mary Elena. He began with Lily, the childlike alter who had been seen on the video. She was about the same age Mary Elena had been when she was first assaulted. Lily had some power to shame Oompah with her baby talk and manner, but as a grown man, he often as not overrode her.

Aronson explained that a couple of years after Lily's appearance in Mary Elena's mind, Olivia came into being. Olivia's personality was that of an ingenue who used her so-called feminine wiles to distract potential attackers. But Olivia had limited power as a guardian, and soon after Olivia became part of the group of alters, Loretta appeared.

Dr. Aronson noted, "I've only met Loretta one time, and when I asked her if she knew the other alters, she wouldn't answer. I later deduced that she'd been instructed to keep to herself by a fourth alter, Ana."

Yuki asked, "What is the nature of Ana?"

Dr. Aronson smoothed his hair back with his hand and seemed to search for the right words.

Finally, he said, "Mary Elena told me that Ana first appeared when she went to high school. Ana was older than the other alters and assumed a parental role in this grouping. She is authoritative, angry at what Mary Elena has suffered, and appeared when boys tried to get physical with Mary Elena.

"It was Ana who told me that she stood up to Mr. Cates, explaining to him that Mary Elena had a personality disorder. Ana told me that she'd specifically told Mr. Cates, 'Don't bother her. She is off-limits because she has a mental disorder that makes her much younger than she appears.' But he didn't listen to her."

The defendant, Tyler Cates, interrupted loudly, "Oh come on. This is crap," as Schneider added, "Hearsay, Your Honor."

The judge slammed down the gavel and cautioned both Cates and his lawyer. Yuki looked at the jury box. As she expected, she saw shock on the jurors' faces. If they bought that Mary Elena, in the person of Ana, told Tyler Cates that she was psychologically impaired, Cates was cooked.

Yuki asked, "Dr. Aronson, how long have you been treating Ms. Hayes?"

"Currently, for about the last six months. But I was at Handel-Reeves, a noted psychiatric hospital in San Francisco, and treated Mary Elena when as a teenager she was admitted to Handel-Reeves on five separate occasions and diagnosed with dissociative identity disorder, post-traumatic stress disorder, mixed personality disorder, and amnesia."

"Did she know Mr. Cates before the attack?"

"She told me that she did not. She does not know him now."

"Thank you, Dr. Aronson. I have nothing further."

Judge St. John turned to the defense and asked, "Mr. Schneider, do you wish to cross-examine the witness?"

CHAPTER 51

YUKI WATCHED ED SCHNEIDER stump across the well to the witness stand. He greeted the witness, getting his name wrong.

"Dr. Aronstein, how do you know that Ms. Hayes has this DID as opposed to faking it for her own benefit?"

Dr. Aronson didn't correct Schneider's mistake. "I first became her therapist when she was a teenager. Her core personality has aged to match her chronological age, but she still manifests the traits of DID and a few other disorders as well."

"So, you diagnosed her based on traits you observed in a therapeutic environment," said Schneider.

"Yes, that's right."

Schneider took a half turn toward the jury, then pivoted back to the witness. He said, "So you're telling us that the diagnosis of DID is based on hypothesis and/or a theory of intermittent behavior, as opposed to a physical illness like, say, cardiomyopathy."

Aronson asked, "Is there a physical marker for DID? Is that what you're asking me?"

He'd twisted the question just enough to make Schneider sharpen his point to Mary Elena's psychological condition.

"Yes, doctor. That's my question."

Aronson said, "In some cases, there can be a brain anomaly or physical damage that dictates abnormal thoughts and behaviors. But DID is a complicated disorder that is pieced out through interviews over a period of time."

Yuki hoped that Aronson was explaining the disorder in such a way that the jurors, even those who had not had therapy, could understand. He talked about the principal marker of the disorder, the two or more distinct personalities as well as depression and gaps in memory that Dr. Birney had also outlined.

Said Aronson, "These memory gaps cannot be attributed to substance abuse or any other physiological diagnosis."

Schneider said, "So this diagnosis is formed by the attending psychiatrist's analysis, but two such professionals could arrive at different diagnoses, isn't that right, doctor?"

Aronson smiled. "Absolutely. But, in my years with Mary Elena, I've not only observed her. I have been with her when she dissociates, and I have conferred with other psychiatrists at the hospital where we worked. This is how DID is diagnosed."

Yuki shut down her urge to shout, "Yeah!"

Aronson looked calm and competent, but Schneider's expression showed that he hadn't given up trying to discredit the doctor, and by extension, Mary Elena Hayes.

Schneider said, "Question, Doctor. Did Ms. Hayes have

control of her body and her conduct on the day in question at Xe Sogni?"

"Yes. But the guile and the physical strength of the attacker would strongly determine the result."

Schneider smiled with his mouth but the rest of his face was stony.

"Dr. Aronstein. It's perfectly clear from what you've told us already that diagnosis of DID is somewhat arbitrary, made of observation, gut instinct, or guesswork—not lab tests or radiology or chemistry. In other words, not provable."

Yuki was on her feet. "Objection, Your Honor. Argumentative."

The judge sustained the objection.

But Schneider talked over the bang of the gavel and the judge's voice.

"—and because psychiatry is not considered a true science, the claim that any single person could know what another person suffers from, if anything . . ."

Yuki, in her best and loudest courtroom voice, said again, "Objection, Your Honor. Not only is counsel's commentary argumentative, it is irrelevant, immaterial, and clearly prejudicial."

Schneider shot back, "Your Honor, this evidence is central to showing that the case against my client is faulty and based on unprovable theory . . ."

The judge, in an equally elevated tone, pounded his gavel harder, saying, "That's enough, Mr. Schneider. The jury will disregard."

Despite the judge's gaveling, Dr. Aronson now joined the free-for-all.

"I don't agree that the diagnosis of DID and psychiatry itself is arbitrary. Studies are made over decades, consensus is formed, and diagnoses made that are evidenced by statistics and improvement and relief for the patient, sometimes with medication, sometimes partially, sometimes entirely, for the rest of their lives."

Schneider said dismissively, "I have nothing else."

Yuki's voice rang out in the courtroom. "Your Honor, I move to strike . . ."

At Yuki's loudly voiced objection, the judge told the clerk to strike Schneider's cross-examination and the doctor's response. He added, "There is a time for closing arguments and this wasn't it. The jury is instructed to disregard Mr. Schneider's commentary. I will see both counselors in my chambers, now.

"Court is adjourned until tomorrow morning at nine o'clock."

CHAPTER 52

JOE AND BAO had been sitting in Joe's car, watching the ferry terminal for over an hour. Ferries had docked, boarded, and launched. In all, ferries had arrived from five points across the bay and hundreds of passengers had disembarked.

Bao had her laptop open. She had uploaded Thordarson and Wooten's threat-catcher program, which indicated computer signals that hopped over oceans and continents. Presently, it showed an enlarged image of Northern California and was alive with pinpoints of light forming clusters and breaking apart. Not a single light came toward or departed from the ferry terminal. There were no hits on St. Vartan's Hospital that were also tagged as having hit on an office building in Amsterdam.

Joe said to Bao, "I'm calling Thordarson and Wooten."

Peter Wooten answered the video call.

Bao said, "We can see you. How's our reception?"

"First-class," said the red-haired cyber tracker from his office on Fremont Street.

Joe said, "Pete, if I'm St. Vartan's, I'm asking, can't you just unplug the hospital network to stop the bleeding?"

"We've taken a few computers off the servers. But if we disconnect the system, there are two possibilities that are as real as death. One, if Apocalypto has booby-trapped the system, it will trigger a complete shutdown and the damage will be biblical. Also, if we disconnect the server, we can't track the signal back to the attackers."

"Okay. My background in cyber threats is out of its league," said Joe.

"Not mine," said Bao.

"Nor mine," said Wooten. "I know you feel like nothing is happening, Joe. We need more time and this is our best chance to pull the line and hook them."

"Got it," Joe said. "All's clear at the ferry terminal."

"Keep the faith," said Wooten. "We're tagging incoming searches, so if they come up again . . ."

Joe left the conversation to Bao. She lived and breathed cyberterrorism. He wondered why Steinmetz had pulled a risk assessment specialist into a cyberwar with lethal consequences. He listened with one ear as tech talk flowed between the woman sitting beside him and a man who'd spent the last six years of his life becoming a cyber threat catcher.

He heard Wooten say, "We're making progress by process of elimination," then goodbyes, and Bao cut their connection.

"Had enough?" she said to Joe.

"Mmmm. I say we grab a slice then go back to Mission Street."

Bao said, "How do you like your pie?"

"Extra pepperoni with jalapeños."

"I wish I'd bet on that."

Joe laughed.

The pizza was hot and good enough, Bao was great company on a dull gray day, and it was good to have a partner again, especially one who understood the nuances of cyber warfare. But the clock was running out on the patients at St. Vartan's, and the clock was loud and persistent.

Joe let out a sigh, and Bao looked up as they cruised toward FBI HQ.

"Joe? It's good that we manned the ferry terminal, but it was a long shot. Wooten and Thordarson have the big guns. If or when they call us with a hit—"

"I like 'go' a lot more than 'wait.'"

Bao said, "I know. Get ready. Get set. Stand down." She dropped her eyes to her laptop, where the threat-catcher program displayed attacks in real time.

Joe crossed Market Street, took a left on McAllister Street to Polk to Mission, and was backing into a spot when his phone buzzed.

"It's Steinmetz," he said, pressing the button on his console. "Craig? We're parking a block from the office. You're on speaker."

CHAPTER 53

STEINMETZ'S VOICE FILLED the front compartment.

"Something just came in," the chief said. "There's an abandoned house on Turquoise Way, a teardown. It's been empty since the crypto market crashed. Suddenly, young guys, five or six of them, college age, start coming and going from this shack. Cars are parked all over.

"Our tipster peered into one of the windows just now. Saw these boys passed out on the floor and on furniture, and several expensive industrial-grade computer setups on the dining table. The neighbor's name is Wade McEnroe. He's a former Silicon Valley engineer and what he saw lit up his nervous system. He called Chief Clapper, who called me."

Joe said, "So, a bunch of college-age kids are holed up in an abandoned building. They could be taking control of a hospital network for twenty million—or watching porn in 3D."

Steinmetz said, "You have a better lead?"

"No. Give us the address. We're going to be outnumbered. Send backup."

Steinmetz agreed, read off the address, and clicked off.

Bao said, "It's just weird enough to be possible."

Joe unlocked the trunk, got out of the car, put on his Kevlar vest, and hung his badge on a chain around his neck. He gave a second vest to Bao, then got back behind the wheel and headed toward the house on Turquoise Way under occupation by a handful of squatters who might be holding hundreds of hospital patients for ransom.

CHAPTER 54

THE HOUSE ON Turquoise Way was faded blue, wood frame, one story high, squeezed in between two taller, bigger houses, and set back on its small wooded lot. Joe knew this area well. The small front yard meant that the rear of the house backed up to the top of a hill at the edge of Glen Canyon Park, a steep drop hundreds of feet above the floor of the valley below.

Joe parked across and up the street from the target house. His mood had picked up significantly since Steinmetz had given them this assignment. He took out his phone and got out of the car. He walked up and down, taking photos of the tags on vehicles. Bao tucked her gun into her waist holster, put her suit jacket on over the vest, and when Joe came back to the car, she said, "We need backup before we go into . . . that."

Joe called Steinmetz. It was midafternoon and the chief was out. His assistant picked up his call.

"Agent Molinari, it's Farah. Chief Steinmetz left you a

message that SFPD is on the way. And also you got a call from a Sveinn Thordarson, twenty minutes ago. He said it's not urgent."

Joe thanked Farah and clicked off.

He said to Bao, "Car's on the way. So we still wait?"

"Who's in charge here?" she asked.

"You are. I'm freelance."

"We watch and wait."

Time passed without either speaking, then Bao reached the limit of her patience. "Okay," she said. "Let's move."

The street sloped up from the car toward the house but the driveway was a parking lot to four used American cars. They walked slowly, a nice-looking couple taking in the view, wearing badges, packing. They reached the poured concrete walk leading to the front door of the shabby blue house without seeing another soul on foot.

"We're not too conspicuous," she said, "but I do feel eyes on me."

Joe said, "I'll be opposite you in the doorway with my gun out. You knock."

"Oh, boy," she said.

As the agents started up the walkway in front of the house, a tall, dark-haired man wearing a ball cap, jeans, and a Giants windbreaker came out of the house next door and walked quickly toward them.

"I'm Wade McEnroe," he said. "I'm the one who called the police. You're FBI?" he said, looking at the badges.

Bao said, "SFPD called us in."

"Good," said McEnroe. "There's about a half dozen of them. Maybe they're just rich kids with nothing to do but sleep all day, drink all night, and play video games. But I spent twenty-five years in Silicon Valley and I recognize the tens of thousands' worth of industrial-grade computer hardware they've got there. It's all new, arrayed on the dining table."

Joe thanked McEnroe and gave him a business card, saying, "We're just checking things out. But for your safety, please go home. And thanks for calling the police."

CHAPTER 55

AFTER LEAVING THE Fricke house, I'd flagged down a cruiser, thrown myself against the back seat, and tuned in to my unanswered question. *Who killed the Frickes?*

I pictured their dead bodies on the street. Compared them. Both lying on their bellies, shot from behind. Holly's face was turned to the left. Jamie was cradling his face with his right arm.

Differences without distinction.

I pictured our array of possible subjects: Arthur, Rafe, Patty, and Jamie's other lovers from here to New York. Of course there was also the mystery man in black, who the neighbor had seen shoot Jamie and drive off in his Jaguar. A lot of work had been done, but we were still at square one. Maybe someone would walk into the station with a hot clue or a confession? It happened. But very rarely.

I got out of the cruiser at the Hall of Justice at 850 Bryant, took the main entrance, and, after putting my gun aside, went through the magnetometer. I bypassed the mob at the elevator bank and took the fire stairs to Homicide on four. I stopped at the front desk to check in with our gatekeeper, Bobby Nussbaum.

He said, "While you were out, some goon confessed to killing Jamie Fricke."

"You've got butter on your chin. Also, you are the world's worst liar."

He laughed, swiped at his chin, and told me that three dozen tips had been phoned in. "Here ya go."

He handed me a half inch of messages.

"Thanks. Where's Conklin?"

"He and Alvarez are in Interview One with"—he checked his log—"Patricia Delaney."

I texted Conklin and Alvarez that I would be in the observation room the size of a walk-in closet that shares a two-way mirror with Interview One. The mic and cameras were on. My attention was drawn through the glass to Conklin and Alvarez, who sat in plain gray chairs at a plain gray table. Across from them, facing the mirror, was Patty Delaney. She appeared to be melting over the tabletop. Her face was flushed and her chest heaved as she sobbed over folded arms. This woman of thirty-five was the picture of depression, petulance, and grief.

Team Fricke had gathered a lot of background on Patty from interviews with her and others in the Fricke household after Holly's murder. She'd tested negative for gunshot residue then and no doubt was negative today. When we ran her prints and photo through FBI criminal databases, they'd netted nothing, not even a *beep.* No one we'd questioned about her thought she had motive for or had taken part in executing Holly Bergen Fricke. I felt sure that went double for Jamie.

I pictured Patty in her floral quilt a few hours ago, distraught, angry, and shedding real tears. Jamie was dead. Her entire dream was dead.

My phone buzzed. Alvarez was texting me notes from the interview room, details from her interrogation of Patty to date. The subject was Patty's finances. She was well paid, and most of her paycheck went into her savings account. Her credit cards showed purchases of the Victoria's Secret variety. Cappy had previously checked her bank statements, and her income, expenditures, and savings all added up.

I looked up from my phone. Alvarez had gotten out of her chair. The mood had changed significantly inside the interview room.

CHAPTER 56

ALVAREZ WAS STANDING over Patty. Having dropped the good cop role, she was grilling the subject.

She said, "Are you listening, Patty? Holly and Jamie. Did they have a common enemy?"

Patty lifted her head to say, "You've already asked me that. I don't know. Jamie wouldn't have told *me*."

"Patty, I've asked you this before, too. It's important. Think. Have you heard any gossip since Holly's death? Someone sounding a little too pleased that Holly—"

"Oh for God's sake," Patty spat. "Am I under arrest?"

Conklin said, "No, of course not."

"May I go?"

"Yes, but hang in for another minute or two and I'll get you a ride home."

Alvarez said, "Excuse me," and left the room. She entered the observation room and said, "See anything interesting, Linds? Because, in my humble opinion, if she's behind either murder, she's wasting her life in the kitchen. She can act."

"She could do both, but I don't see her as cold and cunning. In fact the opposite. But that doesn't make you wrong."

I looked again at the wreck of Patty Delaney, who was pulling on her cardigan. Conklin was asking her to sign her statement, wrapping up the interview.

I said to Alvarez, "How do you see Delaney as a killer?"

Alvarez said, "Jealousy as motive? Get Holly out of the way, and then here comes shock and fury when Jamie doesn't make good on his promise."

"How'd she do it?"

"Hired a bad man with a gun."

I said, "Without money?"

"Guile. Promises."

I could almost see it. Patty was fetching. And for some people she'd be a soft place to land. I said, "She is due to inherit a boatload."

Alvarez said, "Huh. From Jamie? How much?"

"Three million."

"Whoa. If she knew, that's enough to pay a boatload of bad guys."

I turned my attention to Conklin: smart, kind, a great cop with women. He was saying, "I feel bad, Patty, about how much pain you're in. We're doing this now to clear you and because you know everyone who lived in or visited the Fricke house for—what is it, ten years you've worked there?"

"Eleven."

"Right. Eleven. So, we need your help."

I watched Patty relax her shoulders, unclench her hands, sit up in the chair.

She said, "What happens to me if I tell you something, and it gets out?"

Conklin said, "Your name will never be mentioned."

A long silence followed. Then Patty said, "I can't prove anything. Not a thing. But if I were you I'd look at photos from Holly's funeral. I wasn't there, but Arthur was, and he took a lot of pictures."

"You're saying the killer was there?"

Patty said, "I would think so. Maybe a woman."

"Tall? Thin? Young? Old?"

She stared at Conklin. Clearly she had finished speaking.

"Okay. Thank you, Patty."

My partner stood up, walked behind the subject, and helped her out of her chair, saying, "I'll get you that ride home."

CHAPTER 57

ALVAREZ AND I moved to the observation room attached to Interview Two and watched the formidable Jackson Brady interrogate Arthur Bevaqua. He tried to pin the Frickes' majordomo with an icy-blue stare from across the table, but the well-dressed house manager couldn't meet Brady's eyes.

Brady said, "Tell me again, Ah-thuh. From the beginning."

Arthur had loosened his tie, and I could see the sweat on his brow from where I stood in the observation room.

"Well, he looks shaken," I said to Alvarez. "Sorry I missed most of this."

"We can watch the tape," she said to me.

Now Bevaqua was saying to Brady, "I've told you the same thing over and over. I only have one story."

"I'm not bored," said Brady. "Run it again."

Arthur sighed. "I was up and dressed at seven, as usual. Mr. Jamie came downstairs at eight. Patty made coffee and brought it into the office for us. While she was making his omelet, Mr. Jamie's phone rang. Same time, Patty leans in through the doorway and says, 'Breakfast is served.' Mr. Jamie turns his back and says into the phone, 'Seriously? Yes. I'll meet you there in five.' And he says to me, 'Have Rafe bring the Jag around.'

"I passed Mr. Jamie's message to Rafe, assuming he'd drive Mr. Jamie where he wanted to go. But then I saw Rafe through the front window walking back to his apartment as the Jag was pulling out of the drive."

Brady said, "Fricke didn't say who was on the phone?"

"No, he did not. He left his breakfast uneaten and a draft of his will on his desk. I gave it to Sergeant Boxer."

"You've told me you liked Mr. Fricke."

"I've been with him for twenty years. He's been very good to me and I'm grateful to him and I miss him . . ."

Brady leaned across the table, grabbed Arthur by the forearms, and shook him. "Steady, Arthur. Say your life depends on it. Who shot him?"

Arthur tried to break free of Brady's grip and said, "Let go. I'm all right."

Brady released his hold on Arthur, who rubbed his forearms and asked, "Do I need a lawyer?"

"Do you?"

Arthur shook his head. "Don't do that again, Lieutenant. I'm cooperating."

Brady sat back in his seat. Arthur leaned forward and lowered his voice. He said, "One thing I've never mentioned. Jamie had been seeing Mrs. Holly's younger sister, Rae."

"'Seeing' meaning having an affair with her?"

"Yes. When Mrs. Holly was alive, she never said anything about it to me. I never saw any sign of betrayal on her face."

"Tell me about Rae."

"She's wealthy. Has a place in Malibu. She writes screenplays, one of which, according to *Variety,* she sold. Also, I've heard that she parties with big names in Hollywood. That's all I know."

"But Rae came to see Holly, right?" Brady said.

Arthur sighed. "Yes. Sorry. She came a few times a year on holidays. Mrs. Holly always said, 'I love my sister.' "

Brady said, "Arthur, I asked you who shot Jamie. This is your answer? You suspect Rae Bergen? Why?"

Arthur said, "Lieutenant, I don't suspect anyone. I'm desperate to know who killed Mrs. Holly and Mr. Jamie. But the way I do my job is to not see or hear things I shouldn't. What you're getting from me is blindfolded doodling under intense police pressure. Mr. Jamie was seeing Rae Bergen. That's a fact. And Mr. Jamie was seeing her right up till the time he was murdered. He'd call her when I was in the office. On occasion, he had Rafe drive him to the airport to meet Ms. Rae and travel elsewhere. If Mr. Jamie made 'forever after' promises to her, I don't know. I was privy to Mr. Jamie's personal life, but I was not his confidant. I answered the phone. I took messages. I opened the mail. I supervised the staff. Et cetera."

"Do you think Rae Bergen had a motive to kill her sister?"

"I did *not* say that. I'm hypothesizing because you're leaning on me. I think it's possible that someone, Ms. Rae or someone else, called Mr. Jamie and said, 'Hey, I've got something for you. Meet me on Steiner Street.' Again, I'm making up scenarios."

"Okay," said Brady. "I think we're finished. Thanks, Arthur. I appreciate your cooperation."

Brady pushed back his chair, showed the Frickes' house manager out of the interview room, and hooked him up with a ride home.

I said to Alvarez, "See what you can find out about Rae Bergen."

Alvarez said, "Are we looking to bring her in?"

"Dig around. Talk to me. If there's a case to be made, we'll talk to Brady."

Crossing her fingers, Alvarez left the observation room.

CHAPTER 58

IT HAD BEEN a long day and I was flagging. I needed coffee, heavy on the sugar. Cappy and Chi were in the break room, conversing over coffee when I walked in and poured myself a mug of dregs. I pulled a chair up to the table.

I was asked for an update and I was eager to share with the team. I briefed Chi and Cappy on what I'd learned that day about Jamie's financial manager, his house manager, his driver, and his cook—all of whom they knew—and that Jamie had been in the process of revising his will.

"How'd you know that?" Cappy asked.

"Bevaqua showed us the new draft Jamie left out in the office."

I told them about Arthur making a reluctant admission to Brady that Rae Bergen had been seeing Jamie Fricke romantically, both while Holly was alive and after she'd been buried.

Chi raised an eyebrow.

"That's new."

Cappy pushed a tin of sugar cookies toward me and I helped myself to one and then another.

After I'd downed some coffee, I said, "Patty Delaney told me to look at the pictures Bevaqua took at Holly's funeral. You guys were there. Did anyone make it into your notebook?"

"There was a lot going on," Chi said. "Retired Olympians breaking down, gut-wrenching eulogies, but when it came time to lower the casket, no one was allowed to stand by the grave except family."

Cappy said, "Rae was there with her twenty-year-old son, Brock Picard. College kid. She's been divorced from her husband for ten years. It's all in the file."

Chi said, "Brock gave a pretty moving eulogy about his aunt Holly. Jamie choked out something heartbreaking about losing his soulmate. He was so sincere. If you didn't know better . . ."

"And Rae?" I asked.

"Rae was a mess. All she could get out was, 'I'll always love you, Holly.'"

Chi looked pensive, and to me that always meant a big idea was coming up. "Paul," I said. "What are you thinking?"

"That a few of us should go to Jamie's funeral."

"Which is when?"

"Friday. Private service at the family chapel in Pacific Heights."

"Volunteers?" I asked.

Chi and Cappy raised their hands.

"Good. You've got it."

"What was in the will?" Cappy asked.

"I'll show you if you give me half your sandwich."

"You like pastrami? I didn't know," he said.

"Deal or no deal?"

Cappy laughed and pushed half a pastrami on rye with mustard across the table.

"Looks, uh, yum," I said. "Can you spare the pickle?"

He gave it to me. When I'd finished my half of Cappy's sandwich and my past-dead coffee, Chi handed me the whole Fricke family file: two thumb drives and a three-hole binder of tabloid clippings. I gave him the draft of Jamie's will and took the files down the hall to begin reading up on Holly Bergen Fricke's family.

CHAPTER 59

I WAS DETERMINED to find a hook, a clue, something that looked wrong that would lead me to a double murderer. But the material in the files was meant for popular consumption. Party photos, award ceremonies, the material all fell under the heading of "Enquiring Minds Want to Know."

Cappy's notes were on one of the thumb drives, Chi's on the other. I'd seen most of this information before, when we'd been working daily on Holly Fricke's murder, but some of Chi's notes were new to me: Holly and Rae's parents, Bill and Susanne "Sassy" Bergen, had both come from old money going back three generations in New York. They served on a number of not-for-profit boards, had a few hospital wings named for them, but also were rumored to party in shades of gray.

Chi's notes included a crisp professional photo of the Bergen sisters at a Hollywood award after-party. It had been taken no more than two years before. Rae wore a thigh-high gauzy white dress and Holly was standing beside her in a sleek gold catsuit with a low neckline. Chi had attached Rae's thin arrest record as a photo file. She had been caught and released with a few ounces of marijuana when she was in high school. She'd later been pulled over for speeding several times and cited once for having an open glass of vodka in her car.

I found other photos of Rae Bergen: party and award show photos where Rae was with A-list movie stars, looking happy and beautiful in every shot. The only exception was one that had been taken at Holly's funeral. Rae's mascara had run below her lashes, her black dress clung to her thighs, and her hair was unruly. She was still beautiful but resembled a rose that had been caught in a late snow.

If there'd been a clue in Holly's "murder book," Chi and Cappy would have found it. Still, the last photo in the book seemed promising: a party photo of a number of well-turned-out guests posed on the Frickes' back lawn. Chi had listed the guests, typed their names on a separate sheet.

I spent some time learning the names of people I hadn't met or who hadn't yet come up in the investigation of Holly's death. For the same reason Patty had said that we should check out the mourners at Holly's funeral, I felt I might see someone in this shot who might take us off square one.

I was still scrutinizing the photo when Alvarez appeared in the doorway. She looked distressed.

I asked, "You spoke to Brady?"

"Lindsay, Rae told Brady she's not coming to San Francisco unless he has a warrant. She has nothing to say about Jamie's death. She just wants to be left alone. The end."

"You have her number?"

“I sure do.” Alvarez wrote it down on my notepad.

When Alvarez had left the room, I made some calls. Cindy, Claire, Yuki. I needed to schedule a Women’s Murder Club dinner at Susie’s with bottomless pitchers of beer.

But first, I wanted to talk to another of Jamie’s recent lovers. I needed to speak with Rae Bergen. She hadn’t been interviewed. She was Holly’s sister and had had an intimate relationship with Jamie. A nexus. A possible doer. And for sure a real source of information.

I rang her number three times. No answer. Left my number each time. No callback.

CHAPTER 60

IT WAS JUST about quitting time. Claire Washburn was in the autopsy suite with her assistant, Bunny Ellis. Also present was the shot, cut, and stitched-up body of James Fricke III lying on a stainless-steel table, covered in a blue drape. Mostly covered. His right arm lay over the drape, the hand loosely wrapped in gauze.

What about Fricke's knuckles? Was the answer right there? Claire whispered, "Please, God."

A tag lettered with the deceased's name and the number of his drawer hung by a string from his right big toe. Bunny tucked the hem of the drape around the body and wheeled the table through the swinging doors to the storage area.

Claire called out, "After you stow him, Bunny, please stick around until Loomis picks up Mr. Fricke's effects. The carton is under the reception desk."

"The swabs need to be processed immediately," Bunny said.

"Right," Claire said. "Warp speed."

Bunny laughed. "You've only told me six times."

"And now, seven," said Claire. "You understand, right, Bunny? If I have to stop his funeral, I'd like to be correct."

"I totally get it," said Bunny. "I'll make sure Loomis gets it, too."

"They're usually a little early, so stay where you can hear the buzzer. I have a couple of things to do in my office but if I'm needed, come get me."

Inside her office, Claire skimmed the death certificate and the three copies. *Cause of death, five .40-caliber rounds. Manner of death, homicide.* She signed and dated them all.

She turned on the light box behind her desk and put up Fricke's X-rays, which she'd already reviewed at least a half dozen times. Had she overlooked something? Did the five matching shots in the same locations on both Holly and Jamie's bodies mean something to their killer, and if so, what? Was this the mark of a serial killer just getting started in Pacific Heights or was this personal?

She studied the X-rays, animated the murder in her mind. The shooter had taken the first shot to Fricke's back and the bullet had lodged in the fourth rib, grazing his spine. Theorizing now, Claire pictured Fricke spinning around reflexively—a reaction to the shot. She could imagine him seeing the shooter and throwing a punch to his face. Then Jamie Fricke had dropped to his knees. The shooter put a second round in Fricke's heart, then his groin, his liver. And as Fricke rolled onto his side or back, he shot Fricke in the forehead. The coup de grâce. The bullet was still in Fricke's head when she'd gone in after it. The head shot killed him, but Fricke wouldn't have survived the others.

Claire placed one copy of Jamie Fricke's X-rays into a

large envelope that she would have hand-delivered to Jackson Brady in the morning. She slipped the second set of files into another large envelope, this one addressed to Dr. Humphrey Germaniuk. Dr. G., the night shift ME for the last fifteen years, specialized in trace evidence. She left the envelope on his desk.

She filed the original of Jamie Fricke's films and paperwork in her open case file drawer, right next to Holly Fricke's. Then Claire stripped off her gown, cap, and gloves, put it all in the trash.

Earlier, Claire and Lindsay had commiserated about the lack of visual evidence in Holly's death. No witnesses. No security camera footage. There was one known witness in Jamie's murder: Dan Fields, the neighbor who'd seen the shooter. His view was partial, seen from three stories overhead with some obstruction from trees and the corner of the building next door. Fields had not seen the shooter's face. He'd said that the killer was wearing black, and he'd seen no identification on the clothing. And he hadn't seen if the victim had punched out at the shooter. Fields had been shocked by the killing and didn't move until after the shooter drove off in Jamie's black Jaguar. It wasn't much, but it was something.

Claire changed from her rubber-soled shoes to street shoes and was ready to go.

She found Bunny straightening up in the autopsy room.

"Bunny. Have you seen Dr. G.?"

"He just texted me. He's parking his car."

"Good."

Claire was eager to compare notes with the good doctor.

CHAPTER 61

DR. HUMPHREY GERMANIUK was not just a highly regarded medical examiner, but he'd taught at UCLA Medical School before joining the medical examiner's office. After retiring from teaching, he came back to the ME, night shift, and he and Claire were friends.

He was just coming through the ambulance bay when Claire said, "Thanks, Bunny. Put in for overtime. Dr. G. will take it from here."

Bunny didn't have to be told twice. She went to the ladies' room and came out shortly in street clothes, hair loose around her shoulders, lip gloss. As she left the ME's office, Claire and Dr. Germaniuk both wished Bunny a good night.

Claire gave Dr. G. a couple of minutes to gown up, then open his office door and ask her what was lying in wait for him. She got right to it. "I left Jamie Fricke's files on your desk. A million dollars for your thoughts."

He said, "You look tired, Claire."

"Is that your professional opinion or a little help from my friend?"

"Both," said Dr. G.

Claire nodded. "I hear you. I'm a brain wreck. Come with me, Dr. G. If you don't mind," she said, going through the swinging doors to the cold storage room. She opened Fricke's drawer and slid his body out.

"What do you think of this here?" Claire asked Dr. G., unwrapping Fricke's hand with great care. Dr. G. cleaned his thick, black-rimmed glasses and, when James Fricke's right hand had been entirely freed from the bandage, peered at the dead man's hand.

Claire told him her theory of the injury and Dr. G. looked closely at Fricke's skinned knuckles.

"Hmm. It sure looks like he got a punch in before the curtain dropped. You swabbed it?"

"I swabbed the hell out of it," said Claire. "I've got the swabs packaged and I called Hallows to make sure he gives it priority treatment. Rapid DNA could be back tonight."

Dr. G. nodded approvingly.

Claire went on. "Contents of the box for the lab: fluids from the tox screen, clothes bagged, fingernail scrapings, slugs, all in the carton under the reception desk with the swabs, five of them in individual tubes. Loomis is careful. I just hope they come early tonight."

"I'm taking over, okay, Claire?"

"Triple okay," she said. "If the lab calls back with the DNA, wake me."

"You're off duty, Claire. I'm in charge and I'm not going to let you down."

CHAPTER 62

BAO WAITED WITH Joe in his car parked on the shoulder of Turquoise Way three hundred yards downhill from the blue house. The road was flanked by homes with small yards overlooking the steep hillside below.

Bao was focused on Thordarson and Wooten's threat-catcher program. She hadn't found a match from Eastern Europe to San Francisco but was not giving up.

Joe was fixated on the east side of the sorry-looking blue house at the top of the road. At nearly five in the afternoon, the sky was overcast, building up to a soaking rain. The target house was dark and silent, shadowed by its taller neighbors, trees, and the darkening sky.

A little while earlier, Joe had peered into the house through a gap in a window shade. He'd counted five, possibly six, fit young men sleeping on the floor and sofa. But there could be others in the adjacent, windowless room. Joe pictured what else he'd seen—the array of computers on the dining table and the box of .40-caliber ammo on the windowsill. And it was the second item that was keeping him in the car.

He checked his watch again to see how much time had elapsed since Steinmetz's assistant had told him that backup was on the way. It seemed like half a lifetime passed before Bao looked up from her phone and turned to Joe.

"Incoming backup," she said.

Joe got out of the car and stood against the door looking down the road. A white police van turned onto Turquoise Way and came up the hill. Joe held up his badge and the van braked hard next to him.

The passenger door slid open and a uniform stepped out, introduced himself as Sergeant Brian Whalen and his partner, behind the wheel, as Inspector Ray Lipari. Joe introduced Bao and himself and nodded to the three cops wearing tactical gear seated in the rear of the van.

Whalen said, "Wait a minute. Molinari. You're not a cop. You're an independent whatchacallit. Contractor. Boxer's husband, am I right?"

Whalen had crossed swords with Lindsay in the past. This operation was Joe's responsibility. He was working from a phoned-in tip, and with manpower he didn't know. The outcome for St. Vartan's could be apocalyptic. So, he did what he had to do.

"Whalen, let me be clear. This is an FBI operation. I'm in command. Are you in or out?"

"I was never out. What's the plan?"

Joe pointed out the blue house a few hundred yards uphill. He told Whalen, "I saw five or six sleeping males in that house, mid-twenties, four used cars out front. We have a short time frame in which to unwind a cyberattack on a hospital. There are industrial-grade computers set up in that house's main room and I saw a box of .40-caliber ammo on the windowsill."

"So they're armed."

"Very likely. At the moment they're camping in a property that's not theirs. We can bring them in on trespassing alone."

Whalen said, "We have tac gear and search warrants."

"Good. I've roughed out a plan," said Joe. "It's basic. Form a perimeter around the house. Your men knock and announce, then enter through the back door. If the subjects don't drop to the floor, flush them out the front. Director Wong and I will be waiting for them. If they shoot, we shoot. But we prefer live captives who talk."

Whalen had questions and Joe answered. He described the layout of the house, its location on its lot, and the long drop down a hillside at the rear boundary line.

Joe said, "The van is now our command post. Once the perimeter is in place, Lipari calls you, and you drive up the hill, block off the driveway, trapping their vehicles from leaving the property."

Whalen said, "I've got it, Molinari. Make arrests, transport this gang of whatever to booking, go home."

Joe said, "Right. I think we can wrap this up in under an hour."

Whalen was nodding when everything changed.

The lights in the run-down blue house went on.

The occupants were awake.

CHAPTER 63

JOE'S BRAIN WENT into overdrive, assessing the ways things could go terribly wrong. The young men could see the van and grab their guns, resulting in a Wild West–style shoot-out. Or they could leave the house before the perimeter was set, take off through the canyon, and get lost until night. Or it could go the other way. These kids might be a college study group, armed with nothing more than their cheat sheets. People could get hurt right here in the next few minutes.

Five cops, including Whalen, secured their tactical gear and huddled with Joe near the van as he gave them their orders.

On Joe's go, the team moved out.

It started to rain as Joe and Bao reached the front door of the house. Through a crack in the door, Joe saw that some of the young men were on their feet, pulling on their clothes. Two sat in front of computers. They hadn't seen the cops. Then a bullhorn sounded, and a voice announced, "This is SFPD. We're coming in. Toss your guns. Drop to the floor. Hands behind your heads. Do this now and no one gets hurt."

There was shouting inside the small house. One of the men disappeared from Joe's view. The others fell to their knees. A tall kid with leadership presence shouted to his guys, "Front door. Front door. Let's go."

"Ready, set," said Joe to Bao.

Joe put his shoulder to the front door, which splintered as it broke open. Four half-dressed young men pushed aside strips of wood and ran through the doorway with drawn guns, muscling past Bao and Joe.

Joe fired three shots into the air and shouted orders to halt.

The four dropped to the walkway. The cops seized their guns, wrenched their arms around their backs, and cuffed them. Joe heard, "You have the right to remain silent . . ." and watched as the captives were marched to the van.

Bao entered the house with Officer Boyd Jamieson to make sure the house was cleared while allowing her to check out the computers.

Joe felt a rush of satisfaction, a feeling he'd missed since he last worked a case in the field. He holstered his gun and was calling Steinmetz's office—when a shot sounded from the canyon to his left.

Joe yelled, "Everyone down!"

The bullet had hit Officer Devon Brown, who was standing just to Joe's left side. Blood spouted from Brown's left thigh as he dropped.

The van pulled up, blocking the cars in the driveway. Whalen got out, wove between the cars, put his arm around Brown's shoulders, and helped him into the van's passenger seat.

Whalen said to Brown, "We'll get you some help, Dev."

"All I need is a Band-Aid," said Brown.

Joe stood behind an open car door, using it as a shield. He was searching the canyon with his eyes, looking for the shooter, when Bao ran out of the house to where he stood.

Joe turned to Bao thinking she didn't look right. Her eyes were red and there were raw spots on the backs of her hands. She smelled of smoke.

"What happened, Bao?"

She said, "I was doing a cursory check of the computers while Jamieson cleared the house. Joe. Those guys were selling drugs. Online. Mail delivery. The house is full of courier envelopes. There were two pill presses in the spare room. Binding chemicals. Plastic bags. The works."

"Anything on Apocalypto?"

"I was moving fast but I saw nothing but lists and addresses and ledgers of receipts. No ransomware. No hospital anything. These are not our guys."

CHAPTER 64

JOE LIFTED BAO'S right hand and then looked at the right side of her neck.

"What happened to you? Are you burned?"

"One of those guys just appeared, Joe, I don't know from where. Next thing I know, he's at the stove and there's a frying pan on the burner. He turned on the gas and dumped the grease onto the burner and the fire got a good start. I'm okay, but it could have been worse. I smothered the flames with wet dish towels. Jamieson got the curtains out of the way and the guy ran out the back door."

Joe asked Bao, "Do you see the guy here?"

As Whalen and Lipari stuffed the modern-day drug dealers into the van, shackled them, checked them, checked again, Jamieson jump-started a rusted Ford sedan in the driveway.

"Dev, hold on to me," he said to the injured cop as he transferred him from the van to the Ford and headed out to the hospital with him. As the used car lot in front of the house thinned, Bao saw a flash of red in the nearby canyon.

She said, “Look,” as the red flash disappeared behind a rock.

“That’s the guy who set the fire,” Bao said. “That’s him.”

Joe pulled Bao down to the ground just as the guy showed his gun and fired. Joe returned fire and hit the shooter, who howled in pain.

Joe ordered the uniforms into the woods, but they returned to the blue house empty-handed.

Joe said, “Damn. He didn’t get away, did he?”

Lipari said, “We identified ourselves loud and clear. But this dude ran behind the house. There’s a drop-off back there and the ground was muddy. Look.” Lipari showed Joe his mud-caked shoe sole.

“So the jackass slipped. Cafferty and I ran to the edge. Jackass grabbed on to a root about twenty feet down the slope. We couldn’t reach him. We got hold of a good branch to lower down to him, and by then it was pouring. Guy calls out to God, slips, hitting rocks and roots and whatever on his way down.”

Joe said, “Is he alive?”

“Doesn’t look like it. He’s motionless. I yelled. Told him to hang on, we’d come get him. He didn’t answer. I think he broke his neck. He lost his gun near the top of the slope. We have it and his wallet. His name is Keith Ballantine.”

“Can’t leave him there,” Joe said.

He got back on the phone with Steinmetz, told him he needed a search-and-rescue team. “We need it now.”

Joe said to Steinmetz, “We have to retrieve the guy who got away. He attacked Director Wong and then fired on us, hitting Officer Brown, who’s on the way to the ER. The shooter slid down a steep canyon beyond reach. Alive or dead, I want to bring him in."

Steinmetz agreed and signed off. Joe saw Bao picking out cops by name, telling them she needed help getting the computers out of the house. Joe called out to her, "Wait for me. I'll be back."

He didn't hear her say, "I'll be right here."

THURSDAY

CHAPTER 65

AT SIX O'CLOCK the next morning, Nick Gaines crossed Bryant from the All Day Parking lot to the Hall. He turned so that he was facing the gray granite face of the Hall of Justice building and called Yuki.

"Yuki, sorry to wake you. The gaggle is stopping traffic on Bryant and starting to pack the sidewalks. Uniforms are outnumbered."

Yuki said, "Aw jeez," thanked Gaines, and slipped out of bed without waking Brady, made coffee, and called Mary Elena.

"Mary Elena, are you awake?"

"Maybe. I'm not sure I was asleep. What's wrong?"

"Nothing. Not yet. Just every journalist in the country is surrounding the Hall. Please get dressed. I'll pick you up in about forty-five minutes."

"Party dress or jeans?"

"Your blue skirt suit, Mary Elena. Or the gray jacket and trousers . . . I want to get you into the building ahead of the press and they're already stopping traffic."

"I'll be ready," Mary Elena said.

Yuki went to her closet and pulled out the first suit still in a dry cleaner's bag. No one was going to be looking at her. She showered. Soaped her hair. Dried off and dressed. She put on her watch that had once belonged to her mother. Seven o'clock plus a few seconds. She tiptoed back to the bedroom and kissed Brady goodbye. He startled awake.

"What's happening? Are you okay?"

Yuki soothed him back to the pillows and blankets, told him she had to be at court early, kissed him again.

She stepped into her shoes and left the apartment. Yuki's mother's voice warned her, *Drive safe, Yuki-eh.* She said, *Okay, Mother, I'm good,* as she drove her car out of the garage and up the ramp to the street. Checking the time, she was sure she'd be at Mary Elena's place in ten minutes. If the lights were with her.

This was a big day. Mary Elena was going to testify about the assault again, but this time Schneider would cross-examine her. Unordered thoughts flashed through Yuki's mind, but chief among them was this: Would Mary Elena hold up on the stand? Would she stay in her main personality?

Yuki thought over the questions she was going to ask, added one, subtracted another, braking her car as she nearly ran the light on Geary Street. After that close call, she turned on the radio to a light jazz station and kept her eyes on the road.

CHAPTER 66

WHEN COURT OFFICER Louie Mack opened the double doors to Courtroom 8G, journalists and the trial curious stampeded through the wide opening and lunged for seats in the gallery. Cindy fought for the last seat nearest the door, throwing her computer bag onto the chair that she called hers, and nailed it.

Britney Waller, a reporter from the *Sacramento Ledger* who also wanted that seat, stamped on Cindy's instep with her high heel, hard enough to bruise bone. Cindy yelped and cursed at Waller, who was taller, older, and heavier than Cindy. Still, Waller saw something in Cindy that caused her to back off.

Once seated, her computer cord plugged into the socket behind her, Cindy opened her laptop. About then Bailiff Riley Boone entered the courtroom from the side door, filled his lungs with air, and called out, "Alllll riiiise."

The audience stood noisily as the judge came through the narrow doorway from his office and took his seat at the bench.

Even from the back of the room, Cindy noted that His Honor Henry William St. John had had a bad night, or maybe hadn't slept at all. It was clear from the bench that the gallery was packed to the walls, chairs squeezed close together. His Honor was not pleased. He banged his gavel repeatedly, calling out "Quiet," until the volume of voices dropped to a low buzz.

Cindy looked up at the judge as he shouted, "You people in the gallery who've rearranged the chairs. What we have here is a fire hazard. Bailiff, please clear the aisles and everyone standing at the back of the room. That's it. Show the nice people out to the corridor, Officer Mack. No one else comes into the courtroom unless they are part of the proceedings."

While Cindy was drafting her column, a man standing in the rear of the room called out, "Your Honor, Your Honor, I'm Cory Leach from the *Grand Rapids Badger*—"

"Sorry, but no, Mr. Leach. No standing room."

Cindy kept her head down, fingers on the keys, setting the scene, describing her observations, quoting the quotable. She was working fast and well when Bailiff Riley Boone brought in the jurors from their room behind one of the oak-paneled walls of 8G. Once they'd been seated, court was called into session. Judge St. John delivered the rules on court decorum quickly, paused to pass his eyes over the room, then turned to Yuki.

"Ms. Castellano, please call your witness."

Yuki stood, keeping one hand on the back of Mary Elena's chair.

"Your Honor. The People call Ms. Mary Elena Hayes."

CHAPTER 67

MARY ELENA, LOOKING smart and put together in cobalt blue, stepped out from behind the counsel table and set course for the witness stand. She put her left hand on the Bible, raised her right, and swore before God to tell only the truth. And that wouldn't be hard for her. It had been well established that Mary Elena had no memory of being beaten and raped.

As late as last week, after another consultation with Parisi, Yuki and Nick Gaines were convinced that if they didn't call Mary Elena to tell her story in her own words, the defense surely would aggressively present their side; namely, *You asked Mr. Cates for sex, didn't you? The sex was consensual, isn't that right? You hold an important job, don't you, Ms. Hayes? How is it that your psychological disorder hasn't disrupted your job performance in the human resources department at Raymond James over, what is it, four years? Seems a little handy to have a breakdown at Xe Sogni, wouldn't you say?*

It was Schneider's job to bury Mary Elena. When Yuki introduced Mary Elena, she'd present her as credible and the victim of terrible crimes perpetrated by the defendant, Tyler Cates.

When Mary Elena had settled into the witness box, Yuki asked her to state her name, which she did. Then, "You feel comfortable testifying?"

"Perfectly. I could get used to all this attention," Mary Elena said with a smile. She even got a few laughs from the gallery.

"Mary Elena, you remember what His Honor the judge asked me to tell you?"

"Sure. It's about my alters. If they come out, each has to be sworn in individually."

"That's right," Yuki said. "Okay, what do you remember about the afternoon when you entered a restaurant called Xe Sogni to use the ladies' room?"

Mary Elena said, "Well, when I walked in, lunch was being served. I asked the maître d' if I could use the ladies' washroom."

Yuki nodded and asked Mary Elena to go on.

"He pointed me to the stairs and when I got to the second floor, I was inside a locker room, and the ladies' room was to my left. But there was a man near the lockers. I remember that he asked me my name and I didn't like his tone of voice. I told him my name and kept walking toward the door marked 'Ladies.'"

"What happened next?"

"This . . . this guy said he wanted to have sex with me—demanded it—and I just . . . freaked out. He had no right to come on to me like that, and he frightened me. One of my alters came forward and tried to protect me. I lost time. I don't know how much time or what was happening to me, but I've been told that when the police came, I was on the floor, mostly naked and quite bruised. And I do remember this: I hurt everywhere."

Yuki stepped aside so that Mary Elena had full view of the courtroom and asked, "Do you see the man who attacked you?"

Mary Elena said, "There. He's right there." And she pointed to the defense table.

"Are you indicating the defendant?"

"Yes. Wearing a blue jacket."

Tyler Cates didn't flinch.

Yuki asked, "He was a stranger to you, isn't that right?"

"Yes. A large, aggressive stranger."

Tyler Cates shot to his feet and shouted out, "*Liar! You're a stone liar!*"

Mary Elena froze. The judge told Cates to sit down and for Schneider to restrain his client or the defendant would be removed from the courtroom and returned to lockup—indefinitely.

Yuki thought Mary Elena's change of tone and expression were extreme as if one of her alters had taken her over. Her eyes were locked on Cates and she looked angry and afraid.

Yuki said gently, "Mary Elena, don't answer him. Answer me."

"Okay. The first. And *only.* Time in my life. I ever saw that man. Was in the restaurant changing room. Six months ago."

Cates jumped to his feet again and yelled, "*Pants on fire, Mary whatever your name is! Try telling the truth. Tell about Brookside Psychiatric!*"

Yuki felt it. The case was falling apart. Mary Elena was no

longer Mary Elena. Now, she pulled her knees up to her chest, closed her eyes, and screamed. She took a breath and screamed again. Loudly. Painful to hear. She was Lily.

Yuki called up to the judge. "Your Honor, we need a recess, please."

When Mary Elena's feet touched the floor, Yuki put her arms around her and walked her to the counsel table. Behind them, the judge used his gavel with meaning.

CHAPTER 68

THE EMPTY OFFICE on the thirteenth floor of the FBI's San Francisco branch had been a spare, unadorned space with two metal desks facing each other, a narrow credenza, and a large picture window with a view of the traffic on Mission Street.

Since taking over the office, Joe and Bao had spread out to the four corners. The heavy-duty computers with fifty-inch screens covered the desks, a borrowed table, and most of the credenza. Since they had returned from the blue house on Turquoise Way, the sun had risen over the city skyline.

Joe got up, adjusted the shades.

"Coffee, Bao?"

"Thanks, no. I'm still working on the last one."

Her phone tootled and she picked up, said, "Hey, Sweetie."

Joe left the room to give Bao privacy, and as he headed toward the vending machine alcove, he thought about how rare it was to fit this well with a new partner.

He and Bao had maximized every minute, going from a

hospital meeting to a shoot-out, a gas stove fire, a cop down, a dead perp, and four arrests. But while that was all good, they were no closer to putting St. Vartan's back in business than they had been at minute one.

And they were still on it. They'd scrolled through uncountable gigabytes of files as time ambled by. They'd found nothing in all those hours about ransomware, hospitals being held hostage, or Apocalypto. Patients at St. Vartan's were still in danger. The agreed upon forty-eight-hour window was closing despite a well-meaning tip that hadn't paid off.

Joe got coffee from the vending machine along with a bag of M&M's. When he returned to the office, Steinmetz was sitting on a few spare inches of the credenza.

He said, "Fine job you two did yesterday. How about a briefing?"

Joe said, "As it happens, I'm writing up a summary right now. Do you want details or just the bottom line?"

"Cut to the chase. If I need more, I'll ask."

"Okay, then. Starting after our phone call with you from the scene," Joe said, "one of the five squatters took shots at us, hit Officer Devon Brown from Glen Park Station . . ."

"He's the one in Emergency?"

Joe nodded and said, "It was a through-and-through, inner left thigh. Worse than it sounds. The slug hit a juncture of arteries called the femoral triangle. We tied off the wound at the scene and still Brown nearly bled out. As of now, he's out of surgery, but he's still in critical."

"It's not on you," Steinmetz said.

Joe nodded, but he thought it was. He said, "The shooter is at the morgue."

"He's the one went over the drop-off? Has the body been ID'd?"

"Keith Ballantine, twenty-eight. Technically unemployed. Glen Park Station contacted his parents. Bao, you're up."

Bao swiveled her chair so she was facing Steinmetz.

"These are the six computers that were in the house, and they each have enormous storage capacity. I've strip-searched four of them so far. There is nothing in them referencing Apocalypto or ransomware, nothing about hospitals at all."

"So, what did you find?"

Bao said, "Well. The young entrepreneurs in the house were in the drug manufacturing and distribution game. All of their business records were on their computers."

"Drugs?" Steinmetz asked. "You're sure?"

Bao said, "I have another two computers to go through, Craig. But we found pill presses and the chemicals needed to fabricate the pills and package them in the house. A vast mailing list of bulk buyers and repeat customers. They take orders over the web, ship the product out through any courier service. Incoming funds are auto-deposited in one of six banks. Glen Park has processed the four still standing. No sheets, no outstanding warrants. They're geeks, sir, now with serious goddamn drug and money laundering charges."

Joe looked at his phone, which had pinged with an incoming text.

He said, "Sorry to interrupt, Bao. Chief. Message from CS Inc. They've tracked an incoming signal from Eastern Europe that is seeking a target in San Francisco."

"Brilliant," said Bao. "The IP address of the target should belong to an Apocalypto-operated computer."

CHAPTER 69

BAO WONG CALLED Pete Wooten's direct line and Wooten picked up.

He said, "We have high confidence that this is it. The coordinates are on target—"

Sveinn Thordarson joined in, saying, "There's a Starbucks on Divisadero Street at the corner of Bush Street. Joe, you know it?"

"Very well," Joe said. "Their Wi-Fi is strong."

Wooten said, "I'm guessing their operator is going to look perfectly natural in there. Probably young."

Ten minutes after the call with Cyber Security Incorporated, Joe and Bao drove past the Divisadero Street intersection with Bush and parked across the street from the coffee shop. Bao called Pete Wooten for the second time since leaving the FBI offices.

"Pete, we're across the street from Starbucks now."

Wooten said, "Bao, assuming you're still wearing a suit, Joe should go in, buy something, sit down, and text me. The code from Apocalypto is on the subjects' computer right now."

Joe said, "Copy," and headed across the street to the coffee shop. Bao slid over to the driver's side in case they had to move fast. And then she watched and waited.

A few customers drifted out of the store with coffee containers in hand, but five minutes passed and Joe was still inside the shop. What was keeping him? This could be their only shot at Apocalypto. Bao patted the gun on her hip, then opened the car door.

CHAPTER 70

BAO WAS WAITING for a break in the traffic so she could dash across Divisadero Street—when she saw Joe moving rapidly toward her. He was carrying something under his arm. Once he reached Bao, he showed her a laptop.

"You've got it? That's the one?"

"Better be," Joe said. "But we still need the operator."

He got back into the driver's seat and buckled up, as did Bao.

She said, "I'm dying, Joe. Talk to me."

"I'll tell you everything. But first, we have to find the owner of this laptop."

Joe flipped on the flashing emergency lights and pulled out onto the road. When the car was in the clear, he turned the wheel hard and headed slowly up Divisadero toward Pine Street. A soft light filtered through the trees that lined the wide two-lane street. Traffic was sparse.

"Joe?"

"So when I walk toward the front door, I see through the window that there's a laptop sitting on a table by itself."

"Noooo."

"I head for the laptop, but someone beats me to it and takes it up to the barista on the other side of the room. Now there's another person between us in the line. So when I get to the front, I pull my badge. I signal for the laptop and ask the barista does she know the guy who left it. Could she describe him? Yes, she could. What was his name?

"She didn't remember what name he gave for his order, but she described him. White male, five ten or so, chunky build, in his early thirties, wearing jeans and a green windbreaker. I realized I saw that guy leaving Starbucks as I was coming in. I saw him, Bao. But since he wasn't wearing an Apocalypto sweatshirt, I didn't think anything of him. Now, we're going to look for him."

A driver behind them honked his horn.

"Bao," said Joe. "Flip that guy the bird, okay?"

She snorted and said, "Joe, slow down, in case we pass a thirty-something in a green jacket."

Joe smiled. "Have faith. After I got the laptop, the barista—her name is Sophie—said, 'There's a note inside.'"

Bao picked the computer up off the floor, opened the lid, and saw a Post-it note with a couple of lines of handwriting stuck to the screen. She read it out loud.

"'I was here. Where were you?'"

CHAPTER 71

YUKI AND GAINES sat at the prosecution table with Mary Elena in the chair between them. She was quiet and as cold as stone.

His Honor Henry William St. John had once again adjourned court for the day, excused the jury, who were returned to the deliberation room. He offered Mary Elena his chambers until "this mess is resolved."

Gaines wrote the word "mistrial" on Yuki's pad and she put a checkmark next to it.

Yuki asked Mary Elena, "Would you prefer to wait in my office?" She nodded her head vigorously.

"If the judge agrees, I want you to sit in my office until he is through with me, then I'll drive you home."

With permission, Yuki approached the bench and told His Honor her plan. Moments later, Yuki's assistant, Deirdre Palmer, was at the double doors. Deirdre was a kind and resourceful person and Mary Elena had met her before. The transfer was handled quickly, and as soon as the doors closed, Yuki returned to her table. That's when the judge called Tyler Cates, Schneider, and Castellano to the bench.

His Honor stared .50-caliber rounds through the defendant, saying, "Mr. Cates, this is where your presence in the courtroom ends—with one condition. You swear you will make no more comments unless you are on the stand and under oath. Do you understand?"

"I understand, Your Honor. I promise."

Judge St. John wasn't finished.

"If I continue this trial, you will spend the rest of it in a holding cell. No lunch break, no visitors except your attorney. You are dog meat until the jurors have made a decision. Or I will determine that we will have to start all over again. If so, back to jail with you until a new trial is scheduled. So count the months on your fingers. And no discount for time served if you are found guilty. I have a lot of cleaning up to do before I arrive at trial or mistrial."

The judge turned his head a few degrees and said, "Mr. Schneider, you've been a criminal defense attorney for as long as I've been a judge. Today you risked a contempt citation by not shutting down your client and removing him from the court."

"I'm very sorry about this, Your Honor."

"Sorry doesn't cut it. My staff is going to look into this charge your incredibly reckless client has made. We should know by tomorrow if there is such a place as Brookside Psychiatric, and whether or not Ms. Hayes was a patient there—and same for Mr. Cates, and if so at the same time. The results of that research will help me determine how we proceed."

Cates said, "Your Honor, I'm sorry I blurted out what I did. She's making horrible accusations."

Schneider pinched Cates's arm.

The judge turned his back on the sorrys and excuses and disappeared through the door to his chambers. As guards took Cates to holding, Gaines and Yuki gathered their things, left the courtroom, and headed toward the DA's offices.

At the same time, Red Dog was coming toward them in the corridor. In Yuki's current state, Len Parisi looked like a bristling, rust-colored heart attack.

Yuki said to Red Dog, "Len, Gaines will fill you in. I have to make a call. Deirdre is keeping Mary Elena company for a few minutes in my office and then I'm going to drive her home."

Turning away from Parisi, Yuki spoke into her phone. "Dr. Aronson, its ADA Castellano. I need your help."

The frightening scene in the courtroom played over and over again in Yuki's mind as she drove a silent Mary Elena to her apartment. Yuki felt that she had set a bear trap for herself then walked right into it. Could she have known?

Yuki stayed with Mary Elena before, during, and after her tele-session with Dr. Aronson. She made tea and then helped Mary Elena into bed.

CHAPTER 72

JOE PARKED HIS car at the intersection of Divisadero and Pine, giving him a 360-degree view of the street and cross streets. If the guy who'd left the computer was on foot, Joe might recognize him. If he was driving, Cyber Security Incorporated was St. Vartan's best or only chance to get the ghosts out of the machine.

Bao said, "I still don't get it. Why did he leave his laptop? 'I was here. Where were you? What's that?"

"What do you think?"

"He was stood up."

Joe laughed. "Thanks, I needed that."

He really did need a laugh. He was tense, tired, hungry, and exhilarated. If they succeeded, they'd be elated. People would live. If they failed, St. Vartan's was going to have to find millions and Apocalypto would still be in business.

Bao leaned toward him. "Joe. See that?"

"What? Where?"

"That dark SUV parked across the street. The driver just flashed his lights. Joe. Flash ours."

Joe turned on the lights and flashed them.

Bao said, "He's waving. To us. I think he could be wearing a green windbreaker."

"Great freaking catch, Bao. I recognize him."

Bao had called CS Inc. and spoken to Pete Wooten, who'd pinged the laptop she'd put in the footwell. He'd confirmed that it was the one Apocalypto was seeking. Joe reached Craig Steinmetz and brought him up to date. "I'll call you if we nab him."

Bao held the laptop. She would coax, untangle, trick, and in every way deploy her technological chops on that box. CS Inc. could extract the key to the malware implanted in St. Vartan's network. But they still needed the Apocalypto operator to give up what he knew.

"Joe. I think we should go talk to green windbreaker before he drives away. What about you?"

"Okay. Bao, you go around to the passenger side of his car. I'll go to the driver's side. Keep your gun down at your side."

Joe got out of the car. Keeping his eyes on the SUV but totally aware of where Bao was coming up on the passenger side, he stepped up to the driver.

"I'm Joe Molinari, FBI. We need to talk. Raise your hands. I'm opening your door now. Don't make any sudden moves."

Joe opened the driver's-side door with his left hand and showed the driver his Glock.

The driver asked, "You have my laptop?"

"Maybe," said Joe. "What's your name?"

"Robert. Nicholson. Bob."

"Bob. My partner to your right is Director Wong of the FBI. I need you to keep your hands up and get out of the car."

"Okay, I'd like to talk to you, too."

Joe's inner voice asked, *Why?* Was this the Apocalypto connection? Or had he just taken some kid's homework?

Bob said, "I'm not armed. I'm going to roll my legs out and try to stand."

Joe watched Bob awkwardly angle his way around the door frame. He tightened his core muscles and eased his legs out until he was standing.

Bao joined Joe as he threw Bob across the hood and frisked him. The guy had no weapons. His wallet held his driver's license and another picture ID. Bao first pulled Bob's right arm behind his back, then the left, and Joe cuffed him.

"Hey, take it easy," Bob complained. "And by the way, where's your warrant?"

"You had no expectancy of privacy, Bob. You left the laptop on a table in a public place. Look it up."

Now Bob Nicholson was laughing.

"Wait until I tell my friends I got arrested by the FBI for leaving my laptop at Starbucks. Oh. Am I under arrest?"

Bao said, "We're bringing you in as a person of interest in an ongoing case."

Bob said, "Starbucks is open. Why don't we—"

Bao said, "Let's talk here, Bob. What are we going to find on your laptop?"

"That's why I want to talk to you. Depending on what you

can do for me, you're going to be able to liberate St. Vartan's Hospital. And I can expose Apocalypto—all you want to know. Locations. Active operations. Weak links. Okay? But, right now, I'd say the deal is that I stay a free man, and the FBI makes sure that I don't get murdered."

CHAPTER 73

BAO WONG, JOE MOLINARI, and Bob Nicholson, the self-described negotiator for a global ransomware enterprise, sat in a semicircle of office chairs facing Craig Steinmetz's desk. The section chief was dressed in sweatpants and a gray cardigan with a cowl neck and leather buttons, loafers, no socks. Joe knew that Craig, who'd been in bed when he'd called him, had thrown on after-work clothes and made it to his office PDQ.

All of the lights were on. Papers were stacked in neat piles on Steinmetz's desk, which was bracketed by two standing flags; one the Stars and Stripes, and the other a plain blue banner with the insignia of the FBI at the center. Beyond the plate glass window, the evening sky was broken by streaks of headlights thirteen floors below. No beverages were served nor offered. Nicholson struggled out of his jacket and, with Joe's help, hung it on the back of his chair. Did he know Apocalypto's secrets or was Bob just full of crap? Craig would know.

After forty years with the Bureau, Steinmetz couldn't have been more ready for this critical interrogation. He straightened a line of pens in front of him and spoke.

"Mr. Nicholson, you're employed by a firm called Apocalypto?"

"Not exactly, sir. I work for a toy company in Amsterdam that markets toys internationally. But that's their cover. On one floor of their building, about a hundred software geniuses run the real profit center. That's Apocalypto."

"Got it," said Steinmetz. "And how did you come to work for this toy company in Amsterdam when you're a US citizen?"

"They scoped me out. Found out my grades at Caltech. My skills in advanced software technology. My job history with HP and Intel. Then I was recruited by remote interviews with flattery and mounds of shiny objects and I fell for the pitch. This was about four years ago, sir. My US citizenship doesn't come into it because I live, work, and pay my taxes here. Also, Chief, the job wasn't fully explained to me. I thought it was experimental. I typed code into my laptop—like always. Then, it got real. Am I talking too much?"

"No," Steinmetz said. "Please go on."

Bob nodded and continued the story of his life as a criminal.

"Over a few years, I was given increased incentives to negotiate with targeted firms. Most of them were industrial, but not pivotal to anything. Lawn mower manufacturer. Aluminum cans. This was all a tryout but I didn't know. The job seemed great. Creative. Challenging. I got rich. For me. But this year with the hospitals . . . Well. I'm disgusted with myself, sir."

"Convince me."

"Okay. I want to clarify, Chief. I don't select the targets. I don't create or deliver the malware. I'm just what they call the closer. I negotiate the ransom with the target, and after the payment is secured, it goes to the first of many banks who wire it to other banks. I am not part of that, sir, but eventually it gets back to a bank in the Netherlands. For a while I rationalized that once we were out of the victims' hair, we left them more secure than when we broke in."

Bao said, "Big of you, Bob. Did you assign a value to the people who died because of the malware?"

"No. No. I tinkered with the program, I talked to executives by internet, but when I asked about a human toll, I was iced. 'Not your job. Hospitals are insured . . .'"

Steinmetz said, "All right. I get it, Bob. You're a go-between, you're saying, an upstanding citizen with computer skills who got duped by terrorists."

Joe was watching Bob carefully. It seemed to him that Bob had never imagined a moment like this. He was scared. Leaving his laptop at Starbucks hadn't prepared him to confess to the Federal Bureau of Investigation's top man in San Francisco. He wiped his eyes with his sleeve.

Steinmetz rooted in his center drawer, found a packet of tissues, and slid it across the desk.

Bob was stammering now. "Sir . . . I was willfully blind and I don't forgive myself . . . But for context, this was very heady stuff for a fat kid from a factory town who got scholarships and grades and a way out of Nowheresville . . . I want to earn a clean reboot . . ."

Steinmetz said, "So you're going to quit your job, whether or not you get protection from the FBI?"

"Yes, sir. But without protection, I'll be killed. And Apocalypto will live."

CHAPTER 74

CLAIRE AND I drove separately to Susie's and parked about a half a block away. Just the sight of those windows blazing with light was enough to buck me up. I linked arms with Claire as we walked toward the entrance. I did all the talking, as Claire was unusually quiet.

"Something eating you, Butterfly? Talk to me."

Claire's sigh was long and deep.

"Claire?"

"Sorry. I was thinking about some results I'm waiting on. I was collecting scrapings from under Jamie Fricke's fingernails yesterday and noticed that his right hand was a little swollen and the knuckles were slightly abraded. Like he'd punched someone. Probably just before he dropped dead."

"Claire, this is huge. You're thinking he slugged his killer?"

"Or he scraped the sidewalk. All I know right now is that he skinned his knuckles. Anyway, I swabbed each knuckle, segregated the swabs, covered his hand with gauze, and asked the lab to rush it through rapid DNA. Maybe it'll match to his killer."

I asked the air, "How did we miss this?"

"Linds. When I got to the scene, there were ten people inside the perimeter—say, a hundred square feet. And twice as many true crime addicts were outside the tape, taking pictures, shouting questions. Fricke was lying face down in pooling blood. We got him into the van quick—"

I said, "No, it's okay. I'm feeling some hope . . ."

"Me, too," said Claire. "Some. But I'd advise you to keep it in check."

And then we were at Susie's front door.

I pulled it open and the aroma of spice billowed out to the sidewalk along with light, laughter, and the jazzy beat of steel drums. I held the door for Claire and she smiled as the Yellow Bird Band launched into an original tune. The room itself calls up the image of a yellow bird. The walls are the color of ripe mangoes and hung with hand-painted market scenes in the Jamaican style.

Susie was setting up the main floor for the limbo competition and the long bar to our right was packed with regulars who were tossing 'em back without falling off their stools. The barkeep was half-past thirty, played trombone, had a mop of yellow hair, and was wearing a flowered shirt with a name tag reading "Fireman."

He waved and called out to us as Claire and I pushed through the main room, then took the corridor that skirts the kitchen's pass-through window and opens into a smaller, quieter dining area.

Susie's back-room waitress, our friend Lorraine O'Dea,

whistled to get our attention and pointed to "our" booth. Yuki was already seated there, scrunched back in the corner wearing a designer suit and a smile that fell short of happy. Claire slid into the booth next to her. I took the bench seat across from them.

Claire said, "Let's get something to drink. I'm ready."

Lorraine read our faces. She brought over menus and a pitcher of draft plus three frosty beer mugs, and asked Yuki if beer was okay.

Yuki's "go wild" drink is a fruity margarita—she downs tequila like soda water. Then she giggles and sings. I was glad when she said "Sure" to the brew.

I said, "Lorraine, chips and dip until Cindy gets here?"

"You bet."

Claire waited for Yuki to put down half her beer, then placed her hand on Yuki's arm and asked, "You got something to share, sweetie?"

Yuki said, "Oh, boy. I hate to have to say this."

I said, "This is about Mary Elena?"

Yuki nodded. "Wasn't her fault. It was all going well. She was fine in court and on the stand. Then Tyler Cates, that SOB, jumps up and says that he *knew* her. *That they were in a mental institution together.* Brookside Psychiatric. And he hadn't been sworn in. He was at the counsel table when he got to his feet and bellowed this crap out to the jury."

CHAPTER 75

MY JAW ACTUALLY dropped as I pictured Tyler Cates blowing up Yuki's case with his news that he and Mary Elena had both been patients at Brookside Psychiatric.

Then I sputtered, "That's bull, right?"

"We don't yet know," Yuki groaned. "It's near impossible to get hold of medical information. But I googled it. There's a Brookside Psychiatric in Bangor, Maine; in Louisville, Kentucky; and in Pensacola, Florida. Also a Brookside Wellness—a chain of clinics—and a couple of Brookside Mental Health Spas. Those are all in different states, with different laws, and given HIPAA rules, the patient has to sign on the dotted line or you can't find out beans."

I heard myself say "Oh, man" just thinking of the legal hurdles that would have to be cleared to get protected information.

Claire said, "Hold up a second. Just so I understand. If Cates really did know Mary Elena—just sayin'—how does that affect the charges of an obvious violent rape and beating?"

Yuki said, "Mary Elena's credibility is at stake. There were no witnesses to the crime, so it's 'he said, she said.' Yes, she was brutalized, but she also said she didn't know Cates. She said under oath that a stranger demanded sex. He said she's the one who asked for it. So. If she demanded sex from someone she used to know, some people would say it wasn't rape. Aggravated assault? Very possible. Still. One vote could hang the jury, and Cates could get a hall pass."

I asked, "Can Cates document his time at Brookside?"

"No idea," Yuki said.

"And what about Mary Elena?"

"She says it never happened. No way." Yuki went on. "Red Dog would have to move mountains to get this information if Brookside was in San Francisco. Even then, he'd have to pull a million strings. He's barely speaking to me because he said this case sucked from the beginning."

Yuki, Claire, and I had all been at the scene of the crime. This was a case that had to be tried and won, and I said so.

Yuki continued, "Our best chances are with Judge St. John. He's fierce and he's furious. He also doesn't want to lose this jury and have to start over. We're hoping he instructs the jurors to ignore all references to Brookside, as there's no actual evidence or sworn testimony."

"Or?"

"Or he can call a mistrial. Even Red Dog would rather get a mistrial and forget it. We'll find out in the morning. I wish Cindy was here to give you the eyewitness journalist's version. Where is she, anyway?"

In an exception to the "no phones" rule, I turned on my phone, as did Claire. There was a text for me from Joe.

I'll be home late, Blondie. I called Mrs. Rose and she's got the kiddo and the doggo.

That's when Claire called out over the restaurant racket, "Here she comes."

I turned to see Cindy dressed in a pretty floral dress coming down the corridor and into the room.

She wasn't alone.

CHAPTER 76

CINDY HAD BROUGHT her mother.

Darcy Thomas was right behind her daughter as they entered the Women's Murder Club special dining room. We'd all met Darcy before at a party for Cindy's first book, *Fish's Girl.* We'd had dinner together with paper plates in hand at Book Passage in Corte Madera, and had unanimously liked her. The family resemblance was there. Darcy had the same bone structure and curly hair, and she also had an easy laugh over stubborn determination.

Lorraine moved a chair to the end of the table so we could all fit at the booth. Darcy slid in next to me and reached out for a hug, which I was glad to give and receive. She reached across the table and bumped fists with Yuki and Claire.

"So good to see you all. Am I interrupting a serious Murder Club meeting?"

Claire spoke up, saying, "Not at all, Darcy. We were summing up. We know the menu and can make recommendations."

"No time to eat," she said. "Time for a drink, maybe."

Lorraine had her pad in hand and took our dinner orders, Darcy's order for a glass of Chardonnay, and Cindy's request for a mug of beer, then disappeared as if in a puff of smoke.

Darcy said to the table, "This was a one-day turnaround trip. I'll have dinner on the plane, but I do have a problem for the club's consideration, and I hope you all can help out."

Cindy groaned, "Oh, God."

Lorraine brought wine for Darcy, a mug for Cindy, and I used the moment to call Joe. He picked up.

"Can't talk now, Linds. Sorry."

"Later?" I said. "I'll be home in an hour. Or so."

"Don't wait up," he said. "I've got no idea when . . . I gotta go."

He clicked off and I hung up on dead air.

Lorraine came back quickly with our food, and as Darcy was dipping chips, I said, "Darcy, you wanted to brainstorm with us?"

When Cindy's mug was topped up, Darcy said, "Let me say first, no guns are involved. No one gets injured. No ambulances are needed."

CHAPTER 77

DARCY WAS A natural comic, and the three of us laughed, of course, until Cindy said, "Mom, spit it out, will you? You're being overly dramatic."

"Cindy, you tell it, okay? I'm exhausted," said Darcy.

"We went shopping!" Cindy said. "For wedding gowns."

"Ohhhhhh," two or three of us said in unison.

Darcy jumped back in. "There are three semifinalists down from thirty. Cindy is not even committed to a type of dress. You need to write a column about this, Cynthia. Find out how other women deal with the life-and-death decision of buying a wedding gown."

Yuki started to laugh, her bell-like chortle so full of glee, it was impossible to hear without joining in. Even Darcy, who was clearly all worn out, blew wine out of her nose, and Claire slapped the table repeatedly as she guffawed.

When we were all breathing normally again, Claire asked the table, "Where's the rub? Cindy looks good in anything. And for the something borrowed, wear my pearls."

Yuki said, "Please put me on the gown jury. Do you have pictures of the contenders?"

"Why, yes we do," Darcy said.

While we dug into our dinners, Darcy passed around her phone with its picture gallery open to the three top choices. Cindy peered at the time on her phone, then asked her mother if she should call her an Uber.

"That would be great, honey," Darcy said.

Cindy requested the ride and got a confirmation. She wasn't in the mood for fiery food or more interference in her gown selection, but she bore up, and made comments about the last three standing: "That one," she said, "makes me look pregnant and I am definitely not. Number two," she said, "looks like it was made on the cheap in a sweatshop."

Darcy said, "Designer gown, by the way."

Cindy ignored her mother. She said, "This, the third loser, looks good on Mother, but it's a closeout and it's two sizes too big for me."

Darcy scoffed.

Just then, Cindy's phone pinged.

Cindy said, "Your ride is here, Mom."

"I should go, too," I said.

I gave Claire some folding money to cover my share, said good night to her and Yuki, then Cindy and I walked Darcy Thomas out to her ride. I gave Darcy a good hug, told her I'd see her at the wedding.

"Cindy will be wearing white," I said. "I guarantee it."

"Cross your heart?"

"Uh, no."

Cindy gave me a soft punch in the arm.

I was laughing again as I opened the car door for Darcy and waved goodbye. I hugged Cindy, too, saying, "Let's talk tomorrow."

We kissed cheeks, then I jogged down the block to my blue Explorer, the third nearly identical model I've had in the last several years due to on-the-job gunfire. Yes, this is truly what I do for a living.

Skipping past that, I focused on how in twenty minutes I'd be bringing Julie and Martha home from day care with their nanny, our neighbor Mrs. Gloria Rose, and that I'd be home for Joe when he came through the door. Whatever time that was.

CHAPTER 78

JOE WATCHED BOB SWEAT.

Bob Nicholson was speaking from his heart, but he hadn't seen around this corner and the consequences had just gotten real. He asked for a glass of water and Steinmetz shook his head no.

"Keep talking, Bob."

"I see it like this," Bob said. "I can show St. Vartan's protection team how to put the hospital behind a virtual wall. I can destroy the Apocalypto program from the root, and I can tell you how to shut down the decision-makers. All tonight."

Steinmetz sat forward in his chair, said, "Did you negotiate with Oakland Pediatrics?"

"Yes, sir. Sorry to say. I saw the headlines. And the photos. Before you ask me 'Then, why St. Vartan's?' there was no way to turn down the assignment. One guy I know did that, and I heard that he'd gotten a bullet and a wood-chipper funeral."

Steinmetz grunted his ambivalence, but Joe knew that he had decided.

Steinmetz said, "And what you want from us is a new identity and location in exchange for putting the hospital's computer network back together, protecting it, and destroying Apocalypto."

"Yes, sir."

Steinmetz said, "Okay, Bob. I've had you checked out. Quantico. Interpol. Seems you are who you say you are."

He turned his chair a few degrees and said, "Bao, call Wooten and Thordarson and have them get LaBreche down to the hospital."

Joe said, "And the IT guy, Walters."

Steinmetz said, "Fine. Joe, US marshals are waiting downstairs to take you three to St. Vartan's. Call me when you're on-site. Marshals will be responsible for Bob. You and Bao stick with him until CS Inc. confirms that the hospital is in the clear. I'll be here and available. Joe, I need a few minutes with you alone when the job is done. Bob, if you fail, you'll be detained and charged. Understand?"

"Yes, sir."

Steinmetz took a sheet of paper from a folder on his desk and offered it to Bob, saying "This agreement protects both parties. You do your part to our satisfaction and you get a new ID and relocation to a small town in Bulgaria."

Bob laughed. "Let me see."

Steinmetz handed him the agreement. Joe saw by Bob's nods and uh-huhs that he accepted the terms that he would be relocated to a city in the USA with a new identity. Bob picked up a pen from the line of them on the chief's desk. He signed the document, Steinmetz signed, and Joe witnessed the signatures. Steinmetz put the document back in his drawer.

Steinmetz said, "Take care of this tonight, Bob. Save some lives. Redeem yourself."

FRIDAY

CHAPTER 79

AT 2:00 A.M., five hours after the meeting with Steinmetz, Joe was back in the chief's office with vending machine coffee and cinnamon rolls in front of him.

Steinmetz said, "Bao called. She says it all went like quicksilver. St. Vartan's network has been repaired, tested, and approved. You agree?"

Joe said, "Craig, I watched. I looked the part and asked questions, but really, my technical knowledge has its limits. Bao and CS Inc. were satisfied. I'd say more than satisfied."

"Tech speech is irritating, isn't it?"

"Yep, language from outer space. The marshals have Bob in lockup while we work out his part of the deal."

"Very good. And I've got something for you," Steinmetz said.

He opened his drawer and took out a folder and handed it across the desk to Joe. There was a number two envelope inside the folder, Joe's name typed on the front.

Joe wondered if it was another job offer. Steinmetz had tried to lure him back full-time, but so far Joe had resisted.

Steinmetz said, "I fast-tracked this."

He sat back in his chair and had a bit of a grin on his face. Joe put his thumb under the flap, pulled it across the back of the envelope, then fished out the enclosed sheet of paper. There was one double-spaced paragraph.

"Craig, thank you. I want to discuss this with Lindsay."

"Fine. I need an answer by this time next week. Okay?"

"Thanks again, Craig. I'll let you know."

The two men stood up, shook hands, and took the elevator down to the street together.

CHAPTER 80

I WAS STARTLED awake at some time before dawn. My bedside clock tells the day and the weather as well as the time. Six forty. Friday. Overcast, no chance of rain. My clock never lies.

I closed my eyes, hoping I'd fall back asleep, but no. I was thinking about Jamie and Holly Fricke, their bodies spread out on the street, killed only six months apart.

I had a nine o'clock meeting with Rae Bergen. Holly's younger sister had resisted cooperating with the investigation but had finally agreed to meet with me and Rich at the Frickes' house before the funeral service at ten. Not much time for us to question Rae, who'd known Holly her entire life and was also one of Jamie's longtime lovers.

I was determined, though, to get what I could from her in the time allowed, with Conklin's help. We had under an hour to put a dent in the case, but Rich was an ace at interviewing women.

I rolled over and reached for Joe.

"You awake?" I whispered.

"No," he said. "What day is it?"

"Friday. How'd it go?"

"Hmmmmm?"

"Laptop guy?"

"He saved the day, hon. He wants to make good."

"For St. Vartan's?"

"Sure. He was Apocalypto's. Man with Oakland. Pediatrics. Too."

"Seriously? And you caught him?"

"He grew a connn . . ."

"Conscience?"

"Mmmmm."

"Joe?"

He had slipped right back to sleep. I kissed my fingers and touched his cheek and whispered, "I've got to hustle. Got a funeral to go to."

Joe smiled and held up crossed fingers without opening his eyes, then, "Gloria's coming at eight."

"Excellent."

I gave him a full body hug and got out of bed.

Getting a too-short explanation of how or if Joe had closed the Apocalypto business down was like having the power go out while watching a thriller. Joe had said that the ransomware guy had saved the day. Good to know, but I could have used a few more details. Where did things stand now?

I was still thinking about the possibilities, trying to solve the crime with nothing to go on, as I got ready for the day. I spent five minutes in the rain box, then blow-dried my hair. I stepped into pointy shoes for the first time in so long, my feet protested. I slid my smart black dress over my head and hung a gold cross on a chain around my neck. I was brushing my hair when the doorbell rang. I greeted Gloria Rose, our saving grace. She was early.

We had one of our shorthand conversations where I ticked off the few items on the Molinari to-do list. I wrote a note to Joe, and when Julie stumbled out of her room with Martha I was grinning. Julie's curls, black like Joe's, fell over her blue eyes. She put her arms around my waist. I kissed the top of her head, ruffled Martha's ears, and last, asked Mrs. Rose how I looked.

"Like you're going to a funeral."

We laughed, and sandwiching Julie between us, I hugged Mrs. Rose. I kissed Julie again and told her how much I love, love, love my little girl.

"When Daddy wakes up I'm going to teach him a new game," Julie said.

"Make sure he's had his breakfast first, Bugs, okay?"

"Put on some lipstick," said Mrs. Rose.

Copy that.

CHAPTER 81

ONCE I WAS buckled up in my Explorer and headed to Pacific Heights, I replayed my waking thoughts around and around on a closed loop. The Fricke conundrum. The Holly and Jamie executions. The clueless house staff. Claire's sharp observation of Jamie's skinned knuckles. She'd pulled a rabbit out of her scrubs pocket.

And I thought about Rae Bergen, divorced mother of one, seen in Los Angeles's hottest playgrounds, known as a party girl with writing talent that might eventually pay off.

I was dying to meet this woman who'd been having a long-term affair with her sister's husband. It wasn't unheard of but it was uncommon. Is that why Rae had put me off until now?

I reached the Frickes' house about fifteen minutes after leaving home. A moment later, Richie's old Bronco rolled up the house's curving driveway and braked behind me. He got out of the car, handed me a container of coffee, and I smiled. The kindness of this man.

I said, "You didn't sleep, either?"

"It wasn't the case," he said. "It was Cindy."

"What about her?"

"She was flipping. Flopping. Getting out of bed. Coming back. Kicking the mattress. Talking in her sleep."

"It's not about you, Richie. It's about marriage in general. She never imagined it for herself. You know this."

"You didn't sleep, either," he said to me.

"Joe had a big assignment from Steinmetz. He didn't get home until about three."

"Apocalypto?"

"Bingo," I said. "All good. St. Vartan's is back in business."

"Thank God."

Richie crossed himself, sighed. "Details?"

"I wish. Joe fell asleep while talking."

We both laughed.

"I'm going to sleep all day tomorrow if I have to go to a hotel," he said.

I said, "Great idea. Meanwhile . . ."

"Yeah. Will Rae talk to us? Or will she not? Do you get why she wouldn't talk?"

"I think so. My guess is, she loved Holly and Jamie, both at the same time. Or, the obvious: something she doesn't want to tell us. We'll find out, but it would be easier if she didn't live in Malibu."

I took a deep breath, then said to Richie, "After the funeral she's going home."

Rich put an arm around my shoulders and gave me a little squeeze. "She'll talk to us," he said.

Most of the time, Rich was right. He had sharp instincts and could tease out the truth from a sphinx. But no one scored 100 percent on breaking down a suspect without having leverage and in a short time. Not even my partner.

We walked up the pathway to the front door, then I reached out and rang the doorbell.

CHAPTER 82

ARTHUR BEVAQUA OPENED the front door.

"Sergeant, good to see you."

"Same here, Arthur. You remember my partner."

"Of course. Inspector Conklin. Come in."

I asked Arthur, "How are you doing?"

"I feel lost. Do I have a job?"

"This is a big one, Arthur. See what Rae has in mind. And I suggest don't make any sudden moves."

He showed me that his hands were empty, prompting us to grin. We three walked together down the long carpeted hallway lined with old masters that today held no magic for me. I knew the way from the hallway to the domed glass room with its exotic plant life and wide view of the Pacific.

There were a dozen small round tables in the solarium, one of which was set for three. A dark-haired woman in black was sitting at one of them with her back to the entrance. We followed Arthur to the table. He said, "Ms. Rae, this is Sergeant Boxer and Inspector Conklin from the SFPD."

I thanked him, and Rich and I took our seats. I heard Arthur calling Rafe on the phone, asking him to move the cars. I told Rae that we were sorry for her tragic loss, after which Arthur took our order and disappeared.

I said, "Ms. Bergen."

"Call me Rae."

"Rae. I'm the lead investigator on James Fricke's murder. I know we have very little time today, so with your help, we'd like to get some basic information, and any ideas you may have on whoever killed James and Holly."

"I want to help, Sergeant. You don't have to persuade me."

"Good."

I took out my phone and showed her what I had for her address in Malibu, her phone numbers and email addresses, and she confirmed them.

"I'm going to record this interview, Rae. It will save a lot of time. You can ask me as many questions as we have time for. And we can follow up on the phone, or here, or in Malibu."

"Fine with me. May I have your card?"

I passed a card to Rae, and Conklin asked, "I'd like to hear this from you. What was your relationship with James Fricke?"

"I loved him. He loved me. Yes, he was married to my sister, a complicated story. But my sister knew about his free-ranging social life. And that went both ways. Holly had lovers, too. She didn't love Jamie anymore. Or even like him. Or so she told me."

I asked, "How often did you and Jamie see each other?"

"When we could. I live some six hours away by car. I don't like to fly. So, I only saw Jamie about once a month."

Rae told us what she knew about Jamie's schedule since Holly died, that his sons from his first marriage were living in Switzerland as was his first wife, Talia, and that Arthur would have the soccer schedule.

Conklin asked Rae if she knew of anyone who'd threatened Holly or Jamie, if either of them had made big changes in their lives, if Jamie had gambling debts, if Holly could have been the target of a rejected lover.

Rae answered the questions credibly and without hesitation. Four nos one after another. And when she looked at her watch, I knew that our breakfasts of tea and freshly baked rolls would go untouched. That in five minutes or less, our interview with Rae would be over, we would be inside the Frickes' private chapel, and we might not have a chance to speak with Rae in person again.

I put my hand on her forearm and asked, "Rae. Where were you on this past Tuesday morning?"

"When Jamie was murdered? I was at home," she said. "My ex-husband, Christophe Picard, had stayed overnight."

I said, "I've read about Christophe. He has a restaurant here in Presidio Heights."

"Yes," Rae said. "He lives here in San Francisco. On Monday, the day before Jamie was shot, Christophe drove down to LA. We spent the day at Venice Beach with our son, Brock, and then Christophe stayed over with me, which was fine with Jamie. There were no issues there. I can introduce you to Christophe at the funeral."

We thanked Rae for her time, and on my way out the door, I stopped to have a few words with Arthur. He liked Rae.

But although he'd known her for twenty years, he didn't know her well.

"Arthur, yes or no? Would you trust her?"

"I couldn't say," said Arthur.

That meant no.

CHAPTER 83

YUKI BUTTONED THE jacket on her red "closing statement" suit. The case against Tyler Cates had been going as well as Yuki had hoped; she'd been steady, believable, hadn't dropped a single stitch—until Cates had set off an H-bomb saying that he had known Mary Elena when they'd both been patients at a mental institution called Brookside Psychiatric. That was his explanation for why she'd asked him for sex in the changing room at Xe Sogni. He said that they were old friends, both of them crazy.

An advanced computer search showed no fewer than thirty mental institutions with "Brookside" in its name, and as she'd lamented to Lindsay and Claire, they crisscrossed the United States from Bangor to Pensacola, from Baton Rouge to Seattle. Mary Elena had no living relatives who could support or deny Cates's whopper, and if either the DA or the defense found a Brookside Mental anything, the institution would be highly unlikely to turn over records to any lawyer without a subpoena. And there were too many reasons to count why no subpoena would be forthcoming in her lifetime.

Red Dog had been against Yuki taking this case, but he was sympathetic to her current dilemma.

"You did your best. No. Yuki, you did great. And after you give your closing, it's out of our hands."

At 9:00 a.m. Yuki and Nick Gaines took their seats at their counsel table in 8G. Normally, Gaines was as put together as an actor playing Young Dad in a cereal commercial. Today, he looked as though he'd slept in his car. Too much lack of sleep.

Returning Yuki's appraising look, Gaines said of her suit, "Red for the win?"

"I also have my toes crossed and a four-leaf clover in my pocket. I don't think Mary Elena will feel better by lunch recess."

"Is she actually sick?"

"She was re-traumatized, Nicky. There was the original trauma by her grandfather, the attack in Xe Sogni, and now Cates shouting his stinking trash and calling her a liar. Do you think she was actually in a mental institution with Cates?"

"I didn't say that," Gaines said.

But Yuki knew he'd thought it. If Brookside was a real place, and Mary Elena Hayes and Tyler Cates had both been patients there, Mary Elena's multiple personalities would protect her from the shock if Tyler Cates was found not guilty. But her attorneys would have no protection against the crushing disappointment. The loss. Six months gone. Trust in their client gone.

This wouldn't be the first or last time they'd be whacked by a case that had gone upside down without warning. The feeling was certainty that you'd screwed up, despite the facts and the hard work, and it never got easier. Hell.

But Yuki believed in that woman. She'd put her money on Mary Elena over that shit Cates any day.

CHAPTER 84

THE COURTROOM WAS packed, just shy of standing room only. Officer Louie Mack signaled a guard to close the double doors, then he escorted the jurors into their box and swore them in. When they were seated, the door cracked open between the courtroom and the judge's chambers, and the Honorable Henry William St. John entered and took the bench.

Yuki turned her head a few degrees to the left, surprised to see that defense counsel Ed Schneider wasn't yet seated when every other day he'd been early. She said so to Gaines.

He said, "Maybe he's talking sense to Cates."

"Hmph," said Yuki. "So, what's he saying?"

"'Retract this Brookside garbage or you're going to have a lifetime in a cell to regret it.'"

Yuki said, "Maybe. Cates is vile, but to this day, I don't think he gets it."

Gaines said, "Makes him a psychopath, doesn't it?"

Just then, their conversation was derailed by a rising buzz

in the gallery. Judge St. John slammed his gavel down, demanding quiet, which he got. Everything about him, from his precise haircut and trimmed mustache to his controlled scowl and the neat pleat of his robes, said that this judge meant what he said. Quiet.

When the room was silent, the judge cleared his throat and the bailiff called the court to order.

Yuki and Gaines turned their heads at the sound of the double doors opening. Louie Mack opened them wide and Ed Schneider stumped through, unapologetic as he took his seat at the defense counsel table.

The judge acknowledged him with a nod, then called on Yuki. "Are the People ready with their closing argument?"

"We are, Your Honor."

Yuki got to her feet and stepped out into the well to face the jury. At the same time, the counsel for the defense stood and asked if he might address the judge at the bench.

"Mr. Schneider, Ms. Castellano, please approach."

Two minutes later, the judge ordered the courtroom cleared.

CHAPTER 85

DURING THE RECESS, Cindy grabbed two cans of sparkling water plus a sandwich and a fruit salad from the snack cart outside the Hall and brought them up to Yuki's office.

"Chicken and bacon with mayo okay?" she asked. "If not I'll trade you for my fruit salad."

"Either way," said Yuki. "I don't think I can taste anything."

Yuki seemed to have no appetite but looked glad to have Cindy as company. Cindy was thinking of the *Chronicle*'s six o'clock deadline and had hopes she could update the Hayes v. Cates story in time. It was rare for Yuki to give her exclusive news on the record, but today might be one of those days.

Cindy passed a can of sparkling water to Yuki, pulled the tab on hers. She slid the sandwich to Yuki's side of the desk and unsealed the container of fruit salad, took a bite of melon, and dialed down whatever feverish expression might be giving her real hunger away. Yuki took a bite of her sandwich, apparently determined not to let Cindy bully her for any front-page tidbits.

Cindy, sitting across the desk from Yuki, was finding it hard not to interrogate her friend. What did Yuki know? And would she tell her? She watched Yuki take her sandwich apart, push a strip of bacon around with her fork, pick it up with her fingers and chew on it for a while. Cindy drank her seltzer and waited. And then, she had to ask.

"Yuki, what caused St. John to call a recess? Schneider asked to talk to the judge, then the judge asked for the prosecution, too. You all spoke for exactly two point seven seconds. You and Schneider went back to your tables and St. John said, 'Court is adjourned until further notice.' I was there, Yuki. I can write that."

"Sure, Cin. Not a problem."

"So, Yuki. Judge says, 'Court is adjourned.' But you and Schneider don't leave when the room is emptied, so I think there's some story here."

Yuki said, "Cin, I would give you a *kidney,* but this is . . ."

Cindy said, "Let me guess. Off-limits. But. What if I give you one of *my* organs? How about my liver?"

Yuki laughed, and Cindy was laughing too when Len Parisi's shadow crossed the doorway.

Yuki looked up. "You need me, Len?"

"Judge wants to meet in chambers. Now."

CHAPTER 86

THE FRICKE FAMILY chapel, circa 1853, had been built on a treed quarter-acre lot behind the Frickes' house. The white, wood-frame structure was hidden from the road below by the house and a large copse of trees. There were stained glass windows on the long sides, a red painted front door, and a simple cross at the top of the steeple.

By a quarter to ten, Fricke friends and family had gathered on the freshly mown chapel lawn while Conklin and I stood at the edge of the tree line. I had brought Cappy's annotated photo from Holly's funeral and we were attaching names to faces and getting a feeling for the gathering. Some of the mourners were dabbing at their tears or crying out loud. Some were enjoying themselves. Looked like they were at a class reunion or party of old friends.

After scanning the crowd, I put the photo away in my bag and we waded in. Conklin went over to Patty Delaney and cut her from the herd. I couldn't hear their conversation, but she wasn't hysterical the way she'd been a few days ago. I found

Judy Borinstein, looking smart in a navy-blue suit and gold accessories. She was speaking to a tearful woman I recognized as Marilyn Stein, a.k.a. Marly, Holly's assistant and another of Jamie's lovers, now living in New York City. Borinstein was in business mode as was I, and I broke into their conversation. Marilyn stiffened her face to me and started to move away.

Borinstein caught her by the arm and said, "Marly, we're lucky to have Sergeant Boxer leading this investigation. Spend a few minutes with her, why don't you?"

Then Judy was called away.

Marly asked me, "Have you gotten anywhere in Holly's death?"

"Not yet. It's possible that this investigation into Jamie's death will turn up a clue in Holly's."

Marly shrugged and looked past me, her expression meant to convey, *Whatevah. I couldn't care less.*

I said, "Ms. Stein, I know that Mr. Fricke cared about you very much. We need your help."

"I can't tell you anything. I left the Frickes' employ after Holly was murdered. It's been six months."

The lawn had emptied and this might be the last time I'd spend time with this woman.

"Marly, very simply, who wanted Holly dead?"

"Holly would say that I did."

Conklin came over in time to hear this exchange. He said to Marly, "Why do you say that?"

"I knew too much about her," Marly said. "I signed a six-page NDA but that didn't stand up to how much Jamie loved me. I was a servant by day and a madly in love idiot a few nights a month when he and I were together. Holly knew all of that. It's a humiliation that will cost me thirty years in therapy and I doubt I will ever trust a man again. But I didn't kill Holly or Jamie. I have a job and a roommate and a doorman in New York, all of whom can testify to where I was when Jamie was killed."

I asked for names and numbers and Marly gave them to me. I had other questions. Had there had been any hate mail or threatening phone calls to Holly, any aggression from Jamie toward Holly, anything that at that time, or in retrospect, made her suspect that Holly or Jamie might be in serious danger?

Marly said no to everything, her face frozen to stop her emotions from breaching the banks of a lake of bitterness. She emphatically claimed that she was and had been an ingenue when Holly hired her, unprepared to handle the complex emotions of both of the Frickes.

"Arthur can back up everything I've said," she spat. "There are no secrets from Arthur Bevaqua. He knows everything. Good luck, Sergeant. I'm a dead end."

CHAPTER 87

I WATCHED MARILYN STEIN walk away; stiff, angry, and not afraid to show it. I wondered if she was the one who'd made the phone call to Jamie on his last morning, if she had summoned him to his death. Had she hired someone to put him down? Had she done it herself? It would take a few phone calls to airlines to see if Marilyn Stein had flown from New York to San Francisco earlier this week.

I looked around for Richie, saw he was still working the crowd. I also saw brooding women, men drinking alone under shade trees who looked away as I caught their eyes. There was a touch on the back of my arm. I turned around. Rae Bergen was there with a tall, good-looking man of about forty.

She introduced me and Conklin to Christophe Picard, her ex-husband and companion of two decades. Christophe, a chef, said, "By the way, I have a bistro on Sacramento Street—Chez Bonhomie. You are both welcome to drop by and speak with me anytime. I doubt I know anything useful, but I'll definitely serve you a meal you won't forget."

Rae said, "See that gloomy young man over there by the drinks? Gray jacket? That's our son, Brock."

I looked and saw a college-age boy standing beside the bar area. Brock was taller than Rae, had an athletic build, and had a look on his face I couldn't read.

I mentioned wanting to speak with Brock, get his impressions of his uncle.

Rae said, "Good luck. Brock barely even talks to us. I had to plead with him to come to the funeral for my sake. Don't be offended if he just walks away from you."

Christophe said, "Sergeant, Brock's generation would rather text than talk, and he's in his own world at school—four hours from here."

The door to the chapel opened, and the guests filed inside. I took Richie's arm and followed the mourners into the chapel, where we took two seats on the aisle at the rear.

The service was ecumenical. The officiant was Judge Susan Anderson. She had not known James Fricke III, but she spoke as a woman who understood the loss felt by those saying last goodbyes to the dead. Anderson exhorted them—us—to think of the good life Jamie Fricke had lived.

She asked who would like to speak, and hands went up. Arthur Bevaqua stood, took the podium, and spoke of Mr. Jamie as a man who'd shaped his life and taught him to strive for excellence in all things. Arthur said that he loved Mr. Jamie and Mrs. Holly and always would.

Most of the eulogies were given by people I didn't know well. I noted that neither Jamie's first wife nor his sons had flown in to attend his funeral. Not even by Zoom. Rae took the podium to say that she'd known Jamie since before she'd been maid of honor at his and Holly's wedding.

"Although I don't believe in an afterlife, if there is one, Jamie will be having a party for Holly, for their friends who have passed. God bless Jamie and Holly. God bless us all."

I took note of these rehearsed speeches, especially those from Jamie's former lovers, and excepting Patty Delaney, no one fell apart or crossed a line. A prayer was offered by Judy Borinstein, and Sage Dugan, a member of the staff, sang a hymn in French, "J'irai la voir un jour." At one point her voice had cracked, but she'd taken a breath, then picked up where she'd left off.

Conklin and I paid our respects to Jamie in his casket at the front of the chapel; a man no longer powerful, narcissistic, charming, unfaithful. We signed a visitor's book, and I left my phone number and email address in the space provided.

We left the chapel before the hearse and the limos took the long drive out to Cypress Lawn in Colma. Rafe Talbot brought our cars around to the front of the house.

"Good luck, Sergeant," Rafe said to me. "You still have Greta's number? My girlfriend? Please call me there if I can help in any way."

I wondered again about Rafe, this pleasant middle-aged man who'd done time for car theft at nineteen. He lived on the Fricke property and was closely tied to Jamie's movements. We would need to talk to Rafe Talbot again.

As Conklin and I walked down the path to our cars, I composed a short email on my phone to Team Fricke, copied Brady, and pressed Send.

CHAPTER 88

THE JUDGE'S CHAMBERS were lined with bookshelves, carpeted in Oriental rugs, and appointed with mid-century modern furnishings. Judge St. John himself looked as though he'd stepped off the cover of a plump 1955 *Life* magazine featuring the California Department of Justice.

He sat behind his desk facing the door, with the window behind him looking out on Bryant Street. Red Dog sat to the judge's right. Yuki Castellano and her deputy sat at right angles to Parisi. Schneider sat across the room from the prosecution, with an empty seat beside him for Cates.

Also to the judge's right was a thirty-two-inch TV on a stand, Tyler Cates's image on the screen. Cates was sitting on a metal slab bed, with a blanket, no mattress. His head was in his hands and his body language told all. The young man was depressed or worse. On the screen, court officer Robert Wells, who was well-known around the Hall, approached the holding cell.

Cates asked, "What's up?"

Wells said, "You, your attorney, and the prosecution are meeting with the judge now. If I were you, I'd behave."

"Who asked you?"

"Do as you wish," said Wells and unlocked the gate. He cuffed Cates and walked him out of the holding cell.

His Honor turned off the CCTV and phoned his assistant.

"Susan. When Wells arrives with Cates, ask them to wait outside with you for a few minutes. I may ask you to take them to conference room A."

CHAPTER 89

THE JUDGE TURNED back to the attorneys in his chambers.

He said to the defense counsel, "Ed, because of Mr. Cates's eruption in court, I had to check it out. I put every free hand in the justice department on duty yesterday, last night, and early this morning. They made calls to every mental institution with 'Brookside' in its name. There are thirty in the country. And we hopped over the Canadian border while we were at it. None of the institutions had ever had a Tyler Cates or Mary Elena Hayes as patients, ever. One or two of them had closed, but we chased down heads of these defunct places who were working at other mental institutions. As Mr. Cates produced no documentation of his time spent in a mental institution, we not only went as far as we could go. We went farther.

"In my heavily researched opinion, Tyler Cates lied to confuse the jury, to get them on his side. I can't let it stand. I could call a mistrial but it would only serve to encourage your client to repeat this performance in a new trial.

“Ed, when Cates gets here, I suggest you talk to him in the conference room. Tell him this is a come to Jesus moment and if he doesn’t tell the actual truth, I’m going to put him in jail and throw away the key for all of eternity.

“Len. If Cates confesses, will you consider giving him a break?”

“Meaning?”

There was a knock on the door. Court officer Susan O’Connor opened it about ten inches, looked back toward the judge, and said, “They’re here.”

Judge St. John said, “Give us another couple of minutes.”

Susan went outside the room. The judge answered the DA.

“Len, I’m suggesting that the rape and aggravated assault sentences run concurrently so we can lop a few years off if he satisfies you with his full-throated ‘I did it, and accusing Ms. Hayes of knowing me was a vicious thing to do to her on top of the other vicious things I did to her.’

“Mr. Cates should apologize to her and ask her forgiveness. Something approximating all of this. And, let’s say, he’ll be eligible for parole in thirty years. Sound all right?”

Red Dog said, “I’m open to it.”

CHAPTER 90

DEFENSE COUNSEL ED SCHNEIDER left the judge's chambers and followed Susan O'Connor to the conference room to have his stern talk with Cates, repeating what the judge had offered almost verbatim.

Tyler Cates, having had a brief taste of life in a cell, wasn't convinced that his lawyer was fairly representing his interests. And he said so.

Schneider said, "Tyler, this is the point of no return. Confess. Apologize and you'll be eligible for parole sometime in the very distant future. Otherwise, life in prison is your future with a life sentence for rape and the additional sentence for aggravated assault. If you don't confess, you will never be free again. I'm going back to the judge's chambers, where I will try to keep that deal in place. Ms. O'Connor will bring you back to chambers in two or three minutes, so think fast."

Schneider returned to the meeting, took his seat, and a few minutes later, Susan brought Officer Wells and Cates into the judge's chambers. Cates looked defiant. Even the last few hours in a cell hadn't softened him. Still cuffed, he took the chair beside his stern and florid attorney. Wells sat on a window ledge behind Cates so that he could reach him instantly if needed.

Yuki and Gaines sat opposite Cates and Schneider. Red Dog Parisi sat in the side chair beside the judge's desk. The table was set.

Tyler Cates was on the menu.

Judge St. John said, "Mr. Cates. You've had time to reflect on your actions. Do you have anything to tell the court?"

"Like what?"

"Like, do you take responsibility for your actions against Ms. Hayes?"

"I have nothing to say that I didn't already tell everyone in court and probably on national news. Were you listening?"

"Yes I was, Mr. Cates. Mr. Wells, will you please take Mr. Cates back to his cell."

The attorneys remained in place and when the door was closed, His Honor addressed the room.

"Court will resume Monday at nine."

CHAPTER 91

I'D HOPED THAT by going to Jamie's funeral, his killer or a lead to that person would reveal himself, but the opposite had happened. I'd cleared no one, while adding additional potential suspects: Marly, Rae, and Christophe, to name three, and possibly Rafe, to add another.

I thought about Arthur: his attachment to Jamie, his twenty years of loyal service, his access to all things Jamie, and not least, his inheritance of more money from Jamie Fricke's estate than he would earn in three lifetimes as house manager.

I was so absorbed in reviewing the funeral attendees that the fifteen-minute drive home felt like it had only taken a minute. Lake Street was just ahead. I parked around the corner on Eleventh and entered our building, hoping that Joe was awake, his feet on the ground, watching *World News Today.*

Inside our place, I locked my piece in the gun case in the foyer and by then Martha had found me and greeted me with wagging and slobbering and shoving me backward by planting her front feet on my waist. I told her she was a good girl and called out to Joe.

"Help!"

Julie shouted back. "Mom! I'm giving Dad combat training. We need to concentrate."

Meaning, *Don't interrupt us, okay?*

Okay.

CHAPTER 92

INSIDE OUR BEDROOM, I stepped out of my black silky everything and changed into jeans and an SFPD T-shirt. Back in the living room, I dropped into my Mom chair. I wanted to talk to Joe and knew he wanted to talk to me. But this was Dad and Julie time, and Julie wasn't giving that up without a fight.

"Daddyyyyyy. This is important. No talking."

I saw what was happening and stifled a laugh. Julie is one of the funniest people I know, but she takes herself very seriously. When it came to combat training, Julie Ann Molinari, clothed in lavender unicorn pj's, was in charge.

She called out her moves.

"Daddy. This is called 'kicking and punching.' "

Joe covered his eyes and our little combat trainer kicked him in the shin with one bare little foot, then socked him in the biceps with the opposite fist.

"Ooo. Oww, Julie," Joe called out in mock pain.

"Now," she said, "this is what I call 'dodging.' "

She leapt from side to side making, I guess, war cries. "Yah. Pow. Powee. Yahoo." Joe played his part as victim until a laugh escaped him.

"Don't laugh, Daddy. These moves could save your life! Now, this one is 'karate chopping.'"

"No, no more, Julie," Joe said, falling over sideways. "You've killed me."

"Okay. Last one today," Julie announced. "This is advanced training. It's 'using weapons.'"

Julie picked up her plush stuffed cow she'd named Mrs. Mooey Milkington and swung it around her head singing out, "Whoop, whoop, whoop," then slapping those few ounces of fluff and foam rubber against Joe's forearm.

"Julie, I can't take any more. Pleeease stop."

"We're done," Julie crowed. "I promote myself to combat trainer level two," she said, and jumped into his arms. Joe hugged her until she squeaked, "Dadddddyyyyy, you winnnn."

"Thank you, Julie. I can take on anyone now: kung fu fighters, even Superman," said the actual G-man in the family.

I said, "Julie—"

"Mom! You want combat training?"

"Not now, sweetie. I need to talk to Dad. It's confidential police business. How about we set you up with a movie in your room so Dad and I can catch up?"

"Okay. This time. What movie, Mom?"

She ran across the floor, climbed into my lap, and threw her arms around my neck.

I said, "You tell me."

"*House of Cats*," she told me.

Done.

CHAPTER 93

I SET JULIE up in her bed with Martha, a glass of milk, and the extended two-hour version of a cartoon musical filling her TV screen. When she was calling out advice to multicolored dancing cats, Joe and I went to our bedroom and got into bed.

We hugged and rolled around, and I got up to check that the door was locked. Then I got back to bed. Joe was quiet for a full minute. I thought he may have gone to sleep. I shook his arm and he said, "Steinmetz offered me a job."

"Again?"

"This time in writing. And it's a great offer."

"Oh, my God. What did you say?"

"That I wanted to talk to you."

"And here I am. Listening . . ."

"Well. There'd be a very decent raise, other perks. It's a full-time job. Which doesn't mean nine-to-five. You remember."

"Vividly."

I remembered, too, gunfights, touch-and-go nights in the ER, the "Chinese wall" between us, meaning talking about our cases was forbidden, Joe's absence for days at a time, and the worst, still animated in my mind—the evening when a museum made of glass and steel had exploded with Joe inside.

He said, "I could turn down the job again, and keep doing what I've been doing for a few more years. There's a lot to be said for that."

"Like what?"

"I'm the boss. No-brainer work. Afternoon naps. Long walks with Martha. High-fat, salty snacks in the kitchen. Drop off and pick up our little girl at the school bus. But that's not all. Did I mention afternoon naps?"

His delivery was priceless and I laughed out loud.

"No screaming," he said, then tipped my face to his and kissed me long and hard. I kissed him back and then his hands were under my clothes and I was tugging at his.

"Hey. I love you," he said.

"I love you, too."

We made sweet love, panting but not screaming, aware of the little girl in the next room watching a movie that would soon be over.

We dressed reluctantly but stayed in bed and made a circumstances-permitting date for tomorrow night: dinner out, home again, same place, and with some screaming allowed.

I rolled onto my back. It would be good for Joe to go back to work, but we both knew that everything would change.

Joe spoke. "Steinmetz wants a decision next week."

"That stinks. How about we talk again about this a few more times? I have to get used to the idea of it, but the decision is yours."

"Ours."

I squeezed his hand. I rubbed his head and traced the scar from the Sci-Tron explosion that had parted his hair.

It was a rare pleasure to be in sync like this. In the same circadian rhythm with my husband. Even tired, our minds racing from the other's touch, from anticipation, from knowing, loving, trusting each other. Joe and I just had a great, memorable night together.

The best in a long time.

SATURDAY

CHAPTER 94

JOE HELD THE front door for me and I felt transported back to a more elegant time, at least as it was portrayed in black-and-white movies.

The jazz was hot, the patrons looked cool, and Joe and I held hands as we took the grand staircase to the mezzanine floor. To my eye, Joe looked a little bit like Clark Gable without the mustache, and I'd swept up my hair, worn my red, scoop-necked cocktail dress, giving me a glam Ginger Rogers look.

Bix had been named for Jazz Age musician Bix Beiderbecke, and the restaurant in a brick building in an alley off Gold Street felt like a 1930s supper club or speakeasy. The waiters wore white jackets, and ours, a young man named Randall, said, "Welcome back to Bix." He showed us to a table with a view of the ground floor dining room and handed us the menus. In fact, we ordered from memory and Joe and I were alone again.

Over a light white wine, I updated my combat-trained husband on the recent high points of the Fricke case.

I said, "We got an unbelievable break, Joe. Maybe."

"Let me have it. I'm braced."

I told him about Claire's eagle eye, that the first shot at Jamie Fricke was a .40 fired at close range to his left shoulder. That Claire suspected he'd been adrenaline-charged enough to turn around and punch the shooter in the face.

"That's plausible . . ." Joe mused.

"The next four rounds killed him but the DNA on Jamie's knuckles told the tale on the shooter. He's male and get this, Joe. He shares DNA with James Fricke."

"Nice catch on Claire's part," said Joe. "I guess the lab was unable to ID anyone from the DNA comparisons?"

"Not yet."

"Hunh. So if a suspect has no Fricke DNA, he's out of the running. On the other hand, Jamie Fricke was such a hound with women . . ."

"I was thinking the same," I said. "Who knows how many offspring he's produced in the last thirty years . . ."

We paused as the waiter brought our entrées.

When he had left the table, I prompted Joe to tell all about his stress-packed save-the-hospital week. He told me about his partner, Bao Wong, whom he liked and admired.

"How much?"

"Hmmm?"

"How much do you like and admire her?"

Joe pinched my knee. "You goofball. She's a high-tech agent, cyberterrorism director, actually. Lives in DC, but if I take the job, she may move here with her family to work with me and Craig. We make a good team."

CHAPTER 95

OVER DUNGENESS CRAB and sautéed asparagus, Joe described the shoot-out at the blue house. And then described the thirtysomething coder with the green windbreaker who'd left his computer for the Feds, then helped save St. Vartan's Hospital.

Joe said, "I really like that guy. I hope I'm right about him." And then said nothing for a full minute. I shook his arm and then he gave me his straight-on, blue-eyed gaze and said, "So, I'm thinking I should take the job. Here are the whys and why nots . . ."

"Joe, it'll be good for you."

"Not so good for you, though."

"Here's how I see it. If it makes your life more interesting, challenging, and you don't get killed, I'll be happy enough. We'll offer Mrs. Rose a full-time job."

"Well. I'll be getting a good raise, more than enough to cover Gloria's salary and fun for the kiddo. As for the job, it's full-time. Which doesn't mean nine-to-five. You remember."

"I sure do," I said. "It was like living inside a sci-fi thriller and getting out of the theater is not guaranteed. That said, I think it's now or never."

Joe showed me his palms, first one, then the other. "On the one hand, assuming Gloria says yes, it could be the perfect life. On the other, early retirement, and I'm already bored with myself."

"Go for it, Joe. With my full support. Tell him yes."

We held hands under the table, kissed, spooned up criminally delicious chocolate mousse with our coffee, and kissed again. We made it home before Julie was in the sack. Mrs. Rose wanted to hang out for Julie's review of *Super Mario Bros.*

"Four rotten tomatoes," Julie said. "No. Four and a half!"

We thanked our good friend Mrs. Rose, tucked our little girl into her big girl's bed with my old friend Martha. Then Joe and I went to the room next door. We dressed in pajamas and crawled under the covers in the dark and snuggled in for a long night's love. It was Joe who screamed into the pillow. As for me, I held him tight and I prayed to God that we had made the right decision. That all of us would be safe.

I fell asleep remembering nights when Joe hadn't come home. But we were together now. Amen.

MONDAY

CHAPTER 96

I SAT AT the head of the scarred oak conference table, Jackson Brady to my left, Claire Washburn to my right, eight Homicide inspectors filling the remaining chairs. The Frickes' autopsy photos were taped to the far wall. There was also a list of suspects tacked to the adjacent corkboard.

Although our persons of interest list had dropped in number, the energy in our shabby war room was high. By process of elimination, we might be getting closer to Jamie's killer. And maybe Holly's.

Brady said, "Claire, why don't you start us off."

Dr. Washburn was ready. She opened the folder in front of her, then told the group about the Fricke DNA/knuckle connection.

"So far, it's just a good idea," she said. "Which it will be if we have a viable suspect with Fricke DNA. The samples I took from Jamie's hand are now at Quantico. The FBI's database might spit out a name."

It looked to me like Claire's explanation hit Sergeant Paul Chi like a shot of adrenaline, straight to his brain.

"I want to be in on this, Doctor," he said. "Let me know how I can help."

Then Cappy, wearing his undercover leather jacket, denim cap, and jeans, reported that Holly's Bentley had been discovered, sold to a dealer in Acapulco; Jamie's Jag had also been found, demolished. He took off his cap, placed it over his heart, and said: "Every window was broken, the upholstery slashed with a carpet knife. The electronics were gutted, the VIN numbers had been burned off, but one was legible enough to identify it as Jamie Fricke's vehicle. The hundred-thousand-dollar sports car was deliberately run into a brick wall and totaled. Looked personal to me. I'd call it a hit. By proxy. Or to make sure it was really dead."

Chi added, "The perp was wearing gloves. There were no, none, zero prints in the remains of the car."

Conklin then spoke for a couple of colorful minutes about Fricke's funeral, and when he paused for a sip of coffee, I stood, apologized, and said that I had to dash off for what might become an important interview.

I said, "I'm having lunch with Christophe Picard. Like Arthur Bevaqua, he's been entwined with the Fricke family for over twenty years—through his former marriage to Rae Bergen, their son, and his friendship with the Fricke clan. Plus. He wants to talk."

"Free food, Sarge?"

That was Cappy, being a wise guy.

I said, "I hope. I skipped breakfast this morning. I get the sense that Christophe likes to talk. So, he's either going to give me a lot of bull or steak frites."

Folks laughed, wished me luck, and soon I was in my car headed northwest on Seventh Street toward Christophe Picard's trendy, four-star-rated Chez Bonhomie.

At a stoplight, I opened a text from Claire: "FYI. Three new homicides came in this week. Unrelated to Fricke, but still murders."

Feeling time slipping away, I burned some rubber when the light turned green. Inevitably new homicides would drag us away from Jamie Fricke just as had happened with Holly. New cases had come in with an urgency that had turned Holly's case cold. A week in, Jamie's case was still fresh. But every day that passed would lower the odds of finding his killer.

That much was clear.

CHAPTER 97

CINDY WAS IN her protected seat inside the doorway of Courtroom 8G. The placement of furniture and people, the time court was due to go into session was all normal, but at the same time it didn't seem normal at all.

The room was packed and the tension in the air gave Cindy goose bumps. Something was about to happen.

Yuki was at the prosecution table just beyond the bar with Gaines and Mary Elena Hayes in the seat between them. Red Dog entered the room, and a split second later, Bailiff Riley Boone called court to order.

The door behind the bench opened and Judge St. John entered his court as Boone called out, "All rise." The hundred-plus people in the gallery and the lawyers came noisily to their feet. The judge took his place at the bench, looked across the oak-paneled room, and asked the gallery to be seated. The bailiff ushered in the jury, all twelve of whom looked somewhat dazed, as if they'd been sleeping in a closet or under their beds.

Cindy focused her eyes on Mary Elena Hayes, but her face was turned toward the front of the room. Cindy typed a silent note on her tablet that the victim in this case seemed at ease. Mary Elena had information about what was to come while court was in session that Cindy could only guess at, so she typed a line of question marks across the midline of her electronic page.

Judge St. John asked for quiet. It took several long moments and a bang of the gavel to get it. The jury had already been sworn in. The assemblage now sat quietly. No one coughed or dropped a handbag or a phone charger.

When he was ready, the judge addressed the jury, saying, "The court wishes to thank the jury for their time and diligence in hearing the case regarding the defendant, Mr. Tyler Cates. The time you've spent on this has not gone to waste. There will be further proceedings forthwith and the jurors are invited to leave or to remain in their jury seats and observe these proceedings. The press will be admitted. If you are neither a juror nor the press, regrettably, I must ask you to exit the courtroom."

Cindy unclenched her jaw and checked to see that her battery charger was still snugly in the wall socket as the guards moved the grumbling audience through the double doors.

When the doors were closed again, the judge said, "The defendant, Mr. Cates, has confessed to both the crimes of rape and aggravated assault. Mr. Cates and Mr. Schneider, please stand."

"Mr. Cates, to the charge of rape, how do you plead?"

"Guilty, Your Honor."

The judge asked the defense counsel to verify his client's plea, which he did.

Judge St. John addressed the defendant again.

"Mr. Cates. In the charge of aggravated assault, how do you plead?"

Cindy saw the defendant shift his weight from one foot to the other. The judge opened his mouth to speak and Cates preempted him speedily.

"I plead guilty to that charge, also."

"Mr. Schneider?"

"Yes, Your Honor. My client accepts the responsibility and the penalty for his actions, and he would like to say a few words to Ms. Hayes from their respective seats."

Judge St. John asked if that was all right with Ms. Castellano. Yuki bent her head toward Mary Elena, and they exchanged two or three words. Then Ms. Hayes stood and faced her rapist and abuser. She was rigid. Not as at ease as Cindy had thought.

The judge said, "Go ahead, Mr. Cates."

Cindy typed as Tyler Cates turned and faced Mary Elena and whichever of her personalities, maybe her own, had stiffened her spine.

"I'm very sorry," said Cates. "You didn't do anything to bring down my anger and violation on yourself. I hope someday you can find a way to forgive me although I will never forgive myself."

The judge asked all to sit while he pronounced the sentence.

"Mr. Cates, for the charge of rape, you are sentenced to thirty-five years in prison with the possibility of parole. For the charge of aggravated assault, you shall receive an additional fifteen years in prison, also with the possibility of parole."

Ed Schneider asked the judge to waive time, which Cindy understood and noted. It meant that imposition of the sentence would begin immediately.

Looking at St. John, Cindy saw that his expression had been fixed for the length of the trial. In this, the afterword, he finally cracked a small smile. He thanked the jury again and after they had filed out of the jury box and had been returned to their room, Judge Henry William St. John left the bench. Guards escorted Tyler Cates out of the courtroom by the side door, and Cindy stood in the aisle until she could throw her arms around her dear friend Yuki.

"Great job, Yuki. Great job and on the record."

CHAPTER 98

LATER THAT MORNING, Sonia Alvarez got a call from Rob Bailey, a former Las Vegas cop she knew and trusted. Bailey had connections with official CIs and unofficial snitches and now had what he called "a smoking hot tip" for her: A known but unindicted killer-for-hire named Samuel Rochas, who went by the unlikely street name of "Padre," was being held in South Lake Tahoe, Nevada, today before extradition tonight to Mexico City, where he was wanted for killing a high-ranking politico.

Padre was known to have associations with James Fricke via gambling and had been dropping hints to gang members and petty thieves that he may have been involved in the Fricke murders.

Rochas's blabbing to local criminals, insinuating that he had killed the Frickes, seemed suicidal—or maybe his way of evading Mexico's court order. Returning to Mexico was dangerous for Padre. Convicted or not, someone would get to him and put him down.

On the other hand, Bailey had sent an attachment—a mug shot of Padre. Alvarez had a very strong and somewhat supportable hunch that Padre had been at Holly Fricke's funeral, something for which she might have evidence.

Alvarez had the mug shot side by side on her phone with Cappy's color photo of mourners at Holly Fricke's funeral gathered outside the chapel and a black-and-white copy of that same photo with Cappy's handwritten names of the individuals in the shot.

Not all the individuals had been identified. Even with Arthur Bevaqua's help, there were a dozen individuals without names. And Alvarez was particularly interested in the one who might be Padre.

Her eyes had settled on an unidentified Mr. X. He looked to be fortysomething, white, average height and weight, with medium-length dark hair. His sunglasses obscured a quarter of his face and his clothing was unremarkable: a dark sports jacket and trousers. He was standing alone, looking out at the bay, his face in profile to the camera. No matter how much Alvarez enlarged the photo, she couldn't say with a real degree of confidence whether or not this person was the man in the mug shot she had on her phone.

But Bailey had said, "Alvarez, Padre's a psycho. If you want him for killing Jamie Fricke you need to get to Tahoe today and stake your claim before he's transported back to Mexico City."

There was a flight to Tahoe leaving in an hour and a half, but Alvarez needed authorization to make the trip, stay in a motel, buy breakfast.

She'd left a message for Brady, who was in a conference and hadn't called her back. Even Brenda couldn't reach him.

Likewise, she'd left messages for Conklin, who was at the crime lab in Hunters Point, and Lindsay, who might have turned off her phone during her meeting with Christophe Picard, Rae Bergen's ex-husband. At any rate, none of the three had called her back and she couldn't make the plane wait for her.

Alvarez was still at her desktop, her eyes fixed on the screen while obsessively checking the time on the blinking clock app. If she didn't get a call back, Padre Rochas would be in Mexico City tonight and she wouldn't be able to question him.

As point person for the SFPD, it looked as though Alvarez was going to have to bring Rochas in on her own.

CHAPTER 99

THERE WAS MOVEMENT at the halfway point in the bullpen. Alvarez looked up to see Cappy arriving at his desk, dropping his weight into his chair.

She called out, "Cappy. Can you please take a look at this?"

He called back, "Sure, okay. Ten minutes. I have some stuff I have to do."

"Cappy, this will be fast. Two minutes. I swear."

Cappy muttered, "Whose definition of two minutes?" He hoisted himself out of his chair, went to Alvarez's desk in the pod she shared with Conklin and Boxer. He took Boxer's seat, rolled the chair closer to Alvarez's computer.

She said, "I got a reliable lead on a hired gun, gambling pal of James Fricke. Given name, Samuel Rochas. Goes by Padre. Apparently, he says 'Rest in peace' when he pulls the trigger."

"I don't know the guy," Cappy said.

Alvarez said, "Look here, Cappy. That photo you took at Holly's funeral service, the one on the chapel lawn."

"Ya-hunh. That's mine."

Alvarez pointed to a man in the photo who might be Sam "Padre" Rochas, standing alone, staring into the distance in profile. She zoomed in on his face.

Cappy peered at the color image. "I don't recognize him. I don't even remember seeing him. There were swarms of people moving around. Circling swarms."

"I have a mug shot," said Alvarez. "Check this out."

She opened her phone, scrolled through her photo gallery, and opened the mug shot of Sam Rochas. Was he the no-name guy who'd been at Holly's funeral? She had to know.

Alvarez filled Cappy in on Rochas's background. Bailey had told her that Padre was from Chicago, had a sealed juvie record, including gang activity, misdemeanors. Later, he'd been accused of shooting a liquor store owner, raiding the cash register, and getting away. Next stop, Nevada. More shootings, and although no one had made a successful case on him, the Mexican police wanted him for killing a popular politician.

Extradition papers had been submitted and signed up the line, and this shooter, with a reputation as a first-class silent killer for hire . . .

Cappy said loudly, "Alvarez, you saying this guy shot the Frickes?"

"Cappy, I'm going by this. A close source of mine from Vegas PD, now in Tahoe, told me that Padre hung with Jamie when they did a tour of the hotels and casinos. That Padre was a big fan of the Bleus and bet on Jamie's team to win. He went all in. And lost. Big-time. And Padre held a grudge."

Cappy said, "I want to look at some of the other shots I

took of the funeral party. Find a different angle on this guy's face."

"Can you do it now?" Alvarez asked. "There's a flight leaving any minute. I've gotta meet with some cops I know about whether Padre was the last person Jamie Fricke saw before he died."

Cappy said to Alvarez, "How would anyone know that?"

"I guess he said so."

"Fine. Let's see that mug shot again."

Alvarez scrolled down in her photo gallery and passed the phone to Cappy, who began memorizing the man's features.

He took out his phone and looked at the four shots he'd taken of the crowd outside the chapel at Holly's funeral.

He said, "My last shot catches this guy's head from the back. No help. But I'll say this, Alvarez, he's not seen talking to anyone here. Not even Jamie, who was the bereaved. If this dude was checking out the family, Holly's funeral was a scouting operation. In my opinion, Padre's worth a look-see and a chat with the arresting officer and the CO."

"Okay. I'm going. I need you to say, 'Go for it, Alvarez,' and sign off on moderate expenses, okay?"

"Go for it. I'll sign a requisition and email it to Brady. Just call home. And if you think he's the doer, call Clapper and demand to be put through."

"Thank you, Cappy."

"Sonia, be careful. Call me every couple of hours and let me know where you are."

"Will do."

CHAPTER 100

I'D KNOWN OF Christophe Picard's jewel of a bistro in Presidio Heights for years. I'd never been inside but had driven past its outdoor café and thought that someday I'd come here with the girls for dinner. Yet now, I was sitting at a small square table by the fireplace without the girls, dressed in my usual work clothes, badge hanging from a chain around my neck, holstered gun at my waist. I was appropriately dressed. I was working.

While waiting for Christophe to leave the kitchen and join me, I listened to French folk music and thought about Rae Bergen's ex-husband. I was hoping that I was going to learn something from Christophe that would lead to an arrest. He'd invited me to drop by and talk with him. Maybe he wanted to gauge what I knew about the killer. Either way, he'd opened a door and I'd walked through.

While waiting, I mentally reviewed Paul Chi's earlier interview notes with the restaurateur, which ended with "Christophe Picard; alibi checked out, not suspected." I was tapping my feet, twiddling my wedding ring, when Christophe slipped into the chair opposite mine wearing chef's whites and a red scarf knotted around his neck. We shook hands.

Christophe asked if I trusted him to order for me.

"Wouldn't have it any other way."

"Excellent."

Minutes later, a waiter delivered the first course.

Oranges? I looked up at my host.

"Blood oranges," he said. "With caraway seeds and a Champagne vinaigrette. Have a taste, Sergeant. I think you're going to like it."

He was right, and I told him so.

"Just getting started," he said.

"Me, too. I think you invited me to lunch so you could tell me something."

"Did I?"

"Yes. Talk to me, Christophe. Do you know or have any idea who hated Holly and Jamie enough to have killed them?"

"You get right to the point, don't you?"

"Yes. I hope you do, too."

"Shoot," he said. "I mean . . ."

"I get it," I said to the good-looking guy in blazing white sitting across from me. "I've spoken with Rae, but briefly, and she was guarded. I just want to understand her, and you, better."

"Ask me anything."

"Here we go. Where were you on Tuesday morning last week, between eight and eight thirty?"

"That's when Jamie was murdered? That's easy," he said. "I

was in LA, and a lot of people can vouch for that. Also, I paid tolls with my card."

I had my phone in hand and typed notes as he spoke. He went on.

"I drove down to LA on Monday night and stayed with Rae in Malibu. On Tuesday we picked up Brock on campus at Pepperdine University and went to Venice Beach for the day. Look." He removed his watch so I could see a tan line.

I didn't look impressed.

"And then?"

"Then we all went out to dinner, Chinese restaurant en route. I'll have the name on my credit card receipt if you want it. Then we drove the kid back to school. We didn't know about Jamie's death until we got back to Rae's place. I had another overnight with my ex-wife and we talked about Jamie's death all night. I was in the kitchen here by eleven fifteen. I can account for my time and Rae's."

I asked him to go through his wallet now and give me the toll and restaurant card receipts and he did it.

"I'd like these back, okay?"

"I'll get them back to you this afternoon. Now, I'd like to know more about Rae and James Fricke."

"That's a very long and old story. Let me put some more food in front of us, before I start talking."

He called the waiter over, spoke a dozen words in fluent French, and turned back to me.

Christophe said, "Sergeant, most of what I know about Jamie comes from Rae. We were brothers-in-law, of course, but I didn't socialize with him, especially after the divorce. It's whatchacallit, hearsay, Sarge. Personal stuff through Rae, or what I read in the media. Theory seems to be that the same person killed both Holly and Jamie? Is that true?"

"It's still a theory. We have no proof."

A waiter removed our dishes, then put down more surprise food from Christophe. It was a baked ravioli dish. "What is it?"

"Go ahead, Sarge. Taste it," he said. "Then, you tell me."

I took a taste and guessed. "Ravioli stuffed with some kind of squash."

"Very good. Butternut squash."

"Delicious. So, Christophe . . ."

"Chris is fine."

"So, Chris. What do you know about the relationship between Jamie and Rae?"

CHAPTER 101

CHRISTOPHE SAID TO me, "Too late for that long old story now. See that pretty woman who just came in?"

"Short print dress. Long wavy hair?"

"That's the one. Moira Benet."

She was coming toward us, right up to the table, when Chris stood up, gave her a good hug, and introduced us.

"Moira Benet," said Chris, "meet Sergeant Lindsay Boxer. Sergeant, Moira is the heart of gossip central, right, Mo? And Sergeant Boxer is the top cop on the Fricke murder cases."

"Lindsay Boxer," Moira said. "Nice to finally meet you."

"Moira is an old friend of Rae's," said Chris. "You two should talk. I have a nice table opening up on the patio. Lunch is on the house."

We moved to seats at a teakwood table under a striped umbrella outside. Chris moved Moira's handbag out of the aisle and said, "You need anything, just ask."

"He's such a dear," Moira said of Chris.

Turned out Moira wasn't one for banter. She took the reins

and talked through the first course. Her key point was that she and Rae were tight.

"We share many friends, have attended many red-carpet events together, countless parties and after-parties."

Moira told me that she wrote a column for the *Tribune* and also had a podcast that was offered by invitation only and not available at any app stores.

There was no way to say it modestly, so Moira smiled broadly as she told me that she had the inside track with the rich and famous. I hoped that was true. I didn't know enough about Rae Bergen to keep her name on the persons-of-interest list or cross her off. And doing that was my number one goal.

Moira had no questions about me and our investigation, and I was relieved. I wanted information from her, but I wouldn't be able to tell her anything.

When the main course came to our table, Moira left a space between words. I grabbed it.

"Moira, what can you tell me about Rae and Jamie Fricke?"

"I thought Rae told you. She utterly loved Jamie and he loved her, too. Since the day they met. It was complicated, of course. Rae got together with Jamie whenever it was possible. He sent her to the moon and drove her back to the airport. She is devastated that some mofo blew him away."

I said, "Yes, I know. But did Rae's love affair with Jamie cause trouble in her relationship with Holly?"

"Oh," said Moira. "I get it. You're asking, was Rae so jealous of Holly that she killed her? No, no, no way. Not ever in this world." She pushed her chair back a few inches from the table.

"Moira, don't judge the question. I'm a cop trying to solve

a very bloody puzzle and the longer it takes, the less chance we have of finding out who killed Holly and Jamie Fricke.

"Yeah, yeah, yeah, I get that. But you don't know Rae. She and Holly were so close, they were like twins."

"Please go on," I said and meant it.

Moira said, "Well, do you know about Christophe and Holly?"

"I don't know about that. Please fill me in," I said as I typed "Chris + Holly" on my phone notepad.

Moira put down her fork and leaned in toward me.

"It's not a secret," she said. "Not anymore. May I call you Lindsay?"

"Sure."

"Well, Lindsay. Once, a couple of years ago, Christophe and Holly ran off together for a week to an absolutely amazing hotel in the South of France. Cannes, I think. Rae showed me the pictures. Frisky ones. I had to look at those images over and over because Rae and Holly look so much alike. But it was Holly, confirmed by Rae."

That was a bombshell—and news to me.

I said, "Did Jamie know?"

"Sure, he did."

"That must've ticked him off."

"He wasn't that way. Neither was Holly and neither is Rae. I, too, thought there would be ramifications. I'd forgotten how the Bergens, the Frickes, and their social peers played around and how they were raised. It was all allowed."

I could imagine rampant promiscuity, maybe. But had I learned anything germane to cold-blooded murder?

"How long did the Holly and Chris, Rae and Jamie

crossover last?" I asked, even using my hands to do a crisscross pattern.

Moira said, "In Rae's case, she was with Jamie off and on for twenty years. Before Holly and Jamie were married, and during, and after she and Chris were divorced. But those two, Chris and Rae, are still the best of friends and Brock loves them both."

I followed Moira's comments onto a track of my own and when I tuned back in, she was saying, "Brock's a complicated kid. Smart and clueless at the same time. He was smoking, drinking, failing classes. Rae got him into rehab, and then back into school."

"That's why Rae lives in Malibu."

"Exactly. And Chris is very devoted to his son. What a wonderful man he is."

CHAPTER 102

ON MY WAY back to the Hall, I had a dark thought about a missed opportunity. One that threw shade on Moira. It had taken me too long to figure out how to pose this question and still keep her at the table.

Her phone had rung. She'd answered and had gotten into a lengthy conversation with her producer about people I didn't know, movie people, events and designer names that hadn't even grazed my consciousness.

Meanwhile, I was wondering how well Jamie and Moira knew each other. Sexually? And if so, what would that mean? I tried to imagine Moira as a double murderer. I couldn't picture it.

Moira had said over her phone, "Thanks, Peggy. I'll call you after I do the podcast."

Then, she clicked off, saying, "Lindsay, I have to go. Here's my card. Send me your contact info."

She gathered her bag, phone, sunglasses. She blew me a kiss and waved down the driver of her smart-looking car.

She opened the back door and with a flip of her skirt, a kick of her heels, disappeared into the back seat. The door closed.

And Moira was gone, leaving me with a headache and a lot to think about.

CHAPTER 103

I HAD JUST parked my car in the All Day lot off Bryant across from the Hall when my hip pocket chirped out my ringtone. I looked at the screen. Arthur Bevaqua calling.

"Arthur?"

"Sergeant, I'm walking on Bay Street. Heavy traffic."

"Same here," I said, locking my car, picturing the former Fricke house manager I'd talked with so many times in the last year.

"You okay, Arthur?"

"Pretty much, Sergeant. Feeling sad about, well. You know. Listen, I got a call from Ms. Borinstein this morning."

"Something wrong?"

"Mr. Jamie's will, the draft I gave you when we were in his office."

"Uh-huh. What about it?"

"Well, Ms. Borinstein and Mr. Jamie both signed the original and she's a notary. So it's stamped. It's good."

"Arthur, may I call you back? I'm going into the Hall—"

"Mr. Jamie left the house to Ms. Rae."

I paused a few beats to take in this news, and it surprised me. That Jamie had loved Rae had been established. *But how did that affect Arthur?*

I asked, "Arthur. How does that affect you? Did you think Jamie would leave the house to you?"

"Hold on, Sergeant. Garbage truck. Okay. I'm here. I was just surprised, you know? That he didn't want it sold. Money for his sons. Or turn it into a school or a soccer camp."

"Is Rae at the house now?"

"No. She's back in Malibu. She'll be coming next week to look around. I'm just letting you know in case this changes anything."

"I wonder if Christophe knows. He didn't tell me."

"And I haven't spoken with Ms. Rae. It's all so sudden. Call if you want to talk about this," he said.

"Arthur, you sound worried. Why?"

"Ahh. So many questions. No answers."

"Welcome to my world, Arthur."

"I don't think I would have guessed Ms. Rae was his principal heir. Well, Mr. Jamie always did follow his heart."

I climbed the steps, pulled open a decorative steel and glass door, and walked toward the security station.

I was still on the phone with Arthur.

"Please keep your ears open and your phone charged. Call me anytime day or night. Yes, night's okay."

Then we signed off. I had known Arthur for six months and, strangely, I both cared for and mistrusted him. He was distressed.

I didn't know why. And he hadn't really told me.

CHAPTER 104

DETECTIVE SONIA ALVAREZ sat across from her former colleague, Sergeant Robert Bailey, at a plain metal desk on the second-floor squad room of the Tahoe police station. Bailey was forty, shaggy-blond-haired, steel-blue-eyed, a former middleweight boxer, high school math teacher, undercover cop with the Las Vegas PD and now at the police station in Tahoe. He had called her this morning with a lead that went straight to the front of the line.

According to Bailey, Samuel "Padre" Rochas was a known contract killer who'd been dropping hints just short of taking credit for the Frickes' murders. Why? Was he the doer? Did he want to get caught to forestall his imminent extradition? Or was he stupidly attaching himself to the crimes in order to muddy the opaque waters of these sensational murders and boost his street cred?

Either way, Alvarez was charged up by this unexpected development. She had questions when Bailey picked her up at the Tahoe airport about how much Padre had told his street buds.

"Just crumbs," Bailey said. "Based on facts."

He filled in Alvarez on the details of Padre's claims.

"Witnesses of the seedy kind tell us that Padre definitely knew Jamie Fricke well. He dropped names, knows a lot about soccer . . . But mostly he described Holly Fricke as an addict and a whore and Jamie Fricke as a spiteful bastard, which Fricke certainly could be. Have you seen any of the clips of him chewing out various team players? Fricke was a brute. He fired one of the assistant coaches right off the field a couple of years ago. Got into fistfights in locker rooms and hotels—he really thought he was some kind of god."

Alvarez said, "I never thought about Jamie Fricke at all until his wife was killed, and soccer was definitely never on my mind. I'll study up."

Bailey grinned at her. Good-natured teasing went both ways in their partnership and Alvarez had almost forgotten the fun they had injected into their dangerous undercover work.

"No," Alvarez insisted. "I will. Study up."

"Okay. I'm convinced." As they pulled into the station, Bailey said, "So we have Rochas in the cage on the third floor getting his shit together for his flight tonight."

"I need to talk to him if there's a chance he's our shooter."

"No problem, Sonia. If you need coffee, the machine is down the hall, turn left. It's right there. But you'll want to talk to Rochas first and fast."

"Lead the way, Bailey. And stay close. If I get into trouble, I'll give you our help sign."

Bailey put his thumb on his forehead, fingers splayed out like a fan, and he wiggled them.

He and Alvarez both laughed at their old gag. Then Bailey said, "That's it. I think we're good to go."

Alvarez was expectant as she followed Bailey up the stairs to the jail. Padre, serial killer for hire. And she was going to interview him within a hand's length of the bars.

When they reached the landing, Alvarez caught up with Bailey and grabbed the crook of his arm.

"You okay?" he asked.

"Good to go," she said, smiling into Bailey's face. "I really am."

CHAPTER 105

THE INTERVIEW ROOM was a ten-by-ten screened cage at the far end of the cell row. It wasn't private, like the interview rooms Alvarez had become accustomed to, and the acoustics on the tier were crystal clear. She walked alongside Bailey and as they approached the cage, Alvarez glimpsed the prisoner.

Bailey said to Alvarez, "I'm armed. And he's not. He's shackled and we're not. He's ruthless but you'd never know it. His charm is charming, but—well, you'll figure him out, Alvarez."

Rochas was sitting at a table inside the cage. His ankles were shackled, his hands were cuffed in front of him, and a chain ran through the cuffs, then a metal loop in the tabletop, and fed down to connect with his shackles.

Bailey led Alvarez to the door to the cage, opened it to let her inside. He said, "Padre, this is Inspector Alvarez from the San Francisco PD."

Padre turned to look up at her. He gave her a second look and whistled through his teeth.

Alvarez ignored the whistle and took the seat facing the prisoner, with a clear view of Bailey, who was standing to her right outside the cage.

"Mr. Rochas—"

"You can call me Padre."

"And you may call me Inspector Alvarez," she said.

"*Como esta?*" he said with a smile.

"Pretty good, Padre, and you?"

"I guess we'll both know after we talk. If I board a plane to Mexico City tonight, I'll be hanging by my neck in my cell in a week. What do you want me to say?"

Alvarez said, "I'm going to tape our conversation, Padre. Save us a lot of time."

Alvarez set up her phone on the table and pressed the button to record.

"Let's start over again, Mr. Rochas. I'm Inspector Alvarez, SFPD Homicide. Sergeant Bailey has reported comments from confidential informants—"

"Snitches."

"—that you had a relationship with Jamie Fricke. Did you go to his wife Holly's funeral service in Pacific Heights about six months ago?"

"Says who?"

Alvarez picked up her phone, went to the photo gallery app, and opened Cappy's photo of someone who may have been Rochas. She held it up to his eye level, out of reach of his cuffed hands. "Is this you?"

Rochas laughed. "I was there."

"But you didn't know the deceased."

"I went out of respect for her husband."

"Did you have anything to do with Holly Fricke's death? Did you know about a plan for her death or take some role in a plan? Did you pull the trigger?"

Rochas grinned. For a second, gold teeth flashed under the fluorescent lights.

"Inspector, you think if I had anything to do with that whore's death I should tell you?"

"Up to you, Padre. If you took part in her murder, you might not be going back to Mexico and life in prison. Life might be as long as a few days."

Rochas laughed. "What you might call an interesting proposition. I have a better one. Take me back to the City by the Bay for questioning. See what I say."

Alvarez said, "Answer the question, Padre, or I'm saying, '*Vaya con Dios.*'"

"Okay, okay, I had nothing to do with Holly Slut's death. Nothing. Not word. Not deed."

"Thank you," Alvarez said. "Same questions about Jamie. The street is talking, saying you feel James suckered you into a sports bet on the Bleus while you were cruising around Vegas. That you held a grudge against him because he wouldn't make you whole."

"What does 'make whole' mean?"

"It means to reimburse you, pay you back for your loss."

"Right. I lost a quarter of a million dollars. He wouldn't pay me back. He was a snake and everyone knew it. You want me to confess to killing him, so we go back to Frisco? I await trial. And maybe go free? Maybe take you to a good restaurant to celebrate."

"Did you have anything to do with Jamie Fricke's murder, Padre? Yes or no. If yes, tell me your role."

"I wish. I wish I had seen his face when he knew he was about to die. I wish I could have caused him mortal pain. I heard about it on the block."

"On which block?"

"This one. Cell block. I was here when he was gunned down, babe. I mean, Inspector. I was in a cell when Jamie Fricke was killed, and I had no foreknowledge or nothing. Snitches were playing a game with Detective Bailey. I think so."

Alvarez looked up at Bailey, who came over to the cage and said, "Padre. You shitting me?"

"You weren't here," Padre said. "But I was. Corcoran picked me up the night before. *Estupido*."

Bailey opened the cage door and said, "Come on outta there, Alvarez."

To Rochas he said, "Be right back."

Alvarez followed Bailey down to booking on the first floor.

The desk sergeant opened a computer file, said, "He's right, Rob. Checked in on Sunday, never checked out."

"I love to look stupid in front of a dirtbag. Sorry about this, Sonia."

Alvarez laughed. She said, "Tell Padre I said it was good meeting him. And he has a perfect alibi for Jamie's murder."

"What about you? What are you going to do?"

"Ask you to run me out to the airport." She reached up, tousled his hair, and said, "Good seeing you, Bailey. Going home without a suspect, a confession, any kind of evidence, or even lunch, but it's been great."

"We'll have to do this again," he said.

Just before Alvarez boarded her plane, he kissed her goodbye. She stowed her carry-on bag in the overhead rack. She thought about Padre. There was nothing, not even circumstantial evidence, suggesting that he'd killed Holly. He hadn't killed Jamie, either, having the perfect alibi. He was in jail at the time. Now he was going to jail in Mexico . . . where he would surely get jailhouse justice.

TUESDAY

CHAPTER 106

CHRISTOPHE TEXTED ME the following morning, inviting me to lunch again, saying he needed to talk to me. The word "need" hooked me. I was 95 percent sure that the restaurateur had fobbed me off on Moira the day before so that he could avoid telling me something I had to know. I hoped we would have time alone without distraction and bull. If Christophe had inside knowledge of the Fricke murders, I was determined to learn something that would advance the investigation. Or God willing, close these open cases.

I agreed to be at Bonhomie at one. I spent the morning meeting with the team, a somber group of detectives who had nothing to bring to the war room but hope. Even Brady was pinning hope on me getting the name of a killer from Christophe Picard.

I arrived at a crowded Bonhomie on time and Chris greeted me at the door. He looked different than he had a day ago. The ebullience was gone. His face was drawn and he had dark smudges under his eyes.

He led me to an inside table, in a nook between the kitchen and the dining room. The table was up against the wall and the light was low. Chris opened a bottle of wine. I refused the drink but encouraged him to go ahead. Not a problem.

Once Chris had downed his glass and poured another, I crossed my arms on the table, leaned in, and said, "Chris. I need you to tell me the truth. What do you know or surmise about Holly's and Jamie's killers? No ping-pong—"

"Ping-pong?"

"No games. No diversions. I need information. Understand?"

He nodded miserably. Filled my glass with something I'm sure was rare and wonderful, but I pushed the glass aside and waited.

"If I knew," he said, "I would tell you."

I placed the flats of my palms on the table, pushed off, and got to my feet. "That's too bad, Chris. If something comes to you, call or write."

I edged out of the privacy booth and was heading to the exit when he said, "Wait. Please."

I turned and looked into his sorry hound-dog face and walked back to the booth.

When we were both seated, Chris said, "I don't know who killed them, Sergeant, but this I know. I loved Holly. I've loved her for decades. What happened to Holly destroyed me. Thinking how she was gunned down! That she had time to realize she was going to die. I wake up every morning wanting to kill myself."

His voice broke and tears came. He covered his eyes with his hands and cried. I didn't speak. I. Just. Waited. Him. Out.

After he mopped his face with a cloth napkin, he said "Sorry" three times.

"It would be a relief to join her in death, but I can't," Chris said. "People depend on me."

A waiter put a charcuterie board of cheese and sausage in front of us. Aromas from the kitchen filled our small space. I quashed my hunger pangs and did a gut check.

I believed Chris had told me the truth about his feelings for Holly and his grief at her loss. But I felt just as strongly that he was leaving out the answer to who killed her and Jamie.

I tried him on as the killer.

If Chris had killed Holly for rejecting him, if he'd killed Jamie for winning the prize so long ago, it was hardly even a theory. I had nothing to support it.

That really ticked me off.

CHAPTER 107

I STOPPED OFF at MacBain's for a take-out BLT and cursed myself for declining a meal at Bonhomie. I had a small brown bag with the sandwich in hand when I breezed through the gate to the squad room. I said "Hey" to Bobby Nussbaum, our gatekeeper, as I passed his desk on my way to our pod just beyond him, but he stopped me.

"Sarge, I've got a message for you." I turned and he told me, "Anonymous tip."

I groaned, "Great."

He said, "I think this one's good."

"Hit me," I said.

"It was a woman. Her voice was muffled, like she was whispering or blocking the receiver with her hand. She asked for you, then gave me a message but not her name. Says she saw you at Bonhomie and won't ID herself."

"I'll take any old scraps, Bobby."

He said, "I know, I know, Lindsay, so I took it down verbatim. I didn't hear every word, but . . ."

He handed me a sheet torn from a message pad.

The handwritten note read, "Chris is shielding his son who's threatened people at school. You should check him out."

Bobby asked me, "Does this help?"

"Maybe. Is Brady in?"

"He'll be back in five."

I thanked Bobby and set course for the pod, where Alvarez and Conklin were having sandwiches together. I squeezed in behind Alvarez and claimed my spot between them.

"Is Christophe the man?" Alvarez asked me.

I leaned back in my chair and rocked a little. "I can't nail him and I can't clear him," I said. "But a tip came in for me while I was out."

I handed it to Alvarez and she passed it across the desks to Conklin.

"Check out Brock," he said. "Uh. As our killer? Why? Christophe gave him an alibi for Jamie's shooting, didn't he?"

"Right," said Alvarez. "Christophe told you that he and Rae and Brock were together. Venice Beach."

I said, "Yep. So says Chris."

"I'm sure Brock was at Holly's funeral," she said. "He gave a eulogy."

Conklin said, "He was also at Jamie's funeral, for sure. Rae pointed him out."

I agreed, saying for Alvarez's benefit, "Rae said he attended only because she asked him to be there."

Conklin said, "I'll run his name. Brock Picard?"

"This is like my Padre lead," said Alvarez. "It almost fits but doesn't fit at all."

She passed me her favorite snack, the family-sized bag of

truffle oil potato chips. I snatched it before she changed her mind—and that's when a scuffle started at the front desk. Bobby was tackling someone who'd tried to charge past the desk. Bob had been a court officer before coming to the Homicide desk and he still knew how to jujitsu a man.

Through the shouting and thudding of bodies hitting the floor, I heard my name being shouted from under Bobby's thick body twenty feet away.

"Sergeant!"

I launched myself toward the sounds of men fighting and saw that it was Christophe, red-faced and struggling to get out from under Bobby's weight.

I was joined by Conklin and then Brady appeared, coming through the bullpen entrance. He told Bob to step aside.

Brady is instinctively battle-ready. He grabbed a frenzied Christophe Picard with both hands, jerked him to his feet, threw him against the wall, and pinned him there. Then Brady stared around furiously until his ice-blue eyes found me.

"Who is this man, Boxer?"

"Christophe—"

I didn't finish the introduction. Chris interrupted me, pleaded to talk only to me, and in a fashion he did. His voice was a hoarse, paralyzing scream.

"Rae is dead! She was murdered!"

CHAPTER 108

CHRISTOPHE'S SCREAMS NEARLY stopped my heart. I'd seen him less than an hour before, and he'd told me how much he loved Holly. And now he was here, reporting Rae's murder.

Was it true? Or had he mentally skidded off the rails into a ravine? No one moved. His next directive broke the spell.

"*I sent you the video!*" Chris shouted at me. "*Open it!*"

I shifted my eyes first to Conklin, then Alvarez, then Brady. Christophe was keening.

Brady said to me, "Go ahead. I'll keep him here."

A torrent of dread washed over me. I went to the pod, took my chair, and opened my inbox. I stared at the long stack of email on my screen but I made no move to open any of them. Alvarez got up and walked behind me. She reached over my shoulder and found incoming mail from CP@Bonhomie. She clicked on it with a forefinger.

Alvarez is fearless.

The email was blank with a video attachment. Alvarez

stood beside me as I opened it. I was looking directly at Rae Bergen's face, full screen and animated. She was alive, in what looked like a home office, speaking to Christophe, visible in a small window in the corner of the screen.

Chris was saying, "You can't baby him anymore, Rae—"

There was movement behind Rae's image. It was the camera's-eye view of a male torso, from waist to right shoulder, coming into the frame. The figure pointed a .40-caliber at the back of her head and fired.

Rae's eyelids flashed wide-open for a split second as the bullet sped from the back of her head through her forehead, blowing out a hole the size of a golf ball.

Instinctively, my eyes slammed shut and when I opened them a second later, Rae's head and upper torso had fallen forward across her laptop. I heard Chris's voice coming over Rae's computer. He screamed "Rae!" and the picture went black.

The image of Rae's last breath had burned into my brain, and I couldn't blink it away. I heard Alvarez repeating my name. Christophe bellowed from the wall beside the front desk.

"He killed her, Sergeant. Rae is dead."

"Who? Who did it?"

That was Conklin crossing in front of Bobby, calling to Christophe.

Christophe's answer was an anguished, wordless cry. I sat with my elbows on my desk, palms over my eyes, knowing that I would never forget what I'd just seen. It was as if I'd been sitting across the table from Rae Bergen myself, watching as a bullet tunneled through her head.

CHAPTER 109

BRADY SAID, "BOXER, I'm calling the LA Sheriff's Department. Get ready to move out." I snapped out of it, as Bobby called for medical assistance and Brady dialed the LASD and asked for the sheriff. He waited as the desk sergeant hunted him down and then explained what he wanted to do. Ten minutes after placing the call, Brady hung up the phone.

He came to our pod and summarized ground zero for me and Conklin. He'd reported the murder to the LA sheriff, who knew Clapper and was happy to cooperate with us. LA's CSU would leave the scene intact until we arrived, then they would process it, give us the results. Uniformed officers were being dispatched to Rae Bergen's apartment now.

I told Brady I wanted to see Christophe while we waited for transportation to the airport. I took the elevator up to the seventh-floor jail, where I asked desk sergeant and old friend Bubbleen Waters where I could find Christophe Picard.

"I'll let you see him, Lindsay, but EMTs just gave him a

tranq to knock him out. He was hysterical, banging his head against the bars."

"He's unconscious?"

"Yup. I know you're going to ask for how long, and I asked and was told that time out differs from person to person."

I said, "When he wakes up, call Brady."

"Copy that, Sarge," she said, saluting me.

It was the first time I'd smiled that day.

I peeked in on Christophe, who was lying on his back on a slab inside a cell. He was out cold. I tried to rouse him by calling his name, but he was way under.

Because Rae Bergen's murder was attached to the Fricke murders, and all three had happened in California, the case was ours. Rae Bergen went on the board back in our squad room.

A few minutes later, Conklin and I were in a patrol car speeding toward SFO, and from there we shuttled to LAX, where a pair of uniforms were waiting for us when we landed. They also had the keys to a loaner squad car and handed them to me.

Once we were on Pacific Coast Highway, heading to Malibu, I dialed up the radio, introduced myself to dispatch, and got a dedicated channel. Conklin typed Rae's address into the GPS while I had a conference call with Brady and a sheriff's deputy.

Two teams were assigned to us as backup and once the administrative formalities were buttoned up, an APB was put out so that every officer in LA was on alert to a murder with no actual suspect. Our squad moved out and, with all lights on, sirens blaring, we headed to the murder scene: an apartment building in Malibu.

CHAPTER 110

FOUR PATROL CARS were already parked outside a three-sided grouping of town houses on a bluff in Malibu. They were all white with red tiled roofs and decks with a view of the ocean. The building where Rae had lived was the first condo in the A block, the one closest to the street.

Conklin double-parked and our backup teams got out of their cars and cordoned off the street. We badged the uniforms at the entrance to the compound. The ranking officer was Chief William Taverno. I introduced Conklin and myself and asked him if he'd seen the crime scene.

"I was there. Left my lunch in the toilet." I nodded as he added, "We're waiting for the ME."

A CSU mobile was parked at the curb unpacking their gear. I wanted to get into Rae's apartment right now and get out, leaving everything as I found it. I hoped that before I left Rae's place, I would uncover a clue to the identity and whereabouts of Rae's killer.

Taverno said, "Don't worry, Sergeant Boxer. Nothing but nothing moves until after you've seen it."

As if Taverno had conjured it up, the ME's van rolled up the street and double-parked.

Taverno said, "That's Dr. Camille Gray, the ME."

The ME exited from the rear of the van with her bag and camera. She looked to be in her early forties and lithe, moving with speed and purpose. I intercepted her as she reached the sidewalk.

"I'm Sergeant Lindsay Boxer. My partner, Inspector Conklin," I said. "I'm the primary officer—"

"The sheriff called me," said Gray. "Good to meet you, despite the circumstances. I hear that the cause of death is apparent. Let's see the scene. After we've got pictures, I'll take the victim to my offices and send you a full report after the autopsy."

Dr. Gray, Taverno, and two uniforms headed into the A building. Conklin and I followed them to 1A, Rae's apartment. Rae's office was too small to accommodate all of us at once. The others stayed back as Conklin, Dr. Gray, and I approached the nightmare that had been Rae Bergen.

The manner of death was as shocking now as when I had seen the shooting in action earlier, because now there was no screen separating us. A massive amount of blood had poured over the laptop keyboard and desk, dripping onto the floor and forming a pool the size of a kitchen sink. I stepped around the puddle to the opposite side of the desk and saw brain matter and fragments of bone, the shattered remains of Rae Bergen's skull.

I turned away and tapped Brady's direct line into my phone.

"We're in Rae's house," I said. "Did Christophe give up who killed her?"

"He wouldn't talk to me. So I sent in Paul Chi."

Brady is heavily muscled and rarely smiles. From a perp's point of view, Brady looks like he could mash human flesh into pulp. Chi, on the other hand, is about five six and cagey. So regardless of whether or not Christophe could read people, Chi could likely outfox him.

And he did.

CHAPTER 111

CONKLIN TURNED THE car off Pacific Coast Highway south to John Tyler Drive, the entrance to Pepperdine's Malibu campus. There was a parking area at the junction where the road split and continued along the perimeter of the campus while the other road forked into one of the parking lots.

We were looking for a late-model silver Porsche convertible registered to Brock Picard. We had to track him down.

First, locating his car would tell us if he was on campus. There was no place we could park where we could see all the cars in the main lot. So, we drove between the rows, weaving a path, passing many expensive cars, some of them silver, all with parking stickers on the windshields, many with Greek affiliation bumper stickers on the back.

I saw the car at the end of the row we were plowing.

"Slow, Richie. I think that's it."

My partner braked behind the Porsche, blocking it in. There were vehicles on both sides of the car and, since it was the last row in the lot, a curb behind it with landscaping in an enclosed bed. The Porsche was a convertible, and the top was down. A young man wearing a brown jacket was lying in the front seat, his knees bent, his feet on the passenger-side upholstery, his head on the driver's-side armrest. His eyes were closed.

It was Brock Picard, Rae and Christophe's son. I recognized him from Jamie's funeral.

Using hand gestures and one-word sentences, Conklin and I unlocked and opened our doors. Brock was a light sleeper or maybe not sleeping at all. He bolted upright, saw Conklin, and vaulted out of his car. He ran alongside the Porsche, through the curb-contained plantings, and ducked under the branches of a sapling. And he kept going.

My partner and I yelled at Brock to stop running, that we were police, but a bullet whizzed past my ear as he headed uphill toward a block of buildings. We chased him up the twisting walkway from the parking lot, where he ran across the street and into a large building marked ADMINISTRATION. Conklin and I were of the same mind. We split up, Conklin following Brock into the admin building while I circled around the right side of it in the hope of cutting him off, should Brock attempt to escape through the back entrance.

It was a large building and circling around it was no joke, but I forced myself to move as quickly as I could without stumbling and falling to the ground. As I finished circling the building, I saw up ahead to my right a semi-cylindrical building that looked like a large tube lying on its side.

I spotted Brock running down the steps of what appeared to be a small amphitheater with Conklin several lengths behind him. Brock was making for the semi-cylindrical building and was able to reach it before I could cut him off or Conklin could overtake him from behind.

Brock opened the heavy double doors in the tubular structure and entered just as Conklin and I converged a few steps from the doors and a few seconds late. Out of nowhere, two campus cops appeared.

I flashed my badge and shouted, "We're detectives from San Francisco! The guy in the brown jacket. He's wanted for murder. Please clear students from the area."

One of the campus cops dropped away. The other stayed with us as backup. I peeled off my jacket as I ran and left it on the grass nearby. The Kevlar vest I wore under my coat was stenciled SFPD front and back, ID in case of gunfire.

As I turned to the campus cop and asked him what building this was, I was struck by the wall facing the amphitheater. It consisted entirely of stained glass.

The policeman said, "That's Stauffer Chapel."

Conklin asked him about ways inside.

"There is a pair of double doors, heavy ones, inside the grillwork protecting the glass. But there are also a couple of service doors down toward the other end that open near the altar."

"Please lead the way," I said. Conklin was quick off the mark. I was still breathing hard and I had somehow turned my ankle. The pain was catching up with me. Even so, I ran toward the chapel with the campus cop and kept my partner in sight.

CHAPTER 112

CONKLIN FOLLOWED THE path Brock had taken toward the glass wall of the chapel. I had fallen behind Conklin, and the campus cop—twenty years my senior—was jogging behind me.

"Hey, hey, slow down," he called out.

"Catch up!" I shouted back.

"I'm Jerry," the campus cop shouted to me. "Stay with me."

"I'm with you," I panted.

Jerry caught up then took the lead. We ran along the length of the chapel. He reached the side door, opened it, and went in and I followed him inside. We were standing on the dais at the far end of the chapel facing the enormous wall of stained glass. There were four people in the pews facing us, praying, meditating. I told them to please leave quickly by the side door to my left and that there was no time to answer questions.

The students jumped up from their seats, whispering and clutching at one another, and quickly filed out the side door.

I saw Conklin at the far end of the chapel from me, but I didn't see Brock.

And then I did.

One of the side doors was kicked in and Brock entered pushing and dragging a female student, a brunette with two braids, wearing a cardigan over a long blue skirt. She was one of the girls who'd been praying moments ago, and when she made her exit, Brock had scooped her up. His left arm had a vice grip around her neck. A gun was in his right hand. The girl struggled and cried out and begged him to let her go.

Conklin, having hidden behind a pew, now came up behind Brock, his gun drawn, yelling, "Release her, Picard! Let her go. Drop your weapon and no one will get hurt."

Jerry and I had both pulled our guns and moved toward Brock and his hostage at the front of the chapel. Including Conklin, the three of us triangulated Brock Picard. He didn't look frightened. Rather, he had a twenty-year-old boy's bravado.

"Move back," Brock said. "Move back and drop your guns or I will put a bullet in this girl and we won't need to talk."

At that moment and in these circumstances, there was only one thing to do.

We backed off. No guns were dropped.

CHAPTER 113

WE WERE IN a standoff with a killer who had blown his mother's brains out. Now he had a hostage in a choke hold. If we didn't pull a miracle out of our hats, more people were going to die.

I called out to Brock down the length of the chapel.

"Brock. I'm Sergeant Lindsay Boxer, SFPD."

"Yeah. I know. What do you want?"

"I want you to release that young lady and let her walk out of here. She has nothing to do with any of this."

Brock, haloed by stained glass, loosened his grip on his hostage, who was red-faced and gasping for air.

"Get out of here, okay?" he said to the girl. "Sorry I had to do that to you, Becky."

Becky stumbled for the door closest to her and pushed it open without looking back. The door slammed behind her, and for a full ten seconds, no one moved or spoke.

Then, I said to Brock, "Thanks. Now, what do you want?"

"I want to know why you're after me."

I said, "Okay. Christophe recorded his video conversation with your mother this morning. You know what I mean? Bloody horrific in-real-life images of what you did to your mother."

"Aw, Jeez. That's not good. I guess that's what you call direct evidence."

I shot a glance toward Conklin. Had Brock really not known that we'd seen him fire a cannonball through Rae Bergen's head?

Brock asked me, "Now what?"

"There's no reason to keep Jerry here."

Brock nodded, then said, "Go, Jerry. Hurry."

"Are you sure?" the campus cop asked me.

"Go ahead. We're good. Don't let anybody in here. Okay?"

"Okay," he said. He holstered his gun. "Brock. You know me. Take my advice. Don't fire that gun."

"Okay, Boomer."

Jerry shook his head and left the chapel.

I said, "Brock, this is my partner, Inspector Conklin. Let's all of us put our guns down and talk, all right? You okay with that, Rich?"

Conklin nodded. What could he say? Disarming a volatile, violent killer could be done, but it was a calculated risk. I was showing Brock that he was safe. That killing us wouldn't get him anywhere. Would he surrender? Or kill us because right now he had nothing left to lose?

I thought the odds were even. We hadn't hurt him. Maybe he would give up once his gun was out of the picture.

I walked past the altar to the edge of the dais and sat down with my legs hanging over it. I put my gun down, and pushed it away, out of my reach. What would Brock do?

Conklin said, "Now you, Picard."

"Put yours down first," said Brock.

If this maneuver didn't work, my last thoughts would be about what I was leaving behind: my husband, our daughter, my partner, and how Brady wouldn't have done this in a thousand years. Conklin walked to the first row on the aisle, ten feet away from where I sat on the dais floor.

He sat in a pew with his gun still in his hand.

Haloed again in a rainbow of many-colored glass, Brock Picard walked the aisle to the front of the chapel. He took a seat in the first row across from Rich Conklin. From my position on the dais, backed by the altar, I had a twenty-twenty view of both my partner and a young man who, in the next few moments, could end both our lives.

Brock said to Conklin, "Put your gun on the floor, then kick it over to me."

Conklin's expression was clear. He didn't want to drop his weapon, but at the same time, Brock could shoot him dead where he sat, now or anytime. He was trusting my judgment and I had no idea if I was right. But "Keep the guy with the gun calm" was one of the first rules when the gunman was ready to die.

Conklin put his gun on the floor, raised his right foot, and kicked his gun across the aisle to the twenty-year-old killer.

CHAPTER 114

BROCK SAID TO Conklin and me, "Well, you got me on shooting Moms. But you might like to know, Chris isn't my father."

"How do you know?" I asked him.

"Because my father is Jamie Fricke. I thought Chris told you."

"No," I said.

I thought about Moira Benet, Christophe's friend, the gossip queen. She'd told me that Rae had had an ongoing multi-decade affair with Jamie before, during, and after she married Christophe.

Brock said, "It's fucked up, right? You grow up thinking that this sweetheart foodie dude is your father. You call him Dad, hang out at his cool restaurants. I thought maybe one day I'd work for him. Maybe one day I'd take over the business.

"You know who told me the truth?" Brock asked.

I shook my head no.

He was passing his gun from right hand to left. I thought about reaching for my piece, just out of reach, firing on Brock.

I was a good marksman. But unless Brock's gun was empty, he didn't have to reach. He could shoot me where I sat. My ride-or-die partner—he, too, would die.

I tuned back in to Brock Picard, who was talking easily to us.

"It was Holly. Yeah. That Holly. I loved her to death. She was my beloved aunt Holly, former Olympic champ. We played tennis together from when I was five. Then when I was sixteen, she took me to bed. I didn't protest. I was the luckiest guy in the world and Holly was my dream come true.

"One morning about a year ago, we were in bed at the Ritz hotel. Holly says to me, 'You know you should ask your father to take you to Switzerland. See if soccer appeals to you.'

"She was half asleep. I figured she misspoke. I joked around. Like, 'I don't think my dad knows much about soccer,' something like that, but funnier. Holly didn't laugh. She realized what she'd said and got dressed. She kissed me goodbye and just like that, she dropped me. I called her, texted her, asked her to talk to me. She says, 'I'm sorry. I don't love you anymore.'"

I think I said, "Oh, no." Brock didn't hear me.

He said, "No more lovely Holly in my arms. No more funny food daddy. You getting this? Jamie Fricke was my father."

He was angry now, saying, "All those years. All those lies, and I didn't know it."

I heard him, but I was working out the DNA puzzle. Jamie had punched Brock. It was Brock's DNA on Jamie's knuckles. Brock had Fricke genes. Brock had killed his father.

"I killed Holly first," Brock said. "I called her to tell her that I had something of hers and wanted to give it back. She came out to meet me. When she got out of her car, I shot her.

Took some things off her to make it look like a robbery. Diamond jewelry. Her car.

"I was still furious at everyone, still couldn't get over it or make it stop. Months later, I called Jamie. Told him I was in town and Mom had a book for him, asked me to give it to him. He met me on the street and I gunned him down. Are you getting all this, Detectives? These people played huge roles in my life but never gave a shit about me."

Conklin said, "And your mother?"

"What can I say? She was loose and selfish. She kept Chris hanging all those years and he's screwing Holly. I love Chris, though. Still, he was a dummy in a lot of ways. My mom told him Jamie was my biological father, but never told me. There's your capital murder offense and punishment.

"Heard enough?" he said. "Any more questions? Because I'm not sticking around to answer."

"Brock, we appreciate you telling—"

He said, "You're welcome."

He put his gun on the flat of his right hand and stretched out his arm to Conklin.

"I won't be needing this anymore," he said. "Oh, wait. I forgot something."

He got a grip on his gun, pointed it at his temple, and as Conklin and I shouted "*No!*" in unison, he fired a round into his head and fell off the pew and onto the floor.

I checked. No pulse. No breath. No heartbeat.

Brock was dead.

EPILOGUE

CHAPTER 115

CINDY HAD A question for me.

"Will you be my maid of honor?" She looked shy, hesitant, as if she was afraid I would say no.

"Aww, Cindy. You know I will."

But when I looked her square in the eyes, she squirmed and looked down. I had to ask, "Are you sure you're ready?"

"Lindsay, I am. Of course I am. I think I am. I'm sure, right? How can you know more than that?"

As my expression changed from hope and happiness to doubt and consternation, she cracked up and said, "You should see yourself. Don't you know me by now? Don't you know how much I love him?"

Yes, I did. But. Richie was an honest and kind man who loved Cindy entirely, and I really wouldn't forgive her if she hurt him now in front of God and everyone. At the same time, my stubborn friend Cindy had been building her writing career and doing it very well. She'd said from the beginning that she had to devote herself to her work. And Richie had been supportive even though it had hurt him, and he was pretty sure that Cindy might never move off that position.

"So, Linds," she said. "Is that a promise?"

I said, yes, yes, yes, and after she hugged me she asked Claire and Yuki to be bridesmaids, and now here we all were, flanking Cindy in the Chapel of Our Lady at the Presidio.

Cindy was wearing a white gown even her mother loved, with buttons and bows and satin to her toes. I was standing to Cindy's left, Yuki beside me, Claire beside her. Richie was standing to Cindy's right and four of his brothers were lined up beside him.

The officiant was a young reverend named Michael Romano, and he smiled as he asked if Rich and Cindy had prepared vows. Richie said they had and Cindy, clutching a small white square of paper, said, "Right. Here goes."

"I, Cindy Thomas, take you, Richard John Conklin, to be my partner in marriage and in life. To love you, to give thanks for you, and to honor you, with my wit and my strength—"

Cindy stopped speaking, shook her head, and, veering off script, crumpled the note card. She looked at Reverend Romano and said to him, "That was my first draft. May I start over?"

"Of course," said the reverend. "Go right ahead."

"Thank you." Cindy cleared her throat. She looked up at her groom and said, "Richie, I've loved you since our first date at Ruby Tuesday, no lie. I want to tell you . . . I'm sorry I've been so difficult—" Her voice broke. She took some breaths and swallowed, then said, "—but I can be stubborn, you know."

I laughed first but not last. All the people on the left side of the aisle, Cindy's family and college friends and coworkers at the *Chronicle,* joined in. Cindy turned her head to the audience as the groom's side also fell apart—and she laughed along with them.

Cindy had always been a good sport, and watching her crack up at the altar filled me with more love for her than I'd ever felt before. I knew she was all in.

"Richie," she said, "I want to thank you for picking up after me, putting up with me, going out to my car in the rain to get my radio, sitting up front for my little readings in tiny book clubs, rolling with my shenanigans, letting me cry in your armpit, giving me funny nicknames, and for saving my life. There are a million other things I'll tell you later. But right now, I want to say, I love you so much. You can count on me to support you every day and in every way. I believe in you deeply and will always do so, even when you doubt yourself. I promise never to take you for granted but to let you know that you're a giant and my hero. I promise that I'm yours, Rich. All the way, in all ways, and for all time. I swear to you and to God."

Richie laughed, hugging this precious woman who was just tall enough to come up to his shoulder.

"You're one of a kind, Cindy," Rich said. "And I love that about you. I love you for more reasons and in more ways than I can say, and I trust you with my heart and my life. I promise you, Cindy, it doesn't matter how many rainy nights I go out to the car or run the dry cycle in the washing machine or call you Bunny Toes, I am grateful that today you are making me so very happy. And I will be by your side, always."

Applause broke out in the chapel. Darcy Thomas got to

her feet and clapped hard, and so did Cindy's dad. Henry Tyler, Cindy's boss at the *Chronicle*, gave her two thumbs up while Richie's brothers roughed him up, messed up his hair, and called him their own pet names as the laughter rolled from front to back before returning again to the altar, where Rich and Cindy grinned while looking deeply into each other's eyes.

Standing between Lindsay and Claire, Yuki was also grinning along with the bride and groom. She then turned toward the congregation, and as if he were sitting under a spotlight, Yuki's eyes fell on her own fair-haired, good-doing husband, Jackson Brady, Homicide lieutenant, who winked at her as he clapped for Rich and Cindy.

Yuki had never asked Cindy if she'd had sleepless nights when Richie hadn't answered his phone, when he hadn't come home, or had come home in the morning so tired he couldn't sleep or tell her what was wrong. And then having to rip herself away from him and go to work.

Yuki smiled at the sounds of approval from the congregation. She fingered the angel skin coral necklace that Brady had given her as a wedding gift, and she thought about their honeymoon—on a cruise ship that had been boarded by pirates, all armed and dangerous. Every person on the Finnstar could have died but for Brady's sharp thinking and courage. Richie, too, had those qualities.

Claire, standing beside Yuki, reached out and took her hand, nodding once as if she could read her thoughts. Or maybe she just saw the worry on Yuki's face. Yuki tried but couldn't wish the worry away.

She recalled the day she married Brady. Yuki had had little experience with men, and for the most part, had kept to herself. On her wedding day, she'd had a vision of her mother, Keiko, saying to her, *He is love of your life, Yuki-eh. This life and next one. Tell him that.*

Yuki had said those words to Brady, who'd hugged and kissed her, lifting her off her feet and telling her in his soft southern-tinged voice, "Sweetheart. Ah'll be right here with you."

Now Yuki beamed those words and feelings at Rich and Cindy.

Claire took in the full sight of the handsome couple, her friends who were about to make official a marriage that had already put down deep roots during their years together. She thought that Cindy and Rich were more alike than they knew; courageous, committed to their careers, loyal to their friends.

Cindy had never shied from anything. Claire remembered well when Cindy had fatally shot a killer who'd had Lindsay in her gunsights. Claire had done the autopsy. No charges had been pressed against Girl Reporter, who'd never looked back.

Claire also remembered a time when Rich had taken a .38-caliber round through his right shoulder at close range. It had been a painful injury that could have cost him the use of his arm or even killed him. But Rich had been stoic.

Claire had conferred with his doctors and had spent seven hours with Cindy in the hospital waiting room while Rich underwent surgery and was still under anesthesia.

When the surgeon had come out and asked for Mrs. Conklin, Cindy hadn't corrected him, but she'd been visibly shaken and had sobbed when she'd lost her fight to stay with Rich at Metro Hospital overnight.

Now, Claire watched Rich and Cindy stand together as the minister asked Eddie Conklin, best man and Richie's oldest brother, for the rings. She dropped Yuki's hand, covered her mouth as if to stop herself from shouting, "Whoo-hooooo!"

CHAPTER 116

REVEREND ROMANO NOW posed the two show-stopping questions.

"Do you, Richard, take Cynthia to be your lawful, wedded wife, for richer or poorer, through sickness and in health, as long as you both shall live?"

Rich said, "I do," and before the minister had fully repeated the question to Cindy, she replied, to the delight of the audience, "I do, *too*."

The rings were exchanged, and Reverend Romano said, "I now pronounce you husband and wife. Richard, you may kiss the bride."

The bride didn't wait for the maid of honor, her dearest friend, to lift her veil. She pushed it back herself. Richie kissed Cindy and buried his face in her curls, while nearly hugging the breath from her. Then he kissed her again to more applause.

*

As the organ started up, Claire felt as elated as she had on the day she'd married her own best friend. And after all these years, and four blessed children, she thought that they should celebrate their good fortune by renewing their vows. She wanted to get married again and would propose it to Edmund tonight.

Without knowing exactly why, Claire felt warm tears on her cheeks.

As the recessional music continued and the pews emptied from the rear first, Cindy felt the entirety of the wedding flooding through her and with it, a deeper awareness of herself. She was no longer afraid.

The long years of turning away from marriage to Richie and his longing for children were all about fear. Hers. She'd had a fear of failing, fear of giving up her independence, fear of not living up to Richie's belief and faith and love for her.

She also felt a sadness for all the years that she'd denied and delayed. She looked up at her new husband, who looked concerned as he gazed down at her.

"You okay, Cindy?"

"Yes, of course. It's just that I'm sorry for being such a jerk for so long, Richie. But I'm a hundred times better now.

"Thank you for waiting for me to wise up. I think I needed each of those years to learn to believe in myself as a wife. Your wife. To accept that we could be a team and that I could make you happy."

"Cin, we used those years to benefit our future."

Cindy nodded and reached up on tiptoes to kiss her husband as their guests surrounded them, enclosed them in a tight knot moving toward the door. Her parents worked their arms around them, and so did their friends and siblings as they left the small chapel through the narrow doorway and gathered on the front steps.

The photographer was waiting and quickly lined up her shots of the brand-new married couple and the wedding party. Cindy gripped Richie's hand. He squeezed and released hers so he could wrap his arm around her waist.

The photographer said, "Cindy, Rich, look at me."

Enveloped by love, a beaming Cindy posed for many pictures, all the while keeping her one precious secret. She would wait until tonight when she and Rich were in bed. That's when she would tell her best friend, her dear, sweet husband, what only she knew.

Tonight would be the beginning of her married life with the only man she'd ever loved.

ACKNOWLEDGMENTS

Our thanks to these experts who shared their experience with us in the writing of this book. Philip Birney, retired judge, and chief trial attorney for his San Diego law firm, WFGH&B, has practiced law for more than fifty years. Laurie Catherine Birney, licensed clinical psychologist and Phil's daughter, advised us on the mental disorders depicted in this book. As always, we are grateful to the real-life Richard J. Conklin, assistant chief of police, in charge of investigations at the Stamford, Connecticut, PD.

We also want to thank Professor Pierson Clair, instructor of cybersecurity and digital forensics at the University of Southern California, and Oli Thordarson, business executive, ransomware restoration expert, family man, and race car enthusiast. And we thank seven-year-old Lucy Murray for her lessons in combat training. Ingrid Taylar, wildlife photographer and rescuer, our researcher for a dozen years, has once again virtually guided us around San Francisco and its environs. And thanks, too, to Mary Jordan, traffic controller of innumerable parts and pieces, for whom we are always grateful.

Dedicated to our readers, the unofficial members of the Women's Murder Club, with our thanks.

Why everyone loves James Patterson and the Women's Murder Club

'It's no mystery why James Patterson is the world's most popular thriller writer. Simply put: **nobody does it better**.'
Jeffery Deaver

'**Smart characters, shocking twists . . .** you count down to the very last page to discover what will happen next.'
Lisa Gardner

'No one gets this big without **amazing natural storytelling** talent – which is what Jim has, in spades.'
Lee Child

'**Boxer steals the show** as the tough cop with a good heart.'
Mirror

'**Great plot, fantastic storytelling** and characters that spring off the page.'
Heidi Perks

'Patterson boils a scene down to the single, telling detail, the element that **defines a character** or moves a plot along. It's what fires off the movie projector in the reader's mind.'
Michael Connelly

'James Patterson is **The Boss**. End of.'
Ian Rankin

Have You Read Them All?

1ST TO DIE

Four friends come together to form the Women's Murder Club. Their job? To find a killer who is brutally slaughtering newly-wed couples on their wedding night.

2ND CHANCE
(with Andrew Gross)

The Women's Murder Club tracks a mystifying serial killer, but things get dangerous when he turns his pursuers into prey.

3RD DEGREE
(with Andrew Gross)

A wave of violence sweeps the city, and whoever is behind it is intent on killing someone every three days. Now he has targeted one of the Women's Murder Club . . .

4TH OF JULY
(with Maxine Paetro)

In a deadly shoot-out, Detective Lindsay Boxer makes a split-second decision that threatens everything she's ever worked for.

THE 5TH HORSEMAN
(with Maxine Paetro)

Recovering patients are dying inexplicably in hospital. Nobody is claiming responsibility. Could these deaths be tragic coincidences, or something more sinister?

THE 6TH TARGET
(with Maxine Paetro)

Children from rich families are being abducted off the streets – but the kidnappers aren't demanding a ransom. Can Lindsay Boxer find the children before it's too late?

7TH HEAVEN
(with Maxine Paetro)

The hunt for a deranged murderer with a taste for fire and the disappearance of the governor's son have pushed Lindsay to the limit. The trails have gone cold. But a raging fire is getting ever closer, and somebody will get burned.

8TH CONFESSION
(with Maxine Paetro)

Four celebrities are found killed and there are no clues: the perfect crime. Few people are as interested when a lowly preacher is murdered. But could he have been hiding a dark secret?

9TH JUDGEMENT
(with Maxine Paetro)

A psychopathic killer targets San Francisco's most innocent and vulnerable, while a burglary gone horribly wrong leads to a high-profile murder.

10TH ANNIVERSARY
(with Maxine Paetro)

A badly injured teenage girl is left for dead, and her newborn baby is nowhere to be found. But is the victim keeping secrets?

11TH HOUR
(with Maxine Paetro)

Is one of Detective Lindsay Boxer's colleagues a vicious killer? She won't know until the 11th hour.

12TH OF NEVER
(with Maxine Paetro)

A convicted serial killer wakes from a two-year coma. He says he's ready to tell where the bodies are buried, but what does he want in return?

UNLUCKY 13
(with Maxine Paetro)

Someone returns to San Francisco to pay a visit to some old friends. But a cheerful reunion is not on the cards.

14TH DEADLY SIN
(with Maxine Paetro)

A new terror is sweeping the streets of San Francisco, and the killers are dressed in police uniform. Lindsay treads a dangerous line as she investigates whether the criminals are brilliant imposters or police officers gone rogue.

15TH AFFAIR
(with Maxine Paetro)

Four bodies are found in a luxury hotel. Lindsay is sent in to investigate and hunt down an elusive and dangerous suspect. But when her husband Joe goes missing, she begins to fear that the suspect she is searching for could be him.

16TH SEDUCTION
(with Maxine Paetro)

At the trial of a bomber Lindsay and Joe worked together to capture, his defence raises damning questions about Lindsay and Joe's investigation.

17TH SUSPECT

(with Maxine Paetro)

A series of shootings brings terror to the streets of San Francisco, and Lindsay must confront a killer determined to undermine everything she has worked for.

18TH ABDUCTION

(with Maxine Paetro)

As Lindsay investigates the disappearance of three teachers, Joe is drawn into the search for an international war criminal everyone thought was dead.

19TH CHRISTMAS

(with Maxine Paetro)

Lindsay's plans for a quiet festive break are undone when she receives a tip-off that the biggest heist ever to hit San Francisco is being planned for Christmas Day.

20TH VICTIM

(with Maxine Paetro)

When simultaneous murders hit LA, Chicago and San Francisco, SFPD Sergeant Lindsay Boxer is tasked with uncovering what links these precise and calculated killings.

21ST BIRTHDAY

(with Maxine Paetro)

When a young mother and her baby daughter are reported missing, Lindsay takes up the investigation to find them.

22 SECONDS

(with Maxine Paetro)

Lindsay investigates an illegal shipment of drugs and weapons crossing the Mexican border, risking both her badge and her life.

23RD MIDNIGHT

(with Maxine Paetro)

Detective Lindsay Boxer must stop a copy-cat killer who's after fellow WMC member Cindy Thomas before it's too late.

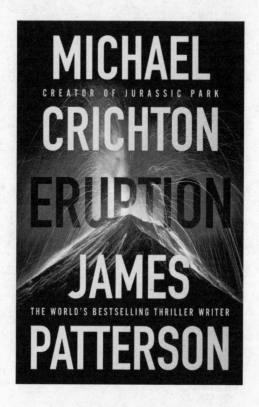

CHAPTER 1

Honoli'i Beach Park, Hilo, Hawai'i
Thursday, April 24, 2025
Time to eruption: 116 hours, 12 minutes, 13 seconds

Dennis!" Standing on the beach, John MacGregor had to yell so the surfer would hear him over the sound of the waves. "How about you don't go all *kūkae* on me, if that would be all right with you."

The kids that John MacGregor was coaching had heard the expression from him before, and they knew full well that it wasn't a compliment. *Kūkae* was a native Hawaiian word for "kook," and when John MacGregor said it, it meant that someone in the water was acting as if he'd never been on a board before. Or was about to end up underneath one.

Mac was thirty-six years old and an accomplished surfer, or at least he had been when he was younger, before his knees started sounding like a marching band every time he got into a crouch on his board. Now his passion for the sport was channeled into these tough fourteen-, fifteen-, and sixteen-year-old kids from Hilo, half of whom had already dropped out of school.

They came to this beach just two miles from downtown Hilo four afternoons a week, and for a few hours they were part of what islanders called the postcard Hawai'i, the one from the TV shows and the movies and the Chamber of Commerce brochures.

"What did I do wrong, Mac man?" fourteen-year-old Dennis said as he came out of the water.

"Well, to start with, that wasn't even your wave, it was Mele's," Mac said.

The two of them stood at the end of the exposed reef beach. Honoli'i was known as a good beach for local surfers, mostly because the strong currents kept swimmers away and the kids had the beach to themselves.

The last one out on the water was Lono.

Lono Akani, who had grown up without a father and whose mother was a housekeeper at the Hilo Hawaiian Hotel, was sixteen and Mac's favorite. He possessed a natural talent for this sport that Mac only wished he'd had at his age.

He watched Lono, into his crouch now on one of the Thurso Surf lancers Mac had purchased for each of them. Even from here Mac could see him smiling. Surely someday this boy would find fear in the ocean. Or fear would find him. Just not today as he flawlessly rode the inside curve of the wave.

Lono paddled in, put his board under his arm, and walked to where Mac waited on the beach. "Thank you," he said.

"For what?"

"For reminding me to always see the sets coming," the boy said. "It's why I was patient, *ya*, like you tell me to be, and waited for the wave I wanted."

Mac patted him on the shoulder. "*Keiki maika'i.*"

Good boy.

They heard the rumble from the sky then. Heard it and felt the beach shaking underneath them, making them both stagger.

The boy didn't know whether to look up or down. But John MacGregor understood what had happened—he knew a volcanic tremor, often associated with degassing, when he felt one. He looked up at the sky around the Big Island. All the kids were doing the same. It made Mac remember something one of his college professors had said about volcanoes and "the beauty of danger."

When the earth quieted, he felt the phone in his pocket buzzing. He answered and Jenny Kimura said, "Mac, thank God you picked up."

Jenny knew that when he was coaching his surfers, he didn't like to be disturbed with minor details from work. The press conference wasn't starting for another hour, so if Jenny was calling him, it wasn't about something minor.

"Jenny, what's wrong?"

"We've got degassing," she said.

No, not a minor detail at all.

"*Hōʻoʻopaʻoʻopa*," he said, cursing like one of his surfer boys.

CHAPTER 2

Mac's eyes were drawn to the twin peaks again and again. They were like a magnet for people who lived here.

"Where?" he asked Jenny, feeling his chest tighten.

"At the summit."

"On my way," he said. He hung up and called out to the surfers, "Sorry, boys, gotta bounce."

Dennis whooped. "Bounce?" he said. "Never say that again, Mac man."

"Well," Mac said, "I need to haul ass and get back to work—how's that?"

"Rajah dat," Dennis yelled back at Mac, grinning. "You go grind, brah." All the boys occasionally slipped into pidgin; it was part of the teenage pose.

Mac walked toward his green truck, and Lono caught up to him, board still under his arm, wet hair slicked back. His eyes were serious, troubled.

"That wasn't Kīlauea, was it?" Lono said, referring to the smallest volcano on the island, keeping his voice low.

"No," MacGregor said. "How do you know that, Lono?"

"Kīlauea quakes—they're all shivery and quick, *ya*? Like a set of waves, one after another, then dying off. That was the big one, wasn't it?"

MacGregor nodded. "Yeah, kid," Mac said, "what we just heard came from the big one."

Lono leaned in and spoke in a low voice, even though no one was close enough to hear him: "Is there gonna be an eruption, Mac?"

MacGregor reached for the door of his truck. On it was a white circle with the letters HVO in the center and the words HAWAIIAN VOLCANO OBSERVATORY on the outside. But then he stopped. Lono looked up at him, eyes more troubled than before, a kid trying hard not to act scared but unable to carry it off. Lono said, "You can tell me if there is."

Mac didn't want to say anything that would scare him even more, but he didn't want to lie to him either. "Come with me to my press conference," he said, forcing a smile. "You might learn something."

"Learning all the time from you, Mac man," the boy said.

Of all the kids, Lono was the one Mac had most aggressively encouraged to become an intern at the observatory, recognizing from the start how fiercely bright this boy was despite average grades in school. He was always in search of approval from Mac that he'd never gotten from his father, who'd deserted him and his mother. It was why he'd done as much reading about volcanoes as he had and knew as much as he did.

But Lono glanced back at the other boys and shook his head. "Nah. You can call and tell me about it later. You gonna be here tomorrow?"

"Not sure right now."

"This is bad, isn't it?" Lono asked. "I can see you're worried even if you're not saying it."

"You live here, you always worry about the big one," Mac said, "whether it's your job or not."

MacGregor got in the truck, started the engine, and drove off toward the mountain, thinking about all the things he hadn't said to Lono Akani, primarily how worried he actually was—and for good reason. Mauna Loa was just days away from its most violent eruption in a century, and John MacGregor, the geologist who headed the Hawaiian Volcano Observatory, knew that and was about to announce it to the press. He'd always known this day would come, probably sooner rather than later. Now here it was.

Mac drove fast.

Also By James Patterson

ALEX CROSS NOVELS

Along Came a Spider • Kiss the Girls • Jack and Jill • Cat and Mouse • Pop Goes the Weasel • Roses are Red • Violets are Blue • Four Blind Mice • The Big Bad Wolf • London Bridges • Mary, Mary • Cross • Double Cross • Cross Country • Alex Cross's Trial (*with Richard DiLallo*) • I, Alex Cross • Cross Fire • Kill Alex Cross • Merry Christmas, Alex Cross • Alex Cross, Run • Cross My Heart • Hope to Die • Cross Justice • Cross the Line • The People vs. Alex Cross • Target: Alex Cross • Criss Cross • Deadly Cross • Fear No Evil • Triple Cross • Alex Cross Must Die

THE WOMEN'S MURDER CLUB SERIES

1st to Die (*with Andrew Gross*) • 2nd Chance (*with Andrew Gross*) • 3rd Degree (*with Andrew Gross*) • 4th of July (*with Maxine Paetro*) • The 5th Horseman (*with Maxine Paetro*) • The 6th Target (*with Maxine Paetro*) • 7th Heaven (*with Maxine Paetro*) • 8th Confession (*with Maxine Paetro*) • 9th Judgement (*with Maxine Paetro*) • 10th Anniversary (*with Maxine Paetro*) • 11th Hour (*with Maxine Paetro*) • 12th of Never (*with Maxine Paetro*) • Unlucky 13 (*with Maxine Paetro*) • 14th Deadly Sin (*with Maxine Paetro*) • 15th Affair (*with Maxine Paetro*) • 16th Seduction (*with Maxine Paetro*) • 17th Suspect (*with Maxine Paetro*) • 18th Abduction (*with Maxine Paetro*) • 19th Christmas (*with Maxine Paetro*) • 20th Victim (*with Maxine Paetro*) • 21st Birthday (*with Maxine Paetro*) • 22 Seconds (*with Maxine Paetro*) • 23rd Midnight (*with Maxine Paetro*) • The 24th Hour (*with Maxine Paetro*)

DETECTIVE MICHAEL BENNETT SERIES

Step on a Crack (*with Michael Ledwidge*) • Run for Your Life (*with Michael Ledwidge*) • Worst Case (*with Michael Ledwidge*) • Tick Tock (*with Michael Ledwidge*) • I, Michael Bennett (*with Michael Ledwidge*) • Gone (*with Michael Ledwidge*) • Burn (*with Michael Ledwidge*) • Alert (*with Michael Ledwidge*) • Bullseye (*with Michael Ledwidge*) • Haunted (*with James O. Born*) • Ambush (*with James O. Born*) • Blindside (*with James O. Born*)

• The Russian (*with James O. Born*) • Shattered (*with James O. Born*) • Obsessed (*with James O. Born*) • Crosshairs (*with James O. Born*)

PRIVATE NOVELS

Private (*with Maxine Paetro*) • Private London (*with Mark Pearson*) • Private Games (*with Mark Sullivan*) • Private: No. 1 Suspect (*with Maxine Paetro*) • Private Berlin (*with Mark Sullivan*) • Private Down Under (*with Michael White*) • Private L.A. (*with Mark Sullivan*) • Private India (*with Ashwin Sanghi*) • Private Vegas (*with Maxine Paetro*) • Private Sydney (*with Kathryn Fox*) • Private Paris (*with Mark Sullivan*) • The Games (*with Mark Sullivan*) • Private Delhi (*with Ashwin Sanghi*) • Private Princess (*with Rees Jones*) • Private Moscow (*with Adam Hamdy*) • Private Rogue (*with Adam Hamdy*) • Private Beijing (*with Adam Hamdy*) • Private Rome (*with Adam Hamdy*) • Private Monaco (*with Adam Hamdy*)

NYPD RED SERIES

NYPD Red (*with Marshall Karp*) • NYPD Red 2 (*with Marshall Karp*) • NYPD Red 3 (*with Marshall Karp*) • NYPD Red 4 (*with Marshall Karp*) • NYPD Red 5 (*with Marshall Karp*) • NYPD Red 6 (*with Marshall Karp*)

DETECTIVE HARRIET BLUE SERIES

Never Never (*with Candice Fox*) • Fifty Fifty (*with Candice Fox*) • Liar Liar (*with Candice Fox*) • Hush Hush (*with Candice Fox*)

INSTINCT SERIES

Instinct (*with Howard Roughan, previously published as* Murder Games) • Killer Instinct (*with Howard Roughan*) • Steal (*with Howard Roughan*)

THE BLACK BOOK SERIES

The Black Book (*with David Ellis*) • The Red Book (*with David Ellis*) • Escape (*with David Ellis*)

STAND-ALONE THRILLERS

The Thomas Berryman Number • Hide and Seek • Black Market • The Midnight Club • Sail (*with Howard Roughan*) • Swimsuit (*with Maxine Paetro*) • Don't Blink (*with Howard Roughan*) • Postcard

Killers (*with Liza Marklund*) • Toys (*with Neil McMahon*) • Now You See Her (*with Michael Ledwidge*) • Kill Me If You Can (*with Marshall Karp*) • Guilty Wives (*with David Ellis*) • Zoo (*with Michael Ledwidge*) • Second Honeymoon (*with Howard Roughan*) • Mistress (*with David Ellis*) • Invisible (*with David Ellis*) • Truth or Die (*with Howard Roughan*) • Murder House (*with David Ellis*) • The Store (*with Richard DiLallo*) • Texas Ranger (*with Andrew Bourelle*) • The President is Missing (*with Bill Clinton*) • Revenge (*with Andrew Holmes*) • Juror No. 3 (*with Nancy Allen*) • The First Lady (*with Brendan DuBois*) • The Chef (*with Max DiLallo*) • Out of Sight (*with Brendan DuBois*) • Unsolved (*with David Ellis*) • The Inn (*with Candice Fox*) • Lost (*with James O. Born*) • Texas Outlaw (*with Andrew Bourelle*) • The Summer House (*with Brendan DuBois*) • 1st Case (*with Chris Tebbetts*) • Cajun Justice (*with Tucker Axum*)• The Midwife Murders (*with Richard DiLallo*) • The Coast-to-Coast Murders (*with J.D. Barker*) • Three Women Disappear (*with Shan Serafin*) • The President's Daughter (*with Bill Clinton*) • The Shadow (*with Brian Sitts*) • The Noise (*with J.D. Barker*) • 2 Sisters Detective Agency (*with Candice Fox*) • Jailhouse Lawyer (*with Nancy Allen*) • The Horsewoman (*with Mike Lupica*) • Run Rose Run (*with Dolly Parton*) • Death of the Black Widow (*with J.D. Barker*) • The Ninth Month (*with Richard DiLallo*) • The Girl in the Castle (*with Emily Raymond*) • Blowback (*with Brendan DuBois*) • The Twelve Topsy-Turvy, Very Messy Days of Christmas (*with Tad Safran*) • The Perfect Assassin (*with Brian Sitts*) • House of Wolves (*with Mike Lupica*) • Countdown (*with Brendan DuBois*) • Cross Down (*with Brendan DuBois*) • Circle of Death (*with Brian Sitts*) • Lion & Lamb (with *Duane Swierczynski*) • 12 Months to Live (*with Mike Lupica*) • Holmes, Margaret and Poe (*with Brian Sitts*) • The No. 1 Lawyer (*with Nancy Allen*) • The Murder Inn (*with Candice Fox*) • Confessions of the Dead (*with J.D. Barker*) • 8 Months Left (*with Mike Lupica*)

NON-FICTION

Torn Apart (*with Hal and Cory Friedman*) • The Murder of King Tut (*with Martin Dugard*) • All-American Murder (*with Alex Abramovich and Mike Harvkey*) • The Kennedy Curse (*with Cynthia Fagen*) • The Last Days of John Lennon (*with Casey Sherman and Dave Wedge*) • Walk in My Combat Boots (*with Matt Eversmann and Chris Mooney*) • ER Nurses (*with Matt Eversmann*) • James Patterson by James Patterson: The Stories of My Life

• Diana, William and Harry (*with Chris Mooney*) • American Cops (*with Matt Eversmann*) • What Really Happens in Vegas (*with Mark Seal*) • The Secret Lives of Booksellers and Librarians (*with Matt Eversmann*) • Tiger, Tiger

MURDER IS FOREVER TRUE CRIME

Murder, Interrupted (*with Alex Abramovich and Christopher Charles*) • Home Sweet Murder (*with Andrew Bourelle and Scott Slaven*) • Murder Beyond the Grave (*with Andrew Bourelle and Christopher Charles*) • Murder Thy Neighbour (*with Andrew Bourelle and Max DiLallo*) • Murder of Innocence (*with Max DiLallo and Andrew Bourelle*) • Till Murder Do Us Part (*with Andrew Bourelle and Max DiLallo*)

COLLECTIONS

Triple Threat (*with Max DiLallo and Andrew Bourelle*) • Kill or Be Killed (*with Maxine Paetro, Rees Jones, Shan Serafin and Emily Raymond*) • The Moores are Missing (*with Loren D. Estleman, Sam Hawken and Ed Chatterton*) • The Family Lawyer (*with Robert Rotstein, Christopher Charles and Rachel Howzell Hall*) • Murder in Paradise (*with Doug Allyn, Connor Hyde and Duane Swierczynski*) • The House Next Door (*with Susan DiLallo, Max DiLallo and Brendan DuBois*) • 13-Minute Murder (*with Shan Serafin, Christopher Farnsworth and Scott Slaven*) • The River Murders (*with James O. Born*) • The Palm Beach Murders (*with James O. Born, Duane Swierczynski and Tim Arnold*) • Paris Detective • 3 Days to Live • 23 ½ Lies (*with Maxine Paetro*)

For more information about James Patterson's novels, visit www.penguin.co.uk.